THE THREE RELIGIOUS LEADERS
OF OXFORD AND THEIR
MOVEMENTS

JOHN WYCLIFFE   JOHN WESLEY
JOHN HENRY NEWMAN

THE MACMILLAN COMPANY
NEW YORK · BOSTON · CHICAGO · DALLAS
ATLANTA · SAN FRANCISCO

MACMILLAN & CO., LIMITED
LONDON · BOMBAY · CALCUTTA
MELBOURNE

THE MACMILLAN CO. OF CANADA, LTD.
TORONTO

THE THREE RELIGIOUS LEADERS OF OXFORD AND THEIR MOVEMENTS

JOHN WYCLIFFE   JOHN WESLEY
JOHN HENRY NEWMAN

BY

S. PARKES CADMAN

New York

THE MACMILLAN COMPANY

1916

Norwood Press
J. S. Cushing Co. — Berwick & Smith Co.
Norwood, Mass., U.S.A.

To

WALTER COUTANT HUMSTONE

OF BROOKLYN

IN TOKEN OF GRATITUDE FOR YEARS ILLUMINATED

BY HIS MANY ACTS OF WISE AND

TENDER FRIENDSHIP

THIS BOOK

IS RESPECTFULLY DEDICATED

PREFACE

THIS book was suggested by a course of lectures delivered under the auspices of The Brooklyn Institute of Arts and Sciences during the Lenten season of 1913. It has since been revised with some care, and would have been issued earlier but for the pressure of pastoral and public duties. It deals with three great Englishmen, great Christians, great Churchmen, and loyal sons of Oxford, who, as it seems to me, are the foremost leaders in religious life and activity that University has yet given to the world. Many prophets, priests, and kings have been nourished within her borders, but none who in significance and contribution to the general welfare compare with Wycliffe, the real originator of European Protestantism; Wesley, the Anglican priest who became the founder of Methodism and one of the makers of modern England and of English-speaking nations; Newman, the spiritual genius of his century who re-interpreted Catholicism, both Anglican and Roman.

Hence I have named the volume " The Three Religious Leaders of Oxford and their Movements," a title which appears to be vindicated by the facts so far as I have been able to ascertain them. It will probably be said that I omit some of these and misconstrue others. This is more than likely, and if it be so, I must be held wholly responsible. I can only plead in extenuation that I have tried to be as disinterested and as just as my standpoint and the information at my disposal would permit, and that throughout I have sincerely intended to give an impetus to that fraternal spirit which leads to a more complete apprehension of divine truth. I shall be amply rewarded if those who have any sympathy with the men and the movements I have attempted to portray, whether Roman Catholics or Protestants, are drawn more closely together in the bonds of a common faith and fellowship.

My thanks are due and are here respectfully extended to the Reverend Doctor Herbert B. Workman, Principal of Westminster College, London, who used his unsurpassed knowledge of Wycliffe and of Wesley to correct the first eight chapters; to my colleague at Central Church, the Reverend David Loinaz, for his constant research in the subjects discussed; to my friends, the Reverend Doctor W. L. Watkinson, formerly Editor of *The London Quarterly Review*, the Reverend John L. Belford, rector of the Roman Catholic Church of the Nativity, Brooklyn, and the Reverend Doctor Joseph Dunn Burrell, pastor of the Classon Avenue Presbyterian Church, in the same borough, for the loan of valuable volumes and documents; to Professor Edgar A. Hall, of Adelphi College, and the Reverend Charles Waugh for their fruitful suggestions and verification of quotations; and to the Reverend Oscar L. Joseph for his scholarly assistance and preparation of the Index.

The reader is asked to remember that the lectures were given before an audience composed of different religious denominations, and this circumstance rendered necessary explanations and details which otherwise might seem superfluous.

S. PARKES CADMAN.

CENTRAL CONGREGATIONAL CHURCH,
BROOKLYN, NEW YORK CITY.
September the first, 1915.

PROLOGUE

AMONG many other benefits for which History hath been honoured, in this one it triumpheth over all human knowledge, that it hath given us life in our understanding, since by it the world itself had life and beginning, even to this day: yea, it hath triumphed over Time, which besides it nothing but Eternity hath triumphed over. For it hath carried our knowledge over the vast and devouring space of so many thousands of years and given so fair and piercing eyes to our mind, that we plainly behold living now, as if we had lived then, that great world, magni Dei sapiens opus — 'The wise world,' saith Hermes, 'of a great God' — as it was then, when but new to itself. By it, I say, it is that we live in the very time when it was created; we behold how it was governed; how it was covered with water and again re-peopled; how kings and kingdoms have flourished and fallen, and for what virtue and piety God made prosperous, and for what vice and deformity He made wretched, both the one and the other. And it is not the least debt which we owe unto History, that it hath made us acquainted with our dead ancestors, and out of the depth and darkness of the Earth delivered us their memory and fame. In a word, we may gather out of History a policy no less wise than eternal, by the comparison and application of other men's aforepassed miseries with our own like errors and ill-deservings. — From the Preface: *History ; Its Rights and Dignity.*

SIR WALTER RALEIGH.

PROLOGUE

THE study of history cannot give mathematical certainty; yet, rightly pursued, it should instill the serious and reverent temper which lessens the danger of partisan blindness. A sense of the largeness and complexity of the experiences of the past is an aid to the recovery of their vital phases. The more deeply these experiences are pondered, the more completely they are stripped of the accidental and non-essential, the more clearly manifest becomes their fundamental relation to the process of human development.

Such considerations are always of value, but never more so than in the period before us. For during the medieval epoch Church and State were intimately related, and those who would gain a just apprehension of the era must endeavor to attain the state of that practised observer

> " . . . whose even-balanced soul,
> From first youth tested up to extreme old age,
> Business could not make dull, nor passion wild,
>
> Who saw life steadily, and saw it whole."

Again, throughout the Middle Ages the limitation of man's power over his environment is everywhere strikingly apparent. Of means of expression for aspiration and ideal there was no lack, but any practical realization was obstructed by the difficulties and complications imposed by circumstances. How philosophical theories influenced statesmanship and politics, how their seeming triumphs so often ended in disaster, and what qualities either in them or in their advocates clothed them with influence and insured

xii THREE RELIGIOUS LEADERS OF OXFORD

permanent benefits, solidifying government and people,
the career of Wycliffe may perhaps serve to illustrate;
for the Reformer embodied much of the genius of medieval
England. The attempt to reproduce the life of the period
is materially hampered, however, by the obscurity of perspective in which many lines of action and the chief personalities of the age are alike enveloped. The original
authorities upon whom historians must rely for information were, as a rule, advocates of some particular cause.
They knew little or nothing about reducing vexed questions
of the time to definite limits, nor did they study them in
the light of their initiatory circumstances. Swayed by contemporary views, they seldom subordinated their partisan
proclivities to fairness of statement, and their work bears
the impress of the passions rather than of the intellect.
Private opinion or special sympathy biased their judgments,
and the chroniclers sought in their records to vindicate policies and individuals agreeable to their peculiar persuasions.
Where one group could find nothing but the beneficial,
another perceived the portents of grave disaster. Even
the best among them did not recognize the superiority, as a
historical method, of close observation over empty argument. Their writings ranged from the grotesquely imaginative, credulous of physical prodigies and disdainful of facts,
to vapid and colorless recitals without pith or meaning.
Evidences of predetermination were rife in the widely differing estimates of pontiffs, princes, prelates, and scholastics
whose careers were woven into the tangle of current controversies. And the well-poised, many-sided historian who
might have bequeathed to us a detached and comprehensive
survey of the ecclesiastical events around which medieval
civilization centered, and from which modern ideas were
projected, was then scarcely a possibility. Eminent scholars,
however, such as Freeman, Stubbs, Creighton, Seeley, and
Lord Acton, have recovered the gains of long past centuries
and have enabled us to understand medieval men and affairs,

not only when they were swayed by unusual circumstances, but also by those common sentiments which influence all ages alike. The process has dwarfed some heroes and robbed some events of a spurious greatness, but the disillusionment was as necessary as it was wise.

Ranke's axiom, which he himself exemplified, "simply to find out how things occurred," requires far more than the perusal of ancient manuscripts. The knowledge of the main lines of history; of the motives at the root of steadfast national purposes; of constantly interfering factors of influence; and a vivid realization of the continuity of the historical process, and of the shaping power of vigorous personality, are prime requisites for the successful interpretation of the past. Our gratitude is due to the historians who have conformed to these principles; they recall the Greek adage that truth is the fellow-citizen of the gods.

It was a notable achievement to bridge the gulf made by the Renaissance between the Medieval and the Modern era. The faith and laws, the ideals and practices, the conceits and fancies of our remoter progenitors still appear strange and perplexing to the unaccustomed eye. But the trained and patient interpretation of the nineteenth century scholar has brought them nearer to us, moralized the entire method of research, and taught us to moderate alike our denunciation and our eulogy. The occupants of that era confronted obstacles too great for their resources to surmount. The influx of a larger, freer life had seriously weakened many venerable customs and institutions, and while these slowly succumbed the reconstruction of the social fabric was delayed by treachery, violence, and war. Yet even in this disdainful passage of the irresistible tide, preparatory to impending change, the primal elements of human progress were not submerged. Amid the chaos, the pretensions of the aristocracy and the delusions of the proletariat were checked; clericalism measured itself against the rapacity and pride of kings and barons; municipalities arose, en-

riched by the growth of trade, the magnates of which sometimes thwarted the rulers they lavishly entertained, and
for whose campaigns they were financially responsible.
Guilds of artisans and tradesfolk, unified by mutual interest
and external opposition, flourished in the chief cities of
Europe. When clerics were recalcitrant, or where merchants and workmen did not preponderate, their respective
organizations still served as counteracting forces, and their
union was a factor monarchs and lords were compelled to
respect. Feudalism reluctantly yielded to the social impact, while the disguise of chivalry availed it less and less.
Slaves became freemen, freemen became burghers, burghers
acquired a firmer hold on the sources of national revenue and
the control of the State. Education was no longer a clerical
monopoly,.and the few learned laymen who had then secured
recognition were pioneers of that distribution of knowledge
which eventually characterized Humanism. Justice between man and man was not simply exact conformity to
preëxistent and obligatory law. Legal relations were sifted
in the light of advancing intelligence. That vague, uncodi-
fied borderland which is now called social justice, as distinguished from the statutes of the realm, was sufficiently
defined for the periodical introduction of laws which incorporated some of its claims and validated certain personal
and property rights. The baneful dogma which assumed a
natural servitude for the vast majority became politically
inexpedient among the bold insurgents who threatened
Richard the Second's reign. Foreign intercourse disturbed
the insularity of England; the Crusades brought the West
face to face with the East, and men began to be aware of the
breadth and splendor of the world. The nationalism which
arose after the defeat of the Holy Roman Empire by the
Papacy vanquished in its turn the schemes of the latter for
a consolidated Christendom. No country gave a more
generous reception to the new consciousness of the integrity
of the State than did England. Her geographical situation

and the temper of her people had always separated her from
the currents of continental opinion, and, while this was a
loss in some respects, in most it proved a decided gain. The
stages in human evolution are seldom noted until they
stand out in the bold relief of a crisis. Their occurrence in
the thirteenth and fourteenth centuries was registered, and
their changes accomplished, through such intermediaries
as St. Francis, Innocent III, Grosseteste, Edward I, Wycliffe,
and other great personalities, who focused and intensified
the tendencies of their day.

These observations also apply to the eighteenth and
nineteenth centuries. John Wesley expressed the spiritual
aspirations and transformed the character of his age more
profoundly and permanently than did any other contemporary Englishman. Even the younger Pitt, who defeated
Napoleon the Great, and added India to the British Empire,
is now seen to have been inferior in lasting influence to the
apostolic evangelist who revived the consciousness of a
redeeming God. Newman quickened a sense of ecclesiastical
universalism which his insular countrymen had deemed
obsolete. He linked Anglican to continental Christianity.
This achievement has largely determined for the past sixty
years the conceptions of the Establishment concerning its
ministerial and sacramental efficiency, its forms of worship,
and its relations with other Communions. The reader will
expand for himself the consequences following such major
events as the American Revolution, the French Revolution,
the growth in politics and in morals of those plain and fundamental principles which a series of tragical experiences
discovered to be the basis of just government. The ever-
increasing conviction that sovereignty must reside with the
people gave rise to the American Republic, regenerated
France, democratized the British nation and its colonies,
and still strives for an intelligent formulation in other countries of mankind. Nor were these later centuries deprived
of publicists whose passion for leadership was an energetic

activity both for good and evil.   The interregnums between Walpole and Gladstone, Bolingbroke and Russell; between Louis XIV and Napoleon the Great, or Washington and Webster, filled as they are with prominent personalities and achievements, can be surveyed to-day with a more impartial eye.   Few, if any, of these monarchs and statesmen escaped "the contagion of the world's slow stain."   At the same time they were in closest fellowship with the erring millions they led in peace and war.   And if some among them sacrificed principle to power and ambition, ever and anon others appeared who redeemed the credit of the race and showed what could be effected by untrammeled character and service.

CONTENTS

BOOK I

JOHN WYCLIFFE AND LATER MEDIEVALISM

BOOK II

JOHN WESLEY AND THE EIGHTEENTH CENTURY

BOOK III

JOHN HENRY NEWMAN AND THE OXFORD MOVEMENT OF 1833–1845

BOOK I

JOHN WYCLIFFE

AND

LATER MEDIEVALISM

GIVE me a spirit that on this life's rough sea
Loves t' have his sails filled with a lusty wind,
Even till his sail-yards tremble, his masts crack,
And his rapt ship run on her side so low
That she drinks water, and her keel plows air.

GEORGE CHAPMAN: *Tragedy of Charles,
Duke of Byron.* Act III, Sc. I.

CHAPTER I

HERALDS OF REFORM

HEAVEN doth with us as we with torches do,
Not light them for ourselves; for if our virtues
Did not go forth of us, 't were all alike
As if we had them not.   Spirits are not finely touch'd
But to fine issues, nor nature never lends
The smallest scruple of her excellence
But, like a thrifty goddess, she determines
Herself the glory of a creditor,
Both thanks and use.

      SHAKESPEARE : *Measure for Measure.*   Act I, Sc. I.

CHAPTER I

HERALDS OF REFORM

I

THE paramount interest of Wycliffe's work as a reformer centers in his courageous stand for religious and political freedom during the quarrel between the English government and the Papacy. This recurrent conflict had its sordid and repulsive phases, which were relieved by the devotion of the few who, concentrating their energies on the principles involved, gave the dispute a moral significance, and largely determined the outcome. A brief résumé of the points at issue in this protracted strife is in place here.

The origin of the struggle is traceable to the extravagant claims of the Holy See and the characteristically independent spirit of the Anglican Church.   This age-long rivalry explains the powerful yet ineffective protest of Wycliffe, and also the later revolt under Henry VIII, which, unjustified as it was in some respects, met a national demand and culminated in an English Reformation.   The degree of liberty enjoyed from the beginning by the English hierarchy should not be exaggerated, for there was a connection with the Papacy which served distinct purposes and was neither feebly nor thoughtlessly established.   Nothing is gained by trying to prove that the relationship never existed, any more than by disregarding the substantial reasons for its severance.

Hildebrand, who gave a definite enunciation to the Papal claims, was elevated to the throne of St. Peter in 1073 and assumed the title of Gregory VII.   As an ecclesiastic he was at once philosophical and practical, large-minded enough to conceive or revive far-reaching policies, and possessed of a penetrative knowledge of mankind and a prophetic understanding of the spirit of his age.   The purity of his personal life, the strength of his character, and the force of his will coöperated with his zeal for service to make him a born leader of men.   Before his lofty vision arose the stupendous ideal of a theocratic State, embracing the entire world, over which, as God's Vicegerent, he asserted his sovereignty.   Civil or religious rulers might not question the prerogatives of his office, since they were conferred by the Deity Himself, to Whom alone the Pontiff was responsible.   Far from being content to leave these august designs in the realm of remote theory, Hildebrand strove to make them actual, and to bring them into closest touch with those days of violent disruption and constant change.   No man could have been selected as the Vicar of Christ who was better fitted by nature and circumstances to act for the cause with which his name is associated. Sagacious and ardent, he knew how to conform to the immemorial traditions of the Papacy, and also how to stamp upon its fabric and diplomacy the impress of his commanding nature. Although he failed in certain directions, he nevertheless succeeded in investing the Holy See with a spiritual influence which overawed and yet in a measure cemented the continental nationalities. He accomplished by the subtle suggestions and definite claims of sacerdotal authority a task which armed hosts would have found impossible. But the defects latent in Hildebrand's statecraft began to appear even during his own administration, and increased in after times. He could not induce England to bow to his spiritual autocracy: then as now she was sheltered by that splendid isolation which has always guarded her from continental ecclesiasticism. The inherent sense of freedom which the Anglo-Saxon people cherished survived even the Norman Conquest and prevented the feudal system from taking deep root on English soil.

Hildebrand knew that Englishmen would not willingly permit the imposition upon them of any system, however impressive in its scope and purpose, which jeopardized their national autonomy; and in the hope of counteracting this sentiment he had advised his predecessor, Alexander II, to bestow his blessing upon the expedition of the Duke of Normandy in 1066. The desires of the two ecclesiastics were frustrated by the Conqueror himself, who so quickly absorbed the leaven of his new realm that when the three legates were despatched from Rome by the Pope to demand homage from the king for his new island dominion, they met with the severe rebuff, — "Homage to thee I have not chosen, nor do I choose to do. I never made a promise to that effect, nor do I find that it was ever performed by my predecessors to thine." The Norman bishops who were appointed to English sees were careful to adopt their monarch's policy. The Primates of Canterbury and York had always been supreme in their archiepiscopates, and there were no indications in the tenor of previous Papal decrees or edicts that the Pope claimed the right of overlordship. Thus sustained by precedent, the civil power, both before and after the Conquest, retained certain rights in England which it did not possess in Germany. It should be added, however, that the Anglican Church was far from being locally independent, and that no one was more anxious than the Conqueror to bring it into touch with continental Catholicism.

Hildebrand resorted to other measures: in 1075 a bull was issued denying to the laity the right of investiture for churches; three years later investitures were pronounced invalid when thus bestowed, and the penalty of excommunication was passed upon those disobeying the edict. Lay investiture originated when bishops and abbots became temporal lords and bestowed upon laymen extensive church properties in return for military service. Ecclesiastical office was then held to be of the nature of a fief for which homage was due to the king. If a Chapter's choice of its bishop or abbot was displeasing to the monarch, he could refuse to ratify the election, whereupon during the interval the income of the benefice reverted to the Crown. William Rufus, the unscrupulous son and successor of the Conqueror, was a notorious transgressor in this respect. He kept the see of Canterbury vacant four years that he might appropriate its emoluments. In a fit of remorse, due to his fear of death, he nominated to the Primacy the saintly and learned Anselm, abbot of Bec in Normandy, a thinker, a sensitive pietist of the character which Englishmen seldom appreciate sympathetically, but one who, to quote the phrase of Ronsard, "had traveled far on the green path that leads men into remembrance." Upon the king's recovery from sickness his compunction vanished, and he resumed an open and shameless barter of spiritual dignities. Anselm's gentle and sincere nature was not devoid of sterner qualities: he opposed the despotism of Rufus, and defended not only the clerical order, but also the imperiled rights of the subject. Finding it unsafe to remain in residence, the Archbishop appealed in person to Pope Urban II. It was during his absence from Canterbury that the prelate, who was predominantly the quiet scholar, found leisure to write his celebrated treatise, "Cur Deus Homo." After the death of Rufus, he refused to do homage to Henry I, or receive investiture at his hands. Pope Paschal II sanctioned the Primate's action, and eventually a compromise was effected.

After the vexed reign of Stephen, during which the armies of the bishops fought against those of the king, the next open breach with the Papacy occurred under Henry II. The clergy now demanded trial in their own courts, which, in accordance with the unwise legislation enacted at the Conquest, were separated from the regular jurisdiction. The flagrant partiality of the clerical judiciary, its frequent miscarriages of justice, and the number and influence of those tonsured miscreants who were thus exempt from the common law, constituted a grave menace to peace and order by making the sacerdotal office a haven for criminals. The higher clergy surrounded themselves with retinues of armed retainers, among whom were warrior priests and not a few of the baser sort. In the ranks of the lower clergy were numerous rascals who had escaped punishment for offenses of which they were palpably guilty. While the controversy was at its height Henry bestowed the archbishopric upon his chancellor, Thomas à Becket, succinctly described by William of Newburgh as one "burning with zeal for justice, but whether altogether according to wisdom, God knows." Becket at once became the champion of the extreme clerical party, and his sturdy resistance of Henry's efforts to subdue it strained their friendship to the breaking point. In January, 1164, a Great Council was convened at Clarendon, near Salisbury, to reduce the friction between Church and State. The resolutions then framed, and subsequently placed upon the statute-book, were termed the "Constitutions of Clarendon." They provided that accused clerics, when condemned and degraded by their own courts, should be transferred to the King's court to receive sentence; to which Becket properly objected that this would be trying a man twice for the same offense. Civil cases involving their members were to be adjusted before the ordinary tribunals. The clergy were forbidden to leave the country without the monarch's consent, neither could appeals be taken to Rome without the royal license. The agreement concerning investiture, under the terms of which the Pope allowed bishops and abbots to do homage to the king for their temporal properties, was confirmed. After repeated quibblings and equivocations Becket gave a reluctant assent to these changes, and then, speedily repentant, refused to affix his official seal. Pope Alexander III encouraged the Archbishop's refractory attitude, and Becket fled to France in November, 1164, to escape Henry's anger. There he remained six years in exile. Upon his return to Canterbury the townsfolk went in procession to meet him outside the city, and escorted him in triumph to his church.

The jubilations were scarcely ended before the smouldering fires broke out again, only to be quenched by the assassination of the fearless prelate in one of the chapels of the Cathedral. The crime excited universal horror and execration: the four knights whose ferocious daring in the king's service prompted the murder had absolutely ruined their master's projects. Henry quailed before the storm of indignation which swept over Europe; he submitted to the Papal decrees, annulled the Constitutions of Clarendon, and made an open expiation in his dolorous pilgrimage to Becket's tomb. The popular admiration which had followed Becket during his later life was due to his courageous determination and steadfast zeal for what he held to be justice against king and barons. Nothing could have enhanced that admiration more than the manner of his ending. No Englishman of the Middle Ages made so indelible an im-

pression on his countrymen as did Thomas of Canterbury.
It has been well said that if Anselm was a saint whose superiority to ordinary motives made him a statesman, Becket
was a statesman whose political audacity was transformed
by the popular imagination into sainthood.

II

A deeper humiliation awaited the Crown in the reign
of the second Henry's son John, whose folly and wickedness
plunged the nation into turbulence and dishonor. After
the death of Archbishop Hubert Walter, which occurred on
July 12, 1205, a dispute arose between the king and the
Chapter of the see in reference to Walter's successor. The
younger monks met in haste before the deceased Primate
was buried, and without applying for the royal warrant
elected their sub-prior Reginald. They even went so far
as to install him, and then secretly dispatched him to Rome
to obtain the Papal confirmation. During his passage
through Flanders, Reginald violated the confidence of his
brethren by publicly announcing himself as the Archbishop-
elect. In the ensuing tumult the king nominated John de
Grey, Bishop of Norwich, the bishops and the older monks of
the Chapter acquiescing, and a second deputation at once
set out for the Vatican to push the claims of the king's
candidate.

The Pontiff, Innocent III, was a consummate administra-
tor, in counsel wary, in fidelity to his office impregnable, and
an unflinching advocate of absolutism as enunciated by
Hildebrand. "Regal dignity," said Innocent, "should be
but a reflection of the Papal authority and entirely subordinate to it." He was not prone to deceive himself, and
he was not liable to be deceived by others. His fame has
been clouded by the contention that he originated the
Inquisition, and it is beyond question that he gave impetus
to the extirpation of heresy by physical violence, deeming

it high treason against Heaven. The Livonians and the Albigenses felt the weight of his hand; the continental rulers bent before his inflexible sway, and he was more than a match for the irresolute and demoralized John.

During the week before Christmas, 1206, the rivals for the archbishopric were heard at the Papal court, where the king's duplicity precipitated his defeat. While openly protesting that the Pontiff's decision would be acceptable to all, he attempted to bribe the officials of the Curia, and enjoined the monks whom he had commissioned to elect no one but Grey. The futility of such double dealing was demonstrated in this negotiation with the astute Innocent, who could neither be cajoled nor affrighted by it. The election of Reginald was quashed as informal, that of Bishop de Grey was pronounced illegal on the ground that it occurred while the appeal was pending; [1] and Cardinal Stephen Langton, an Englishman by birth, and the first scholar in the foremost university of Europe, was named by Innocent for the see. The representatives of the Chapter concurred, regardless of their secret pact with John, and accordingly Langton was chosen. It is beyond reasonable doubt that Innocent was aware of the treachery of the English monarch, and he seems to have been sincerely solicitous that the throne of Augustine should be filled by a man of Langton's worth and caliber. He proceeded cautiously and declined to complete the election by consecrating Langton until the king had given his approval. This John emphatically refused to bestow, and, notwithstanding his previous professions of admiration for the Archbishop, he now complained that he did not even know the obscure person who was being thrust upon him. At this unblushing prevarication, the Pope took the initiative and consecrated his nominee, whereupon the fury of the reckless king fell upon the monks who had dared to disobey his mandate. Innocent countered his assaults

---

[1] Bishop William Stubbs: "Historical Introduction to the Rolls Series"; pp. 467–468.

with an impressive manifestation of the Papal authority which recalled that made by Hildebrand at Canossa. In the spring of 1208, the realm was suddenly deprived of its religious instruction and ministry, and those holy offices of faith and consolation which were believed necessary to eternal salvation were simultaneously withdrawn. This stupendous sentence, a formidable but also self-destructive weapon of the medieval Church, filled the heart of the nation with grief and dismay. What effect it had on the king can only be conjectured; at any rate he offered Langton the royalties of his see and gave him permission to visit England. But overtures for peace were at an end by the time the Archbishop arrived at Dover; the bishops fled the country, the parochial clergy were outlawed from their charges, and the monasteries and nunneries were brought to the verge of starvation. The Papal interdict prevailed until 1212, and John took advantage of the general distress by appropriating ecclesiastical benefices and funds to his own use. Finally the Pope excommunicated him, and when he retaliated with renewed defiances and plunderings, Innocent declared his deposition from the throne. Contemporary accounts of the calamitous struggle assert that a prophecy of Peter of Wakefield played upon the king's superstitions and ended his resistance. However that may have been, it suddenly collapsed, and on May 15, 1213, he made an abject and total surrender in which he ceded the kingdoms of England and Ireland in perpetuity to Innocent and his successors, agreeing to hold them in fief from the Pope at an annual tribute of one thousand marks. By this act John endeavored to enlist the Holy See against the baronage, which was restive beneath the consequences of his misrule. Innocent insisted upon a guarantee of good behavior from the king, and in the final adjustment many significant constitutional changes were effected. But the people refused to place their confidence in a monarch who had dissipated every resource of loyalty and respect, and when the barons brought him to bay at Runnymede they compelled him to sign the Great Charter, which was the chief token and instrument of the growing national consciousness.

The shortcomings and disasters of John's malignant policy stimulated England's resolution to avoid such contingencies in the future. For although the prelates and lords acted in the place of the people, they did so in a representative capacity and to a certain extent with their consent and allegiance. The Charter long remained valuable for what it promised rather than for what it actually performed; since those who drafted and signed it were either unable or unwilling to enforce its articles. Yet its presence in the political life and history of the realm was a gain which neglect obscured but could not destroy. After eighty years of comparatively inoperative existence, one of the greatest epochs, the thirteenth century, which produced Dante, St. Francis, St. Louis, and the first Edward, witnessed its vitalization under the prince last named, a king as faithful as John was perfidious. Its provisions were incorporated into the principles of his government, promoting that harmony and justice which were its steadfast bulwark.

The reign of John brought about the consummation of Papal supremacy in England, the kingdom being formally annexed as a province of the spiritual empire, whose capital was the Vatican and whose disposer was the Pope. Reform within the Church was impossible so long as it was controlled by the Curia, and Englishmen composed themselves to make the best of a situation to which they were far from being reconciled. The Charter with which Stephen Langton had been largely identified made no mention of Papal suzerainty. The implicit alliance between the throne and the clergy was severed for a long period, and notwithstanding the backset due to John's reprehensible conduct, independency reasserted itself, not only in secular affairs but also in the more personal and religious life of the nation.

III

It was a tribute to the unquestioned heroism and picturesqueness of Becket's life that Stephen Langton should have been proud to reckon him among the fathers of English liberty. Both Archbishops resented foreign intervention, and when Matthew Paris sought to make Langton a national saint he based his biography on the model of Thomas, maintaining that the two were representatives of the kingdom of England. Langton's importance is further shown by the fact that he was the connecting link between Becket and Edmund Rich and Robert Grosseteste. Rich was far removed, however, in the mildness and simplicity of his temper from the haughty and imperious Becket. The Saint of Abingdon was better fitted for the cloister than for the archiepiscopal throne, and, while his writings were full of spiritual insight and charm, he was incapable of accurate estimate or vigorous action in reference to men and affairs. Although as Archbishop he was unable to arrest the laxity and intrigue of the day, the affection of his intimate friends led to his canonization within seven years from his death.[1]

Robert Grosseteste, Chancellor[2] of Oxford University, and afterwards Bishop of Lincoln, equaled Becket in firmness and surpassed him in wisdom. His vast diocese included the present sees of Lincoln, Peterborough, Oxford, and part of Ely, and his administration affords an outstanding proof of human capacity, not only with respect to the conduct of the business of his bishopric but also to its manifold relations with the Roman Curia and the Church at large. Wycliffe, chary of his praise, gave it to Grosseteste without

[1] W. H. Hutton: "The English Saints"; p. 266.
[2] The reader should not identify the university chancellorship of that period with the office of the same name at the present time. As Bishop of Lincoln in which diocese Oxford was, Grosseteste was of course the ecclesiastical head of the University; the title of 'Chancellor' would not be given to him, however, but to his representative at Oxford.

stint. The versatility of his gifts and the extent of their exercise made him the most alert and universal intelligence in Britain. Among many appellations applied to him which indicated the admiration and love of his contemporaries were "The Lord Robert," "Robert of Lincoln," "Lincolniensis," "St. Robert," and "that great clerk Grosseteste." Roger Bacon averred he was the only man living who was in possession of all sciences, and had his warning been heeded, the University might have been diverted from its profitless plowing of the sands of later Scholasticism. He composed French verse, was well informed in law and medicine, and wrote with authority upon a wide range of subjects. His knowledge of Hebrew has been disputed; but the translations from his Greek manuscripts made by John of Basingstoke and Nicholas the Greek are not questioned, and show that Grosseteste was proficient in this language. None could deny his large and varied learning, his surpassing intellectual capacities, his consecration to duty, or his immense working powers. These endowments and attainments were evinced in his supremacy as a bishop, a theologian, and a preacher. He strove to harmonize the respective truths of natural and revealed realities, and urged his pupils and clergy to study physical science in addition to the sacred literatures in their original tongues. The vibrant energies he imparted thrilled his diocese and were felt throughout the land. But the crowning proof of his superiority was the fact that his intellectual and moral growth continued to the last. Every year found him more necessary to Church and State than before. So deserved was his reputation for determining the essence of vexed questions that those who were divided on many other matters were a unit in their reliance upon his arbitration. For his exposition and defense of public rights, for his fearless protests against foreign tyrannies, whether temporal or clerical, for his disinterested patriotism, he was venerated by his countrymen. His occasional indiscretions, which were due to defects of temperament and incurred merited rebuke, were not sufficiently grave to mar his work or limit his adaptability and usefulness; and an acquaintance with his achievements is indispensable for those who would understand the religious development of his age in the direction of freedom and of self-control.

Previously to 1247, Grosseteste had either favored or submitted to the ecclesiastical claims for which Becket died. This policy cannot be rightly judged by those for whom the Holy See is a standing conspiracy against the liberties of mankind or by those for whom it is always and everywhere an infallible organization for the regeneration and moral control of the world. An unprejudiced criticism will recognize even more clearly than the plenitude of partisan erudition that the weight of testimony is against these extreme opinions. Rome's authority, although far from perfect or desirable in every case, was not actuated solely by selfish motives, nor was it always inimical to the welfare of medieval society. Mr. Frederic Harrison's tribute to Innocent III is applicable to other Pontiffs: "His eighteen years of rule from 1198 to 1216 were one long effort, for the moment successful, and in part deserving success, to enforce on the kings and peoples of Europe a higher morality, respect for the spiritual mission of the Church, and a sense of their common civilization. We feel that he is a truly great man with a noble cause." [1] The Papacy's better side will appear again in these pages; nevertheless, when the supremacy it claimed came into conflict with the spirit of awakened nationalism, it encountered an opposition so formidable that it was driven to the devious courses of an intriguing diplomacy which it has since pursued. Without debating whether Hildebrand or Wycliffe was correct in his interpretation of the Divine presence in human affairs, we may agree to so much as this: that where absolutism once reigned it

---

[1] "The Meaning of History"; p. 150.

c

reigns no longer, and that the decentralization of its former powers is the present result of an extended and arduous experience.

When in 1250 the Crown and the Papacy again coöperated for the subjugation of the English clergy, Grosseteste condemned the alliance, and even contemplated resigning his see. But his love for the Church prevailed, and he continued his labors in extirpating abuses and promoting reforms. His loyalty to Rome never recovered from the shock it then sustained, and he openly denounced the financial expedients which Innocent IV adopted to defray the cost of his campaign against the Emperor. It was this Pontiff who demanded of Grosseteste a prebend at Lincoln for his nephew, Frederick De Lavagna, an Italian who could not speak English. The Bishop's famous reply, later known as the Sharp Epistle, is a valuable document for the study of the tendency of Anglicanism at this period.[1] He said, "It will be known to your wisdom that I am ready to obey apostolical commands with filial affection and with all devotion and reverence, but to those things which are opposed to apostolical commands, I in my zeal for the honor of my parent, am also opposed. By apostolical commands are meant those which are agreeable to the teachings of the Apostles and of Christ Himself, the Lord and Master of the Apostles, whose type and representation is specially borne in the ecclesiastical hierarchy by the Pope. The letter above mentioned is not consonant with apostolical sanctity, but utterly at variance and discord with it." Innocent was so enraged by this bold unprecedented censure from one whom he regarded as a renegade, that his Cardinals had difficulty in dissuading him from pronouncing excommunication upon the most beloved bishop in Europe. The members of the Curia, notwithstanding the fact that

[1] The Sharp Epistle was not written to Pope Innocent, but to Master Innocent, the Papal Legate in England, a fact which alters the whole drift of the document.

Grosseteste had blamed them for the oppressions he denounced, participated in the veneration freely offered to the aged and saintly churchman of spotless integrity, and besought Innocent to let him end in peace. His enemies had not long to wait; on October 9, 1253, he passed to a well-earned rest. "The Church," said the dying man, "will not be free from her Egyptian bondage except at the point of the blood-stained sword." His valiant affirmation of the apostolic rule against those who sought to degrade it had ended in a seeming failure which saddened his last hours. Actually it played a considerable part in destroying the evil she mourned, and went far to fulfill Adam Marsh's enthusiastic prediction that "it should, by the aid of God, benefit all ages to come."

The ideas and aims of Grosseteste were further developed in the writings of his friend Henry de Bracton, the well-known authority on English common law, who in his celebrated work carefully defined the always sensitive relations between Church and State. He treated clerical claims to patronage as an unwarrantable interference destructive of the regularity and equity of the civil power and administration. Decidedly national in temper and reasonable in statement, Bracton's argument was an additional example of the nature of the opposition to Papal supremacy.

Another friend and junior contemporary of the Bishop of Lincoln was Simon de Montfort, Earl of Leicester, the leading member of the oligarchic party during the Barons' War. He was regarded by the populace[1] as a saint and martyr and was eulogized as such by the Scottish chronicler of Melrose, whose comparison between him and Simon Peter, the prince of the Apostles, was probably traceable to the monk's animosity against Edward I, for whose career that of de Montfort served as a heroical but tragic prelude. His father, Simon de Montfort the elder, was noted for a crusade of persecution against the Albigenses.

[1] See Wright's "Political Songs of the Middle Ages" in the Rolls Series.

The son, born in France about the year 1200, succeeded to the earldom of Leicester in 1231, and his marriage in 1238 allied him with the royal family. Jealousies and intrigues on the part of many of the nobility caused a breach between him and the king, and for a time drove him out of England. On his return and reconciliation with Henry in 1241, however, the barons, who had hitherto regarded him as a foreign interloper, joined him in his opposition to monarchical misrule. In a song which commemorated his victory at Lewes in the year before his death the Earl was hailed as the deliverer of the Church and the avenger of her wrongs, while the king's responsibility for his own acts and his liability to correction were also proclaimed. This was a partisan tribute, but the fact that Simon became famous among English patriots and was a hearty supporter of Grosseteste's ecclesiastical reforms is established by his action in signing the protest of 1246 against the exactions of Rome. He was a practised warrior, a man of ascetical temperament and religious spirit, who championed the lower clergy and the commonalty, sought to abolish arbitrary procedure, and to promote government upon laws framed by the representatives of the people. In 1264 Henry the Third's hostility to these changes provoked a rebellion which issued in the battle of Lewes, when Simon vanquished and captured the king and his sons, Prince Edward and Richard of Cornwall. He utilized his advantage to establish a triumvirate of which he was the head, and the Council which he summoned in 1265 succeeded to some extent in controlling public affairs. This legislative body may be looked upon as the germ of the modern British Parliament, and, notwithstanding repressions and retroactions, since Simon's day England's government has never lacked a constantly increasing element of popular representation. When the natural reaction set in he was accused of having designs upon the throne, and Edward, the young heir apparent, marched against him with an army which Simon himself ᴵhad trained in military strategy. "By the arm of St. James!" he exclaimed, with a touch of soldierly pride, as he watched the advance of the royalist forces at Evesham on August 4, 1265, "they come on in wise fashion, but it was from me they learned it." He knew that the die was cast against him, and, commending his soul to God, fell fighting to the last.

The prince who redeemed the credit of his House in war renounced its favorite policy when the victory was won. Edward I discarded for the time being the Papal alliance upon which his Plantagenet predecessors had relied, and showed himself capable of appropriating the best ideas of his age. Far from abolishing representative assemblies, he saw in them the means of securing the stability of his throne and the welfare of his subjects. These objects he made his own, despite the embarrassments of his position, the exigencies of national defense, and the necessary reconstruction which followed the distractions of civil conflict. He chose in word and deed to be king of England, and the choice brought him honor and renown. His wise and zealous maintenance of law and order have earned for him the title of the Justinian of the Empire. He made that resistance to Papal interference with the affairs of the realm which was a salient characteristic of its best statesmen and rulers. In 1297 he gave his confirmation to the Charter, which had previously been neglected or openly violated, and its articles were applied with a firmness of faith and an intellectual lucidity that caused his reign to become a fountain of justice and equity, the currents of which continue their course into the present age. Boniface VIII tried out the issue when in 1296 he promulgated the bull "Clericis Laicos"[1] which forbade the taxation of ecclesiastics except by consent of the Holy See. Edward promptly retaliated by depriving the clergy of legal protection, arguing that if

[1] For a translation of the Bull "Clericis Laicos," see E. F. Henderson: "Select Historical Documents of the Middle Ages." (Bohn) pp. 432–434.

they would not contribute to the national exchequer they could not expect to share the benefits of the commonwealth. The clergy themselves were in sympathy with this position, and Boniface temporarily gave way only to reassert his authority in the case of Edward's relations to the throne of Scotland. The reply of the English Parliament to the Pope's letter indicated the extent to which the nation resented ecclesiastical supervision of its civil matters; it announced that the monarchs were not, and never had been, answerable for their political acts to any judge but their conscience and their people. Thus, at last, under Edward's directing hand, England converted into stepping-stones the obstacles placed in the path of her progress, and before the end of his reign became a united nation. Although the king was harsh and domineering, he cherished a warm affection for his subjects, who responded in kind. He revived and applied the useful measures he found in abeyance with a sense of honor and of fairness and an earnest desire to advance every legitimate interest. In this he succeeded, and his unique place in the history of England is attributable to that success. He reduced and incorporated Wales; and, had he lived and succeeded in the conquest and settlement of Scotland and Ireland, the three kingdoms might have escaped centuries of turmoil and misery. But the racial barriers between the peoples were too strong to be shattered even by his terrific impact and it was left for after ages to complete his designs of consolidation and expansion. He was fortunate in that he escaped the toils of the French wars, which enmeshed the administration of his grandson, the third Edward. He created a national parliament, a national system of justice and of taxation, and a national army. The years from 1272 to 1290 were more fruitful in historic legislation than any other period of English history before the nineteenth century, and for these laws Edward supplied the initiative. He was in truth a great monarch, second to none in the long array of those who have occupied the throne of the kingdom wherein he stimulated the development of that constitutional procedure and respect for precedent which have made modern Britain an example of practical wisdom and justice among the governments of mankind.

The disastrous career of Edward II terminated in the tragedy of his assassination at Berkeley Castle on September 21, 1327. His name is associated with famine, conspiracy, tumult, civil war, and the decisive English defeat at Bannockburn. Yet the Court which surrounded this weak, self-willed and frivolous monarch was a solidly organized institution, with traditions and resources of government that enabled it to direct every department of the State. Professor Tout argues with considerable force against the popular estimate of the second Edward's reign, and attributes its earlier failure to the policy of his father, which was on the verge of collapse at the moment of the great king's death.[1] The reasons for this statement are given in some detail and afford room for thought. On the surface, however, there was a wide and sobering contrast between the two reigns which indicated the change then sweeping over Christendom.

IV

The new spirit arose with the transfer of the Papal seat to Avignon in 1309, an event which destroyed the absolutism Hildebrand had elaborated, and which his successors, with the possible exception of Innocent III, were unable to maintain. The thirteenth century had been one of buoyancy, enthusiasm, and promise, rich in the number and character of its leaders, and memorable for their achievements in religion, philosophy, statesmanship, and art. Pulsating with conscious mental vigor, animated by high hopes and rejoicing in widened horizons of experience and reflection, rulers and peoples

[1] "The Place of the Reign of Edward II in English History."

received with gladness the stimulus of the mission of the friars to European Christianity. The colloquial speech and homespun wit of the Franciscans rescued the faith from an esoteric seclusion and communicated its joys and inspirations to the daily life of the multitude. In England they were more learned than the Dominicans, who hardly counted there, though they exercised a profound influence in continental Europe. Many schools and universities were then founded, in addition to those already existing, and a keen zest for the conquests of the mind was everywhere manifested. But the golden epoch passed into eclipse with dramatic suddenness; a strange apathy fell upon these short-lived energies; a fatal prosperity divorced the friars from their self-abnegation and from the plain folk, and diverted their zeal into material and selfish channels. It should be added, however, that during the Black Death in 1348,[1] they showed by their devoted service that an unparalleled calamity could recall them to the spiritual significance of their order. Nor were they responsible for the moral fatigue which was a universal distemper, paralyzing individual and collective efforts for betterment. Humanity in general was daunted by the melancholy retreat of courage and optimism, and refused any longer to follow the path over which shone "the high white star of truth." What had seemed to men the dawn of a new day proved to be a false light, as evanescent as the pale radiance which gleams across the northern skies.

In this gloomy environment of negation and disappointment, due to exhaustion rather than design, John Wycliffe appeared as one born out of due time. The exact place and date of the Reformer's birth are uncertain. The antiquary Leland states that he "drew his origin" from Wycliffe-on-Tees, a locality celebrated by Sir Walter Scott in "Rokeby," and in another passage he says, "John Wycliffe, Hereticus,

---

[1] The year 1349 is usually given as the date of the Black Death, though it actually began in 1348.

was born at Ipreswel, a small village a good mile off from Richmont." Neither is there now, nor was there ever, a place of this name in the vicinity of Richmond. The mistake is due to a misprint in Hearne's printed copy of Leland's "Itinerary." Ipswell, the modern name for Ipreswel, is at least ten miles from Richmond, which even Leland could hardly call a good mile, and the reference shows that he is recording gossip. There can be little doubt that Wycliffe was born at Wycliffe-on-Tees, where the tomb of his father Roger, the lord of the manor, may still be seen. The year 1320 is the earliest that can be assigned for his birth,[1] and he may have been born several years later. The differences need not detain the narrative: it is at least certain that he was a Yorkshireman, and possessed the independence and resolution native to that province. Little enough is known concerning the earlier stages of his career and some of its subsequent periods are equally vague. The last decade of his life is, however, an exception, for there his processes as a thinker and a theologian can be traced with much greater certainty than elsewhere, owing to the clearness and fullness of our knowledge of the closing phase. But centuries of neglect have obscured the external conditions of the man to whom Shirley refers as a "dim image which looks down like the portrait of the first of a long line of kings, without personality or expression."[2]

It is perhaps useless to speculate upon the circumstances and influences which shaped his formative period, although they are not without considerable interest. He received the impressions of a static community, whose lonely existence was undisturbed by the echoes of the city's crowded ways. This seclusion had compensations: it afforded him opportunity for the cultivation of sterling worth, candor,

---

[1] According to the genealogical tree in Whitaker's "Richmondshire," Roger Wycliffe and his wife Catherine were married in 1319. The eldest son would seem to have been William Wycliffe, who, however, was dead before 1362.

[2] H. B. Workman: "The Dawn of the Reformation"; Vol. I, p. 107.

and integrity; virtues which, as a rule, are better inculcated in rustic retreats than in the centers of population. The yeomanry of the Yorkshire Ridings have retained under all changes certain refreshing qualities, a goodly heritage from their progenitors. Their provincial speech, energy, determination, prudence, courage, and hatred of any form of injustice stamp them as a peculiar people, whose temper has never been disposed to indulge the arrogance of caste. A better passport to their favor is that assertive individualism which, however distasteful to the assumptions of arbitrary rank, and even injurious in some directions, has hitherto been the sustaining source of democracy. In this respect Wycliffe was a true son of the North, blunt and incisive in address, with an unconscious equality of manner, and a passionate sympathy for the unfortunate and the poor which inspired his disconcerting fierceness of attack upon their oppressors. That such an advocate of the cause of the proletariat in religion and in politics should have emerged from the remotest dales of a shire, at that period rude and unvisited, is another of the many vouchers for the debt the race owes the wilderness and its children.

Living as he did in so retired a spot, Wycliffe's early instruction was probably received from the village priest, who usually dwelt with the manorial family and taught the rudiments of Latin, rhetoric, dialectics, arithmetic, and geometry. The conjecture that he was educated at a monastery school cannot be substantiated, since these institutions no longer opened their doors to outsiders. Nor is there any evidence that he attended one of the schools maintained by collegiate churches, by chantry priests, and by the guilds of various towns.

Lechler surmises that he was fourteen or possibly sixteen years old when he entered Oxford. That some students were no older is evident from the comment of Richard Fitzralph, Archbishop of Armagh, who complained that many youths under fourteen years of age were already con-

sidered members of the University. Lechler's reckoning is
based upon 1320 as the year of Wycliffe's birth, but if
this date is too early, the surmise is incorrect. It is highly
probable that he was still in his nonage when he began
the southward journey along the great Roman road which
ran from the Cheviot Hills to London and passed near his
father's house. He would not lack for company: students,
like other wayfarers, banded together for mutual protection
against lusty rogues and outlaws who infested the high-
ways, and sometimes robbed them of their baggage and
entrance fees even in sight of their destination. After
ten days of more or less excitement and peril, the intrenched
and walled fourteenth century town, with its encircling waters
and massive Norman keep commanding the approaches
which converged from the surrounding hills, would be in full
view.

V

Oxford is situated in the middle reaches of the Thames
valley, and shares that beautiful pastoral scenery for which
the river is noted from Richmond to Sonning Bridge. The
ruins of its ancient fortifications remain to show its
former strategical importance, and its venerable appearance is enhanced by the gray fronts of halls and colleges
along "the High" and other thoroughfares. But the
thriving borough did not arise, as many have imagined, in
response to the needs of the colleges; the place enjoyed
five hundred years of municipal and commercial prominence
before any student was seen in its streets. Equally erroneous
are the popular beliefs regarding the beginnings of the
University itself. That the great seat of learning had its
inception in one of the schools established by Alfred the
Great is only another of the many legends which historical
research has compelled antiquaries to relinquish. Nor
did the fame of churches and monasteries of Oxford have
anything to do with the origin of those schools which were

afterwards merged into the University. It is far nearer the truth to say that Oxford's classical reputation was an outgrowth of its geographical location and civic strength. The earliest mention on which reliance can be placed refers to the nunnery founded by St. Frideswide during the turmoil of the eighth century, on or near the site of the present Cathedral. A brief entry in the Anglo-Saxon Chronicle for 912 states that Edward the Elder, the successor of Alfred, "took possession of London and Oxenford and of all the lands which owed obedience thereto." [1] The ravages of the Danish wars afterwards fell heavily upon the town, which was then a frontier fortress of the Mercian and West Saxon kingdoms, and involved it in burning and destruction. The citizens repaired the mischief wrought by fire and siege in 979, 1002, and 1010, and subsequently Oxford continued to be a theater of national gatherings.

The security of tenure which followed the Norman Conquest promoted the town's growth and trade, and transformed the architecture of its religious and public buildings. In 1074 the collegiate church of St. George arose within the recently constructed castle; the priory, afterwards called the Abbey of Austin Canons, was erected in the next century; the palace of Beaumont was built by Henry I in the fields to the north. The church of the monastery of St. Frideswide, which at the Reformation became the Cathedral of the new diocese, dates from the same period, and these indefatigable masons also renovated the existing parish churches. One of the wealthiest of English Jewries was planted in the center of the town: a settlement having its own religion, language, dress, laws, customs, and commerce, independent of local authorities and subject only to the Crown. There is no doubt that Oxford's general progress was promoted by the financial loans of wealthy Hebrews, and that indirectly its academic methods felt the influence of their rabbis, whose volumes aided the first researches of

[1] James Parker: "The Early History of Oxford"; p. 116.

physical scientists and gave Roger Bacon access to the older world of material inquiry.[1]

While it is not our immediate purpose to deal at length with the interesting details of those educational facilities which were mainly due to the faith and energy of the thirteenth and fourteenth centuries, they should receive the consideration commensurate with their importance. Their larger beginnings have been ascribed to a migration of scholars from Paris, which took place about the year 1169. Such migrations were perfectly congruous with the nomadic habits of medieval clerks, and those universities in Northern Europe which did not arise in connection with some prominent collegiate church were the offspring of a similar exodus. The history of the University of Paris has emerged from the uncritical period when the foundation was attributed to Charles the Great, although his fame as a founder is still celebrated thoughout the colleges of France by an annual festival named in his honor.[2] What the Emperor actually did was to establish collegiate schools in the municipalities of his dominions,[3] and of these the "École du Parvis Notre Dame" eventually won a high reputation, surpassing its rivals at Chartres and Laon. With the widening of intellectual activity the curriculum broadened, while the growth of culture and the decay of monasticism increased the demand for new sources of education and for the better training of the secular clergy. During the eleventh century learned theologians taught there and also at the adjacent school of St. Genevieve, among them being Gerbert, afterward Pope Sylvester II, Fulbert, and Beranger of Tours. But to the brilliant pupil of William of Champeaux, Abailard, and to the successors he trained,

[1] John Richard Green: "Oxford Studies"; p. 9.
[2] This new lord of the world was not a Frenchman, but a German, a fact which the French appellation Charlemagne has frequently obscured.
[3] He designed to have collegiate churches in which the clergy should live together with one of their number, called the Chancellor, responsible for education. Hence arose the title of Chancellor in universities.

men who "grew straight in the strength of his spirit," Paris owed her academic prestige, and the natural evolution of the University out of her schools. Abailard, at that time a layman, commenced a school of his own near to that of St. Genevieve, where not less than five thousand scholars are said to have attended his lectures.[1] His youth and genius, illimitable lore, and audacity were assets of a magnetic personality which drew to itself many future dignitaries of the Church, including a pontiff, nineteen cardinals, and fifty bishops; within a short period after his death the University became the Mecca of European students, scholars, and doctors.[2] Again, Abailard's prominence fifty years after the death of Anselm, the greatest of monastic teachers, showed that higher education had escaped the control of the regular clergy, and that their essential selfishness was gradually driving it to seek other leaders. Moreover, the conflict between the claims of reason and those of faith, which was always imminent, was precipitated by the fears of the clergy that in his efforts to unify all knowledge Abailard would minimize the importance of theology. He finally became a Benedictine in 1119, but this did not save him from condemnation by the Church.

In 1201 Philip Augustus, who reigned from 1180 to 1223, and was in many respects the reincarnation of the far-seeing spirit of Charles the Great, gave the schools exemption from civil jurisdiction. Masters and scholars were placed under the control of ecclesiastical tribunals. In 1212, when the Chancellor, as the Bishop's representative, sought to compel all masters to take an oath of obedience to himself, Innocent III interposed, defeated the scheme of the local hierarchy to control the schools, and forbade the oath. During the

[1] Medieval statistics should be received warily. Wycliffe, for instance, states that there were thirty thousand scholars at Oxford, when its population was not quite five thousand.

[2] The Isle de Cité never was the center of University life; St. Genevieve was the place where the University grew, and became the rival of the School of Notre Dame.

carnival of 1229 a riot arose in a Paris tavern, like unto the quarrel which began the "Great Slaughter" at Oxford in 1354, whereupon the police of the provost savagely suppressed the students, leaving several of their number dead. The masters demanded redress for the outrage, and, failing to obtain it, dissolved the University for six years and retired with their scholars to Oxford, Cambridge, and Angers. Eventually Gregory IX exercised his good offices, the court and the municipal authorities promptly assisted him, and in 1231 the University returned to Paris, confirmed in its former charter and with the grant of additional exemptions. It was finally incorporated by St. Louis, who succeeded to the throne in 1226.

Among the distinguished foreigners who visited or studied at Paris were John of Salisbury, St. Thomas Aquinas, Roger Bacon, Raymond Lully, and Stephen Langton. Dante is reputed to have attended lectures there in 1309, Petrarch boasted of the crown the University proffered him, and, as late as the sixteenth century, Tasso came to the schools of France, Normandy, Picardy, and Germany, situated in the Rue du Fouarre. At the center of the city stood then, as it now stands, Notre Dame, the spiritual citadel of the capital. The Sainte Chapelle, inclosed by the ancient palace of the kings, arose hard by, the most definite, delicate, and graceful monument of French Gothic architecture. The area extending from the south bank of the Seine up Mont St. Genevieve had been surrendered to the expanding schools. From the hill of the patron saint its buildings, gardens, and open spaces sloped steeply down past the ruined residence of the Roman emperors to the river and the Isle de la Cité.

At the height of its power and throughout the Middle Ages, this place was the intellectual center of Christendom, as Rome was its political and ecclesiastical metropolis. The University practically dictated the theology of the Church, and even the Popes were careful about controversy with the doctors of Paris concerning dogmatic statements. It was more completely cosmopolitan than any modern seat of learning; scholars from all parts of Europe repaired there for instruction from its gifted teachers, and, since those who came could, and doubtless did, return in great numbers to their respective homes, there is no difficulty in accepting the statement that a body of English students left Paris and built up a studium at Oxford when recalled by their monarch, Henry II, during his dispute with the French king. Again, the presence in Oxford of such teachers as the legist Vacarius, Thibaut d'Estampes, and Robert Pullein, which anticipated this incursion, had served to raise the city's reputation. Vacarius visited it during the reign of Stephen: he lectured there in 1149, and prepared a compendium in nine books of the Digest and Code of Justinian. When the king ordered him to desist from lecturing, Vacarius is said to have been rewarded with a prebend in the church of secular canons at Southwell.[1]

Beyond the events narrated, the causes which operated to make the already ancient town the seat of the second university in Europe are far from obvious. For some time after the exodus from Paris it was naturally overshadowed by that seat of learning of which it was the offspring, and which played a noble part in European civilization. Yet forty years after the time of Vacarius, Oxford's scholastic standing was well won; at the opening of the thirteenth century she was supreme in her own country, and had also obtained the recognition of older continental foundations.

The medieval meaning of such terms as university and college should not be confused with their modern connotation. The Latin word *universitas*, from which the English derivation comes, originally denoted any collective body, regarded as such. When employed in a strictly educational sense it

---

[1] The name of Vacarius does not appear in Le Neve's "Fasti," the index of which has been examined by the author at the British Museum. This would cast doubt on the preferment of Vacarius to the prebend.

was supplemented by an additional phrase, the current expression being, "Universitas magistrorum et scholarium." In late fourteenth century usage the term university was defined as a community of teachers and scholars whose corporate existence had secured the consent and approval of either or both civil and ecclesiastical authorities. The term *studium* and later *studium generale*, denoting a center of instruction open to all, was the more customary designation of these communities. The studium generale slowly evolved into the universitas at such well-known places as Paris, Bologna, and Oxford, and in the case of the two former cities the change was confirmed by Papal bulls, issued in the reign of Nicholas IV. The word college was simply the old Latin *collegium*, which signified any organized guild, religious, educational, industrial, or political, applied in course of time to secular priests living in common, and afterwards to those residences at Oxford where secular students did likewise.

The distinctive features of the English college system are found in the final form of the Statutes of Merton bearing the date 1274 and the seals of the first Edward. The original code, which perpetuates the name of the ecclesiastical statesman, Walter de Merton, Chancellor of England, was drawn up ten years earlier, in 1264, and was itself the result of previous schemes for the maintenance of indigent scholars at Malden in Surrey. The generous endowments provided by Merton were employed for the benefit of twenty students and two or three priests for whom a hall was to be set apart at Oxford, or elsewhere, if such a lodging was procurable at a more flourishing seat of learning. This design was afterwards expanded, rules of collegiate discipline were enacted, and eventually Oxford became the permanent home of these students. The intellectual freedom of the college marked a departure from the monastic idea, prevented it from being a nursery for the advocates of Papal supremacy, and enabled it to train a succession of graduates who rendered

D

efficient service to Church and State. These measures, as bold in their innovation as they were beneficial and far reaching, became the sources of a normal policy of administration under which colleges superseded monasteries and halls as the residences of students and strongholds of discipline. It was apparent that they could not realize such aims without buildings which should be a nucleus for the accumulation of the best traditions of the past and of worthy purposes for the future. In this undertaking Merton's efforts were seconded by the foundation of New College in 1379, under the patronage of William de Wykeham, Bishop of Winchester. The last of the great episcopal architects of the Middle Ages, Wykeham, was perhaps more renowned for his structures than for his statesmanship. He adorned the bare Norman interior of his cathedral with the Perpendicular style, and the school he established in the former capital city shares with Eton the honor of being a college in the true sense of the word. But his rank as the second founder of the college system is determined by the grandeur and regularity of the noble quadrangle and still nobler chapel which were the most dignified and beautiful of their kind Oxford had yet seen. That which Merton had accomplished in the statutory regulations of the colleges, Wykeham furthered by their architectural dignity and domestic comfort as compared with the older hostels.[1]

VI

In any attempt to recall the Oxford of Saxon, Norman, and later eras, the modern city must be dismissed from the mind. There was little in the outward aspect of its humble genesis and slow development, retarded by violent periods of war, riot, and pestilence, to suggest those mystical enchantments which owe much to the hand of Time. The bewitching vision, steeped in sentiment, of graceful towers,

[1] G. C. Brodrick: "History of the University of Oxford"; pp. 32–33.

quiet cloisters, embowered gardens, immemorial elms, and lawns of living green,

> "Where a thousand gray stones smile and sigh,
> A thousand rustling trees,"

is very largely the growth of later days. When Wycliffe entered the place he plunged into a bewildering maze of mean, filthy streets, lined with dingy hovels and crowded with a jostling, brawling throng of townsmen, priests, scholars, and vagrants. Within the houses the floors and halls were strewn with rushes, beneath which accumulated refuse decayed, the windows were unglazed, the chambers airless and pestiferous, the atmosphere reeked with foul odors. Single rooms served for the common purposes of cooking, dining, visiting, and sleeping. Sanitation was unknown, and frequently dirt was regarded as a sign of sanctity. Even the homes of the better classes were not exempt from these conditions; and the churches and church-yards were indescribably noisome. Courts and lanes, in which darkness prevailed, were knee deep with feculent matter and rendered dangerous by open cesspools. The recurring pestilences which decimated Europe can be understood when it is remembered that these barbarous habits were characteristic of continental and English towns. The wonder is, not that so many died, but rather that so many escaped death. Yet, notwithstanding the toleration of such evils, there was in Oxford, as in many other municipalities of the later Middle Ages, a sense of civic virtue and of social obligation which eventually established better conditions.

In the meantime, religious duty, though vaguely conceived in many practical directions, was the source of genuine corporate life and unity. Master and man, teacher and student, trader and artisan, knew how to think and act together because they were held in the bonds of a catholic faith. The thirteenth century was distinguished by the founding of University, Balliol, and Merton Colleges; the fourteenth, by that of Oriel, Exeter, Queens, and New Colleges. Thus Oxford's high water mark in architecture and other material provisions for education was attained in an era when the country at large was devastated by plagues and insurrections.

We have already noted the dissimilarity between the intelligent energy and design of the twelfth and thirteenth centuries and the comparative confusion and barrenness of the age of Wycliffe. For nearly two hundred years the uniform depression of the Middle Ages had been broken by an interval, the enthusiasms and aspirations of which were too generous to be permanent. The revulsion which followed sprang from an utter weariness of soul, accentuated by bitter disappointments, painful uncertainties, and widespread distrust. Men were not willfully disobedient; they were sorely spent, and unable any longer to realize the vision which disappears when it is neglected. Such enervation is still the human fate: the cycles of day and night persist, and though the one is not so welcome, it is as natural as the other. Yet we are not at liberty to suppose that every good cause was wrecked or forsaken. The edifices and endowments which are now not only a national but practically a world-wide heritage were, in part, the products of the period many historians have unsparingly denounced. They cannot be dissociated from their authors, who, if the buildings are a guide, well knew that they were dealing with the fortunes of an enduring institution. They may have foreseen that these structures would help to convey to future generations the changes, the conflicts, the questionings, the reactions, and the advances which have been experienced in the past six hundred years. The sway of such personalities as Walter de Merton and William of Wykeham is still felt within Oxford's precincts, and all its founders share in the honor, the gladness, the suffering, and the achievement of the life of scholarship. Some deeds these men did are best buried with their bones, but their toil for the first University of the English-speaking nations should be gratefully remembered, not only there, but also here in the New World, of whose mission they were the forerunners. It was wrought when immense impediments had to be overcome, in an age of sparse and ignorant populations cursed by poverty and superstition. And the greatest glory of these men and of their buildings was not in stone nor gold, but in that essential spirituality, that stern watchfulness, that meritorious sympathy, that approval or condemnation, of which John Ruskin speaks, and which is felt, if anywhere, in such places as Oxford, whose walls have so long been "washed by the passing waves of humanity."

VII

The absence of personal references in the writings of Wycliffe compels us to glean our ideas of his university life from the academic conditions of the period. As a northern man he would probably find his way to Balliol College, and the belief long held that in 1356 he was a fellow of Merton, together with the fact that his name was enrolled among the commoners of Queens, is best explained by the contemporary presence in Oxford of two other John Wycliffes with whom he has been confused. Workman states that one of these was an almonry boy at Queens;[1] the second a portionist at Merton.[2]

Balliol was founded between the years 1263 and 1268[3] by John Balliol of Barnard Castle, Yorkshire, the father of the nobleman to whom Edward I assigned the crown of Scotland and whom he afterwards deposed in 1292. The northern and southern "nations," whose feud disturbed for centuries the order of the place, had their headquarters

---

[1] Almonry boy: one who in return for elementary instruction served in the chapel choir or rendered other services. He was generally lodged under the care of the Almoner.

[2] Portionist: A scholar supported on the foundation of the college.

[3] The most assured date is shortly before June, 1266, when a hall was

at Balliol and Merton respectively, and the lines were so sharply drawn that from 1334 onward Merton refused to admit northern scholars into its society. Minor rivalries inflamed the quarrel, which influenced academic action, and especially the election of the Chancellor, whose assistants were known as the northern and southern proctors. The frequent fights and riotous behavior of these and other factions led in 1274 to the adoption of the "Concordia," the precise articles of which read like those of a treaty of peace between hostile powers rather than an act of university legislation. But they did not prevent the disturbances against which they were enacted: a fierce uproar in 1297 and a brutal affray of the student clans in 1319 evidenced the militant lawlessness of such groups. The "Great Slaughter" of 1354, although a town and gown affair, gave further proof of the anarchical conditions which then prevailed. The scholars were herded together in miserable chambers and lecture rooms, where care and comfort were unknown; college governance was still very primitive, while that of the University had scarcely begun. The frank and intimate relations which afterwards became the cohesive bond of varying classes were then all but impossible by reason of the existing provincialism and poverty. The latter state obliged medieval students to obtain manual labor for support, and at intervals they even took to the road and begged for a pittance.

The resources of knowledge were few and unsatisfactory; museums and libraries which are now at the service of all were then beyond the wildest dreams. Wycliffe and his fellow clerks pored over the faded characters of worn manuscripts in chambers deprived of the sun by day, and in a nightly darkness faintly relieved by flickering oil lamps or rushlights. The nature and extent of their learning were

founded for sixteen poor students. John Balliol died two years later, in 1268, and the College received its greatest aid from his wife, Dervorgilla, whose benefactions date from 1284, when Balliol first obtained a house of its own.

amazing; their industry probably surpassed that of any later scholars. They lived a separated life, avoiding the ordinary recreations and athletic exercises of the youth of England, with no outdoor pursuits or pastimes to vary their arduous study. Yet its tasks were illuminated by the ambitions which burned within them the more steadily because of their privations. Regardless of the din and revelry of drunken roysterers in alley and lane, the best of these men plodded steadily onward, memorizing or copying mysterious phraseologies which are now meaningless, but were then accepted and conned as primary truths that might at any turn in their pursuit reveal a universal law prevailing throughout the whole realm of knowledge. Those who were able to endure the necessary exertion of body and mind knew the joy of the strong; their intellectual capacities became firm and flexible, and, had these students enjoyed the advantages of the scientific method, they would have demonstrated their superiority over successors who have been more fortunate in their environment, but not in native or acquired ability. It ill becomes their heirs to mock at efforts which, though wrongly directed, still merit the recognition due to heroic striving.

That men of the type of Wycliffe sometimes fell short of the goal is nothing against them, since they accomplished all that was possible in the nature of their studies. Meanwhile, their failure cleared the ground for the New Learning of the next century. Only as the theories they painfully evolved proved worthless, could thinkers be made to understand that their system was insufficient, and thus be set free to pursue more correct methods of investigation. In this way they helped to transfer the center of gravity from deduction to induction, from dogmatic assumption to experiment and hypothesis. The progress of human affairs owes something to these indirect courses, in which steadfast men strove to attain truth by means of conceptions which, although in themselves imperfect, eventually pointed to the substance of which they were the shadow.

Again, the monastic influence at Oxford had steadily waned from the days of Edmund Rich, whose beautiful and pathetic story heightened the religious temper of the University, but could not check its tendency toward secular inquiry. Where monasticism as a spiritual ideal separated itself from the world, it frequently fell a victim to the forces it despised; on the other hand, where it linked itself with other systems it invariably lost its professed sanctity. In its purest form it was averse to unhampered development in any direction save that of mystical speculation, and when the laity asserted their title to a place in the sun of assured knowledge, the gradual emancipation of learning from clerical tutelage was unavoidable. These causes explain the fact that the monastic colleges are of minor importance in the history of education. The monks never heartily applied themselves to the scholastic philosophy, and the older monastic orders did not produce a single first class theologian from St. Bernard's time to the closing days of medievalism. The coming of the friars gave a fresh impetus to clericalism, and the Benedictines [1] strove to remedy the shortcomings of their order by sending a few selected members to the University.[2] But they could not repress the laical spirit in the colleges which grew apace under the sheltering protection of the Church. Their general contact with an ampler existence began in the latter half of the twelfth century, and despite the contraction of the syllabus in the direction of dialectics, before the close of Edward the Third's

[1] As a matter of fact there never was any monastic control of education at Oxford, nor did the monasteries make any effort to set up foundations there until the Chapter General of the Benedictines held at Abingdon in 1289, which imposed a levy of two pence in the mark to build a hall. In 1284 temporary provision was made for the Benedictines in a house on Stockwell Street. The first real monastic college was Gloucester Hall, built in 1291.

[2] These were few indeed. Christ Church monastery at Canterbury rarely found that it could maintain more than four students at Christ Church, Oxford, and the total number of monks at the University was always small.

reign they had become sufficiently national to justify the description of their secular aims contained in the third book of Gower's "Vox Clamantis." This temper fostered conceptions which questioned those accepted dogmas that had hitherto been the staple themes of instruction. Nor can there be any doubt that it influenced Wycliffe, the bent of whose mind harmonized with its aggressiveness.

It was not as a semi-ecclesiastical corporation, but as a center of religious vitality and positive thinking that the Oxford he knew contributed to the shaping of character both in men and in the times. It had been said of Paris that whatever was read and taught there was sooner or later read and taught in Oxford. But, with the rupture of the once close intimacy of the two institutions, this subserviency had ceased, and the younger no longer shone in a borrowed light. She boasted doctors of her own, whose daring and versatility outdistanced those of the older and more conservative body at Paris.[1] Wycliffe's relations to these thinkers and the subjects they discussed can be set forth later; meanwhile it should be noted that some of them were in latent opposition to the orthodox systems of the Middle Ages. Their feudal presumptions depended on the segregation of human groups, and necessarily decreased when arbitrary distinctions of blood and birth lost ground. Their alignments had hitherto been determined by the accidents of temporal boundaries and by the paramountcy of those material forces which are generally recognized as subversive of the social order. Against this condition as a whole the European schools were at once a protest and to some extent a remedy. The students who frequented them were known as the "nations," and the universities earned the credit of creating and welding together the most liberal and international of fraternities. Notwithstanding their internal bickerings and jealousies they shared a classical

[1] H. Rashdall: "Universities of Europe in the Middle Ages"; Vol. II, pp. 519–520.

language which, however badly construed and spoken, was at least freed from the strife of variant tongues. Intellectual kinships throve apace, the doctrines of celebrated masters were diffused in widely separated communities, and leavened the fear and dislike which had rendered every foreigner suspect.[1]

Chaucer's familiar lines indicate the good impression which the best type of student made on the people at large:

> " A Clerk ther was of Oxenford also,
> That un-to logik hadde longe y-go.
> As lene was his hors as is a rake,
> And he nas nat right fat, I undertake;
> But loked holwe, and ther-to soberly.
> Ful thredbar was his overest courtepy;
> For he had geten him yet no benefyce,
> Ne was so worldly for to have offyce.
> For him was lever have at his beddes heed
> Twenty bokes, clad in blak or reed,
> Of Aristotle and his philosophye,
> Than robes riche, or fithele, or gay sautrye.
> But al be that he was a philosophre,
> Yet hadde he but litel gold in cofre;
> But al that he might of his freendes hente,
> On bokes and on lerninge he it spente,
> And bisily gan for the soules preye
> Of hem that yaf him wher-with to scoleye.
> Of studie took he most cure and most hede,
> Noght o word spak he more than was nede,
> And that was seyd in forme and reverence,
> And short and quik, and ful of hy sentence.
> Souninge in moral vertu was his speche.
> And gladly wolde he lerne, and gladly teche." [2]

His unpretentious appearance, mute evidence of the hardships of a life devoted to knowledge and to the memories of pious founders, not only disarmed prejudice, but commended him to public esteem and confidence. Monks and

[1] The "nations" at Paris were fourfold: those of France, Picardy, Normandy, and England. The English "nation" included the Scotch and Germans. At Oxford there were but two nations, the Australs and the Boreals.

[2] Prof. W. W. Skeat's edition.

friars no longer secured the donations of the great and
wealthy for their religious houses. Instead, these gifts
were bestowed upon the secular clergy, who were rapidly
formulating an ethical and political system deriving its
principles elsewhere than from the Church, and setting up
a rival authority not yet clearly defined, but nevertheless
sedulously maintained. In summary, it can be said that in
an age of change and doubt, when human life was deprived
of the light of a former faith, the gloom was pierced at intervals by the radiance which streamed from the colleges.

VIII

We obtain a glimpse of Wycliffe at Oxford between the
years 1356 and 1360, when he was elected Master of Balliol,
an office not then by any means so considerable as now, but
for which he could hardly have become a candidate had he
not been a fellow of that institution. In 1361 he relinquished it for the college living of Fillingham in Lincolnshire; in the same year "John de Wyclif of the diocese of
York, M. A." petitioned the Roman Curia for his designation
to a prebend, canonry, and dignity at York, "notwithstanding that he holds the church at Fillingham." The
prayer was answered, though not as Wycliffe desired, and
on November 24th, 1369, he received the prebend of Aust
in the collegiate church of Westbury-on-Trym, near Bristol.[1]
It is probable that Wycliffe occupied this benefice; and the
latest investigations show that the connection of his name
with the Wardenship of Canterbury Hall, although deemed
erroneous by some, has substantial evidence in its favor.
The Hall was planned to shelter both seculars and monks,
an intention frustrated by their endless wranglings from

---

[1] There was nothing unusual in this preferment on the part of the Pope;
it was really a medieval equivalent of the modern fellowship, and was
granted to such masters as were selected by the Pontiff from the lists which
the universities submitted.

1365 to 1371. Small importance, however, is attached to Wycliffe's association here, save that in after years his enemies attributed his attacks upon the religious orders to the severe treatment he was then supposed to have received from Archbishop Langham. The diocesan registers of Lincoln state that in 1368 Bishop Buckingham granted Wycliffe two years' leave of absence from his church in order that he might devote himself to the study of letters at the University. About this time he exchanged his living at Fillingham for the rectorate of Ludgershall, in Buckinghamshire, which brought him within sixteen miles of Oxford. In 1372, after sixteen years of incessant preparation, he obtained the coveted degree in divinity which gave him the right to lecture on theology, and in the following year the Pope conferred upon his "dilectissimus filius" a canonry of Lincoln, while allowing him to retain the prebend he already held at Aust.

From these fragmentary records, some of which are far from explicit, two facts distinctly emerge. The first is that he was a pluralist and an absentee rector, accepting and practising the customs he afterwards denounced ; the second, that his return to Oxford was utilized for the further enrichment of his learning. His controversy with the Papal authority had not yet arisen, and the mistaken assertion that he published his "Determinatio Quædam de Dominio" in 1366 as a protest against the tribute levied by Urban V, is without admissible support. This work contained only hints of his doctrine of "lordship," and was not written until at least seven years after the Pope's levy. During the interval before the storm, wind and tide were with him, no untoward circumstances sapped his strength or diverted his attention from that philosophy in which, as Knighton avers, "he was second to none: in the training of the schools without a rival." Arundel, the relentless foe of the Lollards, bore testimony to the purity of his personal life, acknowledging to Thorpe that "Wycliffe was a great

clerk, and many men held him a perfect liver." Some of his
lectures have been preserved in an unrevised notebook
where the display of their range and erudition is only equaled
by their complete mastery of the Holy Scriptures.[1]

His endowments shed a departing gleam upon the philosophical system of which he was the last exponent, and
from the fascinations of which he never freed himself. In
the perspective of history he stands forth as one of the
dominant figures in "a mighty and astonishing style of
scholarship which, doubtless from the absence of the proper
social conditions, will never be seen again." [2] It has already
been affirmed that in the fourteenth century Oxford's
philosophers surpassed those of any European university,
and that in increasing numbers they were not cloistered but
secular clergy. Certainly at no earlier time could the
seculars have claimed three such doctors as Thomas Bradwardine, Richard Fitzralph, and John Wycliffe. The
Reformer's political employments and controversies were
not without detrimental effects, but they came late in life,
when the gaze of friends and foes alike was fixed upon his
formidable power of advocacy. The massive intellect of the
man, his strong personality, his gift of lucid and weighty
utterance, immediately brought his colleagues in the University under the spell of his influence, and eventually won
him preferment in the Church and an international reputation.

[1] H. B. Workman: "The Dawn of the Reformation"; Vol. I, pp. 113–114.
[2] John Fiske: "Darwinism and Other Essays"; p. 250.

CHAPTER II

SOURCES OF WYCLIFFIANISM

WHEN religion and the interest of the soul are the subjects of debate, the sparks of human energy are kindled as by a charm, and spread with the rapidity of an electric fluid. Opinions work upon actions, and actions react upon opinions; the defense of truth or error stirs up the moral powers, and leads men on to deeds of vigor, and the effects of active zeal reflect upon the opinions and systems of men, and raise them to those heights of speculative and logical abstraction, which are the wonder of beholders and the engima of future generations.

Life of St. Germanus.

CHAPTER II

I

AT this time Wycliffe had achieved the desire of his heart; his associations with Oxford were destined to be prolonged and memorable, and from there his prolific pen gave forth those larger works on philosophy and theology which are now seldom read. Many of his pamphlets and treatises on papal claims and imposts, the political status of the clergy, indulgences, and other contentious issues were also written at the University. His friendship with its teachers and doctors was a welcome aid and a protection in his hours of loneliness and danger. And when in his declining years its leaders forsook him, their desertion was a severe blow to his propaganda. In the interval, if the practical affairs of the nation were benefited by his diversified yet systematized knowledge, those which related to religious and clerical questions were quite as fortunate. His utterances and writings were very unequal in merit,

E   49

but the best of them were not mere turgid rhetoric pro-
fusely poured out; they crystallized around an axiomatic
and intrepid reasoning which was the imperative working
principle in many of his intellectual and literary efforts.   His
premises may not be ours; indeed, we may think them often
obscure or incomplete, and at times unwarranted.   Yet it
is patent that some were carefully chosen, and while in the
absence of the inductive method the matter of his argument
was frequently at fault, its form was usually correct.   In
brief, Wycliffe was a Schoolman, whose strength and weakness were alike due to an inherited system which should
be explained in order that his merits as a thinker may be
appreciated.

Scholasticism was an able and praiseworthy attempt to
reconcile the dogmas of faith with the dictates of reason,
and thus formulate an inclusive system on the presup-
position that the creed of the Church was the one reality
capable of rationalization.   As the product of Christian
intellectualism, it acted under the Aristotelian method,
and was governed by the fundamental assumption that all
phenomena must be understood from and toward theology.
The early Fathers had bequeathed to their successors a
well-articulated and comprehensive theological dogma,
and also the philosophical apparatus which determined
and shaped its content.   When the Schoolmen realized the
nature of the bequest they endeavored to recover the spirit
of inquiry which lay behind its results, and consequently
the Church entered, almost automatically, upon a period
of stress and strain similar to those she had previously
experienced.   Now, however, additional factors intervened
and intensified the situation.   The organization and growth
of the Papacy reinforced the predicates of authority, catholicity, dogmatism, and the predominance of spiritual claims,
while the imperial influence of St. Augustine was widely
diffused in contemporary theology.

The Scholastic system can be surveyed in two nearly

equal divisions of the period extending from the ninth to the
end of the fifteenth century. The first of these divisions,
which terminated with the twelfth century, was represented
by Erigena,[1] Roscellinus, Anselm, William of Champeaux
and his pupil Abailard; the second, by Albertus Magnus,
Thomas Aquinas, Duns Scotus, and William of Ockham.
The science of these scholars, in so far as that term is applicable, dealt almost exclusively with divinity. Yet theirs
was an age of reason as well as of faith, and no part of their
work could be canceled without a shock to the continuity
of progress. It is easy for the disciples of later intellectualism to say that their pursuit of truth was a mockery, since
they started upon the journey carrying their convictions
with them, or that they fabricated absurd and ridiculous
problems and then proceeded to demonstrate their validity
or invalidity. The Schoolmen do not deserve these gibes;
they keenly felt the spiritual experiences on which they
discoursed, and craved an adequate defense for them.
Careless criticism of their action has been displaced by
the weighty judgment of Harnack, that their system "gives
practical proof of eagerness in thinking and exhibits an
energy in subjecting all that is real and valuable to thought
to which we can find, perhaps, no parallel in any other
age."[2] If their philosophy was not an effective means for
enriching knowledge, it was a method for the training of the
intellect which strengthened the reasoning powers and prepared them for penetrative and comprehensive work. In
these respects the metaphysic of the Middle Ages is closely
related to that of later experimental schools; its mission was
to expand and invigorate the human mind until the boundless fields of the natural sciences were opened to research.

[1] Erigena was really of the spiritual tradition of the Christian Mystics
and intellectually a Neo-Platonist, rather than a typical Scholastic. He
may be regarded as a connecting link between these schools and the more
pronounced Scholasticism which predominated from the eleventh to the
fourteenth centuries.

[2] "History of Dogma"; Vol. VI, p. 25.

The two camps of Realists and Nominalists furnished the material for scholastic discussion. The Introduction to the "Isagoge" of Porphyry, the Neo-Platonist, anticipated the differences which afterwards separated them. "Next concerning genera and species the question indeed whether they have a substantial existence, or whether they consist in bare intellectual concepts only, or whether if they have a substantial existence they are corporeal or incorporeal, and whether they are inseparable from the insensible properties of things, or are only in these properties and subsisting about them, I shall forbear to determine, for a question of this kind is very deep." The majority of his readers will undoubtedly cheerfully acquiesce in this decision.

The Realists contended that reality belonged only to universal conceptions, and that particulars of any kind were merely mental conveniences. For example, the term "house" did not denote the thing itself, but only the immaterial idea. This reasoning was also applied to man, for whom reality consisted in the humanity shared with all men and not in a distinct ego. Individuality was entirely dependent upon its participation in the general essence of the species. Everything in heaven and on earth was primarily of one substance with the all-comprehending Universal Being. The germs of the Pantheism of Spinoza can be detected here, and also those of later forms of Idealism. The Nominalists maintained that universals were merely terms, and that reality had no meaning apart from the individual and the particular; intellectual conceptions and universal relations being purely mental processes without any actual existence. These unqualified assertions were sufficiently damaging to orthodoxy to alarm its supporters. Their instincts revolted against a doctrine of which, as Dr. Rashdall comments, the skeptical sensationalism of Hume and the crudest forms of later materialism were but illogical attenuations. Yet, while Nominalism did not secure any permanent hold upon the accepted theology of the Church, its insistence that the particular and the individual were the only realities paved the way for the inductive method in physical investigation.

II

Realism received its greatest exposition and defense from St. Thomas Aquinas, an Italian of rank and the Schoolman par excellence, who lived from 1227 to 1274. The pupil of Albertus Magnus in the Dominican school at Cologne, in 1245 he followed his master to Paris, where he graduated in theology, after which he returned to Cologne to become assistant to Albertus. Aquinas surpassed all other teachers as the embodied essence of Scholasticism and the most admirable example of the spirit and doctrine of the medieval Church.[1] His "Summa Theologiæ" is an unequaled effort, in which the mysteries of the Christian faith and the certitudes of the human reason are defined as the two sources of knowledge. While they are distinct in themselves, revelation has the indisputable priority, since, as the fountain of absolute truth, it manifests the life of Deity, and its sovereign precepts are the causes and not the results of that manifestation. Both faith and reason must be received as they are given, in their completeness and unity, with no part advanced at the expense of the rest. The Holy Scriptures and Church tradition being the appointed channels of Divine verity, the student should know the doctrines of the Bible and the interpretations of the Fathers, together with the decisions of the Councils thereupon.

Reason, as Aquinas conceived it, was infinitely more than the product of any single brain. It was the presiding and inspiring attribute of the collective human mind, which hitherto had found its freest vent in the meditations of Plato and the methods of Aristotle. The life of reason did not remain in a state of disintegration and confinement to

[1] H. B. Workman: "The Dawn of the Reformation"; Vol. I, p. 132.

separate points, but resulted in the formation of a common
intellectual harmony. Both revelation and reason were
under the direction of the living and creating energies of
the Eternal Being. They shared one origin and one goal,
and their offspring in theology or philosophy presented
that compatibility which was one of the main tenets of
Scholasticism and, indeed, practically monopolized its
argument. The prepared and diligent seeker might himself
become a vehicle for their communications, and thus, in
his turn, add to the definite gains which benefited history
and society. But he was admonished that they contained
a superior knowledge forever beyond the grasp of man,
who was compensated by a secondary knowledge to which
he could attain. The truths within human reach were but
the foothills of an inaccessible height where God reserved
the pattern of His omniscient will. Toward that lofty
region revelation and reason converged, and there found
their perfect reconciliation. While Aquinas regarded
Christian theology as the sum and crown of all inquiry,
he included the Greek philosophers in his spacious survey
and was influenced by Averroes and Avicenna, the Saracenic
interpreters of Aristotle. For he held that far from being
explicable by natural processes, as these are usually understood, the generalizations of non-Christian thinkers were
traceable to the authority of those sacred writings which
really controlled every intellectual movement, and their
teachings were specified by him as the axioms of an all
pervasive spiritual life. His superb learning was evinced
in the "Catena Aurea," where, under the form of a
commentary on the Gospels, he gave a succinct summary
of the traditional views concerning them. His more direct
exposition of the Psalms, the prophecies of Jeremiah and
Isaiah, and the Epistles, was equally clear and concise.
From these studies he turned to the Greek thinkers, supremacy among whom he accorded to Aristotle, whose dialectic
suited the complexion of his own mind.

Indeed, it can be said that the philosophy of St. Thomas is Aristotle Christianized, and that the doctors for whom he was the spokesman looked on nature and man through the medium of the Stagirite's formulæ. Principal Fairbairn remarks that "if churches always canonized their benefactors, Aristotle would long ago have been at the head of the Roman Calendar. There were many Schoolmen, but they all had one master, and they built by his help and to his honor systems that even he would have acknowledged to be encyclopedic and marvels of architectonic craft." [1]

The ambition of Aquinas that his "Summa" should be the totality of learning, fused into a living unity and subject to ecclesiastical guardianship, was seconded by the spirituality which interpenetrated his work. It was, and still is, for the Papacy and the Curia, the standard theology, and its efforts to prove "that religion is rational and that reason is divine, that all knowledge and all truth, from whatever source derived, must be capable of harmonious adjustment," [2] deserve the attention of those who accept the sentiment of Aubrey Moore that whatever is truly religious is finally reasonable. The moderate Realism which the "Angelic Doctor," who is the patron saint of many Roman Catholic institutions of learning,[3] so triumphantly interpreted became a shining mark for the attacks of the Nominalists of the next generation.

Foremost among its assailants was the Franciscan John Duns Scotus (1275 ?–1308). The broken and uncertain records of his unique career assert that he died when only thirty-four years of age. If this is correct, the rapidity

---

[1] "Christ in Modern Theology"; p. 119.

[2] H. Rashdall: "Universities of Europe in the Middle Ages"; Vol. I, p. 367.

[3] The Franciscans have never completely acknowledged the supremacy of St. Thomas, although Pope Leo XIII practically made his teaching the official authority of the Church. It is also interesting to note that his doctrines have been echoed in the theories of Bergson. Both thinkers use the method of analogy and their concept of order is essentially practical and theological. The Bergsonian views are anticipated in the "Summa" to a limited degree, but it would be absurd to claim their wholesale agreement.

and extent of his literary output, to say nothing of its microscopic detail and tortuous processes, are among the marvels of human achievement. His controversial attitude was swayed by the current antagonism between the Franciscans and the Dominicans. Aquinas was constructive, Scotus destructive; the former was essentially a philosopher, the latter a critic whose dexterous turns earned him the title of "Doctor Subtilis." He insisted that his great predecessor erred in founding theology upon speculation rather than practice. Faith was an act of the will and not an outflow of the mind, and the intellect could not easily find what was loosely called a rational basis for the phenomena with which faith dealt. The most careful defense of this position was open to the attacks of the skeptical. Revelation and dogma were the only reliable guardians of anything noble and true, and the ontology of Aquinas was therefore worthless as an apologetic. The existence and nature of God could not be proved by reason. Even the Gospels were unworthy of credence save on the authority of the Church, and the tenets of religion were accepted and obeyed, not in deference to human understanding, but under the immediate impulse of divine necessity. God commands what is good because it is good, argued Aquinas; the good is such because God wills it, rejoined Scotus; had He willed the opposite, the fact of His doing it would constitute its righteousness. In the one case the determinant was an ethical volition; in the other an arbitrary affirmation which had no necessary ethical quality.

The tendency of the philosophy of Scotus was, as Dr. Rashdall phrases it, towards "an emotional prostration before authority popularly called faith," and its ultimate drift lay in the direction of doubt. His extravagant advocacy of ecclesiastical supremacy, his superfluous intricacies and imaginary entities were more than merely fanciful; they marked the fast approaching decay of

medieval thought, and this was hastened by his less palpable but graver error in divorcing faith from reason,
thus threatening the citadel of the wisest Schoolmen.
Neither his zeal for higher doctrine nor his identification of
faith with a blind submission to the Church could repair
the havoc he had wrought by weakening the distinctions
between right and wrong.   He made moral action dependent
on the unconditioned arbitrary will of God, and reduced
duty to a mere matter of prudent calculation.[1]

The inevitable reaction found its advocate in William of
Ockham, the "Invincible Doctor" whose new interpretation
of Nominalism heralded the dissolution of Scholasticism and
repudiated its historic loyalty to the Holy See.   "Universals," for Ockham, existed only in "the thinking mind," and
no theological doctrines were rationally demonstrable.   The
modern scientist could accept many of his statements without serious modification, and in the light of later philosophy
he was not so much a Nominalist as a Conceptualist.   But,
while he revived Nominalism of a qualified sort, he could
not overcome the current of Realism which "dimly and
blindly testified to the part mind plays in the constitution of
the objects of our knowledge — to the truth that in all our
knowledge there is an ethical element which comes not from
any supposed 'external object' but from the mind itself." [2]
His forceful individuality was felt in his leadership of the
Spiritual Franciscans, who, so long as he was their head,
observed both by precept and example the vows of their
order.   This policy revealed the latent antagonism between
the political autocracy of Hildebrand and the etherealized
aspirations of the Saint of Assisi.   When Ockham with others
inveighed against the Papal decisions on property, Pope
John XXII pronounced condemnation on the Franciscan
doctrine relating thereto, an act which led to further differ-

[1] H. Rashdall: "Universities of Europe in the Middle Ages"; Vol. II,
p. 534.
[2] *Ibid.*, Part II, pp. 356–357.

ences until the order was denied official recognition and placed under the ban of the Church.

Ockham's contention that the State was a divine ordination, and should therefore be freed from ecclesiastical control, aggravated the discontent which provoked the conflicts between the Pope and the Emperor. From these in turn sprang the nationalism to which reference has been made, and which nurtured the theories of religious freedom and the rights of civil government. Through Wycliffe and Hus the protest against the temporal claims of the Papacy passed into the keeping of the sixteenth century Reformers. Yet Ockham's courageous impeachment was exceeded by that of his pupil Marsiglio de Mainardino (1270–1342),[1] whose "Defensor Pacis" was the most original political treatise of the Middle Ages. As the title indicates, it was intended to establish the concord of society upon a democratic basis, maintaining that the source of law was in the people themselves, who should elect the chief executive of the nation, be the judges of his administration, and if it were found errant or corrupt, hold him liable for its failures and crimes. The fictitious supremacy of the Papacy was denounced as the root of the troubles which afflicted the State; the Pope, his bishops and clergy, were denied all right to promulgate interdicts or excommunications, or in any way insist upon the observance of what they deemed the divine law. This power was vested in the Church alone, acting in unity and with the consent of the entire body of believers, and to that end General Councils ought to be composed of clerics and laymen alike. The Bible was the sole authority of faith and doctrine, and Papal decrees should be subjected to its teachings. Such was the quality of Marsiglio's plea for constitutional freedom, which gave him a prior claim to the honors afterwards bestowed on Wycliffe; indeed, in the bull directed against

---

[1] Marsilius of Padua is distinguished by the best critics from Marsiglio de Mainardino, though in the British Museum Catalogue they are identified. Marsiglio de Mainardino was a Canon of Padua in 1316.

the English schismatic, Gregory XI declared that the heresies of the Reformer but represented with a few terms
changed "the perverted opinions and ignorant doctrine of
Marsiglio of damned memory, and of John of Jandun."
Yet this execrated thinker alone divined the secret of an
age unborn, and laid down in all essentials the principles
which were to mold the political institutions of the distant
future.[1]

III

The strange neglect which seemed to follow these men to
their graves prevented any just appraisal of Marsiglio's
services. The enemies of Roger Bacon, the most illustrious
English scholar and thinker of his day, who moved heaven
and earth to come into direct contact with reality, almost
succeeded in destroying his reputation, and only within a
comparatively recent period has it emerged from a long
eclipse. Similarly, in the case of Wycliffe, his voluminous
works, with few exceptions, remained in manuscript for
over five hundred years. Even now many of them are still
unpublished, and, so far as their present interest is concerned,
are likely to remain so. Enough have been rescued from
oblivion, however, to show that he stood in a philosophical
sequence to the scholars already named.

Although the great movement which had illuminated
the spiritualities of life from the time of Anselm and Abailard
virtually ended with Wycliffe, it nevertheless retained sufficient virtue to enable him to rank as a learned clerk versed
in the labyrinthine windings of scholastic philosophy.
The majority of his predecessors were unanimous in their
devotion to the Papacy, but that allegiance was now shaken
and the Holy See openly assailed. This hostility was one
among other symptoms of the restlessness which pervaded
Oxford and Paris, and was encouraged in the former

[1] Archibald Robertson: "Regnum Die"; p. 313.

and repressed in the latter University. At Paris the theologians were at their wits' end to quiet the doubts and questionings which fermented beneath a correct and prosaic surface. Oxford, with the rest of England, enjoyed immunity from the terrors of the Inquisition, which were unknown there until Henry IV needed the support of the Church because of his beclouded title to the crown. The University was therefore undeterred in those courses which inspired and reflected the national will. Her doctors were not only expounders and defenders of metaphysics; they were also the organ voices of the secular government and its claims. Thus while Latin Scholasticism was for political reasons prevented from occupying the wider and more genuinely intellectual interests, the English type increasingly assimilated an independency evoked by the events of the thirteenth and fourteenth centuries.

Wycliffe turned this conditions of affairs to good account: the unembarrassed speculative and practical tendencies of his life as a scholar offset to some extent the difficulty he experienced in dealing with a decadent system which was rapidly degenerating into a philosophical quarrel. While this situation forbade originality, it drove him to other spheres of inquiry, in which he was the founder of a school of his own, the chief authorities of which were the Fathers of the early Church. He possessed in an unusual degree the power of seizing upon and adapting the products of creative minds in such a manner as to secure for them a favorable hearing. His leading ideas were either restatements or modifications of tradition; his minor principles were truths recovered from long obscurity. He acted without the precedents he afforded to Hus, and in this sense he may be regarded as a discoverer.[1]

As between the Realists and the Nominalists Wycliffe stood with the former, albeit with some concessions to the objections urged by the opposing school. His position was

[1] C. M. Trevelyan: "England in the Age of Wycliffe"; p. 173.

a protest against the extravagances of the Scotists and of the revised Nominalism of Ockham; for his thorough-going disposition the substratum of their creeds was an impossibility. His Realism, though modified, ran counter to any theory of illusion: he ascribed reality to mental ideas, and denied the subjectivism which treated them as mere phantoms of the imagination.[1] The Realists' faith in the validity of knowledge was grounded upon reason and upon the actuality of the objective world. But reality also pertains to subjective consciousness, and it is only when both are taken into account that a reconciliation can be effected.

Wycliffe's doctrine of the Deity showed a leaning toward that philosophical Pantheism which characterized all varieties of Realism. "God is all and in all. Every existing thing is in reality God itself, for every creature which can be named is, in regard to its 'intelligible,' and consequently its chief, existence, in reality the word of God." Perceiving the dangerous side of these propositions he amended them by adding, somewhat illogically, that they gave "no color to the conclusion that every creature whatsoever is God." [2] The will of God "is His essential and eternal nature by which all His acts are determined." Creation is conditioned by it, and is neither an arbitrary selection nor a process of emanations, but the only possible universe and an immediate work at a specific time. This was directly contrary to the affirmation of the Scotists that God does not choose to do anything because it is best, but that whatever He does is best solely because He pleases to do it. He regarded Divine Omnipotence as self-determined and morally regulated by the inner laws of God's Being. Omniscience argues an eternal Now: that which is to be in point of time is and ever was in relation to the Supreme Mind. His discussion

[1] H. B. Workman: "The Dawn of the Reformation"; Vol. I, pp. 139–140.

[2] Quoted by G. V. Lechler: "Wycliffe and his English Precursors"; pp. 253–254.

of the Trinity proceeded on lines laid down in part by the Fathers and in part by the Schoolmen. Its main interest centers in the doctrine of the Son as the Logos, the substantive Word; an inclusive theory which embraced all "realities that are intelligible," that is, capable of being realized in thought, and of which the Logos was the mediating element or member between God and the Universe.[1]

He compromised on the question of predestination and free-will, using for the purpose the Aristotelian distinction between that which is absolutely necessary and that which is necessary on a given supposition. When he faced the fact of sin in the light of his own statement that God wills only that which has being, he replied that sin was the negation of being and therefore could not be willed by the Deity, Who necessitated men in their deeds, which, in themselves, were neither right nor wrong, and took of morality only through man's use of them by means of his free agency.[2] Here Wycliffe forsook the teaching of Thomas Bradwardine (1290–1349), the "Doctor Profundis" with whom he had an intellectual kinship to which the development of his own ideas was indebted.

Bradwardine's importance has been overlooked by modern writers, and he deserves more than a passing reference. Neander does not mention him and Gieseler does so only to misconstrue his teaching. More recently, however, such authorities as Lechler and Workman have given him the attention he merits. He was a native either of Hartfield in Sussex, or of Chichester, and a student at Merton College. In 1325, the year when the University was largely freed from the control of the Bishop of Lincoln, Bradwardine was appointed its proctor. In 1339 he became chaplain and confessor to Edward the Third, whom he accompanied to the French Wars. His earnestness and benevolence procured for him the Archbishopric of Canterbury, to which

[1] G. V. Lechler: "Wycliffe and his English Precursors"; p. 253.
[2] Encyclopædia Britannica, XI Edition, Article on Wycliffe.

he ascended unsullied by the slightest stain of selfishness or worldly ambition. After a journey to Avignon to receive consecration, he returned to London only to be smitten with the Black Death at Lambeth Palace, where he died on August 26, 1349. Few prelates have been so widely and deservedly loved and esteemed; his untimely decease was a national sorrow in which king, lords, and people alike shared. A spiritual awakening he had experienced while still a student at Oxford regenerated his entire life, and was the secret spring of his religious insight and moral distinction. Anticipating Bunyan and Wesley, he narrated this visitation in words of the heart, ascribing his conversion to elective grace rather than to his own volition. "So then," he quoted from St. Paul's Epistle to the Romans, "it is not in him that willeth, nor in him that runneth, but in God that showeth mercy." It is hardly surprising that his theology was profoundly necessitarian; his treatise "De Causa Dei" became the fountain of Anglican Calvinism, which asserted that in the act of sin there is a complete exclusion of freedom of choice, since the Everlasting Will infallibly determines man's conduct, and consequently human free will has no existence.

This was too radical for Wycliffe, who objected that any criminal, however desperate and wicked, would be justified in saying "God determines me to all these acts of transgression, in order to perfect the beauty of the Universe." [1] Such a conclusion totally condemned the suppositions from which it was drawn. Hence, although influenced by the obdurate predestination theory which was embedded in Bradwardine's theology, Wycliffe swerved from its more pronounced position, and while he agreed with the Archbishop that everything which takes place does so of necessity, and further, that the Divine Being coöperates in all actions of the human will to the extent of determining them, he tried to save man's freedom of choice from any prejudice

[1] Quoted by G. V. Lechler: "De Dominio Divino"; I, c. 15, p. 265.

due to the coöperation. In particular he repudiated the arbitrary notion that if any man sins it is God Himself who determines him to the act, contending that the motive which prompts the evil deed, and is the main element of transgression, did not proceed from God.

IV

Wycliffe's unique contribution to later medieval thought is found in his treatises "De Dominio Divino" and "De Dominio Civili." The former was an extension of Richard Fitzralph's phrase that "dominion is founded in grace" and the latter a corollary of the former. Fitzralph, who has already been quoted in reference to the age of the undergraduates of Oxford, was a fellow of Balliol College about the year 1320, appointed Chancellor of the University in 1333, and in 1347 consecrated Archbishop of Armagh. He employed his theory as a weapon to assail the Franciscan doctrine of evangelical poverty, arguing that to abjure all holding of property was to run counter to the laws governing social relations, and also to those between God and man. In this Wycliffe favored the austerity of Ockham and the Fraticelli as against Fitzralph's interpretation. Further, Wycliffe's treatment of lordship was powerfully affected by Augustine's views on the nature of sin. According to these "sin is nothing, and men, when they sin, become nothing. Evil is a negation and those who yield themselves to it cease to retain any positive existence. Clearly, then, they can possess nothing, can hold no lordship. That which they seem to possess is no real or proper possession at all; it is but the unjust holding of that which they must one day restore to the righteous. 'From him that hath shall be taken even that which he seemeth to have.' As thus the wicked hath nothing, so on the other hand the righteous is lord of all things." [1]

[1] Quoted in "Social England," Vol. II, pp. 163–164; edited by H. D. Traill.

Wycliffe's discussion of this and corresponding matters is still in manuscript form, the only extant copy of which is kept at Vienna. It filled three volumes, which were preliminary to his major and collective work, the "Summa in Theologia." Lechler regards these volumes as the indication of his transition from the philosophical to the strictly theological phase of his career, and it is conjectured that he wrote them shortly after he had completed his studies in theology at the University. The contemporary disputes between Philip the Fair and Pope Boniface VIII, and between the Emperor Louis of Bavaria and Pope John XXII, raged around the vexed questions of Papal supremacy over the State, and thus directly concerned lordship or dominion. These quarrels may have been a contributing cause in determining Wycliffe's views with regard to lordship; another cause was the controversy of the Holy See with the Spiritual Franciscans, who sought to enforce that rule of their order which forbade it to hold either personal or corporate property. Out of this dispute arose the larger issue whether or not Christ and His Apostles had individually or collectively authorized such a regulation. The obligation of poverty as a vow of the mendicant friars clashed with the policy of John XXII, who personally was far removed from such drastic renunciations, and declared against them in a series of bulls ending in the sentence of excommunication upon those who opposed his decision.

Whatever was the effect of these events upon Wycliffe, there is ample proof that he gave prolonged consideration to the general question and carried it forward into a practical communism, the perils of which were somewhat mitigated by his implication of lordship with service. In his opinion each was essential to the other. The Lordship of God Himself began only when He created beings to perform His service. Moreover, the Supreme Lordship was distinguished from that of man by the fact of its domination over all creatures, and by the same condition of service; for every living

F

being owes it to his God to serve Him with his whole being. "God rules not mediately through the rule of vassals who serve Him, as other kings hold lordship, since immediately and of Himself He makes, sustains, and governs all that which He possesses, and assists it to perform its works according to other uses which He requires." [1] Nor does He give any lordship to any of His servants "except He first give Himself to them."

The principle that in the sight of God all men are equal had been recognized from early times; but Wycliffe, not content to leave it in the sphere of sentiment, built it into his political philosophy. In feudal phraseology he would have said that all men held from God on the same terms of service. From this he argued that the standing which a man has before God is the criterion by which his position among men must be determined. If through transgression a man forfeited his divine privileges, then of necessity his temporal privileges also were lost. Even the Pope himself, if morally unsound, retained his right of lordship no longer.

The entire theory was attached to the article that the creature could produce nothing save what God had already created. Anything He granted to His servants was first a part of Himself, and when bestowed He was still suzerain and retained the ultimate disposition of the gift. It followed from this that the Divine Lordship was forever and in all respects supreme, and that upon it human lordship was dependent. Men held whatever they had received from God as stewards, and if found faithless could justly be deprived of what may be called their fief. A subtle distinction was made between lordship and actual ownership; nothing of the former was of the nature of property, for property was the result of sin; hence Christ and the Apostles would have none of it.

Wycliffe met the obvious possibility that all men were

---

[1] "De Dominio Divino," I, c. 5: quoted in "Social England," Vol. II, pp. 162–163.

liable to dispossession for breach of tenure, in that all had
sinned, by urging that his theory required a pure social ideal,
and, while in actual practice "dominion was denied to the
wicked, power might be permitted to them to which Christians should submit from motives of obedience to God."
His emasculated conclusion was quickly seized upon by
opponents, nor could Wycliffe prevent it from passing over
into an absurdity.

The paradoxical nature of this part of the argument did
not interfere with its general application to the Church as
the standard of universal faith and morals. Wycliffe
agreed with Ockham's contention that she should hold no
property. He urged that endowments had an injurious
effect by involving her in temporal affairs. Her work
lay within the sphere of the soul, and her influence
should be restricted to spiritual supervision. He rejected
the policy of Hildebrand and his successors, declaring that
the Papacy had nothing to do with civil government,
and that it ought to regain its old ideal of supremacy
over men's hearts and consciences; "for to govern temporal possessions after a civil manner, to conquer kingdoms
and exact tribute, appertain to earthly lordship, not to the
Pope; so that if he pass by and set aside the office of spiritual
rule, and entangle himself in those other concerns his work is
not only superfluous but also contrary to Holy Scripture." [1]
He further declared that it was the duty of the State to
vindicate its right of control over its own affairs. Territories and revenues held by the Church should revert to the
nation. The likelihood of the Church's retaliation upon its
plunderers led to his well-known utterance on the matter of
excommunication. If she should use such a weapon, it
could be of no effect unless by his own sin a man had excommunicated himself and cut himself off from all spiritual
communion. No external decree pronouncing spiritual
banishment could overcome a man's consciousness of his

[1] "De Dominio Civili," I, 17, quoted in "Social England," Vol. II, p. 164.

continuation in a state of divine grace.   Wycliffe studiously avoided saying anything derogatory to the reigning Pope. On the contrary, he expressed himself in terms of loyalty, but with the reservation that such loyalty did not obviate the duty of resistance to the Pontiff if his claims were in contravention of Holy Writ.

The readiness with which he passed from scholastic theology to complicated political and social conditions showed that instinct and feeling were the trusted guides of his mind.   He occasionally forgot that the logic of metaphysics was one thing and the logic of life another.   His lack of moderation and his contentment with a technically correct dialectic sometimes betrayed him into an unreal and almost fantastic discourse, in which he viewed the issue at stake as one wherein pure theory could operate, regardless of any other consideration.   This weakness was apparent when he insisted that the Church, and the Universities as a part of the Church, should cease to hold real endowments; and that the clergy should confine themselves to theological studies.   In the first instance he pushed to the extremes of formal disputation opinions he had imbibed from the mendicant friars; in the latter, his postulate that the Holy Scriptures were perfectly sufficient for a clerical education was advanced beyond reasonable boundaries and unsupported by his personal example.   Yet these extravagances and inconsistencies were redeemed by the warmth of his natural sympathies, which generally were rightly bestowed and gradually led him to become aware of something nobler and more vital than the exactitudes of Scholasticism or the unquestioning zeal of partisanship. When force of reasoning failed him he was frequently aided by that insight and prevision which enable prophetical men rightly to value the germinating power of apparently hopeless but pregnant ideals.   His solitariness as the last of the Schoolmen intensified both this faculty of vision, and also his faults as a thinker.   The ages which preceded his own had produced great figures who stood forth from among their contemporaries upon the higher levels of thought and achievement. It was a sign that disintegration had already begun when he was fated to stand alone. The richer the summer, the greater the decay of autumn. Wycliffe came to the vineyard at the eleventh hour, when Scholasticism's day was departing and its sky was already imbrowned with shadows. Chill mists had begun to fall upon those fields in which were found no fellow laborers of equal capacity to correct his peculiarities or counteract his excesses.

Fortunately for himself he was fertile in distinctions and expedients, yet not so fortunate in his facile handling of the abstract as though it were the concrete. The former gift combined with the substantial justice of the causes he undertook to overcome the difficulties of his temperament, training, and isolation. He formulated a series of propositions which other leaders defended and furthered against the claims of the Holy See. The avowal that the King was God's vicar as well as the Pope, and that the State had a natural right and dignity which should not be impaired by ecclesiastical trespass, was carried beyond the theoretical stage as early as 1366, when Parliament finally refused payment of the annual Papal tribute. The report of the debates on this action was strongly influenced by Wycliffe's views; and such could not have been the case except for his acquaintance with public affairs, which saved him from mere syllogistic manipulation and prevented him from beating the air.

His critics should bear in mind that, had not his more daring conceptions and innovations been couched in the formal phraseology of the Schools, they would probably have been instantly rejected. Their nakedness was clothed with a garb academically correct, which concealed the fact that they constituted a revolutionary departure from the authorized tenets then current, and embodied a new theory of the relation between Church and State. Hence the main results of his efforts are not to be found, as some of his readers have contended, in those inventions which were largely the surplusage of his genius. On the contrary, they appear in the broadening of that individual and national freedom for which an unbroken lineage of scholars and doctors had striven. Marsiglio had demanded that the Church should limit herself to her own province; Ockham had vindicated the necessity and justice of an autonomous secular power; the Spiritual Franciscans had exemplified the evangelical poverty which the Gospels inculcated; Grosseteste had denounced pluralities and provisions; Fitzralph had insisted that dominion was founded in grace; and Wycliffe blended these separate ideas into a measurably consistent unity.

V

Pope Urban V has come down to us as the best of the Avignon popes, so far as purity of character and religious fervor are concerned. His labors to repress simony and corruption were creditable, and it was he who in his desire to escape the vicious life of the French seat made an unsuccessful attempt to reëstablish the Papacy in Rome. Equally futile was his ill-timed demand for the homage of England, which Wycliffe, at the command of Edward III, answered, as we have seen, in 1366.[1] The Reformer was still teaching at Oxford when he summarized in his reply the arguments which had already been advanced in Parliament against Urban's action. The temper of the national legislature, as reflected in these arguments and speeches, indicated a strong antipapal sentiment in England, which increased as the fourteenth century progressed.

Apart from the royal mandate, the causes of Wycliffe's diversion to politics may have lain in his weariness of the endless hairsplittings of the philosophical schools. Their members essayed to elucidate eternal mysteries by logic

---

[1] Whether the date is 1366 or 1374 is very doubtful. Some authorities favor the later date. The Pope's demand was repeated in 1374.

while they enshrouded plain everyday truths in a dense mist. Political action offered him a broader path and firmer footing than theological discussion. Again, not only were philosophy and theology an intellectual unity at that time, they also stood in close relation to every public question. The theologian and the metaphysician were political economists of a sort, and Wycliffe's attainments in the first two sciences fitted him to deal with questions of State policy.

By far the most distinguished of his patrons at this stage of his career was John of Gaunt (1340–1399), the ablest and most unscrupulous Englishman of the time; a prince who shared the qualities and ambitions of the Plantagenets, and devoted his talents, as the leader of a small but compact and active party, to the aggrandizement of the Lancastrian dynasty and its supporters. When he and Wycliffe conjoined, the gloom of impending national misfortune had begun to darken the last years of Edward III; the renewal of continental peace had flooded England with a stream of returning soldiers, whose training in the wars had rendered them unfit for civil life; France was preparing to wrest herself free from the yoke of her enemies; and the Black Prince, whose knighthood mirrored departing chivalry, was nearing the end of his brilliant military career. It seems to the student of to-day that there were more natural portents of evil, more droughts, famines, pestilences, seasons of abnormal suffering and degradation than the world has ever known since.[1] Aristocratic and territorial prerogatives remained unrestricted, and society was drifting towards the thunders of the cataract. Strange combinations of somber circumstances were forming when Parliament in 1371 petitioned the throne that secular men only should be employed in the royal court and household.

The Duke of Lancaster's alliance with Wycliffe was prompted by selfish motives on the part of the prince. He

[1] This sentence was written before the outbreak of the great war in Europe. It might now possibly bear revision.

was in hearty agreement with the Reformer's proposal that "the king and his witty lords" should take back the wealth and endowments of the Church "by process of time"; that prelates should vacate their secular offices and that the extensive ecclesiastical estates should be forcibly recovered from those guilty of their misuse. But here the concurrence ended. Wycliffe would have applied the proceeds of such restitution to the welfare of the realm; Gaunt was bent on securing them for partisan ends. Meanwhile the compact remained unshaken, although Wycliffe was disappointed at the pusillanimous conduct of the new administration. When the Papal collector of tribute, Arnold Garnier, visited England, the royal officials merely extracted from him the customary oath that he would do nothing contrary to the laws and liberties of the kingdom. Their mildness angered Wycliffe, who indignantly remarked in one of his pamphlets that it could not be otherwise than subversive of the laws and liberties of the realm that a foreign potentate should plunder it at will.

He was perversely slow to suspect Gaunt of less commendable aims than his own, and Gaunt was quick to make good use of the Schoolman's trenchant pen. In April, 1374, he was appointed by the Crown to the living of Lutterworth, bestowed upon him, not primarily because he was a learned and pious clerk, but rather as a reward for his services to the government. The authorities took advantage of the minority of the regular patron, Henry de Ferrers, to assign the benefice to their nominee, and Wycliffe's enemies circulated rumors that further preferments were in store for him, and that he was to be elevated to the see of Worcester on the death of its occupant, William de Leme.

The wrongs which patrons of benefices suffered at the hands of the Pope through the constant violation of the Statute of Provisors continued to be the subject of protests in Parliament, and finally it was arranged that the matter should be discussed at Bruges with the commissioners of

Gregory XI. Accordingly on the 26th of July, 1374, John Gilbert, afterwards Bishop of Bangor, was made the head of the English delegation, with Wycliffe as a subordinate member.[1] The outcome was discomfiting to them. The six bulls which the Pope dispatched in September, 1375, while deploring past irregularities, gave no promise of future redress. The promotion of the Bishop of Bangor was looked upon as a payment for the betrayal of the interests of the Anglican Church, and Gaunt was suspected of similar treachery in his negotiations with France.

In order to furnish some idea of the grievances that were aired at the conference, it is necessary to revert to the time of King John's humiliation at the instance of Innocent III. After that event the Holy See steadily drew to itself the patronage of the highest ecclesiastical offices and emoluments in England, acting in connivance with the reigning monarch, whose interests generally coincided with those of the Pontiff. "Were the king of England to petition for an ass to be made a bishop, we must not refuse him," was a piece of sacrilegious effrontery attributed to Clement V. An example of the innumerable abuses which sprang from this sinister association, and from the ramifications of the extortionate system and the helplessness of the Anglican bishops to check it, is afforded by the diocesan annals of Salisbury. Here twenty-eight out of fifty prebends in the gift of the Bishop had been provided for by the Popes, while not more than three of the holders resided in them. Eight additional candidates were on the waiting list with the promise of preferment at the first vacancy.

[1] The latest researches by Dr. Workman show that Wycliffe was not a member of the official Conference at Bruges which settled the terms of the Concordat with the Pope. He was only there for seven weeks and was in no sense a chief figure. Bishop Gilbert was practically supreme, and the Concordat, which was so disastrous for England, was not determined upon until 1376, when the moving spirits were Simon Sudbury and John of Gaunt. The statement of Lechler that John of Gaunt and Wycliffe met at Bruges is a fiction. Wycliffe had finally left Bruges long before John of Gaunt went there to participate in the Conference.

At length this senseless rapacity was restrained by the English government, which defied the Papal court at Avignon as the head and fount of unblushing simony, "where a caitiff who knows nothing and is worth nothing is promoted to churches and prebends to the value of a thousand marks." The Pontiff's hitherto unquestioned right of nomination to bishoprics rendered vacant by translation had also been wantonly exercised. Their occupants were removed from one see to another as often as possible in order that the usual fees and first-fruits, *i.e.*, the first year's income, might be collected from the outgoing and incoming prelates. The nominees were more often than not absentees as well as foreigners, content to receive the revenues of offices they had never seen. The shameful spectacle of these adventurers enriching themselves out of the treasury of the national Church and the funds gathered from the gifts of the poor and the faithful excited strong indignation. Wanton avarice had reached its climax and battened on its ill-gotten gains until the notorious evil sharpened the popular appetite for reform. Thus, apart from doctrinal and intellectual developments, the Wycliffian movement suited the resolution of his countrymen, exasperated as they were by clerical parasites who drained the financial resources of communities to which many of them were entire strangers.

The Statute of Provisors of the year 1351 was designed to prevent the Pope from providing English livings for foreign clerics, from making provisions for benefices during the lifetime of the incumbent, and from reserving them for Papal use and benefit while their occupancy was delayed for that purpose. It also prohibited the acceptance of Papal letters of provision, and vested the patronage thus bestowed in the king. Further, by this Statute the free election of candidates for the higher offices reverted to the ancient procedure of their choice by the Cathedral Chapter, and the dignitaries thus chosen were allowed to have free presentations of the benefices under their jurisdiction. The fact that the Statute had to be supplemented two years later by the first Statute of Præmunire showed that it had failed to accomplish desirable results. After thirteen years more stringent legislation was passed, applying the inhibitions of the latter Statute to the Curia, which it boldly named. Finally, in 1393 the Great Statute of Præmunire subjected all appellants to Rome to the forfeiture of their case. This succession of enactments, six in all, during the period from 1350 to 1393, proved the ineffectiveness of the various measures designed to end the Avignon tyranny. But if such means did not avail to abolish foreign ecclesiastical control, they supplied the precedents which gave color to Henry the Eighth's plea that he was acting within the law when he destroyed the independence of the Church and monopolized for the Crown and the nobility the estates and incomes hitherto shared with the Papacy.

After what has been said it is not inexplicable that the Commission of Bruges should have truckled to the Pope and the king, or that its negotiations were as fruitless as the English court no doubt intended they should be. The claims of corrupted usage continued to fetter the liberties of Anglicanism, and the few concessions agreed upon were only meant to save the face of the commissioners. The Bishop of Bangor was appointed to certain benefices by means of the very "provisions" he had been instructed to denounce; Wycliffe remained merely a parish priest in rank, and held the living at Lutterworth until his death. Yet he was prominent in the country, and his alliance with Gaunt kept him in the political arena. The declining health of Edward III and the death of the Black Prince made the Duke of Lancaster supreme, while his reactionary influence served to undo the legislation of the "Good Parliament." Wycliffe resided at Lutterworth and at Oxford, making frequent journeys to the capital, where by this time he was equally well known as a trusted adviser of the Crown and as a preacher whose ardent eloquence fitted him to inspire and direct public opinion.

His labors during this period were only exceeded by those which followed between the years of 1378 and 1382, when his efforts for reform literally consumed him. They seem to have been prompted by the belief that physical decline could not long be deferred, and that what he had to do must be done quickly. Within six or seven years he not only wrote all his English works, of which, according to Shirley's catalogue, there are sixty-five,[1] but revised or completed at least half of his Latin writings, of which the same authority enumerates ninety-seven, and these herculean tasks were augmented by his share in translating the Bible. He also originated the pamphlet as a weapon of controversy. The Scholastic doctor, esteemed by his contemporaries as excelling in profundity and subtlety, now doffed the cumbersome armor of abstruse propositions couched in syllogistic forms and a dead language. His tracts, addressed to fellow citizens in their own speech, were clear in substance and style, with many a racy aside and pungent sally which disclosed in the writer a union of rare qualities of heart and brain. They were terse, pithy, incisive, vehement in feeling; not without antics in which the most learned were capable of indulging on occasion; and relieved and emphasized by the play of sarcasm, banter, and raillery. Some of these broadsides were not more than a couple of pages in length, yet in that brief compass they frequently conveyed a masterly exposition bearing directly upon the matter in hand.

The lack of other literary models than the Bible and a few Latin authors threw him back upon his own originality. The classics were preserved in the libraries of St. Albans, Glastonbury, York, and Durham. Richard Aungervyle, better known as Richard de Bury, author of the "Philobib-

---

[1] The English are much inferior to the Latin works both in bulk and importance.

lion," which dealt with his favorite pursuit of book collecting, was the owner of a great library secured at infinite pains. He bequeathed it to Durham College, a munificent endowment indeed, since such libraries were rare before the time of Duke Humphrey. Peter Lombard's "Sentences" and Gratian's "Decretum" were the better known repositories of learning, and Wycliffe's acquaintance with St. Augustine and St. Chrysostom was probably due to Gratian.

No interpreter of Wycliffe's writings can rate the Reformer an optimist. The world he saw was sorely distressed; the inconstancy of human things ever inclined them toward the great abyss; the common people were bad, the civil rulers worse, the clergy, and especially the higher ecclesiastics, worst of all. Perilous times had come, in which offenses abounded. Their mischief was the more vexatious by contrast, for they directly followed a period of superabundant energy which once bade fair to rejuvenate society. All authorities were now recreant in that they had forsaken Christ, surrendered to human maxims, and become the slaves of tyrannical greed and caprice. The following quotation from one of his sermons shows how far short of Wycliffe's expectations Christendom had fallen, and how freely he reprimanded the religious dearth and coldness of the age. "It is as clear as day that we so-called Christians make the creatures to be our gods. The proud or ambitious man worships a likeness of that which is in heaven (Exodus xx. 4), because, like Lucifer, he loves, above all things, promotion or dignity in one form or another. The covetous man worships a likeness of that which is in the earth beneath. And although, arrayed in sheep's clothing, we hypocritically confess that our highest of all service is in the worship of God, yet it would very well become us carefully to inquire whether we faithfully carry out this confession in our actions. Let us then search and examine whether we keep the first and greatest commandment, and worship God above all. Do we not bend and bow ourselves before the rich of this world more with the view of being rewarded by them with worldy honor or temporal advantage, than for the sake of their moral character or spiritual help? Does not the covetous man stretch out now his arms and now his hands to grasp the gold, and does he not pay court untiringly to the men who have it in their power to hinder or to help his gains? Does not the sensual man, as though he were making an offering to the idol Moloch, cast himself down with his whole body before the harlot? Does he not put upon such persons worldly honor? Does he not offer to them the incense of purses of gold, in order to scent the flow of sensual delight with the sweetest perfumes? Does he not lavish upon his mistress gift upon gift, till she is more wonderfully bedizened with various ornaments than an image of the Holy Virgin? And does not all this show that we love the flesh, the world, and the devil more than God, in that we are more careful to keep their commandments than His? What violence do we hear of the Kingdom of Heaven suffering in our times (Matthew xi. 12), while the gates of hell are bolted? But alas! broad and well-trodden is the way which leadeth to hell, and narrow and forsaken the way which leadeth to heaven! This it is which makes men, for lack of faith, love what is seen and temporal more than the blessings which they cannot see, and to have more delight in buildings, dress, and ornaments, and other things of art and man's invention, than in the uncreated archetypes of heaven." [1]

Whatever may be thought of the justice of this wholesale condemnation, its sincerity is beyond dispute. Self-deception is not dishonesty, though it is often mistaken for it, and the fact that a man's opinions and practices do not always square with his words does not necessarily prove him to be a charlatan. We may be sure, however, that history is not written in such pronounced colors as black

---

[1] Liber Mandatorum (Decalogus): c. 15, fol. 136, col. I; fol. 137, col. 2. Quoted by Lechler, "John Wycliffe and his English Precursors"; pp. 303–304.

and white, and certainly not in black alone, but in the half tints and manifold shades which are necessary to depict the varieties of human character. The unqualified terms of Wycliffe's homily were employed for the sake of mental convenience as well as moral correction, and those who are given to the use of such terms, as he was, generally have in mind the increase of the good and the defeat of the evil in their surroundings.

CHAPTER III

THE QUARREL WITH THE PAPACY

HAD it not been the obstinate perverseness of our prelates against the divine and admirable spirit of Wyclif to suppress him as a schismatic and innovator, perhaps neither the Bohemian Hus and Jerom, no, nor the name of Luther or of Calvin, had been ever known: the glory of reforming all our neighbors had been completely ours.

MILTON, Areopagitica.

CHAPTER III

Wycliffe and Church institutions — William Courtenay, Bishop of London — Wycliffe's trial in 1377 — Gregory XI's five bulls against him — Second trial in 1378 — Wycliffe's polemic against the friars — Sketch of rise, development, and decadence of monasticism — Contrast between monks and friars — Popular accusations against the latter — The Great Schism and its effect on Wycliffe — His defense of Gaunt — His change of attitude towards the Papacy — Wycliffe's doctrine of the Church — His teaching upon Transubstantiation — Development of the dogma — Wycliffe's friends forsake him.

I

WYCLIFFE was in all respects a typical Englishman, independent in thought, jealous for the honor of his country and consistent in his patriotism. He was seldom wanting in self-confidence; a maker rather than a creature of precedent, with a high spirit unaffected by the external circumstances which sway weaker characters. His practical bent made him impatient of dreams and ecstasies. As to his rank in learning, he was "in theology most eminent, in philosophy second to none, in scholastic exercises incomparable." [1]

The conscious authority of these distinctions invested his bearing with an austerity age did not perceptibly soften, and lent his temper a brusqueness that tolerated no dallyings. He lived near enough to conscience to be discontented with things as they were, and when the test was applied he passed into social and political retirement rather than surrender his convictions. His integrity arose out of a solicitude for what he conceived to be spiritual religion. Excessive care

[1] Bishop Mandell Creighton: "Historical Essays and Reviews"; pp. 173–174.

for received dogmas did not deaden his moral sense; he impeached any ecclesiastical ascendency that depended upon resistance to the lawful authority of the State, and encountered no adversaries sufficiently strong to silence or even deter him. He was positive, militant, and eager for direct action because apparently doubtful concerning any self-righting principle in human development. While faithful to his own beliefs, he was not always just toward antagonistic views, and in the heat of controversy sometimes forgot that unbalanced truth is itself untrue. He was far more willing to be hurried than idle; the familiar German proverb, "Ohne Hast, ohne Rast," was scarcely descriptive of a career the moderation of which was altogether disproportionate to its restlessness and resolution. These traits were displayed to the full in his disputes with the Cæsarean clergy, the friars, the Papacy, and finally, in regard to the doctrine of Transubstantiation. Little allowance was made by the stern remonstrant for the inevitable shortcomings of human nature that found expression in these organizations and this dogma. The refinements of analysis which can detect potential good in some present evils were beyond him; in brief, sailing close to the wind was for him an impossible art. Thus one of the exhilarating aspects of his record was its moral intrepidity, which, apart from his connection with John of Gaunt, was seldom deflected from desirable ends.

The denunciations and the virulence of his quarrels grew as the Cæsarean clergy gave place to the friars, the friars to the Papacy, and the Papacy to Transubstantiation.[1] He found abundant incentive in existing conditions; European politics were suffering from the consequences of the later Crusades, which had lapsed into ruffianism, leaving small choice between the conduct of the infidels who held the Holy City and that of the adventurers who strove to wrest it from them. France lay broken and bleeding beneath the weight

[1] The question has been raised whether or not Wycliffe's attack on the friars preceded that upon the doctrine of Transubstantiation.

of the first half of the Hundred Years' War.‾ In Italy and Germany the conflicts between the Empire and the Papacy had shaken the foundations of society, and their cities were overrun with a rabble of mercenaries and free-lances. England had been fortunate enough to escape the distractions of civil strife, nevertheless her social state was wretched beyond words. Compared with those of the Continent, her provincial towns were small and insignificant; outside their closely guarded walls and noisome precincts the peasants of the shires groveled before their lords, for whom they were hewers of wood and drawers of water. Yet there still smoldered in these men the ashes of their fathers' wonted fires; ashes which had heat enough left in them to kindle the conflagration that threatened to devour the ruling powers at the time of the Peasants' Revolt.

When the Lancastrian faction forced William of Wykeham to resign the Chancellor's seals, his deprivation and attempted punishment led to further recriminations and impeachments, and the clergy made Wykeham's cause their own. However desirable Wycliffe's abstention from politics might have been, it was now practically impossible: he could not have retreated without loss of honor and injury to his cause.[1] Moreover, his doubts and questionings, as well as his beliefs, were no longer latent. Once released from the habit of absolute submission and obedience, they proceeded apace, and their radical tendencies affected matters of public moment rather than scholastic discourse. He openly avowed in London churches the tenets of disendowment and of the sanctity of clerical poverty which he had formerly taught in the University. Rumors of his sentiments were verified by his actual declarations, and his writings were closely scrutinized for further evidences of his disaffection by those whose practices were unsparingly

---

[1] Wycliffe's connection with John of Gaunt might also have arisen from the fact that the manor of Wycliffe was in the 'honor of Richmond,' one of Gaunt's fiefs.

assailed, and also by others whose honest convictions opposed his own.

Among the latter was William Courtenay, the aristocratic Bishop of London, a member of the family of the Earls of Devon and, on his mother's side, a direct descendant of Edward I. This prelate forced the hand of the temperate Archbishop Sudbury, whom he virtually supplanted as leader of the clerical party, and Wycliffe was summoned early in 1377 either before Convocation, or more probably, according to Bishop Creighton, before the Archbishop as his Ordinary, to answer charges of heresy, which had been preferred against him for his opinion concerning the wealth of the Church. On February nineteenth of that year the Reformer appeared at St. Paul's Cathedral to defend his position, accompanied by four friars of Oxford, and under the escort of John of Gaunt and Lord Henry Percy, who eleven days previously had been made Marshal of England as the price of his support of the Lancastrians and in place of the Earl of March, who was exiled to Calais. The dramatic but useless scene which followed has vividly impressed itself upon the imagination of later generations. Gaunt, who was detested by the freemen of the city for his cupidity and arrogance no less than for the plottings and chicaneries of his followers, stood at Wycliffe's side throughout the stormy interview, fuming and threatening that he would pull down the pride of all the bishops in England. He was aware that Wycliffe was regarded as the instrument of his schemes for the confiscation of Church offices and revenues. Sudbury and Courtenay were not intolerant prelates, but rather ecclesiastical politicians, whose decision to resist the Duke's measures can be ascribed to their vigilance on behalf of the menaced privileges which they held essential to the existence and standing of the Church. Percy's insolent behavior exasperated the spectators crowding the aisles of the ancient church and the adjacent streets, and the disturbance which attended the passage to the Lady Chapel annoyed Courtenay, who declared, had he known beforehand that Percy would act the master in the Cathedral, he would have barred his entrance. The Duke, blind with rage, replied for his retainer that he should do as he pleased. While prince and prelate exchanged defiances, Wycliffe seems to have calmly awaited the hearing. Even Courtenay, the most gifted and resolute of his foes, whose opposition finally crushed the Wycliffian movement, sank into comparative insignificance when contrasted with the last great Schoolman of Europe, the first clerk of Oxford and the noblest and most astute thinker left in a decadent and reactionary age. Lechler's idealized description portrays him as "a tall, thin figure, clad in a long, light gown of black, with a girdle about his body; his head, adorned with a full, flowing beard, exhibiting features keen and sharply cut, his eye clear and penetrating, his lips firmly closed, in token of resolution — the whole man wearing an aspect of lofty earnestness, and replete with dignity and character." [1]

The issue between the two parties was sharply drawn and thorough examination was desirable, since the justice of the case was by no means confined to Gaunt's faction, but the decorum befitting so grave a trial was altogether absent. Heated rejoinders and personal vilifications ended any pretense to judicial dignity, and were so freely used that Gaunt, overmatched verbally, resorted to threats of physical violence. The Londoners, who loved neither Courtenay nor the Duke, had already been aroused by the introduction of a bill into Parliament on that very afternoon which proposed to deprive the city of its municipal rights and vest its government in an official chosen by the Court. This news created such a tumult against Lancaster that the sitting was suspended, while in the riot which ensued he was compelled to flee, and barely escaped with his life. The enraged citizens, disappointed of their prey, sacked his Palace of the Savoy, refusing to desist till Bishop Courtenay interposed to avert

---

[1] "John Wycliffe and his English Precursors"; p. 159.

their further vengeance. The unexpected deliverance of Wycliffe convinced the writer of the English Chronicle that the entire affair was a device of the devil to protect his elect servant.

Courtenay now had recourse to the Holy See, which required little instigation from him to interfere in English affairs, and on May 22, 1377, Gregory XI, who had just restored the Papacy to Rome, promulgated there in the church of St. Maria Maggiore five bulls against Wycliffe, which he dispatched to the king, the Archbishop of Canterbury, the Bishop of London, and the University of Oxford. Three of these bulls were jointly directed to the Primate and the Bishop, and the other two to the king and the University respectively. Eighteen erroneous articles were transcribed from Wycliffe's writings, all of which, with one exception, were correctly quoted from his treatise "De Dominio Civili." They were condemned as theses and their conclusions expounded and repudiated, the Pontiff affirming with truth that their substance was to be found in the works of Marsiglio, the advocate of the imperial cause against John XXII. The doctrine of evangelical poverty, which Wycliffe set forth against the material magnificence of the Avignon Court, together with his theory of lordship, supplied the material which now came under official censure. The bull addressed to the University chided its members for suffering "tares to spring up among the pure wheat of their glorious field"; the one to the king prayed him to grant the Papal commissioners his favor and protection in the discharge of their duty. Sudbury and Courtenay were reproved as "slothfully negligent, insomuch that latent motions and attempts of the enemy are perceived at Rome before they are opposed in England." Plenary powers were granted to the bishops to ascertain whether these pestiferous opinions were actually taught by Wycliffe, and the Pope directed that "the said John" should be arrested and imprisoned in safe custody until further commands were received.

The edicts reached England at an inopportune moment. Edward III died on June twenty-first of that year; the first Parliament of Richard II at once manifested a strong animus against the encroachments of the Papacy, and the regency of the Princess of Wales was controlled by political exigencies which for the time made Wycliffe the leader of the nation at large. He was consulted by Parliament as to "whether the realm might not legitimately stop the export of gold to Rome, considering the necessities of her defense," and promptly answered in the affirmative.[1] "The Pope," he argued, "cannot demand treasure except by way of alms and by the rule of charity, but all charity beginneth at home, for our fathers endowed not the Church at large, but the Church of England." The document concluded with the plea "that the goods of the Church should be prudently distributed to the glory of God, putting aside the avarice of prelates and princes."

The last clause annoyed those who had predatory purposes of their own, and he was enjoined by the young king and the Council to keep silence. But Parliament and people were so enthusiastically in favor of Wycliffe that, while John of Gaunt was excluded from the Council of his nephew, any effort to indict the Reformer would have been an attempt to indict the nation. It is not surprising that the higher clergy acted circumspectly at this juncture, or that the University doubted whether the Papal bull could be received. The Archbishop's request that Wycliffe should appear before the Commissioners in February, 1378, was extremely courteous in tone, and made no mention of the severe measures the Pope had commanded in the event of his resistance. He came to Lambeth,

---

[1] The export of gold from England by the religious orders was a constant drain on the nation. An example is furnished by the forty English dependencies of the French Abbey of Cluny, which in Wycliffe's time remitted annually to the latter place a sum equivalent to $300,000 or more in modern money. There were many other instances of this continual exaction.

but owing to the pleas of the Princess Dowager of Wales and the clamor of the populace, the conclave was speedily dissolved. Courtenay withdrew his clericals, who were probably much relieved to be freed from their thankless task. Many of the Oxford doctors were in sympathy with Wycliffe's heresies; even his enemies hesitated to lay hands on an influential subject at the behest of a foreign ruler, and during the crisis, the ulterior aims of politicians and the patriotic pride of citizens united to sustain the Reformer as the upholder of national honor. Walsingham, chronicler of St. Albans, mourned over such a dearth of zeal, and chided the cowardice of the bishops who were as "reeds shaken by the wind. Their speech became as soft oil, to the loss of their own dignity and the injury of the Church. They were struck with such a terror that you would fancy them to be 'as a man that heareth not, in whose mouth there is no reproof.'" This jeremiad provided the funeral baked meats for the anti-Wycliffians, whose personal attacks on the Reformer virtually ended in the important year of 1378, when the Great Schism turned the attention of bishops and statesmen to heresiarchs of larger magnitude, and to the evils that arose out of their conduct.

II

Wycliffe's emphatic nationalism developed his first heresies round the grievances of the State, but he passed on to discover in Scripture and Apostolic custom a firm basis for his remonstrance against the friars. His former sentiments toward their self-imposed poverty and sanctity were respectful and affectionate. He spoke of them as "those evangelical men very dear to God," and his early distinction between them and the wealthy monastic orders (religiosi possessionati) was accompanied by an unmeasured rebuke of the indolence, mercenary disposition, and pride of the monks. Historians are generally agreed that it was not till the year 1380, when first he attacked the doctrine of the Mass, that he became embroiled with the friars.[1] Be this as it may, his aversion was not pronounced so long as he recognized that the early Franciscans had been established for the edification of the Church. But when he witnessed with all observers their inconceivably rapid degeneration his references ceased to be eulogistic; in 1378 he protested against those practices which were divorced from their vows, and after 1381 he was their relentless opponent. This revulsion was the more complete because of his previous regard for their excellencies. His unbending nature could not forgive their open derelictions, and these profoundly influenced his attitude toward clerical authority and doctrinal orthodoxy. As monasticism in general was thus the second important factor in his controversies with the Church, a word of explanation concerning the origin and progress of the various orders will enable us better to understand their relation to medieval ecclesiasticism and to Wycliffe.

Monasticism arose in the Orient, and was common to antiquity as well as to modern times; to Buddhism and Mohammedanism, as well as to Christianity. In the third and fourth centuries the deserts of Egypt and Syria abounded with hermits and anchorites, who emulated the rigor and followed the precepts of St. Anthony and St. Pachomius. The former was the first Christian monk, and admittedly the father and prototype of Christian monasticism; the latter, its organizer, who founded nine retreats with three thousand inmates and drew up rules for their guidance in fraternity life. Pachomius' cenobitical rules were made still more stringent by Basil the Great in Cappadocia. When the system entered the West, it received a practical impulse and flourished under better forms than in its original home. Benedictine houses and congregations arose spontaneously, with leaders of piety and personal gifts, whose work was adopted, regulated, and utilized by the inclusive policy of the

[1] Bishop Mandell Creighton: "Historical Essays and Reviews"; p. 192.

Holy See. The fundamental laws which governed all alike were labor, poverty, obedience, and chastity; beneath their sway monasticism fixed the standards and absorbed the forces of the Church, her doctrine and her devotion. Notwithstanding the fact that by Wycliffe's time the virtues and achievements of the system had passed into decline and could no longer overcome the self-assertion of the pagan world, its earlier régime had protected an immature civilization, and was useful in the reduction of its brutal tendencies. The monastic cells enshrined the asceticisms and prayers of innumerable lovers of God whose hard pitiless life was illuminated by those emotions and meditations which are the reverberations of eternity within the human spirit, and their visions of infinitude and holiness are now reflected in some of the choicest devotional literature. Cloistral life in its best periods furnished a center for the spiritual aspirations of mankind, and protected them against a Church too often secularized in heart and soul and a world filled with folly, lust, and cruelty. In addition, the first monks were agriculturalists whose holdings were models of thrift and industry. They did for the rural provinces a work similar to that done by the trade guilds for the cities and towns. The regulars were more than recluses occupying retreats where their beautiful structures, clustering around a Norman or Early English church, arose by the side of some quiet stream encircled by woods and meads. Nor did they spend their entire time in a round of ritualistic offices while they depended on inherited or contributed means for support. They cleared the land of bracken and bramble, drained and tilled it, dug the fishponds, reared the barns which housed the harvests of an erstwhile wilderness, and built the fanes they filled with psalmodies. Their economic and religious value for the half-starved, ignorant peasantry was very considerable. This pioneer work taught the rustics to have some care for their bodies and homes, and the monks further instructed them in respect to their souls' welfare. A colonizing habit and a communistic life were the focus for missionary efforts, in which educational provisions and medical dispensaries were included. Hospitality was a sacred duty, embracing all ranks and conditions. The vestiges of art which survived that stormy interregnum were preserved in the monasteries. They were the treasure houses for the traditions and examples of a former learning, and the sacred books and the writings of the Fathers were kept intact in their libraries and copied in their scriptoria.

But the institution which was comparatively irreproachable in the tenth century was questionable in the fourteenth : later monasticism had forsaken some of its healthy occupations, and was no longer kept pure by sacrificial toil. It incurred the adverse judgments of such loyal Catholics as St. Bonaventure, St. Catherine of Sienna, and the great Gerson himself.[1] The details of its decadence are too lengthy for recital here, nor do the learned and apologetic works of such writers as Cardinal Gasquet [2] deal as fully as could be desired with the official arraignments of the regular clergy during the four centuries preceding the Reformation. The statements therein contained are explicit and conclusive, and the Cardinal's explanations are characterized by a partisanship which the careful student is bound to take into consideration. On the other hand, Thorold Rogers' description of the later monasteries as "dens of gluttony and vice" is entirely too severe. Abandoned wickedness was prevalent in some quarters, but it was the exception and not the rule. Where the charges of immorality are true, as are those given in the painstaking accounts of Dr. H. C. Lea, they are likely to be misleading unless regarded in relation to the age in which the offenses were committed. The restraints and licenses of pub-

[1] *John Gerson* (1363–1429), French scholar and divine, Chancellor of the University of Paris and leading spirit in the Ecumenical Councils of Pisa and Constance. He labored to spiritualize university life, reform the clergy, and end the Church schism, and also to abolish scholastic subtleties from the university curriculum.

[2] The Head of the Benedictines in England, elevated to the Sacred College on May 25, 1914.

lic opinion were felt even in the cloister; its devotees were not all of a superior sort; to a great extent they represented the social conditions from which they had been transferred, and they should not be condemned without reference to current practices, which, although they do not excuse, help to explain the failure of religious professions.

Sporadic attacks of sensuality were not the real causes which led to the decline of monasticism. The system ceased to live because it had forsaken its first love and lay engulfed in its selfish introspections. The terms monk and monastery lost their once grateful sound; local comments turned from praise to blame; esteem and affection gave place in the breasts of their tenants and underlings to contempt and hate. The hostels of the lowly Nazarene, in which the poor and the maimed were no longer welcome, housed lordly abbots and their wasteful retinues. The effects of the unseemly change were seen in many directions, and in none more than in this, that whenever local riots arose the monastery or abbey was almost sure to be the first building upon which the people vented their displeasure. When Wycliffe assailed the monks and friars they were no longer formidable. The seculars had begun to supplant them in the cure of souls; the Universities had found them a negligible quantity; the education of the youth of the nation had passed out of their keeping; the people resented their aloofness; the barons hungered for their broad acres, and patriots viewed them as the watchdogs of an alien power.

At this juncture, when the noble impulses of Benedictines, Augustinians, Franciscans, and Dominicans were trembling on the verge of extinction, the ravages of the Black Death destroyed at a blow one half the inmates of the religious houses in England. Then, as we have seen, the friars rendered a laudable service to stricken humanity. But the fearful visitation crushed the monastic establishments. Their broken and dispirited survivors could not fill the vacancies thus created, and their funds went unreplenished by any entrance fees. In England during the fourteenth century only sixty-four new monasteries were established, as compared with two hundred and ninety-six in the thirteenth century, and four hundred and ninety in the twelfth century.[1] Conciliation by means of a more public-minded policy and service was at an end. The state of affairs before Wycliffe came upon the scene has been depicted by Dr. Jessopp: the monk "fled away to his solitude; the rapture of silent adoration was his joy and exceeding great reward; his nights and days might be spent in praise and prayer, sometimes in study and research, sometimes in battling with the powers of darkness and ignorance, sometimes in throwing himself heart and soul into art which it was easy to persuade himself he was doing only for the glory of God; but all this must go on far away from the busy haunts of men, certainly not within earshot of the multitude." [2]

Monasticism had received repeated warnings to set its house in order; nor did the injustice of some of its enemies excuse its own perversity and pride. It evaded embarrassing situations and suppressed realities until doom fell upon the proudest and richest order of its chivalry, the Knights Templars of France, and none could foretell where the next stroke would fall. In May, 1308, fifty knights were hurried to the stake; five years later Pope Clement V decreed the dispersal of the order, and the tragedy was completed, on March 14, 1314, by the burning of Jacques de Molay, the Grand Master, with three of his principal subordinates. A small island in the Seine, at the western end of the city of Paris, where now the Pont Neuf rests between the arms of the river, was the scene of the execution. The flames rose against the dusk of evening and crimsoned the shores, which were lined with spectators. While the Grand Master stood in the fire

---

[1] In the fifteenth century only one or two monasteries were built in England, the chief of which was the Bridgettine Syon, at Isleworth, Middlesex, founded by Henry V in memory of his father.

[2] "The Coming of the Friars"; p. 7.

and slowly roasted to death he summoned the Pope and the French king to appear with him at the bar of the Almighty. Within forty days Clement obeyed the call, and Philip the Fair within the year.[1]

A century and more before these events, monasticism's loftiest ideal had found its most perfect realization in St. Francis of Assisi, the young Italian who for a moment molded the world to his own will, and better still, kept himself unspotted from it. The life of St. Francis is an imperishable example of the divinest elements victorious in human nature, surviving every vicissitude and bringing the race nearer to the goal of righteousness and obedience. The son of a merchant of Assisi, Pietro Bernardone, he is said to have received the name Franciscus because he was born during his father's absence in France in 1182, although some biographers have attributed it to his own residence there as a youth, and to his familiarity with the language of the Troubadours. In 1206 he was brought to the verge of death by successive attacks of sickness, which decided his career. Out of their regenerating purification emerged the transcendently beatific figure of the saint, who turned from his boon companions and their pleasures that he might taste the powers of the world to come. Relinquishing his inheritance, he took upon himself the vows of poverty, and appeared clad in a single tunic of coarse woolen cloth, girt with a hempen cord, the dress which afterwards became the garb of his famous order. The greatest of the Popes, Innocent III, gave him the sanction for which Francis had petitioned that discerner of spirits, and the young devotee settled the constitution of his fraternity upon the threefold basis of chastity, poverty, and obedience. From the beginning the second of these vows was first in spiritual importance and efficacy. The chosen motto of the brotherhood was Christ's word, "Ye cannot serve God and Mammon"; its practice, that each member should esteem himself the least and most unprofitable of all. "He

[1] M. S. C. Smith: "Twenty Centuries of Paris"; pp. 115, 118.

that will be chief among you," said the founder, "let him be your servant." Those whose self-consequence would not allow them to submit to these precepts were rejected, and the remnant became fratres, freres, or friars, who were sent out to proclaim their evangel to the ends of the earth.

The companion order of the Dominicans was established in 1216, the year of Innocent's death and of his formal authorization of the Franciscans. St. Dominic, their founder, was a native of Calahorra in Old Castile, born in or about 1170, the year of Becket's murder. When still a young man of twenty-three he was so well known for piety and learning that the Bishop of Osma appointed him to a canonry, and relied upon his help in the reform of the Chapter according to the Augustinian rule. His missionary labors among the Moslems, and especially among the Albigenses of southern France, convinced Dominic that the cruelties to which these sufferers for their faith were subjected could not convert or even shake the resolution of the victims. "We must meet them with other weapons and greater faith!" he cried. And in the belief that such heresies lured the souls of men to everlasting ruin, he conceived the order which bears his name. On December 22, 1216, he obtained an audience with Innocent's successor, Honorius III, who reluctantly confirmed his predecessor's stipulation that the first Dominican community, then located at the Church of St. Romain in Toulouse, should be called a house of Augustinian canons. The endowments of St. Dominic as a preacher naturally led him to insist on the agency of the pulpit for the silencing of opponents and the instruction of the ignorant.[1] In 1220 the Dominicans, imitating the Franciscans, adopted vows of poverty so rigid that not even as a corporation could they hold houses or lands. The two orders, thus nearly simultaneous in their origin, were known from the color of their robes as the Grey and the Black friars, and their

[1] A. Jessopp: "The Coming of the Friars"; p. 24.

H

mission, while practically the same in its object, was sufficiently varied in methods to suit their distinctive gifts.

Enough has been said to indicate that monks and friars were not simply different in degree, but also in kind. The monk clung to his possessions, the friar had not where to lay his head ; the monk lived apart from, the friar with, the people. The self-abnegation of the latter set him free to spend and be spent in their behalf. While he raised his voice against their lusts and iniquities, he was alive to their distresses and shared their hopes and fears. The story of the first appearance of the friars in England during the year 1224 surpasses romance in its fascinations. The land was just recovering from the religious destitution consequent upon the Papal interdict against King John when they entered it, delivering as they went the message that neither birth, nor station, nor riches, nor learning counted for aught, but rather goodness, meekness, sympathy, and truth. Men could live above the base and the vile, and find their highest selves while pursuing their ordinary vocations. Such words fell upon hearts longing for the truth, and the consistent conduct of the preachers, seconded by their brief and intense sermons, gained an eager response from all classes. The striking resemblance between the earlier friars and the itinerants of eighteenth century Methodism has been widely observed. "St. Francis," comments Dr. Jessopp, "was the John Wesley of the thirteenth century whom the Church did not cast out." Both the friars and the circuit riders saw that the Church was lifeless, that the parochial system had collapsed, and that the only means of recovery was by a return to the spirit and letter of the New Testament Evangel, in absolute, unquestioning obedience to its teachings. This they essayed, without disputing on useless issues, and unhindered by superfluous dogmas or rules. But the parallel was incomplete in one salient particular. The friars were conformable to the general policy of the Roman Church, and when John XXII condemned the strict observance of the vows of their order they even burnt their brethren who clung to the traditions of St. Francis. The Methodist Churches, whether in England, America, or elsewhere, have always been independent of any ecclesiastical authority outside their own borders.

Papal corruption had little to fear from the friars so long as the Curia exercised control. When the Spiritual Franciscans developed their own principles and became the Fraticelli, they drew upon themselves the censure of popes, of kings, and of those who represented the conservative interests of society. The lower minds among them surrendered those ideals which had awed Europe into adoration, and sank down into an organized hypocrisy. The loftier intellects, who did not share St. Francis' contempt for learning, were harassed, silenced, banished, or imprisoned. Foremost among such men was Roger Bacon, whose vast knowledge and investigations in physics enabled him to confront tradition and authority with facts demonstrated by experiment. Time worked its deterioration on the friars' singleness of aim; the exacting regimen of Assisi was honestly believed by many of the saint's followers to be impossible of fulfillment. Spiritual romanticism was followed by sudden and violent disenchantment. The millennial vision vanished after its collision with reality. The consequences were such as might have been expected; those who set up as idealists while at the same time living on the naturalistic level hastened the triumph of the forces against which they professed resistance. "Whether there be prophecies," said the Apostle, "they shall fail;" and those pseudo-prophets who were unable to breathe the rarefied atmosphere of the altitudes attained by seers of the past could no longer utter oracles with any meaning. Yet "Love never faileth," and, although their brotherhood was demoralized, their concord broken by disloyalties and divisions, that wonderful example of a life of holiness and service which at the first the friars placed before the world has been a source of strength and inspiration in every branch of the Church.

III

An expert in adopting other men's ideas, Wycliffe incorporated the friars' doctrine of voluntary poverty into his own teaching and copied their methods of evangelization when he sent out his poor preachers. The more devout among them were always cherished by him, and he coveted their aid in his revival of their neglected practices. Some responded, and many students, failing to notice this, have been puzzled by the presence of four friars as his advisers when he appeared before the Convocation at St. Paul's. But, once he was persuaded that the orders as a whole were lost to their proper aspirations and no longer abstained from all pursuits common to men that they might preach the Gospel of Jesus in word and deed, he set them apart for contempt and scorn. They were outside the pale of decency, reprobate and abnormally wicked. Nor was he alone in these accusations; all classes, save those which profited by the friars' lapse, were a unit in protesting against their outrages, hypocrisies, and lusts. Exempt from episcopal jurisdiction, they were severely censured by the bishops who could not control their excesses. The monastic orders eyed them askance as successful rivals, and fiercely assailed them. But the general and prolonged outcry against them and the nearly universal hatred heaped upon their works and ways can only be explained by the fact that the offenses laid at their door were substantially true. They had fallen to the lowest levels of society, and the height of their first endeavors gave momentum to the headlong descent.

They glossed the Scriptures to extenuate the crimes of malefactors, and heard confessions and granted absolutions with such flagrant disregard for the sanctity of the priestly vocation that the Pope was driven to contemplate its withdrawal. Freed from parochial responsibilities, they wandered where they pleased, refusing with impudent nonchalance to face the results of their evil deeds, and leaving behind them an increasing army of villains and outlaws shriven for a fee and cleansed of all their sins. These sorry specimens of the pardoning power were the despair of the secular priests and of the bailiffs alike. The sober testimony of such dignitaries as Archbishop Fitzralph supports what otherwise might appear to be rhetorical exaggerations. He averred that he had two thousand [1] such in a year "who are excommunicated for willful robbery, arson, and similar acts, of whom scarce forty come to me or my parish priests for confession, preferring to confess to the begging friars who at once absolve and admit them to communion." "Any accursed swearer, extortioner, or adulterer," thundered Wycliffe, "will not be shriven by his own curate, but will go to a flattering friar that will assoil him falsely for a little money by the year, though he be not in a will to make restitution and to leave his accursed sin." He branded them with the name of Cain, spelt Caym, and taken from the initials of the Carmelites, Austins, Jacobins or Dominicans, and Minorites or Franciscans. Their farcical pretensions to religious oversight were satirized in the political ballads of the street, of which the following stanza is a specimen:

"For had a man slain all his kin,
Go shrive him to a friar,
And for less then a pair of shoon
He will assoil him clean and soon."

Chaucer's optimism gave place to irony when he depicted among the Canterbury pilgrims the monk "who had but one fault, forgetfulness of the rules of his order, and an inordinate love for hunting." The smooth-tongued friar; the summoner, with his "fire-red pimpled face, narrow eyes and loose morals; the pardoner of beardless chin, goggle eyes, dark yellow hair and squeaking voice," were an unedifying group of clerical figures in the poet's narrative.

[1] The number varies: some authorities giving two thousand, others two hundred.

Many had degenerated into hucksters; "Charity," wrote Langland, "hath turned chapman." Their profits were too often spent in dissipation. The friars "knew the tavernes well in every town." Popular songs imputed to them the worst of crimes.

> "All wickedness that men can tell
> Reigneth them among,
> There shall no soul have room in hell
> Of friars there is such a throng."

Wycliffe did not accuse them of the grossest forms of immorality, but Langland, widely divergent from him in temperament and outlook, did, and issued his tirade against the mendicants, pardoners, summoners, and other such "caterpillars of the commonwealth." They were chiefly intent on humoring the lewd and the godless and inducing them to open their pockets after their harangues. Nor did they confine their solicitations to the poor. Lady Meed, the incarnation of illicit gain in "Piers Plowman," had scarcely arrived in London when

> "Came there a confessor coped as a friar
>
>   *   *   *   *   *   *
>
> Then he absolved her soon, and sithen he said,
> We have a window a-working will cost us full high,
> Wouldst thou glaze that gable and grave therein thy neme,
> Sure shall thy soul be heaven to have."

So notorious were the infamies of these parasites that the authorities, and especially those of the Universities, were compelled to rise against them. But the friars were aware of their power as a useful organization to be employed in emergencies by unscrupulous superiors. They also had a firm hold upon the ignorant and the refractory, whose prejudices and offenses they fostered or excused, and they could afford to ignore the threatenings of the higher clergy. This defiant attitude was emphasized by the alignment of the orders in opposite political camps. The Franciscans naturally cast their weight on the side of the peasantry, from whose ranks they were recruited; while the Dominicans favored the wealthier groups. Both alike were advocates of Papal claims, emissaries of Rome, and defenders of the highest sacerdotal views of the priesthood and of the Sacrament of the Mass. They shared in the repression of intellectual freedom at Oxford, and hunted down Wycliffe's preachers wherever found.

He attributed their depravity to the inflated notions of clerical power then prevalent, and the wanton abuse of its prerogatives convinced him that it must be destroyed before any permanent reform in the Church could be accomplished. As with many intellectual people, Wycliffe's inexorable reasoning was more consistent than his insight was sure. He did not perceive that the real cause for the breakdown of the Franciscan ideal was to be found in the inevitable reaction which followed Francis' premature attempt to project his scheme on an agitated and wicked age. No such spiritual conception could remain alive and prosper unless the losses to its disciples from death and disaffection were repaired by compensatory gains the adverse conditions of the period did not supply. The saint of Assisi was set on the immediate regeneration of men and society after the pattern of his own transformation. The less obvious and more patient processes which enable the mass of mankind gradually to transcend the limitations of evil in themselves and in their environment were rejected for a frontal attack upon iniquity and selfishness, which, while it was magnificent, was not war. It may be remarked in passing that the decline of the orders coincided with a desirable change in the fortunes of the parochial priesthood. The seculars were no longer to be ousted from their charges, nor deprived of their pastoral standing, nor robbed of their income in order that some fraternity might reap advantage, or an already wealthy abbey be increasingly endowed. The founding of Merton,

Queens, and New Colleges was the genesis of an educational system intended to supply, among other requisites, a godly and learned ministry for the churches of the nation. The necessity for this waited long upon its fulfillment, but at any rate the diversion had been made, and while the regulars decreased the seculars grew in efficiency and serviceableness. Moreover, the Black Death bettered the condition of the survivors among the parochial clergy by increasing the demand for their labors. The registers show that during and directly after the pestilence, the number of priests instituted to livings increased from thirty-seven to seventy-four in every hundred cases. Notwithstanding episcopal edicts, their stipends were raised commensurately, and in this and other ways the disparity between them and the rest of the clergy was reduced. Thus the Black Death did in one year what the Ecumenical Council of Lyons had conspicuously failed to accomplish, although summoned by a reforming Pontiff, and prompted by such disciplinarians as St. Bonaventura and his fellow Franciscan, Eudes Rigaud of Rouen.[1]

From the moment that Wycliffe resented the sacerdotalism which the friars embodied and abused, his severance from Rome was simply a question of time. His hesitancies were dismissed by the Great Schism which six years before his death tore asunder the Papacy, and continued from 1378 to 1417. This event convulsed Christendom and gravely affected the standing of the Holy See. The confusion and distress which resulted from it were an impressive tribute to the historical service of the Papacy as a centralizing and cohesive power. "For nearly eight hundred years," says Dr. Workman, in an eloquent passage, "Rome had stood, not merely for righteousness, but solidarity. Her bishops were not only the vicars of God; they were the symbols and source of a brotherhood that would otherwise have perished. Men remembered their services in the past; how they had tamed the barbarians, enforced law upon the lawless,

[1] G. C. C. Coulton: "Chaucer and his England"; p. 305.

preached the subordination of the individual to society, curbed the lust and despotism of kings, held up ideals of purity and truth in the darkest ages, saved the Church from the triumph of the Cathari,[1] maintained a unity of faith and hope in the days when all creed was in danger of disintegration."[2] Whether or not everything in this list of notable deeds was Rome's actual work, or an appropriation of that of other agents, the people of the fourteenth century neither knew nor cared. It sufficed for the vast majority that they held her claims valid, and her Pontiffs a divinely ordained succession. Any infringement upon the integrity and rights of the throne of St. Peter was therefore a desecration of the controlling authority in civilization. There had always existed in the Church a liberal and legitimate trend of thought and effort, which was not at variance with any vital principle of Catholicism, but, on the contrary, essential to its functions as a unifying force. The representatives of this trend knew that "if in a higher world it is otherwise, yet here below to live is to change, and to be perfect is to have changed often." Yet when sagacious ecclesiastics, recognizing that the human element in the Church stood ever in need of correction and readjustment, made any overtures for reform, a conflict was invariably precipitated, in which the conservatives, with the Vati-

---

[1] *The Cathari*, also known as Paulicians, Albigenses, Bulgarians, Manicheans, etc., were a widely scattered sect both in the East and the West. They believed in the existence of two Gods, one good, the other evil, both eternal, though as a rule they subordinated the evil to the good; that Satan inspired certain parts of the Old Testament, and was the ruler of this world, which was spiritual, not material; that all men would finally be saved, but that those dying unreconciled to God through Christ must return to earth for a further term of imprisonment in the flesh, either in a human or an animal body. They fell into two well-marked divisions: the Catechumens or Believers, and the Perfect, who had received the gift of the Paraclete. The latter, which included women, formed the priesthood and controlled the Church. The influence of the Cathari on Christendom was enormous. To counteract it Innocent III instituted his crusades, and celibacy was finally imposed on the clergy; the great mendicant orders and the sacrament of Extreme Unction were also evolved by way of competing with the teachings and practices of the sect.

[2] "The Dawn of the Reformation"; Vol. I, p. 12.

can at their head, generally won an easy victory. Gerson's plea for a constitutional Papacy deriving its authority from conciliar representation, or the plan advocated by Grosseteste, who asked that methods of raising revenue should be reformed and a stricter discipline enforced, received scarcely less rebuke from Rome than the revolutionary proposals made by Marsiglio and Wycliffe. The outward unity of Christendom was finally shattered, and the reproach incurred by the Holy See for its part in the calamity was the more deserved, because this was hastened by the resistance of the Popes to human progress and by their ambition for temporal sovereignty. The very *raison d'être* of the Papacy consisted in its being the divinely appointed trustee of the legacy of faith and morals bequeathed to mankind by Christ. The fidelity and energy with which this treasure should have been guarded were squandered on earthly affairs, and struggles for political ascendency.

Further, in demolishing the Holy Roman Empire the Papacy irretrievably damaged its own edifice. Conjoined, the two powers were supreme because they were complementary; separated, each was deprived of the federation of secular and ecclesiastical authority which had been a mutual support in their subjection of European tribes and kindreds. Their centripetal forces were spent in what was really a civil war; Gregory IX and Innocent IV even went to the length of proclaiming their conflict with the Emperor Frederic II a crusade, and, on that assumption, demanded funds from the Church and the faithful. The struggle ended in the defeat of the Emperor, once known as the "wonder of Europe," a ruler of high ideals and pursuits. He died in the summer of 1250, leaving many projects unfulfilled; on the subsequent ruin of his house, the Capetians strengthened their dynasty in France and the English monarchy became a still more essential part of that nation. Rome discovered, too late, the nemesis of her triumph over the Empire in the widespread conviction, which she could not shake, that the building up of separate nationalities was the future task of statesmen and the goal of history. Thus a deadly blow was inflicted upon her prestige by those results which she had imagined would increase it.

There was nothing novel in the idea of national autonomy, though it had long been dormant when the dissolution of the Holy Roman Empire and the passing of the medieval principle of internationalism reawakened it and made possible its realization. The Popes asserted anew their claim to authority, only to find that the moral grounds on which the Papacy originally rested its case were no longer tenable and that the lower methods of diplomacy and of war were their only resources. Rulers and peoples were not disposed to readmit spiritual prerogatives or bow to clerical control without the closest scrutiny, and, at times, open defiance. That astute and unscrupulous politician, Boniface VIII, endeavored to remove this antagonism, but he could not depend, as did his predecessors, upon the European princes as his feudatories and the instruments of his will. Where compulsion was unavailing, negotiation was the last resort; by its employment of artifice and strategy the Papacy lowered itself to the level of surrounding governments, and incurred reprisals that were a contradiction of its theories of overlordship. To make confusion worse confounded Boniface plunged into a quarrel with Philip the Fair of France which ended in the defeat and capture of the Pontiff, who was sent to Rome as a hostage, where he was imprisoned by the Orsini in the Vatican, until, on October the eleventh, 1303, death mercifully released him from further humiliation. Such a tragedy had not been known since the fall of Rome; the spiritual sovereignty of Christendom had become a mere adjunct in the administration of one among a group of developing states. The successor of Boniface likewise perished with mysterious suddenness, and the choice of the next Papal candidate was dictated by Philip, who forced the new Pope to give pledges that he would revise the

Vatican's policy in harmony with the king's wishes. This infamous betrayer of his Pontificate, Clement V, was born a subject of Edward I in or about the year 1264. He became Archbishop of Bordeaux, and was crowned Pope at Lyons on November 14, 1305.

After his elevation to the throne of Peter, Clement peremptorily refused to reside in Rome, nor did he visit the capital of Christendom during his sovereignty. In 1309, consistently with the deliberate exploitation of the Holy See by the French Court, he transferred its seat to Avignon. The act was worse than a blunder, it was a crime. The Pope and Rome were inseparably one, a necessary unity for the religious symbolism which was cosmopolitan, not national, and still less sectional; intelligible to all, understood by all. Their unnatural separation startled and repelled Catholics of every land; it chilled the heart and numbed the intelligence of those who ardently cherished divine things.

Avignon is separated from the rest of the world by the legends and histories that haunt its embattled walls and thirty-nine towers. Innocent IV built these fortifications, whose strength stayed for a time the prowess of Bertrand du Guesclin, the foremost warrior of fourteenth century France. In Avignon, Petrarch is said to have looked on Laura for the first time, and the city still claims her tomb. Along its streets rode the beautiful Queen Jeanne of Naples, attended by her courtiers, when she came to answer for the murder of her husband, and to sell the place to Clement VI for eighty thousand gold florins. Rienzi also found his way here, shadowed by his approaching fate. The Palace of the Popes, a sanctuary and a fortress, is enthroned on the Roches des Domes, three hundred feet above the Rhone, and in its hall of audience the politics of Europe centered for a century and a half. The Court of Avignon during this period was a plague-spot of wholesale bribery, simony, and debauchery. Petrarch, whose language should be received with some reservation, described the gloomy stronghold as "the city of the Captivity, the common sink of all vices, false guilt-laden Babylon, the forge of lies, the horrible prison, the hell upon earth." Beyond question its villainies saddened the souls of believers and stimulated the antagonism in which Wycliffe figured. The morale of the Church was impaired by the sight of the Pontiff acting as the ally of France, and subjected by French statesmen to their schemes for dominating the continent. The tribunal which had been the court of arbitration for Western Christianity, and whose judgments, as the one untrammeled and absolute authority above the control or influence of secular states, had been dispensed with so even a hand as to command general approval, now became a hissing and a byword.

In England dissatisfaction slowly passed into open hostility. The reasons were evident: not only was any measure which ran counter to French interests promptly suppressed, but these interests were aided and abetted by Papal decrees. Clement V and his brother supplied the French army with several millions of pounds sterling during the wars of France with the island kingdom, which itself had previously contributed to the Papal exchequer a large part of the grant. The treacherous deed filled England's cup of bitterness to overflowing; it was typical of the conscienceless extortions wrung under every conceivable pretext from all regions within the Papal jurisdiction. The end of such a course could be nothing short of the degradation of the Papacy, the ruin of its standing and authority. And so the event proved. "The Church is pale," lamented Catherine of Sienna, "through loss of blood drained from her by insatiable devourers."

The suicidal proceeding entered its last phase in the Schism, when two rival Popes reviled and excommunicated each other with every insult and calumny unheeding anger could evoke. They were compared by Wycliffe to hungry dogs snarling over one bone. After more than seventy years of the Avignon Papacy, Gregory XI returned to Rome in the winter of 1376–1377, reluctantly taking this step after repeated solicitations from St. Catherine, whose remarkable letters to the Pontiff on various occasions were replete with literary charm and spiritual fervor. He found the city a desolation and the Lateran Palace uninhabitable; an ominous emblem of the irreparable havoc which had been wrought upon the Holy See itself.

This brief summary of the causes and consequences of the collapse of Romanism, as conceived by Hildebrand and realized in part by Innocent III, leaves one occupied with conjectures upon what might have been the future of Christendom if the warnings of Dante, the foremost religious genius of the last millennium, had been effectual. His "Divina Commedia" is the grandest medieval memorial of a completely enfranchised soul, and the chief token of its power. Individual as his work is, it sets forth a universal system, in which he passes beyond the farthest boundaries of man's mind. The great poet sorrowed over the destruction of the Empire and the lost unity of the Church which had been the nexus of the nations. He foresaw that without some auspicious intervention further calamities would ensue. The conclusions of saints of happier times, such as St. Bernard, St. Victor, and St. Thomas, haunted his remembrance. He heard the failings of the Church on earth recounted in the courts above; the splendors of Paradise grew dim while St. Peter denounced the sins of those who had disgraced the Holy See. But notwithstanding Dante's cyclonic bursts of wrath against her iniquities, Rome remained for him the center of the world and the hope of the race. The idea of a supreme divine development in which human institutions, however holy, were but the foam on the wave, did not relieve his distress. He knew only the things of the past; salvation from the disasters he mourned lay, not in the womb of the future, but in the restoration of a departed authority whose grandeur comported with the notions of his own mind.

Believing this he turned to the reconstituted Church and Empire as the only source and anchorage of humanity.

The results he presaged came in full measure, pressed down and running over. The Papacy, which had cowed Abailard, silenced the speculations of Arnold of Brescia, and at every hazard held fast to the orthodox faith, itself fell a victim to the heresies of the Renaissance. Emerging from the French Captivity crippled and shorn, it became degraded even in its own eyes, and the refined sensualism of the later Pontiffs was only purged away by the defection of the half of Christendom. The wounds then inflicted have not been healed; the unity and the universality lost under Boniface VIII and Clement V have not been recovered, nor has the Holy See since resumed its overlordship of the European nations. Nevertheless, though sorely pressed on many sides, and sadly mutilated, it regained the old severe and rigid method, and continued to serve as a great reservoir of influences and powers which have steadily contributed to the organization of modern society.

The splendid dream of Hildebrand, like that of St. Francis, was foredoomed for lack of elasticity. When realized, it was defeated by the expanding life of Christian States which the Church knew better how to evolve than to control. Beneath the moral turpitude, the exodus to Avignon, the treacheries, grievances, complaints, and wars, lay the Papacy's fundamental error: its slowness to perceive that feudalism in the fourteenth century had begun to die and was no longer possible as an organic system. The higher civilization which supplanted it could not be permanently restrained by the lower. While the northern peoples increased in vitality and ethical superiority, the Holy See lost its breadth of sympathy and was unconsciously narrowed by Latin traits and tendencies. It vainly trusted in the glamour of outward rank and circumstance; in the unyielding monitions of a hierarchy, and in the stilted formulæ with which it expressed the major truths of life and faith. These had little meaning for the more powerful communities which eventually gained supremacy in Germany, Holland, Scandinavia, Great Britain and her colonies of the New World. Rome's traditional arguments, which her wisest children would have modified, were not sufficiently strong to support a position rendered patently anomalous by the growth of knowledge and freedom. The outcome was far too complex and extensive for its various aspects to be characterized in a phrase. The mischievous result for the Holy See was the loss of its genuine catholicity. On the European continent the anarchy and war which followed offset the otherwise notable advantages of release from Roman supremacy.

IV

While Sudbury, Courtenay, and their fellow bishops were anxiously pondering how to obey the Pope without offending the English people, Wycliffe escaped scot free. His first appearance in public affairs after the proceedings connected with the Papal bulls of condemnation was in the autumn Parliament of 1378. John of Gaunt had violated the sanctuary at Westminster by sending a band of armed men to seize two knights who had taken refuge there, one of whom was slain in the mêlée which ensued. Wycliffe was requested to write a defense of the Duke's high-handed action; he responded with a state paper which is still preserved and incorporated in his treatise "De Ecclesia." As an argument against the abuse of such privileges the document is creditable enough, but it was not applicable to the case in question. The result was that it gave color to the accusation that Wycliffe was a hireling of the Lancastrian party, and neither helped Gaunt nor increased its author's reputation. Wycliffe occupied a far stronger position when he resumed with unabated vigor his philippic against the Cæsarean clergy. His ecclesiastical protestantism voiced a common feeling of discontent. Its political elements contained the germinal conceptions of modern as substituted for medieval ideas of man and society, and in giving them utterance Wycliffe confirmed his position as a leader of the nation. The luxurious residences and appointments of the wealthier prelates savored of the devil; their flourishing estates were a scandal to the service of Him who had said, "My kingdom is not of this world"; the exactions and sinecures of the hierarchies and the orders were derogatory to the honor of God. Here he halted before assailing the Papacy, restrained by the reflection that it was the animating principle of the Church and the focus of her external forms. Yet the rift between him and the Holy See was made in the first instance by logical deductions from his own theories on lordship and its counterpart in service, which bore heavily upon the Papal claims. Then came the Schism, which demanded force instead of logic, and certainly could not be met by Wycliffe's fixed faith in the virtues of argumentative persuasion.

In this change of sentiment toward the Pontiffs the antithesis of Church and State was implicated, and to such opposition as his the genesis of the Reformation must be ascribed. Yet he earnestly desired the preservation of the Holy See, believing that its dignity and prestige were as essential to the stability of Christendom as its entanglement with matters temporal was subversive of that end. He contended that the spheres of temporal and spiritual sovereignty were necessarily separate and distinct, that the Church should neither influence politically nor be influenced by the secular power.

Impelled by these and similar arguments he slowly drifted from his loyalty to the Papacy. Prior to 1378 he had acknowledged its governance, although denying its unconditional plenary power. As late as that same year he hailed the election of Urban VI with a burst of approbation: "Praised be the Lord who has given to our Church in the days of her pilgrimage a Catholic head, an evangelical man, who, in reforming the Church that it may live in accordance with

I

the laws of Christ, begins in due order with himself and his own household, so from his works we believe that he is our own Christian head." Even after the Schism, Urban was still, in Wycliffe's words, "our Pope." But the death of Gregory XI at Rome changed all this. His successor had to be elected there, and the violence of the populace so alarmed the Conclave that to appease it they chose Urban, an Italian by birth. Five months later he outwitted the French representation in the College and entrenched himself in power by nominating twenty-eight new Cardinals, a majority sufficient to end the Gallican control of the Curia. At this turn of events the malcontents elected their anti-pope, Robert of Geneva, who assumed the title of Clement VII, and was ultimately deposed by the Council of Constance. Thus the Curia itself destroyed the unity of the Church and created that incipient revolt which ended in the upheaval of the sixteenth century. The conduct of Urban and Clement in their violent outbursts against each other soon quenched Wycliffe's praise of the former claimant. Both became for him as "crows resting on carrion," and he advised that they should be discarded, since they had "little in common with the Church of the Holy God." The description was justified; Urban, a man of meager cultivation and harsh manners, behaved with the ferocity of a savage, and Clement, although less cruel by nature, was conspicuously deficient in moral character. Selfish oligarchies had met their usual fate, and, while Christian people looked on, helpless and depressed, both Popes pursued a tumultuous course of personal vengeance, wherein tortures, imprisonments, assassinations, and wars occurred which the Cardinals themselves endeavored to arrest.

Neutrality was impossible, and Wycliffe's detestation extended beyond the rival disputants to the system which they were tearing to pieces. He publicly denounced the Papacy as accursed in root and branch, employing epithets which echoed the fury that raged at Rome and Avignon,

"Christ," said he, "has begun to help us graciously in that he has cloven the head of Antichrist and made the one part fight against the other." The primacy of St. Peter could not be proved; the claims based upon it were mythical; Papal infallibility and the right to canonize or excommunicate were wicked delusions. He placed upon the Curia the onus of blame for the oppression, immorality, strife, and misgovernment that disgraced the Papal court and administration, and referred to the Pope himself as an apostate to venerate whom was blasphemous idolatry. While he traced the source of these grievous misdoings to the Pontiffs, he asserted that their poison had spread throughout the ecclesiasticism they personified. The "twelve daughters of the diabolical leech" were found in the hierarchical grades of the clergy, beginning with the Cardinals, and ending with the doorkeepers who did their bidding. None had scriptural warranty, and least of all those of the higher ranks, who should be plucked out of the seats they defiled. The pastoral offices were safer in the keeping of simple and godly clerks than in that of learned ingrates, and, unless such virtuous men were installed and the Church purged of crafty and ambitious worldlings who had so long been her woe, she could not be restored to her ancient purity and service. It is difficult to determine how much of this objurgation originated with Wycliffe, as distinguished from that attributed to him. Current controversial literature abounded with references to Antichrist, a mysterious, awful being who was regarded as the sum of diabolical iniquity, whose name was employed by all and sundry to heighten their vilification of opponents. Many of the pamphlets then issued have been confused with the writings of Wycliffe, and, later, of Hus. It is fairly certain that Wycliffe did not object to the Holy See so long as it was invested with its essential qualifications. Nor can his adverse attitude be ascribed to the removal of the Papal Court to Avignon, an event which took place before he was born. His abhorrence arose from the disgrace of rival successors of St. Peter frantically issuing excommunications and raising armies against each other. This prodigious evil infected the entire Church, and, so far as Wycliffe was involved, after 1378, the memorable year in his career, he had no dealings with Rome, except as an open adversary.

His doctrine of the Church, when freed from the scholastic abstractions which mystified it, may be divided into three parts: the Church triumphant, the Church militant, and the Church "asleep in Purgatory." The second of these, which alone concerns us, he defined as consisting exclusively of those who were predestined to salvation. This assignment was so arbitrary that the Pope "wots not whether he be of the Church or whether he be a limb of the fiend." The number of the elect was entirely an allocation of the Divine Will, and their indissoluble spiritual union did not require the countenance of hierarchies, nor that of the "sects" of monks, friars, and priests. He showed here, as elsewhere, the deep distrust of human arrangements which he seems to have inherited from Ockham, carrying it to the extent of complete disorganization. Not only might Pope and Cardinals be set aside, but he further asserted that he could imagine a state of society in which the Church should consist solely of the laity. The law of the Gospel, as her sufficient and absolute rule, rendered her independent of such adventitious aids as masses, indulgences, penances, or any other inventions of spurious sacerdotalism. He found it impossible to defend his statements by Christian tradition or by the canon law, and his unhistorical procedure was really retrograde. But, though he did not see the direction in which the Church should be guided, he did see that the hierarchical system which had hitherto commanded his assent had ended in disgrace and failure. And he expressed the national instinct in his approach towards that evangelicalism which has since largely incorporated the religious life of Englishmen and Americans. He further contended that the reigning monarch should be the head of Christ's commonwealth, popes and bishops being subjected to him. This frankly Erastian doctrine could scarcely have withstood the reasons adduced against it from the encounter of Louis the Fair of France with Boniface VIII and Clement V, wherein French treachery was more to be dreaded than German truculence. What might have been its consequences during Edward the Third's later period, when he was in his dotage and John of Gaunt and Alice Perrers distributed the patronage of the Crown, or again, during the troubled years of Richard II, may be surmised from the robberies and confiscations which were afterwards perpetrated in the reign of Henry VIII.

The way is now clear to discuss Wycliffe's teachings upon Transubstantiation, in which he advanced from his opposition against the Papal power to that indictment of all sacerdotalism and of its visible evidence in the Mass which exposed him to the definite accusation of heresy and completely separated him from Catholicism. In the summer of 1381 he first publicly denied that the elements of the altar suffered any material change by virtue of the words of consecration, an avowal which filled his closing years with agitation and eventually cost him the support of the monarchy, the Lancastrian party, and the University. Here follows a survey of the chief landmarks in the history of the dogma he withstood at such risk. The term Transubstantiation originally occurs in a treatise of the eleventh century, by Hildebert de Savardin of Tours, or Le Mans, although the ideas which the term conveys were familiar at a much earlier date, and arose out of the disputation concerning the Eucharist that extended from the ninth to the eleventh century. During this era theologians endeavored to place the holy mystery of the Christian faith upon a philosophical basis. In 844 the learned monk Radbertus Paschasius published a monograph on the "Sacrament of the Body and Blood of Christ," which defined the dogma more clearly and was instrumental in its development. As Radbertus interpreted it, the bread and wine became internally changed into the veritable flesh and blood of the Lord's actual Body. Against this the Benedictine monk Ratramnus contended that the consecrated wafer was simply a memorial or mystery of the spiritual body existing under the vail of the material, but he failed to secure any general agreement with his conception. Materialistic ideas of the Eucharist found such favor that when Berengarius of Tours, who lived from 998 to 1088, declared against them, asserting that the Real Presence was only spiritually conceived and received, the Lateran Council of 1059 forced him, under threat of death, to recant the heresy. One of its indirect consequences was the remarkable statement of Guitmund of Aversa, that the entire Person of the Divine Redeemer was present in every particle of the associated elements. This St. Thomas subsequently amplified into the dogma that the Blood was contained in the consecrated wafer, and therefore the cup could properly be withheld from the laity. Transubstantiation was treated by Lanfranc from the standpoint of the Realists, who sought to refine the coarse materialism in which it was set by the Nominalists. He emphasized the distinction between the universal substance held to be present in any particular thing included under it, and those accidents or sensible properties which appeared only when the pure form clothed itself in matter. Accordingly, by the act of consecration the substance of the elements was changed while the sensible properties remained the same. It is clear from this reasoning how the Roman Catholic belief in the Mass came to be based upon what was held to be apostolic practice, and also that later Realism supplied its philosophical ground.[1] The orthodox standard was officially announced by the Church at the Fourth Lateran Council, in 1215, which adopted the term Transubstantiation as the expression of New Testament teaching. The summary of that teaching, quoted here from Roman Catholic sources, may be stated as follows: Christ is really and truly present

[1] See Catholic Encyclopædia: Article on Eucharist; p. 577.

in the Holy Eucharist, under the appearances of bread and wine, so that His real Body and Blood, His Soul, and His Divinity are present. The living Christ is on the altar, or in the consecrated wafer. The change that takes place at the moment and by the act of consecration is Transubstantiation; a change whereby the substance of the bread and wine passes over into the substance of Christ, who, under that form of bread and wine, becomes and remains present so long as the accidents remain uncorrupted.[1]

This doctrine had been gradually accepted in the Western Church, tacitly held for more than five centuries, and formally and authoritatively enunciated for three. Fortified by the learning of the Schoolmen, it gradually became the citadel of priestly power, which worked a daily miracle before the adoring faith of God's believing children. In the Sacrifice of the Altar they found the offering of Supreme Love, and in the solemn worship that surrounded it the peace, rest, and meditation belonging to eternal realities thus divined and appropriated. From his youth Wycliffe himself had been taught to revere the sacred Ordinance, and, resolute innovator though he was, its hold upon him caused him to place it above the remaining Sacraments as the highest and most honorable of all. He was convinced that no other had so sure a guarantee in Holy Scripture. It was not indeed the Sacrament itself, but rather the doctrine of the change of substance, that aroused his misgivings. His contribution to Protestant theology under this head did not go beyond the destruction of that theory; it was left to Hus to deal with the denial of the cup to the laity, and to Luther to contend against the sacrificial feature of the Mass. For a long time Wycliffe accepted the interpretation of the changing substance, and there are no hints in his earlier writings of any doubt concerning it. On the contrary, he expressly

[1] See Catholic Encyclopædia: Article on Transubstantiation; p. 579. Also " Hierurgia " by Dr. Rock, Chapter I, sections 3 and 4, and Chapter II, section 1.

stated in the "De Dominio Civili" that our Lord, there described as the eternal Prophet, Priest, and King, "was a Priest when in the Supper He made His own Body." The clear inferences of this phrase were twofold : first, that the words of Christ effected the miracle; and again, that the officiating priest, who stood in the apostolical succession, brought it to pass by virtue of the words of consecration which he repeated, and not by his own authority. The belief that the Body of Christ was present under the accidents of bread and wine was then practically universal, and this is precisely the meaning of the dogma as it is now held.

Beneath all his deviations Wycliffe was very much of the Schoolman, and to the last his theological positions were conditioned by his propensity for metaphysical expressions. Hence his denial of Transubstantiation was directly related to the theory that annihilation was a fiction, for "it was not in the power, because not in the nature of God to annihilate anything." This adherence to philosophical theories in theological discussion, together with his contempt for sacerdotalism and his painful experiences with the superior clergy and the mendicants, helps to explain his rejection of the orthodox view of the Sacrament. At the same time he was eager to validate and safeguard the Ordinance in every possible way, but his study of the Scriptures and of the earlier worship of the Church convinced him that the weight of evidence was against its more recent developments.

According to Wycliffe, these were unknown to the doctors of the early Church; medieval sophistry had supplanted Biblical and patristic teachings, and this usurpation had taken place three hundred years previously, when "Satan was unbound for a millennium." The only theories of the Eucharist he knew at his transitional moment were those of Aquinas, already mentioned, and of Scotus, who, on the basis of his doctrine of the omnipotent and unconditioned will of the Deity, formed the conception that accidents existed independently of their substance. If this was so, it followed that the bread and wine existed independently of the Body of Christ. Wycliffe urged in refutation that accidents always presupposed substance, and that to argue otherwise was to indulge a nonsensical plea which overthrew the very nature of the Sacrament. He challenged the defenders of the Mass to define what was properly the element which remained after consecration; one replied, quantity; another, quality; a third, nothing. Such disagreement demonstrated the untenableness of their doctrine, and he capped his opposition with the words of the Gospel: "A kingdom divided against itself cannot stand." Even if such a miracle as they claimed were possible, it was superfluous, for why should bread be annihilated in order that Christ's Body may be present? When a man became a lord or prelate, he remained the same being, notwithstanding his higher rank. So it was with Christ. He did not cease to be God because he became man. In like manner the substance of the consecrated wafer was not destroyed, it was promoted to higher uses.[1]

The Reformer's reasonings showed the weakness of controversy; they were not always consistent, and there are indications that he had at one time sought a metaphysical interpretation which could satisfy the demands of his mind, while conserving his reverence for the Eucharist. In his expositions of its nature he did not allow his militancy to carry him beyond due bounds, nor did he forfeit that refined devotion which is for religion what the perfume is for the rose. Theologically he held that the bread and wine were the Body and Blood of Christ, for Christ had so ordained them at the Last Supper; the words of institution contained in the Gospel were conclusive on that point. But how the Lord of the Feast was concealed in the elements he could not explain, and sometimes lost himself while endeavoring to do so. He saw an analogy between the Person of Jesus Christ, as being neither solely Creator, nor solely creature, and the bread of the altar which was both

[1] G. V. Lechler: "Wycliffe and his English Precursors"; p. 347.

earthly and heavenly; real bread, and at the same time, the real Body. The Real Presence was a reality, occasioned by the words of consecration, which were necessary for the supernormal change. The bread and wine remained such, but also became in verity the Body and Blood of the Redeemer. Not that the glorified Body of Christ descended from Paradise to enter the elements: He was present in an imponderable and intangible manner, as the soul of man was present in his body. "The Sacrament of the altar," he said, "is the Body of Christ in the form of bread — bread in a natural manner, and Body in a sacramental manner," and the communicant spiritually perceived and handled the Lord's Flesh and Blood thus concealed in the Host. Its grace and blessing depended upon the faith of the recipient, and a nice distinction was drawn between the corporeal and spiritual taste of the consecrated elements.[1]   These conclusions, while differing in important details, are closely allied to the Lutheran theory of Consubstantiation.

The abuses connected with the worship of the Altar were condemned by Wycliffe, whose resentment was particularly aroused against the clergy's deliberate use of the Mass to increase their power and importance in the eyes of the simple. "Can a creature," he demanded, "give being to his Creator?" Some who pretended to do so, he continued, were priests of Baal, not of Christ. But though he described their idea of the Mass as a mischievous fable, he did not correctly estimate its place in the medieval Church as the keystone of her doctrinal system and the secret of her organic life. The bishops protested that were it modified or relinquished, the faith and obedience of communicants would be subverted, a statement which is partly justified by the fact that the hold of clericalism is strongest to-day where a high doctrine of the Eucharist is accepted. This assertion is made with the knowledge that there are in Catholicism not less than four permissible ex-

---

[1] G. V. Lechler: "Wycliffe and his English Precursors"; pp. 332–361.

planations of the dogma, upon which there has been as yet no authoritative decision.

The uproar following Wycliffe's revolt showed how deeply entrenched the Mass was in the hearts of believers. As early as 1380 Chancellor Berton and a council of twelve members condemned his theses, and forbade the Reformer to lecture at the University. John of Gaunt hurried to Oxford and besought his advocate not to meddle with the ark of the Lord. The government withdrew its patronage from him, and his friends, with a few exceptions, left him to encounter the hurricane alone. It was a triumphal hour for Courtenay, when, as it seemed, the results of Wycliffe's gigantic labors had instantaneously vanished. Even at this juncture he might have retracted and yielded to Gaunt's importunities, sacrificing conviction to personal gain and remaining the eminent doctor and teacher, and the chosen advisor of princes. There is little doubt that the hierarchy would have welcomed and rewarded the submission of its most gifted and formidable foe. But such was not the mettle of the man who, whatever his failures and shortcomings, now turned his back upon the temptations of place and power. He petitioned the throne that his teachings should be publicly expounded in the churches of the nation, and continued, undismayed, his resolute efforts in behalf of what he believed to be the truth of God.

CHAPTER IV

PRINCES AND PEOPLE

ONCE more the Church is seized with sudden fear,
And at her call is Wyclif disinhumed:
Yea, his dry bones to ashes are consumed
And flung into the brook that travels near;
Forthwith, that ancient Voice, which Streams can hear,
Thus speaks (that Voice which walks upon the wind,
Though seldom heard by busy human-kind) —
"As thou these ashes, little Brook! wilt bear
Into the Avon, Avon to the tide
Of Severn, Severn to the narrow seas,
Into main Ocean they, this deed accurst
An emblem yields to friends and enemies
How the bold Teacher's Doctrine, sanctified
By truth, shall spread, throughout the world dispersed."

WORDSWORTH'S *Ecclesiastical Sonnets.*

CHAPTER IV

PRINCES AND PEOPLE

Political life of England in the fourteenth century — The wars
with France — The Black Prince — Edward III — John of Gaunt —
Social conditions in England — The Black Death and its effects —
Peasants' Revolt of 1381 — Wycliffe accused of complicity — The
Earthquake Council — Wycliffe's translation of the Scriptures — Purvey's version — Wycliffe's Poor Priests — Trialogus — Opus Evangelicum — Cruciata — Wycliffe cited before Urban in 1384, — Illness and
death — Summary of his character.

I

THE history of religion in England during the fourteenth
century is largely a record of debates and differences which
affected the political status of ecclesiasticism. Yet these
controversies and Wycliffe's part in them were but one phase
of the life of the commonwealth. The main currents of
his thought and action can be best ascertained and their
background surveyed by a reference to the fate which that
generation endured in peace, in war, and above all in the
pestilences which came to stay for the next four centuries,
and caused unparalleled suffering throughout Europe. The
one hundred and seventy-eight years which elapsed between
the death of the first Edward and the accession of Henry VII
were distracted by calamity and turmoil at home, by initial
victory and ultimate defeat to English arms abroad. The
Black Death and the Peasants' Revolt and the campaigns in
France were the events of this period which proved to be most
serious and lasting in their consequences. The early triumphs over the French revealed to European chivalry the
prowess of Edward the Third's redoubtable infantry and the
archers and knifemen of Wales, who, under his strategy,

hurled back the attack of the French knighthood at Crécy in 1346, and, though four times outnumbered, remained the masters of the field. Ten years later, the Black Prince, having already fought as a lad of fourteen under his father's eye at Crécy, won a still more astounding success behind the vineyards of Poitiers, where the French King John, surnamed the Good, was taken prisoner. But these adventures proved as useless as they were brilliant; they inflamed that military arrogance which sought occasions for a quarrel; their monetary cost increased by leaps and bounds; and the baronage, which seldom vailed its crest to the French foe, could not long endure the restraints of domestic peace. The scions of the aristocracy, who respected little except physical force, fell foul of one another, and were finally exterminated in the ferocious Wars of the Roses.

The treaty of Bretigny, confirmed on October 26, 1360, by which France ceded nearly one third of her territory to England, ended the first stage of the Hundred Years' War. The rewards of battle enriched the cities and castles of Edward's Kingdom, and his fiftieth birthday was kept with the pomp befitting so unexampled a conquest. His fame rang in all men's ears; no other ruler of the day could equal the regalities of the chief prince of Christendom, contrasted as they were with the distress and humiliation of his defeated foes. For the nonce all went merrily, and the royal court was the scene of stately ceremonials and sumptuous feastings. At this apex of prosperity, when a moribund phase reasserted itself, deeds of valor and knightly defiance were commemorated in the Round Tower at Windsor, where the Order of the Garter was established in the winter of 1347, shortly after the king's return from France.

But the suffering and discontent of the people were in glaring contrast with the artificial exuberance of their rulers. The laborers of six surrounding counties were impressed to build Edward's Tower, and his Order was instituted when nearly every household in the land lay stricken by the Plague. The sycophantic yet observant Froissart gave his readers glimpses of an impending catastrophe. He complained that all was not well with England. Notwithstanding the intoxication of militarism, the plain folk were vindictive, disloyal toward their superiors, and disdainful of foreigners. A nearer view than Froissart's would have recognized that the disaffection, which began as early as 1349, was due to exorbitant taxation, to other economic and political evils, and to the incessant demand for fresh levies to defend the French possessions of the Crown. As an aftermath of these excesses came the useless expedition of February, 1367, when the Black Prince and his troops marched through the snowy defiles of the Pyrenees and restored Pedro III to the throne of Castile. This gallant campaign cost the Prince his health and bankrupted his exchequer, while the monarch who gained a temporary advantage from it was utterly unworthy of its sacrifices. The Prince's Duchy of Aquitaine rose in rebellion against the financial measures necessary to discharge his huge indebtedness. In September, 1370, he turned upon the city of Limoges, where the insurrection centered, and stormed and sacked it with a savagery that left a dark stain upon his memory. The following spring he returned home to languish for six years in the grip of a mysterious malady which defied the primitive remedies then in vogue, and was aggravated by his despair over the ruin of the Plantagenet sovereignty in France. His father, now fast approaching senility, had transferred the management of state affairs to his second son, John of Gaunt, who ruled by the fear rather than the affection of the realm.

Gaunt was unjustly suspected by his brother of designs upon the throne, and these suspicions were heightened by stories of favoritism, corruption, and lawlessness brought to the invalided Prince at Kennington Palace. The nation now knew that its beloved hero was physically shattered. His prospective subjects were dismayed by the somber clouds

K

which spread rapidly over the horizon of their future.   They had relied upon his wisdom and justice no less than upon his prowess in the field.   "Their welfare," said the Chronicler of Walsingham, "seemed bound up in his person.   It had flourished in his health, it languished in his illness, and perished at his death; in him expired all the hopes of the English."   He died on June 8, 1376, in his forty-sixth year, at the Palace of Westminster; his work demolished, his spirit broken, and the kingdom seething with mutiny.   There was no available space among the royal tombs in the sacred mound of Edward the Confessor, and the Prince was buried in Canterbury Cathedral, where the arms he wore in battle are hung above his tomb.   His separation from his house, even in the place of sepulture, betokened his mute protestation against the degeneracy of the father "whose folly he had vainly tried to correct, and the son whose doom he might foresee, but could not avert." [1]   Although his eulogists invested him with some virtues he did not possess, his character transcended the general morals of the time.   It was sullied by the violent outbreak at Limoges, an act foreign to his nature and committed when he was weak and irascible from continued illness.   The eloquent and discriminating Bishop Brinton of Rochester spoke of him in terms of respect and praise, and the majority of his contemporaries indorsed the Bishop's verdict.

Eight years after the rejoicings and tournaments which ushered in Edward the Third's fiftieth birthday, he had lost nearly all his territories beyond the Channel.   The interminable wars with France had broken out again; the English coasts were menaced by pirates; and John of Gaunt's reactionary Parliament provoked the popular wrath.   Alice Perrers, the king's mistress, decked in the dead Queen's jewels, masqueraded at the tilting yards as the Lady of the Sun.   She sat openly at the judges' side in the law courts, interfered with legislation, and dispensed the royal patronage

[1] G. M. Trevelyan: "England in the Age of Wycliffe"; p. 27.

to her flatterers. On the jubilee of his reign Edward granted a general amnesty, which proved to be his last act of government. A few months later, on June 21, 1377, he died at the royal manor of Sheen, robbed by his leman in his last moments of the very rings on his fingers. While he lay in the final agony, moaning for a priest to shrive him, she forsook him and fled; the parasitical ministers also hastened away to greet the new monarch, and the servants of the household plundered the death chamber. Richard II, who succeeded his grandfather, fulfilled the gloomy destiny of the Plantagenets. Beginning as a handsome and promising youth, he ended as a despised, deposed, and murdered king, the moody, fitful, treacherous "Richard the Redeless," in whom none could put faith. His uncle, John of Gaunt, has already figured in this history as the most distinguished political personality who offered protection to Wycliffe. The Duke took his name from Ghent, where he was born at the Abbey of St. Bavon in 1340, when his parents were in Flanders on a diplomatic errand. He inherited the stalwart build and manly features of the Angevins, and with these physical traits their pride and ambition. Flashes of hereditary distinction from time to time broke through his haughty reserve; he was a pleasant companion where he chose to award his preferences, and he had the courage of his blood, a blind courage, however, so far as his generalship was concerned. Poets and dramatists and a series of propitious circumstances have combined to thrust celebrity upon him. Chaucer was wont to frequent his lordly house upon the Strand, and listen to the "softe speeche" of the golden-haired lady of whom he sang in the "Booke of the Duchesse." He may have met Wycliffe there, since the latter's connection with the Duke required their frequent intercourse. Gaunt was twice married, first to Blanche, the youngest daughter of Henry, Duke of Lancaster, whose title and estates he inherited, and next to Constance, the heiress of Don Pedro of Castile, who brought him additional wealth and honors. To these marriages the great feudatory of the

fourteenth century owed that multiplicity of hereditary claims
with which he was ever busy.   For fifteen years he was the
titular king of Castile; for twelve the ruler of England in all
but name; his son Henry IV seized the throne from Richard
II, and his heraldic devices are still found on the arms of
Bordeaux, and are carried on those of the reigning House of
Hanover.

He merited no such preëminence, either as a strategist or as
a statesman.   The people understood him better than did
Wycliffe, and they hated and plotted against him as the foe
of justice and liberty.   The grotesque exaggerations of his
villanies by the Monk of St. Albans, who saw him "playing
Beelzebub to Wycliffe's Lucifer," can be summarily dismissed.   On the other hand, his soldiers spoke kindly of a
captain who seldom led them successfully in battle, and,
while neither cursing nor blessing him, asserted that he was
never guilty of that most serious of offenses, disloyalty.
How narrowly must this the unpardonable sin of medieval
chivalry have been avoided by a leader who at no time won
distinction for fidelity!   Chaucer's favorable judgment of
him is less trustworthy than that of his troops, because it
was dictated by prepossessions arising from friendship and
social advantage.   And if Gaunt was true to the interests of
class and party, he certainly felt no impulse to repress the
tyrannies of which they were guilty.   The regenerating zeal
of his ancestor Edward I was not in him; on the contrary,
he subordinated his policies to the schemes of a selfish and
lordly group which disguised base ends beneath professions of
heroism.   The caste of which he was the representative was
as ignoble as he; not only did it neglect its opportunities for
service, but, alert to suppress effort for betterment from any
quarter, trampled down in blood the rising spirit of progress.   Subsequent generations have forgiven the Duke's
betrayal of the people's cause, chiefly for the reason
that he relieved the poverty of Chaucer and rescued Wycliffe from peril, two generous acts that secured for him the

indorsement of Shakespeare and the resounding name, "old John of Gaunt, time-honored Lancaster." With the exception of Edward I, and even in his case the exception is not absolute, the Plantagenets wasted their substance and energy upon wild escapades. Those who witnessed their ending in Richard II must have recalled the defiant saying of Cœur de Lion, "From the devil we came and to the devil we shall all go." Yet laudable objects were sometimes accomplished contrary to their intention, thus making their evil an unexpected means for good. The rise of self-government in England, of national unity and patriotic resistance in Scotland and France, and the breaking down of commercial barriers between the island kingdom and the continent, should be weighed against deeds which in themselves were high-handed wrongs.

We may now turn from the princes of the period to the plain people, those who really suffer from war and its deadly allies, famine and pestilence, which destroy what war has spared or failed to reach. From the middle of the thirteenth to the close of the fourteenth century, the average price of wheat was thirty dollars a quarter, which was of course prohibitive for the peasantry. Proclamations were issued to cheapen victuals, but without effect. Not only the poor but the more fortunate, including the monks, felt the pinch of want. Starvation induced disease, and the epidemic of 1349 followed, stalking through Oxford during Wycliffe's residence there and blotting out the thought of lesser miseries by the extent and deadliness of its contagion. This overwhelming calamity which befouled England and the European countries arose in Asia, and, according to Walsingham, extended from the shores of China to those of Galway in Ireland. It was first heard of in its western course at a small Genoese fort in the Crimean peninsula, whence it was conveyed to Constantinople by trading vessels whose crews lay dying on the decks, and from that place, traversing the entire sea coasts, was borne to all parts of Europe. A contemporary friar, Michael Platiensis, has left a graphic account of the Plague in Sicily. "A most deadly pestilence," he wrote, "sprang up over the entire island. It happened that in the month of October, 1347, twelve Genoese ships, flying from the divine vengeance which our Lord for their sins had sent upon them, put into the port of Messina, bringing with them such a sickness clinging to their very bones that, did any one speak to them, he was directly struck with a mortal sickness from which there was no escape." [1] Almost simultaneously with its appearance in Italy the pestilence obtained a foothold in France, and was carried from Calais, then an English possession, to the Channel Islands, and finally into England. Beginning at Melcombe Regis, or Weymouth, in Dorsetshire, the horrible disease, now known as the bubonic plague, steadily invaded the southwestern and midland counties, and on the first of November passed within the gates of London. Its symptoms developed with extreme rapidity, and inspired such terror that the nearest relatives of the stricken shrank from the ordinary offices of charity. "The sick man lay languishing alone in his house and no one came near him. Those most dear to him, regardless of the ties of kindred or affection, withdrew themselves to a distance; the doctor did not come to him, and even the priest with fear and trembling administered the Sacraments of the Church. Men and women, racked with the consuming fever, pleaded, but in vain, for a draught of water, and uselessly raved for some one to watch at their bedside. The father or the wife would not touch the corpse of child or husband to prepare it for the grave, or follow it thither. No prayer was said, nor solemn office sung, nor bell tolled for the funeral of even the noblest citizen; but by day and night the corpses were borne to the common plague-pit without rite or ceremony." [2]

The annals of its ravages in England are found in the episcopal registers, monastic chronicles, and town records of the kingdom. The mortality was so enormous that in the

[1] Cardinal Gasquet: "The Black Death"; p. 15.   [2] *Ibid.*, pp. 22-23.

words of a writer of the period, "very many country towns and quarters of innumerable cities are left altogether without inhabitants. The churches or cemeteries before consecrated did not suffice for the dead; but new places outside the cities and towns were at that time dedicated to that use by people and bishops." [1] Conservative authorities agree that the population of England decreased from five millions to two and a half millions. An unconsciously pathetic comment upon these deplorable statistics is found in "Piers Plowman," where Langland conceives that all the people of the realm could be gathered into a single meadow to hear his rebukes and exhortations. His imagination will not appear at fault if we recall that the entire interval of four hundred years between Wycliffe and Wesley was required to repeople England upon the scale of the early fourteenth century. In other words, the England of George I was no larger in numbers than that of Edward II. Still more significantly, the realm over which Henry VII reigned was neither as enlightened nor as humane as that of Edward I; by the time the first of the Tudors united the houses of Lancaster and York in his marriage, repeated wars and their accompaniments had worked their wicked will on the nation. The strong and steady progress of national consolidation during the twelfth and thirteenth centuries received an effectual check in Wycliffe's day, the worst disaster, that of the pestilence, descending upon a country already staggering beneath the burdens of a protracted and indecisive conflict, a luxurious and licentious court, and a turbulent nobility.

Yet the almost universal visitation did not morally chasten its survivors, who manifested a stolid indifference to their miserable surroundings, and in many instances gave way to the lowest passions. Although commerce fared better than some have supposed, the overthrow of es-

[1] B. Mus. Cott. M. S., Vitell., A. xx, fol. 56, quoted by Cardinal Gasquet: "The Black Death"; p. 187.

tablished conditions was so severe that not only the monasteries, but also the Universities, the system of land tenure, the political machinery, the art and architecture of England, alike felt the cataclysmic shock. The working classes, however, were the chief sufferers, and their diminution brought about a complete social change which ramified from the bottom upwards. The selective processes of the Plague introduced a new scale of life and manners, and so modified or revolutionized the agrarian situation that there is hardly a modern economic problem that cannot be traced to them. The study of these effects verifies two conclusions: first, that not all were injurious, and second, that they were met and borne with a reckless courage which did much to relieve the gravity of the situation. Medieval England was disgraced by transgressions, but she was also disciplined by hardships which, bitter though they were, could not obliterate the color, the variety, nor the joy of her life. The twentieth century peasant knows no such zest and gaiety as blessed his ancestors, who, though they lacked facilities for prompt material recovery from the ravages of the scourge, were not hampered by the fear and disillusionment which too often sadden the prospect of the modern laborer. All who outrode the storm had shared a common peril, and the frequency with which they had looked on death made them despise it. Meanwhile the present moment was their own, and they built again the world they knew, undaunted by difficulty or danger. A fatalistic tinge in their outlook taught them that what had perished had perished, and no time was to be wasted in vain regrets. In Europe great names arose out of the darkness, St. Roch, St. Catherine, Petrarch, and Gui de Chauliac. The era bent, but did not break; it was still sufficiently resilient to reassert its vitality and guard the germinal growth of freedom and justice.

If constitutional progress was retarded it was at least preserved. The national consciousness solidified under adversity, and was still resentful of foreign dictation. The men who believed with Wycliffe that the safety and well-being of the kingdom were to be found in independence of the Holy See were patriots. But patriotism was not confined to one sect or faction; it became a conscious passion in all hearts. Love of country throbs in the verse of Chaucer, than whom no poet was ever more intensely English in his character and sympathies. The nine and twenty pilgrims of the Tabard Inn are a vivid company, standing clearly against the misty background of their time. His inimitable descriptions of the men and manners of his native land made Chaucer its premier poet. Society was still comparatively so simple that his narrative was able to embrace most of the types that had survived the Plague. Wandering by the way became the favorite pursuit of all classes. Pilgrims and travelers were everywhere abroad, exulting in the freedom of the king's highway, and presenting at once the unity and the diversity of medieval life. The pedlar and the pardoner, the mendicant and the outlaw, the juggler and the gleeman, the flagellant and the soldier, journeyed cheek by jowl, casting admiring or envious eyes upon the cavalcades of royalty and gentry riding past. Knights and barons entertained one another in castles and manors, and counted hospitality a habit of courtesy and pleasure. Franklins and merchants frequented the better class of hostelries; the alehouses and meaner inns were crowded with foresters and laborers. The roads, good or bad, were the arteries of trade, and every hall or hut a medium for news. There the nobles met in nightly conclave; the "poor priests" kept aglow the flame of a purer faith; the friars fawned or threatened; and the serfs and underlings debated their wrongs, which were so unendurable that at last they assumed decisive shape in the most spontaneous uprising of the laboring folk that ever took place in England.[1]

[1] G. M. Trevelyan: "England in the Age of Wycliffe"; p. 1.

II

During the two years preceding the Peasants' Revolt in the spring of 1381 Wycliffe remained in comparative retirement at Lutterworth. The Great Schism was the crucial point in his public life, when he became to all intents and purposes a Protestant. While he was still busy berating the popes, sometimes unjustly, as in the case of Gregory XI, and again for reasons which almost excused the virulence of his language, the social outbreak occurred which forever destroyed his hopes of any improvement by means of State interference. During one month the volcanic but mercifully brief terror put half the realm in arms; for some days the existence of the government was imperilled by the efforts of the peasants to avenge their injuries. The causes of their rebellion were both near and remote; they extended far into the past, and were too complicated for prolonged examination here. One third of the working population had perished in the Plague, and, as already stated, this abnormal depletion disorganized agrarian and commercial relations. The survivors were determined to get rid of oppressive usages and secure higher wages. The lords were equally resolved to prevent free competition in labor and to tighten their hold on the situation with bonds of their own choosing. Stripes and brandings were inflicted on stubborn offenders. Repressive legislation begot a reckless lawlessness among those whom it affected. In London and other cities the guilds were agitated by internal difficulties peculiar to themselves. The stringent provisions of some charters granted to towns by spiritual lords and abbots added to the friction. The poll tax of one shilling a head on every adult person in the land which had been voted by the Nottingham Parliament of 1380 was the final aggravation in a quarrel that had lasted for more than thirty years. Then came the terrific explosion, astonishing the court and the nobles, stupefying the clergy, and bewildering the administration. But the source of such an organized resistance lay even deeper than civic and economic causes. England was besotted by the lust of militarism, and degenerated by the vices that followed in the train of the French wars. Impoverished, weakened, betrayed, the nation grew desperate, and distrustful of its hereditary leaders. It is but just to observe that the young king Richard II and his murdered ministers, Archbishop Sudbury and Sir Richard Hales, were not altogether culpable for an anarchy which they did not create and could not control. The line of Horace,

"Not Heaven itself upon the past hath power,"

could be appropriately applied to many troubles and obstacles that threatened the new reign. John of Gaunt, who had been identified with the enormities of his father's court, was the first man the insurgents singled out for punishment. He was absent in Edinburgh when they broke loose, or he would have shared the fate of Sudbury and Hales; as it was, his Palace on the Strand, stored with the richest treasures of foreign spoil, went up in flames. The insurrection defeated his policies, the disendowment of the Church was postponed to the time of an equally rapacious and more powerful prince, and the Duke's influence as a publicist sustained irreparable injury.

The immediate results were a callous mockery of the fine promises and unconfirmed charters which Richard readily gave to induce the rebels to return to their homes. His advisers knew that parliamentary action was necessary to redeem these pledges, and also that it would be impossible to secure any such consent. Wat Tyler was killed at Smithfield in the presence of the king; John Ball, a forerunner of modern reform, together with thousands of his disciples, paid for their untimely efforts with their lives. For the moment, under the pressure of a universal danger, the regulars and seculars forgot their enmities, and the bishops made peace with the friars. Church and State united in the task of torturing and hanging their victims, many of whom were executed without process of law. Nobles returned to their castles from their hiding places in the woods, and resumed their former practices. The exhausted passions of the defeated and hunted peasantry left them helpless, and the nation sank back into apathy and neglect. The proletariat forgot that spasm of outraged self-respect which had caught the barons off their guard. Chaucer's glad morning song, so surprising in this dark epoch, waited long for its antiphony in

"Those melodious bursts that fill
The spacious times of great Elizabeth
With sounds that echo still."

Serfage revived, despite the brave attempt to do away with its abominations. Yet the beneficiaries of feudalism had received a wholesome lesson, not the less impressive because unaccompanied by the nameless horrors of the Jacquerie in France. It taught the proud, self-sufficient aristocrat to beware of his underlings, and he at least understood that fearful possibilities were lodged in men he had hitherto despised. He moved more cautiously among his dwindling claims; the system of villeinage feebly lingered on and came to an almost unobserved end in the days of the Tudors.

Wycliffe did not escape without charges of implication in these movements; his enemies averred that he had been "a sower of strife, who by his serpent-like instigations had set his serf against his lord." Notwithstanding the dying confessions of John Ball and Jack Straw, which involved him, there is no proof of the truth of their accusations.[1] He had little appreciable influence upon the purely secular aims of the insurgents, who were bent on deliverance from practical grievances in which spiritual affairs played no part.[2] University doctors were not found among them, and John Ball's

[1] We hear nothing of these confessions until twenty years afterward. They are not found in any contemporary chronicle, and were probably extorted by the rack.
[2] C. Oman: "The Great Rebellion of 1381"; p. 27.

itineraries in behalf of the peasants had commenced while Wycliffe was still an undergraduate at Oxford. But his sweeping declaration that "every righteous man is lord over the whole sensible world" could easily be distorted by impulsive orators who paid no regard to the refined subtleties with which he qualified the statement. In any case he did not desert the persecuted patriots in their emergency. They had no conception of the communism which was latent in his theories, but he openly avowed his sympathy with their demand for individual freedom and his anger at their oppression. He stood alone in his plea for clemency, and by this unselfish attitude still further separated himself from the ruling powers and the nobles, and was condemned to political impotence. His consistent conduct furnished an instructive contrast to that of Luther under somewhat similar circumstances during the sixteenth century. The Zwinglian heresies, the Rising of the Anabaptists, and the Peasants' War of that era were the logical outcome of Luther's theory of the right of private judgment and dissent. This theory had served him well in the severance of his allegiance from Rome. Yet when others used it for their own purposes he seceded from the people to the princes, complaining loudly of the preachers of blood and treason whom the devil inspired to seek his destruction, and impressing upon his followers the necessity of passive obedience to the State. The popular phase of his Reformation was quickly abandoned, while he took refuge in the arms of the civil power, and purchased the safety of his doctrine by the sacrifice of its freedom.[1]

If Luther's idealism gave place to compromise, Wycliffe steadily refused to surrender his convictions or be silent upon them. "The heresiarch of execrable memory" was cut off from all but a small minority of his supporters, and the unfortunate coincidence of his protest against the endowments of the Church and the pretensions of clerical power with the insurrection of the peasants gave Courtenay an opportunity

[1] Lord Acton: "Essays on Liberty"; pp. 155–156.

to suppress opinions which he believed were responsible for the death of his predecessor, Archbishop Sudbury. Wycliffe, so far from being abashed by the connection of his opinions with these depredations, reaffirmed his position on questions of controversy. He denied Transubstantiation afresh, after having appealed to the king in 1381 for secular help in a purely theological issue. In reply to Gaunt's earnest request that he should rest his case, he memorialized Parliament in 1382 with a lengthy petition, wherein he recited a list of grievances and asked that the Statutes of Provisors and Præmunire be enforced against the Pope, above all urging that "Christ's teaching concerning the Eucharist may be openly taught in churches."

The Archbishop retaliated by convening the "Earthquake Council" on May 21 of that year at the House of the Black Friars in London. The assembly derived its name from the occurrence of a seismic disturbance during its proceedings. This was construed by the Wycliffians as a sign of Heaven's wrath against the higher clergy, and by the prelates as a token of its approval of their efforts to expel heterodoxy from the bosom of the Church. Of the twenty-four Articles examined ten were pronounced heretical, and fourteen erroneous. The Council, in condemning the Reformer's doctrines, also struck at the University which had nurtured them. Courtenay and the regulars, aided by Richard II, won the fight against the doctors and students who prized religious and intellectual freedom. Dr. Rigg, the Chancellor, who had hitherto favored Wycliffe, was summoned to Lambeth and warned by the bishops and the Privy Council that his support of the Lollard Repyngdon as against Stokes must cease, the disaffected be subdued, and concord restored. The seculars who had exhorted the University authorities to expel all friars and monks were themselves excluded. A Convocation for the suppression of heresy met at Oxford; the royal writ ordered a monthly inquisition upon the followers and the works of Wycliffe, and within half a year the second school of the Catholic Church was recovered to orthodoxy at the expense of her academic standing in Europe. The inquisitors made a desolation and called it peace, and Courtenay unwittingly became one of the greatest enemies to Oxford's reputation for scholarship she has ever known. The University sank into stupor and decline; speculation was throttled; Cambridge was regarded by cautious parents as the place unvexed by reactionary ecclesiasticism, and Paris regained the intellectual eminence Oxford had so long disputed. Thus the later medieval period of the University's leadership ended with Wycliffe; Courtenay could not cope with the vigorous dialectic of the last of the Schoolmen, but he could and he did unreservedly destroy Oxford's capacity to produce another like him.

Cast down, but not dismayed, Wycliffe was now beyond the pale of the Church and of the Schools. Yet he was of that type of men who hope,

"And see their hope frustrate,
And hope anew."

He was enough of the ascetic to despise the lures of the world; of the man of affairs to know the deceptions of political strife; of the saint to regard that which he held as truth as more important than place or power. The material side of life was for him reduced to a minimum, and, although ambitious, he desired no influence which required him to subject his conscience to the incitements of temporary convenience or success. His last days at Lutterworth were spent in appeals to the people at large, in which his further separation from sacerdotalism was evident in the unwise declaration that preaching is of more value than the administration of any sacrament. He forsook learned clerks and titled supporters for the weavers and artisans of Norwich and Leicester, and devoted the remainder of his life to its most notable achievement, the translation of the Holy Scriptures. Henry of Knighton, a canon of Leicester during the second half of the fourteenth century, and a fierce hater of the Lollards, complained that Wycliffe's action in translating the Scriptures "which Christ gave to the clergy and doctors of the Church" had scattered abroad the pearls of the Gospel to be "trodden under foot by swine"; "the jewel of clerics was turned to the sport of the laity." [1]

The Reformer's previous insistence upon the supremacy of the Sacred Writings had obtained for him, while still at Oxford, the title of "Doctor Evangelicus." In his attack upon dogmatism or in defense of his own conclusions, he unhesitatingly used quotations from the Old and New Testaments as final proofs, setting aside the weightiest traditions in their behalf. "Neither the testimony of Augustine nor Jerome, nor any other saint, should be accepted except in so far as it was based upon Scripture," and to this he added the assertion that every man had the right to examine the Bible for himself.

The quotation from Knighton contains the substance of similar animadversions against Wycliffe's enterprise, which, nevertheless, was justified by the example of primitive Christianity. For the right of religious independence must have been tacitly assumed by the early Christians to justify their position, and the publicity of the Hebrew Scriptures was presupposed in the works of the apologists of the second century. Even so late as the fourth century no dignitary of the Church dreamt of forbidding the reading and interpretation of the Bible by the laity. On the contrary, Origen held that it was the purpose of the Holy Spirit in the Scriptures to be intelligible to those who were uneducated and insignificant in the eyes of the world. Theodoret, who shared the current presumption that the Scriptures needed defense as literature, in a burst of eloquence turned this lack to gain, declaring that "all the heralds of the truth, to wit the Prophets and Apostles, though unendowed with the Greek gift of eloquence,

---

[1] At that time Knighton was dead. The author whose records are quoted here is known as his "Continuator."

were yet filled with true wisdom, brought to all nations both Hellenic and Barbarian the divine doctrine, and filled all lands and seas with their writings, whose content is virtue and piety. And now all men having renounced the follies of the philosophers, feast upon the doctrines of fishermen and publicans and reverence the words of the Tent-maker." [1] Chrysostom recommended that the sight of the Bible should be so familiar to children as to form a necessary part of their home scenery, and poetically remarked that "the very touch of the Book of the Gospels of itself awakens the heart." [2] Had these counsels been heeded in after times, the false step taken by the Church when she began to withdraw the Scriptures from the laity and place them in the custody of ecclesiastical tradition might have been avoided. Nor could the unchecked sacerdotalism that ensued have escaped the restrictions imposed by a better acquaintance with the Bible.

The entire Old Testament and the greater part of the New were translated into the French language before the middle of the fourteenth century. England was not so fortunate: the Anglo-Saxon versions, some manuscripts of which are as late as the twelfth century, had become unintelligible by Wycliffe's time, with the result that, although the Bible was fairly well known among the clergy and superior laymen, the masses were utterly ignorant of it, and had no means of being otherwise. Anglo-Norman was then the speech of the schools, the colleges, the courts of law, and polite society. English prevailed among the humbler classes and the tillers of the soil. It is not certain that Edward III could address the Commons in the vulgar tongue, as Henry IV took pains to do when he appeared before them to claim the throne. Yet by the end of the fourteenth century, French had become a sickly exotic and English had supplanted it as the official language, first in the courts, and

---

[1] Harnack: "Bible Reading in the Early Church"; p. 90.
[2] *Ibid.*, p. 101.

L

later in Parliament. A doctor of laws confessed in 1404, "We are as ignorant of French as of Hebrew." John de Trevisa attributed its sudden disappearance to the Plague, but the decline antedated this event, and, despite legislative efforts to arrest it, the use of French gradually diminished. It may have survived in Parliamentary debates, however, for fifty years after Chaucer's death.[1] The statutes of the realm continued to be published in French until the reign of Henry VIII. One of the main factors which contributed to the spread of English was the friars' preaching in that language throughout the country, a habit which goes far to explain their hold upon the people. Another factor was the important aid Chaucer rendered by welding the strength of both into one speech different from either, superior in the richness of its vocabulary and the simplicity of its structure, and which became the life blood of the new nationalism. From his day to our own the development and expansion of English have gone steadily forward; but the poet's largest service to the mother tongue was the preference he awarded it during a bilingual period, a literary precedent which later writers were constrained to follow.

This transition from French to English deprived the versions of the Bible in the earlier language of their usefulness, and an attempt was made to meet the needs of the situation by partial translations, including the Psalms, which were made into English in 1320 and 1340. The first of these is ascribed doubtfully to William of Shoreham; the second, to Richard Rolle, the hermit of Hampole.[2] Both men used the Vulgate as a basis, and their work was provincial in dialect

---

[1] Parliament was first opened with an English speech in 1363; and with an English sermon by Courtenay, in 1381. This will indicate that the debates may have been in English, although their reports were actually published in French.

[2] Rolle was born in Yorkshire about 1290, and died at Hampole in 1349. He was one of the first religious authors to write in the native language, which he used for the instruction of those who knew no Latin. His poetical manuscript, "The Pricke of Conscience," is freely quoted by Warton in his "History of English Poetry."

and circulation. But to Wycliffe and his coadjutors in the task belongs the credit of first setting forth the whole Scriptures in their own speech, an indescribably meritorious achievement, and the first fruits of a series of versions which have to a large extent molded the nature and determined the course of English civilization. From the literary standpoint, Wycliffe's translation was a contribution to that movement in which, as we have seen, Chaucer was the central figure, and his version should be viewed in that relation. Of necessity a translation of such intrinsic worth, and one which so closely affected the spiritual interests and ideals of the nation, could not have been woven into its life and character without considerable benefit to the language. But Wycliffe was not a stylist in the larger meaning of the term, and the relatively rudimentary condition of the language made it impossible to produce a finished rendering like that of the translation of 1611. Indeed, the Authorized Version stands apart from all others, "equally untouched by the splendor of Elizabethan and the extravagance of Jacobean prose," and marked by the noble simplicity of ancient times. Wycliffe's version owed much to its later revision by his curate Purvey, who, in or about 1388, smoothed out the harsh literalness of the original and substituted short marginal comments, many of which were taken from Nicholas de Lyra, for the frequent glosses of the text. The desire of Wycliffe and of Nicholas of Hereford, who was his chief assistant in the rendition of the Old Testament, to be scrupulously faithful to the Latin of the Vulgate was the source of the pedantries and obscurities which are found in their work. Others besides Nicholas and Purvey must have coöperated in an enterprise of such magnitude, and the multiplication of copies proceeded so rapidly that of the one hundred and seventy existing manuscripts the majority were written within forty years after the completion of the translation.

Purvey's version, which should be carefully distinguished

from Wycliffe's, was eagerly sought and read by all who could obtain it. The princes of the royal house and the sovereign himself did not disdain to possess it. Nor was there any formal condemnation of the first English Bible. The assumption of sectarian writers that the medieval Church prohibited the translation and circulation of the Scriptures is contradicted by the fact that manuscripts were plentiful both in England and on the continent. Although printing was not yet invented, Germany had fifty complete and seventy-two incomplete versions. Seventeen printed editions of the Bible preceded the great version of Luther. The French translations extensively used in England have been named. Archbishop Arundel, the burner of heretics, commended Queen Anne of Bohemia, consort of Richard II, for having owned in English "all the four gospels with the doctors upon them." Wycliffe's reiterated appeals to the support of the Scriptures, uttered long before his translation was made, would have no meaning for a clerical body unacquainted with them. Such were the principal circumstances connected with the memorable versions of Wycliffe and Purvey, the earliest rendering of the complete Bible England possessed in her own language.[1]

Cardinal Gasquet[2] has advanced the theory that the so-called Wycliffe translation is really a "Catholic Bible," and some extreme Anglicans have taught this supposition. He emphasizes the fact that there was nothing in Wycliffe's writings to show that he had either translated or attempted to translate the Holy Scriptures. While this is true, it should also be noted that those writings are full of passages advocating such a translation. His intimacy with the Bible had been one of the governing forces of his life, and his grow-

[1] For Wycliffe's and Purvey's Bible see the account in the preface to Forshall and Madden's edition.

[2] This distinguished prelate and scholar was appointed in 1907 by the late Pope, Pius X, President of a Commission for the revision of the Vulgate, to restore it, as nearly as possible, to the pure text of St. Jerome; a task which is not likely to be completed for many years.

ing sense of dependence upon its sanction finally obtained an absolute control over his intellectual processes and religious views. It also dictated his rejection of the venerable dogmas and solemn mysticism of his Church, a course which found its justification in his belief that "the New Testament is full of authority and open to the understanding of simple men, as to the points that be most needful to salvation." Lechler's surmise that the perilous conditions of the time imposed a prudent silence on those responsible for such an undertaking is not convincing: secrecy and subterfuge were foreign to Wycliffe's character, and he had scanty regard for men who differed from him. His courage drew him from the set paths which pierced the jungle of medieval life, and he thrust his way in new directions, accompanied by some who, although they lacked his audacity and endurance, were prepared to help him.

Moreover, while the claim that Wycliffe translated the version attributed to him is not invalidated by arguments derived from silence, its probability is confirmed by contemporary evidence, corroborating the testimony of Knighton already given. At the Synod held at St. Frideswide's, Oxford, on November 28, 1407, an edict was passed adverse to any version of Scripture texts "by questionable hands without authoritative sanction." The provisions enacted at the Synod and afterwards promulgated at St. Paul's, London,[1] granted the bishops power to control the circulation of the volume without positively proscribing it. Archbishop Arundel and his suffragans, addressing Pope John XXIII in 1412, accused Wycliffe, "the child of the old serpent and fosterling of Antichrist," with having devised, in order to fill up the measure of his malice against the Church, the plan of a translation of the Scriptures into his mother tongue. John Hus affirmed in a polemical tract issued during 1411 : "It is plain from his writings that Wycliffe was not a German, but an Englishman ; for the English say that he translated the whole

---

[1] The date of the promulgation is given as January 14, 1409.

Bible from Latin into English." These and other quotations of a similar character support two conclusions: first, that Wycliffe's reputed work was actually his own; and again, that it escaped, to some extent, the inhibitions of the ecclesiastics.

Cardinal Gasquet's further contention that an earlier English version than that of Wycliffe existed is founded on refutable statements. Sir Thomas More, who is his authority for this assertion, remarked in his "Dialogue" that he had seen "Bibles fair and old written in English, which have been known and seen by the bishop of the diocese and left in laymen's hands . . . who used them with devotion and soberness." He added that the "Holy Bible was long before Wycliffe's day by virtuous and learned men translated into the English tongue." [1] Since More did not know Purvey's version when he saw it, it is very probable that he mistook that version for an earlier work. He strongly condemned this translation of heretics who purposely corrupted the holy text, as he accused Wycliffe of doing, while he was totally unaware that the English Bibles of his friend Bishop Bonner and of other orthodox persons and of numerous churches and convents were copies of Purvey's version. More was not alone in his confusion of the two editions of Wycliffe's Bible as distinct translations. Until a comparatively recent period all writers mistook Purvey's revision for a translation anterior to Wycliffe's. The assurance that Wycliffe and his associates translated the Bible into English, that their translation was the first complete version thus made, and that Purvey revised it to its great benefit, is too well attested to be easily disturbed.

Bishop Westcott shows that the history of the English Bible, as we now have it, began with the work of William Tyndale, rather than with that of Wycliffe. Tyndale him-

---

[1] Light has been shed upon the question of the Old English Version by a work of A. C. Paues, entitled "The Fourteenth Century English Biblical Version" (1902), showing that there was an independent translation of some parts of the New Testament made before Wycliffe.

self stated that he was not "holpen with English of any that had interpreted the same or such like thing in the Scripture beforehand." Yet the two men, though separated by a century and a half of time, were of the same spiritual genealogy, and one in the loving veneration for the Scriptures which actuated their labors. The translation by Wycliffe stands apart, like a mountain separated and remote from meaner ranges, bearing the marks of primeval origin; in its solitary and rugged grandeur a fitting monument and witness to the 'Doctor Evangelicus,' to his unwearied patience and prodigious toil.

III

His separation from Oxford isolated him as a scholar; the lack of mechanical means for the diffusion of his teachings, and his conflict with the hierarchy drove him to copy the methods of St. Francis, and his ripening experience convinced him that the organized societies within the Church were backslidden sects which could not prevent her decay. To obviate this he adopted the extraordinary measure of instituting an order of poor priests, who were sent out to declare the message of the New Testament in the rejuvenated spirit of the earlier friars. Lutterworth became the headquarters for these evangelists, some of whom were Oxford graduates who had felt the impulse of Wycliffe's influence while he was still at the University, but the majority were unlettered men. Although at first ordained, the demands of their mission superseded clerical limitations and laymen were soon found among them. In Wycliffe's later writings they were no longer called "simplices sacerdotes," but "viri apostolici" or "evangelici." A remarkably effective preacher himself, Wycliffe carried the betterment of preaching upon his heart, and many of his sermons and addresses were directed to that end. He complained that useless speculations, legends, tales, and fables were substituted for Scriptural instruction, and that ornamented rhetoric marred the pulpit utterances of the better sort of clergy. Had he not been constrained to examine and reject the intellectual foundation of Catholic belief, he might have shared the honors of St. Francis and St. Dominic as the founder of another order of preaching friars. His own prototypes of Wesley's helpers were superior to the regular ecclesiastics in self-effacing zeal. They shared that collective sagacity of the Anglo-Saxon folk which has sometimes outwitted the designs of the wise and the noble. Poverty and plainness of speech gave them ready access to their countrymen. Clad in a rustic garb of undressed wool, dependent on charity for their daily bread, provided only with a pilgrim staff and a few pages from Wycliffe's tractates or sermons as the staple of their brief and pointed homilies, they survived the contempt of the hierarchy and secured the good-will of the people. Courtenay, whose aversion to such men and measures can be imagined, referred to them as wolves in sheep's clothing. Their success, which exceeded the most sanguine expectations, was confessed in the exaggerated avowal of Knighton that the "sect was held in the greatest honor and multiplied so that you could scarce meet two men by the way whereof one was not a disciple of Wycliffe." [1]

Under such auspices, the heart of the rector of Lutterworth seemed proof against the frosts of age, or that more deadly blight which the world's harsh treatment so often inflicts upon hope and faith. He saw the good ends his evangelists served, and the restricted areas of his concluding period only intensified its energies. Released from the intrigues of political cabals, his desire to project new activity into the morals of his age found another outlet in the stream. of pamphlets that flowed from his pen, both in Latin and in English. Two of his larger works, the "Trialogus," most erudite of all his productions, and the unfinished "Opus Evangelicum," were also written at this time. Nor did his seclusion render him indifferent to those issues of the State in

---

[1] G. G. Coulton: "Chaucer and his England"; p. 307.

which he had so recently been conspicuous. When Henry Spencer,[1] Bishop of Norwich, obtained a commission from Pope Urban VI to lead a crusade against the adherents of his rival at Avignon, Clement VII, Wycliffe published a small Latin treatise entitled "Cruciata," in which he exposed and condemned Spencer's proceedings, probably the more readily because that bishop had become notorious for his brutal treatment of the peasants during their insurgency. In Wycliffe the prelate encountered an opponent not so easily subdued, who characterized his action as a prosecution unbecoming true Christians, and an invasion of the faith. Not content with this, Wycliffe addressed a letter to the Primate covering the same grounds. The scheme he arraigned failed; on Spencer's return to England the temporalities of his see were withdrawn, and he was cited before Parliament to answer for his conduct. Courtenay had tightened the reins to no purpose if he meant to curb Wycliffe. Yet the Archbishop was reluctant to push matters to extremes, and although this hesitation has been generally credited to the status of the Reformer as a renowned doctor of Theology, his immunity from personal attack may have been due in some measure to more generous motives on the part of Courtenay. The evangelists themselves received no consideration; they were harassed on every side, expelled from the University, forced to abjure their opinions, and to renounce their allegiance to the arch-heretic. One after another submitted, but a faithful group, chiefly composed of men of humble position and relatively small attainments, refused to recant, and displayed that fortitude for which the English yeoman has been justly esteemed.

Their leader was neither banned nor excommunicated, and the fable of his recantation is too flimsy for serious discussion. He had realized his freedom, the outside world had lost its charms and terrors for him, and he was not re-

---

[1] Also known as Henry le Spencer or Despenser; born in 1341 or 1342, died in 1406; a soldier rather than a churchman.

strained from stimulating to the fullest extent the adaptation of his teaching to actual conditions. In the inquiry which Courtenay had set on foot no mention was made of any individual. The doctrines condemned were not attributed to any particular party; ecclesiastical discipline has seldom, if ever, been maintained with more moderation. On the other hand Wycliffe was not so much a Reformer with a numerous and determined body of supporters as an earnest seeker after truth who, although he could no longer accept things as they were, had no deliberate system of his own to offer in their stead.

Thus in a comparatively peaceful eventide, his hitherto unwearied day drew near its close. A paralytic seizure in 1382 had warned him that his incessant toils could not be long extended; still, except in so far as physical debility imposed restraints on him, he gave no sign of relinquishing his duties. The consciousness that his race was well-nigh run could not induce him to retire from the field, in which he labored against the friars and the Holy See with unabated mental and moral force. Some of his biographers assert that the friars appealed to Rome in protest, and that in 1384 Urban summoned Wycliffe to appear before the Papal Court. His reply to the Pontiff, they inform us, showed that the emaciated recluse, "spare and well-nigh destitute of strength," while mellower in tone, could still use the speech of controversy with old-time skill and promptitude: "I have joyfully to tell to all men the belief that I hold, and especially to the Pope, for I suppose that if my faith be rightful and given of God the Pope will gladly confirm it, and that if my faith be error, the Pope will wisely amend it. Above this I suppose that the Pope is most obliged to the keeping of the Gospel among all men that live here, for the Pope is highest vicar that Christ has here on earth. For the moreness (superiority) of Christ's vicar is not measured by earthly moreness, but by this, that this vicar follows Christ more closely by virtuous living. Now Christ during the time He walked here was the poorest of men, and put from Him all manner of worldly lordship. From this I take it as a wholesome counsel that the Pope should abandon his worldly lordship to worldly lords, and move speedily all his clerks to do the same. For thus did Christ, and thus He taught His disciples, until the fiend had blinded this world. And if I err in this sentence (opinion) I will meekly be amended, yea even by death, for that I hope would be a good to me."

This was the last flash of his expiring fires; a few weeks later, "on the day of the Holy Innocents," said John Horn, a priest and an eyewitness, "as Wycliffe was hearing Mass in his church at Lutterworth, at the time of the elevation of the Host, he fell down smitten by a severe paralysis." Three days afterward, on Saturday, December 31, 1384, his transcendent spirit, whose great gifts, activities, and aspirations commanded the admiration of friends and enemies alike, entered into rest with the departing year. The manner of his decease, after all he had said and done, might well be described in the language of Dante's "Convito": "Natural death is as it were a haven and a rest after long navigation. And the noble soul is like a good mariner; for he, when he draws near the port, lowers his sails and enters it softly with gentle steerage. For in such a death there is no grief nor any bitterness; but as a ripe apple is lightly and without violence loosened from its branch, so our soul without grieving departs from the body in which it hath been." [1]

Wycliffe was buried at Lutterworth, but by a decree of the Council of Constance, dated May 4th, 1415, his remains were ordered to be exhumed and cast away. Thirteen years later, Bishop Fleming, the founder of Lincoln College, Oxford, carried out the order. When Charles V stood beside the tomb of Luther at Wittenberg, those about him suggested that the body of his triumphant enemy should be disinterred and burned at the stake in the market place. "I war not with the dead," was the Emperor's reply, a chivalrous word

[1] Dr. Carlyle's translation.

which stands in contrast to the malevolent uselessness of Fleming's deed.

In any attempt to present a unified view of Wycliffe's character and service as the first English prophet who smote the rock of medieval ecclesiasticism, first place should be given to that spiritual insight which outlasts the transient value of his intellectual efforts. The forms of his thought have perished with the age that gave them meaning, but the spell of his soul's presence is with us still. "Feeble unit in a threatening infinitude" though he was, his reliance was upon Christ, Whom he set forth under terms of high political phraseology, as the supreme Head of the race, the "Cæsar semper Augustus," the Saviour of the whole number of the elect. Yet the esoteric strain was seldom apparent in Wycliffe; he expressed little of that poignant sense of individual transgression which is the plaint of such men as St. Paul, St. Augustine, and St. Bernard of Clairvaux, nor does a rapt communion with God seem to have been vouchsafed to his religious experience. His intellectual habits to a large extent controlled his devotional attitude. He closely identified knowing with being, and the legalistic rather than the strictly evangelical appropriation of divine grace found favor in his sight. This was expressed in his article that "working by a right life ended after God's will maketh a man God's child," a statement which, however true in itself, stood unrelated to the doctrine of Justification by Faith. Indeed, despite Wycliffe's familiarity with the New Testament, he did not give that emphasis to St. Paul's teaching which was the mainspring of the sixteenth century Reformation. Notwithstanding his incessant appeal to reason, his words are suffused with a direct earnestness, a passion for truth, and an unaffected sincerity which lift them above the chilling mists of mere abstraction. Moreover, the operations of Puritan theocracy were foreshadowed in his religious development. If reason and the exposition of holy doctors approved by the Church were his earlier guides in the interpretation of the Scriptures, in his later writings he insisted that the Spirit of God alone could expound the Bible to the individual Christian. He only can hope to understand aright who seeks the truth therein contained in holiness of heart and humility of mind. "He that keepeth meekness and charity hath the true understanding and perfection of all Holy Writ," for "Christ did not write His laws on tables, or on skins of animals, but in the hearts of men!" "The Holy Ghost," he adds, "teaches us the meaning of Scripture as Christ opened its sense to His Apostles."

Milton praised Wycliffe in the "Areopagitica" as a "divine and admirable spirit," and, if his rectitude and integrity, his enthusiasm for the cause of religion and his ardent longing for the purification of the Church are recalled, it cannot be gainsaid that the austere poet's eulogium was on the whole deserved. Some of his theological convictions have sunk to the level of curiosities, and men have turned away from others because they have ceased to retain any interest. The rest were held by him in an intelligent and a spacious way, and were full of enlightenment and hope. His theory of the lordship of God was more than an indefinite aspiration or a supreme feeling for the loftiest object of human contemplation. He was not content with the idea of a Deity Who was the mere creation of metaphysics, and whose attributes were so arbitrarily expressed as to baffle those who sought His aid. By deriving human from divine lordship, and by making the former dependent on character and service, Wycliffe but employed feudal language to sweeten the lives of suffering multitudes and lift from their shoulders the burdens that bowed them down. The didactic phraseology of his constructive thinking was seldom without an application to the problems of actual life.

His granitic character was unmantled by superficial tenderness, and as a celibate he could not enjoy the domestic intercourse which contributed to Luther's humanness and popularity. Yet his temperament, though naturally inclined to forcible action, never knew those revulsions of sentiment which frequently accompany such a disposition. He was in a great ethical sense a lover of God, of goodness, and of his fellow creatures; especially such as were deserted and forlorn; victimized by the outrageous evils which a merciless caste system inflicted on the poor. These he cared for as though they were his own, and the more persistently because of their wretchedness. For love is not only the impulse of natural affection, it is also that moralized devotion which seeks the highest welfare of its object. This passion prevailed in Wycliffe; it made him solicitous for the nation, the Church, the Bible, and for those helpless members of the State who could not ward off hunger, cold, and misery. "Poor men," he cried, "have naked sides and dead walls have plenty of waste gold." The recurrence of such abject conditions has brought back these and similar phrases into modern speech. They have not yet escaped the stir made five hundred years ago by his opinions, opinions which, while somewhat inchoate, nevertheless had a real influence for their own age, as the Peasants' Revolt sufficiently attests.

Even friendly observers have complained of his constant invective against the established order, and certainly he indulged an unseasonable readiness for scathing rebuke. Believing, because of his sensitiveness to more commanding interests, that property was the capital offender against the common weal, he scorned its inheritors, and propounded impossible schemes for their elimination from the social organism. His hate of greed and of the despotisms which it dictated was the militant aspect of his ecclesiastical and political righteousness. Yet these explanations do not justify his language in controversy, which was harsh, imperious, and vituperative. His opponents returned it in good measure after the fashion of the era. Dignitaries of the Church and of the University were prone to scurrilous abuse as well as stiff argumentation, and were seemingly oblivious of the fact that such methods lowered the merit of their debate. A witty Frenchman satirized Geoffrey's vitriolic criticisms by announcing that he died as the result of having inadvertently tasted the tip of his own pen. But Geoffrey was mild and soporific when compared with the fourteenth century doctors and disputants, whose picturesquely blasphemous epithets need not be recounted here. Courtesy and fairness were then unknown, and his admirers cannot claim that Wycliffe did aught to discover them.

But the principles of tolerance were known; and the men of that age never thought of persecution as right; they used it as a necessary instrument in the maintenance of the churchly organization as a vital factor of the State. Even so enlightened a scholar as Gerson entirely declined to recognize, except for his own purposes, his avowed principle of the non-coercion of opinions, and when Hus applied it to the revival of spiritual religion it at once became heretical.[1] Wycliffe did not suggest physical violence against his adversaries, but he did recommend that they should be stripped of their honors and emoluments. He might have said in the words of Goethe, "I can promise to be sincere but not impartial," and his unlicensed speech injured his cause and exposed him to the just accusations of his enemies. On the other hand, a judicial attitude was scarcely possible in contentious matters which went to the root of a semi-civilized life. Both he and his adversaries struck for a definite object, and received hard blows in return. Moreover, the clergy upon whom he poured out his anger were not forgiven by following generations. A century and a half later the laity of many countries revolted against them, and to-day no progressive people would tolerate them for a moment.

All conquests are, more or less, the prize of courage, and it is essential for the forward march of the race that deeds of daring should grapple boldly with fate. In this respect Wycliffe has received no blame and requires no defense. He had other characteristics; moral earnestness, a horror of

[1] Bishop Mandell Creighton: "Persecution and Tolerance"; pp. 100–101.

hypocrisy, honesty that did not shrink from the confession of failure, and the temper which brought opinions to the test of practice; qualities expressed in an undaunted bearing which never flinched, and made him the foremost citizen of England while he was a simple clerk at Lutterworth.   To attempt, to persist, to affront unjust power, and to stand in his own place faithful to what he believed, was habitual with him, and constituted him an example of genuine greatness. He was further distinguished for an indomitable will, which harmonized his strong and varied gifts and directed them upon specific lines of action.   Amid the mire and malignancy of his environment, he pushed onward and cleared the ·path for those who had less initiative.   His contemporaries were aware of this determination, and his ablest opponent, Archbishop Courtenay, was wary in his dealings with one whom he knew to be as immovable as himself. If there was in Wycliffe any reluctance to face obnoxious circumstances, he seldom permitted it to appear.   Indeed, he preferred those dangerous pursuits from which prudence would have retreated, and the greater the risk, the more ready seemed his undertaking.   This hardihood was not stimulated by any optimistic outlook; few clear-eyed men were optimists after the Black Death and its consequences. Langland asserted that "the last stronghold of Christianity had already succumbed to the assaults of Antichrist and the teachings of the friars.   Henceforth his pattern of simple faith, Piers Plowman, must shake the dust of the past from his feet and wander forth alone in search of the Christ that is to be." [1]   Even Chaucer, who stood alone in his inexplicable buoyancy, struck a less cheerful note in his latest song.   Wycliffe anticipated Langland, and declared that the Church would never be reformed except by the conjunction of an irresistible movement from within and a heroical pressure from without.   Half the truth of this assertion was preceptible to his vision, but the remainder was not.

[1] G. G. Coulton: "From St. Francis to Dante"; p. 350.

He saw that men had begun to pass their accustomed boundaries and to find other fears and hopes far exceeding the griefs and joys they knew. But he did not foresee their expansion into a freedom which could dispense with narrow creeds and scholastic interpretations, nor rise to an apprehension of that search for good before which such formularies fade away. Yet dejection never impeded his efforts, and, so far as the immediate future was concerned, his wisdom was justified by his accurate prediction of the troubles which fell upon Christendom.

Material for volumes of disquisitions upon justice and righteousness, or upon ecclesiastical and political plots and counter-plots, can easily be obtained from a study of his writings. Their treatment of these issues is far more akin to the problems of our generation than are his acquirements in the Scholasticism he expounded, and from which he could never separate his modes of thought. But though he was not the intellectual equal of the greater Schoolmen, and it is vain to compare him with the premier thinkers of the Middle Ages, nevertheless, in the opinion of those best qualified to judge he was chiefly important because of the weight and extent of his learning. He soared far above others in the range of his genius and surpassed them in the profundity of his knowledge. Sufficient evidence to confirm this has already been quoted from his contemporaries, who were agreed that in philosophy, theology, and familiarity with the Scriptures he had no living equal. Scholasticism was in its recession when he arrived upon the scene; yet Wycliffe's assiduity so redeemed what opportunities were left as to secure him this eminence. The limitations of the metaphysic in which he wrought were shown in the fact that men argued first and thought afterwards. His formal treatment of certain themes moved in a circle, and it was only when he reached the question he desired to prove that he displayed an intellectual vigor and ease which the clumsiness of his methods could no longer

M

conceal. Here the keenness of his mind and his strategical handling of arguments for attack or defense, while derived from the discipline of the Schools, went far beyond them, and transferred him into the region of the reformer.

Passing from his intellectual qualities to his services as a Christian patriot, it is relevant to say that his differentiating principle was the dependence of the individual soul upon God alone. This doctrine, which assigned to every single person an equal place in the regard of Deity, contained the seed of destruction for the carefully graded hierarchies of the Middle Ages. It sounds trite to our ears since custom has deprived it of freshness and force.   But the prelates who resisted it did so because they recognized in its implications the handwriting on the walls of their lordly houses.   Wycliffe transferred the conception from religion to politics, and the result was that he fell into those paradoxes which perplexed his friends and assisted his foes. Yet even here the formula has still to be reckoned with ; for, though it is not the final expression of the truth, it must be held as a depository of what truth it contained, that this may be used as a means for new light upon the relations of character to material possessions.

Wycliffe's thunderings against medieval authority should be estimated in the light of the fact that rulers were unaware of the distinction between civil and religious liberty as a principle and as an actual achievement.   The fact, if not the theory, they were compelled to accept at spasmodic intervals as an unwelcome intruder into a well-ordered condition. Kings and popes granted it, but in reality it was the force of circumstances which gave it, and what were deemed concessions from above were really conquests from below.   The government of Christian States rested on an absolutism which flatly contradicted the democracy of the New Testament, and Wycliffe was too close a Biblical student not to know its plain teachings. Codes, statutes, franchises, charters, dispensations, and similar instruments were frequently extorted by force, or procured by money payments to needy exchequers. Occasionally they were regarded as fragments of a larger freedom not yet evolved out of the surrounding confusion, but never acknowledged by the governing powers as a fundamental social necessity. Wycliffe was shrewd enough to detect this temper in the princes, bishops, and nobles, and if he did not perceive it with the lucidity of Marsiglio, yet his speculations were sufficiently incisive to disturb those who regarded his theory of lordship as a fore-runner of anarchy and madness. Further, these views, however visionary, were the stimulus for those active mental and moral processes by which he sought to attain beneficial results, and which saved him from ending in a morass of impossibilities. He called upon the students of Oxford to renounce the grandiose puerilities of a barren curriculum and occupy themselves with solid and useful verities. The exhortation was enforced by his own researches beyond lordship in the State into the baseless assumptions of a sacerdotal hierarchy, whose pretensions he met, as we have said, with his exposition of the theory of the immediate dependence of the individual soul upon God ; a relation which needed no priestly mediation and to which the Sacraments of the Church, however desirable and edifying, were not absolutely necessary.[1] But powerful minds are not always safe minds, and when he divorced the idea of the Church from any connection with its official or formal constitution, he advocated an impossible radicalism which verified his description of himself as one who "stammered out many things he was unable clearly to make good."

Enough has been said to show that the typical religion which rises above changes of earth, above schools of theology, above conflicting doctrines; the religion which is created by a man's realization that as man he must stand face to face with the Supreme Being, and that God has given him his manhood for this specific purpose, — was

[1] Encyclopædia Britannica : 11th edition : article on Wycliffe.

Wycliffe's, his unfailing source of confidence and of hope. His virtues stood high in the ethical scale, and the motives which inspired his conduct were, as a rule, unmixed. The gross and open immorality then prevalent did not touch him, even by rumor, to sully his priesthood, and apart from politics, no compromise with wrong has been laid to his charge. Among his contemporaries his influence corresponded with the elevation of his character and the largeness of his mind. Yet he could not persuade a comparatively primitive society whose spiritualities had been nourished by that marvel of construction, the dogma, ritual, and liturgy of Roman Christianity in the Middle Ages, to turn at once to his purer and more exacting creed.

But the irresistible forces of Time were enlisted in behalf of his teaching, while the convictions of his countrymen have moved toward its more refined articles and away from dwarfed finalities whose leaden, motionless infallibility arrests change by destroying life. He was brought into contact with issues which could not be discussed without differences nor settled without leaving in the conclusions the leaven of some error. The difficult rôle of the cleric in politics was not undertaken without risk to his reputation, but here the sturdiness which was inimical to his statesmanship served him well, in that it prevented him from making final shipwreck of his honor. Venomous misrepresentation was heaped upon his public acts; he was in no way idealized by what was said about him after he was gone. His memory was either left to the mercies of a rabid ecclesiasticism, jealous for its corporate powers and privileges, or connected with a despised and obscure group of sectaries which dwindled to extinction under persecution and its own fanaticisms. In his earlier days a pluralist, a beneficiary of the Crown, and an associate of the Lancastrian party, in his later years he spurned higher rewards within the compass of his talents because their acceptance would have involved a sacrifice of principle. Thus the gulf between preferment and his own self-respect

had widened, nor would he bridge it by betrayal. He
supported the peasants in their revolt against the festering
abuses and iniquities of their rulers, and the deprivations
which ensued redounded to his credit and usefulness.

The approval of the inward monitor, the translation of the
Bible which he loved and venerated, the ministrations of his
parish and the direction of his poor priests afforded him enjoyments beyond those he had forfeited. Besides, Wycliffe
was built for battle, and for him to renounce patronage was
less difficult than to abstain from onslaughts upon sordid
wrongs. If we are safe in believing the evil which men assert,
not of their antagonists, but of their companions, then clerical avarice, luxury, simony, and similar works of darkness
abounded in high places and under the disguise of spiritual
authority. Against these, the wearisome reiteration of which
would fall short of their actual extent, he waged a good
warfare, and in adversity he kept a high mien which discon-
certed his adversaries. The reaction against the Papacy,
which began in the reign of Henry III, reached its high-water
mark in John Wycliffe, and, though a subsidence followed,
it increased the independence of the nation and created
precedents for a larger freedom. His final months of
earthly life ran their course unvexed; a certain grandeur
overspread the man, who seemed to gather to himself in that
sunset calm those loftier hopes and fulfilments which have
made his memory the treasured heritage of a nation excep-
tionally rich in such bequests. His dust escaped the hate of
ignominious reactionaries and has the world for its tomb,
though he needed neither tomb nor epitaph to guard a name
than which no braver glows in the golden roll of English
sires.

Epilogue

Those who approach the study of the later medieval period
in England through the poetry of Chaucer or the glories of
Gothic architecture may find it difficult to reconcile the joy-

ous and sublime triumph of these master works with the physical and moral wretchedness of the populace we have depicted. The fourteenth century Church which Wycliffe pronounced abandoned and degenerate could still erect those exquisite cathedrals and abbeys which are to-day the monuments of her religious culture. If anywhere there were sermons in stones, capturing the imagination to an extent that can be claimed by few buildings in the world, they were found in Gloucester's reconstructed pile, in Abbot Litlington's additions at Westminster, and in the transformation of the great Hall of Rufus by Richard II. But the marks of decadence were on them, and, though its progress was slow, the change which reduced the free and flowing lines of the earlier Gothic to the stiff utilitarianism of the later style was already in process and continued during the lifetime of Wycliffe. Nor did their fascinations satisfy men's cravings for a more spiritual setting of the Christian faith than "long drawn aisles and fretted vaults" supply. Seekers after God turned from their cloying beauties and from the elaborate rituals they housed, as they had turned from the subtleties of academic argument. Wycliffe, although given to a proper ceremonialism, showed scanty appreciation for these holy fanes. They were memorable achievements, but the world could not live by them. Sculptures, however skillfully wrought, were not the bread of Heaven; not the realities upon which piety must feed to live. Intonings and chantings had not increased the morality of the worshipers. Their constant repetition dulled the hearing of the heart, and sacred offices hardened upon the accustomed mind like a shell. He quoted St. Augustine's dictum — "As often as the song delighteth me more than that is songen, so oft do I acknowledge that I trespass grievously" — against the endless array of vested priests and choristers who enlisted the senses at the cost of the spirit.

But although he was the chief contemporary Englishman who berated such cherished ways of worship, and also opposed the hierarchical control of the State, he did so without rightly estimating their latent usefulness, and his proposals for their abolition failed because they were premature in origin and negative in character. It has been pertinently observed that it was the misfortune of his position to have to attack abuses at a time when their abolition was but too likely to be followed by worse abuses, and to defend the rights of the State at a time when its rights were likely to be asserted in practice for the satisfaction of a clique of nobles more greedy, more unscrupulous, and more incompetent than the respectable ecclesiastical statesmen in whom Wycliffe saw no good thing. The governing classes were aware that the modifications and balances afterwards introduced to adjust the relations of Church and State had as yet found no place in English law. Nor could the towns and cities, those repositories of a larger freedom, advance the Reformer's schemes, since they were fully occupied in protecting their civic interests. The peasants and artisans to whom he appealed in his extremity were deprived of any means for an effective response. Hence he attempted to pluck the fruit before it was ripe; the experiments in democracy which he advocated, if they had been carried out, would have turned back by centuries the hands of the clock. He saw the needs of the present, and to some extent the possibilities of the future, but he did not sufficiently esteem the spirit of the past from which they could not be separated if they were to be satisfied. Constructive policies were absolutely essential in dealing with the great fabric which previous ages had reared with untold pains and sacrifices. These policies were not forthcoming, and the Reformer mediated between the methods he condemned and those he could not fully formulate. Thinker though he was, his first principles were sometimes far from cohesive; on specific questions his was too often the logic that flourished in seclusion but withered in the open. It should be added that he indulged no roseate dreams about victory; on the contrary, he never concealed from himself nor from others the foreboding that their joint efforts would be defeated and driven back. His strength was found in the faith he had in truth and righteousness. And in this temper, more manly and deserving than the artificial courage which is kindled by success, he bore a brave front and wrought valiantly.

Some of his former companions in tribulation were afterward tormentors of the Lollards who inherited his teaching; one of these backsliders, Philip Repyngdon, became Bishop of Lincoln and a Cardinal of the Church. This prelate humanely refused to obey the official order from the Council of Constance commanding that the bones of his old master be exhumed and burned. Nicholas Hereford also recanted his Wycliffian opinions, and, last and most melancholy, John Purvey, who had been so closely identified with the Reformer's dearest hopes and labors, and to whose gifts was due the revision of the first version of the Wycliffe Bible, revealed the untrustworthiness of scholastic Lollardism by his abjuration of the cause in which he had been a leader. He afterwards repented of his cowardice, recalled his recreancy, and disappeared from view. William Thorpe, a more honorable man, kept the faith, enduring imprisonment in 1397 and again in 1407, and on being brought before Archbishop Arundel, gave the Primate a moving account of his own life, and witnessed that historic confession for Wycliffe from which we have already quoted. But the Lollards gradually perished, the University relinquished its hard-won rights and returned to the bosom of the Church, and during the perjured and disgraceful reign of Henry IV the heads of colleges became the persecuting agents of the bishops. Shakespeare made that unhappy monarch, the son of John of Gaunt, denounce his own career, when he cried out that God knew by what crooked means he had obtained the crown, and continued, "I myself know well how troublesome it sat upon my head." He rests beneath the infamy of being the first English king who burned his subjects in the name of religion. This policy could not endure, and after an interval the persecutions of his successor, Harry of Agincourt, and of Archbishop Arundel, were quietly abandoned, although such was not the case until Wycliffe's mission was apparently obliterated in England.

But if his opinions were subdued in his native land, they rose again in Bohemia, and the account of their revival in southeastern Europe is among the dramatic phases of Protestant history. John Hus and Jerome of Prague continued there the enterprise Wycliffe had begun at Oxford and Lutterworth. Hus obtained his forerunner's manuscript works through scholars who came to England with Queen Anne of Bohemia, the consort of Richard II, and, while this influential disciple did not accept all his master's teachings, he raised their essentials to the dignity of a national faith. His tracts, pamphlets and books were copied *ipsissima verba* from Wycliffe's works and freely circulated among the people of that distant land. An Englishman who heard the examination of Hus before the Council of Constance, which condemned and burned him, declared that he thought he saw standing before him "the very Wycliffe." It required little stretch of imagination to see, looming in the background, the majestic shade of that great Englishman "for whose doctrine Hus went to the stake." Their memories, with Luther's, are enshrined in three medallions at the University of Prague, which depict the evolution of Protestantism for a century and a half, from the Anglican Scholastic through the Bohemian martyr to the German Titan. The first shows Wycliffe striking gleaming sparks from a flint; the second, Hus kindling the coals with the sparks; the third, Luther bearing a blazing torch he has lit at their fires.

* * * * * * * * *

Throughout this review we have seen that belief in liberty as an essential part of the good of all things, and dread of liberty as a dangerous innovation, were then, as they are now, the polar instincts meeting there, as everywhere, in ceaseless antagonism. The rulers of the period were intent on securing its aims and ideals in their own way, by the consolidation of Church and State, and the preservation of that loyalty to both upon which, as they held, all welfare here and hereafter alike depended. "Obedience is the first lesson in social progress, and this lesson was well worth learning, even though it took centuries to make it an instinctive motor reaction. By the steady pressure of authority the Church was modifying the very brain tissue of the Christian world, and inculcating habits of thought which lie at the basis of social progress. The Church may perish, but the psychic qualities it created will endure as long as European civilization."[1]

The time came when self-knowledge and self-control were sufficiently developed to attack with success the evils Wycliffe deplored, and the failure of the Roman Church to withstand the onset must be sought in the domain of morals as well as that of religion. Protestantism consecrated the home life of the people, enforced the Ten Commandments, put the ban upon lawless communal pleasures, and reminded men and women that they could attain sainthood by living in the world rather than fleeing from it. The mention of these things does not detract from the inestimable worth and spiritual character of other and more familiar causes that also contributed to the same result, but they are emphasized for the reason that they have not always received adequate consideration. The German Reformation was the outcome of an ethical quite as much as of a theological revolt. When its day dawned and the shadows fled, men saw with astonishment that throughout the long night preceding a few faithful souls had kept their vigil, and that the succession of the truly apostolic order had never been entirely broken. In that succession, always supreme because nearest to God's right hand, John Wycliffe stood first and greatest, as its noblest and most serviceable member during the later medieval period.

[1] S. N. Patten: "Development of English Thought"; pp. 89–90.

BIBLIOGRAPHY

For a scholarly and authoritative study of Wycliffe and his times the student is strongly recommended to consult "The Dawn of the Reformation," by Herbert B. Workman, M.A., D. Lit., of Westminster College, London.

ACTON, LORD. History of Freedom and Other Essays.

ACTON, LORD. Historical Essays and Studies.

ACTON, LORD. Lectures on Modern History.

ARMITAGE-SMITH, SYDNEY. John of Gaunt.

BOASE, CHARLES W. Oxford (Historic Towns Series).

BRODRICK, HON. GEORGE C. A History of the University of Oxford.

CAPES, W. W. The English Church in the Fourteenth and Fifteenth Centuries.

CARRICK, J. C. Wycliffe and the Lollards.

COULTON, G. G. Chaucer and his England.

COULTON, G. G. From St. Francis to Dante.

CREIGHTON, BISHOP MANDELL. Historical Essays and Reviews.

CREIGHTON, BISHOP MANDELL. Historical Lectures and Addresses.

CREIGHTON, BISHOP MANDELL. History of the Papacy.

CREIGHTON, BISHOP MANDELL. Persecution and Tolerance.

CREIGHTON, BISHOP MANDELL. Simon de Montfort.

DENTON, W. England in the Fifteenth Century.

Encyclopædia Britannica. Article on Wycliffe. Vol. XXVIII. 11th edition.

FORTESCUE, ADRIAN. The Mass.

GASQUET, CARDINAL. The Black Death.

GASQUET, CARDINAL. English Monastic Life.

GIHR, NICHOLAS. The Holy Sacrifice of the Mass.

GREEN, ALICE S. Town Life in the Fifteenth Century.

GREEN, JOHN RICHARD. Oxford Studies.

GREEN, JOHN RICHARD. Short History of the English People.

GRIBBLE, FRANCIS. The Romance of the Oxford Colleges.

GUIZOT, M. The History of England, Vol. I.

HARNACK, ADOLF. History of Dogma.

HARNACK, ADOLF. Bible Reading in the Early Church.

HENDERSON, E. F. (Editor). Select Historical Documents of the Middle Ages.

JESSOPP, AUGUSTUS. The Coming of the Friars, and other Historical Essays.

JUSSERAND, J. H. English Wayfaring Life in the Middle Ages. (Fourteenth century).

LECHLER, GOTTHARD V.   John Wycliffe and his English Precursors.
LOCKE, CLINTON.   The Age of the Great Western Schism.
OMAN, CHARLES.   The Great Revolt of 1381.
POOLE, REGINALD LANE.   Wycliffe and Movements for Reform.
RAIT, ROBERT S.   Life in the Medieval University.
RAMSAY, SIR JAMES H.   The Angevin Empire.
RANKE, L. VON.   History of the Popes.   Vol. I.
RASHDALL, HASTINGS.   The Universities of Europe in the Middle
    Ages.   Vol. II, Part II.
ROCK, D.   Hierurgia, or the Holy Sacrifice of the Mass.
SANDERSON, EDGAR.   History of England and the British Empire.
SKEAT, WALTER W.   Geoffrey Chaucer.
STEVENSON, FRANCIS S.   Robert Grosseteste.
STUBBS, BISHOP WILLIAM.   Historical Introduction to the Rolls Series.
TAYLOR, H. O.   The Medieval Mind.
TOUT, T. F.   The History of England.   Vol. II.
TREVELYAN, GEORGE MACAULAY.   England in the Age of Wycliffe.
VINCENT, M. R.   The Age of Hildebrand.
WARD, ADOLPHUS W.   Chaucer.
WORKMAN, HERBERT B.   The Dawn of the Reformation.
WORKMAN, HERBERT B.   The Evolution of the Monastic Ideal.

BOOK II

JOHN WESLEY

AND

THE EIGHTEENTH CENTURY

> I have felt
> A Presence that disturbs me with the joy
> Of elevated thoughts; a sense sublime
> Of something far more deeply interfused,
> Whose dwelling is the light of setting suns,
> And the round ocean and the living air
> And the blue sky, and in the mind of man;
> A motion and a spirit, that impels
> All thinking things, all objects of all thought,
> And rolls through all things.

WORDSWORTH : *Lines at Tintern Abbey.*

CHAPTER V

ANCESTRY AND TRAINING

And yet, as angels in some brighter dreams
Call to the soul when man doth sleep,
So some strange thoughts transcend our wonted themes,
And into glory peep.

Then bless thy secret growth, nor catch
At noise, but thrive unseen and dumb;
Keep clean, be as fruit, earn life, and watch
Till the white-winged reapers come.

HENRY VAUGHAN: *The Seed Growing Secretly.*

"But God, Who is able to prevail, wrestled with him; marked him for His own."

IZAAK WALTON.

CHAPTER V

I

WE deal in these chapters with the history of an almost unparalleled transformation of the English national character effected under the impulse of a revival of Christianity which subsequently spread throughout the British Empire and the United States. That revival was preceded by a period of spiritual decline and moral inertia which itself had followed the brief reign of Puritanism in the seventeenth century. The clergymen who filled the pastoral offices of Anglicanism or of Nonconformity during the eighteenth century were, with few exceptions, convinced that the immediate, direct action of the living God upon the spirits of men was practically impossible in reality and well nigh blasphemous in conception. They differed widely about theological systems and methods of Church organization, but they were united in relegating the intervention of Deity in matters of personal religion either to the far past or to the future that lay beyond the grave. To ward off assaults upon their respective institutions and beliefs seemed to all alike a more imperative duty than to contend against the deplorable vice and crime which afflicted society on every side. The regenerating faith of the New Testament was obscured, while the scholarship and energies which should have heralded it to a needy race were expended in guarding sectarian prejudices and shibboleths, the meanings of which were not always intelligible.

Yet this untoward generation produced out of the heart of Anglicanism the man of Puritan ancestry who reaffirmed the truth of God's presence in His children, and who was instrumental in stimulating and organizing a faith which rested upon Christ's personal word and self-communicated life; a faith that could not be depreciated by controversy, nor shocked by intellectual changes, nor convulsed by social upheavals; an overmastering faith, the progress of which won conquests similar to those of the Acts of the Apostles. Many had perceived the crying need of this faith, but John Wesley became its embodiment and messenger. In him and in his work Anglican and Puritan coalesced — the order and dignity of the one, the fearless initiative and asceticism of the other — and admirably served their mission to his own and succeeding ages. His quenchless zeal enabled him to quicken in multitudes of his fellow men that repentance for sin and sense of the renewed favor of God which had wrought his own deliverance. His labors had a profound and pervasive influence on the evolution of Protestantism, to which Mr. Lecky bears witness in the following words: "Although the career of the elder Pitt and the splendid victories by land and sea that were won during his ministry, form unquestionably the most dazzling episodes in the reign of George II, they must yield, I think, in real importance to that religious revolution which shortly before had begun in England by the preaching of the Wesleys and Whitefield." [1]

This deserved tribute, which has received a tardy yet

[1] " History of England in the Eighteenth Century "; Vol. III, p. 1.

increasing approval, serves to bear out the contention of Goethe, Carlyle, and Emerson, that personality rather than ideas is the determining factor in human progress. But while a character such as Wesley's does infinitely more for the advancement of morals and religion than any abstract theory or mechanical formula possibly could accomplish, it also creates the difficulty of interpreting him adequately. There is a mystery of genius as well as a mystery of godliness, and he shared in both. The Oxford cleric who became the center of the revolution which Lecky described possessed a significance which requires patient and thorough examination. Literary ingenuity can set forth the motions of his gifted mind and the outward expressions of his far-reaching and benevolent sympathies, but it falters in attempting to delineate the secret history of his rich and contagious spirituality. Although his was one of those happily constituted intellects which pierce through immaterial and irrelevant accretions to the core of a question, his nature was complex, and his spirit accommodated many apparently contradictory elements. He shared the sentiments common to saints of every school, and displayed an admirable catholicity toward those who did not hold his opinions. Yet some of his biographers have embalmed him rather than made him vital to our apprehension, and others have treated him as a quarry from which to excavate the building material for the defenses of their orthodoxy. The living Wesley, as one of the chosen vessels of God's grace and a prophet of divine realities whose life and teaching were an inspiration and a blessing to the Church, should not be submitted to these stereotyped processes. Nor can his varied qualities be compressed into those simplifying generalizations which gratify the advocates of a theological system but fail to elucidate the deeper meaning of the man.

He was born at Epworth rectory, in the county and diocese of Lincoln, on the 17th of June, 1703,[1] and came

---

[1] The new style of reckoning would make it the 28th of June.

of a sturdy Anglo-Saxon stock whose later members furnished their quota of scholars and clergymen to the service of the Church.[1] Bartholomew Westley, the great-grandfather of John, was the third son of Sir Herbert Westley, of Westleigh, Devon, and Elizabeth de Wellesley, of Dangan, County Meath, Ireland. An Oxford man, he studied both medicine and divinity in the University where his son, grandson, and three great-grandsons were afterwards educated. In 1619 he married the daughter of Sir Henry Colley of Castle Carberry, Kildare, Ireland, and after an interval, during which little definite is known concerning his career, Westley became in 1640 the Rector of Catherston, and also held the neighboring living of Charmouth in Dorset. When Charles II fled from Cromwell's "crowning mercy" at Worcester in 1651, he attempted to cross the Channel from Charmouth to France. But the delay of the boat chartered to convey the king to the vessel jeopardized the scheme, and he barely escaped. The "puny parson's" bold avowal that he would have captured the monarch had he been present was an indication of the political opinions which speedily involved Mr. Westley in the troubles of the Restoration. In 1662 he suffered ejection from his living under the Act of Uniformity, and thereafter practiced as a physician among his former parishioners and at Bridport. His blameless and benevolent character seems to have been a protection during the persecuting days. He lived to a ripe and honored age, and at his death was laid to rest in the churchyard at Lyme Regis.

John Westley, the son of Bartholomew and the paternal grandfather of the man who bore his name and inherited his spirit, was born in 1636, and graduated from Oxford in his twenty-second year with a reputation as an Oriental

[1] In old parish registers of churches in the vicinity of Bridport, near Dorchester, the name of John Westley appears in 1435 as prebendary and vicar of Sturminster: in 1655 Jaspar, son of Ephraim Westley, gentleman, resided at Weymouth, and in 1691 James Westley was one of the bailiffs of Bridport.

linguist. The Vice Chancellor, Dr. Owen, had imbued him with Dissenting views of Church government, and Westley, probably avoiding Episcopal ordination, exercised his first ministry among the fishermen of Radipole, a hamlet near Weymouth. In 1658 his piety and culture secured for him the pastorate of Winterborne-Whitchurch, in Dorset, and Cromwell's Board of Commissioners, known as "Triers," who pronounced upon the fitness of candidates for the ministry of the Church, approved the selection. In 1661, the second year of the Restoration, he was imprisoned for declining to use the Book of Common Prayer, and a year later was ejected from his living. The remaining sixteen years of his life were marked by repeated labors and hardships; he died when still in the forties, prematurely worn out and apparently thwarted in his aims. But his legacy to the Wesley family was treasured by his widow and children, who transmitted to the sons of Epworth rectory his lofty example of a singularly pure and sacrificial career, ennobled by the sufferings he endured for the sake of conscience.

His wife was the daughter of Dr. John White, the patriarch of Dorchester, a member of the Westminster Assembly and one of the original patentees of the Massachusetts colony. Her uncle, Samuel Fuller, the witty divine and church historian, described her father as "a grave man, who would yet willingly contribute his shot of facetiousness on any just occasion." Mrs. John Westley received the sympathy of those who had admired her husband's adherence to his convictions, and by their assistance she was enabled to educate her children. Her son Matthew became a physician in London; Samuel, the father of John and Charles Wesley, was intended for the Dissenting ministry, and was sent to Mr. Martin's Academy on Newington Green in that city to obtain his training.[1] The lack of genuine religion and

[1] These academies were established after the passing of the Toleration Act. Prior to that, Dissenting ministers acted as private tutors in families or received pupils in their own homes. Many of the ministers were men of learning and power and linked their schools with the history of Noncon-

the prevalence of sectarian controversy among his fellow-students chilled his Nonconformity, and, notwithstanding his tender regard for his father's memory and for his mother's wishes, he began to examine the questions at issue between the Established Church and Dissent. He naturally felt reluctant to inform his mother and her friends of his impending change; yet he met the emergency with characteristic courage and promptitude, and having carefully considered the situation and invoked Heaven's directing wisdom, he determined to seek admission to the Anglican Church. With this end in view, he set out on foot for Oxford, with little or no provision for his expenses, and on arriving there entered as a servitor at Exeter College. After the completion of his studies, he was ordained deacon on August 7, 1688, and priest in February, 1689; thus reuniting his branch of the family with the Church which had expelled his father and grandfather, and which afterwards looked with prejudice on the efforts of his sons. It may be noted here that the change in the spelling of their name from Westley to Wesley was made by Samuel on the ground that the latter was the original form.

John Wesley was equally well born on the maternal side. His mother was the youngest daughter of Dr. Samuel Annesley, a graduate of Queen's College, Oxford, and an able, genial, and erudite divine whose conspicuous gifts were highly esteemed by his brethren. Ejected from the historic London Church of St. Giles, Cripplegate, Dr. Annesley afterwards ministered to a congregation worshipping at Little St. Helens, Bishopsgate, where his reputation as a trusted leader earned for him the title, "the St. Paul of Nonconformity." Mrs. Wesley, like her husband, was dissatisfied with the Calvinistic tenets of Puritan theology then prevalent, and while still a girl had deliberately renounced

formity. But the intellectual activity of these schools injured their spiritual life, and herein lay the secret of their bickerings and ultimate atrophy. See The Cambridge History of English Literature: Vol. X, pp. 431–432.

them and returned to the Anglican fold.[1]   This renunciation
created a mutual sympathy between her and Samuel Wesley, whose good fortune it was to marry her during the
year of his ordination.   From the first the young couple
struggled under burdens of poverty and debt consequent upon a meager income and a growing family.   After a London
curacy, a chaplaincy in the navy, and a brief tenure in the
small living of South Ormsby, Lincolnshire, they came in
1697 to Epworth, the place destined to be the scene of their
joint labors for nearly forty years.   The new rector, then
thirty-five years of age, received scarcely enough support
for his necessities.   The rectory was a three-storied building
of timber and plaster, thatched with straw; the parishioners were ignorant and degraded farmers and peasants,
bitterly opposed to their parson's Tory politics, and the
majority remained long heedless of his religious exhortations.
They have been described by the Rev. W. B. Stonehouse
as descending from the Fenmen, "a race according to the
place where they dwell, rude, uncivil, and envious to all
others."   In the early eighteenth century these people maintained the bad reputation of their ancestors.   They formed
an insulated group, much below even the pitiable average
of rural intelligence, turbulent and vulgar, profane and
corrupt.   The deference usually shown to superiors in long
settled communities was entirely absent from their behavior,
and they despised and habitually neglected the conventional
observances of religion.

The market town of Epworth, containing a hitherto
stationary population of about two thousand, is situated
on the Isle of Axholme,[2] a strip of land ten miles long and
four broad, once enclosed by five rivers, two of which are
now only marked by the willow trees lining their former

---

[1] Archbishop Laud, to his credit, had always protested against these
tenets.

[2] The Isle of Axholme still retains the chief remaining examples of the old
three-field system which was the ancient Aryan method of tillage, showing
how little the place has been affected by the surrounding order of progress.

banks. The fertile plains of Lincolnshire stretch in green expanse beyond the gentle slope on which the place is located, their stagnant marshes drained and dotted with woodland groves, prosperous farmsteads, and herds of cattle. On the rising ground commanding the town stands the church with its massive tower. The parsonage in which John Wesley was born was destroyed by an incendiary fire on a winter's night in 1709, and although the rector promptly began the work of rebuilding, the new edifice remained half furnished for several years. The present rectory is a Queen Anne structure of comfortable dimensions, with one of those old-fashioned English gardens which harbor peace and contemplation in their bordered walks.

Few clergymen seemed less fitted to minister to such a parish than Samuel Wesley, and even his wife's superior discernment could not prevent frequent misunderstandings between pastor and flock which occasionally involved her also. Yet choleric, stubborn of temper and somewhat eccentric in conduct as the rector was, his shortcomings were offset by his cheerful optimism, his courage, and his fidelity to his calling. He contended with pecuniary difficulties and the indifference and malignancy of his parishioners until his high sense of duty and his independence finally won the reluctant confidence of those whom he served according to his own ideas instead of their desires. His tastes and aspirations as a scholar found expression in voluminous writings, none of which had any particular value. Swift in the "Battle of the Books," and Pope in the "Dunciad," dismissed his versifications with a phrase, and even the favorable eye of his son John failed to detect any signs of poetry in them. His chief work in prose was a Commentary on the Book of Job, in which he brought to the memory of the much enduring Patriarch an accumulation of curious and varied learning. Yet these literary efforts kept alive in his frugal household the traditions of scholarship, and doubtless served to cheer the lonely lot of an intellectually ambitious man who was severed from fellowship with craftsmen of the pen. He weathered the storms of his tempestuous passage, and steadily maintained the Apostolic vision of a world converted to the true faith, himself volunteering for missionary service in the far East that this cause might be advanced. An ardent patriot and a churchman, he never despaired of affairs in the homeland. "Charles," said the father as he lay on his deathbed and addressed his youngest son, "be steady; the Christian faith will surely revive in these kingdoms. You shall see it, though I shall not." To John he had before testified, "The inward witness, son, the inward witness, — this is the proof, the strongest proof, of Christianity."

"I did not at the time understand them," remarked John in after days, speaking of these dying words; yet when viewed in the light of Methodist history, they show the prophetic instinct, and how the far-reaching fibers of the Evangelical Revival were nurtured in the hearts of that family from the days of Bartholomew and John Westley to those of Samuel Wesley and his sons.

His wife exercised the dominant influence in the household, and John was essentially his mother's child. Her Anglicanism was blended with the sterner qualities of her Puritan father, and her zeal was no less ardent because it was equable. Although deficient in some milder attributes of the feminine nature, and without that sense of humor which would have softened the rigidities of her domestic rule, she excelled in simplicity, dignity, practicality, and firmness of purpose, traits which made her affection a source of strength and security. Of the numerous children [1] born to this excellent lady all were gifted, and some were doomed to saddened and disappointed lives, but two of them founded the Methodism of which she was a primal source. Her

[1] Epworth was the birthplace of fifteen of the nineteen children of Samuel and Susannah Wesley. Samuel, the eldest son, who was born in London, was thirteen years older than John, and Charles four years younger.

home was a school of manners, morals, and religion, in which their conversation and intercourse were closely guarded, and turned into the most profitable channels. She taught them letters; their knowledge of the Holy Scriptures and professions of piety were the objects of her unstinted care, from which the duties and privations of her household could not detain her. Although her Spartan régime reacted on some of the children, in later days they referred to her in terms of the liveliest gratitude, seeking her counsel, and making her the recipient of their confidences. The touch of humanness, which would have relieved the austerities of her discipline without lowering its tone, came with the passing of the years; time was generous to Mrs. Wesley in that it mellowed her, adding to her grace and tenderness. Her assiduous defense of the circle she adorned was a revelation of her goodness and wisdom, virtues which her letters to John and Charles abundantly confirm. With such a mother, the Church would have been justified in expecting great things from the sons. To enlarge upon her worth is superfluous, since that has been emphasized by many authors and moralists who have wondered at her tranquil authority over a family so highly individualized, and one which conferred such priceless benefits on mankind. The latent Puritanism to which her sons afterwards appealed with an unerring belief in its desire for God, and which produced its best results in regions beyond the sphere of the State, found no finer or more complete setting for the spiritual phases of Protestant history than that given at Epworth by Susannah Wesley. Content to cultivate in poverty and seclusion the purer ideals which political struggles and changes had failed to maintain, she lived to a beautiful and venerable age, and grew in holiness and influence, until called to the life beyond, when her happy spirit passed from peace to deeper peace with confidence and thanksgiving.

II

The first decade in Epworth was full of vexations. When John was but two years old his father was committed to Lincoln Castle for debt. The rector's enemies not only brought this trouble upon him; they also destroyed his crops, injured his cattle, and after several attempts, burned his home. John, who had been overlooked in the confusion, was rescued from the upper story at the last moment by a man raised on the shoulders of others to snatch the child out of the flames. Immediately afterwards the roof collapsed, and his father, overcome with gratitude, fell upon his knees and acknowledged the providence which had delivered the lad. In later days John frequently recurred to the incident then stamped upon his memory as a proof of God's personal supervision of his life, and desired that his epitaph should commemorate it in the words, "Is not this a brand plucked from the burning?" The capricious escapades of "Old Jeffrey," the ghost which haunted the rectory, were also among the vivid recollections of his youth. He had entered the Charterhouse School when this much discussed visitor from another world began those disturbances which continued during the months of December and January, 1716 and 1717. The real source of the phenomena was never discovered; the Wesleys attributed them to a supernatural cause, but seemed not to have been affrighted by this impression. Whenever prayers were offered for the Royal Household the spirit manifested its Jacobite sympathies by vigorous poundings, a form of remonstrance which greatly amused the children. John's frank acceptance of this and similar marvels, references to which are frequent in his writings, was more than an ordinary recognition of such occurrences; it savored strongly of superstition.

Samuel, the eldest son, entered Westminster School in 1704, became a Queen's scholar in 1709, and went up to Christ Church, Oxford, in 1711. He returned to Westminster as head usher, was admitted to Holy Orders, and in process of time made the acquaintance of a group of notables whose political and ecclesiastical opinions he fully shared. Of that select company were Bishop Atterbury, the stormy petrel of the Anglican episcopacy, Harley, Earl of Oxford, Prior, Addison, and Dean Swift. This Samuel Wesley was a poet of some moment, an accomplished scholar, and a conservative man of retiring disposition who looked with alarm upon the religious "extravagances" of his younger brothers. He was designated in 1732 head master of Blundell's School at Tiverton in Devonshire, well known to readers of Blackmore's "Lorna Doone," and died there on November 6, 1739, without having realized the preferment which might have been his had the Tory party not been defeated by its allegiance to the Stuarts.

John entered the Charterhouse School, London, at eleven years of age, on the nomination of the Duke of Buckingham, and remained there until he was seventeen. The name of this famous school is derived from the French Maison Chartreuse, a religious house of the Carthusian monks, and as such was applied to the various Carthusian monasteries in England. Its familiar and corrupted usage is connected with the Charterhouse, where on a former burying ground near the city wall, Sir Walter de Manny, at whose death all England mourned, and Bishop Northbury, founded in 1371 the Priory of the Salutation. After the dissolution of the great monasteries in 1535 the property passed through various hands until in 1611 the Earl of Suffolk sold it to Thomas Sutton, one of Queen Elizabeth's Masters of Ordnance, who here established a brotherhood for eighty poor men and a school of forty poor boys. The latter has long ranked as one of the foremost public schools of the realm, and boasts among its scholars the names of Crashaw, Lovelace, Barrow, Roger Williams, Addison, Steele, Wesley, Blackstone, Grote, Thirlwall, Leech, Havelock, and Thackeray. The school was removed to its handsome new buildings at Godalming, Surrey, in 1872, but the fascinating place which Wesley loved and frequently revisited stands practically the same to-day, and the gentlemen pensioners whom Thackeray immortalized in "Colonel Newcome" still gather at the sound of the curfew in the stately Elizabethan hall, and worship in the dim chapel which contains Sutton's alabaster tomb.

Public school life in Wesley's England was cruel beyond degree; the elder boys bullied the younger ones, who had to be content with short commons at table, and submit to brutal treatment on every side.[1] The discipline of the rectory had prepared John for his ordeal; he did not complain of the food, nor resist the rough handling of his companions, as Charles did at Westminster when he thrashed one of his worst tormentors. Yet his quiet persistence and advanced knowledge gained him a standing even in that ruffianly crowd, and he always attributed his abstemious habits and longevity to the scanty diet and abundant exercise of the Charterhouse. The Rev. Luke Tyerman makes the portentous announcement that "John Wesley entered the Charterhouse a saint, and left it a sinner."[2] What particular kind of saint or sinner he had in mind the vigorous biographer of Wesley does not define; and the statement can be dismissed as one of those vagaries which are due to theological prejudice. It is highly questionable if the boy suffered any loss of genuine faith or purity. He had come from a sheltered existence at home, where his early interest in religious matters induced his father to admit him to Holy Communion when he was eight years old. His fastidious scruples had already attracted the attention of those about him, and needed no further encouragement, while the drastic treatment he received from his schoolfellows probably saved him from becoming a pious prig by discouraging any dis-

[1] Leech's "Winchester College" and the article on Eton in the Victoria County History of Buckinghamshire give striking accounts of the harshness and ill usage of eighteenth century public schools.
[2] "Life and Times of John Wesley"; Vol. I, p. 22.

position towards artificiality. During his six years in London he kept in close touch with his parents and his brother Samuel, who had oversight of Charles at Westminster and of John at the Charterhouse throughout the four years the three brothers were together in the capital. Surrounded by these influences, John maintained his private devotions and communicated on the appointed days.

He entered Christ Church, Oxford, in the summer of 1720, having already gained solid advantages in the breadth and sincerity of his character and a thorough drilling in the classics. As a Carthusian scholar at the University he received an annuity of forty pounds, an income which made it almost impossible for him to keep out of debt. His father's finances were too straitened to be of much avail, and his mother's letters contained frequent advices on the need for economy. Yet the monetary drawback did not hinder his serious use of those opportunities which his fellow students for the most part neglected.

The University was at a low ebb, too careful for the interests of the banished Stuart dynasty, and so indifferent toward scholarship as to provoke Wesley's exclamation — "Oh! what is so scarce as learning save religion?" Edward Gibbon described a typical tutor of the day as a man who "remembered that he had a salary to receive, and forgot that he had a duty to perform." [1] Separated from the life and progress of the nation, supercilious toward the Hanoverian succession, which, despite its foreign extraction, was the safeguard of constitutional liberties, and without any effective internal supervision, Oxford had fallen on evil days, the more pronounced because of its perverse blindness to any defects. Students evaded their classes, wasting their time in drinking and gambling. Idleness, ignorance, and deception abounded. Candidates for degrees could purchase a dispensation freeing them from attending lectures, some of

[1] It should be noted that Gibbon's impressions of Oxford were received when he was a youth of fifteen.

which were never given, and had others been omitted no serious loss would have been incurred. This betrayal of trust and the general immorality intensified Wesley's sense of separateness. Twenty years later he rebuked them in a sermon preached before the University and exhorted the colleges to mend their ways. In the meantime the religious devotion of his adolescence began to weaken under the stress of his studies and social engagements. But he was far removed from the gross pursuits of many of his fellow students, thoroughly reputable and conscientious in his dealings, and justly respected for the propriety of his conduct. His earliest diaries show that he read popular dramas, took a special interest in the gay Horace, and studied the graver works of Homer, Virgil, Juvenal, Spenser, Shakespeare, and Milton.

He spent the Christmas of 1725 with college friends, at the rectories of Broadway and Stanton, villages situated under the Cotswold Hills, in one of the loveliest valleys of England. Here he met Miss Betty Kirkham, probably the "religious friend" who had first induced him in the preceding April to enter earnestly upon a new life.[1] Another of his companions was Mrs. Pendarvis, of the Granville family of Buckland, a third place in the vicinity. This fascinating young widow, the niece of Lord Lansdowne, afterwards the wife of Dr. Delaney of Dublin, was one of the accomplished women of the time, to whom Edmund Burke paid an unusual tribute for her culture and conversation. Wesley maintained a correspondence with both ladies, addressing Miss Kirkham as Varanese and Mrs. Pendarvis as Aspasia. He danced at a wedding which took place during the vacation and also with his sisters at Epworth upon his visits there, and returned to Oxford to reproach himself for his susceptibility to the charms of a bewitching circle. It was his custom on Saturday evenings

[1] "The Journal of John Wesley": edited by Rev. Nehemiah Curnock; Vol. I, p. 15.

to record the events of the moving hours, and confess his faults. "Have I loved women or company more than God?"[1] he asked, shortly after his return from Stanton. The inquiry showed that while enjoying the pleasures of a refined taste, he also felt that to fear God and to have no other fear is the principle which not only safeguards religion, but asserts its truth and wisdom in all affairs of life. In retrospect he was unsparing toward himself, and sometimes demanded more than his nature or circumstances could then afford, striving after a degree of excellence well-nigh unattainable in those who have to mingle in the current of human affairs. With guileless and unreserved candor he exposed the inmost secrets of his soul, and his sincerity led him to reflect, "Who more foolish and faithless than I was?" He did not insinuate his experiences nor gloss them; he proclaimed them from the house-tops. "I still said my prayers, both in public and private; and read, with the Scriptures, several other books of religion. . . . Yet I had not all this while so much as a notion of inward holiness; nay, went on habitually and, for the most part, very contentedly, in some or other known sin; though with some intermission and short struggles, especially before and after the Holy Communion, which I was obliged to receive thrice a year."[2] This confession disquieted him more than it need disquiet others. While we should not refuse to admit the inferences which lie on the surface of his statement, we must not suffer the phraseology to mislead us. The "known sin" of which Wesley speaks can be judged in the light of his maturer experience, when a leaning toward asceticism rendered him sensitive to what may have been at their best harmless amusements, and at their worst mild indiscretions. Assuredly, he did not easily yield to the temptations of a University career. He was remiss in his expenditure

[1] "The Journal of John Wesley": edited by Rev. Nehemiah Curnock; Vol. I, p. 52.
[2] L. Tyerman: "Life and Times of John Wesley"; Vol. I, p. 24.

of money, considering its scarcity at Epworth, and his parents properly warned him to be more careful in this respect, but he never deliberately disregarded the obvious distinction between good and evil. The content of the term sin varies with acuteness of spiritual perception; where this faculty is unduly alert, acts are included in the category of sins which by no means fall within the proper meaning of the word. Spiritually-minded men and women are the severest arbiters of their own past, and are always prone to depreciate their motives and deeds. Their writings teem with accusations against themselves, which not infrequently are the shadows cast by an intense yearning to know and do the will of Heaven, that they may enter into its more perfect fellowship. It should be understood that from his earliest youth Wesley had been attached to noble ideals, and that throughout a long life he seldom swerved from the hard and narrow path of duty.

During the first four years of his residence at Oxford he gave no indication that he proposed entering the Anglican ministry, although there is little doubt that his parents had always hoped such would be his decision. His father frequently expressed the desire that he should do so, and in 1725 Wesley began to read the works of Thomas à Kempis and Jeremy Taylor, with the result that his religious life became more pronounced, and he gave himself to prayer and meditation. His correspondence with his mother, who was then, as always, his guide and confessor, shows that he seriously questioned his fitness for Holy Orders. The ideal of the writer of "De Imitatione Christi" repelled him as being too cold and austere, and he complains in a letter to his mother of à Kempis for "inverting instead of disciplining the natural tendencies of humanity." Taylor's exhortation to humility seemed to him to clash with the claims of truth.[1] Notwithstanding these criticisms, both authors

---

[1] Julia Wedgwood: "John Wesley and the Evangelical Reaction of the Eighteenth Century"; p. 33.

o

introduced Wesley to depths and reaches of the spiritual realm hitherto unknown to him. They stimulated his faith, and placed him under an obligation he afterwards acknowledged. Taylor's "Holy Living and Holy Dying" had exceedingly affected him. He remarked, "Instantly I resolved to dedicate all my life to God—all my thoughts, and words, and actions,—being thoroughly convinced there was no medium; but that every part of my life (not some only) must either be a sacrifice to God, or myself, that is, in effect, the devil." [1] His mother did not always satisfy his inquiries, but she admirably summed up the question of his general relation to the world in the following manner, "Take this rule — whatever impairs the tenderness of your conscience, obscures your sense of God, or takes the relish off spiritual things, that thing is sin to you, however innocent it may be in itself." [2] Her anxiety for his safe emergence from theological perplexities prompted similar counsels which reveal her at her best both as a Christian and a thoughtful student of current doctrinal statements. "But if you would be free from fears and doubts concerning your future happiness," she wrote on July 21, 1725, "every morning and evening commit your soul to Jesus Christ, in a full faith in His power and will to save you. If you do this seriously and constantly, He will take you under His conduct; He will guide you by His Holy Spirit into the way of truth, and give you strength to walk in it. He will dispose of the events of God's providence to your spiritual advantage; and if, to keep you humble and more sensible of your dependence on Him, He permit you to fall into lesser sins, be not discouraged; for He will certainly give you repentance, and safely guide you through all the temptations of this world, and, at the last, receive you to Himself in glory." [3]

---

[1] L. Tyerman: "Life and Times of John Wesley"; Vol. I, p. 36.
[2] Julia Wedgwood: "John Wesley and the Evangelical Reaction of the Eighteenth Century"; p. 34.
[3] L. Tyerman: "Life and Times of John Wesley"; Vol. I, p. 38.

As his ordination approached, the Thirty-nine Articles were scrutinized, particularly those relating to Predestination, and Mrs. Wesley comments on its extreme interpretation in a letter dated August 18, 1725. "The doctrine of predestination, as maintained by the rigid Calvinists, is very shocking, and ought to be abhorred, because it directly charges the Most High God with being the author of sin. I think you reason well and justly against it; for it is certainly inconsistent with the justice and goodness of God to lay any man under physical or moral necessity of committing sin, and then to punish him for doing it."[1] Their interchange of sentiments occupied eight months, at the end of which time Mrs. Wesley wrote, "I approve the disposition of your mind, and think the sooner you are deacon the better." With such commendation, and after exercising every care in preparation for the office he was about to assume, John Wesley solemnly offered himself for the Christian ministry. He was ordained deacon on Lord's Day, September 19, 1725, by Doctor John Potter, Bishop of Oxford, who three years and three days later admitted him to priest's orders.

III

This event marked the beginning of an era in Wesley's religious development. Hitherto he had known some relaxation from his studies, and an acquaintance who must have shared his hours of ease described him as "the very sensible and active collegian, baffling every one by the subtleties of logic, and laughing at them for being so easily routed; a young fellow of the finest classical taste, of the most liberal and manly sentiments. He was gay and sprightly, with a turn for wit and humor."[2] His excellent character and scholarship, combined with his social gifts, obtained for him a fellowship of Lincoln College in the

[1] L. Tyerman: "Life and Times of John Wesley"; Vol. I, p. 40.
[2] John Telford: "The Life of John Wesley"; p. 33.

spring of 1726, an honor indeed for one so young, who had not yet received his master's degree. With his entrance there at the beginning of the October term, he imposed a stricter rule upon himself and wrote to his brother Samuel, "Leisure and I have taken leave of one another." Mondays and Tuesdays he gave to Greek and Latin; Wednesdays to logic and ethics; Thursdays, to Hebrew and Arabic; Fridays, to metaphysics and natural philosophy; Saturdays, to oratory and poetry; Sundays, to divinity. He was appointed Greek lecturer and moderator of the classes, which assembled six times a week for disputation on stated themes, his duty being to preside over and conclude the debates.[1] While he always disliked needless controversy, by means of this occupation he acquired a dexterity in argument which was afterwards of no small service. His general reading was well chosen and showed him to be a scholar of a substantial sort, without that fear for the corrosive effect of intellectualism on faith which has beset so many advocates of religion. Writing to one of his pupils in August, 1731, he tendered the following advice: "You, who have not the assurance of a day to live, are not wise if you waste a moment. The shortest way to knowledge seems to be this: 1. To ascertain what knowledge you desire to attain. 2. To read no book which does not in some way tend to the attainment of that knowledge. 3. To read no book which does tend to the attainment of it, unless it be the best in its kind. 4. To finish one before you begin another. 5. To read them all in such order, that every subsequent book may illustrate and confirm the preceding."[2]

His father, then verging on old age and enduring many afflictions, rejoiced over the preferment of his "dear Mr. Fellow-Elect of Lincoln. What will be my own fate God only knows, *sed passi graviora*, wherever I am, my Jack is

[1] The disputations were the relics of that medieval system which insisted on logic as the main part of a University training.
[2] L. Tyerman: "Life and Times of John Wesley"; Vol. I, p. 81.

Fellow of Lincoln."[1] The college was founded in 1427, by Richard Fleming, the recreant Lollard who, as already stated, became Bishop of Lincoln, burnt Wycliffe's bones, endeavored to extirpate his teachings at Oxford, and ordered that "any fellow tainted with these heresies should be cast out, like a diseased sheep, from the fold of the college." Wesley's fellowship on Fleming's foundation once more demonstrated the folly of such provision against the inevitable changes of time. The crass materialism and neglect which demoralized the University during the eighteenth century were not so prevalent at Lincoln as elsewhere in Oxford. The atmosphere of the college was more congenial to Wesley's intentions than Christ Church had been, where he resented those companionships of which he afterwards said, "Even their harmless conversation, so-called, damped all my good resolutions. I saw no possible way of getting rid of them, unless it should please God to remove me to another college. He did so, in a manner utterly contrary to all human probability. I was elected Fellow of a college where I knew not one person. I foresaw abundance of people would come to see me . . . but I had now fixed my plan. I resolved to have no acquaintance by chance, but by choice; and to choose such only as would help me on my way to heaven. . . . I knew that many reflections would follow; but that did not move me."[2] The men of Lincoln were "well-natured and well-bred," yet their polite intercourse palled on him; he repelled their advances, and shut himself up to his own pursuits. Even at this the world was too much with him, and he looked with longing upon the prospect of a mastership in a Yorkshire school, "so pent up between two hills that it is scarce accessible on any side, so that you can expect little company from without, and within there is none at all." For such solitude he was prepared to sacrifice his position at Oxford. In a less bal-

---

[1] L. Tyerman: "Life and Times of Samuel Wesley"; p. 399.
[2] Ibid., "Life and Times of John Wesley"; Vol. I, p. 55.

anced nature than Wesley's the consequences of this inordinate craving for a cloistered retreat would have been injurious, and as it was the desire determined the course of his private life. Yet his companions did not charge his seclusive habits to any lack of geniality; on the contrary, those who were admitted to his friendship lauded his amiability, and one of them wrote to him, lamenting his enforced absence from the college as a deprivation for them.

After spending the summer of 1726 at Epworth, where he acted as his father's curate, he passed a year in residence at Oxford, returning again to Epworth in 1727, when he assumed charge of the obscure parish at Wroote, which formed a part of the living. In this lonely hamlet of the fenlands, surrounded by bogs and tenanted by a hopeless peasantry, he spent the next two years and three months. His ministrations were addressed to "unpolished wights" as "impervious as stones," and the innate aristocracy of the Wesleys, which denoted, not a class, but a creed, was exhibited toward these stupid parishioners both by John and by his lively sister Hetty. Few details of his curacy are available, and those that are have no particular interest. It was evident he did not then possess the secret of that marvellous power which enabled him to kindle an unparalleled enthusiasm in town and hamlet when he rode the length and breadth of the three kingdoms during later days. He tells us, "I preached much, but saw no fruit of my labor. Indeed, it could not be that I should; for I neither laid the foundation of repentance, nor of believing the Gospel; taking it for granted that all to whom I preached were believers, and that many of them needed no repentance." [1] His relaxation was found at Epworth, where a renewed intercourse with the family rendered the tedium of his unprofitable days less irksome. While in the disenchanting hermitage of Wroote, and probably when he began to feel that distaste for the limitations of parochial work which he

[1] L. Tyerman: "Life and Times of John Wesley": Vol. I, p. 57.

always retained, he reverted to his religious meditations. William Law's "Serious Call," to which later references will be made, was published in 1728, and shortly afterwards Wesley obtained the volume and read it with eagerness. It is notable for its religious fervor and for the insight and skill of its contrast between the life of the flesh and the life of the spirit — qualities the more admirable when the general lukewarmness and formalism of eighteenth century devotional literature are recalled. Law's book followed no contemporary models. It ploughed up new ground, and restored to an age of barrenness in religion, to a church that had become a mere adjunct of public life and which confounded the Body of Christ with the Anglican Establishment, and to a Puritanism submerged in Socinian theology, some forgotten ideals of Evangelical Christianity. The writer's sway was evidenced by the thoroughly appreciative tributes of leading minds far different from his own. He lived with the Gibbons at Putney, near London, where he acted as tutor to the father of the historian. A rubicund man, jovial in appearance, Law gave little indication of the devotee and the philosopher, yet such he was, and one of the very few who then bestowed specific attention upon religious problems. His discussion of these was sympathetic and illuminating, and many who were troubled with spiritual or doctrinal difficulties resorted to him for help.

The Wesleys, John and Charles, valued his counsel so highly that on several occasions they walked from Oxford to London to obtain it. After John's unseemly quarrel with Law the latter remarked, "I was once a kind of oracle to Mr. Wesley," and at least one saying of the oracle was fastened in the recollection of the younger man: "We shall do well to aim at the highest degrees of perfection if we may thereby attain at least to mediocrity," — a remark destined to accelerate that deeper belief in the divine possibilities of human nature which Wesley did much to implant.

"If some persons," wrote Law, "should unite themselves in little societies professing voluntary poverty, retirement, and devotion, that some might be relieved in their charities, and all be benefited by their example, such persons would be so far from being chargeable with any superstition that they might be justly said to restore that piety which was the boast and glory of the Church when its greatest men were alive.[1] The early Franciscans might have been the inspiration of this statement, which flatly contradicted the grosser ideals of Hanoverian Protestantism. It was not by any means Law's greatest conception, but certainly it was reflected in Wesley's conduct and in that of the Holy Club, to say nothing of its palpable effect upon the life of Evangelical Methodism.[2]

IV

Charles Wesley, who was elected a student of Christ Church, Oxford, from Westminster School, about the same time that John became fellow of Lincoln, was the more sanguine and emotional of the two brothers. His affectionate disposition was instanced by his refusal to leave his parents when Mr. Garret Wesley, an Irish gentleman of fortune who was in no wise related to the family, offered to adopt him as his heir. The individual who accepted the offer, one Richard Colley, assumed his benefactor's name and became the grandfather of the Duke of Wellington, who appears in the army list of 1800 as Arthur Wesley. — During his residence at Oxford, Charles indulged buoyant habits which, although harmless, were not conducive to sudden and serious changes, and he resented John's overtures in behalf of ascetical piety by impatiently declining to become a saint all at once. But this mood soon passed, and his letters during his brother's sojourn at Wroote showed

---

[1] Julia Wedgwood: "John Wesley and the Evangelical Reaction of the Eighteenth Century"; p. 39.

[2] The best account of Law can be found in Canon Overton's volume on the Non-Jurors.

that habitual deference to John's superior judgment which nothing could disturb in Charles except his pronounced Anglicanism. He now began to shun his former companions, communicated weekly in the college chapel, and persuaded a friend whom he had reclaimed from doubtful society to do likewise. This was the germ of the fellowship of Oxford Methodism which Charles instituted and John directed. The latter states that "in November, 1729, four young gentlemen of Oxford, Mr. John Wesley, Fellow of Lincoln College, Mr. Charles Wesley, Student at Christ Church, Mr. Morgan, Commoner of Christ Church, and Mr. Kirkham, of Merton College, began to spend some evenings a week reading, chiefly the Greek Testament." To these were subsequently added among others George Whitefield, John Clayton, Benjamin Ingham, John White-lamb, Westley Hall, John Gambold, and James Hervey, the author of "Theron and Aspasio" and "Meditations among the Tombs." The friendships then begun were afterwards ended by death or separation or dissimilar views. Clayton, the Jacobite and High Church rector of Manchester, eventually shunned the Wesleys; Hervey opposed them in his writings; Ingham forsook them; Gambold avowed he was ashamed of his youthful relation with them; and White-field, after being their colleague in labor and persecution, was for a time alienated from them by doctrinal differences.

In their college days they were a harmonious group of kindred souls, and when in 1729 Wesley, at the request of Dr. Morley, the rector of Lincoln, resumed his residence as fellow of the College, he at once became the "curator of the Holy Club." The wicked wit of the University sporting fraternity was spent in vain upon these "crackbrained enthusiasts." Behind John and Charles stood the rector of Epworth and his wife, who advised them "in all things to endeavor to act upon principle," and not to "live like the rest of mankind who pass through the world like straws upon a river." Nothing was further from their purpose;

the foremost member of the band never knew the meaning of retreat, and until he left Oxford in 1735, John remained the controlling spirit of the organization. Wesley's predominance in a group which included Hervey, Clayton, and Whitefield, was an indication of his gifts as a leader of men. The Club flourished or declined according as he was present or absent; its permanent adherents were less numerous than the timid backsliders who could not endure the obloquy which membership entailed. All alike were tenacious of order; scrupulously observant of the statutes of the University and the ordinances of the Church. Their community life and frugality afforded a surplus from their united incomes which they devoted to the relief of the poor and of prisoners. Regular seasons for prayer and fasting were observed, and frequent attendance on the Sacrament of the Lord's Supper, with other means of grace and self-denial, was made obligatory. A systematic visitation of the slums and jails of Oxford and its surrounding villages was undertaken at the instance of William Morgan. Neglected children were instructed in the Bible; debtors confined in the "Bocardo" [1] and felons under sentence of death received the consolations of religion. Upon Wesley's solicitation, prompted by his father's advice, the bishop of the diocese gave his approval to these works of mercy and charity, and a few of the clergy followed his example.

But such thirteenth century practices were bound to meet the censure of a pleasure-loving generation. Fogg's *Weekly Journal* protested against the presence of these sons of sorrow who had committed themselves to an absurd perpetual melancholy designed to make the whole place a monastery. While they passed for religious persons and men

[1] The "Bocardo" was a prison over the North Gate of the city on what is now known as Cornmarket Street. It may have been so named from the form of syllogism called Bocardo, which presented certain logical difficulties; or again, from Brocardia, a legal term signifying a contentious and difficult matter.

of extraordinary parts among themselves, to outsiders they appeared as madmen and fools. The galled jade winced; careless professors and undergraduates of open moral lassitude were incensed by this return to the sacrificial devotion of typical Christianity, and their contempt was poured upon a few fellow members of the University whose offense lay in their regularity and piety. Efforts were made to breed dissensions among them; abuse and calumniation raged apace. Nicknames were plentiful; in addition to those already given, these young men were known as Bible Bigots, Bible Moths, Sacramentarians, and Methodists. The last term was supposed by Wesley to have been derived from Bentley's allusion to the Methodici, as opposed to the Empirics, two ancient rival schools of medicine. This was far-fetched; the waggish student with whom the epithet probably originated may have found the name of the largest English-speaking Protestant Church among the sectarian disputes of the previous century. In 1638 a sermon preached at Lambeth contained the following passage, "Where are now our Anabaptists and plain pack-staff Methodists, who esteem all flowers of rhetoric in sermons no better than stinking weeds?" and in 1693 a pamphlet was published entitled, "A War among the Angels of the Churches; wherein is shewed the Principles of the New Methodists in the Great Point of Justification."[1] When applied to the Oxford men who dared to be singular, the appellation, if not new, was aptly descriptive; it at once clung to them, and was afterwards bestowed on the Church which inherited some of their characteristics.[2]

If Wesley needed further support, the rector of Epworth certainly gave it. He wrote in ringing words to his sons, "Go on, then, in God's name, in the path in which the Saviour has directed you and that track wherein your father went

[1] L. Tyerman: "Life and Times of John Wesley"; Vol. I, p. 67.
[2] For a full discussion of the term see the Oxford English Dictionary; also H. B. Workman's "Handbook on Methodism."

before you." Their brother Samuel interposed a mild objection to their "being called a Club, a name calculated to do mischief." "But," he continued, "the other charges of enthusiasm can weigh with none but such as drink away their senses." He lived to make similar charges himself when Methodism shook off its academic chains and essayed the conquest of a wider field. There was nothing in the bearing of Wesley and his friends leaning toward sensationalism, neither were they whimsical nor unnecessarily precise. They looked inwardly and outwardly with a gaze which was pure and intent on increased purity. Wesley's defense of their habits was almost invariably wise, calm in tone, and modest in statement. His presentation of the case was unmarred by any arrogant assumptions, and showed he was sincerely convinced that the renunciations they made were essential to Christian character. Yet St. Francis himself could scarcely have surpassed his asseveration that no man was in a state of salvation until he was contemned by the world, and unfortunately the prevailing attitude toward those who sought to exemplify their faith in deeds largely confirmed his opinion.

This earlier Oxford movement made no impression on the University when compared with that led a hundred years later by Rose, Keble, Pusey, Hurrell Froude, and Newman. Some of its followers, as already observed, became the censors of the later Methodism of which it was a foretoken rather than a cause. Indeed, but for Whitefield and the Wesleys, Oxford Methodism would have been no more than an ephemeral outburst of pious devotion; an earnest inquiry for the heart of the Gospel rather than a manifestation of the Gospel's subduing grace. Its isolation and environment would have successfully impeded any propaganda, since Oxford at that time could scarcely maintain, far less originate, vitality in morals or religion. Nor were the few who enlisted in the premature attempt as yet equipped for a crusade in behalf of spiritual regeneration.

In fact, the majority retained throughout life the sense of clerical separatism and excessive deference to churchly authority which formed an effective barrier between them and democracy. The enterprise was commendable because it rebuked a moribund University. Yet it proved that such religious efforts, although taking their rise in centers of learning, must find a speedy outlet in the unhampered service of the people, or dwindle and perish at the source.

The venerable rector of Epworth was now approaching the end of his ministry, and in January, 1735, he suggested to John the propriety of becoming his successor. In a later letter he put the matter more definitely and urged it as a personal request. Wesley's reply revealed his need of emancipation from the notion that he was only safe when sequestered. He gave a lengthy but irrelevant list of reasons for remaining where he was, their burden being that he was determined to shun the world and its distracting activities, in order that he might preserve intellectual growth from the blight of material concerns, and shield religious contemplation from the assailments of hypocrisy or wickedness. He could be holier in Oxford, he asserted, than anywhere else. Mingled with this ambition was his love for the University, a sentiment not readily appraised by those who have not felt its force. His father was bewildered by the scruples John raised, and his reply seems to have removed them. "It is not dear self," he wrote, with mature wisdom, "but the glory of God, and the different degrees of promoting it, which should be our main consideration and direction in the choice of any course of life"; and again, "I cannot allow austerity, or fasting, considered by themselves, to be proper acts of holiness, nor am I for a solitary life. God made us for a social life; we are not to bury our talent; we are to let our light shine before men, and that not merely through the chinks of a bushel for fear the wind should blow it out." [1] This was a healthy breeze from the fen

[1] C. T. Winchester: "The Life of John Wesley"; p. 39.

country which John's enervating atmosphere sorely needed, and after further discussion he made a belated and unsuccessful application for the Epworth living.

The rector died on April 25, 1735, joyous and hopeful to the last. Thirty-eight of the forty-six years of his pastorate had been spent in the one parish, and he took leave of it and of his dear ones with a holy confidence which his son Charles, who was with him at the time of his decease, must have had in mind when he composed some of his matchless hymns upon the triumph of the saints in their mortal hour. John was still bent on "saving his own soul," and this resolution dictated his acceptance of an invitation to establish a mission in Georgia. The longed-for consciousness of his personal relation to God through Christ Jesus, which he had hitherto failed to gain, might, he thought, be achieved by his consecration to the task of converting the Indians. He set everything else aside for the primitive and unpromising conditions of a recently founded settlement in the New World. As Dr. Workman pithily observes, "In words that would have charmed a Rousseau he dreamed of a return to nature as a return to grace." "I cannot hope," said Wesley, "to attain the same degree of holiness here which I may attain there." Charles shared his sentiments and joined his mission, and also agreed with John's unsophisticated ideas concerning the innate virtues of the Indians among whom they proposed to dwell. Having obtained their widowed mother's consent and blessing, they sailed for Georgia in the month of October, 1735, accompanied by Benjamin Ingham, a member of the Holy Club, and Charles Delamotte, a friend and also an Oxford man.

General Oglethorpe, the founder and first governor of Georgia, the youngest of the English colonies in North America, was the son of Sir Theophilus Oglethorpe of Godalming in Surrey. His varied career was full of interesting events as a soldier, legislator, pioneer, philanthropist, and patron of literature. Dr. Johnson was his intimate friend, and

Hannah More, the high priestess of the Evangelicals, spoke of Oglethorpe as "a delightful old beau." Touched by the miseries of the English prisoners for debt he determined to give the unfortunate inmates of the Fleet and the Marshalsea another opportunity beyond the seas. He required a chaplain for the expedition who would care both for the whites of the proposed colony and for the Indians. Dr. Burton of Corpus Christi College recommended John Wesley for the post. The Epworth family was already known to the General; he had been the largest subscriber to the rector's volume on Job, and by this and other timely assistance had won the author's affectionate gratitude, who declared that had he been a younger man he would have joined Oglethorpe's enterprise. Under these favorable circumstances John and Charles were offered the position. Their acceptance was actuated by their desire for personal sanctity, and by a solicitude for the cure of souls and the extension of God's kingdom.

Other clergymen had anticipated their missionary effort; their father, as we have noted, had his dreams of a more aggressive Christianity in foreign parts; and Bishop George Berkeley preceded them and their comrades in his attempt to establish the Gospel among the people of Bermuda, leaving an attractive position in England only to return a disillusioned and defeated man. The college he had planned was still unbuilt, and Oglethorpe obtained his consent to petition Parliament that the funds assigned for its erection should be diverted to the Georgian scheme. The Society for the Propagation of the Gospel also supported the General's undertaking, and public grants and private gifts were contributed toward the necessary expenses. During the westward voyage of the *Simmonds* the Oxford men faithfully observed their religious exercises, and when some of the ship's officers took umbrage at this they drew upon themselves a severe rebuke from Oglethorpe. Among the passengers were twenty-six Moravians, headed by their bishop, David Nitschmann, who were about to join their brethren already settled in Georgia. Their acquaintance with Wesley and his companions was fraught with important consequences, which necessitate a brief account of the Church they represented.

Count Zinzendorf avowed it had not been founded by him, but was "the most ançient of the Protestant Churches, if not their common mother," since its origin dated from the movement of John Hus in the early fifteenth century. After numerous vicissitudes the Brethren, as they called themselves, attained a numerical growth which in 1609 included half the Protestants of Bohemia and more than half those of Moravia. But the Thirty Years' War practically abolished their congregations, and for a century afterwards they were an almost extinct body. The renowned bishop, John Amos Comenius, whose work, "The Great Didactic," is still one of the textbooks of historical education, had preserved, however, the episcopal succession and discipline, and after decimating persecutions in Moravia the Church was resuscitated in Germany. Its members, descendants of former German immigrants, retreated to the Fatherland, crossing the border into Saxony, and were received at Herrnhut [1] by Count Zinzendorf, who had to satisfy the State government that the community could be brought under the conditions of the peace of Augsburg, and also quiet the misgivings and suspicions of the Lutheran clergy. The refugees belonged to more than one sect; oppressions had made them cling pertinaciously to small differences of belief, worship, and polity, and it was with the utmost difficulty that the Count induced them to live together harmoniously. Despite his high personal example and tireless energy, their conduct was so fanatical that they combined in his own house to denounce Zinzendorf as the Beast of

[1] Zinzendorf offered them an asylum on his estate of Berthelsdorf, where he built for them the village of Herrnhut (the Lord's keeping). The refugees came thither in various groups between 1722 and 1732.

the Apocalypse, and his helper Rothe as the False Prophet. Presently a better temper obtained, and they conformed to the Count's wishes. Instead of reviving Moravian orders they professed themselves as pietistic Lutherans, and attended the services of the parish church. But after an extraordinary unifying experience at a Communion Service on August 13, 1727, they renewed their allegiance to Moravianism, and that date has since been celebrated as its birthday.

Two conflicting parties were now found among them. The first regarded Zinzendorf as their head, and built their settlements on the estates of friendly noblemen, where they lived a retired life and enriched the spirituality of "the scattered" in the Church at large without attempting to proselytize. The second was recognized in 1749 by the British Parliament as an ancient Protestant Episcopal Church and played a significant part in the religious revival of the eighteenth century. The importance of the Moravians must be measured by their influence upon Christendom at large, and upon such individuals as the Wesleys, Schleiermacher, and, in a measure, Goethe. Their contribution to the missionary spirit of Protestantism is notable for the fact that they were the first to revive the duty of the Church to present the Gospel to all nations. This achievement, together with their blameless conduct, has given them an ascendency in Europe and America altogether out of proportion to their numbers, which, as late as 1909, showed no more than 444 congregations with 62,096 communicants.

Their first appearance in England dates from the early seventeenth century, when, during the first stages of the Thirty Years' War the Bohemian Protestants were routed at the battle of White Hill, fought in 1620, and the Brethren, driven from their homes, took refuge in various countries.[1] Their simplicity and fraternity, expressed in a social life of ordered piety, were singularly attractive; and they

[1] Encyclopædia Britannica, 11th Edition, Article on The Moravians.

P

made a deep impression on devout and meditative people weary of a hard and superficial age. Julia Wedgwood fittingly speaks of the "cool mysticism of these monks of Protestantism" which "afforded a welcome shade from the prosaic aridity of rationalism."[1]

During the tedious voyage of the *Simmonds*, Wesley had ample opportunity for the close observation of a people whose Christianity was both unusual and exemplary. Their patient willingness to serve the sick, their humility, untainted by self-consciousness, and their tranquil behavior during the fierce storms which swept the Atlantic, won his respect and confidence. "Were you not afraid?" he queried, after a hurricane. "I thank God, no," replied the one addressed. This insensibility to the peril of the ocean, which was not permitted to interrupt their stated worship, aroused Wesley's curiosity and his repeated references to the Moravians revealed his interest in them and their affairs. After landing at Savannah, he sought them out again, and asked one of their elders, August Gottlieb Spangenberg, to advise with him about his new field. "Have you," said Spangenberg, "the witness within yourself? Does the Spirit of God bear witness with your spirit that you are a child of God?" Wesley faltered before these pertinent inquiries, whereupon the Moravian elder pushed them home. "Do you know Jesus Christ?" he continued. "I know that He is the Saviour of the World," rejoined Wesley. "True, but do you know He has saved you?" "I hope He has died to save me," was the hesitating answer. "Do you know yourself?" his inquisitor demanded. Wesley was nonplused by this pointed address, couched in terms afterwards familiar enough, but which were then strange to him. He could only express a faint affirmative, and subsequently doubted whether he was justified even in that. He lived for a time with the Brethren, and discovered in them other

[1] "John Wesley and the Evangelical Reaction of the Eighteenth Century"; p. 94.

vital elements of religion till then foreign to his conceptions. Their election and ordination of a bishop prompted the following reflection: "The great simplicity, as well as solemnity, of the whole, almost made me forget the seventeen hundred years between, and imagine myself in one of those assemblies where form and state were not, but Paul the tentmaker or Peter the fisherman presided, yet with the demonstration of the Spirit and of power." [1] It was indeed a far cry from stately Oxford and the latitudinarian Georgian clergy to these few radiant souls on a lonely shore where the light of a hitherto unsuspected phase of Christian experience began to play upon Wesley's sacramentarianism. He did not yield to it, however, without a severe and prolonged struggle, and he was never more active as a champion of ecclesiastical formalism than during his sojourn at Savannah, which lasted from February 5, 1736, until December 2, 1737. But he had seen, if only as through a glass darkly, the great truth that the divine order is not perfectly fulfilled till the soul has believed, not because of indirect evidence, but because of its regenerating contact with the living Christ. And that glimpse must be remembered by those who would understand Wesley's career.

[1] "The Journal of John Wesley"; edited by Rev. Nehemiah Curnock, Vol. I, p. 170.

CHAPTER VI

DARKNESS AND DAWN

Oft when the Word is on me to deliver,
Lifts the illusion, and the truth lies bare:
Desert or throng, the city or the river,
Melts in a lucid Paradise of air, —

Only like souls I see the folk thereunder,
Bound who should conquer, slaves who should be kings, —
Hearing their one hope with an empty wonder,
Sadly contented in a show of things; —

Then with a rush the intolerable craving
Shivers throughout me like a trumpet call, —
Oh to save these! to perish for their saving,
Die for their life, be offered for them all!

Give me a voice, a cry, and a complaining, —
Oh let my sound be stormy in their ears!
Throat that would shout but cannot stay for straining,
Eyes that would weep but cannot wait for tears.

Quick in a moment, infinite for ever,
Send an arousal better than I pray,
Give me a grace upon the faint endeavor,
Souls for my hire and Pentecost to-day!

     F. W. H. MYERS: Saint Paul, XVII and XX.

CHAPTER VI

Wesley in Georgia — Religious condition of the settlers — Charles returns to England — Miss Hopkey — Williamson's suit against Wesley — Wesley's return to England — Effect of Georgia mission on his later development — Peter Böhler — Wesley's dispute with William Law — His conversion — Its results — Social condition of England in the eighteenth century — The effect of Methodism on English national life.

I

WESLEY's residence in Georgia is described at length in the new edition of his Journal, for which the Christian Church is under lasting obligation to its painstaking editor, the Reverend Nehemiah Curnock.[1] It gives a graphic picture of the social and religious conditions of the colony which have only to be comprehended to explain Wesley's comparative failure there: indeed, the wonder is that he did any good whatever for so motley and turbulent a throng. It is noteworthy that the Brethren seem to have been equally unsuccessful; despite their evangelical teaching they were unable to overcome the indifference and reserve of the emigrants, whose scanty numbers embraced various nationalities and beliefs, with few things in common except ignorance and prejudice. The Moravians and Salzburgers did not need Wesley's oversight, having their own Bishop Nitschmann. The Scotch Highlanders clung to their priestless worship, and offended Wesley's sense of decorum by assembling in a barn. French Huguenots, Italian Waldenses, and Spanish Jews formed the fringe of a population of broken Englishmen, including insolvent debtors and disappointed adventurers, of

[1] Died, November 1, 1915.

215

some of whom the Motherland was well rid, whose chief
pursuits were found in the ale-house or in low intrigues
against the parson who denounced rum and slavery.   Such
parishioners would doubtless have afforded a more moderate
man a welcome excuse for being cautious in his dealings with
them.   But Oglethorpe craved Wesley's aid, and he abandoned his mission to the Indians, who showed no propensity
for anything better than tribal wars and the vicious habits
of the white settlers, that he might enforce upon the latter
a meticulous code of ordinances in accordance with the
literal directions of the Book of Common Prayer.   His
requirements were so exacting as to suggest that he was not
altogether assured in his own mind of their legitimacy or
usefulness.   "He that believeth shall not make haste";
and Wesley's ardor in imposing this regimen, which he
himself observed by going unshod, reading prayers thrice
every day, fasting, communicating, and refusing to bury
Dissenters, or baptize children save by triple immersion,
may have been an indication of the secret longings of a
spirit which found vent but not satisfaction in the minutiæ
of punctilious ecclesiasticism.   The Moravians, who were
also in that Apostolical Succession which he held necessary
to faith and order, and upon which he believed the stability
of the Church and the Gospel depended, did not encourage
his sacerdotalism nor make experiments similar to those
which inevitably led to his disappointment.   Yet they lived
in the strength of a calm and constant joy, while he, ill at
ease and restless in spirit, "drenched his flock with the
physic of an intolerant discipline."   Many rebelled against
his lack of wisdom ; others, however, disarmed by his personal
piety and his incessant labors in their behalf, at length
yielded him a reluctant support.

Equally tactless was Charles Wesley's connection with
the mission.   During a six months' stay at Frederica, a
small township south of Savannah, he alienated nearly
everybody, and ended by quarreling with Oglethorpe, where-

upon he returned home. John's disillusionment was now complete, and the impending hostility between him and the colonists was precipitated by his love affair with Miss Sophy Hopkey. This young lady was the niece and ward of Thomas Causton, the principal magistrate of Savannah, a man of doubtful antecedents, and of an overbearing and boorish disposition which attracted to him acquaintances of a like kind. His home became the resort of dissolute characters, and afforded little protection to a beautiful, modest, and affectionate girl of eighteen. One of her uncle's boon companions, who had shortly before proposed marriage to her, was arrested and thrown into jail. This humiliating experience drove Miss Hopkey to the consolations of religion, and her friendship with Wesley developed rapidly. When she removed to Frederica to escape the Caustons and the threats of her imprisoned admirer, Wesley followed and begged her to return. His persuasions, coupled with Oglethorpe's, induced her to do so, and the two young people made the six days' journey back to Savannah together. While encamped one cold, stormy night on St. Katherines Island, Wesley, moved by a sudden impulse, earnestly declared, "Miss Sophy, I should think myself happy if I was to spend my life with you," at which she begged him not to speak to her again "on this head," but in such a way as to indicate that the declaration was not distasteful to her. On their arrival at Savannah she spent her mornings and evenings with Wesley, the Caustons, who regarded the match as assured, consenting to the arrangement. Devotional exercises and literary studies could not prevent what Wesley ingenuously calls "such intimacy of conversation as ours was." Here began the tragic struggle between love and duty, the alternate phases of which are recorded in the Journal. His friends Ingham and Delamotte for somewhat selfish reasons opposed the marriage, and after the former had returned home, Delamotte implored Wesley to surrender all claims to the lady of his choice. The assertion that the Moravians gave such advice is incorrect; indeed, Toltschig, the pastor, astonished the despondent lover by declaring, "I see no reason why you should not marry her." The affair was another instance of that witless suscepti- bility to feminine society which Wesley had previously evinced in the case of the far less worthy Mrs. Hawkins, whom he met on shipboard. Yet while his heart was deeply affected, his sense of responsibility to the ministry and his conviction that he should live a single life warred against his inclinations. Miss Hopkey naturally resented his vacil- lations, and the methods he adopted to reach an irrevocable decision were not calculated to appease her. After prayer Wesley and Delamotte proceeded to a solemn casting of lots, when the latter drew the paper on which was written the last alternative, "Think no more of it," and Wesley at once accepted this as a divine injunction against the marriage.

Such talismanic dealing with a pure and natural attach- ment was its own condemnation. Determined as he was to find and follow the Highest Will in a matter so important, Wesley's ignorance of the feminine nature and his repre- hensible habit of settling questions of moment in a hap- hazard way were responsible for the unhappiness which ensued. Miss Hopkey was by far the most suitable woman he could have chosen for his wife, and probably she was the only woman he ever really loved. He was then thirty-three years old, and when unembarrassed by his leanings toward celibacy, an insistent and ardent suitor. She, while con- siderably his junior, was unusually mature for her age, and needed the help and guidance such a husband as Wesley would have given. Although not his equal in education, she surpassed him in prudence and courage under difficult circumstances, and her affectionate disposition warrants the assumption that, had he formed a union with her, he would have been saved from the domestic wretchedness to which he was afterwards subjected. His sentimentality over- spread the entire proceedings with a half-fabulous tinge.

The credulity he displayed in arriving at his decision by lot, a trait which sometimes impedes reason and practicality in one who is known as a master of men, was always latent in Wesley, at intervals dimly present, and occasionally far too active for his good or for the good of others.

The sequel of this unfortunate incident was grievous enough. Miss Hopkey, prompted by her relatives, accepted a certain Thomas Williamson as her prospective husband, and, much to Wesley's distress, became his wife a few days after the separation from the man of her heart. Her declaration that she would never marry was thus violated by events which she could not altogether control; whereupon Wesley began to act in a manner indicative of the feelings of the injured lover who was also a domineering priest. Williamson was naturally unwilling that his wife should have any further acquaintance with Wesley, and would not allow her to enter the parsonage. Wesley, on the other hand, exhorted her to continue her religious duties, and upon her failing to do so with regularity, proceeded to rebuke her. On the strength of a talebearer's gossip he further upbraided her; and at length, about five months after her marriage, publicly excluded her from the Lord's Table. Her husband, justly outraged at this inexcusable action, brought suit against Wesley for defaming her character. The malcontents of the town, with Causton as their leader, ranged themselves on Williamson's side of the quarrel, and desired nothing better than such an opportunity for getting rid of a pastor who had frequently offended them for righteousness' sake. However, when the charges against him were sifted from the scandals and calumnies with which the small and self-centered community abounded, no case was left against Wesley. He had acted within his clerical rights, although in such a way as to impair the confidence of the best people of the settlement in his motives, and the agitation which followed ended his usefulness in Georgia.

Delamotte agreed with him that his best course was to return home, and accordingly he posted a notice in the public square of Savannah that he was about to leave the colony. Mr. Williamson at once announced that he had sued Wesley for one thousand pounds damages, and would prosecute any one who aided his escape. The magistrates also forbade him to leave until the case had been heard. Wesley reminded them that he had attended seven sessions of the Court, at none of which had he been allowed to answer the charges against him. Nevertheless they demanded that he sign a bond, pledging himself, under a penalty of fifty pounds, to appear in Court whenever required to do so. He refused to give either bond or bail, and the magistrates retaliated by ordering the officers of the law to prevent his departure. These measures may have been a mere pretense, but, whether seriously intended or not, they failed. After evening prayers, which he conducted publicly before going to the boat, Wesley, accompanied by four friendly men, set out for Purrysburg, twenty miles down the river, and arrived there the following morning. From Purrysburg the party of five went on foot to Port Royal, an exhausting journey through trackless forests and swamps. From Port Royal they shipped to Charlestown, and there Wesley embarked for England on December 22, 1737.

Such were some of the main factors in his Georgian preparation for a greater embassy. When the day of his mission dawned, he observed, "Many reasons I have to bless God for my having been carried to America contrary to all my preceding resolutions. Thereby I trust He hath in some measure humbled me and proved me and showed me what was in my heart." Certainly self-denial, resolute sacrifice, a sense of sin, and a constant hope for deliverance from sin were in that heart, so sad and weary, which turned back from the New World to the Motherland, and was destined there to redress the religious balance of the British people.

These feelings already opposed in him the evils of formalism and of a provincial orthodoxy, and, whatever else was lost or won, he had guarded his integrity as a Christian pastor, even to the crucifying of his natural affections. If a little more humanness would have added to the geniality of Wesley's disposition, it might also have detracted from the completeness of a consecration, the intensity of which has seldom been equaled. His autocratic temper was a fault for which he had to make his own atonement. Of quite another sort were the qualities which enabled him to handle with unrivaled strategy and daring the recruits who enlisted in his crusade. These qualities made him prompt, fearless, decisive, a bold leader in extremity, who kept the marks he followed well within the range of his vision. His later innovations, although deplored by his clerical brethren, were dictated by necessity and prompted by the lessons he had learned when defeat had been the outcome of ecclesiastical regularity. In reality he always maintained the better part of Anglicanism as he conceived it. Swayed by its spirit he expatriated himself for a life of devotion and service. It sustained him during his absence from congenial society, while as a missionary wearing coarse clothes and eating coarse food he wandered through a virgin territory in blistering heat or biting cold. His endurance of these hardships is proof that the things in him which could be shaken were being removed in order that those which were fundamental might remain. Oxford Methodism began to languish among the chaotic morals of a turbulent community, but the world's Methodism was already in process of gestation; and the pains Wesley endured were the birth pangs of its deliverance. In Georgia he did nothing more than experiment with a pietistic individualism rooted in ritualistic Anglicanism, which showed small understanding of the central truth of the New Testament. The outcome was disastrous, but would his determined soul have submitted to anything less disastrous? For while these traditions of his earlier religious life, as permanent elements in his nature, were blended with the more complete experience of his conversion and his subsequent growth in divine grace, they never again controlled his energies or invalidated his action. His narrowness and indifference to the interests of the Church universal, and his trust in the merit of good works, had received a definite challenge. Extreme notions regarding ecclesiastical prerogatives and sacramental grace were no longer so acceptable as they once had been. The quietism of the Moravians and the ignorant apathy of the colonists, although nothing akin, had shown Wesley that his exclusive ideas of the Gospel were not its most efficient interpretation, a discovery which gave rise in him to chastening reflections. Yet those who cannot recall his career without a sense of gratitude will not too hastily judge his stay in Georgia a fruitless period. It was a necessary stage in his evolution, and Whitefield, who followed him there, wrote enthusiastically that "the good Mr. Wesley has done in America is inexpressible." This was perhaps the exaggerated tribute of one who seldom had difficulty in believing what he wished to believe. Nevertheless good had been done, and in no direction so much as in this, that Wesley's larger self emerged from uncongenial surroundings which rebuked his fastidiousness and pride, and taught him the lessons of patience and wisdom. The illumination of his powers for serving men to the full was preceded by the consciousness of a failure which finally wrought in him a more productive faith. His confessions during the homeward voyage corroborate these sentiments. "I went to America to convert the Indians; but oh! who shall convert me? . . . I have a fair summer religion. I can talk well; nay, and believe myself, while no danger is near. But let death look me in the face, and my spirit is troubled. . . . Whosoever sees me, sees I would be a Christian. . . . But in a storm I think, what if the Gospel be not true? Then thou art of all men most foolish. For what hast thou given thy goods, thy ease, thy friends, thy reputation, thy country, thy life? For what art thou wandering over the face of the earth? — A dream, a cunningly devised fable! Oh! who will deliver me from this fear of death? . . . A wise man advised me some time since, 'Be still, and go on.' Perhaps this is best, to look upon it as my cross." [1] Doubtless these melancholy soliloquies were prompted by his wounded affections as well as by spiritual disquietude. Miss Hopkey's hand in marriage had been, to quote his own words, "the desire of my eyes and the joy of my heart; the one thing upon earth I longed for." Such a love, unsealing as it does the nethermost springs of life, creates, when thus repressed, a grief likely to become permanent. But notwithstanding these grave discouragements, he accepted the wise man's word, and went on, not knowing that his greater heritage was near.

II

Wesley landed at Deal on the first of February, 1737, just a few hours too late to receive the greetings of his friend Whitefield, whose whole-souled companionship would have been especially acceptable at this time. But after a victorious experiment in field-preaching, Whitefield was then sailing down the Channel on a voyage to Savannah. During the first months after his return, Wesley passed through a period of restless discontent, not to say vehement agitation. Clerical complacency was a banished sentiment; conventional beliefs had lost their authoritative note; he chafed beneath that sense of impotence so distressing to men who are intent upon noble ends and have not yet found the means for their attainment. The account of this interval and of his efforts to meet its emergencies, as given in the Journal, is in all respects a clear, manly,

"The Journal of John Wesley": edited by Rev. Nehemiah Curnock; Vol. I, p. 418.

and candid narrative. He was entering upon an epoch where extensive changes were to prevail, and he had a tough struggle to break through the barriers of prejudice and habit. His emotions and aspirations were such as led him to deeds of capital consequence. Beyond doubt he was a Christian and practically at one with all Christians on the fundamental questions of morality and worship. But hitherto his advanced sacramentarianism and legalism had been the trusted vehicles for communication of divine life, and the revolution now imminent in him was such a complete displacement of those doctrines, and one so entirely due to the royal faculty of faith, that it became a signal event in the history of evangelical methods. His entire being verged upon a new world, wherein he was to become supreme, overcoming by the weight of his witness those Anglican ideas which had previously governed him.

Meanwhile he hastened to London, and reported to the Trustees of the Georgia Settlement. There he found his brother Charles, who entered heartily into his projects, and they began to attend the gatherings of the Brethren. Peter Böhler, a native of Frankfort, a graduate of Jena and a convert to Moravianism, had been ordained in Germany and commissioned by Count Zinzendorf for missionary work in the Carolinas. During his stay in London he was introduced to the Wesleys, who were much edified by his quiet and persuasive preaching. Although ministering through an interpreter, his words were suffused with a mystical influence which subdued and elevated the secluded audiences he addressed, and his connection with the Wesleys has since cast a solitary beam of splendor upon his brief sojourn in England. Charles gave him lessons in the language; John cross-examined him on the matters which prevented his own peace. Böhler's answers consisted, in the main, of quotations from Scripture, specifically those passages which deal with regeneration. He showed that salvation is of God, through Christ Jesus, and by means of

His Death and Resurrection; the sole conditions of its bestowal being repentance and faith on the part of the recipient. These graces are supplied by the Holy Spirit, Who inclines believing hearts to respond to the overtures of mercy, and confirms in them the assurance of their filial relation with the Heavenly Father. The content of this creed, sanctioned as it is by Holy Writ, is summarized in the text, "He that believeth on the Son hath everlasting life." The challenge Luther hurled at the conscience of Christendom was due to his vivid apprehension of the declaration, "Now the just shall live by faith," and his conversion furnishes an instructive parallel with that of Wesley. In both cases a large space of time is covered with a series of confessions which reveal important points of change and progress apparently inconsistent, and, to those not in spiritual sympathy with the men, somewhat perplexing. Luther's mind was eminently intuitional, glancing with an eagle's eye at truth whenever it rose before him. Wesley's mind was eminently logical, arriving at conclusions by argumentative processes. Luther's theology sprang directly from his experience; Wesley's was illuminated and applied by his experience. He learned the doctrine of Justification by faith before he exercised the faith which brought him consciously into a justified condition. Both were alike in that they did not at once gain certitude without wavering, but tarried for a fuller revelation which secured their unreserved consent, and induced in them a state of exaltation and of praise.

The placid but observant Böhler saw that the Wesleys had come to the parting of the ways, and in a letter to Zinzendorf he gave his impressions of their state. "I travelled with the two brothers from London to Oxford. The elder, John, is a good-natured man; he knew he did not properly believe on the Saviour, and was willing to be taught. His brother, with whom you often conversed a year ago, is at present very much distressed in his mind, but does not know how he shall begin to be acquainted with the

Q

Saviour. Our mode of believing in the Saviour is so easy to Englishmen, that they cannot reconcile themselves to it; if it were a little more artful, they would much sooner find their way into it. Of faith in Jesus they have no other idea than the generality of people have. They justify themselves; and therefore, they always take it for granted, that they, believe already, and try to prove their faith by their works, and thus so plague and torment themselves that they are at heart very miserable." [1] On the journey, and while at Oxford, Wesley began dimly to apprehend the secret Böhler strove to impart. This in substance was the verification by actual experience of the principal teachings of the New Testament. These were also embedded in the doctrinal formulæ long familiar to Wesley, but he had not yet abandoned himself to them with that resolution which surmounts every obstacle, or in that faith which is disengaged from all supplementary considerations and fixed on Christ alone. Dependence on the outward form instead of the inward vitality of the Gospel was seldom more palpably shown, yet it is only too frequent in professed Christians, and operates so subtly that they think of it as little as of the air they breathe. A Laodicean contentment arising out of superficial assent to mere dogma deprives many believers of real fellowship with their Risen Redeemer. Here, as elsewhere, the witness of Christian consciousness, which extends not merely to abstract or speculative opinions, but to the whole current of feeling and of action in the regenerated soul, is left stranded on the shore of oblivious years, while men forget the solemn warning that "the letter killeth but the spirit giveth life." Justification by faith is an historic phrase covering the profound depths of religious experience, of which the content cannot be expressed in any statement, however full or apposite. The tides of that experience began to stir in Wesley, and though they ebbed, they ebbed to flow again, bringing on their returning crest a strength

[1] L. Tyerman: "Life and Times of John Wesley"; Vol. I, pp. 181–182.

of will, a courage, and an assurance which made him a wonder to himself and to others.

Decisive moments which affect the wider circles of human existence are rare indeed, and Wesley now approached one that has seldom been surpassed in interest or importance. God's intervention drew near, when the manifestation of love divine ended the travail of this seeker after the highest life and truth, and endowed him with gifts for the strengthening of his brethren. The crisis showed that even the best and most sincere men are never the masters of their highest destiny : that heaven in recognition of their single-mindedness takes their wood and gives them iron ; their iron, and gives them gold.

Between February the first and the date of his conversion he preached at least eighty sermons in London, Oxford, Manchester, and other centers, to congregations so widely separated as the prisoners of the common jails and the students and professors of the University. Although not averse to this duty, he was still in bondage ; and he tells us that he spent March the fourth with Böhler, " by whom, in the hands of the great God, I was on Sunday, the fifth, clearly convinced of unbelief, of the want of that faith whereby we are saved." "How can I preach to others who have not faith myself ?" was his pathetic query. In his bewilderment he turned again to Böhler, who counseled him, "Preach faith till you have it, and then because you have it you will preach faith." Implicit reliance upon the Moravian's precept was not a simple process for the High Churchman. It involved the consummation of beliefs he already held, but which did not as yet hold him in their resistless grasp ; yet, once they were freed from opposing elements, his soul was drawn to them as flame is drawn to flame, and faith became the definite, preponderant ingredient of his personal relation with God in Christ Jesus. This explanation suffices to show the impropriety of Samuel Taylor Coleridge's stupid comment on Wesley's dilemma. The Highgate

philosopher avowed that Böhler's suggestion was tanta-
mount to saying: "Tell a lie long enough and often enough
and you will be sure to end by believing it," a cheap and
shallow criticism devoid of application and lacking moral
insight and sympathy for a situation of peculiar delicacy.

On Monday, March the sixth, Wesley put Böhler's doctrine to the test by proclaiming to a felon awaiting execution
eternal life and blessedness through voluntary acceptance
of the promises of the Lord Jesus Christ. The condemned
man at once responded, relying with absolute confidence
upon the Gospel as thus stated, and its consolations enabled him to die with a "composed cheerfulness and serene
peace." Wesley's questionings were silenced; he hastened
from the cell of the outcast to a renewed study of the Holy
Scriptures, where he found sufficient evidence that repentance at the last hour was a possibility and conversion frequently instantaneous. On Lord's Day, the twenty-third of
the following month, he heard further testimony from "living witnesses," who declared that these operations of saving
grace were not confined to the Apostolic Age. They had
persisted throughout the schisms and heresies wrought by
rites and ceremonies, symbols and theories, ecclesiastical
claims and counter claims, and were being repeated in his
own day. Thus he was slowly drawn from under the cold
shadows of clerical intolerance and misconception into the
sunshine of the all-sufficient Love Divine. "Here ended,"
he wrote, "my disputing. I could now only cry out, 'Lord,
help thou my unbelief.'" [1] Such were the heraldings of the
dawn which abolished his misgivings, extending and irra-
diating his spiritual horizon, and fixing his faith upon its
central luminary, the Son of God Who loved him and gave
Himself for him.

While the actual moment of his daybreak lingered, it was
anticipated by that of his brother Charles, who lay sick in

[1] "The Journal of John Wesley": edited by Rev. Nehemiah Curnock;
Vol. I, p. 455.

mind and body at the home in Little Britain [1] of a tradesman named Bray, where he was visited by his brother John, Böhler, and other friends. They held frequent conversations with him, and offered prayers for his recovery. Mrs. Turner, the sister of his host, who had recently found peace through believing, consented to bear a message of comfort and command to their guest. Accordingly, on the anniversary of the Feast of Pentecost, coming to the door of his room, she called to him in soft, clear tones, "In the name of Jesus of Nazareth, arise and believe and thou shalt be healed of thy infirmities." Charles at once obeyed the injunction and trusted the promise; at the instigation of an obscure agent began for him his rejuvenated being, and for the Church that enraptured burst of Christian song which has kindled and refined her adoration of the Holiest.

Meanwhile, John's resentment was aroused against the theological guides he had read or consulted, because they had not directed him to the simplicity which is in Christ. He wrote a letter to William Law, arraigning him in terms reminiscent of his old hierarchical temper, bearing down upon his former mentor with a stringency indicative of his inward disturbance, and an immoderation which for the time overcame his charity. "Now, sir," he demanded, in reference to Böhler's views, "suffer me to ask, how will you answer it to our common Lord, that you never gave me this advice? Did you never read the Acts of the Apostles, or the answer of Paul to him who said, 'What must I do to be saved'? Or are you wiser than he? Why did I scarce ever hear you name the name of Christ? Never so as to ground anything upon faith in his blood? Who is this who is laying another foundation? If you say you advised other things as preparatory to this, what is this but laying a foundation below the foundation? . . . I beseech you, sir, by the mercies of God, to consider deeply and impartially whether the true reason of your never pressing this upon me was not this —

[1] A London street still to be found in the eastern section of the city.

that you had it not yourself?"[1] Law met this fulmination with the reply that his instruction had been in substance, though not in expression, identical with that of Böhler, and concluded with the timely admonition, "Let me advise you not to be too hasty in believing that because you have changed your language you have changed your faith. The head can as easily amuse itself with a living and justifying faith in the blood of Jesus as with any other notion, and the heart which you suppose to be a place of security, as being the seat of self-love, is more deceitful than the head."[2] Law was not appreciated by the deists of his generation, nor could this be expected; for, as Sir Leslie Stephen remarks, "A mystic in a common sense atmosphere can no more flourish than an Alpine plant transplanted to the Lowlands." But he had a claim to Wesley's grateful respect on the grounds both of his personal character and his teaching. Even Gibbon, who showed scanty appreciation for Christianity, referred to Law in his Autobiography with affectionate esteem. "In our family," observed the historian, "he left a reputation of a worthy and pious man who believed all he professed and practised all he enjoined." In later days Wesley himself acknowledged that Law's writings first sowed the seed of Methodism, and stemmed the torrent of infidelity and immorality which had submerged the English people since the Restoration. Certainly "it was Law who, alone of living writers, materially influenced Wesley's mind; and gave to universal principles that special form which rendered them suitable at the moment."[3] His subjective treatment of Christian doctrine, particularly of the Atonement and other articles of which Wesley had complained, was characterized by remarkable spiritual originality. Law's superiority to Wesley as a thinker was shown in the correspondence that ensued between them. The

[1] L. Tyerman: "Life and Times of John Wesley"; Vol. I, p. 186.
[2] Ibid., p. 187.
[3] Sir Leslie Stephen: "English Thought in the Eighteenth Century"; Vol. I, p. 158.

honors of the dispute remained with Law, the more so because his opponent injected into it personal charges which should not have been made. The unfortunate aspect of the controversy was that it estranged two sincere servants of God. Of the few glaring indiscretions of the sort which can be charged against Wesley, this perhaps was the most unnecessary. He turned from its embarrassments to consult with Böhler until the latter's departure for the Carolinas, and then went forward to his Peniel alone.

The twenty-fourth of May, 1738, has always been kept by Methodists as the day which ended their Founder's night of wrestling. Wesley rose at five o'clock on that memorable morning, and, opening the New Testament, read these words: "Whereby are given unto us exceeding great and precious promises; that by these ye might be partakers of the divine nature." After a while he again opened the book and read — "Thou art not far from the Kingdom of God." In the afternoon he attended St. Paul's Cathedral, where the anthem was taken from the 130th Psalm as found in the Book of Common Prayer:[1] "Out of the deep I have called unto thee, O Lord: Lord, hear my voice. O let thine ears consider well the voice of my complaint." As the strains of supplication and praise rolled in long melodious thunder beneath the soaring arches and lofty dome of the sanctuary, this humble worshiper found his refuge in the words, "My soul fleeth unto the Lord: before the morning watch, I say, before the morning watch." The choristers sang of trust in His changeless mercy and plenteous redemption: outpourings of a faith which had been the stay of Judaism, and was now the comfort of one who was to become a prince in God's spiritual Israel.

He left the Cathedral to enter upon the experience which he describes in simple, solemn, convincing language, uncolored by hectic emotion, and stamped with reality. His

---

[1] The music for this anthem was probably written by Purcell, the greatest of English composers of cathedral anthems.

words have burned in countless hearts, many of which have known their inmost meaning. "In the evening I went very unwillingly to a Society [1] in Aldersgate Street where one was reading Luther's preface to the Epistle to the Romans. About a quarter before nine, while he was describing the change which God works in the heart through faith in Christ, I felt my heart strangely warmed. I felt I did trust in Christ, Christ alone for salvation; and an assurance was given me that He had taken away *my* sins, even *mine*, and saved *me* from the law of sin and death. I began to pray with all my might for those who had in a more especial manner despitefully used me and persecuted me. I then testified openly to all there what I now first felt in my heart. But it was not long before the enemy suggested, 'This cannot be faith; for where is thy joy?' Then was I taught that peace and victory over sin are essential to faith in the Captain of our salvation; but that, as to the transports of joy that usually attend the beginning of it, especially in those who have mourned deeply, God sometimes giveth, sometimes withholdeth them, according to the counsels of His own will."

His regeneration should not be confused with those renunciations of religious or philosophical opinions at the behest of conviction, under the impulse of which Carlyle left the Calvinism of his youth; Martineau ceased to be an orthodox Unitarian; Mill rejoiced over his social gospel after reading Dumont's interpretation of Benthamism in the "Traité de la Législation"; and Newman passed into the Roman Catholic Church. Wesley's was preëminently a vital change, which, while more or less sharing the intellectual importance of the instances named, surpassed them in the qualities it evinced and the services it rendered. In many respects it closely resembled St. Paul's conversion, and can be more fittingly compared with that classic proof of justifying faith, or with the transformation wrought in Luther, than

[1] This was the Anglican Society in Nettleton Court, conducted by James Hutton, and not, as many have supposed, a Moravian gathering.

with any other individual witness to the saving knowledge of Jesus Christ. Certainly after Wesley's realization of eternal verities his former limitations disappeared: his soul yielded to "the expulsive power of a new affection," and the priest was merged into the prophet. He was no longer compelled to rest his case as a Christian upon human authority, however sacred. His belief in the Church and in the Bible had enabled them to bear an indirect testimony sufficient to stimulate his devout and conscientious inquiries. But he had discovered that any beliefs which hinged upon the word of an earthly witness worked under defective conditions, and varied with his estimate of that witness; that faith so founded could be weakened, and lacked the tenacity and the purity which characterized the faith that came through personal contact with the Son of God. In these experiments he at last seized upon the very essence of the Gospel of his Lord, and occupied a position from which he could not be dislodged. Based upon the rock of an indisturbable assurance, his religion was never again minimized into a mere scheme of probabilities: he felt the results of a living intercourse with Christ, and he might have stated them in the words of the Samaritans to their country-woman: "Now we believe, not because of thy saying, for we have heard Him ourselves, and know that this is indeed the Christ, the Saviour of the world."

The chronic irritation which had given him no rest was banished; he drew from the springs of heavenly love a vital energy, and with his spiritual faculties thus quickened he gained the perception of truth; not the deceptive half-truth of material science that conceals the germs of agnosticism, but the truth that transcends mere intellectual knowledge, the truth which is the objective of such faith as his. In the prime of manhood, he passed at a bound to a high point of being, and carried to the grave untarnished and unimpaired the plenitudes of restoration and of power which then became his own. Neither life nor death was suffered

to take one jot of their meaning from his heart; their regnancy increased with the passing of his years.   His regeneration, apparently spontaneous, was really the outgrowth
of all he had been.   But he was now enlarged, enriched,
illuminated in every province of his nature.   Nor could subsequent changes of feeling or circumstance weaken his hold
on God or on his fellow-men.

It is no detraction from his superior value as a Christian
to recognize in him the egoism out of which his growth
and service were shaped by higher impulses.   If he sometimes spoke, like St. Augustine and Bunyan, as though
the Creator and himself were the only valid ends for
which all things else were the means, this re-adjustment
of his soul's fellowship with its Maker ennobled every
other relation he sustained.   Fixed in his conscious acceptance with God, he was enabled to move with freedom in
the entire region of his reconstructed existence.   The grace
he had received imparted no flawless excellence, but it endowed him with a vigilance, a resolution, and a wisdom
which were typical of Protestant Christianity at its best,
and it rebuked the materialized conceptions and indirect
methods of its appropriation which proceed from external
things.

Our reverence for Wesley is the greater because of the
devotion with which he accepted and acted upon the indisputable fact of his new life in Christ.   Only in the
light of that devotion, and of all it involved, can we
form an adequate estimate of the warm, aspiring saint, as
distinguished from the artificial character, cold as monumental marble, which some have ascribed to him in the
interests of doctrinal theories.   He was deeply aware that
he had been created again in Christ Jesus, and the knowledge gave him rest and gladness.   Yet he offered his sacrifice in humility, as one who was not meet, being careful
to reserve nothing from the altar of consecration.   Moreover, because the Gospel was a sanctifying energy, he re-

sented every effort to belittle or obscure it. Yet the controversialist and the precisionist were no longer welcome to him: he rather laid emphasis upon the grace of God manifested in the forgiveness of his sin and in his deliverance from its shame and guilt. This grace solved the problems which once perplexed him; answered the questions that had not spared his tranquillity; imbued him with a divine sensibility and equipped him for the mission which at once became an inherent part of his life. The vision of Christ as the Redeemer of mankind was the heart of his message; the only Gospel sufficient for the saving of his own soul and of them that heard him.

Such, then, was the nature of Wesley's faith, prepared as it was to forsake derivative beliefs, if by so doing it could secure that immediate access where the finite draws life from the infinite. He pushed his interrogations to the last issue, distinguishing, as he did so, between opinions and convictions, and construing truth in the light of the spirit and word of the New Testament. Beginning with inquiry, he was not content to detect his inconsistencies, or dwell upon his needs, but went forward till he found an all-sufficient object in Christ Jesus, and fastened his trust and obedience upon Him. Cardinal Newman remarked that this was an inverted process: that the Roman devotee begins with belief, and reverently following the divine instincts, draws out their hidden oracles into the symmetry of a holy philosophy. The distinction is worth attention, but the fruits of Wesley's faith are the best answer to Newman's objection. That his extraordinary experience should arouse criticism, especially after it became the type and standard of countless similar experiences, was to be expected. Skepticism could not suffer so startling a rebuke to pass unnoticed; for men resent nothing so much as the unexpected advent of a truth that wrecks their assumptions. Whether cultured or ignorant, imaginative or stupid, they agreed in protesting against the claims made by Wesley and his followers. The transformations of life and character on which they were based confuted those who were forced to admit their actual occurrence, but attached to them their own explanation. Hence Coleridge maintained that Wesley's assurance of salvation was nothing more than "a strong pulse or throb of sensibility accompanying the vehement volition of acquiescence: an ardent desire to find the position true and a concurring determination to receive it as truth." This may be a correct psychological definition of some conversions, but in Wesley's case its sonorous phraseology is misleading. Coleridge evidently took it for granted that the divine element dominant in the change then wrought was not worthy of his consideration. He had no valid ground for any such attitude, and the omission of that element so completely vitiated his analysis that it had about as much bearing on Wesley's actual experience, its nature, intensity, and extent, as the nebulous vapors of the heavens have upon the motions of the planets.

Further, notwithstanding Wesley's occasional lapses into sentimentalism, it must not be forgotten that he was a great Christian who was also a great Englishman. He belonged to a people whose pieties have never been divorced either from reason or ethics, who were Pragmatists before Pragmatism, and whose accepted test for enthusiasm, vehemence, or profession, is practice. Their first question concerning theories or institutions is not, "What can be said for or against them?" but, "How do they work?" Their theology and religion have always been influenced by politics and morality; hence the paradoxical compromises of the English Reformation defied the consistency so dear to the French mind, in order that they might include the main currents of public opinion. Innate conservatism is apparent at every stage of the religious development of the nation in which Wesley became a representative teacher. The mystical fervors found in the Latin race, which ran to extremes even in the Moravians, were moderated by the utilitarian tendency of Anglican saints. They usually related their ecstasies to earthly affairs, economizing them for that purpose; the extravagances of St. Francis, of St. John of the Cross, and even of Boehme were foreign to the more sober but equally intent piety of such men as Lancelot Andrewes, Richard Hooker, and Jeremy Taylor. In a letter written to his brother Samuel, dated November 23, 1736, Wesley says, "I think the rock on which I had the nearest made shipwreck of the faith was the writings of the mystics; under which term I comprehend all, and only those, who slight any of the means of grace. . . . Men utterly divested of free will, of self-love, and self-activity, are entered into the passive state, and enjoy such a contemplation as is not only above faith, but above sight. . . . They have absolutely renounced their reason and understanding; else they could not be guided by a Divine Light. They seek no clear or particular knowledge of anything, but only an obscure, general knowledge. . . . Sight, or something more than sight, takes the place of faith."[1] These avowals of the dangers he had so barely escaped leave no doubt on the point at issue. He clung to the venerable guarantees of historic Christianity, avoiding sensational and gratuitous changes, but adopting those dictated by the expansion of his heart and work.

It is one of the triumphs of originality not to invent or discover what is probably already known, but by a revivifying of former things to make their meaning new and irresistible. Wesley's conversion was a good example of this process. His entire life hitherto had been steadily directed toward the inflatus it then received and the decision with which he received it. Even his doubts and difficulties had contributed to his regeneration. He might have said in the language of a later day,

> "Thoughts hardly to be packed
> Into a narrow act,
> Fancies that broke through language and escaped;

[1] L. Tyerman: "Life and Times of John Wesley"; Vol. I, pp. 133–134.

All I could never be,
All men ignored in me,
This was I worth to God, whose wheel the pitcher shaped."

He was early set apart by his mother's diligent care for his soul, and her reminder that he could be saved only by keeping all the commandments of his Maker. This excited his sense of moral responsibility, making him apprehensive of the approaches of evil and painfully censorious of himself. It prevented him from regarding sin as being nothing more than a general imperfection, and his grief over past failures strengthened in him the presuppositions of the Gospel which delivers men from sin. In his dealings with heaven he could not brook trifling or evasion; every act of worship was candid and absorbing. The despair his previous state had evoked was the prelude to the rapture of his deliverance, and his subsequent ministry was proportioned by his experiences both of sorrow and of joy. His affection for the beauty and appropriateness of the Anglican liturgy remained unchanged. He continued to associate faith not only with worship but with work, and he had no sooner begun to preach than he established an orphanage at Newcastle. Alert to the dangers of exuberant emotionalism, he warned his converts that an uprush of feeling did not necessarily indicate divine sonship. It was to be validated by corresponding deeds, since a profession of religion without its fruits was vanity. Here the young Oxonian of the Bocardo reappeared, and while he preached faith he also maintained that "he who doeth righteousness is righteous." The presumptions of those who imagined they had exclusive rights to evangelicalism were rebuked in the following observations: "I find more profit in sermons on either good tempers or good works, than in what are vulgarly called Gospel sermons. That word has now become a mere cant word; I wish none of our Society would use it. It has no determinate meaning. Let but a pert, self-sufficient animal, that has neither sense nor grace bawl out something about Christ or His blood or justification by faith and his hearers cry out, 'what a fine Gospel sermon!'" In later days he wrote again, "When fifty years of age, my brother Charles and I in the simplicity of our hearts taught the people that unless they knew their sins forgiven, they were under the wrath and curse of God, I wonder they did not stone us. The Methodists know better now." The spirit of the New Testament was nurtured in Wesley by the combination of numerous differing phases and gifts. Many streams fed the mighty river of gracious influence which issued from his personality, a river still flowing, and bearing the life of men toward happier havens beyond.

Julia Wedgwood in her able study of Wesley states that his regeneration transferred "the birthday of a Christian from his baptism to his conversion, and in that change the partition line of the two great systems is crossed." This is true so far as characteristic Wesleyanism is concerned, but it does not take sufficient account of the significance of the religious education of the young, or of the Christian consciousness of the Church universal. Later Methodism has been compelled to acknowledge these factors as in many instances modifying the older conception which limited conversion to an immediate and pronounced experience. Countless hosts of Christians owe their faith to early religious training, or to the Sacraments which have undoubtedly fostered it. These multitudes can neither be ignored nor dismissed by a sweeping generalization. The operations of the Divine Presence in human hearts do not submit to the rough and ready assignments of man. "The wind bloweth where it listeth and thou hearest the sound thereof, but knowest not whence it cometh and whither it goeth: so is every one that is born of the Spirit."

Such then in outline was the inwardness of Wesley's change as he published it to the world, to be read by all who desire to form a sober judgment on this supreme issue. Anything more restrained in temper, more cogent in statement, more persuasive in appeal, it would be difficult to find. In many respects it is the wisest as it is the most impartial modern utterance that has interpreted Christian origins and Christian history by Christian experience. And although some of its suggestions may be open to minor criticism, its value as an apologetic and as an eirenicon is beyond estimate. It recalls the flame from the Altar of Eternal Love which burned in the breasts of the Apostles, the Fathers, and the Martyrs, and afterwards burst forth again in St. Francis and the heroes of the Reformation. How well it fulfilled in Wesley the more perfect will of God is dispassionately stated in a further quotation from Mr. Lecky: "It is, however, scarcely an exaggeration to say that the scene which took place at that humble meeting in Aldergate Street forms an epoch in English history. The conviction which then flashed upon one of the most powerful and most active intellects in England is the true source of English Methodism" [1] — a judgment far too modest in its ascription. That conviction set free the religious genius whose light flashed on England when the moral condition of her inhabitants was aptly summarized in the somber phrase of the Hebrew prophet: "They sat in darkness and the shadow of death." Yet neither England nor English Methodism was the sole beneficiary of Wesley's consecrated faculties; his words have gone out unto the ends of the earth.

III

The vile conditions for which the eighteenth century was unenviably notorious were at their worst in its second quarter, and continued even after the Evangelical Revival had succeeded in abolishing some of their most deplorable features. Mark Pattison describes the age as "one of decay of religion, licentiousness of morals, public corruption, profaneness of language, — a day of rebuke and blasphemy

[1] " England in the Eighteenth Century "; Vol. III, p. 48.

. . . an age destitute of depth and earnestness; an age whose poetry was without romance, whose philosophy was without insight, and whose public men were without character; an age of 'light without love,' whose very merits were of the earth, earthy." [1] Since these essays were published in 1860 we have learned to understand the eighteenth century better; to know that, despite the sordidness and materialism which characterized it, the period was not and could not have been wholly corrupt. Agents and forces of purification are always present in every society, however debased and degenerate that society may seem to be, and they never cease to operate, though at times too far below the surface for their presence to be detected by the superficial observer.

Yet without question the disorder of England during the years included in Pattison's survey was far-reaching and obstinate. Professor Henry Sidgwick has remarked that the national character was such as to make belief in a constitutional government impossible. In the judgment of wise and patriotic men absolutism was necessary, because of the ignorance, materialism, and waywardness of the people. The morality of polite circles was content to express itself in epigrams and maxims, while their rampant vices sheltered behind these useless formulæ. Hume, in an essay published in 1741, complained of the tyranny of political factions, and concluded that, "We should, at last, after many convulsions and civil wars, find repose in an absolute monarchy, which it would have been happier for us to have established peaceably from the beginning." If we may judge from these and many other authoritative criticisms, social stability was by no means assured. License was too frequently mistaken for liberty: the general well-being was hindered by those who bawled for freedom in a senseless mood, and there was a justifiable distrust of popular sentiment. The wise political instinct now attributed

[1] "Essays"; Vol. II, p. 42.

R

to the British people, and the actual establishment of civic solidarity and virtue, are far more recent than is commonly supposed. Levity, caprice, selfishness, and turbulence were prevalent. The fickleness and perversity of the populace, which Milton in his treatise on "A Free Commonwealth" regarded as dangerous, were due in a measure to the sourest and narrowest type of Puritanism. Notwithstanding the short tenure of the Cromwellian Protectorate, the religious enthusiasm it generated, and the triumphs of peace and war it secured, the reaction against it flung aside morality altogether, and had not spent its force in Wesley's day. Men still spoke with detestation of the attempts to enforce virtue and suppress vice by penal statutes, and the orgies of the court of Charles the Second were perpetuated in the dissoluteness of the aristocracy and the degradation of the masses. The reign of the saints was succeeded by the revels of the sinners; the profligates of the Restoration had produced a progeny almost worse than themselves, whose cynical brutalities it would be difficult to exaggerate. Rational goodness seemed as impossible as art to a nation smitten with color-blindness. The highest elements in human existence were cast away; conduct drifted into wrong channels; conscience was defiled; then indeed was

"Time a maniac scattering dust,
And life a fury slinging flame."

Yet on the low dark verge might be discerned the twilight of a new day. For there was a saving remnant not unmindful of the honor of God, which waged war on the evils that usurped His claims, however hopeless the undertaking seemed. The earlier reformers who strove to stem the pestilential flood of wickedness voiced their anxiety in the words of Dr. Woodward. Writing in 1699, he declared, "Our great enjoyments in liberty, law, trade, etc., are in manifest danger of being lost by those horrid enormities which have for some years past abounded in this our nation; for indeed they are gross, scandalous, and crying, even to the reproach of our Government and the great dishonor of our religion." The "Proposal for a National Reformation of Manners," issued in 1694, anticipated Woodward's accusation. "All men agree," states its opening paragraph, "that atheism and profaneness never got such a high ascendant as at this day. A thick gloominess hath overspread our horizon and our light looks like the evening of the world . . . vice and wickedness abound in every place, drunkenness and lewdness escape unpunished; our ears in most companies are filled with imprecations of damnation; and the corners of our streets everywhere the horrible sounds of oaths, curses, and blasphemous execrations." [1]

The monarchs of England contributed to the deplorable state of affairs. Thackeray's lectures, "The Four Georges," show that these princes, with the exception of George III, while less openly depraved than Charles II, were infinitely more vulgar. The novelist's masterly portrait of the hero of Dettingen, — the second George, a strutting, self-important, irascible little boor, who corrupted society by his example and coarsened it by his manners, — is not a whit overdrawn in its fearless and repulsive delineation. His Queen, Caroline of Anspach, described by Sir Walter Scott in "The Heart of Midlothian" as a sagacious and attractive princess, although personally chaste and deserving of a better husband than the man to whose puerile eccentricities she sacrificed everything, did not hesitate to jest about his paramours nor to indulge in obscene allusions. The life and thought of the nation were infected by this betrayal of decency in high places: its intelligence, virtue, and seemly demeanor were constantly discouraged; its worst propensities found their instigators among those who were miscalled noble. In spite of his loyalty to the throne, Wesley felt and avowed a healthy contempt for the upper classes. The

[1] Julia Wedgwood: "John Wesley and the Evangelical Reaction of the Eighteenth Century"; pp. 116–117.

barriers which the advocates of an empirical philosophy of cultured common sense strove to oppose against contagious vices were swept away by passions which neither the serene guidance of Addison nor the stern protest of Johnson could withstand. An increase of wealth and trade furnished the means for tasteless profusion and animalistic excess. Folly, filthy conversation, libertinism, and gluttony were the pursuits of the majority. The landed proprietors and the squirearchies took pattern from the reigning house, which was sunk in debauchery until the accession of George III, who allied his court with domestic regularity. Whatever may be urged against him as an incapable ruler whose ambition for executive supremacy ended in the dismemberment of the Empire, in his private character George III was well nigh irreproachable, strongly and simply religious, given to prayer and to observance of the ordinances of the Church. Yet he and his bigoted consort, Charlotte of Mecklenburg-Strelitz, never controlled their unruly sons, who mocked and defied the quiet ways of Windsor, and came near to overthrowing the Hanoverian dynasty in Britain.

The mania for gambling reached its height during this epoch, wielding an absolute sway over rich and poor alike, who turned to its lure as naturally as to food or sleep, and viewed the hazarding of fabulous sums as nothing worse than an indiscretion. Any vice which receives general approval ceases to be looked upon as such, and there were few who escaped the ruinous fascinations of the race track and the casino. All ranks and conditions gambled prodigiously and systematically. "Whist," wrote Walpole to Sir Horace Mann, "has spread a universal opium over the whole nation. On whatever pretext, and under whatever circumstances, half a dozen people of fashion found themselves together, whether for music, or dancing, or politics, or for drinking the waters or each other's wine, the box was sure to be rattling and the cards were being cut and shuffled." [1]   The habitués of St. James's Palace staked nothing less than two hundred pounds apiece at their nightly play, and when Lady Cowper declined to enter the game because she could not afford to risk the wager, she was chided for her lack of courage.   Lord Ilchester lost thirteen thousand pounds at one sitting, a debt of honor he never paid.   Topham Beauclerk, the patron and friend of the literati who met in the taverns of Fleet Street and the Strand, declared that the extremities to which Charles James Fox was reduced after he had parted with his last guinea were pitiable beyond words.   Before this orator and statesman was twenty-four, he had incurred gambling debts to the amount of five hundred thousand pounds, more than a fifth of which sum represented the losses of one evening;   and during his lifetime he squandered a million pounds in the same pursuit.   Instead of being sobered by such wild exploits, Fox jested about them and referred to the anteroom where his Hebrew creditors waited to negotiate his paper as the Jerusalem Chamber.   White's Coffee House was one of the favorite resorts of those who courted the smile of the goddess of chance.   Mr. Thynne won twelve thousand pounds there in one night.   Beau Brummel is said to have won twenty thousand, and General Scott one hundred thousand pounds in the same place at a single sitting.   Nor were these instances extraordinary;   in proportion to their means the majority of gamblers were equally profuse.

The State patronized lotteries until near the close of the century;   the mischief which ensued passes description. Great numbers of people were beggared in mind and body;   the havoc among the tradesfolk, farmers, and artisans was greater than can now be imagined: they were in every sense demoralized.   The racing towns of Epsom and Newmarket swarmed with sharpers, blacklegs, and their dupes. Loaded dice, fullams, and other apparatus for trickery

[1] Sir George O. Trevelyan: "Early History of Charles James Fox"; p. 89.

were carried in the pockets, caps, and sleeves of these knights of the craft, who viewed their calling as the industry of the age. The financial speculations of Exchange Alley victimized thousands rendered gullible by the national pursuit. No project was too ridiculous to win support. The place was filled, according to Smollett, "with a strange concourse of statesmen and clergymen, churchmen and dissenters, Whigs, and Tories, physicians, lawyers, tradesmen, and even females; all other professions and employments were utterly neglected." Companies were formed for discounting pensions, insuring horses, providing perpetual motion, discovering the land of Ophir, and for the manifestly superfluous enterprise of improving the breed of asses. Even when that bloated venture, the South Sea Bubble, burst ·and reduced thousands to poverty and despair, the madness received no perceptible check. Fresh devotees consigned their fortunes to greedy schemers; estates, heirships, trust funds, even chastity and life, were flung into the insatiable maw of this iniquity. The players plunged without stint, laying all they had or could obtain upon the board, while they watched the turns of the game with oaths and imprecations. Flown with wine and rendered desperate by their losses or their lust for gain, men without conscience or honor quarreled and fought, and satisfaction was demanded and given in numerous duels which became infamous for that vulturous ferocity peculiar to the confirmed gambler.

Until Garrick revived the Shakesperian traditions, the stage was monopolized by farces and spectacles of which Congreve, Wycherley, and Vanbrugh were the chief purveyors. Their ribald comedies suited current taste by exalting pruriency and laughing the marriage vow out of fashion. The scenes reeked of the stews; rakes and debauchees were heroes; skepticism of any possible virtue, especially between the sexes, was paraded with sickening reiteration. The dialogues took it for granted that there was an essential antagonism between what was moral and what was witty and admirable. Fielding, who was by no means fastidious about such matters, makes Parson Adams say in "Joseph Andrews" he had never heard of any plays that were fit to read except Addison's "Cato" and Dicky Steele's somewhat prosy "Conscious Lovers." The observation is corroborated by the fact that ladies wore masks at the theaters, a custom which lasted until long after the accession of George III. Tragedies were filled with tedious declamations upon the flagrant crimes of the classic monsters of Greece and Rome, which made little appeal to the mind and less to the heart. This repression of the deeper emotions was inimical to the higher drama: instead of envisaging the sacredness of human fate, resolution, and endurance, it languished in the unrealities of finely polished couplets and rhetorical bravado. Yet these disadvantages could not prevent the triumph of David Garrick's inimitable genius as an actor, nor were they incompatible with the development of a delightful and masterly series of comedies from those two genial Irishmen, Sheridan and Goldsmith, whose treatment of the lighter aspects of life did something to redeem wantonness and intellectual sterility. The fourth Earl of Chesterfield, a pattern of etiquette, inculcated an exquisite bearing and address which was the cloak for a refined impurity much more detrimental to morals than the salacious frankness of Fielding or the grossness of Smollett. Historians may willingly accord him posthumous justice as an able, careful, conscientious statesman who deserved well of his country and despised bribery by money or preferment in an unscrupulous era when Sir Robert Walpole surveyed the benches of the House of Commons and declared "All these men have their price." Chesterfield was not only the representative of his class; he was also a patron of literature, and in a lesser degree an author of some merit. In the former capacity his lack of generosity provoked Johnson into writing one of the best letters of the language; in the latter, his lack of virtue induced him to instruct his son in the arts of intrigue, seduction, and adultery as accomplishments highly becoming a gentleman.

Women of rank appeared at private functions and in public places of entertainment clad in the scantiest garb, and far from incurring disapproval, their immodesty was applauded. Drunkenness was an established custom, with a code of regulations which decreed the order of merit for the bibulous, and arranged the incessant rounds of wine and wit, punch bowl and song. The Prince Regent, hailed by his boon companions and flatterers as the first gentleman in Europe, caroused nightly with Sheridan, Grattan, and other celebrities of the Carlton House coterie. He conspired with his brothers — those stout, well-fed princes whose farmerlike faces look down upon the visitor from the walls of England's Portrait Galleries — to make her premier noble, the Duke of Norfolk, drink a toast with every seasoned toper at the royal board. Norfolk would not refuse the challenge, and the debauch went on till the aged Duke's gray head lay stupefied among the decanters while the wine ran like blood on the table. Lord Eldon was a six bottle man, as were other legal and political luminaries; William Pitt emptied a bottle of port wine at home before going to the House of Commons, and after the debates betook himself to Bellamy's with Dundas and helped to finish a couple more. Addison, Steele, Poulteney, Goldsmith, Fox, and Lord Holland were all addicted to the cup. Sir Gilbert Elliot, writing to his wife in 1787, said, "Men of all ages drink abominably . . . and Gray more than any of them." The beaux of the town, known as "frolics," "bloods," "mohocks" and "macaronies," consumed large quantities of fermented liquor. Byron's letters contain references to the sprees of Cambridge professors and students, and he informed his friend Jackson, the pugilist, of the masquerades at Newstead Abbey, where goblets fashioned out of human skulls were quaffed by young scapegraces attired in monastic robes. Ministers of State reeled to their places in Parliament or at the opera, and sometimes even clergymen, with their wigs awry, went to the sacred desk to hiccough in the pauses of their discourse.

Routs, assemblies, balls and ridottos were thronged with fashionable patrons; Vauxhall and Ranelagh gardens were frequented by the upper and middle classes. *The Spectator* describes Sir Roger de Coverley's visit to the former resort, then one of the sights of the metropolis, which the good knight enjoyed when he came up from Worcestershire. Between the social extremes were the territorial proprietors who shared in the common decadence. The local magnates, parsons, and magistrates of the shires, with their isolation, ignorance, pride, static politics, uncouth speech, and rustic garb, furnished material for the satire of the novelists and the moralizing of the essayists. It was an epoch of hilarious feasting, fiddling, dancing, and buffoonery: in many aspects unmanly, imbecile, and pitiable. The wreck of talent, the untimely ending of individuals who might have been shining lights in a perverse generation, but who left nothing except painful memories of needless error and suffering, fill the observer with a sense of irreparable loss. The hope of the nation's redemption lay in the best of the clergy, the merchants, and the yeomanry, and from their ranks came the leaders of Methodism, who supported Wesley in his efforts to reclaim the debased multitudes.

These neglected hordes were exactly what the ruling powers had made them. Had those who exercised civil and religious authority been wise and just, pure in life, sincere in motive, and honorable in their dealings, the proletariat would undoubtedly have felt the restraint of their example. But such virtues were far to seek, while the vices we have noted spread in virulent form among the workmen and peasants.[1]

---

[1] The editor of the *Gloucester Gazette* wrote: " Is it not mysterious that gambling which has been known to bring calamity on the greatest and richest men should now become common among the common people themselves?" Piety and gentleness must have lived in the shade. Brutality flourished in the daylight. Public executions and whippings were everyday spectacles; bull-baiting, dog-fighting, and duck-hunting — the last

Gin was the chosen beverage of the great unwashed, out-bidding ale, porter, rum, and brandy in competition for popular favor. Hogarth's pictures of Beer Street and Gin Lane were delineations of the neighborhoods of St. Martin's and St. Giles. The first represented John Bull engaged in his national pastime, when the butcher, the drayman, and the blacksmith drained their foaming tankards, flourished a prime leg of mutton, and sang in praise of beer:

> "Labor and art, upheld by thee,
> Successfully advance,
> We quaff the balmy juice with glee,
> And water leave to France."

In contrast to this scene of counterfeit merriment was the nauseating squalor of Gin Lane, where human nature, naked and unashamed, wallowed in the depths of bestiality. The artist vented his wrath on the cursed fiend, with murder fraught, which preyed on the vitals of his countrymen. Nothing in his terrific arraignment of contemporary immorality was more awful in its fidelity than the portrayal of that scene where old and young, and even mothers with infants in arms, greedily drank the potations doled out in return for their coppers. During a debate on the question of drunkenness in 1736, it was reported to Parliament that within the precincts of Westminster, Holborn, the Tower, and Finsbury there were over seven thousand houses and shops which retailed spirituous beverages, — and this in a city which then contained only 600,000 inhabitants, of whom over one fifth were directly interested in the traffic.

two during service-time on Sundays — were usual. Reputable Londoners made it their Sunday afternoon amusement to repair with their families to the Old Bethlehem Hospital, to watch the maniacs who were chained naked to the pillars. At this time some two hundred thousand persons usually gathered in tea-gardens about London every Sunday afternoon, and at the end of the day they were to be classified thus: "Sober, 50,000; in High Glee, 90,000; Drunkish, 30,000; Staggering Tipsy, 10,000; Muzzy, 15,000; Dead Drunk, 5,000." In every circle of life it was unusual for a party to disperse while one masculine member of it was sober.

Distilleries and breweries increased apace, and Mr. Lecky states that, small as is the place which gin-drinking occupies in English history, it was probably, if all the consequences that flowed from it are considered, the most disastrous practice in the eighteenth century.[1] Painted boards were suspended from the door of almost every seventh house, inviting the poor to get intoxicated for a penny, and dead drunk for twopence; straw whereon to lie being provided without charge until they had slept off the effects of the first debauch and were ready to start afresh. Dr. Benson, Bishop of Gloucester, writing from Westminster to Bishop Berkeley of Cloyne on February 18, 1752, says, "Your lordship calls this the freest country in Europe. There is indeed freedom of one kind in it . . . a most unbounded licentiousness of all sorts . . . a regard to nothing but diversion and vicious pleasures. . . . Our people are now become, what they never were before, cruel. Those accursed spirituous liquors which, to the shame of our Government, are so easily to be had, and in such quantities drunk, have changed the very nature of our people. And they will, if continued to be drunk, destroy the very race of the people themselves." [2]

Life and property were menaced by this waste of soul and substance: thugs and footpads, recruited from bagnios and taverns, were quick to take advantage of the unprotected condition of society. Armed with murderous weapons they sallied forth at dusk from their hiding places and skulked in dismal alleys or on the heaths, to rob wayfarers and travelers, beating or killing those who resisted them. The Strand and Covent Garden were infested by these ruffians, and mail coaches were liable to be held up on Hounslow Heath, Gad's Hill, or any other open space. Fraternities of criminals banded together under names which indicated

---

[1] "England in the Eighteenth Century"; Vol. II, p. 101. See also " Memoirs of William Hickey (1749–1775) "; edited by Alfred Spencer.

[2] W. C. Sydney: "England and the English in the Eighteenth Century"; pp. 62–63.

their various depredations; some were driven to theft by poverty, many more preferred it to work, not a few esteemed it a chivalrous occupation. James Maclean,[1] the "gentleman highwayman," and others of his kidney, after they had lost their all in pursuit of pleasure and lust, took to the road with horse, mask, cutlass, and pistols. Cavaliers of plunder invested its sordid realities with a fictitious romance, and had a doggerel of their own, vended everywhere, and especially at the foot of the gallows, where they paid the penalty for their misdeeds. The adventures of Jack Sheppard and Dick Turpin, who were better known to the average Englishman than any other heroes of the hangman's rope, were chanted in alehouses by admiring yokels, and roared in drunken chorus on the streets. The criminal code was a ferocious and sanguinary legal instrument. Sir Samuel Romilly, who commands the admiration of posterity for the enlightened principles of legislative justice and mercy he advocated, on reviewing it, said, "The first thing which strikes one is the melancholy truth that among the variety of actions which men are daily liable to commit no less than one hundred and sixty have been declared by Act of Parliament to be felonies without benefit of clergy; or in other words, to be worthy of instant death." Yet, undeterred by this Draconian severity, crime was outrageous and incessant; the jails were filled with criminals awaiting transportation to the penal colonies or the cart that should convey them to Tyburn; the frequent public executions at Newgate and at the county towns were occasions for a junketing. Men who owed a few pounds they were unable to pay languished in the Fleet Prison; women were hanged for petty thefts.[2] All that has been affirmed here can be

---

[1] Also spelt Maclaine, or Macleane.

[2] Even Oxford students suffered the extreme penalty. Dr. Routh (born in 1756, died in 1855) had seen this. "What, Sir, do you tell me, Sir, that you never heard of Gownman's Gallows? Why, I tell you, Sir, that I have seen the undergraduates hanged on Gownman's Gallows in Holywell — hanged, Sir, for highway robbery." A. D. Godley: "Oxford in the Eighteenth Century"; p. 35.

verified from the pages of Gay, Walpole, Fielding, and Smollett; from the *Newgate Calendar*, the columns of the *Spectator*, the *Tatler*, the *Ledger*, the *London Evening*, and from the caricatures of Gillray and the pictures of Hogarth.

The testimony of these authors, journalists, and artists was largely limited to London, because there the Court, the Government, the social dictatorship, much of the wealth and one tenth of the population of the country were located. But in the provinces and agricultural districts a similar state of affairs prevailed; indeed, Wesley regarded the rural peasantry as the most inaccessible of all the laboring classes. The legislator and the moralist left Hodge out of their calculations, and there seemed to be no remedy for his senseless antagonism to new conditions. Corrupt and contented, his daily life was a dull, sullen, insensate round, his lot a bitter inheritance of deprivation and practical serfdom. Many of the agrarian wrongs which had enraged the insurgents of the fourteenth century were still in existence,[1] and even now the backward condition of these people is a social problem aggravated by their conservatism and apathy. The more active spirits among them migrated to the towns, and settled in congested spots which bred a general depravity. The miners of Cornwall, the potters of North Staffordshire, the colliers of South Staffordshire, Shropshire, Newcastle, Yorkshire, and the Forest of Dean, the stockingers of Northampton, and the weavers of Lancashire, were at once the most unruly and the most promising workmen of England. Their moral deterioration was so marked that respectable members of the community despised them, oblivious of the fact that they had been denied those primary elements and means of knowledge which human beings have a right to expect and acquire. The character of these

---

[1] As a matter of fact, the state of the English peasantry was worse at this time (1760–1820) than during the Middle Ages, owing to the inclosure of the common lands and the injustice and hardship that this wrought.

men and women was in the main shaped by the circumstances in which they were placed and the laws by which they were governed. When these changed they changed, and notwithstanding their faults and profligacies they were at all times vital and responsive. Physical standards of manhood inured them to the hardships of the coalpit and the forge. The wake and the fair were the occasions for their dissipation, affording them relief after exhausting labors which humiliated the body and apparently canceled the last traces of humanity in the soul. Employers, enriched by their exertions, demanded from them an unremitting toil which benumbed their intellectual life and flung them back into paganism. Anything which could uplift them was either forgotten or scouted; when released from work they were left at the mercy of their animal instincts, the reckless indulgence of which, as their only means of recreation, made them thenceforth impatient of moral restraint. The heartlessness and avarice of the masters and the crushing slavery of the workers were a monstrous contradiction of New Testament teaching in a nominally Christian land. The larger part of the inhabitants of the mining and manufacturing districts were without hope, because they were without God.[1] The few lived at the expense of the many. Pay day was preceded by semi-starvation and followed by a saturnalia. The agents and managers of the pits and factories were not infrequently owners or lessees of adjoining taverns where they practically confiscated the hard-earned pittance of the workmen, who must perforce spend it there or suffer for their abstinence. Dog-fighting, cock-fighting, pigeon-homing, and bouts of fisticuffs were interspersed with horse-racing and bull-baiting. Almost any place that could muster a sufficiently profitable crowd to witness the latter spectacle provided accommodation for it, and one of the squares of the city of Birmingham

---

[1] Notwithstanding the increase in population of manufacturing centers, few new parishes had been created. The State Church was so inflexible that it was difficult to adapt it to these growing needs.

still retains the name of the Bull Ring. The *Weekly Journal* for June 9, 1716, advertised that a bear-baiting to the death, with bull-baiting in addition, would begin at 3 o'clock in the afternoon, as the sport promised to be lengthy; a wild bull was also to be released with fireworks all over its body. Nameless torturings and mutilations were necessary in order to attract the largest gatherings. Sometimes, to the huge relish of on-lookers, a cat was tied to the bull's tail; and the delight of the mob knew no bounds when an unfortunate wight was tossed by the frantic beast.

A well known resort of those who matched game cocks armed with steel spurs, was found in Bird Cage Walk, under the shadow of Westminster Abbey. It was here that Hogarth sketched the outline for his picture "The Cockpit," painted in 1759, although he might have obtained material anywhere, since cock-pits were common, even at the public schools, and patronized by all classes. Some mains lasted three days, and not less than two or three hundred birds were killed. The church bells had been known to ring a merry peal when town or county secured the coveted prize. The names of famous pugilists were household words: their portraits were found in the gun-rooms of the wealthy, the students' haunts at the Universities, and on the walls of the coaching hostelries and taverns. Matches were arranged by the nobility and gentry, who presented belts bestudded with gold to the successful combatants. Even royalty did not disdain the prize ring when some first-rate exponent of "the manly art of self defense" occupied the arena, and it is on record that the House of Commons adjourned on February 27, 1770, to attend a contest at Carlisle House in Soho. The gilded youth of Piccadilly and Pall Mall aspired to fistic honors, and lent their countenance to any likely lad for the companionship. Men, and sometimes women, delirious with drink and deviltry, circled around the half-naked pugilists, urging them forward and betting excitedly on the outcome. Comment on such despotisms of fleshly lust is unnecessary: suffice it to say that they further enchained the hapless masses which the rise of industrialism in towns and cities had already brought under its dominion. The people, who delved into every other abyss before they reached that of the grave, literally perished for lack of knowledge.

Yet any survey of eighteenth century England from the ethical standpoint should not fail to emphasize the good qualities which lay dormant beneath such riot and confusion. Because some annalists have neglected to do this, their accounts, while true as to facts, are misleading in import. He would be an unscientific hydrographer who should describe the ocean in nothing more than terms of its surface calms, its currents, its storms, and tempests. Beneath these lie silent depths, the reservoirs of its life and power, in which are contained the remnants of past ages and all those forms of recurring sanitation and renewed existence that help to preserve the habitable globe. The illustration applies to humanity in any period, and especially in such an age as Wesley's, which, apparently so impotent, in reality had a decided capacity for regeneration. There has always been virtue enough in the world when there has been sufficient religious earnestness to call it forth, and always religious earnestness enough when there were strong convictions to arouse it. Individual and social conduct may be reprobate when acting under the governance of swiftly succeeding passions of the baser sort, but it still has to reckon with those fundamental laws of soul and conscience and with those necessities of character upon which the making of Christian civilization depends. The impressionist can find abundant social phenomena in the days of the Georges to justify pessimistic conclusions, but he should correct his observations by extending them to the eras that went before and came after. The very wickedness of the period furnished opportunities for the evangelist and the reformer. Faith had the last word, and during the dreary interval

the few who held fast the beginning of their confidence
without wavering had the consolation that

> "Power is with us in the night
> Which makes the darkness and the light,
> And dwells not in the light alone."

Past and future had large interests at stake in the eighteenth
century: and where such interests are found their rights
and claims must eventually be asserted. More powerful
than all else was the unchanging truth that one Image is
indelibly engraven on the mind of Christendom: the Christ
who reveals the Father in all times and to all His children
was still present with His scattered flock. Those who felt
the inward strivings of divine monition still heard His voice
and followed Him. Wherever any resemblance to the great
Original was perceptible in ideals of charity and deeds of
sacrifice, there the most lawless were subdued and paid a
becoming reverence. The Spirit of the Eternal brooded
then, as He ever does, over the social abyss, to dispel its
apathy and illuminate its gloom. Merchants, miners, and
artisans were mysteriously prepared by His offices to receive
the message and mission of Whitefield and Wesley. After
the long dearth of nearly a hundred years their preaching
was as grateful to these hearers as the return of spring.
Amidst every facility that could be given to treacherous
and ignoble traits, and to leaders in State or Church who
seldom manifested any moral apprehension or spiritual
desire, the revival of religion was born from above, to
strengthen the sinews and the heart of England. It re-
kindled, as already observed, her consciousness of God, and
prevented her from political and social revolution. The
first result was a primal and an unmixed blessing, the
second was by no means without qualifications, — although,
in view of the enormities of the French uprising, which yet
rendered signal service in shattering the corrupt traditions
of the century and in punishing its luxury, frivolity, and

s

oppression, it was perhaps salutary for Europe that England should have maintained her ancient constitutional polity. When in the rush of these fearful events the first Napoleon climbed to power, and, to quote Lord Rosebery, "his genius had enlarged indefinitely the scope of human conception and possibility," it was the resilient strength of the United Kingdom which clashed with his boundless ambition. Aided by the reaction of his stupendous gifts, she defeated the final efforts of the conqueror who had carried the faculties of war and administration to their farthest point and held a continent in awe. Few severer tests could be imposed on any people than those which Britons then met and satisfied. The outcome goes beyond the period with which we are directly concerned, but its causes belong there. Certainly the statesmanship of Pitt and Burke, Clive's conquest of India, the campaigns of Moore and Wellington, and the naval victories of Hood and Nelson, regained in the East the prestige which had been lost in the West, and Great Britain never stood so high in the councils of the world as after Waterloo. That the Evangelical Revival was one of the chief factors in evoking and conserving the solidarity and discipline of the forces thus engaged cannot be seriously gainsaid; and, although domestic reforms were too long postponed, eventually they could not be restrained. The same trustworthy reserves of character which had furnished Wesleyanism with its constituencies, defended the Homeland from invasion, and extended the boundaries of the Empire, also helped to secure the social advantages which have never ceased to accrue to English democracy.

CHAPTER VII

CONFLICT AND VICTORY

LET not that image fade,
Ever, O God! from out the minds of men,
Of him, Thy messenger and stainless priest,
In a brute, sodden, and unfaithful time,
Early and late, o'er land and sea, on-driven;
In youth, in eager manhood, age extreme —
Driven on forever, back and forth the world,
By that divine, omnipotent desire.

RICHARD WATSON GILDER: *Ode to Wesley.*

CHAPTER VII

CONFLICT AND VICTORY

Political development of England in the eighteenth century — Literature of the period — Increasing prosperity of the country — English religious thought rationalistic in tone — Adherence to Locke — Conflict between orthodoxy and deism — Loss of spirituality in the Church caused by undue insistence on rationalizing — Clergy of the Establishment not entirely to blame — Their poverty — Decadence of Dissent — Spiritual awakenings in England and Scotland prior to Wesley — Wesley's visit to Herrnhut — Christian David — Warburton and Wesley — George Whitefield — His field preaching — Wesley joins Whitefield — John Nelson's description of Wesley's labors — Emotional outbursts consequent on Wesley's preaching — Clerical opponents — Bishops Gibson, Lavington, and Warburton — Wesley's relation to the Establishment — Popular outbreaks against the Methodists.

I

THE British dominions expanded rapidly during Wesley's lifetime, their growth being due to the colonizing and commercial activities of Englishmen and also to their numerous conflicts with France. Sixty-four of the one-hundred and twenty-six years between the reigns of James II and George III were spent in a series of wars, the longest of which lasted twelve and the shortest seven years, their general result being that Britain became the mother of free commonwealths in the West and at the Antipodes, whose inhabitants shared with her a common language and law. The revolt of the American Colonists in 1776 showed that communities derived from the parental stock could not be held to their allegiance when unwise legislation offended their love of freedom, and least of all by the threat and employment of physical force. The outcome ensured the elimination from British policy of those structural defects that had resulted in the dissolution of previous empires, consisting of alien nationalities mechanically compressed into a superficial unity. The triumph of Washington and his fellow-patriots was an impressive lesson in the rights of self-government which English statesmen have not forgotten, and it was not less instructive for the founders of the Republic. The world had never known what they proposed to establish, an enlightened and popular authority intended to operate on a continental scale. Hitherto republican institutions had existed only in cities and compact provinces such as the Italian municipalities and the Swiss Confederacy; even ancient Rome failed in her efforts to realize the mean between anarchy and despotism. Hence, from the beginning the American experiment was viewed with disfavor by European rulers whose interests were imperiled by its growing success, and with anxiety by publicists who felt a sincere distrust of democracy. That it succeeded is a tribute to the respect for precedent and for law which animated its leaders.

While Britons arose every morning to hear of new victories on land or sea, they took pains to push the business ventures that provided funds for the costly military projects of the government, and left a handsome surplus to their capital account. Financial interests were carefully fostered by Sir Robert Walpole, who was brought to the front rank of politics in 1721 by the panic that followed the collapse of the South Sea Bubble and involved several ministers of State. He had warned the country against the scheme, and it was to him that the English people looked for guidance and recovery when disaster overtook them. Walpole sprang from the country gentry whose vices he shared without their stupidities. He owed his long continuance in office to a variety of causes, but chiefly to his predominance as a man of affairs when men of affairs were few in the House of Commons. More trustworthy than the gifted but treacherous St. John [1] whom he succeeded, Walpole saw what even Stanhope had failed to see: that the masses were not prepared to participate in affairs of government, which, as yet, must be reserved for the upper classes. His dilatory tactics and pacific temperament staved off the wars for which the nation clamored, while he devoted his wise and useful talents to its material prosperity. In no sense a scholar, a courtier, or a wit, Walpole was nevertheless a statesman of firm temper and unfailing good humor; sane, self-contained, and shrewd in practical concerns. These gifts enabled him to impose his will on the Cabinet, and for twenty years he was the virtual head of the State, the first of a series of Prime Ministers who have gradually limited the prerogatives of the Crown and established the party system which obtains in England. Somers and Montague, Harley and Bolingbroke, were foremost members of administrations which had no premier: Walpole, on the other hand, inaugurated the slow and silent change by which the English constitution was transformed from an hereditary monarchy with a parliamentary regulative agency into a parliamentary government with an hereditary regulative agency. He was accused of wholesale bribery and corruption, but a careful scrutiny of his conduct does not altogether sustain the charges nor justify the reproach that has blackened his reputation. His successor, Henry Pelham, employed methods which Walpole disdained to use, and Pelham's brother, the Duke of Newcastle, who succeeded him, had lower standards of public honesty than either of his immediate predecessors. The wars with France virtually ended Newcastle's ministry, and then emerged the elder Pitt, Lord Chatham, whose lofty appeal to the patriotism of his countrymen enthralled England and marked the beginning of a new era in her affairs. With too much dignity of character to care for the emoluments of office,

[1] Elevated to the peerage in 1712 as Viscount Bolingbroke.

Pitt governed by the force of his tremendous personality and his splendid example rather than by political sagacity. His commanding countenance and bearing indicated the born ruler of men. He was filled with ideals and hopes which, though they could not always be realized, stamped him as something apart from the courtiers and placemen by whom he was surrounded. His chronic and abysmal melancholy deepened this impression on those who knew him, and the tragic scene of his last protest against the policy of George the Third convinced the nation that its true greatness had been safest in the keeping of the dying hero who, "wounded sore, 'sank foiled,' but fighting evermore." The career of his son, "the heaven-born minister of State," was made famous by his resistance of Napoleon I and his life-long duel with his great adversary, Charles James Fox. Above all other statesmen of the period in his eloquent and profound exposition of constitutional questions stood Edmund Burke, the illustrious orator whose hatred of the excesses of the French Revolution prompted those "apocalyptic ravings" which, while they deflected his genius from its true objects, added to his renown.[1]

The endless intrigues and controversies of the century were not conducive to the growth of domestic reform, yet they were interpenetrated with larger, better public aspirations for which the efforts of the more enlightened Whigs and Radical partisans were chiefly responsible. But aristocratic interests were then very powerful: borough-mongering was everywhere accepted, ecclesiastical monopolies were abundant, and equal and speedy justice in ordinary matters was

[1] In his *Lectures on Literature*, Schlegel says: "If we are to praise a man in proportion to his usefulness, I am persuaded that no task can be more difficult than that of doing justice to Burke. This man has been to his own country and to all Europe — in a very particular manner to Germany — a new light of political wisdom and experience. He corrected his age when it was at the height of its revolutionary frenzy; and without maintaining any system of philosophy, he seems to have seen farther into the true nature of society and to have more clearly comprehended the effect of religion in connecting individual security with national welfare, than any philosopher or any system of philosophy of any preceding age."

difficult to obtain. The nation's greatest need, however, was not a social readjustment, nor an educational program, so much as a spiritual regeneration. Many perceived and desired this, but the means they employed were wholly inadequate. They had forgotten that man is an emotional being, and appealed solely to his reason, treating any display of feeling as folly, and branding it with the opprobrious name of enthusiasm, a term which moved into an entirely new atmosphere after the Evangelical Revival, passing from contempt to honor. The preaching of Whitefield and the Wesleys, which was mainly directed to the individual heart and conscience, supplied their clamant necessities and gave to numberless Englishmen a vigorous social coherence through a common religious experience. Wesley's contribution was a powerful organization which, when once established, did not always follow the course of its author, but adapted itself to the exigencies of unforeseen circumstances.

Movements in literature corresponded with those of ethics and religion. They sprang into being from a soil not upturned by any violent convulsion, but in which an irrepressible vitality had been secretly at work. From the age of Milton to that of Wesley, Puritanism had been banished from the superficial life of the world. "Yet, Bunyan had dreamt his dream, and visualized forever his imaginings; Addison had reconciled literature with the earnest purposes of human existence; Defoe had grasped the concrete substance of things and breathed truth into fiction." [1] When deism entered the field it infected with its cold and unsympathetic outlook the school of which Alexander Pope was the acknowledged master. The new birth of Puritanism and the resurrection of emotion reacted against this, and concurred in giving rise to the romanticism of Burns and Scott. They demonstrated that the spirit of man demanded emancipation from a one-sided intellectualism,

[1] "The Cambridge History of English Literature"; Vol. X, pp. 1–2.

and Wordsworth afterwards enforced the demand by prompting that return to nature of which Rousseau's writings were so poor an expression. These underlying principles are merely mentioned here, but they should be taken into serious account in any attempt to appraise and interpret the literary output of the century, which began with Pope, but was really fathered by Dryden.

The work of the high priest of pseudo-classicism, thoroughly imbued as it was with the spirit of his art, furnished current speech with many of its quotable phrases. The "Rape of the Lock" has been termed the most brilliant occasional poem in the language, and as a rule Pope's verse reached the height of polished perfection. When its faultless monotony began to weary the ear of a more earnest generation, Robert Burns appeared, and heralded another epoch for humanity in his spontaneous song. He was so completely the greatest of Scottish poets that no other comes into the reckoning. Sir Walter Scott's genius was more eclectic, but in the essential elements and spirit of the ballad Burns is still unsurpassed. He used the narrow cranny of a rustic dialect to pour out a lyric so unaffected, so compassionate, so clear, and so appropriate, that it rejuvenated his nation. Beginning as the bard of his shire, he became the poet of Scotland, and ended as the singer of love, nature, patriotism, friendship, and courage for the English-speaking race. Thomas Gray and William Collins strove to revive the designs of Greece, both in the fullness and maturity of their style: Gray's "Elegy" remains, as Lord Morley has said, "an eternal delight and solace for the hearts of wearied men," and had Collins lived, he might have rivaled Keats. Oliver Goldsmith vocalized the new feeling for man and nature in his "Traveller" (1764) and the "Deserted Village" (1770). The merits of the humble and obscure, the charms of pastoral environment and the blessings of the religious life were expressed in the works of Cowper, which mark the second phase of poetry in the eighteenth century. In 1782, when past his fiftieth year, he gave forth from a life of sad seclusion his first volume, and three years later "The Task and Other Poems" was published. The strong sense, good morals, domestic piety, and love of rural scenery expressed in them revealed possibilities in poetry which many who worshiped Pope had not suspected.

In other branches of literature influential writers sometimes forgot that works to be enduring must be elevated above contemporary standards and interests. The unscrupulous partisan whose reputation was based upon controversial skill paid little regard to the literary conscience, his principal aim being the proving of his case wholly right and that of his antagonist wholly wrong. Philosophers who hesitated because they held more comprehensive and balanced views were far less acceptable to the popular taste than essayists and pamphleteers who settled vexatious questions with dogmatic assurance, and carried their opinions on religion, ethics, or politics to the last extreme. The century was impatient of the twilight zone in these discussions; it welcomed the man who was entirely positive, clear, and unhampered by misgivings. Jacobites and Hanoverians, Whigs and Tories, Romans and Protestants, Churchmen and Dissenters, Jurors and Non-Jurors, Skeptics and Sectaries stoutly contended for their respective orthodoxies, and denounced the rest with an intolerance ignorant of compromise. When Dean Swift's pen was enlisted in support of Harley and Bolingbroke, he at once turned upon his former friends Addison and Steele and abused them with unseemly violence, looking upon his rivals, not as opponents to be defeated, but as enemies to be driven out of public life. His amazing genius found an opening for its display in his pamphlet on "The Conduct of the Allies," which rendered one of England's most popular wars so odious that the people loudly demanded peace on almost any terms. For inventiveness, ridicule, scorn, and hate, no satires have surpassed "Gulliver's Travels" and few if any political authors have wielded these weapons so effectively. In England, Swift turned the current of feeling against the Whigs, and Ireland's capital still reveres his memory. But although some traits of his singular character were praiseworthy, physical disease and moral deformity united to vitiate his imagination, and he acquired that taste for loathsome ideas which defiled the workings of his powerful but gloomy mind. The most dreaded writer of his age, his vindictive passions prevented him from attaining personal success; he began by attacking partisans, he ended with a fearful and depraved assault upon the human race, "letting irony blacken into savage and impious misanthropy," — and the darkness which finally enveloped him was foreshadowed in his later books.

Of fiction it must suffice to say that Richardson, Smollett, Fielding, and Sterne continued the tradition so delightfully begun by Defoe, and mirrored in a large and varied way the life of their times. The periodical essay was the creation of Steele and Addison: "I have brought," said the latter, "philosophy out of closets and libraries, schools and colleges, to dwell in clubs and assemblies." The claim was genuine, and the humanity, refinement, humor, and instruction of the *Tatler* and the *Spectator* were widely appreciated, although they had little effect upon the corruption and depravity of the period. The historians Hume and Robertson were largely influenced by Montesquieu and Voltaire. Notwithstanding that Hume's History was written from a prejudiced standpoint, its philosophic tone and literary quality partly reconcile the reader to its failings as a trustworthy account. His "Treatise on Human Nature" proved to be the original impulse of the Scottish philosophy, and his "Political Discourses," published in 1752, announced the economic principles afterwards formulated into an elaborate system by Adam Smith in his "Inquiry into the Nature and Causes of the Wealth of Nations." Robertson's "History of Charles V," while less distinguished for style than Hume's work, was more careful as to facts. Extended comment on Gibbon's "Decline and Fall of the Roman Empire" is superfluous: the book was suggested to him in 1764 as he wandered among the ruins of the Eternal City; since 1787 it has been one of the few works that all educated men and women have felt obliged to read, and "still remains unique for its supreme and almost epic power of moulding into a lucid array a bewildering multitude of details." Boswell's life of Dr. Johnson, which is perhaps the best biography in the language, portrays with exactitude and life-like detail the most impressive literary character of the century. Johnson's moral dignity and independence of spirit, so intrepidly shown in his fight against poverty and patronage, was a patch of blue in leaden skies, and gave him a monarchical influence over his contemporaries. Always true to himself, he was more afraid of his conscience than of the world's judgment. R. H. Hutton has justly said, "He towers above our generation because he had the courage to be what so few of us are — proudly independent of the opinion in the midst of which he lived." From the society by which he was surrounded, a society false to God and false to man, the observer turns with relief to this paladin of letters, with the tea-slopped vest, fuzzy wig, and shabby coat, who walked with elephantine motions down Fleet Street to his lodging or favorite tavern, muttering to himself and hitting the wayside posts with his cudgel. His unswerving loyalty to duty, which presented itself to him in the form of certain definite principles, was based, not only upon the general practice of the best of mankind, but also upon the Divine Law as laid down in Scripture. His "Lives of the Poets" and the "Dictionary" attest his critical gifts and his industry as a scholar. His table talk, as recorded by the devoted Boswell, covered a host of convictions, prejudices, axioms, and criticisms on men and events, alike expressed in vigorous and unmistakable speech. It has become an inseparable part of literature, and is in itself a memorial of his tremendous and virtuous personality. An evening spent with Johnson and his chosen friends was an introduction to the inner circle of the most gifted and creative men of the English-speaking world: even Wesley succumbed to the attractions of the Literary Club, and paused in his endless labors that he might enjoy a chat with the oracle of the "Cheshire Cheese."

The period may be likened to a low-lying and arid plain from which ever and anon arose towering mountain peaks. Swift, Gibbon, Chatham, Burke, Johnson, and Wesley were great in the largest sense of that overworked term, and below their height was no dearth of first-class talent. Yet the gracious and elevating elements which make Christian society and conversation were lacking, and one has but to compare such a cleric as Swift with the Founder of Methodism to perceive the gulf which separated them. Wesley's life spanned the century; and he was more familiar with the England of his time than any other man in it. Born in the reign of Queen Anne and dying in that of George III, he saw in his old age, and regretted, the separation of the American colonies from the historical development of English-speaking men; and heard the news that the Parisians had guillotined Louis XVI. The first entry made in his Journal was dated October 14, 1735, the last, October 24, 1790; during the interval his country's religious and social phenomena were perhaps as fully recorded there as in any contemporary volume. Written large in its pages is the evidence of the moral and spiritual obtuseness of the people and the apathy of the educated and clerical classes; dead weights of stupidity and indifference with which he had to deal. No explanation of the Evangelical Revival can be complete unless these adverse conditions are taken into account; no just estimate of the greatness of Wesley is possible without an appreciation of the obstacles he surmounted.

The otherwise disastrous days of the Stuarts had witnessed a steadily increasing commercial prosperity, which, although interrupted by the French Wars, speedily revived after the peace of Utrecht in 1713. The value of exports reached their lowest point in 1705, when it fell to about twenty-six million dollars; ten years later it was nearly forty millions. In the course of the eighteenth century extensive changes took place in agriculture, which was for a long time to come the leading industry. Until the reign of the second George, methods of tilling the soil were extremely primitive, more than half the cultivated land being divided and worked on the old open-field system. The credit for effecting an improvement was due to Jethro Hill and to George the First's Secretary of State, Lord Townshend, who also introduced the turnip root into England, thereby earning for himself the nickname of "Turnip Townshend." The increased productiveness of the soil, which was at least fourfold that of Wycliffe's age, aided the growth of population and manufactures. Statistics are scanty and faulty, but it is generally assumed that the population of England at the close of Elizabeth's reign did not exceed two and a half millions. By the time of James II, Macaulay estimated that it had reached five or five and a half millions. In the eighteenth century there was a large increase, and Professor Thorold Rogers concludes that in 1772 England contained about eight million inhabitants.[1] The people enriched the waste land and drained the marshes. The commons were enclosed and cultivated in order to supply the towns with foodstuffs. In this development, however, the yeomanry were sacrificed; men of slender means could not afford to purchase their holdings at the enormously advanced prices, and for the same reason small owners were induced to sell. These classes either moved into the towns and cities, or became tenants and laborers on proprietary estates. The group of intellectuals, with its salons, its life of cultured ease, of epigram, and sententious wisdom, was apparently as unaware of these changes as were the coteries of fashion

[1] "Six Centuries of Work and Wages"; p. 477.

and of politics. At the very moment when England boasted that she had won half the world and controlled the other half, the once contented workers of the countryside were being robbed of their farmsteads, their ancient rights, their economic freedom, and reduced to the most forlorn condition of all British toilers.

Manufacturing enterprises were also revolutionized during this period. Cotton was scarcely known in England before the eighteenth century, and when it appeared legislation was uselessly enacted to prevent its competition with the time-honored trade in woolen goods. But the most marked improvement resulted from the invention of machinery. Newcomen applied steam power to manufactures in 1712, and James Watt constructed his first steam engine in 1765. Kay's flying shuttle, Hargreaves' spinning jenny, Arkwright's spinning frame, Compton's mule-jenny, Cartwright's power loom, and similar inventions gave Britain her preëminence in textile fabrics. The basic industries, however, were coal mining and iron smelting, in which, until the latter half of the nineteenth century, Great Britain enjoyed practically a monopoly.

These important operations, with others which naturally resulted from them, changed the face of the country. Some neighborhoods lost their wild, shaggy appearance, and began to assume the pastoral aspects which are their present charm. Others were disfigured by unsightly banks of shale and refuse from the mines, while the smoking chimneys of factories and mills polluted the atmosphere. Life in such localities was neither so wholesome nor so happy as when it had been spent on the heath and the upland. Cities and trade grew at the expense of flesh and blood; employers were heedless of the physical and moral well-being of their workmen. At the worst the unsanitary cottages of rustic hamlets were surrounded by fields and forests where the peasants could breathe pure air; now they were huddled together without regard for health and decency. The ugly stories of vice and crime already touched upon were sequences of these abuses. As soon as it was discovered that child labor was profitable, the greedy clutch of capital seized the little ones whom parents or guardians surrendered at a tender age to prolonged hours of dreary and dangerous toil. Enervated hordes, ill-fed, ill-clothed, without education or religion, swarmed in municipalities which supplanted the cathedral towns in commercial importance. Edinburgh, Glasgow, Newcastle, Leeds, Bradford, Sheffield, Liverpool, Manchester, and Birmingham became the centers of the nation, and diverted the volume of trade to the northern provinces.

The dense ignorance then prevalent contributed to the evils attendant upon industrialism and the congestion of manufacturing towns. It also prompted one of the educational movements that stand to the credit of Anglicanism. In 1699 Doctor Bray founded the Society for Promoting Christian Knowledge, which in turn established numerous schools, especially in the larger cities. Thirty years later Griffith Jones organized in Wales a staff of schoolmasters who traveled throughout the Principality and taught adults to read the Bible. In 1775 the Kingdom could muster only 1193 schools with 26,920 pupils. The emergency was so grave that in 1782, Robert Raikes established his first Sunday School at Gloucester. The idea did not originate with Raikes: Wesley held Sunday classes for children in Savannah during 1737; Theophilus Lindsey at Catterick in Yorkshire in 1769; Hannah Ball at High Wycombe in the same year; and Jenkin Morgan near Llandiloes in 1770. These schools combined secular with sacred instruction well on into the next century. Such provisions were of course inadequate; there was no national educational policy until many years afterwards, and Wesley's reiterated insistence upon knowledge as well as piety was due to the fact that in addition to folly and vice he was confronted at every turn by illiteracy and superstition.

T

II

The predominant feature of English religious thought in the eighteenth century was its universal acceptance of reason as the criterion of truth. It might be strenuously contended by opposing schools that a given doctrine or miracle was or was not agreeable to reason, but that the issue was to be decided by reason was never questioned by either party to the dispute. The words of Bishop Gibson in his second Pastoral Letter, 1730, indicate the position occupied in common by all theologians of the period: "It is universally acknowledged that revelation itself is to stand or fall by the test of reason." To the same effect wrote Tillotson, Butler, Rogers, Foster, Warburton, and other divines. They were agreed upon and taught the doctrines of Locke, the father of English Rationalism, that "Reason is natural revelation, whereby the eternal Father of light, and fountain of all Knowledge, communicates to mankind that portion of truth which he has laid within the reach of their natural faculties. Revelation is natural reason enlarged by a new set of discoveries communicated by God immediately, which reason vouches the truth of by the testimony and proof it gives that they come from God. So that he that takes away reason to make way for revelation, puts out the light of both; and does much the same as if he would persuade a man to put out his eyes, the better to receive the remote light of an invisible star by a telescope." [1]

This theory, which Dr. Loofs calls "rational supra-naturalism," deduced religious belief from an intellectual process — just the reverse of its actual history. Primarily all dynamic religious belief issues out of religious experience, and the necessity of coördinating that experience with other contents of one's mental world arises later. In other words, religious experience is the raw material of vital

[1] "Essay"; Book IV, ch. 19, sec. 4.

theology: "men spake from God being moved by the Holy Ghost."

The praiseworthy purpose which inspired the attempt of moralists and thinkers to rationalize religion was twofold. First, they sought to check the growing immorality by preserving in dialectical form the principles of ethical and religious conduct. The problem being one of moral depravity rather than of theological heresy, they labored less in the interests of dogma than in those of virtue. Hence their theme was a prudential ethic, cogently enforced by Scriptural warrants of final rewards and punishments. While this rationalized morality of consequences held the field, dogmatic theology died out, except with a few obscure writers, and it was not long before Christianity, as Mark Pattison observes, appeared made for nothing else but to be proved. Reason, first heralded as the basis of faith, gradually became its substitute. The mind was too busy examining and testing the evidences of Christianity to appropriate its life and power. The only quality in Scripture dwelt upon was its credibility. Dr. Johnson denounced the process as "Old Bailey theology," in which "the apostles were being tried once a week for the capital crime of forgery." It would not be just, however, to accept as true this undiscriminating criticism, for the religious thought of the rationalizing age had varying degrees of merit and fell within two distinct periods. In the earlier, the endeavor was to demonstrate the compatibility of Biblical revelation with reason; in the later, which dates from about 1750 onwards and is mainly represented by the schools of Paley and Whately, attention was confined to the genuineness and authenticity of the Scriptures. Neither, of course, was religious instruction in the real meaning of the term, but the former did in a measure concern itself with vital matters of revelation, and by so much it was superior to the later evidential period, which was incessantly grinding out artificial proofs that proved nothing except the unreality of the whole procedure.

A second cause for the rationalizing process was attributable to its conflict with the deists, who, casting aside the fetters of prescriptive rights, positive codes, and scholastic systems, set themselves to follow exclusively the light of nature. Thomas Hobbes, more radical than Sir Francis Bacon, prematurely conceived a universal construction of knowledge, which would include society and man within its verifiable explanations. His daring inquiries were remarkable for what they suggested rather than for what they accomplished, and their influence can be traced in many directions. Midway between Bacon and Locke, and in contact with each only at a single point, Hobbes gave a decided impulse to the ethical speculation which has since been carried on by his countrymen, and his skepticism evoked those intellectual tendencies which weakened authority and established the supremacy of reason.

The inductive method, as taught by Bacon, and adopted by the Royal Society, the senior association for scientific research in the kingdom, gained ascendency over the ablest minds among the clergy. The six folios of Stillingfleet, who died Bishop of Worcester in 1699, mark the transition from the contention with Rome to the declaration of war against Locke. The deistic controversy raged during the first four decades of the century, and then gradually subsided. By the time of Bolingbroke's death in 1751 interest in the question was practically at an end. His executor, Mallet, published his works three years later, but there was very little demand for them. According to Boswell, Johnson voiced the sentiments of well-principled men when he said concerning Bolingbroke, "Sir, he was a scoundrel, and a coward; a scoundrel for charging a blunderbuss against religion and morality; a coward, because he had not resolution to fire it off himself, but left half a crown to a beggarly Scotchman to draw the trigger after his death."

The controversy was by no means the mere empty sound and folly of words which some have supposed; on the contrary, the objections which occasioned it were acutely felt by many who, though not always equal to sustained thinking, were determined not to be imposed upon by unsubstantiated dogma, whatever name it might assume. As the dispute developed, the sufficiency of natural religion became its pivotal issue. The deists contended that the inherent law of right and duty was sufficient, and so absolutely perfect that God Himself could add nothing to it. On the other hand, Anglican doctors maintained that natural religion required to be supplemented by a supernatural revelation, and that neither excluded or was contrary to the other; indeed, both were essential, the former as the foundation, the latter as the superstructure, of the Temple of Truth. Accordingly, with all the ingenuity and erudition at their disposal, they strove to demonstrate the mutual harmony of natural and revealed religion. Christianity was placed on a philosophical basis, and its claims reconciled, ostensibly at any rate, with those affirmations of the rational consciousness that were unanimously accepted. Their theology and philosophy were blended in an effort of the intellect to become liberalized, comprehensive, even latitudinarian. They wrought in the belief that their doctrines could be demonstrated as being not only products of revelation, but also a body of necessary truths, and apparently they were unaware that such generalizations do not seriously affect the majority, who yield to sentiment rather than to reason.

The willingness of the English theologians to listen to the case for deism, and to meet it with the legitimate weapons of argument, stands in favorable contrast to the obscurantist attitude of Bossuet and his fellow ecclesiastics of the French Church, who were implacable against even the shadow of doubt, and strenuously asserted the authority of the Church, as expressed by Councils and Popes in their definitive agreement, in matters of faith and doctrine. The questions which were answered in England received no sufficient reply in France, where attempts made to suppress unbelief served to propagate it, thus dignifying those heterodoxies which culminated in the works of the Encyclopedists. This resort to force instead of argument in dealing with opponents was typical of the methods of the Gallican Church in that age, and resulted in the calamities which have since befallen her.

The Anglican orthodox party had every advantage that talent, learning, and prestige could bestow, while the deists, although they included Lord Herbert of Cherbury, the originator of the sect, Matthew Tindal, William Wollaston, John Toland, the Earl of Shaftesbury, Lord Bolingbroke, Anthony Collins, Thomas Chubb, and Henry Dodwell, presented a marked disparity of resources. Sir Leslie Stephen refers to their volumes as "shabby and shrivelled little octavos, generally anonymous, such as lurk in the corners of dusty shelves, and seem to be the predestined prey of moths." Against them were arrayed Bentley, the foremost critic of the period; Locke, its greatest philosopher; Berkeley and Clarke, keenest of disputants; Waterland, a scholar of wide range; and Butler, distinguished far above the rest by a largeness of outlook and a moral considerateness diffused over all his work — a series of formidable apologists bent on the destruction of deism. For them fought others, who stood without the Establishment, such as Leslie and Law among Non-Jurors, and Lardner, Foster, and Doddridge among Dissenters. They had little difficulty in finding the vulnerable points of their adversaries, for whom the ordinary feeling was "a combination of the odium theologicum with the contempt of the finished scholar for the mere dabbler in letters. . . . They are but a ragged regiment, whose whole ammunition of learning was a trifle when compared with the abundant stores of a single light of orthodoxy; whilst in speculative ability most of them were children by the side of their ablest antagonists. Swift's sweeping assertion, that their literary power would hardly have attracted attention if employed upon any other topic, seems to be generally justified." [1]

Yet such excellence is sometimes its own deterrent, and so it proved in this instance. The people at large were untouched by the discussion; the Church suffered because her altar fires burnt low; placid insistence upon the externals of faith rather than upon its inward reality worked havoc among the clergy, whose activities were directed toward unprofitable and lifeless discourses which expounded a creed divested of all resemblance to New Testament Christianity, except for a tacit acknowledgment of the veracity of the Gospel narratives and a belief in the dogma of the Trinity. The clarity and atmosphere of ascertained conviction were lacking in the sermons they preached, conscious that few believed them, scarcely believing what they said themselves. The vapid rhetoric of Blair was deemed the ideal of homiletic art even by those who posed as arbiters of literary taste and doctrinal correctness. As the dispute became more trivial and meaningless, the ministry suffered a further decline in zeal, influence, and integrity. It was one task, assuredly not unimportant, to cope with the deists' protest against tradition and with their misrepresentations of history; it was another, and not so easy a task, to withstand their criticisms of Chillingworth's position that "the Bible only is the religion of Protestants"; and the most difficult of all, to quicken the religious instincts of the nation, which had been allowed to remain dormant lest they should prove troublesome. For if the deists failed in their leading design to assert the sufficiency of natural religion, and their cult became a reproach even amongst those who were in no wise defenders of orthodoxy, the Anglicans and their allies made the unhappy mistake of occupying only the outworks of faith, while its citadel, which is the personal experience of the power of revealed truth, was de-

[1] Sir Leslie Stephen: "English Thought in the Eighteenth Century"; Vol. I, p. 87.

serted. This poor strategy left them with little more than the creed of their antagonists, abstract and argumentative, and separated from all that was individual, peculiar, and intense. The substance of theology concerns a world largely beyond the sphere accessible to human reason, and when they proposed to treat their inductions as equivalents for Christianity, they overlooked the danger that in the process the latter might be divested of its vital elements.

The outcome has been succinctly summarized as follows: "Upon the whole, the writings of that period are serviceable to us chiefly, as showing what can, and what cannot, be effected by common-sense thinking in theology. . . . If the religious history of the eighteenth century proves anything it is this: That good sense, the best good sense, when it sets to work with the materials of human nature and Scripture to construct a religion, will find its way to an ethical code, irreproachable in its contents, and based on a just estimate and wise observation of the facts of life, ratified by Divine sanctions in the shape of hope and fear. . . . This the eighteenth century did and did well. It has enforced the truths of natural morality with a solidity of argument and variety of proof which they have not received since the Stoical epoch, if then. But there its ability ended. When it came to the supernatural part of Christianity its embarrassment began. It was forced to keep it as much in the background as possible, or to bolster it up by lame and inadequate reasonings. The philosophy of common sense had done its own work; it attempted more only to show, by its failure, that some higher organon was needed for the establishment of supernatural truth." [1]

That common sense, by which is meant the sense men have in common, has its place in theology and in religion, few will deny. But the fatal defect of the Georgian apologists lay in their sole dependence upon it. They were also too much of one kind, men cast in the same mold, who,

[1] Mark Pattison: "Essays"; Vol. II, pp. 84–86.

while representing positive and conservative opinion, were unanimously agreed that emotionalism was useless and harmful. Mediocrity in all else save what they held as practical wisdom was their habit; and their beliefs, while having a similitude of reasonableness, were at heart narrow and ineffectual. The inexorable march of ideas has deprived their thinking of its pertinency, yet its concentration on the moral aspects of faith inadvertently prepared the way for that reaction of the religious emotions against an exclusively intellectual emphasis which made possible the Evangelical Revival.

The gains of their victory over the deists were relatively meager: after the controversy had collapsed, its negative side came to the front, and to such effect that infidelity, and still more indifference, was commonly avowed in polite circles. Christianity was looked upon as merely an amiable superstition, which served as a desirable safeguard of society, and for that reason should be maintained. In the "Advertisement" to his "Analogy" Bishop Butler says: "It is come I know not how, to be taken for granted, by many persons, that Christianity is not so much as a subject of inquiry; but that it is, now at length, discovered to be fictitious. And accordingly they treat it as if nothing remained but to set it up as a principal subject of mirth and ridicule, as it were by way of reprisals for its having so long interrupted the pleasures of the world." And in his charge to the clergy of the diocese of Durham, delivered in 1751, speaking of the general decay of religion in the nation, he declares that the saddest feature of the age "is an avowed scorn of religion in some and a growing disregard of it in the generality." Testimony of a like kind is furnished by works of other writers. Butler's "Three Sermons on Human Nature," while profound and illuminating, themselves reveal the chief defects of the moral philosophy he expounded. Even the "Analogy" confined itself to the provincial issues of the day, being in this respect greatly inferior to Pascal's "Pensées," which was concerned with speculations upon the higher and more universal reason.   But its chief weakness consisted in reducing religion to a Probabilism unable to control human nature in behalf of spiritual development.   Nor could Butler's style do justice to the native force of his metaphysic: "so far from having the pleasures of eloquence, it had not even the comfort of perspicuity."   The absence of any freedom for flight into the upper regions of revelation prompted Tholuck's criticism: "we weary of a long journey on foot, especially through deep sand."   That is it in a word: the theology of the eighteenth century had no wings.

The studied moderation of Butler's argument was adopted by the clergy, and literature likewise felt the detriment of submission to an undue subjectivism.   The marked difference between the poetry of Dryden and that of Pope, or the prose of Swift and that of Addison, was analogous to the contrast between the pulpit orators of the periods they severally represented.   The persistent needs of human nature found no relief in the presentation of an attenuated Gospel powerless to make new conquests, or appease the spiritual hunger of men, or kindle that enthusiasm which was the bugbear of the period.   Not content with separating themselves from the slightest suspicion of this offense, the clergy were equally eager to protect the good name of the apostles from its defilement.   The substitution of an ethical for a spiritual basis of religion ended, as it must always end, in languor and humiliation; for religion is devitalized the moment it is lowered to the position of a mere purveyor of motive to morality.   Accommodated beliefs and articles were reiterated and argued until they became obscure, justifying the satirical remark of Collins, that nobody doubted the existence of Deity until the Boyle lectures had undertaken to prove it.

The seriousness of the problem was aggravated by the general social degeneracy, though this eventually furnished some means for its solution. The seething, festering masses of unleavened humanity had no native aversion to goodness; indeed at bottom they were incurably religious, and when the surfeit of sin began to be felt they craved a purer life. But skepticism had nothing to offer them, and the ministry was little better off: that which it did offer was not bread, and the parochial system throughout England was ossified. The energy of the clergy was further dissipated by internal strife and by quarrels with rival sects, socially obscure but safeguarded in their freedom by the Act of Toleration. Chief among the controversies within the Church were the non-juror schism and the dispute over the doctrine of "divine right."[1] During the reigns of the first two Georges, these causes of dissension, together with the system of political appointments to the episcopacy, seriously impaired the harmony and lowered the doctrinal standards and religious ideals of the Establishment.

Any indictment of the clergy must be qualified by the fact that thousands of livings were without parsonages and their incomes utterly insufficient for the maintenance of the self-respect, let alone the comfort, of the incumbents. Bishop Burnet states in his History that after Queen Anne's Bounty had somewhat mitigated the poverty of the lesser clergy, there were still hundreds of curacies with an income of less than twenty pounds, and thousands with less than fifty pounds. It is not surprising that non-residence became the rule or that Church fabrics fell into decay. On the other hand, it can be charged against bishops and deans that they made fortunes, and used their extensive patronage for private purposes. The gulf between the rich and the poor clerics was broad and deep; indeed, the rich frequently plundered the Church while the poor suffered the consequences. The

---

[1] This doctrine was the one upon which the Anglican Church was agreed and which it emphasized. It owed its origin to the nationalism which prevailed at the Reformation, and was intended to offset the papal claim to supremacy.

chosen few who moved in the upper ranks of society reserved their attention for the affluent, and the dull round of parish duty was left to their subordinates.

Indolent and worldly ministers were found within and without the Establishment, more anxious to be deemed respectable and rational than to become effective servants of the Gospel to their parishioners. Even the zeal of the more excellent was tempered by their indulgence in material pleasures, which Doddridge attempted to justify because of the benefit to trade. Yet care must be taken not to make the condemnation too sweeping. The sacred memories of such shepherds of the flock as Bishop Lancelot Andrewes, the judicious Hooker, George Herbert of Bemerton, Bishop Wilson, Isaac Watts, and Nathaniel Lardner were treasured in rectories and manses throughout the land. It remains true, however, after all extenuations and exceptions, that spiritual as well as material destitution marked the ministry at large. The parson, with frayed cassock and seedy appearance, was too often the lickspittle of the local magnate, content to purchase favor by enduring his insults and obscenities. His education and manners in most instances were no more than might be expected in an age so sordid that it cut off the supplies necessary for trained spiritual overseers. Some of these clergymen lived godly and useful lives, and many others might have done so had they not been reduced to practical vagabondage. Hired to read prayers in the houses of the great at ten shillings a month, or appointed as private chaplain to some noble family where the master treated him as a menial and the servants despised him as a parasite, the cleric without a benefice was jibed at as a "mess-John," a "Levite," and a "trencherman"; placed below the salt at table, compelled to listen with feigned or real enjoyment to many a bibulous jest, and dismissed when the pastries appeared. Sometimes he was married off to a woman of no social standing or even of damaged reputation. Treated thus by patrons and parishioners, how could the unfortunate man be otherwise than craven or cunning, as circumstances seemed to demand? Nor was it entirely to his discredit that he should have sought to mend his fortunes by dubious courses, and assuredly the ecclesiastics who enjoyed the stipends of pluralities were not the men to remonstrate. The bishops appointed by the Hanoverian Court were first considered with regard, not to their fitness, but to their political sympathies. The cautious worldliness which characterized these prelates did not prevent grave scandals. Some were enthroned by proxy; others never visited their sees; distant parts of the dioceses were left without supervision, and in not a few instances without ministrations of any kind. Generally speaking, the clergy were not in any sense deeply religious, and to this fact is primarily due the tradition of shame which clings to the Church of the eighteenth century.

Puritanism had fallen from its high estate long before that period and was in the most abject years of its deterioration. The glories of such patriots, scholars, and saints as Hampden, Pym, Owen, and Baxter had faded, and the hard angularity of mind of the Dissenters prejudiced the nation against them. Their participation in political embroilments, with the subsequent persecutions and deprivations inflicted upon them, had undermined their influence and destroyed the higher aims which once animated Nonconformity. Chapels and conventicles were frequented by adherents who prided themselves on their independency, but whose doctrines had lost their appeal. The pluralist, the controversialist, the man-pleasing, place-hunting prelate, the priest of disgraceful life, and the sectarian minister who moodily ruminated on his social subjection or preached Socinianism, effectually deprived the nation of religious instruction and guidance.

Passion for work, perseverance, self-sacrifice, tranquil fidelity, magnanimity, devotion to the future, were not unknown, but the Nonconformist divine yielded to the conditions described, which also held the parson of the Established Church in bondage, and forced each to obey the conventional rule. The inertia and blindness of both underlay and accentuated the grievous moral situation. National conduct can be reformed in one way only: by the recovery of the consciousness of the Eternal in a renewed sense of those relations between God and man which make the creature truly devout; and any nation which is not in this meaning a Church will not long remain a State. Herein lay the essential infirmity of the English people: they had forgotten God; and, because they had forgotten God, they fearfully forgot themselves. What freedom they had, subserved the riotous pleasures and pursuits upon which the best and wisest among them looked with grave apprehension. The appreciation of the duties and responsibilities of moral beings, and the ambition to domesti‑ cate the virtues and to purify society with the principles of Christianity, had alike vanished. Religion, in its truest significance, as the life of God in the soul of man, the saving element in creeds and sects, the source of evangelizing aggressiveness and of what Mrs. Humphry Ward calls "a sense of social compunction," was little known by the men and women of the eighteenth century. Because of this fatal ignorance the intellectual classes became the prey of infidelity; the clerical, of indifference; the profane, of blasphemy and license; and the masses, of turpitude and lawlessness.

III

This, then, was the nation which confronted Wesley with its almost insuperable tyranny of wrong thinking and wrong doing. Yet such a state could not persist forever among a people whose past had been deeply ingrained with Christian ideas and whose territories were covered with symbols of religious devotion. In his "Vision of Saints," Lewis Morris sees the "apostolic form" of Wesley "blessing our land," and speaks of his having

"Relit the expiring fire, which sloth and sense
And the sad world's unfaith had well-nigh quenched
And left in ashes."

The flame then kindled by the regenerate soul of this master spirit rose high and spread far. But before he began his work other men had prepared the way for it. Reference has been made to the writings of Law and also to the Moravian teachings that led Wesley into Christian life and peace. Prior to these, however, was the establishment in the Anglican Church of religious societies which had an organic connection with earlier German pietism, and anticipated the class meeting which afterwards became the nucleus of Methodism. These associations were founded by Dr. Smithies of St. Giles' Church, Cripplegate, and Dr. Horneck, Lutheran minister at the Savoy Chapel; their principal features being a close connection with the State Church and a pronounced evangelistic tendency. When they declined in usefulness other kindred organizations arose, less restricted in their aims, which in turn gave birth, in 1670, to the Society for the Propagation of the Gospel in Foreign Parts, and, in 1698, to the Society for Promoting Christian Knowledge.

Such signs and tokens were by no means limited to England. In Northampton, Massachusetts, in 1729, the very year the Oxford Methodists formed the Holy Club, a revival which profoundly affected the entire Colony took place under the ministry of Jonathan Edwards, who declared, "The new Jerusalem had begun to come down from heaven, and perhaps never were more prelibations of heaven's glory given." Simultaneously the provinces of Wales felt a similar impulse, where Howel Harris was, to quote Whitefield, "a burning and shining light, a barrier against profanity and immorality, and an indefatigable promoter of the Gospel of Christ." Scotland also experienced an awakening of which the Reverend James Robe of Kilsyth published an account in 1742, telling of its spread to many cities and towns of the northern kingdom. Thus in places so far apart as Germany and New England, and under pastors and evangelists as widely separated in theology and method as Edwards, Harris, and Zinzendorf, thousands of penitents received blessing, and their lives bore witness to the genuineness of the change.

Almost immediately after his conversion Wesley visited the Moravian settlement at Herrnhut, in order that by further conversation with "those holy men he might establish his soul." On his way thither he was received at Marienborn by Count Zinzendorf. It would appear that each was disappointed in the other, and Wesley proceeded on July 19, 1738, to Herrnhut, where he remained for three weeks, attending the services of the Brethren, and conversing with the teachers and elders upon their doctrines and discipline. He conceived a warm affection for them, and especially for that remarkable saint, Christian David, who deserves a more adequate remembrance. An unlettered man, he was twenty years of age before he saw a Bible; yet at twenty-seven he had become a prominent preacher among his countrymen, afterwards establishing the first missions in Greenland, and making excursions into Holland, Denmark, and England. Wesley, scholar and priest as he was, sat at his feet, and wrote to his brother Samuel, "God has given me at length the desire of my heart. I am with a church whose conversation is in heaven; in whom is the mind that was in Christ, and who so walk as He walked. . . . Oh how high and holy a thing Christianity is! and how widely distinct from that — I know not what — which is so called, though it neither purifies the heart, nor renews the life, after the image of our blessed Redeemer!" Yet a hint of his subsequent rejection of some articles of the Moravian teaching was conveyed in the courteous letter of thanks addressed to Zinzendorf and dated from London on September 16, in which he says: "The love and zeal of our brethren in Holland and Germany, particularly at Herrnhut, have stirred up many among us, who will not be comforted till they also partake of the great and precious promises. I hope to see them at least once more, were it only to speak freely on a few things which I did not approve, perhaps because I did not understand them." [1] What those things were can be surmised from the contents of a second letter, which was not dispatched, complaining of their adulation of the Count and of their communion; of their reserve and dissimulation; in brief, of those failings which are more or less incident to a life of subjective piety unrelated to human affairs.

Wesley now rejoined Charles in labors among the social wreckage of the metropolis, preaching as often as possible, and ministering to the prisoners in the jails. The brothers also obtained an interview with Dr. Gibson, the Bishop of London, that they might explain their methods and secure his approval. This prelate, who was highly respected for tact and prudence, failed to appreciate the opportunity he now had to render a lasting service both to the cause of religion and to his Church. The Anglican episcopacy has often shown an ineptitude for wise and courageous action at similar crises, and in this respect compares unfavorably with the more alert hierarchy of Rome. The Wesleys were in no sense aliens or rebels; in fact both were stricter Anglicans than the bishop himself, whose timid low churchmanship appeared in his answer to their question, "Are the Societies conventicles?" "I think not," he replied; "however, you can read the acts and laws as well as I, — I determine nothing," — an unhappy conclusion applicable to himself and his brethren in more senses than one.

Others, though equally helpless, were not so acquiescent

[1] R. Southey: "Life of Wesley"; pp. 104–105.

U

as Gibson. The doughty Warburton, afterwards Bishop of Gloucester, that "knock-kneed giant" of debate who had distinguished himself in the deistic controversy as a bellicose cleric of whom it may be said

> "That twice he routed all his foes
> And twice he slew the slain,"

now fell foul of Methodism. Writing to an acquaintance, he inquired, "Have you heard of our new set of fanatics, called the Methodists? There is one Wesley, who told a friend of mine that he had lived most deliciously last summer in Georgia, sleeping under trees, and feeding on boiled maize sauced with the ashes of oak leaves; and that he will return thither, and then will cast off his English dress, and wear a dried skin, like the savages, the better to ingratiate himself with them. It would be well for virtue and religion if this humor would lay hold generally of our over-heated bigots, and send them to cool themselves in the Indian marshes." [1] This ranting abuse, of which Warburton was more than once guilty, was the keynote of other attacks made upon the Wesleys, and showed that they had little to expect from the clergy except misrepresentation and slander. By the close of the year John was almost uniformly excluded from the pulpits of the Establishment. While the storm of opposition was closing in upon him and his followers he met with his brother Charles, George Whitefield and others of like mind at Fetter Lane to celebrate the last hours of that annus mirabilis of 1738 in solemn acts of prayer, praise, and renewed consecration.

Whitefield, who has already been named as an Oxford student, a member of the Holy Club, and a close friend and admirer of Wesley, was the youngest and at that time the best known of the three men. He was born December 16, 1714, at the Bell Inn, Gloucester, of which his father was then the tenant. His general worth and gift for elocution

[1] L. Tyerman: "Life and Times of John Wesley"; Vol. I, p. 208.

procured him friends who assisted him in obtaining a University education. He was ordained deacon in 1736, and delivered his first sermon in the magnificent Cathedral of his native city. He then began an itinerary through the western provinces of England, and also in London, where he attracted immense audiences; indeed, his name quickly became a household word in Bath, Bristol, and the capital. After his return from Georgia to receive priest's orders and collect money for the orphanage he had founded there, he was included in the marked disapproval the clergy had shown toward the Wesleys, and with characteristic impetuosity he at once commenced field preaching. When the churches of Bristol were closed against him he repaired to Rose Hill, just outside the city, and there faced the grimy pitmen and laborers who were the terror of the locality, subduing them by his dramatic utterance. The entranced listeners quailed beneath his fervid, searching appeals; their deadened sensibilities were so aroused that, as he afterwards described the scene, tears of penitence channeled "white gutters on their blackened cheeks." As the throngs increased, he wrote, — "The open firmament above me, the prospect of adjacent fields with the sight of thousands and thousands, some in coaches, some on horseback, and some in the trees, and at all times affected and drenched in tears together, to which sometimes was added the solemnity of approaching evening, was almost too much for me and quite overcame me." He left Bristol escorted by a guard of honor composed of his converts and friends and with a handsome subscription for a charity school to be established among them; a project eventually carried out by Wesley at Kingswood.

Before the midsummer of 1739 Whitefield repeated his triumphs in London, where his audiences at Hyde Park, Blackheath, Moorfields, and Kennington Common were the sensation of the town. He asserts that eighty thousand persons assembled at one time; although this estimate was probably exaggerated, there can be no doubt that few have addressed larger gatherings for a similar purpose or served them to a better end. The Thames watermen could not ferry over all the people determined to hear him, suburbs and slums were emptied while his sermons were in progress, and their effect was acknowledged by the educated as well as the illiterate. Foremost among his supporters was Lady Huntingdon, regarded by some as the most remarkable woman of her age and country, an aristocrat whose life was "a beautiful course of hallowed labor" and her death "the serene setting of a sun of brilliant hue." Among others of rank who flocked to hear him were the Prince of Wales, the Duke of Cumberland, the Duchess of Ancaster, Lady Townshend, Lady Franklin, Lady Hinchinbroke, Lord Bolingbroke, Lord Chesterfield, Lord Lyttleton, Lord North, Bubb Doddington, George Selwyn, and William Pitt. David Garrick remarked that he would give his whole fortune to be able to pronounce the single word "Mesopotamia" with the pathos and power he had heard Whitefield put into it. Horace Walpole, who had a keen eye for foibles, noted that "Methodism in the metropolis is more fashionable than anything but brag. The women play very deep at both, as deep, it is much suspected, as the matrons of Rome did at the mysteries of Bona Dea." And again, writing to Sir Horace Mann, his lifelong correspondent, he said, "If you ever think of returning to England, you must prepare yourself for Methodism. . . . Lady Frances Shirley has chosen this way of bestowing the dregs of her beauty: Mr. Lyttleton is very near making the same sacrifice of the dregs of all the characters he has worn. The Methodists love your big sinners, as proper subjects to work on, and, indeed, they have a plentiful harvest. Flagrance was never more in fashion, drinking is at the high water mark."

That a young clergyman not yet twenty-six should have compelled the attention Whitefield received from high and lowly was in itself significant. His facial appearance was not altogether prepossessing, but in earlier manhood his well-proportioned figure and superb voice made him, like Danton, the tribune of the open spaces. Exuberant physical energy, sincerity of conviction and earnestness of manner, lent weight even to his unguarded statements. He could denounce the treacheries of sin, describe the doom of the sinner, enforce the remedies of the Gospel, and comfort the sorrows of the penitent with winged and irresistible words. Dr. Doddridge, Dr. Isaac Watts, and others competent to judge objected to his excessive emotionalism; but, although its modification might have avoided some undesirable results, it would have deprived him of his chief element of power as an unrivaled orator. He was neither a philosopher nor a theologian, but, what was more rare than either, an evangelist whose heart had been fired and his lips anointed to proclaim the saving message of the Cross to a moribund generation.

The most profitable outcome of his work was its formative influence upon Wesley, who not only emulated Whitefield's example as a field preacher, but garnered much of the harvest of his sowing. Early in March, 1739, he received a message from Whitefield urgently soliciting his presence and help in Bristol. Fully employed as he was at the time, Wesley was reluctant to leave London, and his brother Charles vehemently opposed his doing this. In their perplexity they reverted to the customary practice of *sortes Biblicæ*, the results of which were not encouraging until Charles, making a last attempt, opened at the words, — "Son of man, behold, I take from thee the desires of thine eyes with a stroke; yet neither shalt thou mourn nor weep, neither shall thy tears run down." Upon this he withdrew his opposition, and John decided to go to Bristol.

This was the turning point in Wesley's public career. He was about to take a step that would separate him from his ecclesiastical superiors and brethren, and cost him the confidence and affection of the Church of his birth and training, nor is it likely that he was sustained by any pre-vision of the outcome which waited upon his temerity. Preaching on unconsecrated ground, to say nothing of addressing promiscuous gatherings which were never more secularized in feeling than at that time, was considered by even the best of Anglicans a disorderly act, a disturbance of the peace of Church and State. Reluctant to the last, on hearing Whitefield preach in the open air, Wesley com-mented, "I could scarcely reconcile myself at first to this strange way of which he set me an example on Sunday; having been all my life till very lately so tenacious of every point relating to decency and order, that I should have thought the saving of souls almost a sin if it had not been done in a church." Notwithstanding, on April 2, 1739, a date next in importance to that of his conversion, he "sub-mitted to be more vile," and standing on a grassy mound addressed a great crowd from the words, "The Spirit of the Lord is upon me, because He hath anointed me to preach the Gospel to the poor." The appropriateness of the text to the events which had brought him to that place and hour was only equaled by its prophetic character. He deliberately rejected the earthly prizes of his calling that he might proclaim the religion of the New Testament to men and women who were looked upon by the more refined as hopeless barbarians. Yet no Christian statesman could have issued a better justification for this extraordinary pro-cedure than is contained in the opening paragraphs of his "Earnest Appeal to Men of Faith and Religion." After comparing the formal and lifeless professions then prevalent with the renewing energy the Methodists had experienced, he showed how he and his friends had stumbled in the gloom of past days, having none to guide them into "the straight way to the religion of love, even by faith." "By this faith," he continued, "we are saved from all uneasi-ness of mind, from the anguish of a wounded spirit, from discontent, from fear and sorrow of heart, and from that inexpressible listlessness and weariness, both of the world and ourselves, which we had so helplessly labored under for many years, especially when we were out of the hurry of the world and sunk into calm reflection. In this we find that love of God and of all mankind which we had elsewhere sought in vain. This, we know and feel, and therefore cannot but declare, saves every one that partakes of it both from sin and misery, from every unhappy and every unloved temper." [1]

This manifesto, so lucid, emphatic, and unanswerable by those who accepted Christianity at all, is quoted as a first-rate specimen of the statements which exposed Wesley to the censure of Anglican dignitaries and of the learned and the worldly. The ecclesiastical authorities were provoked against Methodism because it violated their rule and rebuked their failure; the devotees of fashion and culture because it disturbed their complacency and pride. Neither had any desire to leave their protected shores and venture after Wesley into the agitated deeps of undisciplined human life. They were repelled by the noise and confusion of its emotional outbreaks and were too punctiliously correct to be anything more than nominally religious. Whitefield was patronized by some among them who endured his opinions for the pleasure of listening to his oratory, but Wesley's putting of the same truths aroused their indignant remonstrance. Yet his "Appeal" and his sermons were in substance the accepted doctrines of their own Church, and better still, a fair presentation of the teaching and spirit of the New Testament. In them he showed himself a master of the proper sentiment and the fitting word. Without straining after grandiloquence, in language the chief notes of which were sincerity, simplicity, and restraint, with every appearance of unstudied utterance, he discovered the secrets of many hearts and applied to them the blessings of pardon and

[1] John Telford: "The Life of John Wesley"; pp. 112–113.

restoration. Old fustian and purple patches were not tolerated, yet the phrase that uplifts, the feeling that is most intense when most repressed, the intellectual rather than the clamorous accent, enabled him to make the deepest impression of any preacher of his age. His speech combined abundance with economy, the little with the much. Its form was concise, its meaning infinite, its character luminous.

There were more accomplished thinkers and rhetoricians than Wesley, but as an advocate of religion and an organizer of its forces he was unsurpassed. The level reaches and tranquil flow of his discourse were sometimes stirred by a divine afflatus of which his hearers afterwards spoke with bated breath; the pillars of the sanctuary seemed to tremble, the Eternal One Himself bowed the heavens and came down, while all the people stood in awe of Him, and the souls of the worshipers were shaken by the winds of God. John Nelson, a well-poised Yorkshireman, has left a forceful description of Wesley which amplifies the difference between him and Whitefield in that respect. "Whitefield was to me as a man who could play well on an instrument, for his preaching was pleasant to me and I loved the man . . . but I did not understand him. I was like a wandering bird cast out of its nest till Mr. John Wesley came to preach his first sermon at Moorfields. . . . As soon as he got upon the stand, he stroked back his hair and turned his face towards where I stood, and, I thought, fixed his eyes upon me. His countenance fixed such an awful dread upon me, before I heard him speak, that it made my heart beat like the pendulum of a clock; and when he did speak, I thought his whole discourse was aimed at me. When he had done, I said, 'This man can tell me the secrets of my heart; he hath not left me there; for he hath showed the remedy, even the blood of Jesus,' . . . I durst not look up, for I imagined all the people were looking at me. Before Mr. Wesley concluded his sermon he cried out, 'Let the wicked man forsake his way, and the unrighteous man his thoughts; and let him return unto the Lord, and He will have mercy upon him; and to our God, for He will abundantly pardon.' I said if that be true, I will turn to God to-day.''

Although Wesley was short of stature and slight of build, his personal appearance was benign and commanding. His carriage was erect and graceful, and in that time of wigs he wore his own hair long, parted in the middle, and falling upon his shoulders with a slight curl. Austerity and benevolence were harmoniously blended in his bearing; his voice, which he carefully modulated, was melodious and penetrating; his movements agile and dignified. The slightly feminine cast of his clean shaven face and robed figure was balanced by the masculine strength of his profile, with its Roman nose and firm mouth. In the gallery of beautiful and impressive faces of renowned men, such as those of Shakespeare, Milton, Goethe, and the youthful Burns, a place has been rightly given to that of Wesley, who resembled Milton more than any other great Englishman, not only in physical appearance but to some extent in spiritual complexion. Richard Watson Gilder in his Ode to Wesley, exclaims:

"In those clear, piercing, piteous eyes behold
The very soul that over England flamed!"

They retained to the last the searching expression which Nelson had noted, and numerous contemporaries spoke of the glance, swift to encourage, steadfast to control, before which the dainty exquisite Beau Nash and the mobs of the Midland shires alike shrank.

Whitefield's energies were divided long before he died, and Charles Wesley's itinerant preaching, which began with promise, practically ended after his marriage, but John continued his beneficent journeyings to the end of life. In them he kept to the centers of industrial population, leaving the remoter regions to be afterwards evangelized by his helpers. London, Bristol, and Newcastle were the points of an isosceles triangle which included the principal areas of his mission. Not a moment of the long day was lost; he rose at four, frequently preached at five, and then rode, or in his older years drove, over wretched roads to his appointments. Nothing was allowed to disturb the schedule, the intervals of which, when he tarried at an inn or at the home of a friend, were occupied in reading or in making notes, in writing tracts and pamphlets and in conducting an interminable correspondence. Duty wisely and scrupulously carried out according to a fixed program never had a more faithful disciple. His love of orderliness, a good index of the mind, was seen not only in the neatness of his dress but in every particular of his life. Wherever he might be, he was satisfied, absorbed, detached, free from vexation of spirit, and able to pursue his meditations, whether among the wild hills of Wales or tossing on the Irish Sea, or in the bleak and inhospitable fastnesses of the Cornish coast. He crossed St. George's Channel nearly fifty times, and traveled 250,000 miles on land — this when there were no turnpikes in the north of England, and the London stage coaches did not run beyond York. In June, 1750, he was nearly twenty hours in the saddle and covered ninety miles in one day; in 1778 he speaks of having made 280 miles in 48 hours, and in the winter weather of Scotland he rode an equal distance in six days. His northern route in February, 1745, was one of the severest he ever undertook. Gateshead Fell was covered with snow, no roads were visible; wind, hail, and sleet, accompanied by intense cold, made the country one sheet of impassable ice. The horses fell down and had to be led by Wesley and his companions, who were guided by a Newcastle man into the town. The following winter he was crusted from head to foot by a blizzard as he struggled on from Birmingham to Stafford. In 1747 the drifts almost swallowed him upon Stamford Heath. In his eighty-third year he was as fearlessly energetic as ever. While travelling in the "Delectable Duchy" he came to Hayle, on his way to preach at St. Ives. The sands between the towns were covered with a rising tide, and a sea captain begged the old hero to wait until it had receded. But he had to be at St. Ives by a given time, and he called to his coachman, "Take the sea! take the sea!" At first the horses waded; ere long they were swimming, and the man on the box feared that all would be drowned. Wesley put his head out of the carriage window to encourage him — "What is your name, driver?" he inquired. "Peter, sir," was the reply. "Peter, fear not; thou shalt not sink," exclaimed the patriarch. When they reached St. Ives, after attending to Peter's comfort, he went into the pulpit, drenched as he was, and preached. The philosophical coolness and brevity with which he recorded these and similar adventures show that he regarded them as merely incidental to that cause he had assigned as the sole purpose of his existence, and to which he consecrated all his gifts. He delivered forty-two thousand sermons in fifty years, an average of over fifteen a week. He was beyond seventy when thirty thousand people gathered to hear him in the natural amphitheater at Gwennap Pit, Cornwall. Ten years later he wrote, "I have entered the eighty-third year of my age. I am a wonder to myself, I am never tired, either with preaching, writing, or travelling." By no preconcerted scheme, nor under the impulse of the moment, but calmly, deliberately, and with the love that endures to the end, Wesley became the most devoted, laborious, and successful evangelist the Christian Church has known since Apostolic days.

He had read with amazement of the physical contortions and convulsions during the New England Revival, little dreaming that his renewed ministry would produce such phenomena. He had no more than begun it, however, when at a service in Baldwin Street Meeting House, Bristol, he could scarcely be heard for the groanings and wailings of stricken penitents. In the audience sat a Friend who was annoyed by what appeared to him unseemly pretense, till he himself was carried away by the same resistless feeling, for the time being losing all self-possession, and declaring on his recovery, "Now I know that thou art a prophet of the Lord." Although the greater number of these seizures occurred in small crowded rooms, there were instances of persons affected in like manner in their homes. John Haydon, by profession an Anglican, and a man of good standing, who had hitherto regarded such outbreaks as of the devil, while seated in his own house, reading a sermon on "Salvation by Faith," suddenly fell writhing to the floor. Wesley, who was in the vicinity, hastened to Haydon's relief. "Aye," cried the smitten one on his recovery, "this is he who I said was a deceiver of the people; but God has overtaken me. I said it was all a delusion; but this is no delusion." These ebullitions were in the main as unsought by Wesley as they were surprising to him, nor did the whole series amount to more than a passing incident. His Journal and letters mention only about sixty cases, an insignificant number when the thousands of his converts are recalled; a few were extremely painful and prolonged, the rest comparatively mild and brief.

His explanation of them was derived from the dreams, trances, and visions of Biblical report. But he added that after a time natural depravity polluted the work of grace, which Satan cunningly imitated in order to defeat its ends; so that, while the hand of Deity was undoubtedly present in these mysterious events, Satan's was no less evident — "a singular coöperation," as Sir Leslie Stephen observes, "between God and the devil." Many subjects of these manifestations, however, proved by their after life the reality of a gratifying change of heart coincident with the seizures. Later simulations, some of which were quickly detected and silenced, modified Wesley's belief in their value. In a letter to his brother Samuel, who was alarmed by the wild rumors which spread abroad concerning John's preaching, he protested that his work should not be judged by outward signs, whatever might be their cause, but by its true element; that quickening spirit, a greater wonder than any other recorded, which remade society, and brought into the Kingdom of God men and women whose iniquity had been notorious. He urged that such regenerated souls were living arguments which could not be successfully disputed.

The psychological aspects of the question merit a fuller treatment than can be given here. It seems strange that this loss of self-control should have first occurred under Wesley, who could not, in the usual sense of the term, be called an emotional preacher. The explanation is probably to be found in his very restraint. While Whitefield, with his torrential eloquence, and Charles Wesley, by his impassioned appeal, deeply stirred the heart, their own tears and ecstasies suggested to their hearers these more normal avenues for the expression of excited feelings. On the other hand, the steady beat of Wesley's plain, measured discourse, expounding hitherto unfamiliar doctrines which searched the consciences of a benighted people as with the candle of the Lord, was enforced by a solemnity of manner and a peculiar yet repressed intensity overwhelming in their influence. Unlike his brother or Whitefield, he discouraged by his outward composure the facile discharge of agitations which he nevertheless aroused in far higher degree than either of them. Hence the only outlet for the volcanic emotions he kindled in the miners of Kingswood and Newcastle was in that sympathetic nervous action which those emotions induced.[1]

The hostility of official Anglicanism towards his mission, which, as we have seen, showed itself from the beginning, was naturally inflamed by these irregularities; and it increased with the rapid growth of the movement. There

[1] For a discussion of this subject see Professor Frederick M. Davenport's volume, "Primitive Traits in Religious Revivals."

was not sufficient expansiveness in a State Church governed by rule and rote to admit, much less assimilate, the extraneous practices of the Wesleys and Whitefield. Macaulay speculates that the Papacy would have absorbed the enthusiasm and adopted the new organization for the benefit of the Holy See. "At Rome the Countess of Huntingdon would have been given a place in the calendar as St. Selina, . . . Elizabeth Fry would have been the first Superior of the Blessed Order of Sisters of the Jails. John Wesley would have become General of a new society devoted to the honor and interests of the Church." Without by any means indorsing another oft-quoted passage, in which Cardinal Newman laments the callous perversity of the Establishment, it was at least more applicable to Wesley than to any other Anglican since the Reformation: "Oh, my mother! whence is it unto thee that thou hast good things poured upon thee and canst not keep them, and bearest children yet darest not own them? . . . How is it that whatever is generous in purpose and tender and deep in devotion, thy flower and thy promise falls from thy bosom and finds no hope within thy arms?" The Church which too often tolerated laxity and idleness promptly stigmatized Wesley's effort to remedy these evils as a breach of ecclesiastical discipline. It could see the occasional extravagances and mistakes of Methodism, but was blind to its religious value. Thus, when Wesley solicited the countenance of Butler, then Bishop of Bristol, even he, the bright particular star of the episcopacy, replied: "Sir, since you ask my advice, I will give it freely — you have no business here; you are not commissioned to preach in this diocese. Therefore I advise you to go hence." Wesley had but one defense: he was a churchman no less than his lordship, with no desire to disturb the order which had been habitual to both, yet, when that order sought to check the influx of spiritual life which he had every reason to believe was divinely bestowed, he was constrained to take his own course. He openly avowed: "God, in Scripture, commands me, according to my power, to instruct the ignorant, reform the wicked, confirm the virtuous. Man forbids me to do this in another's parish; that is, in effect not to do it at all, seeing I have no parish of my own, nor probably ever shall. Whom then shall I hear? God or man? I look upon all the world as my parish; thus far I mean, that, in whatever part of it I am, I judge it meet, right and my bounden duty to declare unto all that are willing to hear, the glad tidings of salvation." [1]

Bishop Gibson, whose interview with the Wesleys is mentioned earlier in this chapter, showed in his later references a more pronounced antagonism to their mission, classing them with "Deists and Papists," and condemning their respective errors as "greatly prejudicial to religion and dangerous to the souls of men." An anonymous tract ascribed to him, and which at least received his approval, vigorously berated Whitefield for violating Church discipline; the Wesleys for having had the effrontery "to preach in the fields and other open places, and by public advertisements to invite the rabble to be their hearers"; and the Methodists in general for daring to remain in the Anglican communion. Gibson returned to his arraignment, describing them as "enemies of the Church who give shameful disturbance to the parochial clergy, and use every unwarrantable method to prejudice their people against them and to seduce their flocks from them." Wesley kept silent as long as silence seemed wise, but, notwithstanding his esteem for the episcopal office and for Gibson personally, he now felt that the bishop had exceeded all bounds, and he published a chastening rejoinder, which, apart from its specific aim, deserves mention. The asseveration that the bishop was "an angel of the Church of Christ, one of the stars in God's right hand, calling together all the subordinate pastors, for whom he is to give an account to God, and directing them in

[1] L. Tyerman: "Life and Times of John Wesley"; Vol. I, p. 235.

the name of the great Shepherd of the sheep, the First Begotten from the dead" — is one of the noblest passages Wesley ever penned. His dignified rebuke was accompanied by an argument which dwelt upon the breakdown of the parochial system, and vindicated Methodism as a source of supply for the religious needs of the people. He concluded with a solemn warning which reversed their positions, leaving the aged diocesan the accused and himself the accuser: "My lord, the time is short; I am past the noon of life, and my remaining days flee away as a shadow. Your lordship is old and full of days. It cannot, therefore, be long before we shall both drop this house of earth, and stand naked before God; no, nor before we shall see the great white throne coming down from heaven and He that sitteth thereon. . . . Will you then rejoice in your success? The Lord God grant it may not be said in that hour, 'These have perished in their iniquity: but their blood I require at thy hands.'"

The next episcopal assailant, George Lavington, Bishop of Exeter, was incomparably inferior to Butler and also to Gibson. Following the usual line of Englishmen of the day, who at once assigned any beliefs or actions they did not understand to the malignant machinations of Rome, he published in 1749 an anonymous pamphlet entitled, "The Enthusiasm of Methodists and Papists compared." This precious production, which was nothing better than a continent of mud, was issued in two parts, the last being worse than the first. His attack sank to its lowest depth of vileness when Lavington pretended to argue that the Eleusinian mysteries, with their gross physical symbolism, were "a strange system of heathen Methodism." Wesley could well have afforded to ignore such scurrility; but the natural man in him prevailed, and he met Lavington with a naked blade, exposing his garbled quotations, limping logic, and bad grammar, and ending by indignantly challenging him to come out from his hiding place and drop his mask. This unusual burst of righteous indignation did not prevent him from having later and friendly intercourse with Lavington. They met in the autumn of 1762, and partook of the Lord's Supper together. The bishop died a few weeks later, and his epitaph in Exeter Cathedral eulogizes him as an overseer "who never ceased to improve his talents nor to employ them to the noblest purposes; . . . a Man, a Christian, and a Prelate, prepared, by habitual meditation, to resign life without regret, to meet death without terror." It would be difficult to identify from this description the unscrupulous controversialist whose prevarications and invectives earned the contempt of right-minded men. Ten years after the Lavington episode Warburton reappeared, and led the van of mitred brethren and college dons against these detestable renegades who menaced the peace of the community. Originally intended for the law, Warburton had drifted into divinity, carrying with him those pugnacious tendencies and arrogancies which were hit off in the phrase, "There is but one God, and Warburton is His Attorney-General." Yet, overbearing, reckless, and abusive as he was, he did not hide under anonymity, and the vigor and honesty of his attacks made him a formidable opponent. The last and the most honorable of anti-Methodist bishops was Dr. George Horne, President of Magdalen College, afterwards appointed to the see of Norwich. He entered the debate when its virulence had subsided, and in any case his amiable and refined disposition made it impossible for him to proceed to the extremes of the earlier disputants. While sincerely believing that Methodism led to Antinomian practices, he was amenable to correction, and thirty years later, on Wesley's asking for the use of a church in Norwich, Horne assured the incumbent that there was no reason to refuse the request.

So far nothing had occurred to separate Methodism from the parent Church; Wesley still regarded his Societies and helpers as existing solely for the purposes of religious

x

culture, and despite the strained relations they, like their Founder, were loyal members of the Establishment. The Nonconformists had their own ministry and ordinances, but Wesley was careful to avoid instituting either, or in any way needlessly offending the susceptibilities of the clergy. He used different names for his organizations, and insisted that they should meet at other than the stated times for Anglican services. Further, his followers were urged to attend their respective parish churches and to communicate there. Unfortunately, in many instances they were rudely treated, and given to understand that they were ingrates and rebels. As they increased in numbers, this deprivation was deeply felt, and the Wesleys were glad to avail themselves of the offer of Mr. Deleznot, a Huguenot pastor, to lend them his sanctuary in Hermitage Street, Wapping, for the administration of the Lord's Supper. A thousand members from the Foundery partook of the Eucharist there; and Charles Wesley was forced to administer it to the Kingswood Society in their school building, declaring, stout cleric though he was, that, if no other place had been accessible, he would have communicated in the open.

In the last decades of Wesley's life a marked reaction was perceptible among the clergy themselves, many of whom found matter for reflection in the marvelous changes for the better which his work had wrought. An attitude of tolerance found its way into their common habits by a process of pacific penetration. Evangelical sentiments began to leaven the Anglican fold, and some who could not adopt Wesley's methods nevertheless yielded to his teaching. This doubtless contributed to his prolonged but impracticable attempt to maintain the fiction of union between Anglicanism and Methodism, in which there could be little meaning so long as the two communions were dissimilar in spirit and practice, and the clergy strove to unchurch the converts who, as they supposed, outraged ecclesiastical procedure. The growing impossibility of such a relation at last dawned on his reluctant mind. He was not less percep- tive than others, though in this instance less willing to admit the distressing but palpable fact of which he wrote three years before his death, "A kind of separation has already taken place and will inevitably spread, through slow de- grees." He also addressed a remonstrance to one of the bishops, and said, "The Methodists in general, my lord, are members of the Church of England. They hold all her doctrines, attend her service, and partake of her sacraments. They do not willingly do harm to any one, but do what good they can to all. To encourage each other herein, they fre- quently spend an hour together in prayer and mutual exhor- tation. Permit me then to ask, *Cui bono?* for what rea- sonable end would your lordship drive these people out of the Church? Are they not as quiet, as inoffensive, nay, as pious, as any of their neighbors? Except perhaps here and there a hairbrained man, who knows not what he is about. Do you ask, 'Who drives them out of the Church?' Your lordship does; and that in the most cruel manner. . . . They desire a license to worship God after their own con- science. Your lordship refuses it; and then punishes them for not having a license. So your lordship leaves them only this alternative, 'Leave the Church or starve.'" [1]

Of all ideas toleration, while so much less than equality, would seem to be the very last in the general mind. When the fervid pioneers of Methodist principles struck directly at the wickedness of their day, they could not long escape the resentment and then the violence of the mob, incited by ignorance and drink, and sometimes by the clergy or their agents. Lawless outbreaks occurred in the Midlands, the North, Cornwall, and Ireland. The local parsons and mag- istrates frequently abetted the persecution, and dealt harshly with its victims. These administrators of petty justice were infuriated by the vehement exhortations which burst upon their neighborhoods, oppressed as they were by

[1] L. Tyerman: "Life and Times of John Wesley"; Vol. III, p. 613.

wrong and sodden in poverty and vice. They looked upon the evangelists as enemies of the peace, or as Jesuits in disguise. Hate and calumny, superstition and bigotry, found vent in many places, and nowhere more than at Wednesbury in Staffordshire, a town which has long since atoned for its outrageous treatment of Wesley by its loyalty to him and to his Church. During the summer and autumn of 1743 houses and shops were plundered and gutted, their contents destroyed, and the occupants maltreated, the members of the Society being in hourly jeopardy. Wesley writes, "I received a full account of the terrible riots. . . . I was not surprised at all; neither should I have wondered if, after the advice they had so often received from the pulpit as well as from the episcopal chair, the zealous high churchmen had rose and cut all that were Methodists in pieces." [1]   The situation, created by the unwise conduct of the preacher in charge, aggravated by the angry protestations of Mr. Egginton, the local clergyman, and by the vicious propensities of the miners and iron workers, who were even worse than those of Kingswood or the keelmen of Newcastle, compelled a suspension of Methodist services for some weeks, and finally required the personal attention of Wesley himself. He rode into the town on October 20, and preached at noon in the open air. Three hours later a turbulent crew appeared before the house where he was staying, and demanded that he should come forth. After some parleying, he accompanied them to the magistrate, who, being in bed, refused to see them, and whose son advised the ringleaders that they should release their captive and quietly disperse. Instead, they trudged on to Walsall, an adjacent town, where another magistrate also declined to interfere. The mob had scarcely left the place before a second and more dangerous one appeared, led by the doughty prize fighter, "honest Munchin," and

---

[1] "Journal of John Wesley"; edited by Rev. Nehemiah Curnock; Vol. III, p. 79.

swept all before it. Wesley was now at the mercy of this contingent, and for a time his life was in grave peril. These "fierce Ephesian beasts," as his brother Charles termed them, cried "Kill him!" and some even attempted to brain him with their cudgels. But his tranquil demeanor subdued those nearest to him, and the rest reluctantly fell back while he passed through their midst and returned to Wednesbury, escorted by a body guard recruited from their own ranks. The next morning, as he rode through the town, he was saluted with such cordial affection that he could scarcely believe what he had seen and heard. Charles, who met him at Nottingham, bruised, tattered, and torn, said that he looked like a soldier of Christ fresh from the fray.

Others were not so fortunate. Thomas Walsh was imprisoned at Brandon, and took his revenge by preaching through the barred windows of his cell to the crowd outside. Alexander Mather's house was pulled about his ears in Wolverhampton, and at Boston in Lincolnshire he was left for dead. At York, John Nelson was beaten into unconsciousness, and afterwards forced to enlist in the army. Thomas Olivers was pursued at Yarmouth, and barely escaped with his life. The list of these veterans of the Cross could be extended indefinitely. From 1742 to 1750 hardly a month elapsed without references in Wesley's Journal to similar scenes. At Penfield a baited bull was let loose on the congregation; and at Plymouth and Bolton howling fanatics, dancing with rage such as had never been seen before in creatures called men, hunted the preacher like a pack of wolves. There is nowhere a hint that any of these humble helpers retreated before such outrages: indeed they showed the same fortitude and courage which were characteristic of the Wesleys. Some, like Thomas Walsh, died while still young; others lived to see the harvests that, in the abundance of their reaping, redeemed the tears and blood in which they had been sown. The meanest peasants rose above the sorrow and confusion of the time, and took a part in the molding of the destinies of the nation. Mob leaders became class leaders, and directed their prowess toward spiritual ends. The pugilist who was foremost in the Wednesbury riot afterwards joined the Society there, and made a good confession of his faith. The services of the growing Church were conducted by lay preachers and itinerants who had once purposed to destroy it, but now gladly yielded obedience to the leader whose genius compacted them into a healthy and harmonious organization.

CHAPTER VIII

CONSOLIDATION AND EXPANSION

THE epoch ends, the world is still,
The age has talk'd and work'd its fill —
The famous orators have shone,
The famous poets sung and gone,
The famous men of war have fought,
The famous speculators thought,
The famous players, sculptors, wrought,
The famous painters fill'd their wall,
The famous critics judged it all.
The combatants are parted now —
Uphung the spear, unbent the bow,
The puissant crown'd, the weak laid low.
And in the after silence sweet,
Now strifes are hush'd, our ear doth meet,
Ascending pure, the bell-like fame
Of this or that down-trodden name,
Delicate spirits, push'd away
In the hot press of the noon-day.
And o'er the plain, where the dead age
Did its now silent warfare wage —
O'er that wide plain, now wrapt in gloom,
Where many a splendor finds its tomb,
Many spent fames and fallen mights —
The one or two immortal lights
Rise slowly up into the sky
To shine there everlastingly,
Like stars over the bounding hill.
The epoch ends, the world is still.

MATTHEW ARNOLD: *Bacchanalia; or the New Age.*

CHAPTER VIII

CONSOLIDATION AND EXPANSION

Wesley's withdrawal from Fetter Lane — The Foundery — Controversy with Whitefield — Sermon on Free Grace and Predestination — Continuance of Calvinistic controversy — Toplady — Thomas and Rowland Hill — Wesley's clerical supporters — Fletcher and Grimshaw — Lay Preachers — Their sufferings — Wesley's care for them — The Class Meeting and other Methodist institutions — First Methodist Conference — Wesley's theological position — Methodism in North America — Philip Embury and Barbara Heck — Bishop Asbury — Bishop Coke — Wesley and Coke's ordination — Deed of Declaration — Death of Charles Wesley — Last Days of John Wesley.

I

BEFORE Methodism was solidified and shaped to his purpose, Wesley had to encounter internal as well as external strife. Nor is this to be wondered at, in view of its recent origin, the dissimilar views of its supporters, and the enthusiasm, not always salutary, of its converts. The Fetter Lane Society, founded on the advice of Peter Böhler, and composed chiefly of Moravians, showed, as early as 1739, the inherent differences which separated German and Anglican types of religious life. For a time Wesley calmed the contentious spirits, but the exuberance of his followers was repugnant to the passivity of the Moravian group, whose leader, Philip Molther, advised the discontinuance of reading the Scriptures, of prayer, and of good works. He urged that expectant believers, undisturbed by such employments, might passively await the assured fulfillment of the promises of the Gospel. Once established in this manner, they were at liberty to observe or neglect the ordinances, as they saw fit. Wesley continued to act as peace-maker, endeavoring by seasonable means to correct an attitude which would have killed his enterprise. But the outcome was such as might have been expected, and he and Charles were at last convinced that any further attempt at union between Moravianism and Methodism would be a surrender of the ideals of both for the sake of a temporary truce. On July 16, 1740, the Society resolved that John should not be allowed to preach there again. On the following Lord's Day evening he arose in his place and read a brief explanation of his position, which among other things contravened the Moravian teaching concerning ordinances. After this he and a few sympathizers withdrew.

They repaired to the Foundery, where their associates gladly received them into a union which became the first distinctive Methodist Society, itself the unit of the future Church. The outcome of these internecine troubles was decidedly helpful to Wesley's efforts, which now had a free course. The Foundery remained his headquarters until 1778, when City Road Chapel was erected. As the name indicates, it was formerly a government ordnance factory which, after being wrecked by an explosion, lay in ruins until purchased by Wesley. Here he established his depot for religious literature; the edifice was consecrated by the presence of his venerable mother, who spent her last days within its precincts, and died there on July 23, 1742. The building stood in Windmill Street, near Finsbury Square, and has long since disappeared; the present Wesleyan Methodist Book Room and City Road Chapel are contiguous to its site, and continue its sacred traditions.

Although his intercourse with the Moravians was now at an end, Wesley always realized his extensive obligation to such men as Peter Böhler and Christian David. The separation was dictated by his conviction that he had gone almost too far for safety in the direction of their mysticism; when this was remedied, he recalled them with gratitude, and his later references to them were kindly and respectful. Nor was his caution unjustified: had he not halted and realigned his forces, he would have forfeited to an artificial peace the responsibilities and results of half a century's war upon sin in all its forms, secret or open. "Stand still!" was their exhortation. "Necessity is laid upon me; I must go forward," was the substance of his reply.

Far more important in its scope and results was the doctrinal dispute between Whitefield and Wesley. In this case the dogma of predestination was the cause of dissension,— that Gordian knot which no theologian nor philosopher can untie; the insoluble problem of Divine Sovereignty and the freedom of human will as bearing on mortal destiny. We have observed that during his preparation for the ministry Wesley had revolted against the extreme interpretation of the Anglican article which treats on the question, and that his mother agreed with him. His view was, that while Omniscience necessarily foreknew men's future state, that state was entirely determined by their own act of personal acceptance or rejection of the Gospel. In 1740, he published his sermon on "Free Grace," preached in the previous summer. It was the utterance of one who saw only a few great principles, but expounded them with clarity and earnestness. The Calvinistic theory of election was summed up as follows: "By virtue of an eternal, unchangeable, irresistible decree of God, one part of mankind are infallibly saved, and the rest infallibly damned; it being impossible that any of the former should be damned, or that any of the latter should be saved. To say that Christ does not intend to save all sinners is to represent Him as a gross deceiver of the people, as mocking His hapless creatures, as pretending the love which He had not. He in whose mouth was no guile, you make full of deceit, void of common sincerity. Such blasphemy as this one would think might make the ear of a Christian to tingle. So does this doctrine represent the most holy God as worse than the devil, as both more false, more cruel, and more unjust."

Miss Wedgwood speaks of the "provoking glibness" of the discourse, and of Wesley's incapacity for perceiving difficulties "which is the characteristic of an early stage of culture." He certainly did not meet the argument that, if the design of Christ is to save all and the result is He only saves some, His work is to that extent a failure. Nor can the horrors of the lost be extenuated by relieving the Almighty of responsibility for their doom. Man's free will is a transparent mockery if, too weak to stand alone, he is placed amidst temptations which inevitably seduce the masses of mankind and consign them to eternal reprobation. Neither reason nor revelation, wisely interpreted, entirely supports the eschatology of the Arminian or that of the Calvinist. They do not warrant the notion of eternity as a perpetual prolongation of time: it is rather one of the attributes of Him Who is incomprehensible, and theologians invade His Being when they thus attempt to measure or announce His judgments. Out of this invasion have arisen certain repulsive conceptions of the penalties of perdition for which there is often but a slight basis of truth. Yet Wesley's chastisement of Calvinism was an effective effort to modify the awful dogma which left nothing to human choice, and to soften the pitilessness of a theology which protected its logic at the expense of every instinct of justice. Notwithstanding Peter Böhler's crude assertion that "all the damned souls would hereafter be brought out of hell," for "how can all be universally redeemed if all are not finally saved," Wesley heartily accepted the orthodox teachings concerning human depravity and everlasting punishment for wilful transgression of the divine law and conscious rejection of the divine mercy. He knew nothing of the modern temper, deeply felt by Protestantism, which assigns rights to man as well as to Deity, conceiving of all divine-human relations from an ethical rather than from an arbitrary standpoint. One of the postulates of contemporary theology is that punishment must be remedial if it is to be just, and must terminate if it is not to be futile. Nor does he seem to have considered the impermanence of evil, as St. John reveals it: a more or less mundane phenomenon which passes away, in contrast to the essential reality of good, which alone abides. He did not hesitate to proclaim the terrors of the Law, although they were not the staple of his preaching. And it must be remembered that a more balanced opinion would have been of little avail for the majority of his audiences, to whom moderation on such an issue might have appeared as a decision for, rather than against, their open wickedness. It is a hard saying but a true one, and not without support in a more enlightened age, that many individuals are only moved by three or four circumscribed fears: those of hunger; of force; of law; or of the dread hereafter. And many who heard Wesley's denunciations with guilty and trembling hearts frequently proved that if the fear of God is the beginning of wisdom, the love of God is its end.

Whitefield, on the other hand, had always leaned towards the doctrinal position originally derived from Genevan sources. Hard and consistent thinking was alien to his nature, and his expositions of Calvinism, the most consistent of systems, were fragmentary and disjointed. He was content in this matter to submit to one of the greatest minds that ever combined power in thought with equal power in speech and action. Jonathan Edwards, the foremost intellect America can boast, was primarily a philosopher rather than a theologian, whose excessive speculations marred his religious thinking, and who used them to bring into painful prominence those severe dogmas of the Puritan theocracy, the reaction against which was found in earlier Unitarianism and later in the transcendentalism of Emerson. Under different circumstances this recluse of New England and Princeton might have developed a metaphysical system comparable for its intellectual influence with that of Hume or Kant; as it was, he derived his chief inspiration from a nearly obsolete theology which, but for the impetus he supplied its flagging energies, would probably not have known the renaissance it enjoyed. A survey of his narrower range shows how steadfastly credal formulæ persist, even after reason and truth seem to have uprooted them. Yet, if prophets have a right to be unreasonable, Edwards was thus privileged, for he grasped the essentials on which real morality depends, though, while expanding the doctrine of the absolute Sovereignty of God on lines necessary to that end, he carefully refrained from dealing likewise with others not so necessary to his main purpose. Even in such superior natures as his the windows of the mind are all too limited for an ample prospect of things pertaining to other worlds than this. And it must not be forgotten that whatever else he did or left undone Edwards knew how to awaken the best feelings and impulses of men, to stimulate their faith, and to kindle and keep alive the religious zeal of the commonwealth. His writings are full of spiritual subtleties and great verities, tinged with the melancholy of a lofty spirit who was much misunderstood.

Whitefield's admirers were frequently more fervent than helpful, and their unqualified homage gave him no hint of any of his defects. Sir James Stephen speaks of him as "leaping over a state of pupilage" to become "at once a teacher and a dogmatist." His convictions upon Calvinistic doctrines must have been strong, or he would not for a moment have sacrificed for them his friendship with Wesley. But election and reprobation as expressed by him were not the scandalous Theism which their worst forms presented. Their presence can rather be detected under such sweet and exultant phrases as the "sovereign," "electing," "distinguishing" love of the Eternal Father, whose "irresistible call" had brought him out of darkness into the light of "the chosen"; "a mere earthen vessel," meriting naught but wrath, but filled with undeserved mercies. This was the language of the impassioned orator, who felt the presence of his audience, but did not comprehend the basic phases of Calvinistic teaching.

In New England these prevailed for a period sufficiently extended to reveal their lamentable consequences. Chiefly because of the sheer fatalism which separated the elect from the non-elect, the clergy opposed the religious education of the young, and proscribed missionary activities. In the Northern States slavery was regarded as a regrettable necessity; below Mason and Dixon's line it was accepted as a Scriptural provision, by which Whitefield, among numerous other clergymen, felt free to profit. The mechanical and lifeless rationalism of this theory, as held by disciples who had neither Edwards' genius nor his devotion, created endless disputings, and drove many people into sects of religious liberalism. Some of these supplanted the impossible and irresponsible egoism which had hitherto been postulated as the determinant of Divine action, with the ideal of God as the Universal Father, and of all men as essentially and permanently related to Him. Others, in their rebound from a relentless system, went much further, and formed that rationalizing caste which has been an influential factor in American Unitarianism. Such, then, were the beliefs which Whitefield proposed to incorporate into Methodism, and had Wesley not anticipated the protests of Bushnell and Beecher, the evolution of evangelical Christianity might have followed very different lines.

Writing from London on June 25, 1739, to Wesley at Bristol, Whitefield refers with alarm to his colleague's intention to print a sermon on predestination. "It shocks me to think of it; what will be the consequences but controversy? If people ask me my opinion, what shall I do? I have a critical part to act, God enable me to behave aright! Silence on both sides will be best. It is noised abroad already, that there is a division between you and me; oh, my heart within me is grieved!" When a copy of Wesley's sermon on "Free Grace" was sent to Whitefield at Savannah, he entered into a lengthy correspondence with the author, which, at first affectionate enough, grew less conciliatory as it proceeded. He prepared a formal answer to the sermon "in the spirit of candid friendship"; but the friendship was not so obvious as the candor. Charles Wesley, to whom he submitted it before publication, advised its withdrawal. Nevertheless it was published, and Whitefield notified John that hereafter he was resolved to preach against him and his brother wherever he went. Wesley remonstrated with him on the unwisdom of such a course, and criticized the pamphlet for its random rhetoric and flippancy. In March, 1741, he wrote: "Mr. Whitefield, being returned to England, entirely separated from Mr. Wesley and his friends, because they did not hold the decrees. Here was the first breach, which warm men persuaded Mr. Whitefield to make merely for a difference of opinion. Those who believed universal redemption had no desire to separate; but those who held particular redemption would not hear of any accommodation, being determined to have no fellowship with men that were in such dangerous errors. So there were now two sorts of Methodists: those for particular and those for general redemption."[1] Happily, however, personal rancor subsided; Howel Harris interposed to reconcile them, and Whitefield made a handsome apology for the allusions in his pamphlet to Wesley's habit of casting lots. On April 23, 1742, they spent "an agreeable hour" together, concerning which Wesley made the self-complacent comment, "I believe he is sincere in all he says concerning his earnest desire of joining hand in hand with all that love the Lord Jesus Christ. But if (as some would persuade me) he is not, the loss is all on his own side. I am just as I am. I go on my way, whether he goes with me or stays behind."[2]

[1] "Wesley's Works"; Vol. VIII, p. 335.
[2] "Journal of Rev. John Wesley"; edited by Rev. Nehemiah Curnock; Vol. III, p. 4.

A less dubious note was struck toward the close of 1755, when Wesley declared: "Disputings are now no more; we love one another, and join hand in hand to promote the cause of our common Master." [1]

But the ties which prevented an irreparable breach between them did not bind their followers, and after White-field's death the controversy broke out again in uproar-ious fashion. The London Conference in 1770 sent forth a counterblast against Antinomianism, which rebuked this deduction from Calvinism for its ethical rather than for its theological errors. Lady Huntingdon, with some of the ministers who inherited the work and opinions of White-field, took umbrage at this, the more so because Methodism was drifting away from the Anglican Church. Her desire that it should remain within the Establishment, and her impatience with Wesley's Arminianism, assumed such violent forms that she vowed she would go to the flames in pro-test against the "infamous Minutes" of the Conference. Whatever may have been her ladyship's cravings for martyr-dom, she was apparently more willing to inflict punishment on others than suffer it herself. Neither she nor her partisans had arrived at the state of intellectual freedom in which, while holding to one's own conclusions, it is possible to believe that others who think differently may be right, or, at any rate, equally honest. Accordingly, she summarily dismissed the learned and able Joseph Benson from his tutorship at Trevecca College, and even the saintly Fletcher was so harassed that he could not remain there. Wesley's magis-terial expostulations with the Countess had no effect: she was just as accustomed as he was to having her own way, and "Pope John" and "Pope Joan" joined issue. The Honorable and Reverend Walter Shirley entered the lists in aid of his titled relative, and sent out a circular letter declaiming against the action of the Conference. Their

---

[1] "Journal of Rev. John Wesley"; edited by Rev. Nehemiah Curnock; Vol. IV, p. 140.

attack ended in a fiasco, the Countess suffered the unusual experience of a decided reverse, and Shirley felt obliged to apologize for his unseemly language.

His strictures evoked the defense of Arminianism by John Fletcher and Thomas Olivers, while Augustus Toplady, Sir Thomas Hill, and his better known brother Rowland became their antagonists. The honors of the acrimonious discussion were with Fletcher, whose "Checks to Antinomianism" were more admirable for their Christian temper than for their philosophical grasp of the difficult problems about which others wrangled while he at least reasoned. Toplady's contributions are best passed over in charitable silence, in view of the fact that he was the author of one of the noblest hymns in the language. The then youthful Rowland Hill's talent was perverted to abusive epithets and studied insolence: Wesley, according to this son of a landowning Shropshire family, was "the lying apostle of the Foundery"; "a designing wolf"; "a dealer in stolen wares"; "as unprincipled as a rook and as silly as a jackdaw," "first pilfering his neighbors' plumage, and then going forth displaying his borrowed tail to the eyes of a laughing world." Such ramping recalled Lavington's escapade, and, like it, had no bearing on the question. Wesley replied to Hill in his pamphlet entitled, "Some Remarks on Mr. Hill's Review of all the Doctrines taught by Mr. John Wesley," in which he also "drew the sword and threw away the scabbard." "I now look back," said he, "on a train of incidents that have occurred for many months last past, and adore a wise and gracious Providence, ordering all things well! When the circular letter was first dispersed throughout Great Britain and Ireland, I did not conceive the immense good which God was about to bring out of that evil. But no sooner did Mr. Fletcher's first Letters appear than the scene began to open; and the design of Providence opened more and more, when Mr. Shirley's Narrative and Mr. Hill's Letters, constrained him to write his Second and

Third Checks to Antinomianism. It was then indisputably clear, that neither my brother nor I had borne a sufficient testimony to the truth. . . . I will no more desire any Arminian, so called, to remain only on the defensive. Rather, chase the fiend, reprobation, to his own hell, and every doctrine connected with it. Let none pity or spare one limb of either speculative or practical Antinomianism, or of any doctrine that naturally tends thereto; only remembering that, however we are treated by men, who have a dispensation from the vulgar rules of justice and mercy, we are not to fight them at their own weapons, to return railing for railing. Those who plead the cause of the God of love are to imitate Him they serve; and, however provoked, to use no other weapons than those of truth and love, of Scripture and reason." [1]

This outspoken document scarcely exemplified the charity it advised, but it eliminated Calvinism from Methodist theology. After the purification and the later secession of some fanatical advocates of perfectionism, Wesley found himself at the head of a homogeneous and aggressive body, delivered from doctrinal uncertainty, and animated by unshaken confidence in its mission.

II

While his independence of the world helped him to know it as no worldling can, and to guard his infant cause against its foes, he was not without the steadfast sympathy and friendship of a group of Anglican clergymen, some of whom stood by him to the last. The first of these was Vincent Perronet, Vicar of Shoreham, Kent, a man of whom it may be said, in Jowett's phrase, that for him things sacred and profane lay near together but yet were never confused. Although seldom in the public eye, he counseled the counselors, and few things of importance were undertaken by

[1] L. Tyerman: "Life and Times of John Wesley"; Vol. III, p. 144.

the Wesleys without his approval. Another was William Grimshaw, vicar of Haworth, a moorland town in the heart of the West Riding of Yorkshire, since associated with the famous daughters of his successor, the Reverend Patrick Bronté. Grimshaw was an eccentric but frank, fearless, and companionable man, large in nature as in stature, and a warm advocate of Methodism so long as it remained within the Established Church. Another was John Berridge, of Everton, in the Midlands, a useful and widely known colleague, whom Wesley loved to visit. But the extravagant conduct of Berridge and the prostrations and ravings of his converts were excesses Wesley found it difficult to explain.

The ripest, most apt and perfect saint of Anglican Methodism was Fletcher of Madeley, a naturalized Swiss of patrician descent, whose holiness of character impressed even Voltaire, and is still an inspiration and a power. His memory is encircled by an ethereal luster which has given him a unique place in the annals of his own Church and in those of Methodism. Many devout men and women of all persuasions have derived their best ideals and conceptions of evangelical Christianity from his personal example. Disregarding his parent's intention that he should enter the ministry, Fletcher, like many of his countrymen, sought employment as a soldier of fortune, and being frustrated in this attempt, repaired to England, where he secured a position as tutor in the family of Mr. Thomas Hill of Tern Hall, Shropshire.[1] While residing with his patron in London, he became an earnest Christian, and at once showed that capacity for the religious life in which he has had few equals. An ardent love for New Testament truth and inward purity possessed him. He was set apart to the pastorate in his twenty-eighth year, and during the first months after his ordination ministered at Atcham Church, an ancient structure of Norman foundation, standing near one of the loveliest

[1] Now called Attingham Hall and the seat of the Berwicks.

windings of the Severn River. In this rural paradise, surrounded by a landscape full of unmarketable beauties of glade and hedgerow, where, beyond the skirting woods of Attingham and Haughmond, the spires of Shrewsbury pierce the horizon and the gray walls of the former Cistercian Abbey of Buildwas are seen in the adjacent valley, Fletcher entered upon the work of his life. Two livings were offered him, one of comparative ease, the other, at Madeley, an industrial parish seven miles distant, small in stipend and overflowing with vice and iniquity. He chose the latter, and there began that ministry which could not be confined to any locality. At first wantonly opposed, at last tenderly loved, in a then obscure village Fletcher led a life crowded with these alternations, but crowned in the sequel by the unbounded reverence of his parishioners and many others who held him well-nigh infallible in the higher matters that pertain to the spirit. His unadorned story, like that of St. Francis, whom he resembled in sanctity, is as fascinating as any romance of medieval religion.

His frail body could not adequately sustain the intensity of his meek but unquenchable soul, and when, at length, it gave way, he spent his last Lord's Day in the sanctuary at the altar of the Holy Communion, and was carried thence to his death-bed amid the blessings of his people. His wife, Mary Bosanquet Fletcher, survived him many years, and was herself counted among the saints of Methodism. Wesley, who had chosen Fletcher as his successor, mourned his decease, and testified of him: "Many exemplary men have I known, holy in heart and life, within fourscore years; but one equal to him I have not known, one so inwardly and outwardly devoted to God. So unblamable a character, in every respect, I have not found either in Europe or America; and I scarce expect to find such another on this side of eternity." [1]

Other assistance came, however, and Wesley soon

[1] L. Tyerman: "Life and Times of John Wesley"; Vol. III, p. 464.

obtained an active corps of workers. In the first days of the movement, preaching was confined to ministers of episcopal ordination, but its spread in wider areas where the Anglican pastors were unfriendly led to developments which eventually separated Methodism from the older Church. On occasions when no such clergyman was present to address the congregations, lay helpers had ventured to do so. Of these were Joseph Humphreys, John Cennick, and Thomas Maxfield. As early as 1738, Humphreys had assisted Wesley at Fetter Lane, and after 1740 the other two were identified with the more distinct Methodism at the Foundery. By the end of that year the Wesleys were isolated: Whitefield was in America; Gambold and Brigham had joined the Moravians; and Anglicans generally had washed their hands of the enterprise. Under these circumstances the forerunners of the itinerant preachers appeared. Cennick was a man of some culture, the Master of Kingswood School, who celebrated his conversion in several well-known hymns, among which are those beginning

> "Children of the Heavenly King"

and

> "Thou dear Redeemer, dying Lamb."

Requested to reprove him for expounding the Scriptures to a congregation disappointed of its minister, on the contrary Wesley so encouraged him that he gave his spare time to preaching and exposition in the neighborhood of Bristol. Yet when Wesley received word there that Thomas Maxfield had also "turned preacher," and in the London Society at that, he was greatly disquieted. One surmises that his dismay was due to the relative importance of the Foundery and to the difference between Cennick and Maxfield, rather than to Maxfield's presumption. A man of unstable disposition, the latter had been converted under Wesley's preaching at Bristol on May 20, 1739, and became the servant and companion of his brother Charles. John now hurried to London, determined to silence him, but there he received an unexpected caution from his mother: "You know what my sentiments have been," said Mrs. Wesley. "You cannot suspect me of favoring anything of this kind, but take care what you do with respect to that young man, for he is as surely called to preach as you are." He yielded to her advice to hear Maxfield for himself, and, after doing so, the matter ended with his hearty sanction. Within a year there were twenty recognized lay preachers in the various Societies, an innovation which again annoyed the clergy of the Establishment. "I know your brother well," remarked Dr. Robinson, Archbishop of Armagh, to Charles Wesley. "I could never credit all I heard respecting him and you; but one thing in your conduct I could never account for — your employing laymen." "My lord," rejoined Charles, "the fault is yours and your brethren's." "How so?" asked the Archbishop. "Because you hold your peace, and the stones cry out," answered Charles. "But I am told," urged his Grace, "that they are unlearned men." "Some are," said Charles, adding with a flash, "and so the dumb ass rebukes the prophet," whereupon the Archbishop asked no further questions.[1]

The truth that laws and institutions are not made, but grow out of necessity, was illustrated by this emergence from the neglected people of their spiritual guides and teachers. Those who were chosen for such offices carried the Gospel into places where Wesley, ubiquitous as he was, could never have penetrated. Their advent into his evangelizing scheme delivered it from the contingencies which might have arisen at his death; the work ceased to hang on the thread of a single existence, and the confident prophecies of its opponents that the movement would soon perish were doomed to remain unfulfilled. Within twelve years eighty-five helpers had already entered the service, of whom six had died, ten had retired, one had been expelled,

[1] L. Tyerman: "Life and Times of John Wesley"; Vol. I, p. 277.

.and sixty-eight were in active employment. At the Leeds Conference in 1755 rules regulating their conduct were formulated and published by Wesley. They were expected to be always earnestly alive to their duty, patterns of self-denial; to drink only water, to rise at four, to fast on Fridays, to visit from house to house, to insist on a definite religious experience in the members, and to make a quarterly report of their labors. No one else could have required such self-effacement with any hope of obtaining it from men characteristically independent. He did not make these demands, however, in the spirit of mere supremacy, but because he was satisfied that they were absolutely essential to the welfare of his workers and the success of their work. On their part, the preachers were content to submit to ordinances which the ruler himself was the first to obey. When he was criticized for investing himself with arbitrary power, he answered artlessly, "If by arbitrary power you mean a power which I exercise singly, without any colleagues therein, this is certainly true, but I see no hurt in it." There was little, because his love for these obscure laborers was that of a father for his children, and theirs for him was blended with a reverent awe. Once his prejudices were overcome, none rejoiced in their presence and progress more than did Wesley. He knew them intimately, read their respective traits with a discerning eye, watched over their temporal and spiritual wants, was patient with their misunderstandings, mourned over their defections, which were few, and covered the pages of his Journal with accounts of their struggles and triumphs. The hardships of their lot were such as even he had not known, save for a brief period. They were subjected to inhuman treatment long after their leader, by general consent, had obtained exemption from the penalties the world is wont to inflict on prophets of the truth. Relentlessly pursued by their enemies, denounced, ridiculed, caricatured, threatened, maltreated; penniless and a-hungered, sometimes sick unto death; and all for no other reason than their exercise of the liberty to testify concerning the Gospel; yet as a rule they were found faithful to the end. A word of praise from Wesley's lips was as eagerly prized as is the cross for valor by the soldier on the battle-field. The testimony of a conscience void of offense and the bliss of a regenerated life were at once the secret of their heroical character and the burden of their message.

Doubtless there were violations of good taste, prudence, and sobriety of judgment, but, when the origin, training and environment of the first itinerants are considered, these mistakes appear relatively slight. It is apparent that they not only met a national religious emergency, but that on the whole they were the best equipped men to meet it. The gulf which separated the lettered cleric from the artisan and the peasant was unknown to them. After the manner of those of the New Testament these democratic disciples consorted with the multitude, and captured many strongholds of sin which had withstood the parochial clergy. They introduced to homes ravaged by vice and crime the thrift and industry, the domestic piety and rectitude of conduct which form the hearth where the soul of a country is nurtured and protected. Wesley's estimate of them was judicious: "In the one thing which they profess to know they are not ignorant men. I trust there is not one of them who is not able to go through such an examination in substantial, practical, experimental divinity as few of our candidates for holy orders even in the University (I speak it with sorrow and shame and in tender love), are able to do." He had his full share of the scholar's hate of ignorance; none knew better the advantages of an educated ministry, and he was at great pains in aiding his helpers to gain knowledge. "Your talent in preaching does not increase," he wrote to one of these. "It is lively, but not deep. There is little variety; there is no compass of thought. Reading only can supply this, with daily meditation and daily prayer.

. . . Whether you like it or not, read and pray daily. It is for your life! There is no other way; else you will be a trifler all your days and a pretty, superficial preacher. Do justice to your own soul; give it time and means to grow; do not starve yourself any longer." He lectured to them on "Pearson on the Creed," "Aldrich's Logic," and similar works; discussed their difficulties, instructed them in the art of correct thinking and speaking, and arranged the course of their studies. His "Notes on the New Testament," taken from Bengel, and the "Rules for Action and Utterance" were written primarily for them, and his "Christian Library," an abridgment of some fifty well-known works, while meant for a larger public, was also intended for his helpers. Whatever came from his pen was eagerly read by them in order that they might become a more efficient fighting unit under his generalship. The time was not ripe for constitutional Methodism: indeed a division of its government at this stage would have been equivalent to placing an army confronting the enemy under a committee of half-trained officers. It was necessary that the preachers should cultivate a talent for administration before they could safely be intrusted with its powers. This was a wise policy, preserving the integrity of the movement from the undesirable elements which a few zealots were eager to introduce. Although an autocrat, Wesley was generally careful to ascertain as far as possible the wishes of his preachers. No Protestant clergyman ever exercised a more fascinating influence over his brethren. The charm was personal, whether diffused through his conversation, his correspondence, or his kindly acts. His preachers, old and young, were free to offer suggestions, which he readily adopted if they commended themselves to his judgment; and Henry Moore, who took advantage of this privilege more frequently than did his brethren, was relished for his freedom of speech. When a younger minister's frank expression of opinion provoked the blunt and militant

Thomas Rankin to chide him for impertinence, Wesley at once interposed in his defense, and added, "I will thank the youngest man among you to tell me of any fault you see in me; in so doing, I shall consider him my best friend." This was his usual bearing in a singular position not easily understood in this day of distributed ecclesiastical authority. While he lived, his absolutism was tempered and adjusted by his paternal conduct; after he died, not even the Conference, in its collective wisdom, could exercise it as he had done without encountering resistance and material loss.

The fact that one great soul made his ideas and convictions the sources of spiritual vitality for generations of men and women is impressive. Wesley's Christian nature, endowed with an intellectual energy unrivaled in its attraction for the plain folk, made him the figure of his century which brightens on the historic canvas while other figures fade. The bishops and statesmen whom he could not persuade nor prompt, who would not hearken to his counsel and despised his reproof, wax dimmer and dimmer, while he looms larger and more influential. But this would have been impossible had he not extended his work through the helpers whom he brought to the rescue of a degraded populace and controlled and directed with singular firmness united with equally remarkable tact. Thus it was not only his renovated forms of theological faith or his unique individuality coinciding with opportunity or necessity, but the fertility of his organizing genius and, most of all, the devotion of his preachers, that accounted for the spread of Methodism.

Some of his subordinates were designated "half itinerants," such as John Haime, William Shent, William Roberts, Charles Perronet, John Furz, Jonathan Jones, Jonathan Maskew, James Roquet, John Fisher, Matthew Lowes, John Brown, and Enoch Williams; others, "chief local preachers," such as Joseph Jones, Thomas Maxfield, Thomas Westall, Francis Walker, Joseph Tucker, William Tucker, James Morris, Eleazer Webster, John Bakewell, Alexander

Mather, Thomas Colbeck, Titus Knight, John Slocomb, and Michael Calender. Southey, in reviewing these lists, describes the appearance of John Haime, the soldier evangelist, dwelling on his mean and common features, his small, inexpressive eyes, scanty eyebrows and short, broad, vulgar nose, "in a face of ordinary proportions which seemed to mark out a subject who would have been content to travel a jog-trot along the high-road of mortality, and have looked for no greater delight than that of smoking and boozing in the chimney corner. And yet," adds Southey, "John Haime passed his whole life in a continued spiritual ague." [1]   True, Haime had his disordered humors, and he was troubled about many things. But his case showed that when religion reaches and uplifts the lowest in the human scale illimitable are the hopes it inspires of what humanity may be permitted to attain. On May 11, 1745, he stood in the stricken ranks at Fontenoy and was among the last to retreat. When the army camped in Flanders, Haime, although he had never seen Wesley, preached his doctrines to his comrades, and led them to the Cross. They went into action singing Methodist hymns, and died on the field praising God for His salvation. John Downes, who left sixpence as his total fortune, and was forced to relinquish preaching because of ill-health, was a mathematician and a mechanical expert, and best of all, a godly and an honorable man. Thomas Walsh, one of the Irish converts of 1749, in some respects the foremost member of the pioneer band, was distinguished not only for his fervid piety, but also for his learning. Wesley regarded him as the best Biblical scholar he had ever known. His proficiency in Hebrew and Greek was such that he read these languages as easily as he did his native Erse, and could tell how often and where a given word occurred in the original Scriptures. "The life of Thomas Walsh," said Southey, "might almost convince even a Catholic that saints are to be found in other communions

[1] "Life of Wesley"; pp. 292-298.

as well as in the Church of Rome. . . . His soul seemed absorbed in God; and from the serenity and something resembling splendour which appeared on his countenance and in all his gestures afterwards, it might easily be discovered what he had been about." [1] He was widely accepted among his own people, to whom he became an ambassador of Christ Jesus for nine years before he died at the early age of twenty-eight.

Among the six preachers admitted at the Limerick Conference of August, 1752, the first held in Ireland, was Philip Guier, Master of the German school at Ballingran. Of the seven thousand Germans who in 1709 had been driven by persecution from the Palatinate of the Rhine to England, three thousand were sent to America, and the majority of the remainder settled in or around Limerick, where Guier taught Embury his letters and instructed Thomas Walsh in the faith. The leader of Methodism at Limerick until his death in 1778, Guier tended the little flock so assiduously that a hundred years later his name was still a hailing sign of the people for the itinerants. John Jane certainly earned a place in the roll of self-sacrificing devotees. Unable to purchase a horse, he undertook his journeys on foot, and Wesley once met him at Holyhead without food or means, but in capital spirits after a long tramp from Bristol, during which he had spent seven nights on the road and managed to exist with only three shillings to his account. Weakened by privations and exposures, he died a few months later, sixteen pence and his clothes being his total estate — "enough," said Wesley, "for any unmarried preacher of the Gospel to leave his executors." The list of these worthies could be enlarged indefinitely, and even so late as the early Victorian period, the Primitive Methodist exhorters and preachers were subjected to similar hardships.

Southey's criticism that as a rule Wesley's men "possessed no other qualifications than a good stock of animal spirits

[1] "Life of Wesley"; pp. 381–388.

334 THREE RELIGIOUS LEADERS OF OXFORD

and a ready flow of words, a talent which of all others is
least connected with sound intellect," would make them the
merest accident in a tremendous moral conflict of which they
were actually the center. On the contrary, their preaching
served to emphasize the fact that the tongue is eloquent in
its own language and the heart in its own religion. That
religion was sheltered in their deepest consciousness, and
for it they wrought and suffered greatly, finding in its ideals
the true life of the spirit and an inspiration to disinterested
action.

III

Wesley's success as an organizer was further due to his
resourcefulness in adopting or modifying methods and plans
already existing as well as those he formulated himself.
Neither the name nor the idea of the Societies originated
with him, and he refers to his own use of them as follows:
"The first rise of Methodism was in November, 1729, when
four of us met together at Oxford; the second was at
Savannah in April, 1736, when twenty or thirty persons
met at my house; the last was at London, when forty or
fifty of us agreed to meet together every Wednesday evening,
in order to free conversation, begun and ended with singing
and prayer." [1] The Society in Aldersgate Street, where
he was converted, was held under Anglican auspices previously to Molther's appearance, and so was that at Fetter
Lane. Three years after the exodus to the Foundery,
distinctively Methodist organizations had spread from
London to Bristol, Kingswood, Newcastle-on-Tyne, and
were soon multiplied throughout the kingdom. A book of
rules for their guidance, which was issued at Newcastle in
1743, and signed by the Wesleys, contained their definition
of a Society as "a company of men having the form and
seeking the power of godliness, united in order to pray

[1] Ecclesiastical History, IV, p. 175, quoted by Canon J. H. Overton:
"John Wesley"; p. 121.

together, to receive the word of exhortation, and to watch over one another in love, that they may help each other to work out their own salvation." They naturally desired fellowship, and in providing for it Wesley reverted to the practice of the Apostolic Church, where he found the authorization of those measures without which his congregations would have been impaired if not destroyed. The institution most typical of Methodism was the class meeting, which began at Bristol in 1742. In order to raise funds for the extinction of the debt upon the Horse Fair Chapel, one Captain Fry proposed that every member should give a penny a week. The objection was made that some were too poor to afford this modest sum, whereupon Fry volunteered to underwrite the contributions of eleven such members, and suggested that others should do likewise. His advice was taken, the entire Society was divided into groups of twelve, the responsible member being called the leader, and the rest his class. In this way originated the fiscal system which has since been employed for the support of the ministry, and also that communion of saints which has had no superior.

The watch night service, which was akin to the *vigilæ* of the early Church, was at first held monthly, but later, on New Year's eve only. The quarterly meeting arose out of the necessity for pastoral supervision of the Societies and class meetings, and gradually became the local church court for the circuits assigned to the preachers, who also gave tickets to the members in good standing. The band meetings and love feasts were intended to cultivate in their attendants a grateful sense of God's mercies, and self-examination concerning their state, sins, and temptations. The penitents' meeting is sufficiently described by its name, the hymns and exhortations being such as were suitable for mourners who had lost their assurance of forgiveness. It is evident that these means for religious growth were more nearly a reproduction of those of the New

Testament than many others then extant, and that nothing had been done as yet to contravene the ideals of Anglicanism concerning the priesthood of the clergy. On this issue even Wesley contended that the priest was a representative character, with derivative functions, and traces of his conception have appeared in some of his ministerial followers. We return to the class meeting because it was the soul of the peculiar fraternity and social worship which have been the cohesive bonds of Wesleyanism. Within its hallowed circle the sinful were warned to "flee from the wrath to come," the careless were reproved, the backsliders recovered, the faint-hearted encouraged, and the presumptuous restrained. As the fundamental part of a polity which was dictated by necessity rather than expediency, it directed spiritual energies, and conserved the divine life out of which these arose. It gave Wesley and his members an inviolable retreat for their souls' safety; it freed them for the most aggressive evangelism England and America have known; it coördinated in one Christian democracy colliers, laborers, artisans, ironworkers, merchants and scholars, and fused them into a brotherhood whose main objects were to live soberly and righteously, and grow daily in the knowledge and love of their Redeemer. It also produced an extensive hagiology, in which for the first time the miner and the plowman had their proportionate numbers and distinction. The majority of its adherents came from a harassing environment to the cherished spot where they learned to endure as seeing Him Who is invisible. "It can scarce be conceived," wrote Wesley, "what advantages have been reaped from this prudential regulation. Many now experience that Christian fellowship of which they had not so much as an idea before." The leaders essayed the difficult task of spiritual culture, and despite many drawbacks discharged its duties with courage, fidelity, and wisdom. Such an intercourse could not fail to be mutually helpful and enriching. It was at once the outer court and the inner sanctuary of that temple of living souls which arose before the unbelieving gaze of bigoted clerics and cynical secularists, and while it was held dear the missionary spirit of Methodism remained invincible.

The first Conference convened at the Foundery on Monday, June 25, 1744, and remained in session for five days. It consisted of ten members: the two Wesleys, John Hodges, Rector of Wenvo, Henry Piers, Vicar of Bexley, Samuel Taylor, Vicar of Quinton, John Meriton, an incumbent in the Isle of Man, and four lay preachers, Thomas Richards, Thomas Maxfield, John Bennett, and John Downes. Although of these last named only Downes remained with Wesley to the end, they were the representatives of the lay preachers who in Britain now occupy ten out of every twelve of the pulpits of Methodism. Small in numbers as the Conference was, this did not prevent it from devising a large program. On the Lord's Day previous to the opening session the Holy Communion was administered to the London Society of over two thousand members. Charles Wesley delivered the official sermon, which was followed by a series of discussions on doctrine and order, when it was resolved to maintain Anglican standards both by preaching and example. The new disciples were urged to build one another up in faith and diligence in order that Scriptural holiness might be spread throughout the land. The itinerants were minutely directed as to their general conduct, and exhorted to remember that "a preacher is to mind every point, great or small, in the Methodist discipline. Therefore you will need all the grace and sense you have, and to have all your wits about you."

These ten men, the majority of whom were Anglican clergymen, created the annual Conference, over forty-seven sessions of which Wesley himself presided, and which has met for one hundred and seventy-two successive years. The Conferences of American and Australian Methodism,

z

both annual and quadrennial, were afterwards modeled upon it. As organizations they have spread a network of jurisdiction throughout the English-speaking world and over missionary lands, becoming the high courts of legislation and executive control, and conveying the spirit and doctrines of their Founder to every quarter of the globe.

The apparent innovation of Wesley's teachings was largely due to the fact that what is seen or heard for the first time, however ancient, appears novel. He did little more than expound the principles of Christianity contained in the Articles of the Church of England, and interpreted by Moravianism. This led him to the regenerated life which is supreme over ecclesiasticism and dogmatism. From Moravianism he also derived some major conceptions of how that life was received and propagated. In its example he saw the possibility of forming vital groups within the Church rather than of founding an independent communion, and enacted his measures accordingly. He deemed the position of the Scriptures impregnable, and wrote of them in the Preface to his Sermons. "Let me be *homo unius libri*. Here then I am, far from the busy ways of men. I sit down alone: only God is here. In his presence I read His book; for this end, to find the way to heaven. Is there a doubt concerning the meaning of what I read? I lift up my heart to the Father of lights, and ask him to let me know His will. I then search after and consider parallel passages of Scripture. I meditate thereon with all the attention and earnestness of which my mind is capable. If any doubt still remains, I consult those who are experienced in the things of God; and then the writings whereby, being dead, they yet speak. And what I thus learn, that I teach." [1]

His language shows that few men have been less hampered in their religious energies by the critical intellectual atmosphere. While he never regarded regularity in minor theological issues as of supreme importance, he

[1] L. Tyerman: "Life and Times of John Wesley"; Vol. I, p. 532.

always insisted upon the necessity of repentance, regeneration, and justification by faith. These, though separable in thought, were quite inseparable in fact. "The moment we are justified by the grace of God through the redemption that is in Jesus, we are also born of the Spirit. . . . Justification implies only a relative, the new birth, a real change. God in justifying us does something for us; in begetting us again He does the work in us. By justification, instead of enemies we become children; by sanctification, instead of sinners we become saints. The first restores us to the favour, the other to the image of God."

His view of regeneration was inconsistent. In his "Treatise on Baptism," published in 1756, he states that "By baptism, we, who were 'by nature children of wrath,' are made the children of God. And this regeneration, which our Church, in so many places, ascribes to Baptism, is more than barely being admitted into the Church, though commonly connected therewith: being 'grafted into the body of Christ's Church, we are made the children of God by adoption and grace.'" Again in his sermon on the New Birth he says, "It is certain our Church supposes that all who are baptized in their infancy are, at the same time, born again; and it is allowed that the whole Office for the Baptism of Infants proceeds upon this supposition. Nor is it an objection of any weight against this that we cannot comprehend how this work can be wrought in infants. For neither can we comprehend how it is wrought in a person of riper years."[1] This was sound Anglicanism, but when Wesley faced the truth that regenerated infants developed into unmistakable sinners, he promptly abandoned it. Becoming impatient with the futility of arguing back to any presumptive change in infancy, he exclaimed, "How entirely idle are the common disputes on this head! I tell a sinner, 'You must be born again!' 'No,' say you, 'he was born again in baptism; therefore he cannot be born again.' Alas, what

[1] L. Tyerman: "Life and Times of John Wesley"; Vol. II, pp. 264–265.

trifling is this! What if he was then a child of God? He is now manifestly a child of the devil. Therefore do not play upon words. He must go through an entire change of heart. . . . Remember that if either he or you die without it, your baptism will be so far from profiting you that it will greatly increase your damnation." Here, as was his custom, Wesley concerned himself with the facts of the case and left the theories to take care of themselves. The two standards are hard to reconcile, nor did he attempt their reconciliation; he preferred to dwell on the transformation which God effects in the soul when He raises it from the death of sin to the life of righteousness, recreating it in Christ Jesus, and renewing it in His own likeness. At that moment the affections were transferred from things temporal to things eternal; pride became humility, and passion meekness; hatred, envy, and malice were supplanted by a sincere, tender, disinterested love for all mankind. He did not insist upon the instantaneousness of this revolution, although he had been told by Böhler that it occurred at a given moment. "I contend, not for circumstance, but for the substance," he observed. "So you can attain it another way, do; only see that you do attain it."

His sermon on "The Duty of Constant Communion," published in 1788, shows that he looked upon the Eucharist as the food of souls, giving strength for the performance of duty, and leading its recipients toward perfection. He held both Sacraments in such reverence that he persistently refused to allow either of them to be administered by any except episcopally ordained clergymen. Nevertheless he was not a Sacramentarian in the sense that permits outward and visible signs to displace an inward and renewing grace; a grace, as he avowed, received by faith, not by material media, and which depends upon the witness of the Holy Spirit and the assurance of the believer's heart, rather than upon conformity in communicating. Again, this assurance differed from the tenet of final perseverance; it could be forfeited by lack of faith or lapse of conduct; it was active only in those who continued steadfast in well-doing, and who brought forth the fruits of righteousness in their daily lives. It was also diametrically opposed to the governing concept of sacerdotalism, Anglican as well as Roman, which repudiates the idea of the believer's certainty of forgiveness, save on priestly authority. In the medieval Church the mystics alone professed this independent certitude; Wycliffe rejected it absolutely; Calvin found no sufficient place for it in his deterministic scheme; Luther, though it was contained in his teaching on salvation by faith, receded from it in proportion as he narrowed the meaning of faith to intellectual acceptance of dogma. The Church of England was committed, by the implication of her Homilies, if not by their specific declarations, to the doctrine of assurance; but this had been completely overlooked, and Wesley's teaching was invested, even in the minds of her leading instructors, with a dangerous if not heretical tendency, "another illustration," as Dr. Workman remarks, "of the familiar truth that the working creeds of a Church are by no means the full contents of its official symbols."

The doctrine of Christian perfection was the crown of Wesley's teaching, and the corollary of his appeal to experience. A genuine consciousness of sonship in the believer implies the possibility that such consciousness may become complete, and this as a present possibility, else the experience would not be in consciousness. Its inward truth has been common, as an experience rather than as a doctrine, to saints of all ages. It has been misinterpreted through regarding time as an actuality rather than as a quality of consciousness, the latter being Wesley's understanding of it. Those who would dismiss it either as an egoistical delusion or an iridescent dream, which, like that of St. Francis, cannot overcome contact with the earth, may perhaps be induced to turn to it again by the observation of Professor Huxley, that perfectibility is the one rational goal of progressive existence. This suggests the further reflection that the life everlasting would seem to demand the final unity of all being in the likeness and will of God. Wesley derived his ideal from those Scriptural passages which enjoin unreserved surrender to Christ Jesus, and a heart overflowing with love toward God and man. He not only expounded these graces without faltering, but also verified the type of Christian life they produced by an open discussion of its results. Wherever they were practiced he noted a quickening among his people, and this caused him to preach perfection more constantly, as of the utmost importance for the growth of believers. Writing to Adam Clarke in November, 1790, he says, "To retain the grace of God, is much more than to gain it; hardly one in three does this. And this should be strongly and explicitly urged upon all who have tasted of perfect love. If we can prove that any of our local preachers or leaders, either directly or indirectly, speak against it, let him be a local preacher or leader no longer . . . how impossible it is to retain pure love without growing therein."[1] To Robert Brackenbury he wrote in the same year, "This doctrine is the grand depositum which God has lodged with the people called Methodists; and, for the sake of propagating this chiefly, He appeared to have raised them up."[2] He commented on the Society at Otley in Yorkshire: "Here began that glorious work of sanctification which now from time to time spread through most parts of England and all the south and west of Ireland. And wherever the work of sanctification increased, the whole work of God increased in all its branches." He had visited the Otley Methodists and examined them one by one. Some of them he doubted, but of the majority he wrote, "Unless they told wilful and deliberate lies, it was plain: (1) That they felt no inward sin, and, to the best of their knowledge, committed no outward

[1] L. Tyerman: "Life and Times of John Wesley"; Vol. III, p. 633.
[2] *Ibid.*, p. 625.

sin. (2) That they saw and loved God every moment, and prayed, rejoiced, and gave thanks evermore. (3) That they had constantly as clear a witness from God of sanctification as they had of justification. In this," he added, "I do rejoice and will rejoice. . . . I would to God, thousands had experienced thus much; let them afterwards experience as much more as God pleases." [1]

In his "Plain Account of Christian Perfection" he dwelt upon it at length, but despite his avowals many devout Methodists have held that while these higher levels are divinely authorized, they are not always humanly possible. Nor was Wesley under any delusion concerning the measure of his own sanctification. He never claimed for himself that the goal was won: on the contrary, it was ever before him, and his language was that of anticipation rather than acquirement. He scrupulously avoided the phrase, "sinless perfection," yet the term perfection was itself susceptible of abuse, both from the indifferent and from those whose zeal outran their knowledge. Standing midway between these extremists was a group of men and women who satisfied his highest hopes. Cardinal Newman's test of the claim of a Church to be in the apostolic succession by its ability to produce saints was not only met by John Fletcher and Thomas Walsh, to whose splendor and serenity the world could offer no bribe, but also by such children of Methodism as Hannah Ball, Nancy Bolton, Hester Rogers, Martha Thompson, William Bramwell, Roger Crane, Ezekiel Cooper, Thomas Taylor, David Stoner, William Carvosso, Thomas Collins, Benjamin M. Adams, Bishop Marvin, William Owen of Old Park, and numberless others — elect souls who verified the reality of Christ's word, "I am come that they might have life, and that they might have it more abundantly."

The contrast furnished by the unseemly ebullitions of a cult of perfectionists in the London Society grieved Wesley,

[1] L. Tyerman: "Life and Times of John Wesley"; Vol. II, p. 417.

and alarmed the more sedate brethren. Thomas Maxfield, among other heady emotionalists, began by professing entire sanctification, and ended in hysterical delusions. Upon being rebuked by the preachers, he displayed a temper anything but holy, and Fletcher, anxious for the preservation of genuine spirituality, wrote to Wesley: "Many of our brethren are overshooting sober Christianity in London. . . . The corruption of the best things is always the most corrupt." When Wesley returned there, in October, 1762, he found the Society rent in twain, and Maxfield and his sympathizers inclined to further mischief. They had withdrawn from fellowship, and one of them, George Bell, a former soldier and a noisy fellow whose obsessions were incurable, became a full-blown prophet of the Millennial Advent, which he solemnly announced would take place on February 28, 1763. God had done with preaching and ordinances, and His presence was now strictly limited to the assemblies of the Bellites. These lurid apocalypses led astray the unwary, and Wesley's patience with them ceased to be a virtue. But Maxfield, who through the good offices of Wesley had obtained ordination from the Bishop of Londonderry, had been prominent in Methodism, and Wesley was reluctant to silence the preacher who had received the commendation of his mother. Finally Maxfield withdrew from the Society, taking two hundred of its members with him, to whom he ministered for twenty years after the schism. It is gratifying to add that toward the close of his life he came to a better mind; friendly relations with his old associates were resumed; Wesley preached in his church, and visited him in his last illness. The dissensions cost the London Society four hundred members, a loss from which it did not recover for a long period. In the sequence, however, the purging was beneficial. Pharisaism was halted, and credulity and irrational exaltation were discontinued. Similar disturbances in later times have raised the question whether the distinction between regen-

eration and sanctification is valid in actual experience, or
whether the latter is simply an intensified expression of
regeneration. In any case, the moral is that doctrines
should be as catholic in scope and simplicity as the
nature of the truths they are intended to set forth will
allow. Methodism was bound to keep alight on its altars
the flame of holiness, though perhaps they might have been
more effectually guarded against strange fires. Be this as
it may, in nothing did Wesley show his sagacity more admirably than in his refusal to yield to senseless vaporings on the
one hand, or, on the other, to lassitude and indifference.

While the heart is not another kind of reason, it is a
recognized faculty for discerning truth. It represents
implicit judgments, the relative values of different sentiments and purposes, and supplies the regulating principles
of life. Upon it Wesley relied for these gifts in the enforcement of his teachings. With Plato and St. Paul and other
prophets, he perceived by its illumination things eternal,
and that these could be attained by mortals. He modified
these implicit judgments, and fashioned them into the
stated beliefs now known as Wesleyan theology. It was
not always easy to do this, but he persevered until he felt
he had alike satisfied the claims of reason and of religion.
His success was apparent in those who received his message:
they were no longer ensnared in a melancholy rotation of
sinning and repenting, but having gained the liberty of the
children of God, became a people "for His own possession,"
unafraid in the day of battle, and who made a specific
contribution not only to the life and thought of Protestantism, but to "the total of truth and vantage of mankind."
He also transferred the basis of the doctrine of assurance from the objective grounds of the Church and the
Sacraments to those of an experimental witness within the
believer. Although he substituted an infallible Book for
an infallible Church, it was not necessary to the structure
of which he was the architect. Methodist theology is not

so highly articulated that its living growth cannot supply the wastes incurred by large variations of thought or advances in knowledge. Its assignment of experience as the final criterion of religious truth guards it from the liabilities of less fortunate systems which dare not yield one premise without endangering the entire argument. But its claim for the validity of introspection and its subordination of the objective to the subjective were kept within bounds, and it is "the conjunction of belief in the authority of an organic Church with insistence upon the value and reality of individual experience as the final test which gives to Methodism its special position in the Catholic Church."[1] The sectarian asceticism which clouded English society with the gloom of bigotry was not unknown in Wesleyanism. Until the Tractarians taught the needed lesson that all life was sanctified in Christ, a suspicion of culture and of the æsthetic conscience was found in Methodism as a natural revulsion against their abuse elsewhere.

Its inner history is a record of the freedom and universality of the Gospel operating on a scale which has seldom, if ever, been equaled since the earliest ages, when, as it seemed to the first missionaries of the Cross, the restoration of all things was at hand. Unquestionably it is the purest phase of New Testament Christianity which has arisen in modern times. One is filled no less with wonder at the measure of its achievements than with the conviction of its origin in the counsels of Eternity. Without adventitious aids or questionable alliances, despised and rejected by the wise and great of the world, employing for its propaganda the unfettered Evangel mediated through Wesley, and relying solely upon the Holy Spirit for its success, the little company which first followed him has multiplied in many lands, and in some is the dominant Protestantism of this era. As such it must be explained, either by the scientific

---

[1] "A New History of Methodism"; edited by W. J. Townsend, H. B. Workman, and G. Eayrs; Vol. I, p. 16.

methods which now prevail in the study of the past, or treated as a religious mystery without any perceptible cause. Theories which limit the conveyance of saving grace to prescribed channels of apostolical succession will have to be accommodated to the magnitudes of this latest offspring from the higher powers, or suffer the fate of hypotheses which ignore integral facts.

The most vivid delineation of the inner life of Methodism is found in the hymns of Charles Wesley, which have glorified Christian worship more than any other similar lyrics, with the possible exception of those written by Isaac Watts. They set forth intimate as distinguished from legalistic religion, radiant with the beauty of holiness and the arts of consolation, and overflowing with tenderness and joy. The cry of penitence, the answer of faith, the defiance of death, the sound as of a trumpet, the opened vials, the broken seals, the solemn doom of Judgment, the triumphant certainty of an immortality of passionless renown, and all the signs and wonders of the Kingdom's triumph, were more persuasively and exultingly expressed in them than in any other productions of sacred literature since the Reformation. Their principal theme was the adoration of the Everlasting Father for His supreme gift in Jesus Christ and for the love He is always seeking to impart through Him to His children.

> " 'Tis Love! 'tis Love! Thou diedst for me!
> I hear Thy whisper in my heart;
> The morning breaks, the shadows flee,
> Pure universal Love Thou art;
> To me, to all, Thy mercies move;
> Thy nature and Thy name is Love."

The peasants who turned from their ancestral fanes to worship in the humble meeting-houses where such praises rang forth were amply rewarded by the strength and comfort they imparted. Here the Real Presence was manifested before their reverent faith while with sacred song they made melody in their hearts. In their insistence upon personal sin, personal forgiveness, and personal assurance, the hymns echo the individualism which is a dominant note of the Gospel in its essential application, but they do not express those larger social aspects of religion which are now monopolizing the vision of the Church. Charles's productiveness was amazing; he wrote over six thousand compositions, of very unequal quality, but numbering some unsurpassed in any language. He was in a marked degree the creature of his inspiration. Sometimes his poetic impulse hardly lifted him above the flatness of doggerel, again it suddenly failed after a burst of promise, but, in those sustained flights of lyrical rapture which it occasionally made, it opened for the poet a passage to the skies and raised him as on seraph wings to the very throne of God. His hymn, "Jesus, Lover of my soul," stands at the summit of odes of its order; that on "Wrestling Jacob" Isaac Watts averred to be among the finest ever written; "Rejoice, the Lord is King" is an entirely different but equally noble example of his powers. These and others of a notably high character have been woven into the very fiber of millions of souls, and in them we come to the sanctum sanctorum of Christian faith. Nor is it too much to affirm that they are one of the strongest bonds of universal Christian fellowship. The limitations under which poetry must always move are more severely felt in hymnal composition than in other forms of its expression. Dr. Johnson declared that metrical songs meant for Christian worship could not be poetry, since it was necessary to exclude from them that play of imagination which would violate orthodoxy. On the contrary, this term has little meaning in hymnology: a sacred lyric need but arouse the devout sentiments that control human nature to secure a place in the services of every sect. There is no better evidence of the underlying unity of truly religious natures than their independence of theological speculations when they find a hymn which blends their spirits with the Spirit of the Eternal. True, they revert to their creeds again, but stanzas that voice with glowing phrase the unconquerable beliefs of men also fashion them, and in this respect Charles Wesley gave the people much of their theology.

John's fastidious taste revised his brother's poetry and modified its exuberances. His own translations of the Moravian hymns, while somewhat bald and literal, were excellent; among them are Scheffler's "I thank Thee, uncreated One," and Terstegeen's "Thou hidden love of God unknown," which has in it "a sound as of the sound of the sea." John Bakewell and Edward Perronett also wrote some choice lyrics, but it was reserved for Thomas Olivers to rival even Charles Wesley in his sublime ascription to the Everlasting:

> "The God of Abraham praise, —
> Who reigns enthroned above,
> Ancient of Everlasting days
> And God of love.
> Jehovah, Great I Am,
> By earth and heaven confest;
> I bow, and bless the sacred name
> Forever blest."

Commenting on this hymn of the little Welsh preacher, whom Toplady ridiculed as an ignorant cobbler, James Montgomery said, "There is not in our language a lyric of more majestic style, more elevated, or more glorious imagery. Its structure indeed is unattractive on account of the short lines, but like a stately pile of architecture severe and simple in design, it strikes less on the first view than after deliberate examination." The realization of divine grace which gave Methodism its first outburst of Christian song had many other far-reaching effects, but none of these compare with the influence of its sacred poetry over all classes, and especially over the poor and illiterate multitudes who were thereby taught to worship God aright. Dr. James

Martineau asserted that the "Collection of Hymns for the Use of the People called Methodists," issued in 1780, was, "after the Scriptures, the grandest instrument of popular religious culture that Christendom has ever produced."

The beginning remains always the most notable moment, and this carries the genesis of Methodism beyond the reach of artificial growths in ecclesiastical order into the heart of primitive Christianity. At the risk of repetition it must be said that its practices were really reproductions of those which first established the teaching of Jesus. And in these lay its authority, for "when a religion has become an orthodoxy, its day of inwardness is over; the spring is dry; the faithful live at second hand exclusively and stone the prophets in their turn. The new Church, in spite of whatever human goodness it may foster, can be henceforth counted on as a stanch ally in every attempt to stifle the spontaneous religious spirit, and to stop all later bubblings of the fountain from which in purer days it drew its own supply of inspiration."[1] There could be no better description of the conditions which Methodism met and overcame in the power of a holier faith and purpose. God has ordained that life should be endowed with an almost unerring discrimination in favor of its necessities and against that which is inimical to its welfare. Applying the ordinance to religion, we find that when any particular form of Christianity seemed requisite, it emerged from the implicit to the explicit stage, was then adopted as a governing factor, and finally passed away with the ending of its usefulness. This process affords an argument for the predetermination of the end which such forms have been made to subserve, and although the theologian and the priest may mourn its operation, it furnishes a basis for belief in a superintending Power. This belief is strengthened by the fact that, beneath these changes in the superficial region of revealed religion, there is always an irreducible body of truth

[1] William James: "Varieties of Religious Experience"; p. 337.

necessary to life. Upon this sure foundation, John Wesley built his theology and his Church.

Before dealing with the memorable legislation of the year 1784, which made the Societies in Britain and America to all intents and purposes self-regulating, it is necessary to speak of the introduction of Methodism into the colonies of North America, since its presence there precipitated its separation from Anglicanism. Wesleyan teaching had been carried to New York by Philip Embury and Barbara Heck, who were among the immigrants from Limerick in 1764 and 1766. Embury's devotion languished in his new surroundings until Barbara Heck revived it,[1] when, together with other friends, they began services in a private house. Captain Webb, an officer of the forty-second regiment of British infantry stationed at Albany, who had been converted under Wesley at Bristol, joined the little company at New York, and in 1768 a chapel was erected in John Street, Embury making the pulpit with his own hands, and preaching the first sermon on October 30. From these origins and those at the log meeting house on Sam's Creek, Maryland, and at Lovely Lane, Baltimore, arose the Methodism which was destined to surpass the parent body in numbers. The English Conference of 1769, held at Leeds, received and responded to an appeal for help from the American brethren by appointing Richard Boardman and Jacob Pilmoor as their pastors, and subscribing fifty pounds towards the debt on John Street Church, and twenty pounds for the expenses of the new ministers. Pilmoor was stationed at Philadelphia, and Boardman in New York. *Lloyd's Evening Post* of London, amused by these bold measures, announced that other promotions would soon be listed: "The Rev'd. George Whitefield to be Archbishop of Boston, Rev'd. William Romaine to be Bishop of New York, Rev'd. John Wesley to be Bishop of Pennsylvania, the

---

[1] Despite common report some modern Methodists have informed the author that Embury did not lose his zeal.

Rev'd. Martin Madan to be Bishop of the Carolinas, Rev'd. Walter Shirley to be Bishop of Virginia and Rev'd. Charles Wesley to be Bishop of Nova Scotia;" a squib in which a clown for once came near to prophecy.

Before the War of Independence, American Methodism had a membership of 3148, yet in 1777 the minutes of the English Conference do not even mention the branch in the colonies. "They inform me," said Wesley, "that all the Methodists there are firm for the Government and on that account persecuted by the rebels, only not to the death; that the preachers are still threatened but not stopped, and that the work of God increases much in Maryland and Virginia." He was strongly opposed to the Revolution; and his pamphlet, issued in 1775, "A Calm Address to our American Colonies," which procured for him the thanks of the British government, added greatly to the distresses and difficulties of his disciples in the West. The pamphlet was an almost literal transcription of that undiluted sample of fatuous Toryism and hackwork, Johnson's "Taxation no Tyranny," and Wesley's wholesale appropriation laid him open to the charge of plagiarism. His friends in America suppressed it, a kindness indeed in view of the fact that its sentiments flatly contradicted some of his earlier utterances. In a letter to Lord North against that minister's policy, he wrote, "All my prejudices are against the Americans; for I am a High Churchman, the son of a High Churchman, bred up, from my childhood, in the highest notion of passive obedience and non-resistance; and yet, in spite of all my long-rooted prejudices, I cannot avoid thinking, if I think at all, that an oppressed people asked for nothing more than their legal rights, and that in the most modest and inoffensive manner that the nature of the thing would allow. But, waiving all considerations of right and wrong, I ask, is it common-sense to use force towards the Americans? These men will not be frightened: and, it seems, they will not be conquered as easily as was at first imagined, they will probably dispute every inch of ground; and, if they die, die sword in hand." [1]

No nobler or more impressive figure rose above the political and religious confusion of the Revolution than that of the great Englishman and bishop of American Methodism, Francis Asbury. Although many of the Episcopal clergy and five of his own colleagues withdrew from their pastoral charges, he refused to follow their example, suppressed his natural sympathies with his native land, and never ceased to preach and toil among his scattered and afflicted members. He was born on August 20, 1745, at Handsworth, near Birmingham, a few miles from the locality where Wesley underwent his fiercest persecution and won one of his most signal triumphs. Blessed in his parentage, and always spiritually disposed, Asbury, then in his fourteenth year, hearing of the Wednesbury riots, went to the scene of the disturbance to find out what kind of piety it was that had aroused and then subdued the hostility of the mob. He returned a Methodist, and a warm advocate of Methodism. About three years later he began to hold public meetings, and when other places were closed against him had recourse to his father's house, where he exhorted and prayed with the neighbors. When he was twenty-one, Wesley enrolled him among his itinerants, and in 1771 sent him to Maryland. Asbury felt some misgivings that he had perhaps undertaken a venture beyond his powers, and wrote in his Journal, "If God does not acknowledge me in America, I will soon return to England." With this resolution he sailed from Bristol, never to see his relatives or Wesley again. But though the seas separated them, the ideals and doctrines of Methodism were embodied and proclaimed by him as by no other preacher except Wesley himself, whom he equaled, if indeed he did not exceed him, in privations and labors. The text of his first sermon at Baltimore was a suitable motto for forty-five years of illustrious service: "I determined

[1] L. Tyerman: "Life and Times of John Wesley"; Vol. III, p. 198.

2 A

not to know anything among you, save Jesus Christ and Him crucified." Sorely grieved and hampered by the quarrel between the two nations, the one the country of his birth, the other of his adoption, he was nevertheless sustained by the ambition that the newly acquired freedom of the United States should be enlightened and purified by the saving knowledge of God. His was that higher patriotism which soared beyond strife and blundering, and, when every attachment to the past became an avenue of pain, and his choice for the future caused many to malign him, he transcended the darkness and dismay and became an historic pleader for the peace and federation of the Kingdom of Christ.

Asbury showed an adaptability for the Republic and its institutions beyond that of any other clergyman of English birth. He came from the artisans and laborers of the Midland shires to the plain folk of the Eastern States, unembarrassed by social or ecclesiastical prejudices. One fears to speculate on what might have been the fate of American Methodism had such a cleric as Charles Wesley controlled it at the critical juncture. Fortunately for his own reputation and for his brother's work, this was not the case. Although Asbury had few intellectual gifts comparable with theirs, he possessed a loyalty, a determination, and a soundness of judgment which enabled him to hold intact the thin lines of his little army until the propitious moment came for advance and conquest.

Tall, gaunt, and ascetic in appearance, clad in a plain drab suit, a stock, and a low, broad-brimmed hat, and married only to the Church, twice yearly he rode along the Atlantic seaboard from Connecticut to the Carolinas, and westward through the mountains to the farther slopes of the Alleghanies, then the frontiers of civilization. He forded rivers and followed trails which led to the solitudes of the virgin forest. Indian savages or white fugitives from justice were frequently his only companions in the wilderness. If his horse cast a shoe, he bound the hoof with bull's hide and pushed on. In a time when steamboats and railroads were unknown and coaches rare, he made his tours of four to five thousand miles annually, preaching at least once a day, and three times on the Lord's Day. The families he encountered in these lonely journeyings were not always decent or hospitable, but he never called on them without prayer, or left them without a blessing. Quarterly meetings, camp meetings, and seven annual Conferences, all widely apart, were the rallying points of his activity, and he visited them at least once a year, besides writing a thousand letters annually to his preachers and helpers. This prodigious exertion was accomplished under constant bodily suffering; yet aches and pains, chills and fever, were mere trifles to his superior spirit, and could not dismay him. A diligent student, he became proficient in Latin, Greek, and Hebrew, was a master of the Holy Scriptures, and had a respectable acquaintance with other branches of literature. In his old age, when weak and crippled by infirmity, he reluctantly consented to use a light carriage. He clung to his office with tenacity, continually ordaining preachers, planting churches, sending fourth pioneers, and like the bird which sees not the casement for the sky, he was slow to learn that neither his ardor nor his austerity could be imparted to others without their consent. But these were only spots on his sun, and, bishop though he was, as all men knew, his spirit of beautiful humility was shown in his charge that after his death no mention should be made of him, nor any biography be written. He died on March 31, 1816, at the house of his old friend George Arnold, near Fredericksburg, Virginia, where he had tarried on his way to the Conference at Baltimore.

Some results of his unremitting devotion are seen in the growth of the movement during his episcopate. At his ordination, in 1784, there were eighty-three itinerants traveling forty-six circuits, and less than fifteen thousand members; at his death there were over seven hundred preachers ministering to more than two hundred and eleven thousand members. Among the noble band of circuit riders, who emulated their bishop's example of sacrificial service, were Jesse Lee, Enoch George, Thomas Ware, Hope Hull, Ezekiel Cooper, Freeborn Garrettson, Benjamin Abbott, John Emory, William McKendree, Robert Roberts, John Dickins — a succession of prophets of God, of whom the Church and the Republic they lived to serve may well be proud.

The Societies were organized under Wesley's plan, and guided by his wishes; the class meeting, the love feast, and the quarterly and annual Conferences being duplicates of those in Great Britain. At first New England was averse to Methodism, but in New York, Pennsylvania, Maryland, the Southern States, and on the ever receding frontiers it had a free field, and soon became an important factor, some of its preachers helping to build cities and commonwealths as well as churches. They came at an opportune moment; the pastoral office in America had defaulted in respect to the Sacraments, the majority of the Anglican clergy had been dispersed by the conflict with Britain, and those who remained were at a low ebb of learning and religion. Bishop White lamented that "the Church of England was becoming more and more unpopular, a useless burden on the community." Dr. Hawks relates that a large number of its edifices in Virginia were ruined, and twenty-three out of ninety-five parishes forsaken.[1] Under these circumstances the Methodists began to inquire why their own ministers should not have authority to administer the Holy Communion. For the time, Thomas Rankin induced the preachers to await Mr. Wesley's advice, but the agitation increased, until in 1779 it widened into an actual breach between the Northern preachers, who pleaded for patient delay, and those south of Philadelphia, who asked for full

[1] For a description of the American Episcopal Clergy in Virginia, see "Richard Carvel," by Winston Churchill.

ministerial rights. The latter were temporarily conciliated by Asbury's promise that he would appeal to the Founder for an adjustment of the matter. The interests of souls were at stake, and the demands actuated by this consideration brooked no further parleying.

Wesley had already met the clergyman whom he was about to designate as Asbury's senior colleague, and whose name is connected with acts which led to the constitution of the Methodist Episcopal Church of America. Thomas Coke, a gentleman commoner of Jesus College, Oxford, became Wesley's first lieutenant, visiting the Societies in Ireland alternately with him and exercising some of his delegated authority. Coke was the founder of the Foreign Missionary Society and one of its most generous supporters, and he wrought earnestly in behalf of Home Missions in England and Wales. Asbury, on hearing of his death, spoke of him as "a minister of Christ, in zeal, in labors, and in services the greatest man of the last century." Notwithstanding his many excellencies, Coke's restless energies were not always judiciously directed. On more than one occasion his ambitions excited resentment, nor does Dr. Stevens's defense of him quite remove the impression that he had entertained designs upon the superintendency to which he was ordained. Yet as an Oxford graduate, a priest of the Church of England, a doctor of laws, and a more gifted preacher than Asbury, Coke would naturally be preferred for that office. Wesley did not proceed in the matter without deliberation, and only after he had failed in his efforts to persuade Dr. Lowth, then Bishop of London, to ordain a preacher that the pastoral necessities of American Methodists might be regularly met. Hitherto he had been correct in his contention that nothing he had set in motion was inconsistent with his position as an Anglican clergyman. But he was now confronted by a condition, not a theory; and one accentuated by political misunderstandings eventuating in war and separation. Nor did he have any means at hand to supply the imperative requirements of his American members. Fletcher of Madeley was so sensible of their neglected state that he would have gone to its relief had his health permitted, and he besought Wesley, by whom he was esteemed above other advisers, to accede to the request of the American Methodists and grant them an ordained ministry. It was superfluous to ask for Charles Wesley's opinion; since he would have sacrificed the Methodism of the Republic to Anglican conceptions of unity and order. Coke only consented to go on the stipulation that Wesley should give him "by the imposition of hands the power of ordaining others." Accordingly, without haste, and in the full knowledge that he was about to incur the lasting disapproval of his Church, Wesley summoned Coke, with two itinerants, Richard Whatcoat and Thomas Vasey, to Bristol, and there on the 20th of September, 1784, in his private chamber, he set apart the itinerant preachers as presbyters, and laid his hands on Coke, consecrating him "to the office of Superintendent of the work in America."

He instructed Coke to take with him the two newly made presbyters, and in like manner set apart Asbury, first as a deacon, then as a presbyter, and then as his associate in the superintendency. Forms of ordination for deacons, elders, and superintendents were prepared by Wesley, which indicated that acts and terms he had purposely avoided at home were now to be authorized in America. Thus he assumed episcopal functions, and, if the ordination of Coke meant anything at all, it signified that he had received the same functions from Wesley, subject to the ratification of the American preachers. It was so understood and approved by them; at the Christmas Conference of Baltimore, on December 27th of the same year, the selection of Coke was confirmed, and Asbury was elected by the Conference and consecrated by Coke, assisted by several presbyters. Several presbyters and deacons were also elected and ordained on the following day. In this manner began the Methodist Episcopal Church in the United States of America. It was the first Church thus established in the young Republic, sharing its hopes and fears, and occupying a continental expanse which gave it ample room for its singular admixture of autocratic and democratic traits in a system approved by Wesley, Fletcher, Coke, Asbury, and its own preachers. In May, 1789, its chief pastors presented an address to President Washington beginning with the superscription "We, the bishops of the Methodist Episcopal Church"; and since then its life and work have been incorporated with those of the nation in which it is to-day the largest Protestant denomination.

After the irrevocable step was taken the hitherto unquestioned rule of Wesley was no longer absolute. The arbitrary change of the title of superintendent to that of bishop irritated him because of the adventitious dignities it suggested, but he was powerless to prevent it. Nor could the liberties he had granted to the ministry abroad be finally withheld at home, and after a prolonged interval they became the unquestioned right of all the preachers there. At the American Methodist Conference in 1789 the first question asked was, "Who are the persons that exercise the episcopal office in the Methodist Church in Europe and America?" The answer was, "John Wesley, Thomas Coke, and Francis Asbury by regular order and succession." Although their office was strictly defined as such and not as an order, these phrases must have sounded grandiloquently impertinent in the ears of ecclesiastics who had hitherto monopolized them. Apart from this they had several advantages; and not the least, that the colorless character and deferential attitude of a hybrid organization were abolished. The language of the New Testament was also used to describe other institutions and offices of the Church, whose episcopacy has since been held, not in any sense as the embodiment of an apostolic succession, but as a personalized and historic center of unity, administration, and efficiency.

Charles Wesley reproached his brother for the bold and un-expected procedure which frustrated his hopes, and appeared to him as "the beginning of a schism as causeless and un-provoked as the American Revolution." His complaints and groanings were vented in a letter to the Rev. Dr. Chandler, dated April 28, 1785: "I never lost my dread of separation, or ceased to guard our Societies against it. I can scarcely yet believe it, that, in his eighty-second year, my brother, my old, intimate friend and companion, should have assumed the episcopal character, ordained elders, consecrated a bishop, and sent him to ordain our lay preachers in America. I was then in Bristol, at his elbow; yet he never gave me the least hint of his intention." Charles further affirmed that Lord Mansfield, the Chief Justice of England, had told him a year before that ordination was separa-tion; and such it was from the standpoint of the church-manship which he represented. To what, then, beyond the necessitous circumstances already related is to be attributed Wesley's conviction that he had a right to discard the prin-ciples his brother so strenuously upheld? He had read in 1746 Lord King's account of the Primitive Church, from which he derived the teaching that bishops and presbyters were originally one order. In his "Notes on the New Testament" he cautiously commented that "perhaps elders and bishops were the same . . . and their names were used promiscu-ously in the first ages." In 1756 he stated that he still believed the episcopal form of Church government to be Scriptural and apostolical, but that it was prescribed in Scripture he did not believe. This opinion, which he once zealously espoused, he had been heartily ashamed of since studying Bishop Stillingfleet's "Irenicon." Canon Overton laments that so well-read and thoughtful a man as Wesley should have attached any weight to the youthful utterances of these two men, King and Stillingfleet, who afterwards re-canted.[1] Nevertheless they leavened Wesley's churchman-

[1] "The Evangelical Revival"; p. 18.

ship, and he now wrote to Charles that he firmly believed himself to be "a Scriptural episcopos as much as any man in England." The uninterrupted succession, he declared elsewhere, was "a rope of sand ; a fable that no man could prove."

The endless debates on this affirmation have no place here ; they have been best summed up in Bishop Lightfoot's verdict that the episcopal office did not arise out of the apostolical by succession, but out of the presbyteral by localization.[1] This conclusion has found powerful advocates in modern scholarship,[2] and if it is valid, Wesley's acts were in keeping with the ancient order. On the other hand, for forty years he had carefully abstained from them, and had even said that for an unordained preacher to administer within his Societies was a sin which he dared not tolerate, although by sending out scores of preachers without ordination, he had really made apostolic succession an anachronism so far as he was concerned. Of course his setting apart of Coke was indefensible from the standpoint of Anglicanism. "What could Wesley confer upon Coke which Coke might not equally have conferred upon Wesley?" queries Canon Overton. And the answer is, if given according to the Canon's conception of ordination, nothing. But a large body of Christians have denied the dogma of apostolical succession; they have resented its imputations, and have liberated themselves from its oppressions. Wesley, at least, gave Coke the premiership in a great Church, with the practical results that followed, and Canon Overton adds, with justice, that the true explanation of his conduct in

[1] See the references to this question in the subsequent chapters on Newman.

[2] For an interesting discussion on this question see "Some Remarks on Bishop Lightfoot's Dissertation on the Christian Ministry," by Charles Wordsworth, D.D., Bishop of St. Andrews ; also "The Leaves of the Tree: Studies in Biography," by Arthur Christopher Benson. Whatever contradiction of misunderstandings Bishop Lightfoot afterwards made he did not retract the main statements of his Essay on the Christian Ministry, found in the Appendix to his "Commentary on the Epistle to the Philippians."

this, as in other things, was the practical character of his mind, which led him to make everything subservient to his work of restoring the image of God in the soul of man.

An unprejudiced review of the matter, which in thought, purpose, and accomplishment covered nearly half a century, shows that any inconsistencies — and there were some — did not affect the integrity of Wesley's main position. He treated ordinances and offices as means of grace which should be held paramount so long as they promoted Christianity. When they ceased to do this they were set aside, and he took occasion, under necessity, to make the freedom and accessibility of God's Kingdom wider than antiquity had decreed. What he said will be long remembered, what he did will be conserved in the general outcome. The vast majority of his sons and daughters in the family of Methodism partake of the Living Bread in their own sanctuaries, unhindered by any consciousness of the warfare he waged with himself and others for their birthright; and those who have reflected upon it partake with no less faith because of the course he adopted.[1]

The Deed of Declaration which was executed on February 28, 1784, and a few days later enrolled in Chancery, has been called the Magna Charta of Wesleyan Methodism. It substituted for Wesley a permanent body of one hundred ministers, selected by him and authorized to bear the responsibilities and discharge the duties of the supervision of the Societies. This instrument was adopted none too soon; he was now an old man, and though still vigorous, could no longer be expected to take oversight of the Church in England, Ireland, and America, which in 1790 numbered nearly one hundred and fifty thousand members. He unwillingly restricted his hitherto incessant journeyings, and approached a peaceful twilight which the night of death

---

[1] See the *Methodist Review* for July–August, 1915, for a very able article by the Rev. Dr. J. M. Buckley on the Methodist Episcopacy; also the *Christian Advocate* for September the 30th, 1915.

lingered to disturb, moving among the people of the three kingdoms as the most apostolic figure of his generation. In Ireland as much as in Great Britain his last appearances were scenes of affectionate farewell and open sorrow at his departure. The accusations that he was a Jesuit, a Jacobite, a fanatic, a former rumseller, and a wily hypocrite, had gone never to return. Many Anglican clergymen and their congregations gave him a respectful hearing, and he received more invitations to preach before them than he could accept. "I am become," he said in 1785, "I know not how, a most honorable man. The scandal of the Cross is ceased, and all, rich and poor, Papists and Protestants, behave with courtesy, nay, with seeming good will." "It was, I believe," wrote Crabb Robinson, "in October, 1790, and not long before his death, that I heard John Wesley in the great round Meeting House at Colchester. He stood in a wide pulpit, and on each side of him stood a minister, and the two held him up, having their hands under his armpits. His feeble voice was scarcely audible, but his reverend countenance, especially his long white locks, formed a picture never to be forgotten. There was a vast crowd of lovers and admirers; . . . of the kind I never saw anything comparable to it in after life."[1] In a farewell letter dated February 1, 1791, addressed to Ezekiel Cooper, an American preacher known as the Lycurgus of his Church, Wesley told of his infirmities and how that time had shaken his hand and death was not far behind. Although eighty-six years of age, he enjoyed comparative freedom from pain: his sight and strength had failed, but he could still "scrawl a few lines and creep though not run." He concluded with the consoling prediction that his work would remain and bear fruit, and that Methodists were one throughout the world and would ever continue one,

"'Though mountains rise and oceans roll,
To sever us in vain.'"

[1] Henry Crabb Robinson's Diary; Vol. I, p. 19.

Whitefield died at Newburyport, Massachusetts, in 1770, about the time Asbury entered the field from which the famous orator was suddenly removed. Charles Wesley, though nearly five years younger than John, died on March 29th, 1788, His unequalled brother, on whom rested the glow of his approaching translation, was preaching in Staffordshire at the time. At the very moment when Charles passed away, the congregation, unconscious of this, was singing his hymn,

> "Come, let us join our friends above
> That have obtained the prize."

Wesley did not hear of his death until the day after the funeral. He deeply felt the separation, and a fortnight later, when attempting to give out another of Charles's hymns on "Wrestling Jacob," he faltered at the lines,

> "My company before is gone,
> And I am left alone with Thee;"

sat down in the pulpit, and buried his face in his hands. The singing ceased, and the people wept with him. In a little while he regained self-control, and proceeded with the service. He hastened to London from the North, that he might console the widow and children of the departed poet. His sermon at Leatherhead, Surrey, on Wednesday the 23d of February, was his last public utterance; the text being, "Seek ye the Lord while He may be found; call upon Him while He is near." With this message of mercy and exhortation his peerless ministry ended as it had begun, in the urgency of compassion, the strength of righteousness, the light of love, and the demonstration of the Spirit. The next day he spent with Mr. Wolff at Balham, and there penned his well-known letter to William Wilberforce, concluding with the stirring appeal, "O! be not weary in well doing. Go on, in the name of God, and in the power of His might, till even American slavery, the vilest that ever saw the sun, shall vanish away before it. . . ." [1]   It was entirely appropriate that the warfare he had waged for sixty years upon the cruelty of society toward the fallen and the helpless should conclude with this impassioned protest against human bondage.

Returning to his house in City Road on Friday, the 25th, he spent the remaining hours in prayer and praise. During an interval he asked those around him that his sermon on "The Love of God to fallen man" should be scattered broadcast and given to everybody. Later, he blessed them, and lifting his hand in grateful triumph, exclaimed, "The best of all is, God is with us!" Shortly afterwards, on March the second, 1791, this splendid being put on immortality.

EPILOGUE

THE history of Methodism beyond its leading events in the eighteenth century has been necessarily excluded from this account. Speaking generally, it followed three main lines of development: the rise and progress of the Evangelical Revival; the organization of the Methodist Churches therefrom; and their more familar expansions of the modern period, which by no means exhaust the results of the movement, for in many instances its palpable and its hidden influences have blended with the life of the nations it affected, purifying and strengthening them for domestic, social, and political reforms. Nor have the limits imposed here allowed us to dwell at length upon the multifarious details of Wesley's personal career, which abound in the biographies of Southey, Watson, Lelièvre, Tyerman, Telford, Fitchett, and Winchester, the books of Workman, and also in Wesley's self-revelatory Journals. He had the serenity of one who is at home in his own mind, who draws his water from his own fountain, and by means of whose inward light the path ahead is always plain. These

[1] L. Tyerman: "Life and Times of John Wesley"; Vol. III, p. 650.

outstanding qualities, and others which have been mentioned, reveal with unusual directness their heavenly sources.
Like the large-minded man in Aristotle's "Ethics" he thought
himself equal to grand moral achievements, and was justified
to the extent that the rare virtue of absolute disinterestedness gradually became a ruling factor in his conduct.   He
lavished all his energies and some of his best years upon the
search for divine illumination.   This obtained, he at once
became the director of a religious crusade which has helped
to upraise the race.   The means he employed were exposed
to reprobation, but they proved stronger than the formidable
display of earthly and ecclesiastical powers arrayed against
them.   Nor is it possible to escape the conclusion that in
all these things his course and destiny were not self-chosen,
after the usual meaning of the phrase, but in a special and
peculiar sense shaped by the guidance of his Maker.   For
God has always been pleased to build his best bridges with
human piers, never allowing their faults to impede the work-
manship when men were solicitous that they should not
do so.

The leisure of mind which followed the stirring epoch in
which Wesley acted so creatively has produced a number
of tributes vindicating him in every quarter of his historical
firmament.   Mr. Augustine Birrell says that "no man lived
nearer the center than John Wesley, neither Clive nor Pitt,
neither Mansfield nor Johnson.   You cannot cut him out of
our national life.   No single figure influenced so many
minds, no single voice touched so many hearts.   No other
man did such a life's work for England." [1]   Macaulay's
better known eulogy is equally generous.   The famous
essayist compared him with Richelieu, whose genius solidified the French nation and stimulated the authority
of its monarchy.   In like manner Wesley's weak chain of
organizations was lengthened link by link, and as they
developed he formulated rules for their guidance, until

[1] "John Wesley," in "Essays and Addresses"; p. 35.

Methodism became nothing less than an army intent on the moral conquest of the race.

An eighteenth century man, he shared in no small degree the strange contradictions of his age. His character was both simple and complex because it was in some measure the reflection of the people in which he moved, whose national texture has been thickly packed and plaited fold upon fold by an endless variety of custom and habit. In a corresponding way he dealt with many-sided truths and situations, undeterred by dread of paradox or the inconsistency of policies which might appear to lead in opposite directions. His experiences were both extensive and remarkable, and perhaps this may explain the supernatural aspect which he gave to them. Yet in matters where he was not directly interested he was capable of a becoming skepticism, and his belief in witchcraft and in the doctrine of particular Providence, which he sometimes carried to great lengths, showed no more credulity than did the notions of Addison, the pride of Oxford, whose " Essays on the Evidences of Christianity " include stories as absurd as the Cock Lane ghost, and forgeries as rank as William Henry Ireland's " Vortigern." Exact and vigorous in his thinking, Wesley's ideas were as far removed from what is meretricious or vulgar as were those of the best classics with which he was familiar. In his case great talents and considerable learning proved their suitability for a world-wide and permanent religious propagandism, and his career as an evangelist, who was also a man of culture, is an effective answer to those who deprecate the value of intellectual attainments in such efforts. There have been many imitators of Wesley, but, as yet, he has had no successor.

His steadfast mind discouraged the fitful gleams of self-deception from which he was not entirely free. Hasty or false assumptions were distasteful to his more robust processes of thought, and any tendency to purely emotional excitement in himself or in others was generally subdued by his innate conservatism. Clerics and philosophers whose prejudices he encountered dubbed him a fanatic; the believers whose faith he aided extolled him as a saint and a sage. He went quietly forward, living down rancor and disregarding praise, examining and restating his doctrinal views and qualifying them by their hold on life. A pervading reasonableness gave weight to his utterance, and its sincerity and restraint enabled him to overcome his critics. In the excitement attending a great revival he did not forfeit his sanity, his poise, his love of books, or his good breeding. His prescience as a statesman preserved that which he had won by aggressive attacks upon degeneracy and vice. And throughout life he readily yielded to truths hitherto neglected, or to aught else when refusal to yield would have been less than right or rational.

Although his conversion was beyond doubt, he repeatedly returned to it, allowing neither foregone conclusions nor deference to pious opinion to check his constant scrutiny of the basis of his assurance. In many of his confessions one knows not whether the feeling is deeper than the reflection, or the reflection deeper than the feeling. If some of his instinctive recognitions of God were in their nature mystical rather than intellectual, it would be difficult to overestimate the corrective value of such a religion of the heart when contrasted with that latitudinarianism which denied the possibility of Wesley's transfer into the boundless realm of the living, moving, progressive Spirit who led him into light, wisdom, and truth; into the very presence and persuasion of the Soul of souls. A sense of spiritual union springing from his voluntary surrender to Christ was strengthened by grave and habitual meditation, until he reached the plane where contradictions cease. Pondering the highest he knew till it became more than his ideal, he appropriated it as a part of himself, thus blending his life with the life everlasting that he might do God's work in the world.

Although he was compelled to act without her approval, and, indeed, in the face of her undeserved rebuke, the Anglican Church was always dear to him, and the liturgical forms of her worship harmonized with his sense of order and of the beauty of holiness. That by her opposition she lost the greatest opportunity she has yet had to strengthen her ranks and become a truly national church is beyond question; but this loss was compensated by the gains to the Kingdom of God which resulted from Wesley's independence of ecclesiasticism. Dr. Joseph Beaumont, in speaking of his attitude toward the Establishment, likened it to that of a strong rower who looks one way while every stroke of the oar propels him in the opposite direction. Further light is cast upon Wesley's relations to Anglicanism by excerpts given here from a letter, hitherto unpublished as fully as here, written by Dr. Adam Clarke to Mr. Humphrey Sandwith, and dated from Bridlington, on October 1, 1832 : —

"I have been a preacher in the Methodist Connexion more than *half a century:* and have been a travelling Preacher 47 years, and I ever found many people in most places of the Connexion very uneasy at not having the Sacrament of the Lord's Supper administered in our own Chapels, by our own Preachers. Mr. J. Wesley *mildly* recommended the people to go to the Church and Sacrament. Mr. C. Wesley threatened them with damnation, if they did not: for even in very early times the contrary disposition appeared in many Societies. In 1783, at the Bristol Conference where I was admitted into full Connexion, I heard Mr. Charles Wesley preach in Temple Church, on Matt. xi. 5. 'The blind receive their sight, and the lame walk,' etc., in which Discourse, and on that part, *the lame walk,* he spoke the following words, which I shall never forget : — 'My brethren, the lame man, that was healed by Peter and John at the beautiful gate of the Temple went into the Temple with the Apostles to worship God : — They who are healed under the ministry of my Brother and myself, go with us into the

2 B

Church: — Abide in the Church — if you leave the Church, God will leave you, or you will go halting all the days of your life, should you even get to heaven at last: — but abide in the good old Ship, and some on Boards, and some on broken pieces of the Ship, and you'll all get safe to Land.'   On this I make *no comment.*

*   *   *   *   *   *   *

It was only when the cry became *universal,* and the people were in danger of being everywhere divided or *scattered,* and a party of *Rich men,* principally *Trustees* in the Connexion, rose up to prevent any concessions to be made to the people, and it was too evident, that those very men aimed not only, as they professed, to *keep the people to the Church,* but to *rule them and the Preachers too,* that the Preachers in general declared in behalf of the Societies; and then, and not till then, did I argue in their behalf.

*   *   *   *   *   *   *

At the London Conference, in 1788, Dr. Coke, thinking we were in danger of losing our people, and that our avowed *connexion with the Church* hindered our work, proposed *in Conference,* that 'the whole Methodist Body should make a formal separation from the Church.'   In this Dr. Coke was not only *earnest,* but *vehement.*   It was stated, 'that it was impossible to keep up the Connexion with it, that all the Churches in the nation could not accommodate our Congregations, nor the Communion Tables receive the members of our Societies, as Communicants; and that as they generally called out for the Sacrament from the hands of their own Preachers, they should have it,' etc.   After the Doctor had said what he wished at the time Mr. Wesley rose up and with great *calmness said:* — 'Dr. Coke would *tear* all from top to bottom — I will not tear, but *unstitch.*'   He had begun to *unstitch.*   Witness the *ordination* for *America* and for *Scotland* and his calling *Mr. Myles* the year after to come within the rails of the communion-place in Dublin, to assist him by *giving the Cup!* — It has been said, 'the members of our Societies were *taken out of the Church*, and in forming Societies out of its members, we made a *Schism in the Church.*' This is a total mistake. I know well what *has been*, and what *is* the composition of our Societies. Our Societies were formed from those, who were *wandering upon the dark mountains*, that belonged to *no Christian Church;* but were awakened by the preaching of the Methodists, who had pursued them through the wilderness of this world to the High-ways and the Hedges, — to the Markets and the Fairs, — to the Hills and Dales, — who set up the Standard of the Cross in the *Streets* and *Lanes* of the *Cities*, in the *Villages*, in *Barns*, and *Farmers' Kitchens*, etc. — and all this in such a way, and to such an extent, as never had been done before, since the Apostolic age. They threw their drag-net into the troubled ocean of irreligious Society, and brought to shore both bad and good : and the very best of them needed the salvation of God : and out of those, who in general had no Christian Communion with *any Church* were formed by the mighty power of the God of all grace the Methodists' Societies. Thus they travelled into the wilderness, and brought back the stray sheep, that, had it not been for their endeavours, would in all likelihood have perished on the Dark Mountains. Our Founders were Ministers of the Established Church, — but what good did they do as Ministers *in* that Church? — They were obliged to go *over its pale*, in order to reach the lost sheep of the house of Israel. Had they continued *regular* in that Church, *Methodism* would not now be found in our ecclesiastical vocabulary. And since we, as a Body, threw aside the trammels of our prejudices, God has doubly, trebly blessed us in our work." [1]

Such was the attitude of Wesley when he stood on the

[1] The extracts are inserted here by the kind permission of the Rev. W. L. Watkinson, D.D., who is the owner of the letter.

verge of the grave. The cry for honorable independence came from an influential minority of his preachers who resented the indignities to which they were subjected and the anomalous position in which they were expected to do their work, but their leader's attachment to Anglicanism for a time prevented the fulfillment of their desires. Whether or not their proposals would have secured the stability and prosperity of the infant Church is still an open question. Those who hold that its Founder made the most intelligent and timely provision possible have to meet the fact that a large minority of the Methodists enrolled in Great Britain are outside Wesleyanism, principally because of schisms concerning the vexed questions of ministerial authority and relevant issues. Doctrinal difficulties were a negligible quantity in these disputes, which, whatever their causes, have greatly hindered Methodism. Its more progressive members sometimes formulated their claims regardless of evidence and experience; the conservatives clung to the status quo with unwise persistence; the consequences were lamentable accusations and disruptions. Many of the demands for advanced legislation which formerly aroused intense opposition have since been granted by the parent body, whose adjustment of clerical and lay authority has only been obtained after many years of cautious experiment. The growth of Methodism in the United States, where it was not overshadowed by a State Church, afforded no sufficient argument for a like policy in Britain, where Wesley's revered name and unique position deferred the advantages afterwards secured at considerable cost.

His rule, while not perfect, was unblemished by the caprice, selfishness, or tyranny which have generally accompanied the sense of unrestrained power, and made so many great men bad men. Never since the eras when the Church held sway over every action has any ecclesiastic possessed a more complete autocracy, or more straitly guarded it as a trust deposited with him by God for the welfare of the people.

Sir Leslie Stephen complains of his disagreeable temper, but there are surprisingly few instances of its exhibition. On the contrary, he knew how to cloak his occasional severity and arbitrariness with an urbane or a patriarchal manner. Audacity balanced by caution, firmness vailed by benevolence, inflexibility compensated by goodness, and a courage that revealed, when necessary, the fire beneath his calm exterior, were the chief features of his administrative capacity.

Some accounts of his unfortunate marriage with Mrs. Vazeille have not been entirely just to that lady, a dispassionate view of whose conduct shows her to have been a much abused woman, who suffered more severely than her husband. Wesley, notwithstanding the best intentions, did not properly discharge the duties of married life, nor devote himself to Mrs. Wesley with the ardor he showed for his mission. He was as mistaken in his conception of her as she was in her jealousies of him; and his bearing toward other women, while morally blameless, was indiscreet in view of her extreme sensitiveness. Wrapped a little too exclusively in his rectitude, he addressed her in terms which added fuel to the flame of her anger, and which were better suited to a rebellious preacher than to a wife who indulged the morbid susceptibilities of her ill-regulated heart. In after years he told Henry Moore that the schooling of sorrow which his marriage brought to him had been overruled for good, since if Mrs. Wesley had been a better wife, he might by seeking to please her have proved unfaithful to his calling.

The light and shade of ordinary existence were as foreign to Wesley as the joys of domestic life. He had to yield to a pressure from all sides which injured his more human qualities. His declaration that he dared no more fret than curse indicated a self-consciousness which was also shown in his lack of humor, and one cannot avoid a feeling of thankfulness that at intervals he let himself go and found relief. Yet the English people, however racy in their exchanges, distrust a jocular clergyman; and Wesley could never have gained their confidence had he scintillated rather than shone. The classes to which he chiefly appealed highly esteemed seriousness in the ministerial character; they would only have been puzzled by such brilliant by-play in Wesley as Sydney Smith indulged, and doubtless would have resented it. Dr. Johnson, craving further conversation with Wesley, and failing to obtain it, growled about his absorption in his work. He abstained from social intercourse, even when it was as an arch through which

> "Gleamed the untravelled world,"

and he was openly bored by the aristocratic circles which Whitefield admired and courted. When he chose, he could be a most delightful companion, but his steadfast gaze was on the religious needs of the race, and on

> " . . . The whole of the world's tears,
> And all the trouble of her labouring ships,
> And all the trouble of her myriad years."

Like St. Paul at Athens, he passed, not unheeding, yet unmoved, through scenes which would have enchained a lesser spirit. This aloofness injured his followers more than it injured him, for while he regarded some things as secular which in essence were sacred enough, he was always a liberal thinker and a sympathetic student of men and affairs.

He lacked the boldness of imagination which could frame philosophical or theological hypotheses and generalizations. His intellect was of the prosaical sort, uninfluenced by those higher but more hazardous motions which characterized his contemporary, Jonathan Edwards. His sentimentalism and taste for the romantic, like his drift toward Moravian mysticism, were finally mastered by his will and his reason. A feeling which did not evince itself in action counted for little: he measured mental and moral processes by their results in conduct; the only indications of a change of heart he felt free to accept were a sensible regeneration and its outward evidence in purity of life and conversation. He perceived that in the great matters of existence people are not convinced by argument. Good logic may remove difficulties which impede belief, but faith has its origin in a moral temper, and when this is absent the most cogent dialectics are wasted. Intellectual operations have never been readily adjusted to those religious impulses, which, though they remain among the deeper mysteries of human being, have yet been powerful enough to transform its entire character, and direct it into new channels. Thus, while there is a Wesleyan theology, a Wesleyan hymnology, and a Wesleyan type of religious experience, there is no Wesleyan philosophy. His system was never endangered by such streams of metaphysical speculation as flowed in Calvinism. For this and lesser reasons certain authors have supported the charges of his earlier opponents that Wesley swung the pendulum from the intellectual to the emotional side of Christianity. What he really did was to demonstrate the values of spiritual experience to such a degree that philosophy was compelled to acknowledge them. That he did this unwittingly does not detract from its importance, and the latest modern thought has confessed that his movement re-enthroned a religious consciousness which must be recognized and respected.

His Journal contains many allusions to literature in general, with reflections and comments upon particular works of numerous authors, as for example, Machiavelli's "Prince," of which he observes that it engendered in European government universal enmity and strife, its policies being bound by no moral obligation to God or man, and thriving on destruction. Mandeville's "Fable of the Bees," a very shrewd and advanced commentary on national hypocrisies, which asserted that private vices were public virtues, was even more abandoned than "The Prince." Marcus Aurelius was "one of those many who shall come from the East and the West and sit down with Abraham, while nominal

Christians are shut out." Rousseau was "a shallow yet supercilious infidel, two degrees below Voltaire." Ignatius Loyola, whose career he studied with care, was "surely one of the greatest of men that was ever engaged in the support of so bad a cause," one who set out "with a full persuasion that he might use guile to promote . . . the interests of his Church, and acted in all things consistent with his principles." Of the Puritans he wrote, "I stand in amaze, first, at the execrable spirit of persecution which drove these venerable men out of the Church, and with which Queen Elizabeth's clergy were as deeply tinctured as ever Queen Mary's were: secondly, at the weakness of those holy confessors, many of whom spent so much of their time and strength in disputing about surplices and hoods or kneeling at the Lord's Supper." There were deeper elements in the Puritan controversy than are indicated by this criticism, which is, however, admissible so far as it goes. On reading Richard Baxter's "History of the Councils," he vigorously denounced their evil side: "How has one Council been perpetually cursing another, and delivering all over to Satan, whether predecessors or contemporaries, though generally trifling, sometimes false and frequently unintelligible and self-contradictory?"

His judgments were not always within the mark, yet the desire to be just made him aware of the good in disputing sectaries, whose religious life was a unity at its source. Anglican, Nonconformist, and even Roman Catholic divines, theologians, and exegetes shared in the approval he generously bestowed where he deemed it deserved. In art, although he saw the weakness of design in the great cartoons of Raphael, his opinions were negligible. Music was always his delight, especially the oratorio, in which England has excelled. In his later years he loved to linger among the monuments of Westminster Abbey, where his own has since received its place.

Wesley could not be called a great scholar, in the present

technical sense of the term, although the University training he received, which was linked with the names of such men as Blackstone, the legal commentator, Lowth, the lecturer on Isaiah, the Wartons, especially Thomas, who was poet laureate, Addison, and Dr. Johnson, can be truly said to have left its mark on England. Oxford's thinkers of the eighteenth century acquiesced in the supremacy of Aristotle, and contributed little to the progress of organized or metaphysical inquiry. Erudition was constantly endangered by the acerbities of political partisanship, and few of the dons shared in the rapid expansion of learning which characterized their rivals at Cambridge. Alexander Knox states, however, that Wesley had an attachment to the English Platonists, including Taylor, Smith, Cudworth, Worthington, and Lucas. His life of ceaseless journeyings and labors gave him little time for literary interests, and it is greatly to his credit that he read as widely and wrote as accurately as he did. His Journal, which is among the first half dozen works of the era, shows the difficulties under which he pursued his studies. Neither tempestuous winds nor dripping skies, summer heat nor winter cold, breakdowns on the road nor impassable highways, threatening mobs nor the necessities of his Societies, could restrain his avidity for books, and, above all, for the One Book with which he was most conversant. Blessed with a compact and sinewy frame, and an equable temperament, he neither hurried nor chafed, nor did he suffer any reaction from his toils. The anxieties which corrode the lives of those who wear themselves out in battling for temporalities were unknown to him: the inspiration of his aims sustained him against every circumstance. During eighty-eight years he lost but one night's sleep, and at all times his composure enabled him to withdraw within himself. His seat in the saddle or the chaise became a cloister where he read and meditated, regardless of his surroundings.

There he planned his sermons and writings and reprints

of other men's works, which had an enormous circulation and influence. The magazine which he established in 1778 is now the oldest periodical of its kind in Great Britain. The entire list of his publications would form a volume in itself, and a glance at their contents enables one to realize the tireless energy and skill of the man. They ranged from the standard doctrines of a growing church to the quaint pre-scriptions of "Primitive Physic," and most of them were eagerly accepted and practised by the multitudes to whom his word was law. His style was decidedly inferior to that of Newman and other masters: he did not have nor did he desire to have the subtleties of thought and expression which were the great Tractarian's. In answer to the query, "What is it that constitutes a good style?" he said, "I never think of it at all, but just set down the words that come first. Only when I transcribe anything for the press, then I think it my duty to see that every phrase be clear, pure, proper, and easy. Conciseness, which is now as it were natural to me, brings quantum sufficit of strength." [1] Sir Leslie Stephen observes, "He shows remarkable literary power; but we feel that his writings are means to a direct practical end, rather than valuable in themselves, either in form or substance. It would be difficult to find any letters more direct, forcible, and pithy in expression. . . . The compression gives emphasis and never causes confusion." [2]

In summary, if culture consists in knowing much of the best that has been thought and said, in breadth of outlook and intellectual sympathy, then it cannot be denied that Wesley was a cultured man. Pagan masters, heretics of the ancient Church, and "excellent Unitarians," like Thomas Firmin, whose biography he commended to his followers, were included in his appreciative review. As early as 1745 he issued a letter to his people which has a message for them to-day. "Have a care of anger, dislike or contempt toward

[1] L. Tyerman: "Life and Times of John Wesley"; Vol. III, p. 657.
[2] "English Thought in the Eighteenth Century"; Vol. II, p. 409.

those whose opinions differ from yours. You are daily accused of this (and indeed what is it where you are not accused?), but beware of giving any ground for such accusation. Condemn no man for not thinking as you think. Let every one enjoy the full and free liberty of thinking for himself. Let every man use his own judgment, since every man must give an account of himself to God. Abhor every approach, in any kind or degree, to the spirit of persecution. If you cannot reason or persuade a man into truth, never attempt to force him into it. If love will not compel him to come in, leave him to God, the Judge of all." "The Methodists," he said at another time, "do not impose, in order to the admission of persons to their Society, any opinions whatsoever. Let them hold particular or general redemption, absolute or conditional decrees; let them be Churchmen or Dissenters, Presbyterians or Independents, it is no obstacle. Let them choose one mode of baptism, it is no bar to their admission. The Presbyterian may be a Presbyterian still; the Independent or Anabaptist use his own mode of worship. So may the Quaker, and none will contend with him about it. They think and let think. One condition and one only is required — a real desire to save their soul. Where this is, it is enough; they desire no more; they lay stress upon nothing else; they ask only, 'Is thy heart therein as my heart? If it be, give me thy hand.'"

He was alive to the defects of many who make much of religious feeling or strict dogmatic statements, yet are lamentably deficient in Christian charity. His own catholicity was accompanied by a chivalrous bearing towards opponents, to be ascribed, not to the indifference which treats doctrines and creeds as superfluous, but to his certitude concerning what he held as of faith, and to the more perfect love which casts out fear. The character such faith and love create is of far more importance than intellectual gifts. Too often highly rationalized convictions are found in men of weak purpose or low motive, and though opinions are an important part of character, and never more so than when they affect sacred matters, they should not be confused with it.

While his complex personality was not faultless, two things were never possible for Wesley: to betray even for a moment his religious vocation, or to hesitate at any sacrifice in its behalf. No one could be less careful of his own interests; he despised mercenary considerations, and the end of life found him as poor as he was at his birth. The narrowing lust of gold was abolished in him by his literal compliance with the word of the Master, a word which has always been one of the very last His followers are willing to apply to themselves. Wesley met it with thoroughness by giving away everything he had, and on his own showing he never possessed a hundred pounds which he could call his own. He brought himself and his followers within the divine injunction, "If thou wouldest be perfect, go, sell that thou hast, and give to the poor;" and his latest discourses contain frequent warnings against the demoralization of unconsecrated wealth. This is but one, and yet how sufficient an illustration of that profoundly religious spirit which dictated his affairs and sought through them to do the Highest Will. During a long and exalted career, of which he himself was the straitest censor, he occupied a height on which the light was always beating; content to be an inexplicable mystery to those who, actuated by a less devout or comprehensive temper, shared neither his convictions nor his experiences, and to fulfill the Apostle's ideal, "I live, yet not I, Christ liveth in me." He believed that God, in assuming human flesh, living sinlessly in its limitations, and dying for sinners, had effected that reconciliation between Himself and man which is the greatest achievement in moral history. This doctrine of the Person of our Lord he unfeignedly accepted; this, and this alone, was for him the unquestioned basis of his confidence and joy. He neither modified nor minimized it. It was "the creed

of creeds, involved in, and arising out of, the work of works."
The Church no less than the individual lived in and by its
central truth; the collapse of religion quickly followed its
abandonment. In that faith is to be found the intrinsic
explanation of Wesley's moral greatness, and the devotion
it inspired has always been the salient characteristic of
those, who, like him, have attained holiness in the patience
of Jesus Christ.

No spirit shines by its own radiance, and none can trans-
mit more light than its purity enables it to receive. The
strength and range of Wesley's illumination reflect the
closeness of his fellowship with the Light of lights. The
faith and works of the saint, the evangelist, the statesman,
the theologian, and the builder of the Church were derived
directly from his risen Lord. Had Christ entered the room
in Aldersgate Street as He did that other room in Jerusalem,
visible to the worshiping gaze of His disciples, and silencing
the doubts of Thomas, Wesley could not have left it more
determined to follow Him in His ministry of mercy and
redemption. From that moment he was borne upward
and onward by a supreme affection to freedom and to power
as the anointed servant of his century and of the nations.
As it is the function of fire to give light and warmth, so it
was the function of his new-found love to spread the sense of
love. His conversion discovered him an ecclesiastic ensnared
in legalisms; it made him the greatest prophet and evangelist the English-speaking people have known. Everything
lived at his touch, and as an agent of religious revolution
he earned the praise and reverence of those who imitated
his example, whether in his own or in other communions.

Undeterred by the appalling contrasts between his tastes
and habits and those of the degraded masses, he entered the
dreary haunts of physical and moral destitution, a spiritual
Archimedes, who had found his leverage and proposed to
upraise the lost and the abandoned, not only to decency,
but to holiness. He foresaw, gathered from these waste

places, an ideal Church of regenerated souls, broadly and securely based on love and social duty. Toward that divine society the faith of mankind is ever steadily growing, a society not of antagonisms, but of concord, not of artificial separation, but of spiritual unity — the Bride for whose coming her Heavenly Bridegroom waits.

If Wesley presented an extraordinary combination of characteristics seldom found in any individual, it is also of the first importance to remember that, unlike strong men in other spheres, he had the satisfaction of carrying out his own ideas. The sequence of events placed him in the unique position for which his qualities were exactly fitted; even the contradictions of his age enlarged his capacity for arousing and handling passional forces that previously had no outlet in religion. He made such diligent use of his entire equipment that the Church which was his own embodiment became to Britain and America the purveyor of his affection, his courage, his prudence, his detestation of sin, his love of the sinner, and his faith in a Higher Power. Memory frequently tells a tale almost as flattering as that of hope, but few characters appear in the teeming fields of retrospect which justify its optimism more than does that of Wesley. Happy is the nation which gave him to the highest possible service. Incalculable are the obligations North America and the world at large owe her for such a gift. Blessed are the people in whose midst he moved, vigorous without vehemence, neither loud nor labored, but as a fixed star of truth and goodness, a pattern of private excellence and public virtue.

And while he is regarded with ever deepening reverence and gratitude, not the least cause for thankfulness is the assurance that He who sent him forth as the angel of the churches, to "turn the hearts of the fathers to the children, and the disobedient to walk in the wisdom of the just; to make ready for the Lord a people prepared for Him," can and will, in His infinite goodness, grant His Israel another prince who shall continue Wesley's work.

IMPORTANT DATES IN WESLEY'S LIFE

1725   Ordained Deacon.
1726   Elected Fellow of Lincoln College.
1727   Degree of M.A. conferred at Oxford, February 14.
1727–28   Curate at Epworth and Wroote.
1729–35   Tutor at Oxford.
1736–38   Georgia, America.
1739–91   Itinerated in England, Scotland, and Ireland.

Presided at the following Conferences:

1744	London	1760	Bristol	1776	London
1745	Bristol	1761	London	1777	Bristol
1746	Bristol	1762	Leeds	1778	Leeds
1747	London	1763	London	1779	London
1748	Bristol	1764	Bristol	1780	Bristol
1749	London	1765	Manchester	1781	Leeds
1750	Bristol	1766	Leeds	1782	London
1751	Bristol	1767	London	1783	Bristol
1752	Bristol	1768	Bristol	1784	Leeds
1753	Leeds	1769	Leeds	1785	London
1854	London	1770	London	1786	Bristol
1755	Leeds	1771	Bristol	1787	Manchester
1756	Bristol	1772	Leeds	1788	London
1757	London	1773	London	1789	Leeds
1758	Bristol	1774	Bristol	1790	Bristol
1759	London	1775	Leeds		

Born at Epworth, June 28, 1703.
Died at City Road, London, March 2, 1791, aged 88 years.

BIBLIOGRAPHY

BIRRELL, AUGUSTINE. Essays and Addresses.
DAVENPORT, F. M. Primitive Traits in Religious Revivals.
Encyclopædia Britannica. Article on Wesley. Vol. XXVIII. 11th edition.
FAULKNER, J. A. The Methodists.
FITCHETT, W. H. Wesley and His Century.
GODLEY, A. D. Oxford in the Eighteenth Century.
GREGORY, J. ROBINSON. A History of Methodism.
INGE, W. R. Studies of English Mystics.
JACKSON, THOMAS. Life of Charles Wesley.
JAMES, WILLIAM. Varieties of Religious Experience.
LECKY, W. E. H. History of England in the Eighteenth Century.
MAINS, G. P. Francis Asbury.
McCARTHY, JUSTIN. The Four Georges.
Methodism, A New History of. Edited by W. J. Townsend, H. B. Workman, and George Eayrs.
OVERTON, J. H. John Wesley.
OVERTON, J. H. The Evangelical Revival in the Eighteenth Century.
PATTISON, MARK. Essays.
RIGG, J. H. The Living Wesley.
ROSCOE, E. S. The English Scene in the Eighteenth Century.
SEELEY, J. R. The Expansion of England.
SIMON, J. S. The Revival of Religion in the Eighteenth Century.
SNELL, F. J. Wesley and Methodism.
SOUTHEY, ROBERT. Life of Wesley.
STEPHEN, SIR LESLIE. English Thought in the Eighteenth Century.
SYDNEY, W. C. England and the English in the Eighteenth Century.
TELFORD, JOHN. Life of Charles Wesley.
TELFORD, JOHN. John Wesley.
TYERMAN, LUKE. Life and Times of Rev. John Wesley.
TYERMAN, LUKE. The Oxford Methodists.
WEDGWOOD, JULIA. John Wesley and the Evangelical Reaction of the Eighteenth Century.
WINCHESTER, C. T. John Wesley.
Wesley's Journal. Standard Edition. Edited by Nehemiah Curnock.

BOOK III

JOHN HENRY NEWMAN

AND

THE OXFORD MOVEMENT OF 1833–1845

AND when the stream
Which overflowed the soul was passed **away,**
A consciousness remained that it had left,
Deposited upon the silent shore
Of memory, images and precious thoughts,
That shall not die, and cannot be destroyed.

WORDSWORTH: *The Excursion,* Book VII.

CHAPTER IX

THE NINETEENTH CENTURY RENAISSANCE

WITHOUT doubt, if religion could remain in the pure realm of sentiment, it would be beyond the jurisdiction of science; but religion expresses and realises itself in doctrines and institutions which cannot be exempted from criticism. These doctrines, which bear upon their face the indelible date of their birth, implicate as to the constitution of the universe, the history of the early ages of humanity, the origin and nature of the writings in the canonical Scriptures, certain notions borrowed from the philosophy and general science of a bygone period of human history. To force them upon the philosophy and science of to-day and to-morrow is not merely to commit an anachronism; it is to enter upon a desperate conflict in which the authority of the past is defeated in advance.

This is why traditional theology appears always to be in distress; one by one she abandons her ancient positions, having been unable to find security or a basis of defence in any of them.

AUGUSTE SABATIER.

CHAPTER IX

No modern religious revival has received more attention from writers of literary distinction than the Oxford Movement of the early Victorian period. The main reason for any further reference to it is that each succeeding generation sees it from a different point of view, and fashions for itself its own conceptions of the issues which the Movement projected into art, poetry, ecclesiasticism, theology, and religion. Moreover, the transcendent personality of John Henry Newman is inseparably associated with that particular epoch in Anglicanism, and has been a perennial source of attraction for representatives of every school of thought. Dr. A. E. Abbott, Thomas Huxley, James Martineau, Dean Burgon, Dean Church, Thomas Mozley, Principal Fairbairn, Wilfred Ward, and Algernon Cecil are distinguished names selected at random from a host of contemporaries and biographers who have been identified in the effort to shape a true history both of the Movement itself and of Newman as its most commanding figure. His pervasive influence upon religion and human life gave rise to endless controversies, in which friend and foe were alike inspired by the sentiment that he belonged not only to his own but to following eras, and though no longer for many of them what he was for the first group of followers at Oxford, still for all, and for those who should come after them, one of the spiritual geniuses of the race.

The memorable year of 1833 marked an awakening in the Established Church of England, due in large measure to the conjunction of Newman with John Keble and Richard Hurrell Froude at Oriel College. That awakening transformed the ecclesiastical ideals of High Anglicanism: it manifestly affected the worship and ritual of churches derived from Puritanism, and it materially modified the attitude of the British nation toward the Papacy. Principles and opinions which seemed farthest removed from the actual surface consciousness of Englishmen were recovered and disseminated with astonishing vigor and success. Doctrines and ordinances that had become well-nigh obsolete and indeed difficult to understand were quickened by the interpretative imagination of this new cult of Catholic Anglicans.

The principal outlines of their propaganda have long been familiar, and although its legitimacy has been seriously questioned, those who write to prove that the Oxford Movement did not confer lasting blessings upon the Church as a whole waste their own time and that of their readers. Yet at its worst it has been a source of strife and schism rather than of peace and unity among believers in one Lord and one Gospel. Its advocates were prone to set aside things evidenced in behalf of things assumed. Their habit of ignoring realities which refused to be accommodated to their peculiar theories, and of wrongly distributing cause and effect, narrowed their outlook, confused their judgments, and cheapened their estimates. However, the one important matter about the sun is not its spots, but its light and heat, and although there were extensive discolorations and false appearances in the radiance which arose at Oxford during the last century, at least it dispelled the indifference and doubt which had hitherto thwarted the progress of the Established Church.

The type of Anglicanism to which Keble and Froude, and, through them, Newman belonged was not common either among the clergy or the laity. It originated, not only from the days of Laud and the Neoplatonists, but also from the teachings of the Latin Fathers, and from the traditions of medieval Christianity in the twelfth and thirteenth centuries. The *depositum fidei* of these periods, though frequently neglected, was always latent in Anglicanism; when given an opportunity by the failure of Calvinistic Evangelicalism, and stimulated by a series of political agitations, it suddenly sprang into prominence, showed an unexpected vitality, and assailed some time-honored theories which had hitherto contained the substance of loyal churchmanship.

But while what may be called the historic leaven of Tractarianism [1] existed long prior to its emergence, its characteristic forms and tendencies were determined by the local atmosphere and by current events. It is therefore necessary to ascertain as fully as may be possible its direct and indirect causes, the motives which governed its initiators, their relative importance, their particular efforts, their relations with other clerical parties, their political, social, philosophical, and religious environments, and the sum total of these various factors. Some such comprehensive survey, which seeks to examine and combine into coherent unity a great variety of elements, many of which are ostensibly unrelated, is never more requisite than when dealing with the operations of the human mind in the realm of religious speculation. For nowhere else does the blended life of thought and action become so subtle and intricate, or spread its roots over such widely separated areas. It draws its sustenance from sources which

[1] Christopher Benson (1798–1868), Canon of Worcester and Master of the Temple, an Evangelical of the more liberal sort, is credited with the invention of the name "Tractarian" as applied to Newman and his colleagues.

betray no kinship among themselves. And even when the lines of research are extended beyond the ordinary, contributory facts are likely to remain outside them. The proposed method of investigation is exacting, and any attempt to follow it must at best be but approximate. Yet it is as indispensable for a veritable history as for a judicial verdict upon its material, and should lead to that last and best result — a sympathetic knowledge of the whole.

Nor can it be forgotten that beyond and far above the assertions and disputes which confront us at every turn is a ceaseless moral force, a divine tribunal, which regulates their claims, and admits or rejects their pleas, so that any effort to find the exact points of continuity between past and present Anglicanism, to connect its apparently isolated eras, and rightly present their meanings, should be reverent in spirit as well as catholic in purpose.

I

During the opening decades of the nineteenth century, Europe was absorbed in the dramatic and overwhelming career of Napoleon the Great. His name was on every tongue, the menace of his measures in peace or war disturbed every heart. Great Britain's integrity was at stake; even the destruction of her commerce and the capture of her outlying provinces and dependencies were contingencies entirely overshadowed by the threatened invasion of the Homeland itself. The energies of the nation were monopolized by the political dangers of a ravaging time. There was neither opening nor inclination for matters of less immediate concern; these, however imperative in themselves, were postponed to a more convenient season. What vitality the Church possessed spent itself in subservience to the antagonisms of theological and political partisanship, or in denouncing the tenets inculcated by the Revolutionists of France. The ideas mediated through Voltaire, Rousseau,

Diderot, and other savants and philosophers to men of fearful and decisive action, such as Mirabeau, Barnave, Danton, Desmoulins, and the Terrorists, were originally adopted from English history, political philosophy, and romance. For enlightened Frenchmen England became the dreamland of freedom of conscience, and those who knew her language of liberty began to evince an independence of thought which foreboded the hurricane that followed. But although the anæmic organism of France had been flooded with life by Scotch and English thinkers and economists, the vast majority of sober if shortsighted Britons heeded Burke's magnificent warnings, and refused to have any dealings with a regeneration disfigured by prodigious cruelties and excesses. Even those who regarded with a measure of approval the doctrines of liberty, equality, and fraternity deferred their consideration. A strong reactionary temper pervaded society and nullified the demand for domestic reforms.

The Crown had been subjected to repeated humiliations by the intellectual, and still more the moral frailty of successive monarchs. Aristocratic circles dictated the wobbling experiments of a Government incapable of self-improvement and without that steadfast support which a policy of justice toward the oppressed might have obtained. The narrow and despotic caliber of such publicists as Sidmouth, Castlereagh, Eldon, and Liverpool displayed a skill that wore many of the aspects of intrigue against the popular welfare and defeated every proposition in its behalf. Even more enlightened statesmen, including Tierney, Brougham, and Mackintosh, who urged legal propriety in the numerous trials for sedition and treason, and less drastic punishment for lawless outbreaks, were prompt to disclaim any relation with the deluded Radicals. The gross and open corruption of an extremely limited franchise by noble and wealthy families; the political and religious disabilities to which large and growing towns and cities were subjected, while insignificant and in some instances nearly extinct constituencies were over-represented in Parliament, aroused the wrath of industrial magnates who owed their positions to their own enterprise and their exploitation of labor. Whigs and Tories were more at variance with the masses than with each other. Nor would this composite and depressing picture of the aristocracy, the landowners, and the merchants be complete without a reference to the official nepotists and place-hunters who

> " leech-like, to their fainting country ' clung,' "

heartily despising the proletariat and defending the ministers who rewarded them with jobs, titles, and pensions.

The universities and the public schools which fed them had too often fostered obscurantism in preference to light and freedom. Reflecting, as they did, stolid prejudices and customs, they became the haunts of ultra-conservatism rather than dispensaries of knowledge at any risk, encouraging that love of truth "for which youth is the inevitable season." At Oxford, as nowhere else, were to be found the last ponderous links of the shattered chains of feudalism, chafing her temper and hampering her advance. The scrutiny of spiritual or secular authority at once offended her well-drilled instincts. Tastes and habits inherited and inborn, arising from the depths of her immemorial past, protested against change of any kind.

At this critical juncture the bishops and heads of colleges were found in alliance with other stable elements of polite society against that painful revulsion to actual life which sharply disturbed their stock notions and comfortable existence. So long as the dread of Napoleon's hegemony lasted, revolt against them and against governmental control by the landed proprietors, although incipient, was held in check. Once released, it became aggressively persistent; allegiance to the monarchy visibly declined, the prescriptive rights of prelates and peers were rudely assailed, and acquiescence in the rule of existing hierarchies of Church and State was withdrawn. From 1812 to 1832 these privileged orders were made the objects of popular attack. The leaders of the onslaught represented nearly every rank and condition of society, and those who made it effective were men of birth and breeding. But its underlying causes existed in the general discontent, wretchedness, and poverty.

Artisans and peasants, crushed by the burden of the largest debt ever yet incurred by any nation, were not allowed to participate in public affairs. The destitution which crowded on the heels of an artificial prosperity, due to war tariffs and inflated prices, led to misery and disaffection among the poor. For the time, labor-saving machinery, which eventually gave England her commercial supremacy, bore hard on the hand-craftsmen. Agriculture was prostrated, farms went out of cultivation, half the inhabitants of many rural parishes were reduced to beggary, and the price of iron, the staple product in manufactures, fell fifty per cent. As a consequence bread riots were frequent, and had to be repressed by the use of the military arm.

This widespread distress was not only accentuated by the selfishness and incapacity of the Government, but exaggerated by the fiery harangues of patriots and demagogues. Among the exponents of a larger freedom whose motives were sincere, William Cobbett was remarkable, rather for his embodiment of the hopes and fears of the yeomanry than for any consistent scheme of reform. Amazing as were his extravagances, his exhaustless store of passionate and picturesque rhetoric, racy of the soil, enabled him to wield such an extensive sway that Hazlitt declared he formed a Fourth Estate in himself. The violence of pamphleteers and orators like Hobhouse and Hunt, and the satirical and denunciatory poetry of Byron and Shelley, excited public indignation until it became permanent and dangerous.

Such a lamentable state of affairs was further aggravated by the eternal problem of Ireland, where those outside the pale of Ulster looked upon those within it as occupants of a stolen territory. The history of the sister island pronounced judgment upon Englishmen as strong, resourceful, but unscrupulous rulers. The wrongs inflicted upon Roman Catholic natives because of their ancestral faith were kept alive by vivid recollection and frequent recurrence. The name and fellowship of Britons were abominated. The news of their supremacy at home or abroad was heard with loathing, the anticipation of their defeat nurtured as the best of consolations.[1] These woes at last found a trumpet voice in Daniel O'Connell, whose pleading for the annulment of the penal laws against their religion entranced his countrymen. His arraignments of this bigoted discrimination marked the turning of the tide of Toryism, which at last had overreached itself and, despite the unique influence of the Duke of Wellington, then the "foremost captain of his time," began to run swiftly in the opposite direction.

The Dissenters now rallied their forces for the total repeal of the Corporation Act and the Test Act.[2] Among other persons of consequence the Duke of Sussex, Lord Holland, and Lord John Russell came to their aid, and insisted upon a complete restoration of the civil and religious rights of three million subjects who belonged to Nonconformist churches. These Acts were an evil legacy from the reign of Charles II, and the question of their repeal had been shirked from 1790 until 1828. In operation they had gradually sunk beneath the level of contempt, and were denounced for injecting the venom of theological quarrels into political discussion, and profaning religion with the vices of worldly ambition, thus making it both hateful to man and offensive to God. Lord Eldon predicted that their removal from the statute-

---

[1] W. S. Lilly: "Characteristics from the Writings of John Henry Newman"; pp. 158–159.

[2] The Test Act compelled all persons holding office of profit or trust under the Crown to take the oath of allegiance, to receive the Sacrament of the Lord's Supper according to the rites of the Church of England, and to subscribe to the declaration against Transubstantiation. The Corporation Act, of like import, militated against the ascendency of Nonconformists in cities and towns.

book, which took place in 1826, would speedily be followed
by a Catholic Emancipation Bill. The event justified his
forecast; O'Connell's election to Parliament in the same year
raised the question in such an acute form that Wellington
and Peel found themselves powerless to quell the agitation
which ensued, and on April 13, 1829, that measure became
law.

The long-delayed abolition of these anomalies was only the
prelude for an extension of the electoral franchise obtained
three years later under Lord Grey's premiership. The
Tories realigned their shattered ranks to save the constitution, as they declared, from the invasions of an insolent
rabble bent on destroying the Crown, the Church, the landed
system, and whatever else made England truly great. The
nobles were impervious to social pressure; the isolation imposed upon them by their position made them contemptuous of changes near at hand; changes they could not
prevent, but which they scorned with the fury of outraged
pride and injured self-interest. Their wild prophecies of
irremediable evil were groundless. The Reform Bill introduced by Lord Grey contained nothing inconsistent with the
principles or practices of England's unwritten constitution,
or that in any way violated the precedents upon which it was
founded. Pitt had contended for the aristocracy as against
the usurpations of the personal rule of George the Third;
Grey contended for the bankers and manufacturers as against
the monopolies of the aristocracy. The democracy which
had borne the weight of the Napoleonic wars lay outside the
range of Whig statesmanship.

Nothing was done to remove the economic grievances from
which the nation suffered, and many other notorious wrongs
were left unredressed. Yet the Bill encountered such determined opposition, prepared to go to any length for its defeat,
that a more comprehensive enactment could not have been
secured without incurring the risks of civil war. If the
formidable and weighty reasonings of Grey and Russell could

not be refuted, the Bill could at least be voted down in that Malakoff of Toryism, the House of Lords; and voted down it was. Twenty-one bishops registered themselves in the total majority of forty-one against it.

Upon its rejection the people rose in resistless strength, and converted Grey's proposals into law. Disturbances at Bristol, Nottingham, Derby, and other industrial centers showed that no faction could hold its own against the will of an aroused commonwealth, and after being presented to the House three times in twelve months, the Bill again passed the Commons. A hundred and fifty thousand men met at Birmingham, formerly the scene of the depredations of a Church and King mob which destroyed Dr. Priestley's house, and petitioned William IV to create as many new peers as might be necessary to ensure the success of the measure. It was no longer a question of what the Lords would do with the Bill, but of what the country would do with the Lords. At the final moment, and just in time to prolong the Hanoverian dynasty for happier days, the King yielded, the Bill passed both Houses, and received the royal assent. The peers, who had withdrawn their opposition, skulked in clubs and country mansions, careless to dissemble their chagrin.

Although this broadening of the suffrage was too restricted to accomplish any immediate revolutionary changes, it renewed the youth of England without forfeiting the advantages of her rich experience. It battered down some strongholds of privilege, released a forward impulse for the causes of religious and civil equity, preserved the realm from internecine strife, and placed its government on a surer basis of confidence and good will. Boundaries were prescribed for the haughty claims of a hereditary peerage, and the encroachments of a self-perpetuating oligarchy received a decided repulse. Best of all, and most conducive to the welfare of the nation, Lord Grey's victory animated the public mind with a spirit of courage, patience, and generous enthusiasm. It enabled men to bide their time and devote themselves afresh to the justice and freedom for which the Bill of 1832 supplied a precedent. Hope rather than realization inspired the rejoicings which everywhere prevailed. Nor was that hope to be made ashamed. It found its fruition in an orderly and lawful development of popular control under which Britain has become the mother and the maker of States, and which has furnished the model for similar constitutional efforts.

II

The political and social conditions which gave birth to those events that precipitated the Oxford Movement were naturally followed by a revival of philosophical speculation, which raised new issues for theology and controverted current orthodoxy with unwonted boldness. Reflective minds, freed from the distractions due to international difficulties, reverted to the more congenial pursuits of intellectual and ethical inquiry. "The several religious parties, disengaged from their civic campaign, were sent home to their spiritual husbandry, and thrown upon their intrinsic resources of genius and character. The time, ever so critical for Church and doctrine, had come at last, — the time of searching thought and quiet work. Other charity than would serve upon the hustings, — a deeper gospel than was known at apocalyptic tea tables, — a piety stimulant of no platform cheers, became indispensable in evidence and expression of the Christian life." [1]

Among the currents of reforming thought which flowed into the stream of nineteenth century philosophy the first in order, though not in merit, was the ethical system of the Benthamites, known as Utilitarianism. No divination of impending changes which arose on the ruins of the Napoleonic régime was more keen and resolute than that of these thinkers, who followed in the wake of Locke's seventeenth century

[1] James Martineau: "Essays, Reviews, and Addresses"; Vol. I, p. 222.

empiricism, and also reproduced the strength and the weakness of eighteenth century philosophy. In the midst of intellectual and social unrest, of doubt, perplexity, and hesitation, the writings of the Benthamites were distinguished for their cool acumen, fearlessness, dogmatic assurance, and for a fastidious integrity which gave them a wide popularity. They were not collections of desultory remarks, but orderly and articulated discussions of absorbing themes which permitted no deviation. Their beginnings had reference to their conclusions, and almost every part had some relation, and frequently a close one, to other parts.

Jeremy Bentham concentrated his attention on jurisprudence, James Mill on psychology, and John Stuart Mill expounded a new political economy. Although the subjects with which they dealt were too full of the contentions brought about by the growth of knowledge for their works to become permanent authorities, nevertheless they were erudite, thorough, far-reaching; notable for skillful capacity and high aims. The writers were principally concerned to discover the meaning and obligation of the moral code under which men lived. Finding, as they contended, nothing save contradictions, they resolved to begin *de novo*. Their unflinching application of reason to moral phenomena led them to a complete abandonment of prevailing ethical creeds. Thus deprived of any assistance from the past, they fixed attention on man himself as the one indispensable reality.

Utilitarianism defined matter as "the permanent possibility of sensation," and mind as "the permanent possibility of feeling." Experience was the sole source of knowledge, and the mind derived its entire fund of materials through the senses, *a priori* and intuitive elements of every kind being rejected. The so-called primary truths or innate ideas were only habits of the mind which time and repetition had rendered irresistible. The mind, the Benthamites averred, contributed nothing of itself to the structure of knowledge. John Stuart Mill went so far as to deny the principle of contradiction, and declared that we were not even sure that we were not sure. When Hume conceded the necessary truth of the axioms of Euclid, Mill rebelled against the concession, and urged that "there might be another world in which two and two make five." "My mind is but a series of feelings," he remarked, "a thread of consciousness, however supplemented by the believed possibilities of consciousness, which are not, though they might be realized."

Although Mill disliked the inference, and tried to escape it, these views were closely affiliated with necessitarianism. "An act of will," quoting from his own words, "is a moral effect which follows the corresponding moral causes as certainly and invariably as physical effects follow their physical causes." This and similar statements which dealt with the subtleties of human nature lacked Mill's customary clearness and accuracy. Their looseness and confusion have since been remarked by more critical philosophers, to whom it was obvious that they aimed a mortal blow at ethical freedom, and annulled that personal responsibility which is the source of moral character.

The attack on the integrity and reality of mind as the nexus of personality and on the will as the decisive factor in conduct has now spent its force. It endeavored to undermine the only intelligent basis for experience, notwithstanding that on experience the Utilitarians rested their whole case. From it alone they sought to derive the laws which govern mental and moral life, but they gave no satisfactory explanation of the unity of consciousness which is presupposed in every form of intellectual activity. Apart from that unity, such self-evident functions of mind as discrimination and combination are altogether impossible. The mind itself, reduced to a mere series of feelings, is destroyed as a real agent. And in his oscillations between idealism and materialism, Mill was frequently compelled to recognize personality, the existence of which he sought to disprove.

The assertion that individual and universal happiness
2 D

according to reason was the most desirable end, was a further and incurable defect in Utilitarianism and also a virtual impeachment of its entire ethical position. The qualitative distinction between one form of happiness and another required a moral sense to discern it. For Bentham push-pin was as good as poetry provided it afforded equal pleasure. Mill shied at this ludicrous deduction, and averred that it was better to be Socrates dissatisfied than a fool satisfied. Many critics heartily echoed Mill's plea, but he could not urge it and remain consistent. His observation displaced pleasure as the standard and goal in itself. Carlyle chuckled over the lameness of Mill's logic in the statement that each person's happiness was a good to that person, and therefore the general happiness a good to the aggregate of persons. Even later Utilitarians, without any admiration for the Sage of Chelsea's somewhat uncouth retort, have felt equally impatient with reasonings that entailed such a sordid and unlovely view of human nature.

A theory which denied the existence of *a priori* ideas and the trustworthiness of the moral sense necessarily obliterated the fundamental distinction between right and wrong, and ended by enthroning social utility, with personal happiness for its inspiring motive, as the paramount law of conduct. The bases of faith were thus swept away, and conscience was merged into enlightened self-interest, the prevalence of which would presently demonstrate that Christianity was superfluous.

In rebuttal, it has been shown that the true relation between the individual and social welfare is not sentimental but rational. On the ground that man is incapable of finding contentment in gratified feeling, but capable of self-realization in a common good, the opponents of Utilitarianism were justified in setting aside arguments founded on comparisons of pleasures. The conviction that the emotional nature provides no ground of authority for moral conduct, and that conscience and reason do this, and do it in all realms, awakened Thomas Arnold's antipathy to Benthamism and Newmanism alike as "the two grand counterfeits forged at the opposite extremes of error. The one merged the conscience in self-interest, the other in priestcraft : the one identified moral and sentient good, the other separated moral and spiritual. Both extinguished the proper personality and individual sacredness of man ; the one treating him as a thing to be mechanically shaped, the other as a thing to be mysteriously conjured with. In opposition to both systems, which sought for human conduct some external guide, the one in social utility, the other in church authority, Arnold held fast to the internal guidance which he maintained God had given to all, and through which His Will was practicable and Himself accessible to all." [1]

The repelling effect of the Utilitarian ethic upon confident believers in a Divine order, who held with passionate intensity definite views of the constant workings of that order in the world, can scarcely be imagined now. Set forth, as it was, in penetrating ways, the creed owed as much to the weakness of its antagonists as to its inherent strength, and released a militant spirit with which the Church seemed unable to cope. Enjoying nothing of that noble intimacy with the inner facts of life which illuminates philosophical speculation, its stark individualism made a powerful appeal to those who delighted in things which perish with the using, and who looked upon pleasure as the sole end of being.

Yet on its better side this philosophy rebuked the indifference of churchmen and religionists to social disparities. It gave pause to the cold-blooded rapture with which some Evangelicals portrayed the doom of the material universe. It originated and set in motion many useful and wisely considered reforms, and by its thoroughgoing treatment of personality it compelled theologians to reëxamine moral and religious intuitions, and to seek less assailable grounds

[1] James Martineau : "Essays, Reviews, and Addresses" ; Vol. I, pp. 73–74.

for their opinions.   They were admonished to remember that
Christianity should be reasonable as well as devout; should
invigorate the intelligence as well as transform character;
that it should neither darken the conscience nor scandalize
the mind.   But behind the efforts of the Benthamites to
explain man lay that belittling estimate of human nature
which impaired their discourse and thwarted their enterprises.   Notwithstanding that their economic teachings have
borne fruit in many directions, their system as a whole is a
warning that a sufficient doctrine of man's essential nobility
must lie at the foundation of any speculation or action which
proposes the betterment of the race.[1]

Among other opponents to Benthamism, the Tractarians
donned their armor and entered upon a campaign in which
they proved, if not invulnerable, at any rate, uncompromising antagonists, who neither gave nor asked for quarter.
Yet John Stuart Mill, the latest oracle of rationalistic inspiration, had much to say for these determined adversaries.   "He
used to tell us," remarked Lord Morley, "that the Oxford
Theologians had done for England something like what
Guizot, Villemain, Michelet, Cousin had done a little earlier
for France; they had opened, broadened, deepened the issues
and meanings of European history; they had reminded us
that history is European, that it is quite unintelligible if
treated as merely local.   Moreover, thought should recognize
thought and mind always welcome mind; and the Oxford
men had at least brought argument, learning, and even philosophy of a sort to bear upon the narrow and frigid conven-
tions of the reigning system in church and college, in pulpits
and professional chairs.   They had made the church ashamed
of the evil of her ways, they had determined that spirit of
improvement from within, which, if this sect-ridden country
is ever really to be taught, must proceed *pari passu* with
assault from without.'" [2]

[1] For a further treatment of Utilitarianism see the author's volume on
"Charles Darwin and Other English Thinkers"; pp. 91–139.
[2] "Life of Gladstone"; Vol. I, pp. 163, 164.

The ethical speculations enumerated were quickened by the inflow of Teutonic thought, whether to deluge or to irrigate, which began about this time at the Universities of Oxford and Cambridge. In Germany Hume's appeal to the world of the five senses had long ceased to charm superior minds. A succession of poets and thinkers emulated one another in brushing aside the sandy sophisms of Locke and the conclusions of his school. They destroyed the after-math of eighteenth century deism which encouraged the notion of an absentee God, and they reinvested His creation with spiritual significance and splendor. The infinite and finite elements in man and nature were reiterated by Goethe and Kant, Hegel and Lessing, Fichte and Schiller. Meta-physics was reëstablished upon an ampler basis, psychology assumed a subordinate place, and the universe was viewed by them as pulsating with the mystery and majesty of endless life and purpose.

Immanuel Kant continued the apologetic of Butler in behalf of supernaturalism, but he went far beyond the Eng-lish doctor's Probabilism, and rejected the mischievous idea that the chief end of religion was to promote morality. His reasoning demonstrated that in the sequence such a notion was inimical to religion. Disinterestedness was the essence of virtue; wherever ulterior motives prevailed, and however derived, they were subversive of genuine morality. The scarcely disguised Utilitarianism of Paley, who defined virtue as the doing of good to mankind in obedience to the will of God, and for the sake of everlasting happiness, made virtue to spring from self-seeking, and found its sanction in rewards and punishments. This other-world selfishness, as it has been justly termed, was set aside by the categorical impera-tive of Kant, which rested morality on duty, and defined religion as the love of goodness for its own sake, and the cheerful acceptance of duty without regard to gain or loss, because it was the manifested will of the Eternal.

On that day in the year when the faculty of the University

of Koenigsberg went to the town church to worship, Kant
paused at the entrance of the sacred edifice and returned
home to his study, thus revealing his attitude toward Lutheran theology and discipline.   Yet inadequate as his interpretation of religion was in the direction of practical devotion, it served to vindicate faith on its philosophical side, and
to rescue it from the oblivion to which some advanced thinkers
had consigned it, transferring it to an invigorating intellectual
climate, in which evasive conformity or patronizing superiority was no longer the accepted mark of culture.

Lessing felt as keenly as Kant the necessity for a rejuvenated ethic and religion.   But realizing that he was without
the capacity to bring this about, he invoked the advent of a
stronger thinker.   The Messiah of the new era was Schleiermacher, with whom Luther's reform returned to its creative
principle — justification by the faith of the heart — and
Protestantism entered upon a new phase.

His Moravian antecedents endowed Schleiermacher with a
warm intense piety, not unduly dogmatic.   His philosophical
caste was fashioned in the dialectic of Plato and Spinoza.
He strove to reconcile sentiment and reason, and to find a
scientific theory for faith.   His "Discourses upon Religion,"
which appeared in 1799, blended the passion for religion,
which is in truth a great romanticism, with the play of a
marvelous sympathy, which, again, is only another aspect of
imagination.   The happy abstractions of the scholar were
varied by the fervid aspirations of the saint.   His readers
felt the emission from his words of something pure and kindling, which evoked their better selves.   Those in whom piety
was at odds with mental temperament and circumstances
were reconciled by the teachings of a prophet who could not
conceive of religion except in terms of the subjective consciousness and apart from anything external.   The divine
life in man had its residence in the emotions, and was as carefully separated from dogmatic authority as it was from ethical
precepts.   Independent, because in itself supreme, religion,

according to the famous German preacher and theologian, was an ineffable communion between the heart and God. "It vindicates for itself its own sphere and its own character only by abandoning entirely the provinces of science and practice; and when it has raised itself beside them, the whole field is for the first time completely filled and human nature perfected. Religion reveals itself as the necessary and indispensable third, as the natural complement of knowledge and conduct, not inferior to them in worth and dignity." [1]

The origin and development of experiences must be analyzed before reliable data could be obtained. Hence the proper subject for religious inquiry was the mind engaged and absorbed in the knowledge that God is all and in all. In brief, the entire question of the nature of religion and its expression was transferred from philosophy to psychology, and its authority was found in no creed nor volume, still less in an ecclesiastical organization, but in the attested experiences of the devout. External standards could not bind the spiritual man; he judged all things; within his breast and nowhere else, the divine law registered those decisions from which there was no appeal. Theology, therefore, was not speculative but expressive. Its subject matter consisted of the facts of Christian experience, and its function was to formulate these without reference to the problems of metaphysics or the discoveries of physical science.

But while every believer's personal consciousness of sin vanquished and overcome by the mediation of Christ constituted for him the ultimate ground of his confidence, it was impossible for him to isolate this experience from that of others similarly blessed. A nature steeped in the life of faith clung to the principle of association, without which it could not reach its fullest possibilities. Furthermore, the immanence of God in humanity, an idea fundamental to Schleiermacher's entire system, was directly related to the

[1] Quoted by Arthur C. McGiffert: "The Rise of Modern Religious Ideas"; pp. 65 et seq.

rise and structure of the Church as its manifestation. On these two immovable pillars he founded her strength and security, conceiving her, not as an institution, nor as an hierarchy, but as the congregation of faithful souls, in whose corporate existence the dwelling of the Divine Spirit forbade schisms, casting out the self-will and discords which created them, and fusing its members into one living body which radiated a glowing fellowship to every part.

This transfer of the seat of religious authority to experience, while still preserving the place and integrity of the Bible and the Church, delivered believers from apprehension concerning those changes which attend expansion in knowledge. The Church, steadfast in the spiritual consciousness of her children, was under no necessity to practice methods which, while they stifled doubt, failed to reach the truth. Her path was cleared of sacerdotal and credal obstacles; vulnerable theories of Biblical inerrancy and ecclesiastical infallibility, which could not survive the tests now being brought to bear upon them, were relegated to the rear. The growth of God's Kingdom was hastened by this spirit of courageous candor, which welcomed truth for its own sake, let it emanate whence it may.

The sources of Schleiermacher's views are traceable to the Greek Fathers of the second century, in particular to Clement of Alexandria. Both in its positive and negative elements Schleiermacher's mind was as entirely Greek as St. Augustine's was entirely Latin. The juristic theology of the latter was dissolved under the imaginative mystical quality of Schleiermacher's conceptions. He resented concrete things, and preferred to think of Christianity as a living organism endowed with the potentiality for continuous growth. Hence, the content of the spiritual consciousness was always being increased, and this increase was the material for a progressive as opposed to a static theology. The Augustinian doctrines of total depravity, atonement in the terms of sacrificial Judaism, and the endless punishment of the unregenerate, were set aside as repugnant to God and man. The conception of God as a Being between Whom and His creatures yawned an impassable gulf was rejected as derogatory to the self-communicating life and love of the Eternal Father. On the contrary, Schleiermacher proclaimed an illimitable range of possibilities as the chief feature of divine and human intercourse. And although such boundlessness was too vague and shadowy for less refined and mystical intellects, or for those which were attached to dogmatic and symbolic forms, it was equally true that in recovering and amplifying the idea of God which had prevailed in the ancient Church, Schleiermacher summoned the leaders of his own and after times to a fountain of suggestiveness which has fertilized many areas of Christian thought and replenished the inspiration for Christian living.[1]

To him belongs, therefore, the honor of giving a fresh impulse and direction to metaphysics and theology. He showed that there could be an experimental science of religion, which observed, classified, and elucidated spiritual phenomena. Thus, in the words of Sabatier, to obtain independence for religion and for the science of religion its uncontested supremacy was the most eminent service which Schleiermacher rendered at once to faith and philosophy. His interpretations were instrumental in emphasizing much that is highest and best in the life of the spirit. Directly or indirectly, he left a permanent impress on Protestantism, both in Europe and America, and even ecclesiastics who have refused to make any terms with Modernism and for whom an unchanging order is the governing power of faith, have felt to some extent the vivifying touch of this luminary of his age.

The new blossoming of the European mind, largely due to the fundamental brain work of German metaphysicians and scholars, began to manifest itself in science and

[1] Alexander V. G. Allen: "The Continuity of Christian Thought"; p. 397.

history.   The publication of Sir Charles Lyell's "Principles of Geology" heralded the advent of Evolution, with its immense range of biological facts, and caused nothing short of a panic in those circles already gravely perturbed by political and theological liberalism.   Its "wild theories and preposterous conclusions," which were more easily denounced than answered, contravened the cosmogonies of Genesis, and the coincidence of the appearance of Lyell's volume with the formation of the British Association for the Advancement of Science seemed darkly ominous to the orthodox.   To make matters worse, the book steadily won approval from experts competent to judge, and marked the beginning of a serious attempt to arrange scientific phenomena in more coördinated forms.   Lyell's work and its extensive implications altered the whole tone of Darwin's thinking, who declared that but for the inspiration derived from Lyell his own conclusions might never have been obtained.   "I have long wished," he wrote in 1845, "not so much for your sake as for my own feelings of honesty, to acknowledge more plainly than by mere reference how much I owe to you.   Those authors who, like you, educate people's minds, as well as teach them special facts, can never, I should think, have full justice done to them except by posterity."   These inquiries, while possessing the romantic interest attached to excursions in hitherto unknown fields, were also conspicuous for their intellectual impressiveness and fidelity to detail.   They were vindicated in a revolution foreshadowed by Newman in his "Essay on the Development of Christian Doctrine," and which gave coherence and meaning to the accumulations of natural knowledge.   The entire field of human effort acquired new promise and dignity.   For although geology and biology were the cradles of the evolutionary hypothesis, its ramifications spread rapidly into many other spheres.   Statesmen, sociologists, reformers, and theologians were inoculated with the theory of progressive development and determined to parallel its story in nature with a similar unfolding in politics, ethics, and religion. In directing the gaze of mankind toward an ideal all the more attractive because its frontiers were lost in the radiance of a possible perfectibility, Lyell and Darwin did the greatest service men can render to their fellows. They showed that creation and man were not isolated units, that the creature had a princely inheritance from an interminable past, the recesses of which were beyond discernment, and its irrepressible energies mobilized in himself.

Thomas Carlyle, who, together with Wordsworth, directed some of these conceptions into popular channels, was perhaps the most important literary accessory in the revolt against tradition. While scornful of conventional opinions, he was at heart hostile toward materialism. As an author, virile, vehement and iconoclastic in temper ; as a thinker, intuitional rather than logical, impatient with the letter and mechanism of history, this shaggy Titan, who was so eager for the realities and forces underneath outward events, gave a more cosmopolitan range to English literature. Carlyle was so constructed that "the prophet who reveals and the hero who acts could be his only guides." He stirred the lethargy and aroused the resentment of his readers by his antagonisms rather than by his sympathies. His habitual eccentricities of style and method, and his absorption in the higher learning of the philosophers who resided between the Rhine and the Oder offended more sedate and careful scholars, who doubted the soundness of many of his conclusions. But these shortcomings and prejudices were compensated by his reverence for truth, his imaginative grasp of facts, and his fascinating humanness. His superabundant vitality and candor gave the first clear expression to the struggling heart of a desolate yet aspiring time, making a clean breast of many repressed unbeliefs and noble hatreds. He generated a tempest which swept away some shams, whether in Church or State, and cleared the ground for affirmative thinkers.

Yet so far from being purely destructive, he was always mindful of the "Everlasting Yea," and if he inspired rather than illuminated, he certainly provided an immediate foot-hold for faith and loyalty at a moment when some ancient landmarks were being removed. The infinite nature of duty was the token of the Divine Presence which never forsook him. Only in submission before that Presence could any worthy freedom be found. The higher self within was the one medium of contact with the Supreme Will. Through obedience and renunciation the soul entered its divine king-dom. It was Carlyle's powerful presentation of such truths as these, far more than his vitriolic objurgations against cant or the pretensions and quackeries, real or imaginary, which he detested, that gave him a tremendous hold upon his admirers. They saw in him the survival of a moral code inherited from generations of honest God-fearing ancestors, at first stifled by doubt and questioning, and then majestically quickened and purified under the stress of deepened insight and the sense of high responsibility. How much they owed to him cannot be easily computed, but that his early writings may be reckoned among the chief forces of liberation working in those years is beyond dispute. "Whilst the schools of the Economists were laboriously de-molishing the homes of prejudice and superstition, Carlyle's battering ram made such a noisy assault upon them that all were bound to listen."[1] His discordant summons to sincerity was heard in every walk of life, rousing opposition as well as discipleship, and further disquieting the ecclesias-tical centers which were already alarmed by what they deemed the impious aberrations of the world.

Thus the period was one of confusion, in which devout men were timid, nervous, and, for the most part, resourceless. The transposition of values had driven Wordsworth from his earlier radicalism into a practical alliance with the Tories. The evolution of his opinions was both straightforward and intelligible, but it affected his productive powers, which

[1] F. Warre Cornish: "A History of the English Church in the Nine-teenth Century"; Vol. I, p. 196.

henceforth were intermittent in their effusions. The social anarchies of France as represented by the "Terror," and William Godwin's "Enquiry Concerning Political Justice," which was calmly subversive of marriage and similar institutions, compelled Wordsworth to abandon his liberalism in behalf of the quiet of an ideal state, in which the bonds of domestic piety were strengthened by the contemplation of God in nature, thus conserving the spirit of the simple society in which he had been bred.[1]

Beset on every side by a renascent philosophy, theology, science, and literature, churchmen in Germany and France, and later in England, saw their systems subjected to severe ordeals; the past, at the instigation of the growth of knowledge, rose up to grapple with its own progenies in the present. The heart of things as they were was ruthlessly torn open and scrutinized. What existing party could abide the hour of reckoning? The polite and titled cliques which loathed democracy were on the defensive. The prelates and dignitaries of the Establishment scented danger everywhere. For dreamers and poets the day of Utopia had dawned. Would the Church herself, as the last hope, prove equal to the emergency, or be made a show of in the open as natively incapable of readjustment to its necessities?

III

The answer must be sought in the condition of the two predominant parties into which Anglicanism, speaking generally, was divided. These were known respectively as High and Low Churchmen. The former included non-jurors, other irreconcilables, and a large proportion of the orthodox, a term applied to those who accepted the Reformation and the Prayer Book, and who, although sacramental in theory, were content with a minimum of ritual and observ-

---

[1] "Dictionary of National Biography"; Vol. LXIII, article on Wordsworth.

ance. The Low Churchmen consisted of both Evangelicals and Latitudinarians. Indeed, at the beginning of the nineteenth century these terms were loosely used, and there was no very wide divergence, either in doctrine or practice, between the two main groups or their subdivisions. Alexander Knox observed that the old High Church race was fatigued, the majority being men of the world, if not of yesterday. They boasted their direct succession from a series of learned divines beginning with Hooker and ending with Waterland, who embodied for them the authentic and unchanging mind of their communion. Passionless, scholarly, contemptuous of zeal, content to take things as they found them, they coveted reasonableness and repudiated emotionalism. Their preaching spent itself in a balanced presentation of Carolinian theology and in a steady effort to avoid every kind of extravagance.

"The better members," says Dean Church, "were highly cultivated, benevolent men, intolerant of irregularities both of doctrine and life, whose lives were governed by an unostentatious but solid and unfaltering piety, ready to burst forth, on occasion, into fervid devotion." [1] Their wholesome though restrained ministry was too frequently counteracted by pluralist and fortune-loving brethren, many of whom were nothing more than country gentlemen in Holy Orders who used the advantages of their calling for the pursuit of personal interests and pleasures. Thanks to the regenerating effects of Tractarianism, this type of cleric has long since disappeared, and nothing more than a misty reminiscence of the sporting parson, or the clergyman who held his office as a sort of perquisite, lingers in rural regions.

Although their number was far smaller than has been commonly supposed, the Evangelicals furnished the prevailing religious and philanthropic tendencies of the first generations of the century. They were related to the Revival from which they took their name, with two very marked differences;

[1] "The Oxford Movement"; p. 10.

that they owned no allegiance to Methodism as a sect, and accepted the Calvinism of Whitefield, Toplady, and Hill as against the Arminianism of Wesley and Fletcher. High Churchmen accused them, not without reason, of being morbid pietists, whose jaundiced vision regarded an enjoyable world as a dreary wilderness overshadowed by impending doom. This antipathy was too often synonymous with a mistaken hatred of all that made life beautiful, combined with a quick appreciation of whatever added to its material comfort. Their favorite teachers and guides were such men as Hervey, Romaine, Cecil, Newton, Thomas Scott, and Charles Simeon. The Evangelicals were students of the Bible, deeply versed in its contents, pronounced literalists, experts in the doctrinal views they accepted, and frequently more than equal to the controversialists they were called upon to meet. Nevertheless, they were too circumscribed in range and deficient in imagination and sympathy to supply an adequate theology for the age. "The history of the Evangelical Revival illustrates the limits of religious movements which spring up in the absence of any vigorous rivals without a definite philosophical basis. They flourish for a time because they satisfy a real emotional craving; but they have within them the seeds of decay. A form of faith which has no charms for thinkers ends by repelling from itself even the thinkers who have grown up under its influence. In the second generation the able disciples revolted against the strict dogmatism of their fathers, and sought for some more liberal form of creed, or some more potent intellectual narcotic. . . . When the heart usurps the functions of the head, even a progressive development will appear to be retrograde." [1] Their instruction was subordinated to the dogma of election and its corollaries, insistence upon which engendered that aversion felt at Oxford toward Calvinism, where it supplied one of the first incentives to the Tractarian

[1] Sir Leslie Stephen: "History of English Thought in the Eighteenth Century"; Vol. II, pp. 431 and 435.

Movement. Their fatalism inclined many of them to Premillenarianism as a refuge from the approaching catastrophes of the present dispensation. The breadth and verve of Luther, or the logical array and incisiveness of Calvin, or the "platform of discipline" of Knox and the earlier Puritans was not in them nor in their followers.

Social conditions had slowly changed their once unbending bearing in an environment which laid stress on what was fastidious or ingenious or genteel: almost insensibly they inhaled the subtle poison of these requirements, and developed an accommodating spirit toward them. Despite deterioration, however, the more intense Evangelicals warred against prevalent evils in Church and State, thus incurring proscription as enthusiasts and bigots. Their preaching lent weight to the charge; it abounded in credal phrases which had lost their significance, and left untouched large and vital needs of human life. References to ethical obligation and the necessity for righteous conduct were disparaged if they seemed to clash with salvation by faith and for the elect alone. The result was that their homilies seldom ventured beyond the rudiments of the Gospel, preferring the well-worn track of a call to repentance and a conditional assurance of pardon.[1] Arrogant exclusiveness, a sure sign of decay, began to show itself among them. They set themselves apart as the truly religious, the chosen depositaries of Christian verity, culture, and experience, with a dialect of their own; and were inclined to regard those who were not of their persuasion as worldlings and soothsayers.

It was but one remove from this temper to the materialism which believed in making the best of both worlds, projecting the theory of rewards and punishments into the future with reckless profusion, and emphasizing it as the chief stimulus

---

[1] Sydney Smith wrote: "The great object of modern sermons is to hazard nothing. Their characteristic is decent debility, which alike guards their authors from ludicrous errors and precludes them from striking beauties. Every man of sense in taking up an English sermon expects to find it a tedious essay."

to godly living. Their progenitors had braved the anger of
Georgian bishops by exhortations and practices that drew
all classes to their churches. The descendants were found
in the rich and fashionable pulpits of London and the
provinces. Yet, notwithstanding this decline in value
and breadth of service, a large contingent of Anglicans
still clung to the Low Church, cherishing its devout inheritance and earnestly expecting a renewal of those gifts
and graces which were now its fondest traditions. Famous
divines strengthened and adorned the wider ranks of
Evangelicalism, but few such were found within the pale of
the Establishment. Robert Hall, John Foster, William Jay
of Bath, Edward Irving, the eccentric genius, and in Scotland,
Thomas Chalmers, represented the vigor and fearlessness of
an earlier day and maintained the excellence of Evangelical
preaching.

It should be added that, notwithstanding its waning fires,
the party conferred upon humanity some of its foremost
benefactors. The men and women whose unstinted labors
and sacrifices were instrumental in founding the foreign
missionary propaganda, in obtaining clemency for the Hindu
and freedom for the slave, in abolishing cruel penal laws
and purifying noisome prisons, as a rule, owed allegiance to
the Clapham sect vividly described by Macaulay, or to its
lesser rival, the Clapton Sect, and were active and influential
members of the evangelical wing of the Church.

Standing apart from High and Low Churchmen were certain thinkers and writers to whom the term Broad Churchmen
has since been conveniently applied. These may be divided
into two sections, the philosophical, which began with Samuel
Taylor Coleridge and passed on to such typical divines as
Frederick Denison Maurice, and later, Brooke Foss Westcott;
and the critical or historical, represented by Henry Hart
Milman, Newell Connop Thirlwall, Julius Charles Hare,
Thomas Arnold, and Arthur Penrhyn Stanley. The Platonic
gospel of Coleridge discarded the apologetic of Paley, which

2 E

found all good in happiness, and the empiricism of Locke, which posited all knowledge in phenomena as derived by reflection from what the senses reveal.   With Schleiermacher, Coleridge traced the sources of religious faith to experience, but he also affirmed the existence of an intellectual organ for the apprehension of God.   This he defined as the *Reason*, which was loftier in nature, and dealt with higher truths than the *Understanding*.   For while the *Understanding* was wholly dependent upon perception for its data, and generalized from the material presented by the senses, the *Reason* was concerned intuitively and immediately with necessary and universal truths.   The former operated in the world of time and space, and was in a measure shared by animals, whose instinct was only a lower kind of "adaptive intelligence." The latter fulfilled its office in the spiritual sphere, and its presence in man proved his affinity with a supernatural order as certainly as the *Understanding* related him to the physical creation.   The *Reason* had two functions : the cognitive, from which proceeded all ontological thinking, ideas of cause, unity, infinitude, and the like ; and the active, from which arose the postulates of moral action, such as obligation, freedom, and personality.

This, of course, was another way of stating Kant's resolution of the *Reason* into its components, the speculative and the practical, and the indebtedness of Coleridge to the founder of the critical philosophy is everywhere apparent.   From Kant and Schelling his metaphysic received its primary impulse.

Both functions of the *Reason*, argued Coleridge, were fulfilled in definite religious faith.   The speculative element could give the conception of an Absolute Being, but since its content was purely ontological it could not predicate His character.   On the other hand the practical element, or moral consciousness, revealed the Absolute as the Holy One, who was "visible" in that degree in which the perceiving heart was pure.   The *Reason* which discharged this double

function was not a detached personal faculty, but the immanence in human apprehension of the Divine Reason, "the light
which lighteth every man," the link between the Creator and
the creature, and the essential medium for that fellowship
which apprises men of spiritual realities. Since the basic ideas
of religion were derived from the *Reason*, thus understood,
it followed that the deistic view of "natural religion" was
precluded as a contradiction in terms.

The psychological analysis of the soul was supplemented by
the reverse process. Having worked upwards from the data
of human consciousness to the Divine Being, Coleridge proceeded on a descending path from the Absolute One to His
manifestations in the finite. The Logos or Son of the Father
was the one mediator between God and the universe, sustaining cosmic relations to all that is, directing the eternal
process in history, and inspiring the soul with moral and
spiritual truth. In Jesus, the Son attained a concrete personal expression, which while specialized in a profoundly
impressive manner, was neither exclusive nor final in
the sense that He had withdrawn from the rest of mankind.
Humanity as a whole felt the throbbings of His light and life,
without Whom nothing could exist. Thus the particular
Incarnation the Gospels recorded revealed and realized the all-
pervading truth that the race was the offspring of God, Who
through self-manifestation and utmost sacrifice ever sought
to reclaim and reconcile His errant children.

The apprehension of this fundamental truth made possible
the new birth which was the chief purpose of the Son's
redemptive mission, and which consisted, not in an improved
self, but in "a Divine other-than-self." The mind of Christ
blended with the mind of believers, and a life of the
Spirit was inaugurated, a life of trust and love, a life of
closest and most intimate communion with the Father,
through the Son. The two paths of ontological dialectic and
psychological examination converged to the point where God
and man met in a living union. The powerless abstractions

of deism gave place to a Holy Father whose love, worship, and service evoked and satisfied the deepest feelings of regenerate hearts, which intuitively demanded a Personal Deity rather than a principle as the source of their salvation and the center of their faith.

If this Christianized Platonism was a reaction from the sterile thinking and materialized necessity of current philosophies, it was no less opposed to some main articles of the reigning Calvinistic theology.   The opposition was interpretative rather than negative.   Coleridge admitted the fact of sin and the consequent alienation of every soul from the Everlasting Will, so that man was always the object of a necessary redemption.   But Calvinism had formulated a doctrine of Original Sin issuing in that hereditary depravity which infected the entire race at birth.   Upon this it proceeded to construct a scheme of atonement, viewed as a propitiation of the wrath of Divine justice by means of the penalty which fell upon Christ.   Sin, contended Coleridge, was a moral not a natural fact, and therefore could not be born in man, but must be the outcome of his own volition: the only Original Sin was that which each man himself originated.   The aim of redemption was not to discharge an ancestral debt which involved all men, but to deliver them from the dominion of iniquity which had its seat in the deflected will; in brief, to recreate them in Christ Jesus.

In the matter of Biblical criticism, Coleridge sympathized with the historico-rationalistic methods of Germany.   His system, like Schleiermacher's, was sufficiently expansive to incorporate the results of the new scholarship without detriment to the objectives of faith, as he understood them.   Too susceptible to impressions of various kinds to be always consistent, too mystical and remote to be always clear, nevertheless Coleridge imparted a needed impetus to the spiritualizing of theology in England, where he was esteemed by his disciples as the greatest religious thinker of his time.   Just so surely as Carlyle widened and deepened the insular channels of literature, so surely Coleridge, notwithstanding his occasional obliquities, challenged the champions of an orthodoxy which had hidden behind the authority of the Church or the Bible and used the medium of a hidebound theology. Newman, speaking for many others who agreed with him in little else, protested against Coleridge's speculations, and said that they took for granted a liberty which no Christian could tolerate, and carried him to conclusions which were often heathen rather than Christian. Yet he admitted that Coleridge "installed a higher philosophy into inquiring minds than they had hitherto been accustomed to accept. In this way he made trial of his age, and succeeded in interesting its genius in the cause of Catholic truth." [1]

Prominent among the critical and historical group of scholars was Henry Hart Milman, who, after a most creditable career at Oxford, became Dean of St. Paul's Cathedral, London, in 1849. While retaining some of the intellectual habits of the eighteenth century, Milman was markedly friendly to the larger ideas of the succeeding era, holding himself free to accept and spread their light, however trying it might prove to older perspectives. His cautious and independent nature allowed nothing to pass without examination, and he was too devoted to truth to accept or reject conclusions merely because of their age or novelty. If he was not exactly the forerunner of Higher Criticism in England, he was a pioneer in that school of criticism which has since developed fruitful inquiries in many directions, and especially in the study of the Holy Scriptures. His "History of the Jews," which appeared in 1829, marked an epoch in the historical scholarship of Anglicanism, and was at least fifty years in advance of the times. Dean Stanley, who was in some respects Milman's successor, described the work as "the first decisive inroad of German theology into England, the first palpable indication that the Bible could be treated like any other book; that the characters and events of sacred

---

[1] "Apologia"; p. 97.

history could be treated at once critically and reverently."
Its inferences and suggestions, even more than its actual
statements, led to such a furore that the publication of the
manuals in which it was one of a series came to a sudden
end. Oxford joined in the outcry against it, and Newman
reviewed it adversely in the *British Critic*. Once the
right of entry into the hitherto inclosed field of Biblical
history was ceded, important consequences were bound to
follow. Philosophers and theologians might indulge in
ceaseless disputes without arriving at any agreement; under
Milman's treatment the records of Scripture were no longer
matters of opinion, but of fact, dependent upon accurate
knowledge derived from the scientific study of their contents.
To men who held that the inspired writings were immune
from research, his method appeared nothing better than an
abomination of German infidelity introduced into the English
Church at a moment when she was imperilled by a crumbling
ethic and a vanishing faith.

The slumbering tenacities of the Universities were now
slowly awakening. At Cambridge those who resented the
dogmatism of arrogant ignorance, and advocated a sound
and reasonable view of life, formed a coterie of better spirits
known as the Apostles Club. Impatient with the banalities
of purblind regularity, Thirlwall, Hare, and Maurice,[1] together with others not already named, such as John Sterling,
Adam Sedgwick, Richard Chenevix Trench, Arthur Hallam,
Alfred Tennyson, and Charles Buller, attached themselves
either to Coleridge or to more spacious beliefs in politics
and religion. They earnestly desired a dispassionate
and penetrative spiritual life and thought, and, while loyal
to the substance of Christian teaching, asked for a searching
revision of current creeds which would render them acceptable to changed conditions. Thus the clerical edicts against
further quest for truth wrought effectively in the opposite
direction.

[1] Maurice belonged to both Universities.

Thirlwall, afterwards Bishop of St. Davids, was conspicuous even among these eminent men as one of the
princeliest intellects of the century. With Hare, who could
not be assigned to any particular theological cult, he
labored to supplant the formulæ then in vogue by more
accurate and progressive principles. Among their many
services in this direction they collaborated in the translation
of Niebuhr's "History of Rome," which Hare supported by
his "Vindication of Niebuhr" against the charge of skepticism. In 1825 Thirlwall published Schleiermacher's "Critical
Essay on the Gospel of St. Luke," containing an introduction that revealed his extensive acquaintance with German
theology, a field of learning as yet hardly known to
English students. Thirlwall's endowments and catholicity of outlook made him a competent and trustworthy
guide for those who cared to follow him. In 1834 he
petitioned and wrote in favor of the admission of Free
Churchmen to university degrees. He also condemned the
collegiate lectures in divinity and compulsory attendance at
Chapel, "with its constant repetition of a heartless mechanical service." This pamphlet was issued on May 21, 1834;
five days later Dr. Christopher Wordsworth, Master of
Trinity, wrote to the author, asking him to resign his appointment as assistant-tutor; Thirlwall at once complied.
In 1840 Lord Melbourne offered him the bishopric of St.
Davids, a see the solitude and retirement of which exactly
suited his philosophical and literary tastes. He rarely
quitted "Chaos," as he called his library, except to attend to
the duties of his diocese.

Seldom was a severer strain of self-suppression necessary
at a moment when the natural desire should have been to
obtain information, and to bring to the common stock whatever of well-considered suggestion or of legitimate criticism
might be available for the attainment of those reforms
on which the future of the Church depended. Thirlwall
was well qualified to further such aims, but his great

qualities as a thinker without passion or prejudice, and the fearlessness with which he expressed his views on disputed questions, separated him from the clergy and the bishops. His first charge was a broadly conceived defense of the Tractarians, then the anathema of all parties.   He was one of the few prelates who refused to inhibit Bishop Colenso of Natal for his heretical expositions on the Pentateuch.   Among important legislative acts that won his approval, of which two at least have since been ratified by the nation, were the admission of Jews to Parliament, the granting of State funds for the Roman Catholic College at Maynooth, and the disestablishment of the Anglican Church in Ireland.   A pervading sanity characterized the workings of his mind; he humanized the episcopacy of which he was an unusual but influential member, and endeavored to secure the inclusive policy and action of the Church in a nation emphatically Protestant, and to preserve it from being controlled by an obscurantist sacerdotalism.   Partisan opposition could not separate him from these resolves.   His devout reasonableness counted for infinitely more with far-sighted men and women than abstract systems deduced from assumed first principles.   His massive intelligence and sagacious judgment were as deserving of reverence as the tender and fragrant piety of Charles Marriott.   The fear which Wordsworth says

> "has a hundred eyes, that all agree
> To plague her beating heart,"

was unknown to Connop Thirlwall.   He believed in man because he believed supremely in God and in the ultimate triumph of His will.

While the genius of German philosophy was welcomed by the Cambridge men, who passed quickly from admiration to penetration of the new soul and an understanding of its meanings, Oxford was alert under other forms; forms less pliable, less evenly just, less open to the inflow of continental thought and the modification of assured facts: more dialectical, dogmatic, and imaginative. Oriel, in particular, stood forth as the center of a succession of more or less perceptive men. Under Provost Eveleigh it was the first college to throw open its fellowships to competition and to ask for the institution of university class lists. From the days of Copleston to those of Hampden it harbored a breadth then unknown elsewhere in Oxford. Its reputation for liberalism was enhanced by a resident band known as the Noetics, who "fought to the stumps of their intellects." They represented the common loyalties and sympathies of Oxonians, intermingled with an extensive variety of gifts and opinions, and accompanied by a mutual concession of the rights of inquiry. The evangelical, sacerdotal, mystical, and rational aspects of religion were freely discussed, and, notwithstanding a certain aridity of mind which characterized some of the Noetics, out of the ferment they stimulated Tractarianism arose.

The most prominent figure among them was Richard Whately, afterwards Archbishop of Dublin, who had an exceptional knowledge of and power over his acquaintances. So far as he may be classified at all, Whately belonged to the Liberal wing, but there was no necessary incompatibility between his position and a definite traditional standpoint. In fact, his theory of the Church was the acknowledged precursor of a more advanced doctrine. But he was too original and self-contained to be a good partisan. Contemporary Evangelicals deemed him a typical Latitudinarian of the previous century; High Churchmen rested some of their conclusions upon his premises; Broad Churchmen have claimed him as one of their founders. His communicating qualities as a thinker were demonstrated by their operation in such divergent directions. Upon none did he exercise them more freely, and for a time successfully, than upon Newman, and the part Whately played in his career will be mentioned later.

Whatever else the Noetics questioned they were convinced that the Church of England must change her course or presently be wrecked. The first to forfend this eventuality, and to articulate the claims of High Anglicanism, was Dr. Charles Lloyd, who had been Sir Robert Peel's tutor, was appointed in 1822 Divinity Professor at Oxford, promoted to the bishopric of that see in 1827, and died in 1829. Those who resorted to his lectures, among whom were Pusey, Newman, Hurrell Froude, and the Wilberforces, heard for the first time an exposition of the history and structure of the Prayer Book as a translation and adaptation of the Missal and the Breviary. Engrossing contentions with rationalistic deism had obscured these antecedents of the Litany, the study of which enabled Lloyd's students to discern that the Church was far more than a mere creature of the State.

He announced in a tentative form the doctrines to which the Tractarians were subsequently converted. These were afterwards more completely stated by Newman, who said: "We were upholding that primitive Christianity which was delivered for all time by the early teachers of the Church, and which was registered and attested in the Anglican formularies and by Anglican divines. That ancient religion had well-nigh faded out of the land throughout the political changes of the last one hundred and fifty years, and it must be restored. It would be, in fact, a second Reformation — a better Reformation — for it would be a return not to the sixteenth century, but to the seventeenth." [1]

This transformation of the nature and claims of the Anglican Communion insisted upon her place in the Church Universal as an organized society founded by her Divine Lord, independently of the will of the State. She was regarded as the one true and sufficient source, in England and among English speaking men, of instruction in faith, worship, and morals. The spiritual authority conferred by Christ upon the Apostles was, under the guidance

[1] "Apologia"; p. 43.

of the Holy Spirit, transmitted by them to their successors, to be exercised in conformity with the original commission. Its discipline and edification were the sole prerogatives of the bishops, who maintained by ordination an unbroken line of descent from the New Testament Church, as a solemn trust belonging solely to them and to the priesthood which, to use the cryptic speech of High Church clerics, had the inalienable power of the keys. They and they alone were entitled to administer the Sacraments as the appointed means of regenerating and renewing grace.

These theories minified the Evangelical principle which treated the community or the Church as secondary and placed the individual face to face with God. They magnified the external and corporate existence of the Church as opposed to the purely internal life of the believer. The fact that attenuated catenas of this kind were out of date as bonds of union was not known to the Tractarians. Their idea of origins has since succumbed to historical evidence, which takes the question no farther back than the cautious statement of the Ordinal that the three orders of bishops, presbyters, and deacons existed from the time of the Apostles. Even at that they were limited to the precedent of St. John and the region of Asia Minor. As to whether the ordination was of the *esse* of the Church or only of the *bene esse*, Anglican divines could be quoted in both directions. Hall, Taylor, Laud, Montague, Gauden, Barrow, Beveridge, Hicks, Brett, Hughes, Daubeny, Van Mildert, and Heber ranged themselves on the side of the necessity of the episcopate. Against them were Hooker, Andrewes, Usher, Cosin, Leighton, Burnet, Sherlock, and Thorp. Non-episcopal orders are now described, even by High Churchmen, as irregular rather than invalid. The difference is significant, and while the Church of England stands for episcopacy with resolute determination, it evinces more reasonableness than did the more ardent Tractarian advocates of the theory.

The bishops of the first decades of the nineteenth century

bore no resemblance to some of the magnates whose names have just been quoted. The long tenure of Latitudinarianism had demoralized their spiritual force and leadership. Many among them had been appointed for political or family reasons: once enthroned, they subsided into their natural insignificance, and it was left to Samuel Wilberforce to become the restorer of their office. The early Tractarians rendered them submissive obedience until it was clear that they did not propose to secure that freedom of speech and action for the Church which was necessary to her welfare. Yet it should be remembered that the bishops shared the temper of the nation, which was frankly Erastian and anti-Catholic. The English people had seen unmoved a series of religious and ecclesiastical revolutions, facilitated and encouraged by their own indifference. Henry VIII, by his will alone, sealed the national faith and prescribed the forms of the Church; Edward VI abolished the Catholic doctrine his father preferred, and brought in an undiluted Protestantism, while Mary's accession was the signal for that rehabilitation of Papal authority against which her sister Elizabeth in turn rebelled. At the time in question, apart from a few scattered clergymen and enthusiasts of Oxford there seemed to be no desire for changes, least of all for such as offended the strongest instincts of the people. The bishops believed it their duty to maintain the dignity of the Crown from which they had received their preferment: to leave authoritative reforms to the government, and to administer the existing order as they found it. Although at fault in their neglect of spiritual affairs and in their excessive subservience to the State, they were not without justification for the policy they pursued.

This fragmentary review of the period when a new heaven and a new earth emerged to view can now be recapitulated. The mighty deeps had been broken up by the French Revolution and its sequel in the Napoleonic wars. Then came a swell of soul at home and abroad which bore forward on its crest a series of poets, prophets, thinkers, and statesmen, with every kind of talent and genius in human affairs. Although they assailed or defended vested interests and creeds, the one constructive project which engaged all alike was the rebuilding of the social structure. The sons of the new liberalism urged this on the basis of religious and political reform. The defenders of rank and privilege preserved as best they could the remnants of their station in life. The traditionalists, whether Roman or Anglican, resumed their pleas for the sanctions of custom and antiquity which had been interrupted by the revolutionary epoch. Serious men for whom religion meant the most awful and most personal thing on earth were dismayed: theologians were either retroactive or cautiously progressive, philosophers were averse to current orthodoxy, and scientists, absorbed in their first vision of the wonder of physical phenomena, were advancing theories which had to run the gauntlet of a bitter opposition. The need for unified processes of thought and action was apparent. But none seemed to have that gift of generalization which could bring the era to a focus, or show its bearing upon the forces of a growing communism to be realized by the spread of intelligent and identical aims among all classes. Yet the difficulties and perils of the situation have been exaggerated. It was not in any sense a widespread crisis; the stern discipline of war or of a common calamity had no place in its history. There was no leveling of the artificial differences which separate man from man. The depths of life were still left unplumbed. The majority of the people remained indifferent to the perpetual strife of the clericals and anti-clericals. The religious instincts and emotions, which are as remote from dogma as they are from politics, asserted themselves independently of the clash of opinions between the clergy and their opponents. Neither the Oxford Movement nor any other stir in the troubled affairs of the time had power to reveal on a large scale the essentials of human being; to obliterate social caste, to transform surface existence to simple sincerity of word and deed, and, as in a day of supreme searching trial, to banish the dross of base desire and ignoble triviality and purify the national character. Neither the High nor the Low Church party was conspicuous for clarity of thought or warmth of sentiment; both were deficient in philosophical essentials; both were deprived of sufficient intellectual guidance. And if their constantly accumulating obligations to the advancing mind of the times found them without the means of payment, from the moral and religious standpoints their condition was even worse. Dean Church declared that Tractarianism to a large measure had its spring in the consciences and character of its leaders reacting against the prevalent slackness in the religious life of their fellow churchmen, many of whom were afflicted with a strange blindness to the austerity of the New Testament. Yet when all these factors have been weighed, the origin and results of the High Church Revival remain somewhat of a mystery, in the interpretation of which hasty judgments are to be deprecated. For the profound changes which have been wrought by modern life and thought were then no more than embryonic. In addition to the political developments named, a system of compulsory education has since been established throughout the British Empire. Ecclesiastical claims that once seemed essential to the interests of religion have been set aside and an unaccustomed breadth imparted to the symbols and standards of theological opinion. The scientific temper which was formerly an outcast is at last dominant in art and literature. The entire conception of society and of the functions and duties of government has been enormously extended. The Tractarians were under the duress of the sacerdotalism already described. In behalf of a divinely authorized Church they were indifferent toward immediate or prospective betterment, and disparaged what was near at hand for the sake of what was afar off. They set forth much that was romantic and, to the British mind, obscure, in terms that sounded like a grotesque perversion of facts and rhetoric. A reaction to Catholicism which seemed to be born out of due time was thus equipped and treated with a homage having in it the note of an older world. Nor were they subject to that discipline which accepted what was prejudicial to previous convictions, if it was true, or rejected what seemed favorable, if it was unaccompanied by substantial proof. Nevertheless, they made headway in an age when science began to vaunt itself as competent to deal with philosophy and religion. Among a people avowedly Protestant, the Tractarians managed to baffle their assailants, overcome apparently insuperable difficulties, and, armed with weapons despised as archaic, to continue the struggle against the rationalism of the eighteenth century.

The chief agent in this achievement was a child of Calvinistic Evangelicalism and a son of Oxford, devoted to the medievalism which prevailed in its institutions as in its architecture. "Destined, like Wesley, to traverse the century; like him to exercise on all who came near him a miraculous influence of attraction or repulsion; like him also to be rejected of his University and his Church, and to set a large movement going in many directions," [1] Newman, though not the actual originator of Tractarianism, was its regal personality, its leader of radiating power. He gave it life, breath, being; apart from him, and his intrepid genius, it is highly problematical whether it could have attained a permanent existence. And after he had ceased to be a member of the Church of his birth his unprecedented predominance was long felt in her history. His Anglican career was another proof that the exceptional man is the solution of problems which yield to nothing else: the man with that touch of heart and brain which cannot be defined, but which all instinctively recognize as sufficient for the occasion. Such was Newman; he flashed through the mass of mediocrity that vital light without which no development of ordinary qualities can prosper.

[1] Dr. William Barry: "Cardinal Newman"; p. 5.

CHAPTER X

NEWMAN'S DEVELOPMENT AND PERSONALITY

THE stage on which what is called the Oxford Movement ran through its course had a special character of its own, unlike the circumstances in which other religious efforts had done their work. The scene of Jansenism had been a great capital, a brilliant society, the precincts of a court, the cells of a convent, the studies and libraries of the doctors of the Sorbonne, the council chambers of the Vatican.

The scene of this new Movement was as like as it could be in our modern world to a Greek πόλις or an Italian self-centered city of the Middle Ages. Oxford stood by itself in its meadows by the rivers, having its relations with all England, but, like its sister at Cambridge, living a life of its own, unlike that of any other spot in England, with its privileged powers and exemptions from the general law, with its special mode of government and police, its usages and tastes and traditions, and even costumes which the rest of England looked at from outside, much interested but much puzzled, or knew only by transient visits. And Oxford was as proud and jealous of its own ways as Athens or Florence, and like them it had its quaint fashions of polity; its democratic Convocation and its oligarchy; its social ranks; its discipline, severe in theory, and usually lax in fact; its self-governed bodies and corporations within itself; its faculties and colleges, like the guilds and "arts" of Florence; its internal rivalries and discords; its "sets" and factions. Like these, too, it professed a special recognition of the supremacy of religion; it claimed to be a home of worship and religious training, — Dominus illuminatio mea, — a claim too often falsified in the habits and tempers of life.

DEAN CHURCH: *The Oxford Movement;* pp. 159–160.

CHAPTER X

I

NEWMAN was an exemplification of his own contention that
the same object may be viewed by various observers under
such different aspects as to make their accounts of it appear
more or less contradictory. To some he was the religious
philosopher, the Pascal of his period; to others he was the
great doctor, whose work on the Arians would be read and
studied by future generations as a model of its kind. To a
certain type of admirers he was the superb preacher, the
Chrysostom of St. Mary's, Oxford, and of the Oratories of
Brompton and of Edgbaston; to a less favorable group he
was nothing more than a cunning master of English prose,
a writer of incomparable artistry and seductive charm, who
made siren words do duty for rational and coherent thinking. Lord Morley, from whom we quote, observes that
style has worked many a miracle before now, but none

more wonderful than Newman's.[1]   Again, some asserted that his knowledge of the first centuries of Church history entitled him to rank among the foremost ecclesiastical historians, while for apologists and disputants his merit lay in his controversial skill.   Both Modernists and Traditionalists have claimed him as their own.   Catholic Anglicans revere his proud yet melancholy memory because he was their great pleader at a critical moment and in an anomalous position.   Perhaps his most notable achievement was this: that he actually raised the Roman Communion to which he seceded out of the contemptuous misunderstanding and deep dislike of his countrymen to a place in their recognition, if not esteem, which before his appearance would have seemed unattainable.   His presence in the midst of her was an incalculable help to the Roman hierarchy, which did not, however, fully appreciate his value.   The fact that the most brilliant and gifted son of the Church of England was content to be the eremite of Edgbaston, because of his exceeding love for antiquity and for a system they had despised and rejected, never ceased to puzzle and chasten eager Protestants.   For them and many besides, John Henry Newman was, and still is, the grand enigma.

He was born in Old Broad Street, London, on the 21st of February, 1801, the eldest of six children, three sons and three daughters.   His father, John Newman, a banker in that city, is said to have traced his descent from the Newmans who were small landed proprietors of Cambridgeshire. They claimed Dutch extraction, and in an earlier generation spelt their name "Newmann," a form which has given rise to the conjecture that they were of Hebrew origin, but there is no conclusive evidence that such was the case.   Although the "Apologia" is silent about the elder Newman, his son's "Letters and Correspondence" contain numerous and affectionate references to him.   He was a Freemason of high standing; a man of the world, prosaic, honest, choleric,

[1] "Miscellanies"; (Fourth Series), p. 161.

enterprising, full of good sense; animated by a love of justice and a hatred of oppression and fraud. Newman eulogized his forbearance and generosity as a father, and while the son's genius was all his own, he inherited from him a taste for classical music and an excellent capacity for business.

Like another famous contemporary, James Martineau, Newman also sprang from Huguenot stock. His mother, Jemima Fourdinier, belonged to the French Protestant family of that name long and honorably established in London as merchants. For her he cherished a filial love, which was not, however, without occasional moods of self-assertion and flashes of an exacting disposition. She had some part in his earlier religious development, but was temperamentally unable to follow his leadership in later days, and he spoke with regret of the differences on religious matters which separated them, and that he missed the sympathy and praise she could not conscientiously bestow.[1]

His introduction to literature began while listening to her reading of "The Lay of the Last Minstrel," and when "Waverley" and "Guy Mannering" appeared, he spent the early hours of summer mornings in bed eagerly devouring them. Scott was always one of his favorite authors, but the Holy Scriptures were his constant companion: from the dawn of his understanding he was trained in their precepts, and it would not be an exaggeration to say that he knew the Bible by heart. In old age he described in beautiful and pathetic language the hold it had upon him and how impossible it was to elude or even lessen the sweet influences of this, his first and last treasured possession.

A fleeting glimpse is caught of him as a child playing in Bloomsbury Square with young Benjamin Disraeli, but his best remembered home was at Ham, then a rural retreat, near Richmond-on-Thames. Its charms always lingered in his recollections, and in his eightieth year he

[1] "Letters and Correspondence"; Vol. II, pp. 176–177.

wrote: "I dreamed about it when a schoolboy as if it were paradise. It would be here where the angel faces appeared 'loved long since but lost awhile.'" His two brothers shared the intellectual endowments of the family, but Charles Robert, who stood next to him in age, was eccentric to the verge of insanity, and the purposes of his life were defeated by his personal habits. Francis William, the youngest of the three, had a more successful undergraduate career at Oxford than John, obtaining a double first class in 1826 and a fellowship at Balliol in the same year. After a diversified and eventful life as a missionary in Persia and professor in several schools, he was appointed to the chair of Latin in University College, London, where he remained from 1846 to 1869, an extended tenure during which his versatility in writing on many and different themes attracted wide attention. Some of these were of such an erudite or fantastic nature as to defy popular apprehension. He was a much misunderstood and disappointed man, whose life and work were in striking contrast to those of his eldest brother. The one drifted toward the shelter of an infallible dogma, the other toward the tempestuous seas of doubt. Carlyle spoke kindly of Francis as "an ardently inquiring soul, of fine university and other attainments, of sharp-cutting restlessly advancing intellect, and the mildest pious enthusiasm, whose worth, since better known to all the world, Sterling highly estimated." [1] Of the three sisters the eldest, Harriet Elizabeth, married Thomas Mozley, the author of the "Reminiscences," a work necessary to students of Newman; the second, Jemima Charlotte, married John Mozley of Derby; and the third and favorite sister, Mary Sophia, died unmarried in 1828.

Harriet's portrayal of John Henry as a young man, while showing a sister's partiality, is significant and candid. He was inclined to be philosophical, observant, considerate of others, dainty in his tastes, and extremely shy; his

[1] "Life of John Sterling"; p. 184.

views were moderate, his judgments measured, his regard for truth absolute. Social intercourse of any kind bored him, and his dislike of praise or blame induced him to practice an unusual reserve which hid even from his parents the fact, not without its pathos, that the son lived in another world than theirs. God intended him, as he supposed, to be lonely, and his mind was so framed that he was in a large measure beyond the reach of those around him. He found consolation in music, and became so proficient on the violin that Thomas Mozley assures us he would have equaled Paganini had he not become a doctor of the Church.

His reveries bemused him, a sense of things ethereal, subtle, remote, haunted him; he loved to surrender himself to vague and formless imaginings: unknown influences, magical powers and adumbrations entranced his youthful spirit. He lay passive and luxuriant in their embrace while they wafted him to an upper realm, wherein, as he says — "I thought life might be a dream, or I an angel, and all the world a deception, my fellow angels by a playful device concealing themselves from me, and deceiving me with the semblance of a material world." [1] This persuasion of the illusory nature of sensible phenomena came early in his life and persisted to its close. He moved freely in the home and the social circle, contributing to their pleasure by his accomplishments, but always separated from them by an imponderable barrier. For the moment in these things, he was never of them. Like an occasional visitant from another sphere, who might choose at intervals to dwell among appearances as unsubstantial as his own experience was vividly real, yet without being deceived by them or capitulating to their charms, so Newman came and went. Life everywhere hid beneath its delusions something better to be gained. This nearness to the invisible aroused his superstitious fears, and he states that for some time previous to his conversion he used constantly to cross himself on going into the dark. [2]

[1] "Apologia"; p. 2.   [2] *Ibid.*, p. 2.

At the age of seven he was placed in a private academy at Ealing conducted on Eton lines by Dr. George Nicholas. Thomas Huxley, whose father was a tutor there, was also a later pupil, and the high reputation of the school was increased by the fact that it helped to shape the lives of two such entirely different men as Huxley and Newman. Although he showed no interest in the favorite pursuits of his companions, his character and gifts soon elicited their esteem and confidence. He was of a studious turn and quick apprehension, and Dr. Nicholas, to whom he became greatly attached, was accustomed to say that no boy had run from the bottom to the top of the school as rapidly as John Newman. Still he lost something by not being a public school man, for, while he acquired an accurate knowledge of mathematics, he was deficient in Latin. He used to regard with admiration the facile and elegant construing which a pupil of very ordinary talents would bring with him from the sixth form of Rugby or Winchester; yet he assisted in rendering the plays of Terence which were frequently given at the school, and acted the parts of Davus in the "Andria" and of Pythias in the "Eunuchus." He wrote both prose and verse with grace and flexibility; at first he imitated Addison; later Johnson's sonorous roll could be detected in his efforts; then the stately cadences of Gibbon manifestly affected him; finally he found himself, and began to show traces of that artistic construction wherein by practice his style became so nearly perfect, so complete, as to suffice for the permanence of his works.

His preternatural religiousness was greatly stimulated after he matriculated at Oxford by his conversion, of which he says in the "Apologia," "I am still more certain than that I have hands or feet." After seventy years had elapsed it was difficult for him to realize his continuous identity before and after August 18, 1816.[1] The sudden uprush and consummation of continuous processes which drew so clear a line

[1] "Letters and Correspondence"; p. 19.

between the two periods is discussed at length in the "Apologia": "I fell under the influences of a definite Creed, and received into my intellect impressions of dogma, which, through God's mercy, have never been effaced or obscured. Above and beyond the conversations and sermons of the excellent man, long dead, the Reverend Walter Mayers, of Pembroke College, Oxford, who was the human means of this beginning of divine faith in me, was the effect of the books which he put into my hands, all of the school of Calvin. One of the first books I read was a work of Romaine's; I neither recollect the title nor the contents, except one doctrine, which of course I do not include among those which I believe to have come from a divine source, viz., the doctrine of final perseverance. I received it at once, and believed that the inward conversion of which I was conscious would last into the next life, and that I was elected to eternal glory. I have no consciousness that this belief had any tendency whatever to lead me to be careless about pleasing God. I retained it till the age of twenty-one, when it gradually faded away; but I believe that it had some influence on my opinions, in the direction of those childish imaginations which I have already mentioned, viz., in isolating me from the objects which surrounded me, in confirming me in my mistrust of the reality of material phenomena, and making me rest in the thought of two and two only absolute and luminously self-evident beings, myself and my Creator."[1] This account of his inmost experiences is important for several reasons. It unveils the secret motives and aspirations which he felt and favored at this juncture; it shows that from adolescence onward his intellectual life was as full of contrasts as his emotional, and that his excessive sensibility was the explanation at once of his frailty and his strength. Even in the moment of their real awakening, his religious instincts found other than normal outlets. In his comparison of the impressive change which supervened in him with other remarkable

[1] "Apologia"; p. 4.

personal experiences which demonstrated Christianity's regenerating effectiveness, he was careful to state that his own had none of their special characteristics. It was without violent feeling: he did not pass through the prescribed stages of conviction of sin, terror, despair, and acceptance of a free and full salvation followed by joy and peace. His emotions were peculiar to himself. While he considered that he was predestined to salvation, his mind did not dwell upon the general fate of mankind, but only upon the mercy displayed toward himself. Indeed, normal Evangelicals doubted whether he had been regenerated at all, and when in 1821 he tried to write a description of the inwardness of this reality he added in a note, "I speak of conversion with great diffidence, being obliged to adopt the language of books. My own feelings, as far as I can remember, were so different from any account I have ever read, that I dare not go by what may be an individual case." [1]

To the unsophisticated believer, triumphant in a newborn realization of his personal Saviour, a logically coherent dogmatic system such as Newman accepted is, for the time being, a secondary consideration. In the words of Thomas à Kempis, the soul which has heard the Eternal Voice is delivered from its opinions; the greatness which is from above does not spend its first strength on such details. The avowed absence in him of conviction of sin and of the consequent enraptured sense of deliverance from sin deepens the mystery of the process. It was an influx of divine life, but that life appears to have been conveyed through channels unknown to the general consciousness of Christians respecting their conversion. If in this crucial hour such was Newman's case, it may help to explain his constant endeavors to defend his faith. Hort remarked of him, "A more inspiring teacher it would be difficult to find, but the

[1] Wilfred Ward: "The Life of John Henry Cardinal Newman"; Vol. I, p. 30.

power of building up was not one of his gifts." [1] "Certainly, books with a system abound in his work, but he does not need much pressing to make him admit the essential brittleness and contingency of these provisional structures." [2] His survey of divine things, begun with much apparent confidence, is often shadowed by reflections that what has been said is "but a dream, the wanton exercise, rather than the practical conclusions of the intellect." "Such," he continues, "is the feeling of minds unversed in the disappointments of the world, incredulous how much it has of promise, how little of substance; what intricacy and confusion beset the most certain truths; how much must be taken on trust in order to be possessed; how little can be realized except by an effort of the will; how great a part of enjoyment lies in resignation." [3] This reasoning is acceptable to those upward striving men of whom Matthew Arnold speaks, who walk by sight and not by faith, yet have no open vision. But it plays a minor part in that warm certitude which is the product of living faith in the revelation of the Lord Jesus Christ.

In summary, as a child Newman felt with unusual intensity the sense of the presence of God. He has already told us in solemn and memorable phrases of the moment when the still pool within his heart became a living fountain, divinely thrilled by the spiritual quickening which blended his innermost being with the love, the omnipotence, and the nearness of the Almighty. Ever afterwards this event was a ruling factor in his religious attainments, but the essence of the Gospel of Redemption did not seem to be luminous to his apprehension.

Among other writers who contributed to his spiritual welfare was Thomas Scott, the commentator, of Aston Sanford, "to whom" he averred, "humanly speaking I almost owe my soul." Scott, who had been won from Socinianism

---

[1] "Life and Letters"; Vol. II, p. 424.
[2] Henri Bremond: "The Mystery of Newman"; p. 330.
[3] "Prophetical Office"; Lecture XIV, pp. 392–393.

by John Newton, the friend of Cowper, denied and abjured the "detestable doctrine" of predestination, and planted deep in Newman's mind "that fundamental truth of religion, a zealous faith in the Holy Trinity." Law's "Serious Call" convinced him of the relentless warfare between the powers of light and those of darkness, and he took for granted the hard-and-fast dualism which was afterwards injurious to his interpretation of life.[1] The doctrine of eternal rewards and punishments he accepted with full inward assent, as delivered by our Lord Himself, though he tried in various ways to soften the truth of endless retribution so that it would be less terrible to his apprehension. He made his first acquaintance with the Fathers through the long extracts from St. Augustine and St. Ambrose given in Joseph Milner's Church History. Simultaneously with these, of which he was nothing short of enamoured, he read Newton's [2] "Dissertations on the Prophecies," and became firmly convinced that the Pope was the Antichrist predicted by the prophet Daniel, and also by St. Paul and St. John. He complains of his imagination being "stained by the effects of this doctrine up to the year 1843; it had been obliterated from my reason and judgment at an earlier date; but the thought remained upon me as a sort of false conscience." [3]

[1] We have already noted the extent of Law's influence over Gibbon, Wesley, and other dissimilar men; it is interesting to observe that Dr. Johnson also testified to the power of that writer. "I became," he says, referring to his early youth, "a sort of lax talker against religion, . . . and this lasted till I went to Oxford, where it would not be suffered. When at Oxford, I took up Law's 'Serious Call to a Holy Life,' expecting to find it a dull book, as such books generally are, and perhaps to laugh at it. But I found Law quite an overmatch for me; and this was the first occasion of my thinking in earnest of religion, after I became capable of rational enquiry . . ." "From this time forward," adds Boswell, "religion was the predominant object of his thought. . . . He much commended Law's 'Serious Call,' which he said was the finest piece of hortatory theology in any language." (Boswell's "Life of Dr. Johnson"; Everyman's Library, Vol. I, pp. 32–33, and 390.) Law was also one of the favorite authors of Richard Hurrell Froude.

[2] Thomas Newton, 1704–1782, Bishop of Bristol and Dean of St. Paul's, London. In 1754 he lost his father and his wife, and distracted his grief by composing these Dissertations.

[3] "Apologia"; p. 7.

From the moment that Newman entered Oxford his life continued to be in the main the record of a series of varied influences poured into his highly receptive nature. His vigorous and expanding intellect displayed an unusual aptitude for imbibing the thoughts and ideas of others. This unique impressionability had an unfortunate bearing on his course both as an undergraduate and a fellow of the University. It was the cause of that perpetual modification or relinquishment of principles which has fastened upon a man of commendable motives the reputation for fickleness and vacillation. The successive formations of his beliefs resembled the accumulating deposits of an alluvial soil. Yet as the strata underneath the soil remain stable, so despite his hospitality toward different views Newman retained a steady and fixed individuality. "Perhaps," says Mrs. Mozley, "no man, passing through a course of change, ever remained more substantially the same through the lapse of years and revolution of circumstances and opinions." [1] He selected from the instructions and advices he received those elements which seemed necessary, and, this done, he did not hesitate, in many instances, to discard the mentor. "John," observed his sister, "can be the most amiable, the most generous of men; he can make people passionately devoted to him. But to become his friend the condition *sine qua non* is to see everything with his eyes and to accept him as guide." [2]

In a University sermon preached on January 22, 1832, he dealt with personal influence as the means of disseminating truth. Commenting on the text "Out of weakness were made strong," he asked, how came it that, notwithstanding persecution, those who first proclaimed the Christian dispensation gained that lodgment in the world which has continued to the present day, enabling them to perpetuate principles distasteful to the majority even of those who professed to

[1] "Letters and Correspondence of John Henry Newman"; Vol. I, p. 1.
[2] Francis Newman: "The Early Life of Charles Newman"; p. 72.

receive them? The answer was that the evangel overcame the vast obstacles confronting it, not because it was upheld by a system, or by books, or by argument, or by any temporal power, but by a few highly endowed spirits who shone in the reflected light of Christ's perfect life, and communicated their radiance to lesser luminaries. They were enough to carry on God's noiseless work, and their successors in holy character and service rescued the generations that followed.[1]

Newman was a first-class example of transmitted influence; both receiving it himself and imparting it to others, sometimes inexplicably, almost always with unusual facility and leavening power. Although this readiness hindered him from dealing adequately with many scattered facts and discriminations lying beyond the range even of his percipient spirit, it contributed to the fecundity of a heart rarely equaled for its skill in contemplating those outflowing tides from the Supreme Being, which men call life when they rise in us, and death when they ebb again to Him.

The "Apologia" is an acknowledged masterpiece of literary portraiture. Certain passages in it are of the highest quality; the characterizations are as fine and close as need be; bold and pitilessly outright. Its self-revelation and self-criticism show much candor and strength, mingled with a delicate evasiveness or an eloquent silence about some persons and events which betrays the author's feelings toward them. A wholly detached and disinterested observation of his own career was hardly to be expected, indeed, was not within his power, yet the volume is of primary importance for those who would understand how this raw bashful youth, who at first seemed likely to dwarf his mental stature through diffidence and modesty, was rescued from his extreme reticence and an overweening anxiety to guard against solecisms. He began his first phase at Oxford as an ardent Calvinistic Evangelical, with a reproachful and pensive view of life

[1] Oxford University Sermons; pp. 75–97.

which drew him away from transitory things toward an exclusive concern for the spiritual side of existence. The University of which he afterwards became an avatar was steeped in the traditions of immemorial generations. Its guarded and venerable precincts represented dignity, wealth, and undisputed place. Its history embraced the hot issues of his own and opposite creeds. The romance of its yesterdays had not infrequently become the reality of its to-morrows. Schoolmen and Medievalists, Roman Catholics and Protestants, Humanists and High Churchmen, Anglicans and Puritans, in turn had contributed to the intellectual and moral atmosphere which was now Newman's vital breath.

Although his scholarly attainments were nothing remarkable, — indeed he was never noted for extensive or profound learning, — yet his first tutor at Trinity, the Reverend Thomas Short, formed a high opinion of his abilities, and encouraged him to compete for the only academic distinction he won as an undergraduate, a scholarship of sixty pounds, tenable for nine years. This proved a timely assistance, for in the following year, 1819, the bank in which his father was a partner suspended payment, and although all obligations were met, their discharge crippled the resources of the family. Nothing remained but his mother's jointure. In these declining fortunes Newman read the call to a higher and more congenial profession than that of the law, for which he had actually been preparing, having kept a few terms at Lincoln's Inn.[1] The loss of opportunity in other quarters naturally increased his anxiety to do well in the final University examination; the result was further disaster. It was scarcely surprising that, although he had passed with credit his first examination, a youth not yet twenty should have fallen short in his efforts to win the highest honors. He was below the average age of candidates for the B.A. degree; he had read too discursively and was unable, in the time that remained, to remedy the deficiency. His energies were never

[1] Thomas Mozley: "Reminiscences"; Vol. I, p. 16.

more diligently employed, but they were misdirected. He worked to the point of exhaustion, and, being called up earlier than he expected, was compelled, after making sure of his degree, to retire altogether. "My nerves," he wrote to his father, "quite forsook me, and I failed." When the lists were published his name did not appear on the mathematical side of the paper, and in classics it was found in the lower division of the second class which went by the contemptuous term of "under the line." Anxious to remain at Oxford, he received private pupils and read for a fellowship at Oriel, then the center of the intellectualism of the University. The coveted election was won exactly a year after his graduation, on the 12th of April, 1822, a day which he ever felt the turning point of his life and of all days most memorable. "It raised him," he says, writing in the third person, "from obscurity and need, to competency and reputation. He never wished anything better or higher than 'to live and die a Fellow of Oriel' and he was constant all through his life in his thankful remembrance of this great mercy of Divine providence."[1] It was then that he met John Keble for the first time. "How is that hour fixed in my memory after the changes of forty-two years, forty-two years this very day on which I write! I have lately had a letter in my hands, which I sent at the time to my great friend, John William Bowden. . . . 'I had to hasten to the Tower,' I say to him, 'to receive the congratulations of all the Fellows. I bore it till Keble took my hand, and then felt so abashed and unworthy of the honor done me, that I seemed desirous of quite sinking into the ground.' His had been the first name which I had heard spoken of, with reverence rather than admiration, when I came up to Oxford. When one day I was walking in High Street with my dear earliest friend just mentioned, with what eagerness did he cry out 'There's Keble!' and with what awe did I look at him."[2]

[1] "Letters and Correspondence"; Vol. I, p. 64.
[2] "Apologia"; p. 17.

The one, however, to whom Newman owed most at this juncture was Dr. Whately, who saw with his accustomed keenness the promise of great things in the newly elected fellow. "He was a man of generous and warm heart . . . particularly loyal to his friends. . . . While I was still awkward and timid in 1822 he took me by the hand and acted toward me the part of a gentle and encouraging instructor. He, emphatically, opened my mind, and taught me how to think." [1] But teacher and scholar were built on entirely different lines. Whately was a loud and breezy conversationalist, brimful of accurate information on many subjects, and by no means loth to impart it. He overflowed with rough humor, and was impervious to self-reproach for his numerous breaches of university etiquette. Imbued with a resolute sense of justice; zealous, courageous, conscientious, he boldly encountered obstruction and misconception, and rendered valuable service to the cause of education and of a reasonable religious belief. In his intercourse he was wont to use others as instruments by which to shape and define his own views, a habit the more readily cultivated because of his freedom from party spirit.

Newman was equally steadfast and uncompromising. By this time the seductive charm of his fascinating personality, so mild yet so invincible, began to assert itself in unmistakable ways. He spoke and acted as the man of interior life who held the secret of an illimitable purpose, which in the eyes of his associates invested him with an indefinable superiority. His combination of gentle manners and responsive kindness with unseizable reserve and incapacity for subordination was a deceptive but formidable obstacle between him and Whately. They began to drift apart: Whately openly, and Newman tacitly, resented interference, and the more the older man provoked the younger one's independence, the nearer they came to the inevitable separation. Newman seems to have forced the issue, and

[1] "Apologia"; p. 11.

2 G

confessed that although he had meant to dedicate his first book to Whately, the intention was abandoned, and that after the year 1834, Whately "made himself dead to me." Dr. Abbott asserts that Newman was mainly responsible for the rupture.[1] He spoke of the anguish which it inflicted on him to pass Whately in the street coldly, but this sentiment was hardly consistent with the tone of a letter which he wrote to the now Archbishop, and in which he said: "On honest reflection I cannot conceal from myself that it was generally a relief to see so little of your Grace when you were in Oxford; and it is a greater relief now to have an opportunity of saying so to yourself." He proceeded to explain at great length his reasons for this extraordinary statement, so charged with personal feeling. Whately's support of the Irish Church Temporalities Act, passed in August 14, 1833, which prospectively abolished two archbishoprics, and reduced the suffragan bishoprics by consolidation from eighteen to ten, had provoked a painful resentment in Newman, who referred with utter aversion to the secular and unbelieving policy in which Whately was implicated. The letter mentioned, which was a mixture of piety and presumption, was written in 1834, when Newman was no more than an ordinary member of the University, while Whately, who had been warmly attached to him, was his senior, his former patron, and a high dignitary of the Anglican hierarchy. Evidently these considerations counted for little. However Newman may protest that "in memory" there were few men whom he loved so much as Whately, the Archbishop was no longer of consequence. Newman's sentiment toward him was not one of personal hostility, but rather of ecclesiastical and theological antipathy. More than a year previously he had said in a letter to Bowden, "As to poor Whately, it is melancholy. Of course, to know him now is quite impossible, yet he has so many good qualities that it is impossible also not to feel for him . . . for a man more void of, what are

[1] "Anglican Career of Cardinal Newman"; Vol. I, p. 304.

commonly called, selfish ends does not exist." [1] Such an attitude explains the fatality which beset so many of Newman's associations. He frequently expressed it in passages similar to that which declares that "every individual soul is a closed world, and that the most intimate friendship does not succeed in penetrating the solid wall behind which each of us, in spite of himself, is hiding." [2] As yet only the surface of his spirit had been ruffled by the first gust which heralded other storms. It had flung up its chill spray, and sunk again to suave placidity. But anger in any form is a great revealer, and no air of high-bred indifference toward those who did not agree with his unyielding certitude could effectually conceal the reservations to which even Newman's admirers have never been quite reconciled. [3]

He was ordained on Trinity Sunday, June 13, 1824, and at the suggestion of Edward Bouverie Pusey, also a fellow of Oriel, he became curate of St. Clement's Church, Oxford. He had felt a preference for foreign missionary work, which accentuated his desire to be free from any domestic relationships, and he began to practice those abstentions in which religious enthusiasm takes shape in sacrifice. The heart which could but durst not love remained faithful to the vow never to surrender to any creature that which was meant for God alone. He questioned the direction of his

---

[1] "Letters and Correspondence"; Vol. I, p. 395. Five years later he and Whately met. "He is so good hearted a man that it passed off well," was Newman's comment. (*Ibid.*, II, p. 238.) A friend looking back to a day when Whately, then Archbishop of Dublin, was in Oxford," remembers accusing Mr. Newman to his face of being able to cast aside his friends without a thought, when they fairly took part against what he considered the truth." (*Ibid.*, Vol. I, p. 88.)

[2] Bremond: "The Mystery of Newman"; p. 29.

[3] The inferences which Dr. Abbott draws from Newman's letter to Whately appear to be somewhat overstrained. The reader is referred to the entire correspondence contained in the second volume of Newman's Letters, pp. 61–63. Mozley says, "He would have been ready to love and admire Whately to the end, but for the inexorable condition of friendship imposed by Whately, absolute and implicit agreement in thought, word, and deed. This agreement, from the first, Newman could not accord." "Reminiscences"; Vol. I, pp. 29–30.

life, whither it was leading him, and of what worth it was to other souls, with a startling perspicacity. These unusual refinements of thought and aim, seldom found in one so young, were reflected in his physical appearance. James Anthony Froude described him as "above the middle height, slight and spare. His head was large, his face remarkably like that of Julius Cæsar. The forehead, the shape of the ears and the nose, were almost the same. The lines of the mouth were very peculiar, and I should say exactly the same. I have often thought of the resemblance, and believe it extended to temperament. In both there was an original force of character which refused to be moulded by circumstances, which was to make its own way, and become a power in the world; clearness of intellectual perception, a disdain for conventionalities, a temper imperious and wilful, but along with it a most attaching gentleness, sweetness, singleness of heart and purpose. Both were formed by nature to command others, both had the faculty of attracting to themselves the passionate devotion of their friends and followers, and in both cases, too, perhaps the devotion was rather due to the personal ascendency of the leader than to the cause which he represented. It was Cæsar, not the principles of the empire, which overthrew Pompey and the constitution. 'Credo in Newmannum' was a common phrase at Oxford, and is still unconsciously the faith of nine tenths of the English converts to Rome." [1]

The clerical cast of his countenance was diminished by its Dantean severity, which indicated an exalted and influential personality,. animated by a passion for divine truth and for a better order of daily life. In his social interchanges he was at once simple and complex, reserved and approachable, constrained and genial. These opposite qualities drew to him many and very different men who found in their variety some common interest. Meanwhile, as Dr. Barry observes, he paid the penalty of genius in a deepening solitude; a

[1] "The Oxford Counter-Reformation" in "Short Studies"; Vol. IV.

shadowy figure in those days, his feet were set upon a strange path toward a goal which few foresaw and from which there was no turning. After Hurrell Froude's death no one took his place in Newman's affections. Never again did he surrender the pass key to his spirit: the strong man armed kept his own house, and during the spiritual conflict of his last phase at Oxford, he excluded even those who stood nearest to him, and went forward almost without witnesses.

II

The reaction from the creed of Calvinism had long been felt when this youthful recluse entered Trinity College. At first the continental reformers won a widening way in Anglicanism, and during the sixteenth and seventeenth centuries the "Institutes" of the Genevan theologian prevailed at Oxford and Cambridge. Archbishop Whitgift had striven to amend the Thirty-nine Articles by inserting in them the salient features of Calvin's doctrines. Those doctrines thrived because they constituted an authoritative standard against the inroads of the Jesuit controversialists, and instilled those religious and political convictions which protected the integrity of the nation and of the Church against the intrigues of the Papacy. But they also usurped the Protestant right of private judgment by an arbitrary theory of Biblical interpretation. The Calvinists deified the Scriptures, the Romanists deified the Church. Both reverenced the framework of religion to the detriment of religion itself. Presently the Independents began to complain that

"New presbyter is but old priest writ large,"

and at the other extreme the hierarchical tendencies of the Church of England reasserted themselves. The episcopate and the Sacraments were elevated until they became repugnant to Puritans of every stripe. Ritual grew more sacerdotal in meaning and more profuse in display. The warfare between the factionists increased in virulence. The stiff-necked individualism of the sectaries was forever associated with great deeds and great men, but it antagonized that veneration for the solidarity of the visible Church and for its governing priesthood which prevailed in the Laudian school. The articles of predestination and election were deprecated by those who argued that Christian life and history, as vouched for by personal experience, rested on a more enduring basis than arbitrary decrees.

These factors in the evolution of Anglicanism had their sources in racial sentiment, in political and religious quarrels, in the statecraft of princes and bishops, and, supremely, in the ceaseless energies which resulted from even a limited degree of the freedom which such leaders as Milton appropriated to the fullest extent. The toleration eventually forced upon Englishmen by their struggles for civil and religious equality led to a placidity and contentment that induced the lassitude and decay of the eighteenth century, which, in turn, gave an opportunity to the Evangelical Revival.

Newman's search for a divine philosophy confronted these peculiarities of opinion in the forms in which they had passed over into his era. The Noetics, who questioned everything in order to ascertain its characteristics and external relations, belonged to the rationalistic group in that they subjected orthodoxy to reason. They had introduced Newman to a larger world where the beliefs of his home life lost their significance. Hawkins, not yet Provost of Oriel, taught him that the Bible was to be understood in the light of a living tradition. From Whately he learned that the Christian Church was a divine appointment, and, as a substantial visible body, independent of the State, endowed with rights, prerogatives, and powers of its own. His pastoral service at St. Clement's convinced him that the faith he had received from John Newton and Thomas Scott would not work in a parish, and that Calvinism was not a key to the phenomena of human nature as they occur in the world. His alienation from these doctrines was a gradual process, extending over his first phase at Oriel, and some traces of their former hold upon him remained visible to the end. But from the moment he came to Oxford the doom of his earliest creed was assured. Its emotional and peculiar content was subordinated to an objective and concrete faith, succeeded by a dogmatic ecclesiasticism that found its logical conclusion in the Church of Rome. His restless spirit showed its dissatisfaction with the specific gifts of these transitory states to his peace and welfare, nor was his assurance so perfected as to be beyond disturbance, even in the final outcome.

As we have seen, he was a dreamer, full of eloquent and radiant imageries, and a poet, having the poetical temperament and mastery of poetic form which exuded an atmosphere redolent of his own personality. The higher loveliness which springs out of poignant introspection suffused his utterances. Dr. E. A. Abbott complained that Newman's imagination dominated his reason; it certainly carried him far away from the charted routes of investigation. The undue subjectivism, not to say egoism, of his nature received no salutary restraint from the best results of modern thought. He had none of that admirable curiosity which would have driven him to inquire of those experts in philosophy and religion who had recreated the ideas of some of his contemporaries. Dean Stanley exclaimed: "How different the fortunes of the Church of England if Newman had been able to read German!" Mark Pattison declared that all the grand development of human reason, from Aristotle to Hegel, was a sealed book to Newman, who himself confessed in old age, "I never read a word of Kant, I never read a word of Coleridge."

Nor was his imagination, when left to itself, at all flexible. Underneath its surface fluctuations he was conscious of a hardness and a centralization which nothing beyond him could touch. "I have changed in many things," he

said, "in this I have not changed. From the age of fifteen
dogma has been the fundamental principle of my religion;
I cannot enter into the idea of any other sort of religion;
religion, as a mere sentiment, is to me a dream and a mockery.
As well can there be filial love without the fact of a father, as
devotion without the fact of a Supreme Being. What I held
in 1816, I held in 1833, and I hold in 1864. Please God, I
shall hold it to the end. Even when I was under Dr. Whately's influence I had no temptation to be less zealous for the
great dogmas of the faith."[1]   For Newman, Christian belief
and character were determined by an unquestioning acceptance of this position. He wrought earnestly to understand
and apply credal statements received upon authority, which
he believed could not be neglected without incurring Heaven's
displeasure. His reliance was increasingly placed upon the
Church and her institutions. Moored to this anchorage, he
felt that he was safe and better able to measure the strength
of the currents which bore mankind either from or toward her
welcome haven. Under her protection, he craved a close
fellowship with God, compared with which the honors and
intercourse of the University sank into nothingness. The
prizes and emoluments others coveted never allured him;
fame itself was but a mere breath, an empty sound, a vibra-
tion of the air in words. The maxims of Thomas Scott,
"Holiness rather than Peace," and "Growth the only evidence of Life," were his chosen guides, the mottoes of a
heart intent on the vision of eternal realities through the
medium of the divine society on earth.

His unquestioning acceptance of the *ipsissima verba* of
Holy Writ was another evidence of the innate conservatism
which blended with his progressiveness, another tribute of his
spirit to the stability of the historic past. From first to last
he treated every text, every expression, every emblem, every
idea the Bible contained as a settled and saving truth, to be
developed later, perhaps, by the Church, but never to be

[1] "Apologia"; p. 49.

doubted. His severe adherence to concrete and explicit authority found an outlet in this notion of Biblical infallibility, which he maintained practically unmodified after his submission to Rome. Unafraid of the inconsistency which is "the hobgoblin of little minds," he carried to the Roman Cardinalate one of the basic teachings of his hereditary Protestantism. Anything savoring of exegetical research and criticism was distasteful to him, and if the results of constructive scholarship trespassed on his theological dogmatism he promptly ignored them. For him, at this stage, spiritual culture was synonymous with absolute trust in the Holy Scriptures and in the Church of England as their guardian. Contradictions could no more be permitted in the prescribed principles of religion than in those of astronomy or chemistry. On the entire issue he might well have held the Authorized Version inspired for any critical use he ever made of it. A keen observer has remarked that whereas the Vatican Council had declared the whole Bible has God for its author, Newman's belief was that God was its editor.

Blanco White detected these strivings between the old and the new, and predicted that Newman's preference for history over experience as the revelation of whatever was true and holy would unfailingly draw him within Latin Christianity, the home of that conception. White was qualified to judge: he had formerly been a priest in Spain, was afterwards an Oxford man, a traveler, a student of literatures, and a powerful writer on philosophical and religious subjects untroubled by the thoughts of yesterday. But his volatile and erratic temperament could exercise no restraint upon Newman, now beset by a host of reflections he revealed to none. On the very day he fulfilled White's prophecy and accepted the rule of Rome, White himself renounced that of Canterbury: thus they separated, journeying in opposite directions. Chief among the reflections mentioned was the persuasion that an inevitable nemesis and reaction permeated life, an idea which rendered Newman sensitive to signs and tokens in whatever happened.   Ordinary events were viewed in the light of a special Providence, which graciously intervened to provide these stepping stones on a dark and perilous road. His daily routine was never in his own keeping, his ordinations were from above.   Confident of this, he became impersonal in his ambitions, cherishing his calling as Christ's anointed messenger beyond any other pursuit, and saying of it:

> "Deep in my heart that gift I hide,
>   I change it not away
> For patriot warrior's hour of pride
>   Or statesman's tranquil sway;
> For poet's fire, or pleader's skill
> To pierce the soul and tame the will."

His break with Whately was due, not as some have asserted, to their disagreement over Sir Robert Peel's candidature at Oxford as the reluctant advocate of Catholic Emancipation, when Newman was found in the camp of vociferous Orangemen and No-Popery zealots, but to his growing separation from the Noetics, whose offense lay in their being the forerunners of a reasonable theology.   Equally dissatisfied with the immovable orthodoxy of Evangelicals and the dull pompous inertness of High Churchmen, the Noetics discountenanced both factions and cultivated a spirit of moderation and sympathy impossible within either.   Newman's Evangelicalism had not deterred them from receiving him with respect and kindness, nor was the broadening effect of their intimacy entirely lost upon him.   On the contrary, Dr. Wilfred Ward states that as a thinker pure and simple, although confined in range, his reputation was never more deserved than when he was under their spell.[1]   But he could not permanently identify himself with what he conceived to be the nebulous theories of a few intellectual aristocrats who did not even agree among themselves.   As an Evangelical, he had far more in common with Catholic

[1] " Life of John Henry Cardinal Newman "; Vol. I, p. 38.

teaching than with a Rationalism, however disguised, which held all formularies at arm's length. The same may be said of other notable seceders: Sibthorp, Manning, Ryder, Dodsworth, Hope-Scott, Noel, Faber, and the Wilberforces "proceeded from Oxford to Rome as they had already marched from Clapham to Oxford."

In 1826 Newman resigned the ,curacy of St. Clement's to become one of the four public tutors at Oriel. And now the friend and companion who finally vanquished his tentative and short-lived liberalism appeared upon the scene, the "bright and beautiful" Hurrell Froude, who was destined to have a part in Newman's inspiration and recollection analogous to that which Arthur Hallam had in Tennyson's "In Memoriam." He was the eldest son of Archdeacon Robert Hurrell Froude, of Totnes, Devon, a High Churchman of the most extreme and exclusive type, who loathed Puritanism, denounced the Evangelicals, and brought up his sons to do the same. The aged President of Magdalen College, Dr. Martin Routh, a relic of the far past, represented this nearly extinct cult at Oxford long before and after the Tractarians had resuscitated it. Hurrell Froude thus conveyed to Newman's mind an indoctrination hitherto alien to its experience; he became the living bridge over which Newman passed from the Evangelical to the Catholic conception of Anglicanism. During the first stages of the Oxford Movement, Froude was its most pervasive force, and the afterglow of his personality lingered long subsequently to his short day. He caricatured and mocked the vacillations and compromises of Erastianism, assailing with unsparing invective its surrender of the heroical attributes of High Churchmanship and its insular and egregious complacency. These defects were contrasted with the bold and consistent policies of the Holy See, for which he openly avowed his affection. A rash and adventurous critic, without accurate information on many issues he presumed to determine, Froude rejoiced in the little he knew about the Puritans, since it gave him a

better right to hate John Milton, whom Newman also reproached as contaminated by evil times and the waywardness
of a proud heart.[1] Froude adored Charles I, and venerated
Archbishop Laud, whose apparition Newman gravely
declared might even then be found in Oxford, anxiously
awaiting the developments of events.

Froude's extravagances were probably intensified by his
prolonged illness, which ended his life when he was not yet
thirty-three. While he lived, the light of battle was in his
eye, and as though prescient of death, he eagerly spread a
feverish restlessness among the Tractarians, who received his
reckless statements with avidity. These he proclaimed in
the temper of a zealot, describing himself as a priest of the one
Holy Catholic Church allowed by her Divine Lord to manifest herself in Great Britain, and engaging his loyalty to her
and to her alone. Other Protestant communions, English or
continental, were the objects of his violent detestation and
abuse. Their great institutions, no matter how beneficial,
were viewed satirically. The variety of his gifts, the vehemence of his ecclesiasticism, and his insatiable craving for
sympathy endeared him to kindred spirits, who could not
resist his unrestrained outpourings, even when these did not
win their entire approval.

Dean Church has suggested that Froude's intemperate
language and demeanor, which in some instances came near
to ill-bred and useless folly, were such as could be easily
misinterpreted by those not admitted to his confidence, and
that his insolent pronouncements were uttered at random and
not intended for the public ear. The Dean added that
friends were pained and disturbed, while foes exulted over
such disclosures of the animus of the Oxford Movement. But
the editors of the "Remains," of whom Newman was one,
asserted that, "right or wrong, they were his deliberate opinions, and cannot be left out of consideration in a complete
estimate of Froude's character and principles. The off-hand,

[1] "Letters and Correspondence"; Vol. I, p. 195.

unpremeditated way in which they seemed to dart out of him, like sparks from a luminous body, proved only a mind entirely possessed with the subject, glowing as it were through and through." [1] The volume speaks for itself and for the incurable provincialism and ignorance that infest its pages, in which violence of assertion was the ideal method, assertion that sought no ultimate proof higher than prejudice. It abounds in flouts, jibes, and sneers; exhibiting those prepossessions which corrupted the history and also cramped the intellectual processes of the entire group for whom Froude was an apostle. Neither he nor they realized that a churchmanship imbedded in dread of democracy, in separatism, and in uncharitableness toward its rivals and opponents, could not withstand the strain of crisis.

James Anthony Froude, the younger brother, described Hurrell as one who went forward, taking the fences as they came, and sweeping his friends along with him. Hugh James Rose distrusted him from the first, and the description of Froude's position as that of a Catholic without the Popery and a Church of England man without the Protestantism made many others distrust him, and irritated those who regarded these as irreconcilable terms. But he penetrated Newman's proud isolation to such a degree that the latter was unable to write with confidence unless he had received the imprimatur of Froude: "He was one of the acutest and clearest and deepest men in the memory of man," avowed Newman. Other equally keen and far more sagacious thinkers were avoided or forsaken because their ability to conserve spiritual interests was distrusted. Newman's self-knowledge was not balanced by a sufficient knowledge of his fellow creatures. Hence he admitted within the sacred walls of his individuality this hectic young dogmatist, who helped to make him a resolute and aggressive Churchman, aglow for the Catholic Anglicanism Newman was after-

[1] Preface, "Remains of the Late Reverend Richard Hurrell Froude"; p. 20.

wards to renounce and ridicule. "He taught me," said Froude's illustrious pupil, "to look with admiration towards the Church of Rome, and in the same degree to dislike Puritanism. He fixed deep in me the idea of devotion to the Blessed Virgin and he led me to believe in the Real Presence."[1] How much farther Froude would have proceeded toward Rome had he lived is a speculation. True to his origin he seemed well intrenched in Anglicanism, and just before his death declared his faith in it as a branch of the Catholic Church, with the right of apostolical succession in its ministry and free from sinful terms in its communion.

But the "Apologia" shows how firmly and how far he planted Newman's feet on the road toward secession. It also delineates Froude as so many sided that it would be presumptuous to attempt to describe him, except under those aspects in which he came before Newman himself. He speaks of this man of dew and fire as gentle and tender; of the free elasticity and graceful versatility of his mind, and the patient and winning considerateness in discussion which endeared him to those to whom he opened his heart. Depicting a very different Froude than the one the "Remains" presents, Newman extolled him as "a high genius, brimful and overflowing with ideas and views, in him original, which were too many and too strong even for his bodily strength, and which crowded and jostled against each other in their effort after distinct shape and expression."[2] Bereaved of his companionship, he took refuge in verse —

> "Oh dearest! with a word he could dispel
> All questioning, and raise
> Our hearts to rapture, whispering all was well
> And turning prayer to praise,
> And other secrets too he could declare,
> By patterns all divine,
> His earthly creed retouching here and there,
> And deepening every line."

[1] "Apologia"; p. 25.　　[2] *Ibid.*, p. 24.

The significant achievement of Froude's brief career, as he himself regarded it, and the one on which he dwelt with satisfaction, is related in the "Remains," where he inquires: "Do you know the story of the murderer who had done one good thing in his life? Well, if I were asked what good deed I had ever done, I should say that I had brought Keble and Newman to understand each other." There was need of this, for Keble had suspected Newman of the taint of Evangelicalism. Nor did they at any time enter into the closest and most sympathetic intercourse; Newman's nature precluded such affinities, and rendered him superior rather than fraternal. Like Napoleon on his way to Elba, his thoughts were his only real companions. He was never fully alive to the fact that a man's life consists in the relations he bears to others — is made or marred by those relations, guided by them, judged by them, and expressed in them. That Christianity from the first had been a social and not a solitary religion, and that aspirants after its ideals cannot run counter to this truth, did not seem to occur to him. The instinct for human fellowship was foreign to his breast. The relaxation, the joy, the refreshment which belong to the fellowship of saints were sacrificed to those grand designs which he carried from childhood up to manhood and on to old age.

Even Froude was far from being Newman's alter ego; in many respects he was of a contrary as well as a complementary temperament, abounding in traits which Newman either suppressed or did not have. Froude, as we have seen, was nothing if not original, daring, thorough, open; delighting in publicity and abrupt effective sallies. Newman's shrewd judgments of the foibles and follies of the many were reserved for the few: and even they were kept in suspense as to what he really thought. Yet like most people who follow an elusive labyrinth, he was deficient in prevision, and did not anticipate the vigorous resentment which his neatly arranged plans excited. Both men were engrossed with the theory of a complete hierarchical system, and of a sacerdotal power which granted the fullest liberty to ecclesiastical prerogatives at the expense of every other kind of freedom. Froude, in particular, had an almost superstitious reverence for the physical despotisms and spiritual transcendencies of the saints of the Middle Ages.

Thus the Oxford Catholics occupied a region filled in its upper ranges with courage, determination, and the spirit of sacrifice, but poisoned on its lower levels by a miasma that has bred misunderstanding and division. The one man who by mutual consent of all parties lived on the heights, secure and serene, was John Keble, vicar of Hursley. Homely and unambitious, it seemed strange that this retiring and sequestered clergyman should have been one of the principal factors in the most important religious movement of his day. His personality was not easy to analyze: and as a result, opinions about him have not been free from confusion. A rigid sacerdotalist, he divided the human family into three classes: Christians, properly so called; Catholics, Jews, and Mohammedans; heretics, heathen, and unbelievers. Yet, while knowing little of the magnitude of mind which is incomparably above any other intellectual endowment, he had generous views of life within certain marked limitations, disapproving the severities of William Law, and remarking that even the "Imitation of Christ" should be read with caution. He adopted Butler's dictum that Probability, not demonstration, is the guide of life, to which he always adhered, and the robust polemic of Warburton was also congenial to the more masculine features of his nature.[1] His writings were as diversified as his intellectual character. They contained the most exquisite passages and stanzas mingled with almost unintelligible references based upon his conceptions of the infallibility of the Church and the Bible. Acting under an impulse that had its source in beliefs which many educated men had abandoned, he endeavored to substi-

[1] "Dictionary of National Biography"; Vol. XXX, pp. 291–295.

tute for the creeds of Protestant Anglicanism those of his
Cavalier forefathers. But everything was forgiven, if not
forgotten, by all Christians to whom his Evening and Morning Hymns had been a benediction, and one of his strongest
opponents described him as "a great and good man whose
memory will last as long as Christian devotion expresses itself
in the English tongue." Born in a secluded country parish
of Gloucestershire just before the close of the eighteenth century, Keble was the fortunate child of an old-fashioned rectory
where his father represented scholarly culture, Prayer Book
piety, Carolinian Churchmanship, and congenital Toryism.
From the first the son was nurtured in conceptions which
afterwards breathed in his poetry and were exemplified in his
character. As Methodism sprang from Epworth rectory,
so the Oxford Movement sprang from the vicarages of Coln
St. Aldwins and Totnes. Keble and Froude were High
Churchmen by ancestral right; the tenets they conveyed to
Newman were theirs by inheritance; his doctrinal antecedents differed in many essentials. But the three men
found a unity of place and of ideas at Oxford; she
refashioned and blended them and gave them to the
Catholic Revival, and with them, Miller, Palmer, Pusey,
Hook, and Ogilvie. Like Froude, Keble remained unshaken
in his allegiance to his Church. When others bent to the
storm, or asseverated from their pulpits that, although faint,
they were still pursuing, or silently stole away to Rome, he
gave full proof of his staunchness as an Anglican priest, and
this notwithstanding that the logic of his beliefs pointed
directly to the refuge in which his friends and protégés found
shelter. But though he admitted the strength of Rome's
canonical position, and objected to her doctrinal corruptions
with a timid and deferential air, he chose the domestic
privacy which suited his pacific disposition, forsook further
preferment in his University, married, and stayed in his lot
to the end of his days.

Testimony to his importance as the actual founder of

Tractarianism has been given by Dean Church and also by Newman. "Long before the Oxford Movement was thought of, or had any definite shape, a number of its characteristic principles and ideas had taken a strong hold of the mind of a man of great ability and great seriousness . . . John Keble." [1] "The true and primary author of it, as is usual with great motive powers, was out of sight. Having carried off as a mere boy the highest honors of the University, he had turned from the admiration which haunted his steps and sought for a better and a holier satisfaction in pastoral work in the country. Need I say that I am speaking of John Keble." [2] Pusey confirmed these statements and so did Dr. James B. Mozley, who was regarded by competent judges as the most stimulating thinker the Church of England had produced since Butler.

When Oriel was the center of Oxford's talent and learning Keble was hailed as the glory of the college, for whom every visitor inquired and expected to see. "The slightest word he dropped was all the more remembered from there being so little of it, and from it seeming to come from a different and holier sphere." [3] Yet such giants as Copleston, Hawkins, Davison and Whately gathered around the fire in the Oriel Common Room; they gave tone to the University, and it was impossible that Keble, a recently elected fellow, could be equal to their skill in disputation. Truth to tell, he was not, and Sir John T. Coleridge hinted that he sometimes yearned for the less exacting society of his old friends at Corpus. His intellectual endowments were inferior to his classical knowledge. In scientific matters he was a tyro. Thomas Mozley recites his amusing argument with Buckland, the geologist, which lasted all the way from Oxford to Winchester. Keble took his stand on the certainty of the Almighty having created the fossil remains of former existences in the six days of Genesis. [4] He was an elegant scholar,

---

[1] "The Oxford Movement"; p. 32.   [2] "Apologia"; p. 17.
[3] Thomas Mozley: "Reminiscences"; Vol. I, p. 38.   [4] Ibid., p. 179.

who could discourse with wisdom to congenial listeners, but
nothing original was in him, nor was he fitted for leadership
in large affairs. He rather served as an embodiment of
usages and institutions first deemed Laudian and then
Apostolic, and as such he was regarded by Froude and Newman. Disliking speculation and the competition of trained
minds, he embraced with childlike trust the teachings of
the Church he apostrophized as his mother, retained untarnished the impressions of his youthful goodness, and relinquished the University eminence to which his consecrated
character entitled him, that he might bury himself in his
curacy at East Leach and Burthorpe. This decision, while
entirely in harmony with his wishes, was a genuine self-
effacement. Yet by it he gained what he most desired,
nearness to his family, escape from the turmoil of a belliger-
ent world, and a suitable environment for uninterrupted
communion with God.

In 1831 he was elected Professor of Poetry at Oxford in
succession to Dean Milman, and held the chair for ten years.
His motives and experiences as an author were indicated by
his definition of poetry as the vent for surcharged feelings or
a full imagination. His muse was a gracious gift dedicated
to the sanctuary and the inner life: serving faith and the
objects of faith with chasteness and purity of speech. "The
Christian Year," published in 1827, was the first literary
expression of Neo-Anglicanism, and the volume made him
the central sun of his then contracted but rapidly enlarging
sphere. Newman mildly remonstrated that its doctrines,
although lovely, were not sufficiently thorough, but he cheerfully conceded that the popularity of Tractarian ideas was
due to Keble's poetry. Those ideas centered around material
phenomena as both the types and the instruments of things
unseen, and embraced in all its fullness whatever was received
by Catholics as well as Anglicans concerning the Sacraments,
the communion of saints, and the mysteries of religion.
Although the lyrics in which these were expressed were

thoughtful and soothing, their awkward meter and construction and occasional obscurity were so marked that Wordsworth offered to correct their English. Nor were they poetry of the inevitable kind: they lacked the highest play of passion or pity, and their placidities were far removed from "the Dantean flame in which all things are transmuted to the colors of a supernatural world." Despite these drawbacks they were favorably received not only by the Church in general but also by the literary world. All felt that Keble had struck an original note and aroused a new music in the hearts of multitudes.

Taking the Book of Common Prayer for his guide, he composed a poetical manual of religious sentiment which, though sometimes degenerating into sentimentalism, became an undoubted source of pious inspiration. The winsome tenderness he displayed toward the ideals of High Anglican worship was couched in moving and unaffected language. Antique prejudices and extreme opinions occasionally protruded, yet they were not so pronounced as to arouse sectarian resentment, which was lulled to slumber by the unction of the writer's melodies. The well-known truth already mentioned in the chapters on Wesley, that sacred poetry is blind to heterodoxy, was seldom better illustrated. His habit, however, of mapping out the slightest allusion in the Gospels so as to have a well defined and appropriate mood of poetry for as many days as possible in the calendar evoked the rebuke of some critics, who complained, not without justice, that the smallest item of historic incident or moral epithet was forced into the service of thin and feminine verse, which was often vague and formless. Bagehot's pungent comment was that it translated Wordsworth for women. The poems contributed to the "Lyra Apostolica" and the "Lyra Innocentium," which followed those of "The Christian Year," added nothing to Keble's fame. This was permanently secured by his best lyrics, which will long be associated with those of Bishop Ken for their fragrant devotion and insistence upon the daily consecration of Christian fellowship. Full of spiritual suggestiveness, replete with sweetness and delicacy, happy in their references to the nobler aspects of Nature, and steeped in the sacramental usages of the Church and in the letter and spirit of the Bible, they have heightened, adorned, and hallowed the praises of the Church.

Resentful of the preponderant intellectualism of the day, with its attendant egotism and sterility in motive power; given to allegorical and fanciful interpretation; subservient to patristic illustrations of ritual and worship; as a rule meek as a lamb, but liable to outbreaks of temper when his pet theories were assailed; and separated from the social existence of the majority of his fellow countrymen; such was John Keble, the saint and singer, who lived to see his principles promulgated in countless parishes and his ministrations extended throughout England and America. His spiritual elevation, his laudable consecration of visible means, his passion for the holiness of Christian adoration helped to remove from the Church the stagnation and dearth he deplored. He passed his days surrounded by the propitious circumstances of an orderly and somewhat aristocratic society, in which he dwelt at peace, yet resentful toward many aspects of the actual life of his time. The loving eulogies lavished on him were not always wise or discriminating, for the Tractarians sometimes used very exalted terms about one another, and few of them could be trusted to sit in judgment on their patron saint. Notwithstanding these misapprehensions, the real man was singularly lofty and unassuming; in most respects worthy not only of esteem but of affectionate reverence. Keble College, Oxford, erected after his death, was raised, said Canon Liddon, "to the memory of a quiet country clergyman, with a very moderate income, who sedulously avoided public distinctions, and held tenaciously to an unpopular school all his life. . . . The more men really know of him, who, being dead, has, in virtue of the rich gifts and graces with which

God has endowed him, summoned this college into being, the less will they marvel at such a tribute to his profound and enduring influence." [1]   In these words we feel the orientation of Keble's spirit; by them we are made aware of his saintliness and of his nobler aspirations, which

> ". . . come transfigured back,
>   Secure from change in their high-hearted ways,
>   Beautiful evermore, and with the rays
>   Of Morn on their white shields of Expectation."

III

One of the first fruits of Newman's friendship with Froude and Keble was a marked increase in the sense of his personal responsibility for the spiritual welfare of pupils committed to his care.   Esteeming his college duties a pastoral privilege, he refused to merge the cleric in the scholar.   A lofty prophetic strain began to pervade his utterances.   The law of the Church, which he construed yet more and more according to the standards of Catholic Anglicanism, prevailed in his conduct and in that of those whom he influenced.   Writing to his mother he informed her that his engagements preempted his time and energy, making him an exile from those he so much loved. [2]   Everything else was eclipsed by his devotion to the immediate service of God, which expelled all lesser affairs as a strong plant in a hedgerow drives out or sterilizes the rest.   Froude, who had been elected to an Oriel fellowship and tutorship in 1826, entered enthusiastically into the propagandisms which were the daily bread of both men, and when he deemed it desirable did not hesitate to urge his companion to still greater lengths.   In relation to his age, Newman may be regarded as a pioneer of the High Anglican movement then gathering its first impetus.   But his was not a happy, full-blooded spirit, and in his struggle

---

[1] "Clerical Life and Work"; pp. 353–354.
[2] "Letters and Correspondence"; Vol. I, p. 115.

against a vigorous opposition, he abandoned himself to that belittling view of human nature which is frequently an evidence of religious fatigue rather than of religious discernment. Other and very different personalities of the nineteenth century shared his despair over a general condition which offered large opportunity for discontent as well as renunciation. Though some new truths which sounded dolefully to him were grateful to them, all alike were distressed by the moral and spiritual enigmas their times presented. George Eliot, who somewhat resembled and greatly admired Newman, distilled through fiction a stoical resignation and a calm resolve to endure the worst. Arthur Hugh Clough gave up the whole problem, yet still clung to it in blank bewilderment. Tennyson eventually succeeded in reaching a stage of faith where, on the whole, the odds were in favor of heaven. Browning's optimism, so often lauded, was sometimes too insistent to be convincing. Newman, like Matthew Arnold, at this moment was dejectedly

> "Wandering between two worlds,
> One dead, the other powerless to be born." [1]

He complained of the present state of things, which his change of opinion obliged him to represent in its worst form, and retreated to an obscure past, over which he threw the legendary halo of an exceeding sanctity. Harassed by modernity, and its supposed preference for material aggrandizement, he resorted to antiquity and its supposed preference for qualitative perfection. The future, being supreme, became as nothing; the past became everything. In journeying toward this goal, he forsook to a large degree the wider areas of human life and forfeited that wholeness of contemplation which becomes the historian and the thinker. The large majority of men who must be content to dwell far below the summits of achievement, but who instinctively renew their youth and perform the cyclopean tasks of the

[1] John F. Genung: "Stevenson's Attitude to Life"; p. 6.

race, were of little moment compared with the few outstanding figures to whom he attached the entire meaning of existence. Beneath his failure to accommodate himself to his surroundings operated a vivid retentive mind, content to dwell in the primitive organizations of Christianity, finding in their persecutions and conquests the example and the stimulus for a present readjustment. The mighty drama of God's ceaseless working was thus woefully circumscribed, and many of the forces which have helped to weave the fabric of Christian civilization were treated as negligible quantities.

He voiced his dissatisfaction with the barren levity and the thirst for false and worthless things and the blindness to all majestic or tragical tendencies in the following sentiments: "We can scarce open any of the lighter or popular publications of the day without falling upon some panegyric on ourselves, on the illumination and humanity of the age, or upon some disparaging remarks on the wisdom and virtue of former times. Now it is a most salutary thing under this temptation to self-conceit, to be reminded, that in all the highest qualifications of human excellence, we have been far outdone by men who lived centuries ago; that a standard of truth and holiness was then set up, which we are not likely to reach; and that, as for thinking to become wiser or better, or more acceptable to God than they were, it is a mere dream."[1] He earnestly wished that St. Paul or St. John could rise from the dead to show this untoward generation that its boasted knowledge was but a shadow of power, and cause the minute philosophers who dared to scrutinize the traditions of the faith to shrink into nothingness. "Are we not come to this," he asked, "is it not our shame as a nation, that, if not the Apostles themselves, at least the Ecclesiastical System they devised, and the Order they founded, are viewed with coldness and disrespect? How few there are who look with

[1] "Parochial and Plain Sermons"; Vol. II, Sermon XXXII.

reverent interest upon the Bishops of the Church as the Successors of the Apostles; honoring them, if they honor, merely because they like them as individuals, and not from any thought of the peculiar sacredness of their office."[1] The dexterity of these statements is apparent, and much they contained enlists approval. But his identification of the Apostles, who were the immortal servants of mankind and the personal sources of an unparalleled reconstruction of religion, with his own ecclesiastical order was a gratuitous assumption which deft phrasing could not conceal. His adoration of former times and depreciation of the present and the future led him to ignore one half of history. The services of justice and freedom, knowledge and philanthropy in nineteenth century England were left outside his consideration. He felt that she had few affinities with Apostolic life and thought, but many with Greek and Roman paganism. That she also had, as have all nations, organs and proclivities for living the life of the spirit apart from sacerdotal governance, he would not concede. The theory of universal depravity he had retained from Calvinism overlooked some better elements which must be present in men's souls if they are to recognize, understand, and obey the overtures of divine love. And in addition, Newman was always liable to an emotional logic which blurred important facts and lamed his conclusions.

A serious illness which befell him about this time left him with a quickened realization of his religious needs. Never robust in body, always an endless toiler, he spent himself until what health he had was seriously impaired. His eyesight failed, his voice grew faint, his form was worn to emaciation. At last he collapsed, but despite everything, he still felt the impulse of his purposes, and the contrition of a genuine seeker after God, who confessed to Him what he would never confess to man, and having done so, renewed his vows and resumed his quest. Then came the death of his

[1] "Parochial and Plain Sermons"; Vol. II, Sermon XXXII.

much loved sister Mary, bringing with it the moral elevation
of a lasting sorrow, and ingeminating those indefinite,
vague, and withal subtle feelings which made the soul
within him forlorn and well-nigh comfortless. Nor did he
find relief in the rural haunts of the west country, where he
spent a brief holiday while convalescing. Tragic occurrences
were associated with pastoral sights and scenes; they reminded him of the dear one who had gone: "Mary," he said,
"seems embodied in every tree and every hill. What a veil
and curtain this world of sense is! beautiful, but still a
veil." [1]

Ilis campaign for the high doctrines of the Church now
became more direct, shaped as it was by these causes that
separated him from other contentions and interests not
germane to the main concern. Alarmed by the negativism
of the rationalists and by the destructive tendency of
philosophers who considered intellect and enlightened virtue
all their own, he passed out of the shadow of liberalism
which had hitherto darkened his orbit into a resentful mood
which confused constructive and sympathetic teaching with
the errors of infidelity and looked upon all theories antagonistic to his own as one chaotic mass. Though unconscious of it, he and his allies were themselves in bondage to
the deistic notion of an infinite separation between the Creator and creation. Schleiermacher's doctrine of Divine
Immanence, and also that developed by Coleridge, seemed
to High Churchmen a presumptuous and pantheistic denial
of the personality of God but one remove from atheism.
The open-mindedness of the German theologian toward the
Holy Scriptures was equally repugnant. Tractarians claimed
that they could understand a Bible miraculously indited and
preserved intact throughout its wonderful history; they
could not understand that the Holy Spirit directed the sacred
authors without emptying them of their individuality. Any
attack upon the accepted position that the Bible was through-

[1] "Letters and Correspondence"; Vol. I, p. 161.

out an unimpeachable revelation of the will of God they vigorously resented. The idea that its contents were the more convincing because the writers were not reduced to the level of automata, but freely exercised their several gifts and graces, was obnoxious to them. In a word, the difference between their viewpoint and that of the new scholarship was the difference between hypnosis and inspiration.

Again, revivals of religion such as the one which swept through Britain and her colonies in the preceding century were denounced by Anglo-Catholics as detrimental to the life and action of the Church: emotional whirlwinds, raising the dust of fanaticism, heresy, and schism. Periodical regenerations had a Scriptural and historic sanction quite as traceable as that of apostolic succession, and one which was by no means as open to valid objections. The power to move men and women to spiritual decision has always been a hallmark of New Testament authority and benediction. Nevertheless clerics of the type of Newman, Keble, Froude, and Pusey, together with many educated and ignorant laymen in the Church of England, were thoroughly set against these manifestations and all that they portended. The Tractarians enunciated the principle that formal law obtains in the spiritual as in the physical realm. Irregular and spasmodic outbreaks of religious fervor contradicted their main premise that the divine life in man was part of an external process, and as such, acted independently of his transient states of mind. They believed that the sources of spiritual renewal and sustenance were as stable and irrevocable as the operations of nature, and, like these, were universal, not provincial; continuous, not intermittent; primarily obtained by submission and obedience to ostensible authority, rather than through inward experience. This sacerdotal rule suited the complexion of minds content to rest on its assumptions, and not repelled by its mechanical and materialized processes. But it destroyed the New Testament democracy of believers by treating the dispensation of Divine grace as a hierarchical monopoly, and by denying the right of approach to God unless mediated through an ordained priesthood. Loyalty to concrete objectives of faith, which asserted unbroken relations with the very presence and word of Jesus Christ while He actually walked on the earth, was substituted for the wrestlings and pleadings of guilty sinners who, like Jacob at the brook Jabbok, invoked for themselves the Everlasting Mercy. Yet, as in his case, the discipline of these more heroical ventures obtained for men their divinest gifts and produced the grand personalities of the Church. They were not as general in their scope as was the easier method which depended upon the guarantees of a visible organization. But though they had no such width of application, their certitudes were enshrined in the human soul, their insecurities were on the surface.

At this moment Romanticism appeared, creating a sentimental appreciation for Catholic peculiarities, and flinging a delusive glamour over the so-called ages of faith. Refined spirits of an æsthetic turn, whether in Germany, France, or England, were enraptured with the sensuous beauty and seemliness of medievalism. Loving every era better than their own, they turned from the rush of surrounding forces which they dreaded to bewitching presentations of the chivalry they adored. Their literature and art idealized the triumphs, the tragedies, the gay loves, the deadly hates of the period, until it began to assume the appearance of a golden age, wherein men wrought greatly because they greatly obeyed and believed. Its strange veneering of both tenderness and ferocity by religious rites and observances gave scope to those whose actual knowledge of the events they treated was too often a thing of shreds and patches but whose fancies were no longer fettered. There was also a revulsion against the debased taste in architecture that had bestudded the land with squat ugly meeting-houses and nondescript Georgian churches, the very hideousness of which was supposed to be a protection against the lure of Rome's gorgeous fanes and ritualistic decorations. The paramount influence of Sir Walter Scott was due to the fact that "he turned men's thoughts in the direction of the Middle Ages. The general need of something more attractive than what had offered itself elsewhere may be considered to have led to his popularity; and by means of his popularity he reacted on his readers, stimulating their mental thirst, feeding their hopes, setting before them visions, which, when once seen, are not easily forgotten, and silently indoctrinating them with nobler ideas, which might afterwards be appealed to as first principles." [1] This rallying to fiction as the storehouse of first principles was the infirmity of some Romanticists, who, had they known more, would have imagined less. Impervious to the verdicts of knowledge and reason, they attempted to turn the tide and again impose upon the church and nation those forms of supremacy that had been thrown off by the resurgent energies of life itself. The degradation, the cruelty, the oppression which characterized medievalism were ignored, while its stately symbolism and sacramental authority were lauded and imitated by clerics, artists, poets, essayists, and novelists who viewed them through the media of pontifical and princely display, knights in shining armor, Gothic minsters, and Dante's poetry. They had much to say which gave verisimilitude to their pleas for the soul of honor and of virtue in past days of mingled good and evil. But what they said was not always substantiated by the facts which divide and compound man's dual nature. Prophets who prophesied falsely, they eluded disagreeable realities; fomented the dissensions which have weakened the structure of English-speaking society and aggravated the religious divisions they proposed to obliterate. Their god was resplendent to the uninstructed eye, but its feet were of clay. Scott was conscious of this misdirection, and, contrary to his predilections, gave the laurel to the Covenanter rather than to his perse-

[1] "Apologia"; pp. 96–97.

cutors. Thus while the work of the Romanticists was in many instances injurious to religion, it was conducive to a renaissance of Catholicism. Professor McGiffert properly observes that "the Oxford Movement gave delayed but somewhat distorted expression to certain elements of the romantic spirit." [1]

Newman, who felt a growing attachment to Christian antiquity, contrasted its unity, continuity, and effectiveness with the hazardous experiments of intellectualism then being inflicted upon the faith. To offset these he returned to the precedents of third and fourth century churchmanship, advocating them without sufficient allowance for the organic changes which had since been evolved. It was not altogether native to his habit to reason in this fashion; for he was instinctively distrustful, and showed at intervals that his belief in the heroic epochs of Catholicism was not only determinative of his new creed, but still more a refuge from the tempestuous doubts and questionings to which his soul was susceptible. He had rebelled against those who, as he conceived, were endeavoring to undermine the principle of authority to which he rendered special reverence. If the Church was not the guardian of ethics and religion, the qualified censor of morals, the natural champion of faith, the mentor of mankind in spiritual matters, what could be said for organized Christianity? Separated from his former companions and from much of the actual life of his fellow men; entranced, as he was, by the ideal of a living, growing Ecclesia either opposing or controlling the world, Newman knew not for the moment where his true strength lay. Beset by such trying circumstances, his subjective faith broke down beneath the weight of externalism. That assurance which is not an energy of intellect, or heart, or imagination, but rather the spontaneous and irresistible vitality which uses these faculties, was not his at the crisis. At the beginning of his ministry, with the doctrines of Evangelicalism retreating into

[1] "The Rise of Modern Religious Ideas"; p. 194.

those subconscious realms from which they were never entirely eliminated, he whose mission it was to proclaim salvation to others was no longer sure of it himself. In his distress he renewed his youthful fondness for the Fathers whom Whately had flippantly termed "certain old divines," and found in them the remaining source of his reconstructed theology. Having little or no confidence in a progressive development that was not controlled by the Church, and an ever-present fear of scientific investigations as entailing moral anarchy, he must needs flee with unspeakable relief to the ancient masters who became his Strong Rock and House of Defense. Beginning with St. Ignatius and St. Justin, he read them in their chronological order until he arrived at the broad philosophy of St. Clement of Alexandria and Origen. Their homilies and meditations carried him back from present evils to their own times, and in his recession he conceived a still greater detestation for modern methods which created more difficulties than they settled. The Fathers' discourses " came like music to my ear," he declared, " as if the response to ideas which I had cherished so long. They were based on the mystical or sacramental principle, and spoke of the various Economies or Dispensations of the Eternal." His search for the heart of Religion ended in the dreams of his childhood, now realized in these Elder Brethren of the household of God whose writings exhibited an ideal of Christian regnancy in impressive contrast with the fears and doubts of Oxford's churchmanship. In them was found the antidote to the baneful practice of resting religion on an intellectualism that was everything in turn and nothing long, for the supernatural order had revealed itself more freely and convincingly in them than in their derelict successors. He was enthralled by such saints as Irenæus and Cyprian, supremely typical of the Christianity which molded society and subdued the hearts of men, and to their guidance he unreservedly submitted his judgment. Hereafter precedent and tradition dictated his arguments; and, individualized though he was, the use of independence became a temptation to be withstood.

This fragmentary story of his momentous change may be regarded as an illustration of the saying that the most singular lapses are those of gifted men. With all his brilliance and insight, Newman had accomplished nothing more than the kindling of his churchly zeal to its utmost. The real battle was not yet in sight; many imperfectly known antagonisms, including the philosophical and moral conceptions of his own day, had yet to be faced, nor could he escape the obligations arising out of that fact. Every system or creed, however ancient and well tried, must be prepared to reckon with new conditions of constantly evolving life. Meanwhile, despite heresy, lukewarmness, and failure, the Church of his baptism was still for him the living representative of the Apostles; she had not lost for a moment her vital nexus; she was still capable of recovery, restitution, and compliance with the divine commandment. Her spirit freed, her confidence regained, the future opened before her with an illimitable prospect.

Thus believing, he pushed the issue to its limits, adding to his conceptions of clerical sanctity and prerogative, and defending them against the learned who derided him. Discerning the perils that menaced faith, he contended that scholarly coteries with strong inclinations toward the rejection of pious heritages were no schools for saints. Their detrimental measures must be overthrown by the doctrines of past ages, providentially preserved, and communicated through chosen men, who, while not acceptable to profane wisdom, had faithfully guarded the deposit committed to them. In a letter to his mother, under date of March 13, 1829, he set forth the situation as it appealed to him. "We live in a novel era — one in which there is an advance towards universal education. Men have hitherto depended especially on the clergy for religious truth; now each man attempts to judge for himself. Now, without meaning of course that Christianity is in itself opposed to free inquiry, still I think it is in fact at the present time opposed to the particular form which that liberty of thought has now assumed. Christianity is of faith, modesty, lowliness, subordination; but the spirit at work against it is one of latitudinarianism, indifferentism, and schism, a spirit which tends to overthrow doctrine, as if the fruit of bigotry and discipline — as if the instrument of priestcraft. All parties seem to acknowledge that the stream of opinion is setting against the Church. . . . And now I come to another phenomenon: the talent of the day is against the Church. The Church party (visibly at least . . .) is poor in mental endowments. It has not activity, shrewdness, dexterity, eloquence, practical power." [1]

From the Fathers, Newman also derived a speculative angelology which described the unseen universe as inhabited by hosts of intermediate beings who were spiritual agents between God and creation, and determined to some extent the character of various peoples. Of these intermediaries some were good, directed by a superior wisdom, and content to serve the Supreme Will in the economy of material worlds; others were neither angelic nor reprobate, partially fallen, capricious, wayward; noble or crafty, benevolent or malicious, as their qualities were evoked by differing environments; the remainder, being farthest removed from divine contact, were lowest in the scale; in essence evil, and an active hindrance to the higher progress of mankind. The Angels proper were the real causes of motion, light, and life and of what are called the laws of nature. Those who were neither banned nor blessed gave a sort of intelligence to nations and classes of men. The case of England was cited as an example of their operations. "It seems to me," he commented, "that John Bull is a spirit neither of heaven nor hell." The third order represented the principle of evil; and it was of infinite moment to man that

---

[1] "Letters and Correspondence"; Vol. I, pp. 178–180.

2 I

he should know how to avoid their seductive overtures and thus keep his religious nature unclogged and unsullied.[1] It is obvious that this attenuated hypothesis had no necessary connection with the faith; it was theosophical rather than Christian in its development, and renewed some features of the heresy which St. Paul rebuked and corrected in his Colossian Epistle. Indeed, Newman's cosmogony was essentially Gnostic, and echoed the teaching of Cerinthus, who is best entitled to be considered as the link between the Judaizing and Gnostic sects.[2]

His earlier intention to become a missionary had now vanished; he felt that his vocation was at Oriel, and this seemed likely enough until Dr. Edward Hawkins was elected Provost of the college. Hawkins, who united a limited power of decisive thinking with great talent for action, held the provostship within four years of half a century, from 1828 to 1874. He magnified his office and introduced many reforms, usually opposing, however, such as did not originate with himself. A man of practical intelligence, he showed his discrimination in the oft-quoted prediction that if Thomas Arnold were elected to be Master of Rugby he would change the face of education all through the public schools of England.[3] But the University in which the distinguished Provost administered was sorely vexed about many things, and its turmoils helped to turn his activity into "a channel of obstinate and prolonged resistance and protest, most conscientious but most uncompromising, against two great successive movements, both of which he condemned and recoiled from as revolutionary — the Tractarian first and the Liberal Movement in Oxford."[4] The last trace of Newman's connection with the Noetics was seen in his support of Hawkins for Provost, whom they had adopted as their candidate in pref-

---

[1] "Apologia"; pp. 28–29.
[2] Lightfoot: "Commentary on St. Paul's Epistles to the Colossians and Philemon"; pp. 71–111.
[3] Dean Stanley: "Life of Thomas Arnold"; Vol. I, p. 51.
[4] Dean Church: "Occasional Papers"; Vol. II, pp. 344–347.

erence to Keble.   When Froude criticized the choice,
Newman replied that had they been electing an angel
he would have voted for Keble; but it was only a Provost. He did not believe that Keble could manage men,
whereas, about Hawkins he had no doubt, and the interests
of Oriel demanded a strong and capable head. A little
later he would probably have reversed his judgment and
selected a candidate of High Church principles. As it was,
Keble retired to Hursley, and Hawkins proved to be far more
aggressive than some desired. The pulpit of St. Mary's,
rendered vacant by Hawkins' transfer to Oriel, now fell to
Newman, who made it his throne of power for some years
prior to the "Tracts for the Times." A considerable amount
of ingenuity has been expended on what might have been had
events shaped themselves differently. Keble as Provost
might have remained unmarried, and would certainly have
been in closer contact with Newman, in which case Dr. E. A.
Abbott surmises that their joint composition of the "Apologia" was within the bounds of possibility. As a matter of
fact, Keble never dreamed of seeking relief in the Roman
communion, and Newman's secession grieved him beyond
measure. Again, if Hawkins had stayed at St. Mary's, he
would have deprived Newman of his matchless opportunity
to set forth, as he alone could, the Via Media so nobly embodied by Richard William Church, as a desirable compromise between the Papacy and Puritanism. This Newman
did, and did marvelously well, until the Anglican Church
ceased to be any longer the prophetess of God for him.
However, these conjectures must not divert us from what
actually happened. Newman's indignation was aroused
by the want of system, waste of effort, and paucity of results
in the responsible affairs of the University. Above all else,
he objected to the religious formalism and lassitude which
left the undergraduates over-shepherded yet shepherdless.
They were compelled to subscribe to the Thirty-nine Articles
as a preliminary to admission to the University, and to attend

the Holy Communion, whatever their state of life and conduct. After these requirements had been observed, they were free to follow their own inclinations, with results that might have been expected. Drunkenness and vice were prevalent; idleness and distaste for scholarly pursuits ended in repeated failures and humiliations. Newman's protests against these abuses enlist approval now: many will share his feeling that tutorial work in an Oxford college implied far more than its leaders were willing to admit, and justified such aims at the growth of virtuous character as might fairly occupy a clergyman.[1] Accordingly he suggested that the tutors of Oriel should divide into groups the men under their care, each tutor being responsible for the religious as well as the educational guidance of those intrusted to him. In conjunction with Froude and Robert Isaac Wilberforce, he sought to remodel the lectures, introduce new textbooks, and revive other important academic interests which were sacrificed by conservatism and negligence. Hawkins rejected these proposals, whereupon the three tutors tendered their resignations. This ultimatum did not daunt the Provost, who promptly called in Hampden to give lectures, and though he could not compel the tutors to relinquish the pupils they had, he announced his intention to send them no more. Out-generaled and defeated, Newman surrendered, and Hawkins doubtless felt relieved that he was rid of a teacher who attempted to act on his own discretion, and whose theological opinions were too radical for the welfare of the college. Newman, on his part, declared that the Oxford Movement never would have been had he not been practically dismissed from his tutorship, or had Keble, not Hawkins, been Provost.

More than half of 1830 had now gone, a year of trials and troubles. "I am desponding," he wrote to Froude. "All my plans fail. When did I ever succeed in any exertion for

[1] E. A. Abbott: "The Anglican Career of Cardinal Newman"; Vol. I, p. 206.

others? I do not say this in complaint, but really doubting whether I ought to meddle." He steadied himself with the reflection that disappointment and self-denial were necessary for the reception and retention of spiritual truth; and, released from his duties at Oriel, awaited other employment. Dr. Jenkyns invited him to participate in a projected Ecclesiastical History, the outcome being, as far as Newman was concerned, his volume on the Arians. In writing it he felt an intense intellectual pleasure he had not previously known. Yet the task was not altogether congenial for so versatile and discursive a mind as his. He had to deal with such unfathomable truths as the Triple Personality and the Divine Unity, those vast and remote ideas in the revelation and philosophy of religion which have taxed even greater spirits. Nor did he enjoy that thorough acquaintance with patristic literature at which his sister Jemima hinted when she reminded him that Archbishop Usher had spent eighteen years in reading the Fathers. In the December of 1831 he wrote, "I was working too hard at the 'Arians.' It was due next summer, and I had only begun to read for it, or scarcely so, the summer past." Froude grew impatient with his "dallying," declared against his "fiddling" any longer with the introduction to the work, and predicted his ending in "a scrape." Newman was resolved, however, to muster all the learning within his reach: he toiled with a vengeance, and where his learning was at fault, his rhetorical gifts admirably served his immediate purposes. Yet two defects could scarcely be concealed: his neglect of scientific research, and the irrelevancy of some of his dissertations. Desirous always of leaning on authority in religious matters, he forgot that history has no prejudices in behalf of ecclesiasticism, and he introduced a sort of reasoning, best described as heart-foam, to supply the lack of that strict historical accuracy which checks undue speculation and is content to set down the thing that actually occurred.

His general treatment of the Arian period was based on St.

Clement's theory that all religion was from God, and that Christianity did not supersede so much as it corrected and sanctified other forms of belief. While divine in its origin, it depended on human agents for its transmission, and consequently suffered some diminution of content and quality. The teachings of the New Testament were limited by the intellectual processes that conveyed them, since these were necessarily unequal to their full comprehension. The creeds likewise were in spirit and essence far below the level of the august propositions they attempted to embody, hence the introduction from time to time of orthodoxy's multiplying and minute articles as a protection against specific errors and heresies. With their growth Christian societies naturally became more complex, and required additional explanation and defense. Exactitude of credal expression was elevated to a theological virtue, requisite for the permanence of primitive Christianity and but for that exactitude the character and meaning of the Apostolic age would have been lost to mankind. Upon these grounds Newman pleaded for a rigid enforcement of formulæ. "If the Church," he averred, "would be vigorous and influential, it must be decided and plain spoken." The corrosive effects of liberalism, so energetic in Arian days, were still in evidence, still demanding precedence and sanction. Left unchecked, they would destroy not only the basis of revealed religion, but ultimately everything that could be called religion at all.

His study of the Arian controversy strengthened his conviction that Apostolic precept and practice were in complete accord with the characteristic conceptions of Anglo-Catholicism. He saw, or thought he saw, instructive parallels between the sees occupied in the fourth century by Arian bishops and those of his own communion. In both instances the purity of faith was preserved by a few valiant reformers, who had confidence in a divine intervention for their cause. Athanasius had arisen in solitary grandeur against the defilers of God's heritage; similarly some holy warrior would be found, equipped, and sent forth, to deliver the distressed Anglicanism of the earlier nineteenth century.

The volume, which was the result of a little over six months' strenuous effort, might well have taken him more than as many years. "Tired wonderfully," he says of himself, "continually on the point of fainting, quite worn out." He had been relieved of a crushing burden none too soon, and at the same time he was also giving up the last of his pupils at Oriel. The cessation left him free to brood in theological gloom over the forbidding prospects of the faith, the result, as he supposed, of the ever widening opposition between the Church and the world.

IV

His pent-up feelings found their outlet in the incomparable parochial sermons which he began to deliver at St. Mary's in 1828. They enforced his contention that things could not stand as they were, that Christ's Church was indestructible, that she must rise again and flourish, when the poor creatures of a day who opposed her had crumbled into dust. As a preacher he was profoundly conscious of the sacredness of his vocation, and in its fulfillment was superior to any other divine of his day. Oxford's foremost pulpit had several famous occupants during the nineteenth century: among them, Pusey, saint and scholar, whose personality for a time overshadowed Anglicanism; Mozley, the deepest yet clearest thinker of the group; Manning, self-conscious, politic, and facile of speech; Liddon, "with the Italianate profile, orator and ascetic." But none approached Newman in his analysis of the human heart, his exquisite rhetoric, his tender or indignant fervor. He united simple earnestness and refinement with a sense of reserved power on the verge of being released. Although his audiences were often small, they were influential, and eventually he brought Oxford to his feet. "His hearers felt," said Principal Shairp, "as

though one of the early Fathers had returned to earth."
He appealed to them with a directness and force, and a
passionate and sustained earnestness for a high spiritual
standard, to be seriously realized in conduct, the more imperative because the nation had come to the verge of religious
dissolution, and was resting complacently in its own pride
and might, while divine judgment threatened its recreancy.
Mr. Gladstone said of him : "Dr. Newman's manner in the
pulpit was one which, if you considered it in its separate parts,
would lead you to arrive at very unsatisfactory conclusions.
There was not very much change in the inflection of the
voice; action there was none; his sermons were read, and his
eyes were always on his book; and all that, you will say, is
against efficiency in preaching.   Yes; but you take the man
as a whole, and there was a stamp and a seal upon him, there
was a solemn music and sweetness in his tone, there was a
completeness in the figure, taken together with the tone and
with the manner, which made even his delivery, such as I
have described it, and though exclusively with written sermons, singularly attractive." [1]   The stamp and seal were,
indeed, manifestly impressed by nothing less than consecrated genius.   His two discourses on " Holiness Necessary
for Future Blessedness," and "The Ventures of Faith," are
worthy examples of a new type of prophetical speech, heard
with strained attention, and long remembered and repeated.
Holiness he defined as an inward separation from the world,
and in answer to the question, "Why salvation is impossible
without this frame and temper of mind ?" he replied : "Even
supposing a man of unholy life were suffered to enter heaven,
he would not be happy there, so that it would be no mercy to
permit him to enter. . . .   He would sustain a great disappointment, he would find no discourse but that which he
shunned on earth; no pursuits but those which he had disliked or despised ; nothing which bound him to ought else in
the universe and made him feel at home, nothing which he

[1] Justin McCarthy : "History of Our Own Times"; Vol. I, p. 142.

could enter into and rest upon. He would perceive himself to be an isolated being, cut away by Supreme Power from those objects which were still entwined around his heart." [1]

The second sermon, "The Ventures of Faith," is a searching and inspiring challenge to all who would direct their heavenward path by that high and unearthly spirit which is the royal, unmistakable sign of the children of the Kingdom. The text, taken from the reply of James and John to the words of Jesus, "Are ye able to drink of the cup that I shall drink of, and to be baptized with the baptism that I am baptized with?" was used to emphasize the wisdom of endeavors after the Christian life even when they are attended by no promise of absolute attainment. "No one among us knows for certain that he himself will persevere unto the end; yet every one among us, to give himself even a chance of success at all, must make a venture." Faith is the essence of a Christian life, and our duty lies in the hazardous directions where faith is demanded, since fear, risk, danger, anxiety, require its presence and attest its nobility and excellence.[2]

"No one," comments Dr. Alexander Whyte, in speaking of other discourses in this series, "can feel the full force of Newman's great sermons on 'The Incarnation' and on 'The Atoning Death of God the Son' who has not gone with Newman to the sources of the sermons in Athanasius, and in Basil, and in Cyril." [3] Nothing in his homilies showed any sign of the youth and comparative inexperience of the preacher, or was immature and technical in treatment. The creeds, confessions, and catechisms were vitalized; reclothed with the beauty and the majesty of genuine sacred oratory. They were poems, and better still, transcripts from the most inspired souls, as well as from the souls to which they ministered; reasonings in a lofty dialectic; views of life and of goodness, of sin and its malefic consequences, which, in

---

[1] "Parochial and Plain Sermons"; Vol. I, Sermon I.
[2] *Ibid.*, Vol. I, Sermon XX.   [3] "Newman, An Appreciation"; p. 125.

numerous instances, marked the beginning of a new life in those who heard them. Their chaste yet glowing diction and spiritual perception were employed to such effect that Newman's followers crowded St. Mary's as the Piagnoni did San Marco at Florence to listen to Savonarola, and exhibited an equal enthusiasm, if not extravagance.

On December 2, 1832, when preaching before the University, on "Wilfulness, the Sin of Saul," he entered upon a sweeping condemnation of English society and a defense of religious partisanship: "The present open resistance to constituted power, and (what is more to the purpose) the indulgent toleration of it, the irreverence towards Antiquity, the unscrupulous and wanton violation of the commands and usages of our forefathers, the undoing of their benefactions, the profanation of the Church, the bold transgression of the duty of Ecclesiastical Unity, the avowed disdain of what is called party religion (though Christ undeniably made a party the vehicle of His doctrine, and did not cast it at random on the world, as men would now have it), the growing indifference to the Catholic Creed, the skeptical objections to portions of its doctrine, the arguings and discussings and comparings and correctings and rejectings, and all the train of presumptuous exercises, to which its sacred articles are subjected, the numberless discordant criticisms on the Liturgy, which have shot up on all sides of us; the general irritable state of mind, which is everywhere to be witnessed, and craving for change in all things; what do all these symptoms show, but that the spirit of Saul still lives? — that wilfulness, which is the antagonist principle to the zeal of David, — the principle of cleaving and breaking down all divine ordinances, instead of building up." [1] It will be remembered that one of the sins of Saul was his refusal to perpetrate a wholesale massacre on the Amalekites, an act which compared very favorably with Samuel's demand that the unfortunate captives should be ruthlessly exterminated,

[1] "University Sermons"; Sermon IX.

or with David's betrayal of the unsuspecting Uriah. The misuse of the word party suggested that our Lord Himself originated religious factions because He employed a small group of His countrymen as the immediate emissaries of His Gospel. The preacher's exaggerated references to the craving for change in all things were characteristic of the University don who is proverbially blind to widespread interests beyond his narrow domains, and on the other hand, so alert to whatever occurs within their boundaries, as to overrate its actual importance. Even as a preacher Newman harbored these incapacitating sentiments, refusing to view from any other standpoint than his own the measures he denounced in adroit periphrasis.

Three days after this deliverance he was at Falmouth awaiting Hurrell Froude and his father, and hourly expecting the vessel which was to take them and him to the Mediterranean. He found it hard to leave Oxford; a brief visit to Cambridge had only intensified his longing for the former place, but rest and recreation were imperative both for him and for Hurrell Froude, who had been out of health for some months. They set sail at a moment when the Anglican Church, in Mozley's phrase, was folding her robes about her to die in what dignity she could. The bill for the suppression of the Irish sees was in progress, and the English bishops were warned by Lord Grey that they too must set their house in order. "I had fierce thoughts against the Liberals," confessed Newman, and again, "We have just heard of the Irish Church Reform Bill. Well done; my blind premier, confiscate and rob, till, like Samson, you pull down the Political structure on your own head." [1] For the moment his attention was turned to less troubled prospects, yet go where he would, he could not escape himself. The subjective world in which he dwelt, into which he fully admitted none — a world quick and intense beyond the ordinary — created its own pain, welcomed its own infre-

[1] "Letters and Correspondence"; Vol. I, p. 310.

quent gleams of joy, and indulged its own reveries. "He changed his climate, but not his mind."

His letters and the poems he composed while journeying abroad give a sufficient account of his sentiments and experiences at this stage. During the voyage he enlarged in his correspondence with his mother upon the pleasures of external things, avowing that he had never spent happier days than those he described. Nature's ministries had evidently refreshed him, and for a brief space his interests ceased to be purely personal. He spoke of the ocean's entrancing aspects and varied colors; of the rich indigo of its placid surface, of its white-edged waves ruffling into foam under a stir of wind, and again, curling into flashing, momentary rainbows. The sun was setting in a car of gold; the horizon above changed from pale-orange tints to a gradually heightening dusky red. As night closed in upon these ravishing scenes the evening star appeared high and pure in the deepening gloom. The Portuguese coast slipped past like a veiled pageant, tantalizing in its dim outline, over which stood the summits of Torres Vedras, where Wellington had kept at bay the valor of France. At the foot of the reddish brown cliffs the breakers dashed and rebounded in crested spume which rose like Venus from the sea; "I never saw more graceful forms, and so sedate and deliberate in their rising and falling."[1] Yet these delights could not long detain him; the mood was transient; his mind soon reverted to its introspective habit, and he began to fear the dangers concealed beneath sensuous perceptions. Penetrating but a little way into reality itself, these might easily distract him from the more pregnant elements of being. The principle of dualism had so infected his reasonings that where inspired psalmists and prophets had seen in Creation the wisdom and beneficence of God, Newman frequently discerned "the craft and subtlety of the Tempter of mankind." He touched on natural wonders not so much for their own sake, as to explain the motions

[1] "Letters and Correspondence"; Vol. I, p. 257.

of his breast. "I have good hope," he writes, "I shall not be unsettled by my present wanderings. For what are all these strange sights but vanities, attended to, as they ever must be, with anxious watchfulness lest the heart be corrupted by them." [1]

He was still on the verge of the thirties, and had only recently undergone his metamorphosis into the extreme clerical form. Yet one might imagine that the ecclesiastic had been organized in this new made divine by a hereditary transmission of long descent. He was a compound of the evangelicalism of his youthful home and the sacerdotalism of his University circle. His negative feeling of antagonism to the sensible world, and his positive feeling of a divinely appointed mission combined to separate him from the most charming surroundings. Even when he is on the track of Ulysses, gazing on Ithaca, and aware that at last his earliest visions were made actual before his eyes, he turned back to the memories of his father's garden at Ham; memories so faint, so shadowy, that they evaded his pursuit; memories of that twilight before the dawn "when one seems almost to realize the remnants of a preëxisting state." [2] The historic landscapes teeming with classic reminiscences which have usually fascinated poets and scholars could not prevail against his inwardness; he was interested in them, but nothing more, and would have been well satisfied to find himself suddenly transported to his rooms at Oriel. [3] "I shrink voluntarily from the contact of the world, and, whether or not natural disposition assists this feeling, and a perception almost morbid of any deficiencies and absurdities — anyhow, neither the kindest attentions nor the most sublime sights have over me influence enough to draw me out of the way, and, deliberately as I have set out about my present wanderings, yet I heartily wish they were over, and I only endure the sights, and had much rather *have* seen than *see*

[1] "Letters and Correspondence"; Vol. I, p. 266.
[2] *Ibid.*, Vol. I, pp. 279–280.   [3] *Ibid.*, Vol. I, pp. 281–282.

them, though the while I am extremely astonished and almost enchanted at them." [1]

This paradoxical state increased his determination to seek afresh the benefits of self-seclusion, and he seized the occasion to write a eulogistic sonnet on Melchizedek, the legendary king and priest, of whom he sings,

> "Thrice blest are they, who feel their loneliness;
> To whom nor voice of friend nor pleasant scene
> Brings that on which the sadden'd heart can lean.
> Yea, the rich earth, garb'd in her daintiest dress
> Of light and joy, doth but the more oppress,
> Claiming responsive smiles and rapture high,
> Till, sick at heart, beyond the veil they fly,
> Seeking His Presence Who alone can bless.
> Such, in strange days, the weapons of Heaven's grace:
> When, passing by the high-born Hebrew line,
> He forms the vessel of His vast design.
> Fatherless, homeless, reft of age and place,
> Severed from earth, and careless of its wreck,
> Born through long woe His rare Melchizedek." [2]

Although such isolation was conducive to atrabilious views and an open rebellion against the conventionalities, nevertheless it was measurably justified.   For Newman was at bottom neither a complacent egoist nor an ambitious ecclesiastic, but an earnest servant of truth, as he understood it. The extent of his influence has been variously estimated, and his career has given rise to numerous and contrary inferences. Yet it would be a desecration to make capital out of the worst of these, nor should it be forgotten that one of his most relentless critics has testified that in his conduct of the Tractarian Movement he showed few, if any, symptoms of a wish to be the head of a party, but, on the other hand, a laudable desire to do anything that seemed likely to please God. [3]   For this end he sacrificed otherwise desirable projects, and ex-

---

[1] "Letters and Correspondence"; Vol. I, p. 282.   [2] *Ibid.*, Vol. I, p. 288.
[3] Edwin A. Abbott: "The Anglican Career of Cardinal Newman"; Vol. I, pp. 256–257.

posed himself to serious misunderstandings, holding his integrity at heavy charges to himself, and facing the issue that in dealing with unseen verities the human mind is bound to accept truths beyond its powers of demonstration. Like the microscopist who carefully separates the organism he investigates, shuts off superfluous light and adjusts his instrument to what light he requires, Newman economized by consecrating imagination, intellect, memory, and utterance to those transcendencies which were, as he believed, jealous of any diversion from themselves.

His reflections soon turned from obvious historical associations to others of Scriptural or Churchly origin. "What has inspired me . . . these two days is the thought that I am in the Mediterranean. Consider how its coasts have been the seat and scene of the most celebrated empires and events which are in history. Think of the variety of men, famous in every way, who have had to do with it. Here the Romans and Carthaginians fought; here the Phœnicians traded; here Jonah was in the storm; here St. Paul was shipwrecked; here the great Athanasius voyaged to Rome." At the mention of Athanasius, he broke into somewhat halting verse, and pathetically asked,

"When shall our Northern Church her Champion see,
    Raised by Divine decree
To shield the ancient Truth at his own harm?" [1]

The ferment in that " Northern Church " from which he was temporarily absent was ever present in his mind. In his highest flights of vision or his most mournful soliloquies he interrupted himself to fling an admonitory parenthesis at "frowning Gibraltar," "infidel Ammon," and "niggard Tyre," alike pressed into the service of the "Bride of Heaven," who was exhorted to be patient and to bide her time. The one thing now needful for her, as for him, was to find the basis of sufficient *Authority* upon which to rest her religious de-

[1] "Letters and Correspondence"; Vol. I, pp. 266–267.

velopment, and no longer be driven to hunt for it indefinitely beyond the bounds of possibility, or attempt illogically to construct it with the aid of *Private Judgment*.[1] Hitherto he had said very little about the sinister side of the Greek or Roman Churches, but the spectacles he and Froude witnessed in Sicily and Naples both men lamented. Froude wrote to Keble: "The Church of England has fallen low, and will probably be worse before it is better; but let the Whigs do their worst, they cannot sink us so deep as these people have allowed themselves to fall while retaining all the superficials of a religious country." [2] Newman seconded Froude's views: "The state of the Church is deplorable. It seems as if Satan was let out of prison to range the whole earth again. As far as our little experience goes, everything seems to confirm the notion received among ourselves of the priesthood, while on the other hand the Church is stripped of its temporalities and reduced to distress." [3]

Rome was reached at last, the city of divine apocalypses; too complex, manifold, contradictory, magnificent, for Newman's understanding. As he walked along the Appian Way over the Pontine marshes and looked upon the metropolis of Christianity, a mingled throng of bitter thoughts and sweet besieged him: he hesitated whether to name her

> "Light of the wide West,
> Or heinous error-seat."

Her titles glowed in the stern judgment-fires which would end earth's strife with heaven and open the eternal woe.[4] Eventually the place of celestial traditions subdued his questionings; the superstitions of his youth that Rome was the "Beast" which stamped its image on mankind, the "Great Harlot" who made drunk the kings of the earth, were dispelled, and he began to regard her as vicariously bearing, in her corrup-

---

[1] Edwin A. Abbott: "The Anglican Career of Cardinal Newman"; Vol. I, p. 240.
[2] "Remains"; Vol. I, p. 294.
[3] "Letters and Correspondence"; Vol. I, p. 310.   [4] *Ibid.*, Vol. I, p. 315.

tion and distress, the sins of the whole world. He wrote to Frederic Rogers, who next to Froude was his confidant, "There is such an air of greatness and repose cast over the whole, and, independent of what one knows from history, there are such traces of long sorrow and humiliation, suffering, punishment, and decay, that one has a mixture of feelings, partly such as those with which one would approach a corpse, and partly those which would be excited by the sight of the spirit which had left it. It brings to my mind Jeremiah's words, . . . when Jerusalem, or (sometimes) the prophet, speaks as the smitten of God. Oxford, of course, must ever be a sacred city to an Oxonian, and is to me. It would be a strange want of right pride to think of disloyalty to it, even if our creed were not purer than the Roman; yet the lines of Virgil keenly and affectionately describe what I feel about this wonderful city." [1] He begged that Rogers would repeat to himself the passage from the Eclogues to which he referred and dwell upon each word:

> "Urbem quam dicunt Romam, Meliboee, putavi,
> Stultus ego, huic nostrae similem," etc.

The quotation describes the change in a rustic of northern Italy who had been presumptuous enough to imagine that Rome was like his own city, but who soon knew that she was to the latter as a cypress tree to a bramble bush. The comparison is informing: Newman never ceased to love Oxford, but another love was now beginning to divide his loyalty. It was not the Rome of the Emperors, nor that of Michelangelo and Raffaelle; it was the Rome of the Apostles and the Martyrs that impressed his prepared imagination, and made a bid for his heart.

The "Apologia" omits some important facts connected with this visit, and, although it states that Newman and Froude twice waited upon Dr. Wiseman, then Rector of the English College, and afterwards famous for his pastoral

---

[1] "Letters and Correspondence"; Vol. I, pp. 318–319.

2 K

letter to England dated "from out the Flaminian Gate," no hint is given of the object or the result of their interviews. From Froude's "Remains," however, we learn that they sought to ascertain whether or not the perversions of the truth, which were adapted for Rome but not for England, could be regarded as non-essentials; and as to what were the fundamental differences between Catholicism and Anglicanism, and whether these were so great as to prevent all hope of union. They discovered to their dismay that not one step could be gained in that direction, unless their Church "swallowed the Council of Trent as a whole." Froude frankly expressed his resentment and disgust in the ensuing note:

"We made our approaches to the subject as delicately as we could. Our first notion was that the terms of communion were within certain limits under the control of the Pope, or in case he could not dispense solely, yet at any rate the acts of one Council might be rescinded by another; indeed, that in Charles the First's time it had been intended to negotiate a reconciliation on the terms on which things stood before the Council of Trent. But we found to our horror that the doctrine of the infallibility of the Church made the acts of each successive Council obligatory for ever, that what had been once decided could never be meddled with again; in fact, that they were committed finally and irrevocably, . . . even though the Church of England should again become what it was in Laud's time, or indeed, what it may have been up to the atrocious Council." [1] "Right pride" in Oxford and the Establishment of which it was the citadel had certainly met with a fall when two Anglican clergymen could seek interviews with a distinguished Roman theologian, afterwards a Cardinal, in order to discuss the terms on which their Church could obtain reconciliation with the Papal See. Froude, as we have noted, made no effort to conceal his feelings; Newman said little, but the probabilities are that he was even

[1] "Remains"; Vol. I, p. 307.

more profoundly depressed. "I ought to tell you," he wrote to his sister Jemima, "about the Miserere at Rome, my going up St. Peter's, and the Easter illumination, our conversations with Dr. Wiseman and with M. Bunsen, our search for the Church of St. Thomas of Canterbury, my pilgrimage to the place of St. Paul's martyrdom, the Catacombs, and all the other sights which have stolen away my heart, but I forbear till we meet. Oh that Rome were not Rome! but I seem to see as clear as day that a union with her is *impossible.* She is the cruel Church asking of us impossibilities, excommunicating us for disobedience, and now watching and exulting over our approaching overthrow." The conversations with Wiseman were one of the significant events of Newman's journey; they afterwards echoed in his heart, and begot that uneasy questioning which ended with his repudiation of Anglicanism. The mental peculiarities which are produced by granting to dogma, resting on a very puzzling structure of evidence, the place and power of primary truth, had already become apparent in him. The wholesome, regulative co-operation of the intellect with the heart by which the impulses of the latter are carefully examined with the view of determining their legitimacy, came to be regarded by him as savoring of presumption. When men, however richly endowed, slip into this state of mind, and require no other passport for theological statements than that they shall accord with their own fixed conceptions of the revelations of Deity, they are apt to search not for facts as such, but for facts that appear to support their position. Adverse evidence can only be encountered by stratagems that demoralize healthy thinking, and the last expedient is to throw the burden upon conscience, thus depriving reason of its proper function and elevating questionable articles of faith to the dignity of religion.

Froude and his father having started for England, Newman, full of uncertainty about the future, returned for a while to Naples. He was repelled by its glitter and glare, which were in painful contrast with the grave melancholy of the capital. "Oh, what a change from the majestic pensiveness of the place I have left, where the Church sits in sackcloth calling on those that pass by to say if any one's sorrow is like her sorrow!"[1] "How shall I describe the sadness with which I left the tombs of the Apostles? Rome, not as a city, but as the scene of sacred history, has a part of my heart, and in going away from it I am as if tearing it in twain."[2] He elaborated this latest opinion in order to dismiss his lingering belief that in some sense the Papal Church was recreant. The city itself, he asserted, had possessed but one character for two thousand five hundred years; of late centuries the Christian Church had been the slave of this character. The day drew near, however, when the captive would be freed. Meanwhile Rome's memory would ever be soothing to him; Jerusalem alone could impart a more exalted comfort. Thus he sums up: "In point of interest I have seen nothing like Ithaca, the Straits of Messina, and Egesta (I put aside Rome), and in point of scenery nothing like Corfu. As to Rome, I cannot help talking of it" . . . and once more he utters the plaintive cry—"O Rome, that thou wert not Rome!"[3] She stood out like a towering mountain on a receding shore and outvied them all in the endlessness and power of her appeal.

He had drawn away from his companions that he might see again the towns and hill country of Sicily, and there plan the campaign on which he and Froude were jointly resolved. When Monsignore Wiseman expressed the courteous hope that they would visit him again, Newman replied, with great gravity, "We have a work to do in England."[4] How seriously they took themselves and their projected crusade appeared in their choice of Achilles' proud speech as the motto for the "Lyra Apostolica": "They shall know the

---

[1] "Letters and Correspondence"; Vol. I, p. 338.
[2] *Ibid.*, Vol. I, p. 336.　　　[3] *Ibid.*, Vol. I, p. 344.
[4] "Apologia"; p. 34.

difference now that I am back again." [1] The saying was not inappropriate to the warfare that ensued, which was to cause so many wounds, and leave so many ugly scars behind.

His heart thus full of the portents of this conflict, Newman fell ill of a fever, a circumstance which he regarded as providential and afterwards repeatedly described in most solemn and searching words. It marked another sovereign moment in his life, appearing to him partly as a judgment on his past faults, and partly as an assurance of heaven's forgiveness and direction. "I felt God was fighting against me, and felt at last I knew why — it was for self-will." The sense of his frailty, the peril of his pride, the burden of his mission, and his insufficiency for its discharge, instigated a severe examination of his motives. Nor was this the result of hasty decision induced by physical weakness, for he remanded the case until he returned to Oxford: his illness occurred in May, 1853, his account of it was not begun until August 31 of the year following, and was continued at intervals as late as 1874. "I felt and kept saying to myself 'I have not sinned against light,' and at the one time I had a most consoling overpowering thought of God's electing love, and seemed to feel I was His. . . . Next day I seemed to see more and more of my utter hollowness, I began to think of all my professed principles, and felt they were mere intellectual deductions from one or two admitted truths. I compared myself with Keble, and felt that I was merely developing his, not my convictions. . . . Indeed this is how I look on myself; very much as a pane of glass, which transmits heat, being cold itself. I have a vivid perception of the consequences of certain admitted principles, have a considerable intellectual capacity of drawing them out, have the refinement to admire them, and a rhetorical or histrionic power to represent them; and having no great (*i.e.* no vivid) love of this world, whether

[1] Iliad XVIII, L. 125. "Γνοῖεν δ' ὡς δὴ δηρὸν ἐγὼ πολέμοιο πέπαυμαι" the assertion of Achilles to Thetes when he returned to the fray that he might avenge himself on Hector for the death of Patroclus.

riches, honours, or anything else, and some firmness and natural dignity of character, take the profession of them upon me, as I might sing a tune which I like — loving the Truth, but not possessing it, for I believe myself at heart to be nearly hollow, *i.e.* with little love, little self-denial. I believe I have some faith, that is all; and, as to my sins, they need my possessing no little amount of faith to set against them and gain their remission." [1]

Studied impartiality was foreign to Newman's character; his strong sense of what was real, or of what he wished to believe was real, prevented him from always doing justice either to himself or others, so that his confessions, like many similar ones, were excessive in their self-depreciation. Assuredly he was prepared for any sacrifice which would benefit his soul; and despite his skeptical tendencies faith was his in abundance, whatever may be urged against some objectives to which he attached it. His love, however, was not of that quality which

> "Gives to every power a double power
> Above their functions and their offices."

Toward men, except for his closest friends, it was narrow and embarrassed, and lacked the glow of sympathy; even when offered to God it did not have that restful response of the heart made perfect in the charity which casts out fear. His dread that essential truth was not his has been shared by devout thinkers whose conceptions of the truth and of the nature of its sanctifying power have widely differed. But "wisdom is sometimes nearer when we stoop than when we soar," and nothing testified more clearly to the genuineness of Newman's religious nature, or to the presence of the life of God in him, than did these admissions and penitences.

Four-fifths of his published poems, if the "Dream of

---

[1] "Letters and Correspondence"; Vol. I, pp. 365–366.

Gerontius" is excluded, were written during his tour in Southern Europe. Many of them first appeared in the *British Magazine* as lyrical compositions of the "proper kind." Although they were spontaneous effusions, springing directly from the thoughts and events of the moment, and dealing with sentiments then present in his heart, competent critics have given them a high place in literature, and Mr. R. H. Hutton asserts : "For grandeur of outline, purity of taste, and radiance of total effect, I know hardly any short poems in the language that equal them." [1] Nor were they without presages of the future. Despite weakness and humiliation, Newman felt that he was being divinely led onward to some enterprise, he knew not what, but for which grace and wisdom would be given. His wistful yet resigned longing to see the way before him, the pathetic but uncomplaining entreaties for guidance of an eager soul caught and confused in the darkness, found permanent form in the beautiful hymn which he wrote on the orange boat that carried him from Palermo to Marseilles, when becalmed in the Straits of Bonifacio. Familiar as the lyric is, it must be transcribed here, since it has long enjoyed the grateful appreciation of a multitude of similarly seeking or sorrowing ones who are content to wait until the day breaks and the shadows flee away.

> "Lead, kindly light, amid th' encircling gloom,
>   Lead Thou me on;
> The night is dark, and I am far from home;
>   Lead Thou me on;
> Keep Thou my feet; I do not ask to see
> The distant scene, — one step enough for me.
>
> "I was not ever thus, nor prayed that Thou
>   Shouldst lead me on;
> I loved to choose and see my path; but now
>   Lead Thou me on.
> I loved the garish day, and, spite of fears,
> Pride ruled my will: remember not past years.

[1] "Cardinal Newman"; p. 44.

"So long Thy power hath blest me, sure it still
  Will lead me on
O'er moor and fen, o'er crag and torrent, till
  The night is gone;
And with the morn those angel-faces smile,
Which I have loved long since, and lost awhile."

CHAPTER XI

TRACTARIANISM AND ITS RESULTS

"OLD customs and institutions, even of the most trivial kind, linger long after their origin has been forgotten and some new justification has been invented for them. Forms of language and of thought have a similar vitality, and persist long after they are recognised as cumbrous and misleading. Every change must originate with some individual who, by virtue of his originality, must be in imperfect sympathy with the mass of his contemporaries. Nor can any man, however versatile his intellect, accommodate his mind easily or speedily to a new method and a new order of ideas."

SIR LESLIE STEPHEN.

" Thou shalt leave each thing
Beloved most dearly; this is the first shaft
Shot from the bow of exile.   Thou shalt prove
How salt the savour is of other's bread;
How hard the passage to descend and climb
By other's stairs."

DANTE.

CHAPTER XI

I

FULLY restored to health and eager for the conflict, Newman returned to England in July, 1833, to find that political developments were helping to mature the projects over which he and Froude had brooded. The long-expected blow at the Establishment had fallen; ten Irish suffragan bishoprics and two prospective archiepiscopal sees were about to be suppressed; a contingency which outraged the feelings of many Anglicans, tended to sever other friendships besides that between Whately and Newman, and crystallized the action of clergymen who were intent on a larger measure of independence for the Church in her relations to the State. They were not agreed on this question: advanced Churchmen favored a practical autonomy; with the rest it was a matter of convenience rather than conviction. The disestablishment of a State Church which did not muster more than half the Protestants south of the Tweed, and an

507

infinitely less number across the Irish Channel, appealed to the sense of justice in many publicists, while to leaders such as Keble, Froude, and Newman the proposition savored of disruption and anarchy.   The problem was further complicated by the rapid growth of population in the United Kingdom during the nineteenth century, a condition that intensified the hitherto neglected demand for additional church accommodation, which zealous men of various parties vigorously urged.   Friends and foes alike were also disturbed by the anomalous inequalities of Church funds.   The income of bishoprics ranged from thirty-two thousand pounds for Canterbury and twenty thousand pounds for Durham to sums which were barely sufficient to cover expenses.   The deaneries of Westminster, Windsor, and St. Paul's netted from seven thousand to twelve thousand pounds each, and a number of rectories from five thousand to ten thousand pounds.   At the other extreme the poorer clergy were miserably paid, not less than four thousand of the livings in England and Wales having a stipend under one hundred and fifty pounds a year.   Large numbers of these fell below fifty pounds, and as a consequence parochial work was pauperized.   One third of the clergy were pluralists, some holding as many as five benefices.   The law that required incumbents to reside in their parishes was openly violated, canons and rectors living where they chose and leaving their duties to curates on a starvation wage.   One clergyman holding two rectories bringing in twelve hundred pounds was said to have paid eighty-four pounds for the work done in both.   Bishop Sparke of Ely, his son, and his son-in-law jointly received annually over thirty thousand pounds of Church moneys.   Archbishop Moore is reputed to have died a millionaire, and that mild but rapacious prelate, Archbishop Manners Sutton, presented seven of his relatives to sixteen benefices besides several cathedral dignities.[1]

---

[1] F. W. Cornish: "The English Church in the Nineteenth Century"; Vol. I, pp. 102–109.

This nepotism and greed became a scandal, and in 1831 a Royal Commission was appointed to report upon its causes and consider what remedies should be adopted. Parliamentary control was responsible for such rank abuses: it now endeavored to abolish them by legislation.

The long-continued evil and their helplessness to eradicate it evoked from indignant hearts the query, Has the Church no voice in her own affairs? Evangelicals were not particularly concerned to reply; as a party they had taken little interest in ecclesiastical changes, so long as the status quo favored or at least did not interfere with their doctrinal preferences. But Oxford inhaled an atmosphere which made it distrustful of all reforms and especially of those which affected the Church or the Crown. Its strictest loyalties centered around the former; idealized as the fond mother, who had inspired the best creations of the past, and who maintained the highest and widest possible relations with religion, learning, art, architecture; while the Crown was revered as the fountain of national honor and security. Both were so interdependent that neither could be touched without weakening the other, and the marauding hand that was raised against them must be prompted by ignorance, impiety, or treason. The misguided or deliberate enemies of settled government who went about to suppress bishoprics antedating the State itself, and to confiscate or redistribute endowments derived from the gifts of pious founders, would presently, without doubt, find in University affairs the next object of their unlicensed interference. Such sentiments were current, not only in Oxford, but in a thousand town and country parsonages throughout the land. They found a historic expression in John Keble, who, despite his disinclination to public controversy, emerged from seclusion, and challenged parliament and the nation in behalf of the rights and liberties of Anglicanism. He believed that the Establishment, although in dire need of purification, was not only a formal recognition of religion by the State, but its bulwark against liberalism and moral degeneracy — conditions which he identified as cause and effect. After repeatedly discussing these and kindred themes in the Common Room at Oriel, Keble and his friends pledged themselves to write and speak for the Church. Their situation was somewhat inconsistent, inasmuch as they conceived their communion to be a divine ordination, and esteemed its spiritualities above everything else, yet these were of necessity closely associated with the temporal authority which nominated deans and bishops, and regulated doctrine and discipline. Moreover, her union with the State made the Church the ally of the powerful and the rich. And for the Tractarians to company with these, while condemning others who ardently desired her regeneration as anti-Christian in their policy, involved the definition of what Christianity really was and how its teachings affected the entire question.

This Keble undertook to some extent in his Oxford Assize sermon, delivered on Lord's Day, July 14, 1833. He felt that the duty and the hour for its discharge had been granted him, and he used the opportunity to the full in his discourse, entitled "National Apostasy." To his utterance Newman attributed the actual origin of Tractarianism, saying that he had ever considered and kept the day as the start of the religious movement of 1833. A superficial view has ascribed Keble's impeachment to the suppression of the Irish bishoprics, but actually its main causes were to be found in the spiritual dearth of Anglicanism, which enabled unscrupulous politicians, as he deemed them, to take advantage of the general weakness. Further, he believed that faith and order were jeopardized when the episcopate was reduced in numbers or in authority by civil decrees. On this matter he and his colleagues were sincere, inexorable, and united. The consideration that no changes in ecclesiastical methods could permanently impair the vitality and energy of the New Testament Evangel had no weight with clerics who were swayed by the influences, good or bad, of their unique surroundings. They invested their sacerdotal claims with the sanctity of an absolute revelation, and held that the totality of God's working force in the world was, in essence, a priestly possession. The ability to see every side of a question, so necessary for comprehensive and safe conclusions, was not a gift of the Tractarians, yet their narrowness of outlook was not due to any conscious paltering with the facts, but to certain mental and moral limitations. That all men are more or less the victims of these limitations is a truism that should restrain impatience at what naturally seems the astonishing infatuation of the Tractarians, and Keble's observations can be judged accordingly.

Churchmen, said the preacher, and by this he meant Anglicans, had hitherto taken it for granted that England " had for centuries acknowledged, as an essential part of her theory of government, that, as a Christian nation, she is also a part of Christ's Church, and bound in all her legislation and policy by the fundamental laws of that Church." This proposition practically asserted that Anglicans should dictate the laws of England, and it could have been extended with equal legitimacy to the Presbyterianism established in Scotland. "When a government and people, so constituted," he added, "threw off the restraint which in many respects such a principle would impose upon them, nay, disavowed the principle itself," such conduct was a "direct disavowal of the sovereignty of God. If it be true that such enactments are forced on the legislature by public opinion, is Apostasy too hard a word to describe the temper of such a nation?" These extracts present the substance of a remonstrance conceived in the strictest partisanship, yet addressed to all England. Its language disclosed no careful study of those stages in national evolution which had rendered unavoidable the changes painfully resented by Keble. It manifested a temper belonging to the genial days of the Act of Uniformity rather than the nineteenth century. Community of interest and sympathy, which is the root of social justice, was

destroyed by such extraordinary prejudices. Contemptuous toward that excellent and persistent spirit operating in
human progress, the strength of which no circumstances,
however adverse, and no creed, however inflexible, can
permanently overcome, Keble and his disciples refused to
credit their generation with any good thing, and mourned
over its shortcomings with a mistaken grief. Some among
them were inordinately lachrymose : deprived of domestic
joys and feeding on the despair of their own hearts, they
were wont to display an ill-regulated emotion over events
out of all proportion to the tears expended on them.

> "No matter where; of comfort no man speak:
> Let's talk of graves, of worms and epitaphs;
> Make dust our paper, and with raining eyes
> Write sorrow on the bosom of the earth."

They applied themselves to their theories with unswerving
vigor, and regarded them as living verities, never to be
doubted, always to be obeyed, whatever the consequences.
History is plentiful in similar examples showing how merciless and unjust theories can be : how they can cut like a
scythe, separating men and nations, once they are allowed
to obsess the mind and to become the watchwords of religious or political cliques.

Twelve days after Keble's sermon was preached, and seventeen after Newman's return from the continent, Hugh
James Rose convened a gathering at his rectory of Hadleigh
in Suffolk, to consider the state of the Church and what
measures should be adopted for its betterment. William
Palmer, Arthur Philip Perceval, and Hurrell Froude accepted
the invitation; Keble and Newman, though absent, actively
coöperated with the rest. "The meeting was the first
attempt to combine for the preservation of great principles,"
remarked Palmer; but small in numbers though it was, its
members were not agreed, and finally they adjourned to Oxford. Those who maintained that sacred beliefs and ordi-

nances were not subject to fluctuations of ideas, or to scientific, economic, and political conditions, and that apart from hierarchical authority there could be nothing but confusion and loss, encountered a show of resistance from the more cautious brethren. Nevertheless, "the Hadleigh conspiracy," as Froude and his foes alike termed it, cleared the way for simultaneous action, and Rose and his companions afterwards spoke of themselves as "the Society." During the long vacation of 1833 they met again at Oriel, and by the third of September or thereabouts, Newman had put forth the first three in the series of "Tracts for the Times."[1]

Resentment against modern thought and a sense of its danger to religion were their main burden. This danger was manifested in the secularization of the Church and the proposed alteration of the Prayer Book in a latitudinarian sense by authority of parliament. Existing heresies and infidelities were to be overcome by archaic shibboleths duly refurbished; the doctrines of apostolical succession and sacramental grace, taking the place of evangelical theories of conversion by means of prayer and preaching, were trusted to put to confusion enemies within and without the Church, which, purged of the one and defended from the other, would return to her ancient beliefs and renew her forgotten services.

Newman's first Tract, respectfully addressed to his brethren in the sacred ministry, struck this note at once. It was an imperative summons to forsake ungodliness, and to set the example of unworldly men taking their solemn office seriously and sacrificially. They were exhorted not to rest upon that secular respectability, or cultivation, or polish, or learning, or rank which gave them a hearing with the many; and to have done forever with the false notion that present palpable usefulness, producible results, acceptableness to the flock are indubitable evidences of

[1] Authorities differ as to this date; Dean Burgon gives September 3d; Dean Church, September 9th; Wilfred Ward, "the December following."

2 L

divine approval. In the last day, Scripture warns us, the recital of such proofs will in many instances be met by the stern sentence, "Depart from me, for I never knew you." The Tract was as intentionally provocative as Keble's sermon, and also as exclusive and uncompromising. It assailed whatever was unworthy and much that was customary in the Church, and boldly exalted the ages of intolerance and asceticism. This backward gaze on denser times was a prevailing trait in the Tractarians. A surprising passage occurs in one of Keble's homilies, entitled "The Religion of the Day," which would have made an appropriate motto for his cause, and wherein he declares that it would be a gain to England "were it vastly more superstitious, more bigoted, more gloomy, more fierce in its religion, than at present it shows itself to be."

The second Tract applied the principles of the first to practical Church politics. Was the State the Church? Had the State the right to create a clergy, to regulate dioceses, to determine in any way the propaganda of the Church? The answer did not tremble; it was emphatic, even defiant. The Holy Catholic Church was a living reality, placed in the Creed as an article of faith immediately after the belief in the Holy Ghost; Apostolic, because founded by the Apostles; Catholic, because it knew no limitation of race; Visible, in its divinely instituted orders of bishops, priests, and deacons; and essentially above all civil authority in matters of doctrine and ritual. Furthermore, communion with the Church, thus defined, was "generally necessary to salvation in the case of those who could obtain it." In short, the Tract was a declaration of war against the right of parliament to any voice in religious matters, and against the Evangelical and Broad sections of Anglicanism. "I stand amazed," wrote Arnold to Pusey, "at some apparent efforts in this Protestant Church to set up the idol of tradition."

In the third Tract Newman deplored a current proposal to revise the liturgy. "In a day like this," he wrote, "there are but two sides, zeal and persecution, the Church and the world; and those who attempt to occupy the ground between them at best will lose their labour, but probably will be drawn back to the latter. Be practical, I respectfully urge you." Any changes in the liturgy would lead, he felt, to controversy and unbelief; the way would be opened to objectors who disliked its teaching rather than its form to tamper with both.

During 1834 twenty Tracts were published, nine of them being from Newman's pen. The theology and practice of the eighteenth century were discarded and denounced, and the clergy were admonished to betake themselves to the Carolinian divines and to their instructors, the early Fathers. In November of the same year the first volume of Tracts, forty-seven in number, was published, "with the object of contributing something towards the practical revival of doctrines, which, although held by the great divines of our Church, at present have become obsolete with the majority of her members, and are withdrawn from public view even by the more learned and orthodox few who still adhere to them." At intervals five more volumes appeared. In the preface to the third of these, issued in 1836, the editors, referring to the first Tracts, remarked that they "were written with the hope of rousing members of our Church to comprehend her alarming position . . .; as a man might give notice of a fire or an inundation, to startle all who heard him . . . to infuse seriousness into the indifferent. . . . Now, however, discussion became more seasonable than the simple statements of doctrine with which the series began; and their character accordingly changed."

Simultaneously with the Tracts other books were sent forth to support the novel theories, in accordance with Newman's plan of giving them a wide publicity. His own works on "The Prophetical Office of the Church," on "The Arians," already noticed, and also on "Justification" appeared

in 1837 and 1838. In the latter year the first volume
of the "Library of the Fathers," of which Charles
Marriott became managing editor, was published, followed
by fifty volumes in succeeding years, the object being
to furnish the clergy with the teaching of the Church
before the division between East and West. About the
same time another series was issued, the "Library of Anglo-
Catholic Theology," comprising the writings of notable
English divines of the sixteenth and seventeenth centuries.
In 1839 Isaac Williams, of whom we shall hear again,
commenced a series of "Plain Sermons by Contributors to
the Tracts for the Times " for the purpose of heartening the
fearful and guiding the perplexed. In the periodical press
the Movement was ably and vigorously represented by the
British Critic and by its successor the *Christian Re-
membrancer.* Among others who contributed to the Tracts
were Keble, his brother Thomas, Benjamin Harrison, George
Bowden, Hurrell Froude, Isaac Williams, Alfred Menzies,
and Pusey. Despite Newman's deprecation of corporate
effort, and his avowal that no great achievement was
ever wrought by a system; whereas systems, on the contrary, arose out of individual energy, Palmer insisted on
further organization; the laymen were enlisted, and an address of protestation was signed by eight thousand Anglicans and presented to the Primate.

These proceedings came none too soon; the third decade
of the nineteenth century found the Established Church
in large measure what she had been when she rejected the
Wesleys and their mission. She was still slumbering and
sleeping when the days of trouble came upon her. "Nothing,
as it seems to me," Dr. Arnold confessed in 1833, "can save
the Church but union with the Dissenters; now that they
are leagued with the Anti-Christian party, and no merely
internal reforms will satisfy them." [1] This widespread
hostility, followed, as it was, by the publication of the

[1] Dean Stanley: "Life of Arnold"; Vol. I, pp. 326–345.

Tracts, alarmed the officials both of Church and State; but they were totally unprepared to meet the emergency, and behaved as men surprised in a moment of fictitious security. Lulled to somnolence by their detachment from the clergy and the people, the bishops at last awoke to the possibility of a collapse largely due to their prolonged neglect and indifference. Even when aroused, some were content to indulge the luxury of moral indignation against Erastian mismanagement, and at the same time to insist that the Church should continue to enjoy the material advantages she derived from State supervision. But to the majority of the bishops and to all the Evangelicals, the Tracts seemed glaringly inconsistent with the doctrine and discipline of the Church; an act of betrayal solemnly perpetrated by grave and reverend men, who violated the sacredness of their calling and the legitimate construction of the Rubrics and the Articles.

In reality, Tractarianism was a development of the freedom which Anglicanism obtained at the Reformation, when Europe was divided into two camps, and scholars and Humanists became persecutors and martyrs. In the long interval that had elapsed, the creative source of the theological opinions enunciated by Newman and his companions had been forgotten. The Semitic mind, which produced the New Testament; the Hellenistic, which produced ecumenical dogma; the Imperialistic, which produced the Papal rule; the Feudal, which produced medieval theories of ecclesiastical governance; the National, which produced Protestantism — were all involved in the chaos of that era out of which the Establishment arose under the supremacy of Henry VIII. How much self-governance was left to Anglicanism had long been disputed. The compact between Church and Crown, if such it was, at any rate presumed that the Church had power to make it. Precisely what it signified, and the interpretations derived from its statements, grants and reservations, became an acute problem which distressed and distorted the thoughts of Churchmen. The Tractarians contended that the Church did not concede, nor was she asked to concede, that her doctrine should be determined or her laws administered by other than her own clergy. Original powers of direction and guidance were carefully distinguished from those relating to constraint and correction. But the distinction was too fragile to withstand the rough usage of revolutionary politics. The sudden appropriation to themselves of the spiritual authority hitherto vested in the Papacy aroused acrimonious discussion among its new possessors. During the Tudor and Stuart periods many valuable prerogatives were left lying loose which despotic rulers and ambitious statesmen were quick to use for their own ends. Neo-Anglicans denied the plea that the Holy See was until the sixteenth century both the source and center of ecclesiastical jurisdiction and the supreme judge of doctrine. Following Laud, Andrewes, Ken, Wilson, and Hammond, they went behind the transfer of headship from the Pope to the monarch; behind the controversies and schisms which succeeded the corruptions of the period; and found their basis for the Prayer Book, its liturgies and forms of ordination, in the purer and more universal faith and practice which flourished from the eleventh to the thirteenth centuries. The ancient jurisdiction of that era, they argued, was restored at the Reformation, without vital injury to the continuity and integrity of the Anglican Church. Mr. Gladstone summed up the controversy as follows: "I contend that the Crown did not claim by statute, either to be of right, or to become by convention, the source of that kind of action, which was committed by the Saviour to the Apostolic Church, whether for the enactment of laws, or for the administration of its discipline; but the claim was, that all the canons of the Church, and all its judicial proceedings, inasmuch as they were to form parts respectively of the laws and of the legal administration of justice in the kingdom, should run only with the assent and sanction of the Crown. They were to carry with them a double force — a force of coercion, visible and palpable; a force addressed to conscience, neither visible nor palpable, and in its nature only capable of being inwardly appreciated." [1] Without commenting on this rather labored discrimination between a force of coercion and one addressed to conscience, it is enough to add that Mr. Gladstone himself admitted that while, according to the spirit and letter of the law, such appear to be the limits of the royal supremacy relative to the legislative action of the Church, in other branches it goes farther, and that the claim of the Crown to determine at any point the jurisdiction of the Church may also be construed to mean that the Crown is the ultimate source of jurisdiction of whatever kind.[2] When Henry VIII delivered the Church from the bonds of Rome, he did not free her; he merely substituted the sole control of the Crown for the dual authority hitherto exercised by the Pope and the monarch.

These scattered hints may serve to convey some idea of the Tractarian position, the validity of which is repudiated by able advocates of opposing schools. Certainly her connection with the State, and the compromises forced upon her by national and religious necessities, enabled the English Church to shelter many shades and varieties of mind and opinion. Whatever has been her bearing toward some outgrowths of Puritanism, and in this she has little on which to look with equanimity, within her own borders she has preserved a commendable breadth. By resisting the swashbucklers of peculiar orthodoxies, who sought to stereotype creeds and forms and thus sever the Church from the life of the nation, she has saved herself from disintegration and conferred great benefits on her members. Her forces have not always been rightly

[1] "Remarks on the Royal Supremacy, as it is Defined by Reason, History, and the Constitution"; *Guardian*, July 10, 1850.
[2] Dean Church: "Occasional Papers"; pp. 8–9.

directed, yet, at intervals, leaders have appeared who refused to fall back from ever-widening horizons upon circumscribed areas. An organization which included Hooker, Thirlwall, Maurice, Robertson of Brighton, Stanley, Jowett, and Tait, together with Laud, Law, Keble, Froude, Pusey, Church, and Liddon, can be said in this respect to have been truly catholic. Cynical observers have criticized the divisions which separated these eminent men, and outsiders entirely friendly to Anglicanism have remarked with justice, that apart from its alliance with the State, it would probably fall asunder into contending sects. The fact remains, however, that its wisest sons, although separated in some beliefs, have generally been faithful Churchmen who were not blind to their inheritance or to the sacrifices of its past and the hope of its present and future. Neither Tractarians, Evangelicals, nor Broad Churchmen have always rightly conceived and used their freedom, but this is not a sufficient reason for its withdrawal, nor for the uniformity which would deaden, if not destroy, liberty of conscience and opinion. Upon that liberty as a sure foundation rests the strength of a Church which aspires to be truly national; in which different types of character and temperament have found a habitation for Christian scholarship, and a center for worship and service.

This digression helps to indicate the obstacles the Tractarians encountered, in which the first question confronting them was, "What is the Church as spoken of in England? Is it the Church of Christ?" Hooker, whose conclusions were the outcome of a nobly temperate mind, had defined it as the nation, viewed in its entirety, and Arnold simply echoed his definition. The Nonconformists declared that it was the aggregate of separate congregations, locally independent and in fellowship one with another. Erastian lawyers and politicians regarded it as the creation of the State, an establishment by law under parliamentary legislation and control. Roman Catholics asserted that it was not, in any apostolic and catholic sense, a Church at all, but a sectarian schism, cut off from communion with the fountain of grace and spiritual authority, and hampered by an ignominious history of subservience to the Crown. Whately's affirmation, already quoted, advanced the proposition that it was a divine religious society, distinct in its attributes from any other. Froude and then Newman adopted and heightened this theory, and a majority of the Tractarians followed suit, teaching that the Anglican Church was the one historic uninterrupted ecclesia, than which there could be no other in England.[1] While this doctrine defied Erastianism, it left the internal life and teaching of the Church in need of further elucidation, which the Tracts endeavored to supply.

Although described by Dean Church as "clear, brief, stern appeals to conscience and reason; sparing of words, utterly without rhetoric, intense in purpose; the sharp, rapid utterances of men in pain and danger and pressing emergency,"[2] they varied in quality, and as literature are now deservedly forgotten. Some, indeed, were meager and desultory, others consisted of quotations from the Fathers, or did not rise above the level of dogmatic assertion, and while those which came from Newman's pen stood out in favorable contrast to the rest, little that he contributed enhanced his reputation. Pusey's coöperation supplied a needed element of scholarship, and what he wrote was afterwards considerably expanded. A spirit of chiding and rebuke breathed in the words of these leaders, which seemed to burn with the heat of their compression. They were exasperated beyond endurance by the lassitude and delusive respectability which deadened the enthusiasm and spirit of the Church. She had become the sanctuary of the "Gigmanity" and "Philistinism" against which Carlyle and Matthew Arnold railed, and nourished within her borders the sort of

---

[1] Dean Church: "The Oxford Movement"; p. 51.
[2] *Ibid.*; p. 110.

gentlemen, lay and clerical, who worshiped the deductions of their own reason and the creations of their own fancy,[1] but who, nevertheless, were warmly attached to the Establishment, a fact which Froude and Newman did not sufficiently recognize. Nor were the times as ready for radical changes as the Tractarians imagined. The University and the nation were widely separated in thought and feeling; the trimming diplomacy of the majority, and the fact that the Church always sailed a little behind the age, pleased the conservatism of those who were free from the dread that she would be stranded upon the shoals of liberalism. Much that the Tractarians addressed to the nation sounded strange, shifty, and unsubstantial. The apostolic origin and catholic nature of Anglicanism as a branch of the one visible Church had no special charm for that generation. A certain bishop declared that he was not sure in what manner his office was derived; others denounced the sacerdotalism which glorified them as chief pastors. Undismayed, however, the Neo-Anglicans inculcated their notions on the alleged unbroken apostolic rights of the priesthood, and the regenerating sacraments. Notwithstanding Dean Church's comment that they appealed to the intellect, they seldom discussed religion from the standpoint of reason or from that of an intimate acquaintance with the comparative study of the various forms Christianity has assumed in the course of its philosophical speculations. Nor did they extricate themselves from a mass of intricate details to rise to large and luminous generalizations. Apart from Pusey, and perhaps Newman, none of them was specially distinguished as an exponent of historical and constructive theology. Solidity and depth of thought were as absent as massive and inspiring eloquence, or as the generous culture which could appreciate the best in other communions. When they proceeded to accuse the common source from which all alike derived, by asseverating that there

[1] Newman: "Idea of a University"; p. 211.

were grievous errors and structural defects in Protestantism, and that the Reformation was by no means as impeccable in principle or practice as was generally supposed, they not only shocked the sensibilities of those fellow-countrymen who had long looked upon the Papacy with unmitigated aversion, but also aroused their permanent distrust. The further statement that the Establishment had many features in common with those Churches which rested their claims on apostolic succession evoked an indignant challenge from men of divergent views, who charged the Tractarians with being guilty of intellectual immorality.

Undoubtedly there were among them spirits as pure and devoted to truth as any who have wrought in the arid region of religious polemics. But some betrayed a decided tendency towards decorated language, word-juggling, and beguiling sophistry, a sort of verbal craft which was a poor substitute for direct speech. They approached their unusual theories with the vanity of inexperience and laid upon them burdens they could not sustain. An immovable preference for reality, at whatever cost, was hard to maintain in an environment agitated by disputes and full of well-nigh reckless anxiety for causes which had now become sacred. It was easy to succumb to the insidious temptation that truth was not sufficient for its own defense, but must also be served by other weapons inferior to its single two-edged sword. The dreadful tangle of economies and reserves; the esoteric interpretations of phrases the import of which seemed obvious enough; the clericalism which read into the Articles and Rubrics a meaning diametrically opposed to the common apprehension, irritated those who had taken Anglicanism on their own terms, and were baffled by this jungle of beginnings and developments. After making every allowance for the bias which deflected the compass of even experienced mariners in these stormy seas, and for the insular prejudices which prevailed among nearly all classes, it must be admitted that the Neo-Anglicans did not set an example of intellectual integrity such as posterity should emulate. Their antagonists also fell under the same reproach. The Evangelicals were more intent on defending their teaching and undermining the position of their adversaries than upon determining with open minds what of substance lay behind these wranglings. Among liberal Churchmen, Maurice, while more truly catholic, was scarcely less subtle and mystical then Newman and Keble. If the latter were driven to doubtful expedients of verbal legerdemain in the task of developing Anglican unity out of the few explicit and the many supposedly implicit Roman elements of the Establishment, Maurice was equally at fault in laboring against reason and facts to reconcile these elements in a common formula. Low Churchmen enlightened nothing, but added to a grave and unfathomable confusion by twisting and torturing the phraseology of the Articles in order to wring out of them their own definite and severe Protestantism.

Far more potent than the Tracts in drawing sympathy and support to the Oxford Movement were Newman's sermons at St. Mary's, in which the preacher cast the spell of his fastidious diction, psychological skill, and spiritual influence over his followers, led upward by him on a golden stairway of sequences to powerful climaxes. Paradoxically enough, they taught that religion is a life of pure inwardness, while they associated its expression with venerable forms which were sanctioned and guarded by an infallible Church. Without the sermons, says Dean Church, "the Movement might never have gone on, certainly would never have been what it was." The living voice of an irresistible personality drove home the meanings and implications of the Tracts. It created the atmosphere in which their statements became incumbent upon all who were susceptible to the appeals of this type of Anglicanism.

The local and personal beginnings of the High Church reaction antedate the appearance of the Tracts by nearly two decades, under aspects, however, which, so far as Newman is concerned, were very different from those of subsequent developments. Thirteen years before the Tracts were advertised, Newman defended the Evangelical side in a controversy on baptismal regeneration, and in 1828 Pusey accounted for the extravagances of German Rationalism on the ground of the intolerable orthodoxy of Lutheranism. He welcomed the aid of Kant and Schelling in behalf of a higher faith, gave great praise to Schleiermacher, recognized De Wette's genuine Christianity, and described the *gratia ministerialis* — the efficacy of the Sacraments and offices, though administered by evil men — as an absurd and pernicious fiction. "For a while," observes Dr. Martineau, "it seemed doubtful which of the two paths the Oxford High Church was to take — Germanism or Romanism — theological advance or ecclesiastical retrogression." [1] Newman supplied an explanation for this remark when he said that "the same philosophical elements lead one mind to the Church of Rome; another to what, for want of a better word, may be called Germanism." [2] In 1829, Dr. Pusey had supported Catholic Emancipation and Sir Robert Peel's unsuccessful candidature as member of Parliament for Oxford University. Newman, as we have seen, opposed both, and voted with the most pronounced partisans of the Protestant faction. Foiled in these earlier efforts, the two leaders were now united, only to be separated later. The devoted Anglican, who stood unsheltered to the end, and whose steadfastness probably saved the Church from schism after Newman's withdrawal, came over from the camp of Liberalism; the future Roman prince from that of the Orangemen. Pusey, like Keble, brought to the Tractarians a type of Churchmanship which he derived through his parental training from Bishop Ken, Robert Nelson, and the Non-Jurors. His mind was formed before Evolution

[1] "Essays, Reviews and Addresses"; Vol. I, p. 230.
[2] "Essay on the Development of Christian Doctrine"; p. 71.

and Development had become the normal channels of thought, and his large and systematic learning is now out of date. It was then enlisted in behalf of the fabric he constructed out of analogies, resemblances, and metaphors, obtained from Biblical, historical, and legendary sources, some of which have no value and abound in fanciful flights and barren ingenuities. Any attempt to disparage these was set down as indicating a want of piety and an unteachable and rebellious nature. The light inseparable from the life of religion, and which is the constant outpouring of the Spirit of God and of Holy Scripture, was feared by those who, like Pusey, declared that faith depended on authority, not on reason, and that the faculty of thinking and conceiving was detrimental to the spiritualities within men. The understanding became a drudge to what was described as the conscience, but was in many instances the unlicensed use of imagination to sustain theoretical speculations upon apostolical, succession and its sacerdotal sequences. Reflection was condemned as inimical to obedience, and thus the balance of reason and faith was disturbed by arbitrary opinions.

Pusey's accession to the Oxford Movement gave it considerable impetus. The second son of Philip Pusey, and grandson of Lord Folkestone, a fellow of Oriel, a German scholar, an Orientalist, and Regius Professor of Hebrew at Oxford, he had a standing and dignity in the University which no other Tractarian could then claim. Newman called him "ὁ μέγας" and dwelt with joyful gratitude upon the immense diligence and simple devotion of the welcome recruit. "Without him we should have had little chance, especially at the early date of 1834, of making any serious resistance to the Liberal aggression . . . he was able to give a name, a form and a personality to what was without him a sort of mob."[1] No man of his age exceeded him in his devotion to duty, which, as he conceived it, was to spread

[1] "Apologia"; pp. 61–62.

among Churchmen the conviction that only on the doctrines of the Fathers and the early Anglicans could Christianity be based. "My life," he says of himself, "has been spent in a succession of insulated efforts bearing indeed upon one great end — the growth of catholic truth and piety among us." His influence for a time was overwhelming, as evidenced alike by the praises of his adherents and the aspersions of his opponents. It cannot be ascribed primarily to his enduring courage, his exhaustive research, or his sturdy blows against indifferentism, deism, and ultra-Protestantism. First and foremost, he was a true saint and minister, whose pronounced defects were offset by a thoroughly original and consecrated character. Those who judged him by his morbidness, his remorse, his penances, his impolitic utterances and abortive efforts, or in the light of their sincere dislike of the practices he inaugurated and the ordinances and means of grace he restored, were not always aware that the unbending ecclesiastic, incessant disputant, and High Churchman *facile princeps*, had a charity toward his critics which begot in him a patience and a hopefulness that never flagged. He once exclaimed, in a burst of tenderness, "I have always had a great love for the Evangelicals." Not many Evangelicals of that day could have said the same about Pusey. He stands out, even in Newman's company, as an impressive figure, strong, rugged, awkward, indomitable. If his style had none of the grace and allurement which were prominent in Newman's prose, his nature disclosed a passion for holiness that tempered the hardness, as of iron, with which he repelled the doubter and the heretic. There was nothing harmonious or artistic in his make-up, and while he defended his section of the Church with great ability, the foes he encountered were largely imaginary, so that he never really faced the forces of essential agnosticism. But he was sincere and single-minded in his refusal to accommodate the perplexities of religion for the sake of those who sought relief therefrom by a process of simplification, and he deplored the utilization of spiritual instincts or institutions for the benefit of the prevailing social order or to serve the fagged moods and jaded tempers of secular minds. "It seems to be thought that those who have faith may always be sacrificed with impunity to those who have none," he wrote when Archbishop Tait showed sympathy with the effort to rid the Prayer Book of the Athanasian Creed. The ghosts of the past were his fond care, and his biography is full to repletion of the history of skirmishes in their behalf, many of which have long since disappeared before the advance of substantial and dangerous enemies of religion. Believing, as he did, that there was an adequate objective correspondence for every faculty of the soul and that to disregard the law which governed their relations afforded ground for wholesome dread of retribution, he sometimes expounded this article in terms which sounded harsh and inhuman. Yet he was a man of heart, pitiful toward the sinner who was repentant and submissive. And for the Church at large he was a defender of traditions which he identified with all that was sacred or salvatory. No matter to what sect or creed such leaders belong, or how widely and justly we differ from them, they usually transcend their boundaries and help to illuminate the life we live. Pusey does not stand among the immortals, but he had felt the spirit of the Highest, and was one of those who

"Cannot confound, nor doubt Him, nor deny;"

who are ever ready to aver,

"Yea, with one voice, Oh World! though thou deniest,
Stand thou on that side, for on this am I."

II

The Tractarians disturbed the stagnancy of Anglicanism, and contradicted the prevailing notion that the Church of

England was as sacrosanct as the House of Commons. The works of divines of the palmy Stuart days were rescued from dusty bookshelves, while those of Paley, Horsley, Hoadley, and Warburton went a-begging. The leaders of the cult knew exactly what they wanted, and in that knowledge lay their strength. Outwardly deferential to the episcopacy, Keble and Pusey and Froude were at heart even more independent than Newman; he trusted the bishops, they depended on the organization. All took their stand upon antiquity and were ever ready to give reasons for the hope that was in them, to define and advocate their position. The Evangelicals had come to the end of their tether, the Broad Churchmen were divided in sentiment and circumstances. Whately had retired to the comparative seclusion of archiepiscopal dignity, Thirlwall was too philosophical for the needs of faction, Arnold's impetuosity marred his usefulness, Hampden was laborious and uncouth. The Tractarians held the field at Oxford, the center of the strife, and shared the interest of onlookers with the Utilitarians and Romanticists. The strong, daring sternness of their opinions was in singular contrast to the composed meekness and submission of their bearing. Statesmen, scientists, and literary people, as well as opposing clerics, began to ask what these things meant. No man among the earlier and wiser Tractarians was better able to answer the question than Hugh James Rose, at whose Hadleigh rectory the Movement had been initiated. For a time he ranked foremost among the university dons and parish priests who, like him, contended for the spiritual supremacy of the Church and the restoration of certain usages which had come to the verge of extinction. His powerful mind readily adopted every means of information offered to it, and his earnest disposition commended him to his companions, who entertained the liveliest expectations for his future. Without a trace of self-seeking, he rose to an unusual place in the regard of the Church as a whole. The German drift of Prot-

2 M

estantism at Cambridge aroused his vigorous objections, and as a graduate of the University, and a Select Preacher there, he endeavored to arrest the ravages of what he deemed a false liberalism. Pusey replied to the strictures of Rose in two volumes, afterwards withdrawn from circulation, in which, as we have seen, he defended and explained continental rationalism. Among Newman's correspondents, Rose alone acted as his born equal, an assumption which Newman allowed without demur, believing him to be the one above all others best fitted to make headway against the difficulties of their day. His cool and cautious judgment and his confidential relations with the higher ecclesiastical authorities prevented him from running with the root and branch Tractarians, so that Froude soon lost faith in him as a possible leader. But his death at the age of forty-three was a heavy blow to those who were averse to ill-considered and extreme action. For some time before his decease he had only a small part in the affairs of Tractarianism, yet had he lived, its course might have been very different.

Newman's verdict that William Palmer was the one thoroughly equipped scholar among High Anglicans was well within the mark. His beliefs were ably expounded in his "Treatise on the Church of Christ," which has been cherished as the most powerful and least assailable defense of Anglicanism from the sixteenth century onward. Romeward inclinations never affected Palmer, whose study of Bellarmine, Bossuet, and other Catholic doctors enabled him to detect and disavow the methods and ideas which allured some of his friends. He identified the fortunes of his Church with those of the State, and was persuaded that both had sunk to their lowest ebb. A communion entirely separated from the Papacy on the one frontier and from Puritanism on the other, with its own inherent life and ministry of grace, was his ideal, and he deplored the apathy and coldness of the public mind toward it. Another elect spirit was Robert Isaac Wilberforce, the second son of the well-known philanthropist. Wilberforce lost contact with Newman after their dismissal from the joint-tutorship at Oriel, but in 1843 he formed a friendship with Henry Manning, then rector of Lavington and archdeacon of Chichester. The amiable character, innate modesty, and accurate sense of right and wrong of Wilberforce were prized by his fellow Tractarians, and especially by Manning, who afterwards turned to him as to a father confessor for relief concerning his misgivings about the validity of Anglicanism. The Gorham Judgment of 1850, which denied that the regenerating grace of Infant Baptism was a necessary dogma of the Church of England, and ratified her subjection to State control even in so cardinal a doctrine, added gall to the bitterness Manning and Wilberforce already felt. On April 8, 1851, the former was received into the Catholic fold, and three years later, Wilberforce followed him, but did not long survive his secession. While journeying to Rome in 1857 to receive ordination, death deprived those who loved and trusted him of an unfailing helper, incapable of unworthy motives; one who shone in many directions with a steady if subdued radiance. He was the recipient of the confidences of partisans whose merits he was well qualified to determine, and he left them an example of intellectual rectitude they did not always sedulously imitate.

In these and other respects Charles Marriott, "the man of saintly life," was much akin to Wilberforce. To Marriott the Oxford students repaired for spiritual direction after Newman had departed. His devotion to Christ, to His Church, and to the Movement, was without stint. No other more completely sacrificed himself, for he placed upon the altar of his offering all that he was and all that he had. Dean Burgon states, in his "Lives of Twelve Good Men," that Marriott's prevailing grace was an unbounded charity, which ministered to those who sat in darkness and in the shadow of death, and enabled him to see the good in everything and everybody. Halting to eccentricity in manner and conversation, nevertheless he usually brought out the core of matters at stake, and his discourse, though scanty, was unfailingly instructive. He was so averse to publicity that his literary labors were not always as widely known as those of other writers who depended on his assistance, and Pusey called attention to the fact that Marriott had entire charge for some years of "The Library of the Fathers." To the last he was unwilling to admit that Rome had captured Newman. When this could no longer be denied he remained steadfast and spent the balance of his brief period and enfeebled physical strength in gathering up the things that remained. Amid the panic that followed Newman's conversion no man, except James B. Mozley, did more to allay the fears and stem the flight of those who believed that Newman could do no wrong. Marriott could not draw large congregations; he did not leave behind him works of genius; he enjoyed few of the pleasures or even the necessities that are found in other fields of enterprise. He labored day and night in the search and defense of divine truth.[1] His reward was with him, in that he distilled upon the heated air of controversy the refreshing fragrance of simple goodness, unshaken hope, and love without reproach.

Isaac Williams, a fitting companion for Wilberforce and Marriott, was the son of a Welsh lawyer and landowner, and a graduate of Trinity College, Oxford. He formed his friendships at Oriel, and after he had won the Chancellor's prize for Latin verse, came under the direction of Keble, who looked upon him and Robert Wilberforce and Hurrell Froude as his special pupils. Although accustomed to lean on others for support, Williams had a will of his own, and on occasion did not hesitate to assert himself. He acted as Newman's curate at St. Mary's, and afterwards gave this impression of his vicar: "I was greatly delighted and charmed with Newman, who was extremely kind to me, but I did not altogether trust his opinions; and

---

[1] Thomas Mozley: "Reminiscences"; Vol. I, p. 448.

though Froude was in the habit of stating things in an extreme and paradoxical way, yet one always felt conscious of a ground of entire confidence and agreement; but it was not so with Newman, even though one appeared more in unison with his more moderate views." The magician ultimately prevailed, and the Tracts 80, 86, and 87 were written by Williams. It was the hard fate of this unsophisticated man that the first of these, which dealt with "Reserve in Communicating Religious Knowledge," brought upon its author a crushing rebuke. The title was misleading because it seemed to justify the charge that the Tractarians were evasive in their methods, but the contents offered no adequate cause for the complaint. Bishop Monk of Gloucester was obliged to admit that he had condemned the Tract without knowing its argument, and his apology was so flimsy that Thomas Keble, more unyielding than his brother, resigned his rural deanery in that diocese, and thus began the quarrel with the bishops. That Williams should have produced an unfortunate document which unjustly exposed him to popular indignation and calumny was extremely distressing to his guileless nature. He strove to retrieve the error of his ill-selected thesis, but this was beyond him, and the meditative poet who was revered by his college historian as too good for this world, was regarded by the Evangelicals as the most perfidious and dangerous member of a wicked band of conspirators. His friend and fellow tutor, William John Copeland, contemplated writing a history of the Movement in which they participated, a task for which his wide acquaintance with its supporters and his retentive memory eminently fitted him. But pastoral duties largely absorbed his energies, and until his death in 1885 he gave what time he could afford to his correspondence and to the editing of Newman's "Plain and Parochial Sermons." Copeland also contributed to the Tracts, and translated the "Homilies of St. John Chrysostom in the Epistle to the Ephesians" for the "Library of the Fathers."

The general current of Tractarianism now began to be ascertainable. It was marked by the rise of forces which swept away the barriers secrecy and caution at first had erected: forces full of a new willingness and striving; forces that threatened to disrupt the doctrinal beliefs upon which recent ideals of Anglicanism and Romanism had been founded, and have since materially modified these beliefs and ideals. They took their shape in repeated disputes which endured for a decade; of small intrinsic importance in themselves; with no more than an adventitious interest derived from their connection with the Oxford Movement and also with the devouring claims of Rome. They were usually trials of strength, engineered now by the High Churchmen, now by their adversaries, not always with conspicuous candor or fairness, nor fraught with any good for either party. Amongst these was the nearly forgotten Hampden controversy, which assumed dimensions out of all proportion to its deserts. Cynics and others who were not cynical have derided it as a tempest in a tea cup, with no attraction except for bigoted fanatics and antiquaries. We are not going to weary the reader with an extended digest of this quarrel. Yet it should be said that it furnished the Tractarians with a prominent object for their attack and a coveted opportunity to state their case. They desired nothing better than to come to conclusions, not with Hampden, but with that for which he stood, and their pent-up energies were released with alacrity. Liberal Churchmen were disgusted by such an unseemly display of High Anglican rancor; Erastians found fresh guarantees for their assertion that the power of appointment to certain preferments in the Church and the Universities was exercised most justly when left in the hands of the civil government. Hampden was a sober, plodding scholar, who owed his elevation to a combination of circumstances rather than to his talents or services. He had made himself obnoxious to High Churchmen because he subordinated dogma to religious liberty, and contrasted the benefits of toleration with the evils of exclusiveness. Few, if any Christians, he asserted, were really at odds; even Unitarians and Anglicans might realize a common fellowship if only faith were no longer hampered by its doctrinal forms. This foretaste of genuine catholicity was a pestiferous heresy to those who could not conceive of religion except as guarded by ecclesiastical monopolies and dogmatic statements. Newman spoke for them when he declared that he would not trust himself to put on paper his sentiments about Hampden's principles. Upon the publication of his lectures on Moral Philosophy, reactionaries of all Anglican schools combined to silence him as an anti-Christian writer and a purveyor of baleful and erroneous opinions. Unshaken and unterrified, he came to grips with them in Convocation, where he proposed that compulsory subscription to the Thirty-nine Articles as the condition of admission to the University should be abolished. The proposal was overwhelmingly defeated, but it called the attention of the Prime Minister, Lord Melbourne, to Hampden's temerity as a liberal in politics and religion, and Melbourne determined to nominate him Regius Professor of Divinity at Oxford. His decision gave the disturbance a fresh start and a wider area, in which the fury of opposition ran so high that Hampden considerately offered to resign and thus relieve Melbourne of the odium attending his appointment. But this the Premier would not permit; and when William IV, who had been petitioned by the Tractarians through Archbishop Howley not to confirm the appointment, attempted to intervene, his outspoken minister bluntly reminded the king that such an action would affect the honor of the national administration and constitute an abuse of the royal prerogative. Quarrels seldom turn upon the point in dispute, and this one became a duel between Newman and Pusey on the one side and Arnold and Archbishop Whately on the other. Newman issued a broadside entitled "Elucidations of Dr. Hampden's Theological Statements," in which quotations from his opponent's Bampton Lectures and other writings were so openly garbled and wrenched from their context as to suggest that he who wills the end wills the means. Pusey came to his assistance with a more careful presentation and criticism of Hampden's views. Arnold gave the reins to his wrath in an article on "The Oxford Malignants," which was published in the volume of the *Edinburgh Review* for 1836. His words breathed the fiery indignation of a wholesome but frustrated reformer whose hopes for the betterment of the Church were clouded by the intrusion of the Tractarians. He averred that Newman's methods implied intentional dishonesty, and Whately stigmatized their product as a tissue of deliberate and artful misrepresentations. There were not sufficient grounds for impugning Newman's moral integrity, but his understanding was such that when disturbed by matters he held paramount it became essentially illogical and inveterately imaginative. Reason and equity were smothered beneath the profusion of his hypotheses and imageries, and, as Sir James Stephen commented, he could not do justice, either to himself or to his opponents. Although every possible influence was brought to bear, nothing availed to annul Hampden's appointment, and, aware of this, the Evangelicals made common cause with the High Churchmen to hunt the wolf in sheep's clothing from the fold. After two attempts Convocation succeeded in depriving him of the right to vote for Select Preachers, and he remained officially censured and theologically discredited by the University in which the Crown had chosen him as the instructor in divinity. The persistency of his enemies might have led some to suppose that he was anything except what he actually was, an orthodox Churchman, albeit one sufficiently enlightened to observe the relative importance of life and dogma and to respect the scruples of the Nonconformist conscience. But the Tractarians reprobated him because of his stalwart Protestantism, and the Evangelicals disparaged him because he extended it beyond their credal confines. The humiliating fight ended with neither side the winner, and when in 1847 Hampden was elevated to the see of Hereford, some of his persecutors had already renounced the Church over which they formerly assumed proprietary rights, and departed to Rome.

The ill-assorted union between the Tractarians and the Evangelicals speedily dissolved; animosities which had been temporarily forgotten during this alignment revived again. The Evangelicals felt that they had overshot the mark, and the publication of Froude's "Remains" in 1838 intensified their chagrin. The book shed a strong light on the worst aspects of High Anglicanism, and placed its leaders under grave suspicion concerning their motives and objects. The Movement began to encounter a power which could be matched even with that of Rome herself: the Protestant character of the British nation. So far from assuming a Catholic demeanor, Englishmen demanded that the secret and undermining foes lurking within the Establishment should be expelled. The first result of this formidable sentiment was seen at Oxford when the University was solicited to erect a memorial to the martyrs, Ridley, Latimer, and Cranmer, who had suffered there during the Marian burnings. The threefold purpose behind the scheme was to marshal the full strength of Oxford's allegiance to the Reformed faith, to provide a counterblast to Froude's volume, and to discover whether there were any vestiges of Protestantism left among the Tractarians. Newman and Keble hated the term Protestant, and much that it connoted. They held aloof from the proposal, and after some hesitation, Pusey and those who felt as he did followed suit. To honor the faith and sacrifice of the three bishops was an impeachment of Anglican catholicity and an indirect indorsement of the Genevan theology which the Tractarians abjured. "Any thing," said Keble, "which separates the present Church from the Reformers I should hail as a great good." The memorial was set up without their aid, to be, in the words of Dean Church, "a decisive though unofficial sign of the judgment of the university against the Tractarians."

It showed that they had nothing favorable to expect from the authorities, and that they were fast severing themselves from the nation. They were still one in their professions of fidelity to the Church, but the last of the Tracts was about to appear and divide them on that question. Its pages glowed with light, heat, color; they were written with the pen of a ready scribe, never crude, always graceful. Yet despite Newman's rare gifts, his in many ways unsurpassed charm, his unique personality, he was not convincing. High intentions conferred on him no sufficient powers of persuasion. "The father of them that look back," he was unable to perceive that

" Creeds pass, rites change, no altar standeth whole :"

in a world of dust and ashes he predicated an almost endless durability for venerable ideas and symbols which were being forsaken when he prophesied. His mind worked under conditions which his age refused to accept and from standpoints it instinctively rejected. The far-reaching extent and apparent antiquity of the Papal Church were always before him. They molded his conceptions of faith as forever associated with secondary, incidental things, with a formula, a hierarchy, an institution. For him there was but one goal, ominous and repellent as it then appeared — *Christianity meant Rome*. The prolonged oscillations of his heart and brain, the innumerable impressions which he had received from widely separated sources, could not divert him from the underlying equilibrium he eventually found in the Papacy.

These inward wrestlings he revealed to none, but Tract

Ninety could not have been written had he not experienced them. They began anew in 1839, when he read the history of the Monophysites, and, as it seemed to him, saw their heresy reflected in the sixteenth and nineteenth centuries. If these ancient sectaries who contended that Jesus Christ was neither wholly divine nor wholly human but in part both, were heretics, so were Protestants and Anglicans of to-day. "The drama of religion and the combat of truth, were ever one and the same. The principles and proceedings of the Church now, were those of the Church then; the principles and proceedings of heretics then, were those of heretics now." The similarity may not have been patent to others, but it was to him; he grieved over it, and spoke of the awful likeness between the dead records of the past and the feverish chronicles of the present. What use was there in continuing his labors if he was only forging arguments for Arius or Eutyches, turning devil's advocate against the much-enduring Athanasius and the majestic Leo? "Be my soul with the saints!" he exclaimed . . . "anathema to a whole tribe of Cranmers, Ridleys, Latimers, and Jewels." [1] During the August of that year he read an article by Dr. Wiseman in the *Dublin Review,* which did not specially interest him until a friend called his attention to the words of St. Augustine quoted by Wiseman, "Securus judicat orbis terrarum." They became for Newman as a nail fastened in a sure place; indeed, driven through the heart of his theory of a Via Media. Although his Anglican principles refused to be silenced, they were mortally wounded. Out of the mists which had so long enshrouded his vision there leaped up a sudden definite presentiment that in the end Rome would be victorious. To use his own phrase, he had seen the shadow of a hand upon the wall. Hereafter he felt a growing dislike to speak against the formal teachings of the Papacy. Yet as a moral, social, and political fabric, it was vulnerable, and in any event he felt bound

[1] "Apologia"; pp. 114–116.

to return to the defense of his mother Church. What she lacked in catholicity she gained in apostolicity. Her rejuvenation was still possible if the vulgar misunderstandings of her Articles could be removed, and the doctrines of the purer faith were permitted to live and speak in her formularies. He felt a grave responsibility for the younger Tractarians, who were bound in the toils of his personality, to whom he was the real primate, the source of light and leading. Some were straining on the leash, others straggling toward Rome. He could neither consent to part with them, nor admit that their threatened defection was justifiable. Its ostensible cause was their resentment against the historic Protestantism of the Articles, and in order to disabuse their prejudices Newman wrote his Tract.

Its governing principle was the interpretation of the Reformed confessions in the most inclusive sense they would admit, entirely subjecting the particular beliefs of their framers to the beliefs of the Church universal. Its object was to assure his followers that they could still find divine life and shelter in Anglicanism. Its fundamental errors were that it contradicted a known historical development and dealt solely with credal mechanisms which were incapable of repairing their own injuries. In pursuance of these principles and aims, Newman attempted the subjective creation of a historic situation by his manipulation of language. None could have made a better attempt, but not even he could achieve success. The license with which he treated historic phraseologies was a blot upon his argument. His shadings, softenings, circumlocutions, special pleadings, careful avoidances of decisive features, were by this time familiar to his critics. Like Napoleon, he had revealed to observant foes the secret of his strategic genius. Dean Church remarked that he pared down language to its barest meaning. His conclusion was that though the Articles were the product of an unCatholic age, they were *patient* of a Catholic interpretation. Since this was the marrow of his contention, other matters which he mentioned can be passed over. Material in proof of his position was compiled from sundry sources without regard for the exceptions and qualifications from those same sources, which, if produced, as they should have been, must have altered the substance of his reasoning. His antagonists based their objections on the history and the words of the Articles. They demonstrated that the Anglican divines of the sixteenth century, although they loved and revered the earlier Church, joined themselves to the continental Reformers against the Renaissance Papacy, and restricted the Rule of Faith to the Holy Scriptures. The precise weight to be ascribed to the literal and grammatical sense of the Articles, which Newman claimed he had given, was not sufficient for their explanation. Had it been sufficient, it bore heavily against his exposition. They were so avowedly Protestant in dealing with Purgatory, Pardons, Adoration of Images, and the dogma of the Mass, that Newman was hard driven to construe them in any other way. A review of the edicts of Councils and Parliaments during the reigns of Edward VI and Elizabeth plainly shows that it was the purpose of those who took part in them to formulate a theological system which should be distinctly Protestant, and at the same time, not incompatible with the retention of Catholic liturgies. This would secure, as they hoped, solidarity for the State Church, and uniformity of religious practice for the nation. So far as the framers of the Articles were concerned, they intended to allow a reasonable latitude for their interpretation without compromising their Protestant determination. That such an intricate process afforded Newman a suitable opportunity for his dialectical cleverness could not be gainsaid. But he failed to convince either friend or foe, or, as it proved in the sequel, himself.

The Tract fell like a bomb shell in the camps of Evangelicals and High Churchmen. Oxford was attacked in the House of Commons as a seed plot of Roman teaching; even the majority of Newman's friends felt that he had advanced too far into a doubtful region : his opponents accused him of false doctrine, false history, false dialectics, and deliberate dishonesty. Ten days after the Tract appeared Churton of Brasenose, H. B. Wilson of St. John's, Griffiths of Wadham, and Tait of Balliol communicated with Newman as the editor of the series, calling upon the author to divulge his identity and accusing him of opening the way for Roman doctrines and practices to be taught in the University. The Hebdomadal Board met and without granting Newman a hearing, condemned the Tract out of hand as evading rather than explaining the sense of the Articles and reconciling subscription to them with the adoption of errors they were designed to counteract. Newman admitted that he was its author, and enlarged upon his distinction between the Tridentine decrees and the Scholasticism on which modern Papal beliefs were founded. The hastiness of his arraignment was a selfish blunder which recoiled on the perpetrators. It brought him sympathy from unexpected quarters and summoned the more moderate Tractarians to his aid. After some correspondence with his bishop, Dr. Bagot, it was agreed that the Tracts should be discontinued, upon which for a brief space the tumult subsided. Newman was gratified at the outcome; the bishops, as he supposed, were anxious for peace, and to this he consented, provided Tract Ninety was not to be withdrawn nor condemned. He decided to surrender nothing which he held on conscience, and did not yet realize that he had helped to kindle a conflagration which was beyond his power or that of any other man to extinguish. The summer of 1841 found him at Littlemore, set upon banishing cares and controversies, and busy with a translation of St. Athanasius.

Such a reaction from overstrained tension must have seemed to him like a dream of the Fortunate Isles. Yet self-centered as he was in everything, not from morbid vanity or pride, but because he stood alone, fashioning for himself more congenial conditions, he had made but little way in his work when his troubles returned, escorted, as usual, by the Arian specter, which came to taunt him with the helplessness of his attempts to reconcile the perplexing disparities between opposing theories or assign their place and efficiency in history. He again perceived, and again retreated from the perception, that the pure Arians were the Protestants of their age, the semi-Arians the Anglicans, and that Rome was now what she had always been. The misery of this unsettlement was heightened by a second blow which seriously weakened his hold upon Anglicanism. The bishops, to use his own language, "began charging against us," and the Tractarians met with the usual fate of those who traffic in new ideas. For three years Bloomfield of London, Sumner of Chester, his brother Charles of Winchester, Phillpotts, known as "Harry of Exeter," Copleston of Llandaff, and other prelates maintained a steady assault upon Newmanism. "Bishops' charges," says Mr. Augustine Birrell, "are amongst the many seemingly important things that do not count in England." But on this occasion they did count, and their warnings, remonstrances, and inhibitions were read and discussed in political and clerical circles. Even Bagot ceased to temporize, and although lamenting the violence and unseemliness of some other attacks, he felt compelled to disapprove interpretations which he said were so full of vagaries that the Articles may be made to mean anything or nothing. Newman knew that public confidence in him was rudely shaken, his place among his brethren lost, his occupation in the Movement gone. He abandoned his attempts to persuade the shepherds of the flock that the Church of England was infinitely more than a mere national institution; that it was a living member of the one Church which God had set up from the beginning; and, weary of Anglicanism, again retired to Littlemore, to be "denounced as a traitor who had laid his train and was detected in the very act of firing it."

Programs, prospects, hopes, friendships changed with startling rapidity. Newman's transparent scorn of the bishops and their followers was expressed in words the more cutting because scrupulously civil; he was wounded to the quick, nor did any truly capable leader appear who might have redeemed him to Anglicanism. On the contrary, the man who, after Newman, was chiefly responsible for wrecking Tractarianism now forged to the front. The audacious brochures of W. G. Ward created consternation in his own ranks, and amazed and gratified his opponents. That which Newman had either left unsaid or cautiously suggested, this unmanageable disciple openly avowed, tearing away his master's closely woven veils of rhetoric, and demanding subscription to the Articles, not as they read, nor according to Newman's reading of them, but in a non-natural sense. Such elasticity of conscience in the region of theological bias is not the least notable curiosity of human nature, but while Pusey deprecated it in Ward, Newman gave no hint of repudiating him. The Via Media, the Tractarian party, the Anglicanism of its irreconcilable members, alike crumbled before the merciless onfall of Ward's logic, an outcome which delighted rather than alarmed its agent. He was the refreshingly candid radical of the Oxford group, in some respects its most estimable and philosophical theologian, a man of splendid and diversified gifts and personal seductiveness. The extensiveness and quality of his acquirements and the good-natured contempt with which he treated his changing fortunes recall the lines of the Archbishop of Canterbury in *Henry the Fifth*:

> "Hear him but reason in divinity,
> And, all-admiring with an inward wish,
> You would desire the King were made a prelate.
> Hear him debate of commonwealth affairs,
> You would say, it hath been all in all his study:
> List his discourse of war, and you shall hear

A fearful battle rendered you in music:
Turn him to any cause of policy,
The Gordian knot of it he will unloose
Familiar as his garter."

Ward exhibited a marked development of the reflective over the imaginative faculty and a capacity for abstract reasoning which made his writings on the doctrines of the Creator and of the free, responsible, and immortal spirit of man, works of the best character. The reaction of an over-wrought brain, stimulated by his huge body, incurable pessimism, and numerous eccentricities, led him to take refuge in occupations not often found in a metaphysician. He was full of contradictoriness and perversity, and would sometimes talk by the hour "with such intense gravity and such elaborate logical sequence, that a stranger would think he must have missed the drift of his words." In religion he was nothing if not controversial, and during the intervals between his incessant debates he found relaxation in music, fiction, and the drama; passing from the gravest tasks to the opera and theater with equal facility, and, as he avowed, with equal benefit. The vigor and acumen of his analytical and critical powers were not cramped, apparently, by his settled orthodoxy. Although he was supposed to reason under confessional restrictions, his agile mind enabled him to convey the impression of consistent argument, which, if not correct, was, as a rule, in clear agreement with its premises. The accepted opinion that intense religious convictions are not easily compatible with the free motions of the intellect, or that purely arbitrary traditions impede the functions of philosophical reflection, was not sustained in the case of Ward. Despite his theological narrowness and avowed sacerdotalism, he was, said Dean Church, "the most amusing, the most tolerant man in Oxford; he had round him perpetually some of the cleverest and brightest scholars and thinkers of the place; and where he was, there was debate, cross-questioning, pushing inferences, starting alarming

2 N

problems, beating out ideas, trying the stuff and mettle of mental capacity. If the old scholastic disputations had been still in use at Oxford, his triumphs would have been signal and memorable. His success, compared with that of other leaders of the Movement, was a preëminently intellectual success." [1]   In his first phase he was a latitudinarian, wavering between the Broad Churchmanship of Tait, Arnold, and Stanley, and the milder Utilitarianism of John Stuart Mill. In this and much else, "he represented the intellectual force, the irrefragable logic, the absolute self-confidence, and the headlong impetuosity of the Rugby School. Whatever he said or did was right. As a philosopher and a logician it was hard to deal with him." [2]   His hesitation ended after his first contact with Hurrell Froude and Newman, although the latter only mentions him once in the "Apologia." The conversations at Oriel and the lectures and sermons at St. Mary's completely separated him from Broad Churchmen and the Millites, and he became one of the most indefatigable, industrious, and yet independent adherents of the Tractarian party.

Beneath his adherence to dialectical forms and his excessive love of æsthetics was a profoundly religious temperament which drove him to seek for a greater assurance in matters of faith than reason could supply. He longed for an authoritative organization to which he could surrender his perturbed mind, and enter into the peace attained by submission. From Newman he derived the conviction that primitive Christianity might have been corrupted into Popery, but that no form of Protestantism could possibly have developed into Catholicism. This led him to the conclusion that the Tridentine decrees were obligatory and that the Anglican Church must reconcile her Articles with them or surrender her claim to Catholicity. The distinction which Newman made between what was es-

---

[1] "The Oxford Movement"; pp. 343–344.
[2] Thomas Mozley: "Reminiscences"; Vol. II, p. 5.

sentially Catholic as opposed to what was purely Roman did not satisfy Ward, who argued that while the Articles were "patient of a Catholic meaning they were ambitious of a Protestant one; the offspring of an unCatholic age, and a hindrance to truly Catholic belief in the English Church." He endeavored to substitute for their accepted teaching his conjectural emendations on their original doctrine, or, at any rate, what in his view that doctrine should have been. Because of this proceeding, at the request of Tait, his friend and fellow-tutor, he was deprived of his lectureship at Balliol, an act which he cheerfully accepted and declared quite proper. His advance toward Rome grieved Newman, who, destined in this to follow instead of lead, suggested prudence and delay. Nothing was more contrary to Ward's temper, and after the older Tractarians saw that he would not yield to their wishes, they turned against him. Keble, Pusey, Williams, and Palmer were now separated from Newman, and yet further from Ward and his admirers. The publication in 1843 of Palmer's "Narrative of Events" voiced the grievances of these conservatives, who complained of their unruly subordinates as contemptuous toward the Church of England and her reformers, and servile in their adulation of Rome. Ward replied by giving forth his "Ideal of a Christian Church considered in comparison with existing Practice." The exuberant gymnastics of the volume, which showed how he could leap from one side of the fence to the other with astounding ease and indifference, earned for him the sobriquet of "Ideal Ward." In manner argumentative, in matter lacking cogency, his production consisted of one syllogism, the major premise being that everything pertaining to Rome was divinely authorized; the minor one, that the common forms, methods, and rules of the Church of England were contrary to those of Rome: hence the conclusion, Rome was right and all else was wrong. Although Ward continued to assure his half-amused, half-outraged readers that he was still an Anglican, he expatiated on the Roman Church in glowing terms, as the nearly perfect incarnation of Christian fellowship, against which the Protestant sects stood out in odious contrast. These exasperating sentiments had their sequel in his degradation, the story of which is postponed in deference to the chronological order of events and to the account of the third shattering blow which awaited Newman.

III

This was the establishment, at the instance of King Frederick William of Prussia, of the Jerusalem bishopric, an act which, together with Newman's misgivings over ancient heresies and their modern counterparts, and the reprisals of the bishops, ended his relations with Anglicanism. The Chevalier Bunsen, a well-known scholar, historian, and diplomatist of the early Victorian period, was commissioned by the Prussian monarch to arrange with the English government for a dual protectorate over the Christians in Palestine who were outside the pale of the Eastern Churches. The origin of the project may have been due to a royal whim, but under Bunsen's guidance, it was brought to a successful issue. He knew and admired England and Englishmen, and was anxious to cultivate amicable relations between his native land and the country in which he spent the larger part of his life, where he was for thirteen years ambassador at the Court of St. James and popular among all classes. The bishopric was founded to be filled alternately by the two governments; a mutual recognition of Anglican and Lutheran orders and creeds was agreed upon; Dr. Alexander was consecrated to the see, and authorized to ordain German Protestants in the Holy Land on their signing the Thirty-nine Articles as well as assenting to the Augsburg Confession. The scheme was approved by Broad Churchmen, some of whom were Bunsen's personal friends; the High Churchmen disliked it; the Tractarians repudiated it; and Newman labeled it "fearful," "hideous," and "atrocious." In July, 1841, he wrote in the *British Critic*: "When our thoughts turn to the East, instead of recollecting that there are Christian Churches there, we leave it to the Russians to take care of the Greeks, and the French to take care of the Romans, and we content ourselves with erecting a Protestant Church at Jerusalem . . . or with becoming the august protectors of Nestorians, Monophysites, and all the heretics we can think of, or with forming a league with the Mussulman against Greeks and Romans together." [1] In November he sent a solemn protest to the Archbishop of Canterbury, and to his own bishop, in which he fulminated against Lutheranism and Calvinism as "heresies, repugnant to Scripture, springing up three centuries since, and anathematized by East as well as West." The assumption that the Anglican Church was in origin and doctrine closely allied to the German Evangelical Churches was abominated by those whom he represented. Once admitted, as it was in this case, such an assumption destroyed the claim of the Church of England to be considered a branch of the Catholic Church, and condemned the theory of the Via Media. From now onward, in Newman's estimate, Anglicanism was "either not a normal portion of that one Church to which the promises were made, or at least one in an abnormal state." [2] It may be added that the "Fancy Church," as Mr. Gladstone called the organization at Jerusalem, had a very brief and ineffective existence, and after the joint arrangement had furnished three bishops it was relinquished.

These three blows which had fallen upon Newman were now followed by three defeats. The Liberal Churchmen, encouraged by their success in the matters of Tract Ninety and the Jerusalem episcopate, resolved to push their advantage, and the contest for the Professorship of Poetry at Oxford, which Keble resigned in 1841, gave them an

[1] "Apologia"; pp. 141–142.   [2] *Ibid.*, pp. 149–150.

opening. Isaac Williams, the Tractarian candidate, possessed some poetical gifts of which his victorious rival, James Garbett, was entirely guiltless. Williams was placed in nomination only to discover how seriously his candidature had been prejudiced by his partisan connections and by his authorship of the Tract on "Reserve." He was further handicapped by an ill-timed circular letter which Dr. Pusey sent out recommending him for the professorship on the ground of his religious views. His failure to obtain the chair so deeply distressed Williams that he withdrew from Oxford to Stinchcombe, near Dursley, where he found consolation in writing those devotional commentaries, poems, and hymns which are still prized by some High Churchmen. Far more important than this, the first setback of the Tractarians as a party, was the attack made on Dr. Pusey and headed by Hawkins, the Provost of Oriel. On May 24, 1843, Pusey preached in Christ Church Cathedral on the Holy Eucharist, and although, according to Dean Church, he used language strictly in accordance with that of other Anglican divines, the sermon was made the basis of action against him for heresy. Its assessors were Hawkins, Symons, Jenkyns, Ogilvie, Jelf, and Faussett, two of whom acted as both accuser and judge. They condemned Pusey and inhibited him from preaching within the University for two years. The proceedings were irregular throughout; Pusey was neither allowed a hearing nor acquainted with the charges made against him. He did not even know who the objectors were, except from rumor, nor to what standards his sermon had been submitted. Consequently, although he offered to sign an explanatory statement, he would not formally retract what he had said, and his illegal and unjust suspension remained in effect. It both confirmed High Churchmen in their obduracy and brought Newman nearer to secession. "Things are very serious here," he wrote to a friend; "the authorities find that, by the statutes, they have more than military power, and the general impression seems to be, that they intend to exert it, and put down Catholicism at any risk." [1]

Ward was the next offender slated for a severe punishment, and one which marked the final overthrow of the original phase of Tractarianism. On the 13th of February, 1845, Convocation ratified formally the action to censure him already adopted by the Hebdomadal Council. He made a unique defense of his opinions, and assured the Convocation that he was still loyal to Anglicanism, while at the same time he held the whole content of Roman doctrine. Such arguments strengthened the resolution of his enemies to silence him : his book on the "Ideal Church" was condemned and his degrees taken from him. Upon this he resigned his fellowship, and although hitherto an avowed believer in celibacy, he married, retired to Rose Hill, near Oxford, and in September of that year, was received into the Church of Rome. The career of this richly endowed but wayward genius has been portrayed in the admirable and impartial biography written by his son, Dr. Wilfred Ward. Tennyson, who was neighbor to him in his last days, composed the well-known epitaph which commemorated a most extraordinary and lovable character.

"Farewell, whose living like I shall not find,
Whose faith and work were bells of full accord,
My friend, the most unworldly of mankind,
Most generous of all ultramontanes, Ward,
How subtle at tierce and quart of mind with mind,
How loyal in the following of thy Lord."

Ward rightly rebuked Protestant harshness towards Rome, but it is questionable whether he was ever in the vanguard of spiritual leadership in Britain, and although he made sport with logic, ultimately logic took its revenge on him. He addressed his appeals to his countrymen, heedless that

[1] "Apologia"; p. 179.

they deprecated the exaltation of any theories beyond their legitimate sphere as working hypotheses, and were wont to apply the antiseptic of common sense to the laudations of those who worshiped an abstraction. Even Ward's skillful handling could not avoid the collision between sentiment and reason, or lessen the distaste of those who held with Burke that nothing absolute can be affirmed on any moral or political issue. Consequently they rejected a religious philosopher who was wanting in gravity, and who, at a pinch, could make the worse appear the better reason. Yet, in the larger sense, Ward's personal life was anything but inconsistent, and, in the lesser sense, many of his inconsistencies were due to the wide sweep of his vision and the greatness of his nature.

His condemnation and secession to Rome marked the exit of other notable converts, amongst whom were Dalgairns, Frederick Oakley, Ambrose St. John, and F. W. Faber. Newman testified in words often quoted: "From the end of 1841, I was on my deathbed, as regards my membership with the Anglican Church, though at the time I became aware of it only by degrees." [1] It was indeed a lingering death and yet one which the events we have cited rendered certain. He relinquished the editorship of the *British Critic* and asked that his name should be kept out of it as far as possible. A little later, in 1842, he left his room at Oriel, and went to Littlemore, where he and a few disciples lived in monastic seclusion, praying, fasting, studying, and repeating the daily offices. In 1843 he made a formal retraction of all the hard things he had said against the Roman Church, and on September 18th of that year he resigned the living of St. Mary's. On the 25th he uttered his valedictory as an Anglican preacher: the sermon on "The Parting of Friends," delivered to a small and grief-stricken congregation in the church at Littlemore. The October following he returned to Oxford, where, on the

[1] "Apologia"; p. 147.

15th, he celebrated the Holy Eucharist at St. Mary's for the last time, when those worshipers to whom he meant more than words could express gathered around the altar with conflicting emotions. He had now come to the margin, but he feared to launch away. Though he "was very far more sure that England is in schism, than that the Roman additions to the Primitive Creed may not be developments, arising out of a keen and vivid realizing of the Divine Depositum of Faith," [1] two years were to elapse before he entered on the unknown regions ahead; an interval during which he wrote his "Essay on the Development of Christian Doctrine."

This was his apologetic for the step he was about to take. Through it he hoped to demolish the objections against Rome because of the accretions of her later beliefs and practices, by proving that these were simply expansions of the original seed of truth committed to the Apostles. The work was begun in 1845, and as it advanced his difficulties vanished; he no longer referred to those who held the views he discussed as "Roman Catholics" but as "Catholics"; he had not completed his task when he resolved to be received into their faith, and the volume remains in the unfinished state in which it was then.[2] He stated that it was his intention and wish to have carried the book through the press before his secession, but he recognized in himself a conviction of the truth of the conclusion to which the discussion led, so clear as to supersede further deliberation. Here followed one of those passages, observes Mr. Hutton, "by which Newman will be remembered as long as the English language endures."

"Such," he wrote, "were the thoughts concerning 'The Blessed Vision of Peace' of one whose long-continued petition had been that the Most Merciful would not despise the work of His own hands, nor leave him to himself; while

[1] "Apologia"; pp. 208–209.
[2] *Ibid.*, p. 234.

yet his eyes were dim, and his breast laden, and he could but employ Reason in the things of Faith. And now, dear reader, time is short, eternity is long. Put not from you what you have here found; regard it not as mere matter of controversy; set not out resolved to refute it, and looking about for the best way of doing so; seduce not yourself with the imagination that it comes of disappointment, or disgust, or restlessness, or wounded feeling, or undue sensibility, or other weakness. Wrap not yourself round in the associations of years past, nor determine that to be truth which you wish to be so, nor make an idol of cherished anticipations. Time is short, eternity is long. Nunc dimittis servum tuum, Domine, secundum verbum tuum in pace, quia viderunt oculi mei salutare tuum." [1]

The "Essay" has received more attention than any other prose work of Newman's except the "Apologia," and in it theologians have found grounds for their assertion that Newman was the progenitor of Modernism. Its constructive statements dealt with the wide divergencies between the teachings of the New Testament and those of Catholicism. These were apparent, not only in degree but in essence, and presented a strong prima facie case against the historical continuity of Roman doctrine. Not only so, but when the authorized creeds current in different ages of the Church were compared, large variations were disclosed. How could these variations be harmonized as actual necessary parts of a homogeneous whole? Newman arrested the argument at this stage to point out that Christianity, however explained, was first and last a supreme fact established in history, and could not be treated as a matter of private opinion. Theories did not create its importance, but its importance created them. Therefore they should neither over-ride nor minimize the reality of a faith which had found its objective existence not in the cloister nor the sanctuary, but in the world. It had been public property for many

---

[1] "Development of Christian Doctrine"; p. 445.

centuries, and to know it men must listen to the records of the past. He was so confident history was at last on his side that he could afford to be careless and over-liberal in allowing a greater weight to its evidence in behalf of his opponents than they could properly claim. "Let them consider," said the polemic who in defiance of history had endeavored to wrest out of the Thirty-nine Articles the Catholic meaning he coveted, "that if they can criticize history, history can retort upon them." It was neither creed nor catechism, but none could mistake its general import in this matter, whether he accepted or rejected it. Its bold outlines and broad masses of color arose in perspective, distant, incomplete, but still definite. And one thing was certain; whatever history taught, whatever it magnified, whatever it extenuated, whatever it said or unsaid, at least the Christianity of history was not Protestantism. If ever there was a safe truth, it was this, and Protestantism had ever so felt it. If not, why had its founders thrust aside historical Christianity, dispensing with it altogether and forming their doctrine from the Bible alone? The long-continued neglect of ecclesiastical history in England, and even in the Anglican Church, was accentuated by the melancholy reflection that perhaps the only English author who had any right to be considered an ecclesiastical historian was the unbeliever Gibbon. The utter incongruity between Protestantism and historical Christianity extended alike to early and later times; it could as little bear its Antenicene as its Post-tridentine period.[1] To be deep in history was to cease to be a Protestant, whereas, on the other hand, the Roman Catholic communion was the heir of patristic Christianity. All parties agreed that did St. Athanasius or St. Ambrose come suddenly to life they would find themselves more at home with such men as St. Bernard or St. Ignatius Loyola, or with the lonely priest in his lodging, than with the teachers of any other creed.[2]

[1] "Development of Christian Doctrine"; pp. 7–8. [2] *Ibid.*, pp. 97–98.

Newman admitted the abstract possibility of changes in the original deposit of the faith, but added that those who advanced the assumption should sustain it, for unbelief must justify itself as well as faith.   And until positive reasons grounded on facts were advanced to the contrary, the most natural hypothesis was to consider that the society of Christians the Apostles left on earth were of that religion to which they had been converted.   The external continuity of name, profession, and communion argued a real continuity of doctrine.   Christianity began by manifesting itself to mankind in a given shape and bearing.   Therefore it went on so to manifest itself.   To take it for granted that the intervening periods had preserved in substance the very religion which Christ and His Apostles taught in the first centuries was not a violent supposition, but mere abstinence from the wanton admission of a principle to the contrary which necessarily led to the most vexatious and preposterous skepticism.   Whatever may have been the modifications for good or for evil which lapse of time and the vicissitudes of human affairs had impressed upon the original revelation, in essence it was the same, yesterday, to-day, and forever.[1]

Conceding the emergence of certain apparent variations in the teaching of the Church, he sought to explain them without hurt to the unity, directness, and consistency of that teaching.   Doctrinal development arose out of the power of Christianity to impress its ideas upon the mind, and these, being subject matter for the exercise of reason, expanded into other ideas, harmonious with one another, and in themselves determinate and immutable, as was the objective Christianity which they represented.   The more vital ideas were, the more manifold their aspects would be.   Too deep and opulent for immediate apprehension, their bearings, multiform, prolific and ever resourceful, kept pace with the changing fortunes of mankind.   The longer they endured, the more clearly they were ap-

[1] "Development of Christian Doctrine"; p. 5.

prehended and expressed. Contemplation and reflection gradually absorbed meanings which, implicit from the first, sometimes persisted through many generations before they became explicit. True everywhere, supremely true of Christianity, this principle overthrew the objection that the inspired writings definitely decreed the limits of Christian doctrine.

The dogmas which Protestants renounced as superfluous, were in reality the latest forms of ideas, which, though not found in the Bible, were incipient in the sacred writers and in their readers. This was a wise provision, for Christianity, as a universal religion, intended for all times and peoples, was bound to adapt itself to different environments or cease to be effective. Its teachings were capable of infinite applications which corresponded with the social demands made upon them. Nor were the straitest orthodoxies of the Reformed Churches exempt from the workings of this law of change. The duty of public worship, the substitution of the first for the seventh day of the week as the Lord's Day, the rite of Infant Baptism, and the affirmation that the Bible alone was the religion of Protestantism, had little if any prominence in the New Testament. They were not derived from the direct usage and sanction of the sacred writings, but from the unconscious growth of ideas fostered by the Christian experience of nearly twenty centuries. Similarly, numerous other questions were found in Scripture which Scripture did not solve; questions so real and practical that they must be answered by a development of the letter of revelation. So much was this the case, that it was impossible to avoid the conviction that post-biblical evolutions of Christian teaching were part of the providential purpose of its Divine Author. The presence of need and its supply in nature constituted a convincing proof of design in the material creation; in like manner the breaches which occurred in the structure of the original creed of the Church made it probable that those developments which grew out of the truths surrounding that creed were intended to fill up its fissures.

This probability was reënforced by the consideration that the entire Bible was written under the governance of the principle of development — "line upon line, precept upon precept." Its revelations were disclosed "in sundry parts and divers manners," ever new, ever old; the new being not a renewal but an expansion of the old. Our Lord Himself declared: "Think not that I am come to destroy the Law and the Prophets, I am not come to destroy but to fulfil." Nor could the exact point be found, either in the Apostolic teachings or afterwards, where the vital growth of dogma ceased and the Rule of Faith was established in finality. No doctrine was so complete in its primary stages as to require nothing in addition. The Apostolic Church received the seed of truth, the nucleus of a coherent system of belief; a living seed, a living nucleus, to be developed by its own potentialities reacting upon society, and beneath the direction of the Spirit of the living God.

Thus far Newman enlisted general assent, and showed how magnificently he could have handled theological problems in the light of the biological learning he unconsciously heralded. But when he entered the next phase of the discussion and tried to justify Roman doctrine and practice as the inevitable outcome of the residual forces, implicit or explicit, of New Testament Christianity, his touch was not so sure. The contrary elements injected by human malignancy and misdirection have sadly interfered with the smooth operation of this theory in the realm of faith and morals. On every hand contending sects arose, alien to one another, each equally confident of its direct and unmixed descent from the parental stock. How was the vexed question of their opposing claims to be adjudicated? Newman replied, by an infallible Church. "In proportion to the probability of true developments in the Divine Scheme, so is the probability also of the appointment in that scheme of an external authority to decide upon them, thereby separating them from the mass of mere human speculation, extravagance, corruption, and error, in and out of which they grow."[1] There is small chance of escape from his conclusion for either Romanists or Protestants who identify religious life with the acceptance of doctrinal formulæ. An infallible revelation committed to the care of fallible custodians is only a large indication of the exasperating risks of ultra-orthodoxy. To the precise and logical intellect of Newman such a revelation, when subjected to the thousand and one interpretations of private judgment, was too variable a compass for safe navigation. He argued that certain Catholic doctrines professing to be Apostolic, and possessing high antiquity, were universally considered in each successive age as the echo of doctrines of the times immediately preceding, and thus were continually thrown back to a date indefinitely early. Moreover, they formed one body, so that to reject one was to disparage the rest. They also occupied the whole field of theology and left nothing to be supplied, except in detail, by any other system. From these statements he drew the inference that the nearest approach to the religious sentiment and *Ethos* of the Early Church, even of the Apostles and Prophets, was to be found in Roman teaching. All would agree, he urged, that Elijah, Jeremiah, the Baptist, and St. Paul were in their history and mode of life more like a Dominican preacher, a Jesuit missionary, or a Carmelite friar; more like St. Toribio, St. Vincent Ferrer, St. Francis Xavier, or St. Alphonso Liguori, than any individuals, or classes of men, that could be found in other communions.[2] Why all *should* agree to this monopoly of resemblance does not appear. John Wesley, Henry Martyn, Adoniram Judson, David Livingstone, Bishop William Taylor, and a host of other Protestant worthies had many external features in common with the Biblical heroes named.

[1] "Development of Christian Doctrine"; p. 78.   [2] *Ibid.*, pp. 99–100.

He next enumerated the features which every genuine development of Christian ideas presented and by which it could be recognized: preservation of type, continuity of principles, power of assimilation, logical sequence, anticipation of its future, conservative action upon its past, and chronic vigor. Neither Thomas Huxley nor Herbert Spencer, who had the advantage of the evolutionary hypothesis, excelled Newman in the invention and suitability of scientific nomenclature. The rest of the volume was devoted to applying these seven tests to the doctrines of the Roman Catholic Church. An extended argument on the first — the preservation of type — was prefaced by the following inquiry: "What is Christianity's original type? and has that type been preserved in the developments commonly called Catholic? Let us take it as the world now views it in its age; and let us take it as the world once viewed it in its youth; and let us see whether there be any great difference between the early and the later description of it. . . . There is a religious communion claiming a divine commission, and holding all other religious bodies around it heretical or infidel; it is a well-organized, well-disciplined body; it is a sort of secret society, binding together its members by influences and by engagements which it is difficult for strangers to ascertain. It is spread over the known world; it may be weak or insignificant locally, but it is strong on the whole from its continuity; it may be smaller than all other religious bodies together, but it is larger than each separately. It is a natural enemy to governments external to itself; it is intolerant and engrossing, and tends to a new modeling of society; it breaks laws, it divides families. It is a gross superstition; it is charged with the foulest crimes; it is despised by the intellect of the day; it is frightful to the imagination of many. And there is but one communion such. Place this description before Pliny or Julian. . . . Each one knows at once who is meant by it." [1]

[1] "Development of Christian Doctrine"; pp. 207–208.

In enlarging upon the second note — continuity of principles — the following ideas were evolved from the doctrine of the Incarnation: *Dogma*, or supernatural truths committed to human media; *Faith*, as the necessary correlative of dogma; *Theology*, which was the output of the human mind operating upon the truths given by dogma to faith; the *Sacramental principle*, which conveyed the supreme gift of God in the material and visible medium of our Lord's physical body; the necessary use of *Mystical Language*, since words were invested with a sacramental office; the *Sanctification of Grace ;* the practice of *Asceticism ;* the possible *Holiness of Matter* as well as mind. Will any one say, asked Newman, that all these principles, directly arising out of the New Testament doctrine of the Incarnation, have not been retained in vigorous action in the Church at all times? and he proceeded to answer the question in a series of historical surveys.

Passing over his discussion of the third note of a genuine development, we come to the fourth, that of logical sequence, with which this review can perhaps best be concluded, since the crux of his argument lies here. If the doctrines of modern Roman Catholicism were logical sequences of the teachings of Christ and the Apostles, there was nothing further to be said; it would only remain for those who received the New Testament to do as Newman did, secede to Rome. In illustration of one doctrine leading to another, he used the instance of Baptism. In the primitive Church, the Sacrament of Baptism was held to convey inestimable benefits to the soul, its distinguishing gift being the plenary forgiveness of sins past. The Sacrament was never repeated. How then, since there was but one baptism for the remission of sins, was the guilt of post-baptismal sins to be removed? Or was there no hope for such sinners? Differences of opinion arose. Some conceived that the Church was empowered to grant one, and only one, reconciliation to baptized transgressors. In the West, idolatry, murder, and

2o

adultery, if committed after baptism, were by many held unpardonable. But as Christianity spread, and gathered converts of every kind, a more merciful rule gradually obtained. Penances were appointed, and by the end of the third century as many as four degrees of penance came into vogue, through which offenders had to pass in order to a reconciliation. The length and severity of the penance varied. Sometimes, for serious transgressors it was lifelong, without any remission; in other cases it was for a period of years. But the bishop always had the power of abbreviating and altering it.

The further question arose, Were these punishments only signs of repentance, or were they also in any sense satisfactions for the sins committed? If the former, then it was in the discretion of the Church to remit them as soon as true contrition was discovered. But if they were also an expiation made to the Almighty Judge, how then? "It cannot be doubted," said Newman, "that the Fathers considered penance as not a mere expression of contrition, but as an act done directly towards God and a means of averting His anger." Suppose, such being the case, that death intervened before the *plena pœnitentia* was accomplished, how and when would the residue be exacted? According to Bishop Kaye, whom Newman quoted, Clement of Alexandria answered this question very plainly. "Clement distinguishes between sins committed before and after baptism: the former are remitted at baptism; the latter are purged by discipline. . . . The necessity of this purifying discipline is such, that if it does not take place in this life, it must after death, and is then to be effected by fire, not by a destructive, but a discriminating, fire, pervading the soul which passes through it." [1] After further references to

---

[1] Clement, Chap. 12. We do not recall, and have failed to find in Clement's works, any passage in support of Bishop Kaye's statement. At the end of the 24th chapter of the fourth book of The Stromata, Clement has the following on post-baptismal sin, but nothing suggestive of purgatory: "There are two methods of correction, the instructive, and the

early Church writers, Newman concluded: "Thus we see how, as time went on, the doctrine of Purgatory was brought home to the minds of the faithful as a portion or form of Penance due for post-baptismal sin;" and again, "When an answer had to be made to the question, how is post-baptismal sin to be remitted, there was an abundance of passages in Scripture to make easy to the faith of the inquirer the definitive decision of the Church."

We are then carried on to the doctrine of Meritorious Works as the corollary to that of Purgatory. For if post-baptismal sins were debts which must be paid to the uttermost farthing, virtues, no less, passed to the credit side of the book of life, and might be drawn upon both for the souls concerned and for others. Finally, Monasticism was brought forward as a logical sequence of Penance. The penitential observances of individuals were necessarily on a larger scale as the Christian community increased in numbers, and the Church, divinely guided, adopted the important principle of economic science that everything should be turned to account and no waste allowed: she gave to penances the form of works, whether for her defense or for the spiritual and temporal benefit of mankind. Thus in cleansing their souls from sin the penitent monks and nuns were at the same time serving the Church and humanity.

Traces of the argument from the theory of development were found in Christian Apologetics long before Newman employed it to wall up the Via Media. Petavius and Mohler had substantially shown him how to use it; Pascal had made references to it, the eighteenth century divines had dwelt on it to some extent, and Gibbon's assault upon it in his history had become famous. But what Darwin afterwards did for the evolutionary hypothesis in biology, in a less degree Newman did for it in theology. He raised its

primitive, which we have called the disciplinary. It ought to be known, then, that those who fall into sin after baptism (λουτρὸν) are those who are subjected to discipline; for the deeds done before are remitted, and those done after are purged."

importance for the purposes of Catholic defense and aggression, and placed High Anglicans in an awkward dilemma. The only way of escape from his inexorable conclusions was to reject his premises, which was exactly what they did not propose to do. Although based on the identical principle of an external and absolute authority, Tractarianism and Romanism were now placed in powerful contrast. As a nominal Anglican, Newman exposed the illogical nature and illegitimate claims of the fellowship he had already inwardly forsaken. Those who did not admit his assumptions, whether Anglicans or Protestants in general, were not involved in their result. Once his basic plea for an inerrant document, which necessitated an inerrant interpreter to unfold its germinal verities, was granted, the force of sequence would carry men all the way with him. Deny him this, or even a part of it, and the whole of his cleverly constructed fabric fell asunder. That Christian experience of the past was of the essence of authority few, if any, of his opponents for a moment doubted, and revolutionary iconoclasm was as repugnant to them as it was to him. Yet such an authority was not so determinate as to exclude them from looking toward the future for light and wisdom, nor could it bring every motion of their minds under slavish subjection to the past. Men must be allowed to make trial of those new ways which are in keeping with the promptings of Christian intelligence and Christian conscience. To make this trial is to incur the risks of misunderstanding; to refuse to make it is either to surrender religion altogether, or to relinquish the hope of assimilating the assured results of knowledge and the slow achievements of moral effort. These considerations point to that kingdom of God within men which Christ Himself proclaimed, and they also imply a divine and ceaseless revelation in the growing human consciousness. The touchstone that discriminates between the true and the false, the essential and the accidental, in morals and religion, is not the sole right and property of tradition, nor of the Fathers, nor even of the Scriptures. Objective authority in religion goes beyond these and is vested in the Person of God and of Jesus Christ, Whom He has sent. In operation, this authority is not a fixture of chronology, nor a matter of antiquity, but the voice and spirit of the Eternal speaking through *all* the media of His life in the race, and not therefore separable from the subjective authority of conscience.[1] This reasoning was fatal to Newman's position; and he would have none of it, nor would he extend the idea of organic development beyond the arbitrary limits he had assigned it. Thus, although his system was the legitimate product of his theory, it ignored some main truths relative to God and the creature. Admissible in the courts of rigid ecclesiasticism, his case broke down in the wider court of human life. He was not strong enough to face doubt and then rise beyond it. In an era which plagued him with justifiable fears he could not lift his faith to those serene certainties which need no confirmation of the reason, and in confusing dogma with faith, he, who was perhaps the finest religious nature of the century, failed the Church universal in the hour of trial. Agnostics saw in him a superstitious mind, accompanied by symptoms of admirable intellectual clarity and depth. Ultramontanes questioned his right to impugn, ever so slightly, the changelessness of the decrees of tradition. The more liberal Roman Catholics afterwards rejoiced in his Essay as the basis for further modifications of dogma in behalf of culture. Tractarians lamented his discharge of what appeared to him an unavoidable duty, linked, as it was, with the semblance of disloyalty and the wrecking of their hopes. In the United States of America the volume was discussed by the Unitarians, and Dr. Brownson quoted it as evidence that the Trinitarian doctrine was not primitive but a development of the third century. The Roman Catholic bishops of the Republic declared that it was half

[1] James Martineau: "Essays, Reviews, and Addresses"; Vol. I, p. 248.

Catholicism and half infidelity. It was scarcely surprising, remarks Sir William Robertson Nicoll, that after his secession the theological guides of the Papacy thought that Newman should be a learner, not a teacher.

The mental and physical strain entailed upon him was evidenced in a letter of June, 1835, which he wrote to Mr. William Froude: "Did I tell you I was preparing a book of some sort to advertise people how things stood with me? Never has anything cost me (I think) so much hard thought and anxiety, though when I got to the end of my 'Arians' thirteen years ago, I had no sleep for a week, and was fainting away or something like it day after day. . . . I have not written a sentence which will stand, or hardly so." [1] As it approached completion he stood at his desk for hours, a pale, thin, nearly diaphanous form, his face almost transparent, his wearied hand revising and correcting what he had put down. The end of his strange, unearthly pilgrimage from Calvinistic Evangelicalism to the shelter he found in Rome was in sight. Father Dominic, the Italian Passionist friar, was expected in Oxford on October 8, 1845; and, although Newman's associates at Littlemore did not deny that he would become a Catholic, they were ignorant of his intentions in detail and wondered when it would occur. That afternoon Dalgairns and St. John set out to Oxford to meet the Passionist Father, and Newman said to Dalgairns in a very low and quiet tone, "When you see your friend, will you tell him that I wish him to receive me into the Church of Christ?" Dalgairns answered "Yes," and no more. [2] The evening drew on dark and stormy, the wind blew in gusts, rain fell in torrents; that night Newman seceded to the Roman Catholic Church. At almost the same time Renan arrived in Paris, bade farewell to St. Sulpice, put off his clerical habit, and renounced the faith

---

[1] Wilfred Ward: "Life of John Henry Cardinal Newman"; Vol. I, pp. 86-87.
[2] *Ibid.*, Vol. I, p. 93.

Newman accepted; an historical coincidence which, as Dr. William Barry has observed, "will register its consequences for a long time to come."[1] The midnight scene in the little chapel where Newman made his confession was deeply impressive: he was so overcome that when it was over he could not stand alone, and his companions led him out of the tiny Oratory. The final separation had been before his imagination continually; he had reflected upon it with such intensity and insistence, he had thought so constantly of the consternation, the dismay, the sorrow, it would bring to his Tractarian associates, that when the deed was done, he had already largely paid the penalties it exacted. The bitterness of his death to Anglicanism was past, the future was tinged with tranquil hope and assurance. Nor did he ever afterwards regret what here occurred. His proud imperious spirit was fated to endure many chastenings, yet in seasons of the most humiliating depression he referred to his second conversion with unshaken confidence, and with an accent of conviction it would be dishonorable to question; Rome was for him the only safe anchorage; Protestantism "the dreariest of possible religions." He never saw Oxford again, except at a distance, until he revisited the city after an absence of more than thirty years. But in one of the rooms of his residence at Edgbaston hung an engraving of the place displaying the Radcliffe dome with its attendant spires and towers, and under it was inscribed the legend from the prophet Ezekiel, "Can these bones live?" According to Newman, they could not, save through acceptance of his theological creed.

The English Church received the news of his departure with mingled feelings. Many openly rejoiced that he was gone, others regarded him as an apostate; his closest friends, although they had expected his action, placed their hope against their fear, lest fear should become despair. Up to this hour they had met with not a few disasters but none

[1] "Cardinal Newman"; p. 64.

seemed irretrievable. The more sanguine spirits still believed that the prospect might change; Anglicanism might retain him; the Movement might prosper. Now they were undeceived, and their party overthrown. "It was more than a defeat," said Dean Church, "it was a rout in which they were driven from the field." Principal Shairp spoke of the event and of the sentiments it evoked both in those who loved and those who feared Newman, in the following words. "How vividly comes back the remembrance of the aching blank, the awful pause, which fell on Oxford when that voice had ceased, and we knew that we should hear it no more. It was as when, to one kneeling by night, in the silence of some vast cathedral, the great bell tolling solemnly overhead has suddenly gone still. To many, no doubt, the pause was not a long continuance. Soon they began to look this way and that for new teachers, and to rush vehemently to the opposite extremes of thought. But there were those who could not so lightly forget. All the more these withdrew into themselves. On Sunday forenoon and evenings, in the retirement of their rooms, the printed words of those marvelous sermons would thrill them till they wept abundant and most sweet tears. Since then many voices of powerful teachers they may have heard, but none that ever penetrated the soul like his." [1]

The limits imposed on this volume prevent us from discussing Newman's after life, and in view of the recent publication of his Biography by Wilfred Ward, to do more than barely indicate its outline would be an impertinence. He faced the critical years when Pius IX was reigning, when Manning was omnipotent in English Catholicism, and the Infallibilists were "an aggressive and insolent faction." The fires of the Vatican Council, kindled on the ruins of the Temporal Power, may have tested Newman's allegiance to the Papacy, but they did not touch his Catholicism. Yet

[1] Wilfred Ward: "The Life of John Henry Cardinal Newman"; Vol. I, pp. 77-78.

he could not have known what awaited him, or that he would become as a discrowned king, and a forsaken prophet amongst his Roman brethren. "Had he died directly after his sixty-third birthday," says Dr. Ward, "at an age which would have fallen not very far short of the allotted days of man on earth — his career would have lived in history as ending in the saddest of failures. His unparalleled eminence in 1837 would have been contrasted by historians with his utter insignificance in 1863. His biography would have been a tragedy." [1] One of the main reasons for the apathy and even open hostility he encountered was his curious reversion to liberalism. Contrary to his Anglican precedents he stood increasingly for a broader policy and looked with distrust and dislike upon the Syllabus and Papal Infallibility. The very firmness of his new foundation granted him unusual freedom; he felt that he could afford to relax and incline toward the shades of opposition. This determination was shown in his ill-timed effort to impress upon the authorities the need of his doctrine of organic development, and by his misunderstandings with the Irish hierarchy, the Roman episcopate in England, with Cardinal Manning, and many others. Everything to which he set himself came to grief. The finest mind of the Catholic faith was consigned to a harshness of exile which seemed to have no chance of release. Accused by Ultramontanes such as W. G. Ward and Manning of lukewarmness toward the Holy See, Newman complained that one who was not extravagant was found treacherous, and that those who frustrated his plans regarded every intellectual man as being on his way to perdition. The fact was, he had been accustomed to command, and now felt it exceedingly difficult to obey. To his superiors, at home and especially abroad, he remained an enigma. Their knowledge of his antecedents was of the vaguest, they felt no particular interest in his philosophical and theological spec-

[1] "Life of John Henry Cardinal Newman"; Vol. I, pp. 10–11.

ulations, they resented his provincial Oxford ways, and the
English of which he was a master was an unknown tongue
at Rome.   He bore himself in silence and outward submission, but the ordeal wore on him; his health declined, his
countenance changed, he even made ready for death.   Then
in 1864 came Charles Kingsley's headlong, random remarks
concerning him, and Newman, finding his honesty assailed,
laid aside the verdict he had previously passed upon himself
as "an evaporating mist of the morning," and told the world
the plain story of his life in the "Apologia."   Fortunately
for his fame, he afterwards deleted some opening phrases
of the volume, and it went forth to bring back to him the
heart of England.   "Thenceforth John Henry Newman was
a great figure in the eyes of his countrymen.   English
Catholics were grateful to him and proud of having for their
champion one of whom the country itself had become suddenly proud as a great writer and a spiritual genius.   He had
a large following within the Catholic Church, who hung on his
words as his Oxford disciples had done thirty years earlier.
Opposition in influential quarters continued.   But his supporters among the bishops stood their ground, and the
battle was on far more equal terms than before." [1]   True,
he did not esteem the dialectics with which he could have
vanquished far abler controversialists than Kingsley, but the
book revealed Newman in all his grandeur and his weakness.
Those who had long been indifferent or angry, turned to
him again, and the generation that had arisen since the
days of relentless war judged him more justly.   He
now lived under kindlier local skies, and once more felt that
responsive warmth of sympathy which was necessary to
his temperament and his gifts.   In 1878, Trinity College
elected him an honorary fellow, and at the same date Pio
Nono, who had long misconceived him, died.   Encouraged
by the Duke of Norfolk and other distinguished Roman

---

[1] Wilfred Ward: "The Life of John Henry Cardinal Newman"; Vol. I,
p. 11.

Catholic laymen, Leo XIII elevated the noble Oratorian to the Cardinalate, the distinction being the more marked because Newman was a simple priest and not resident in Rome. The newly elected Pope thus placed the highest approval on his works, and forever disposed of suspicions as to his fidelity. Manning, who could never be charged with subtlety any more than could Newman with ambition, interfered with his promotion in ways difficult to understand or to forgive. Their antipathy was primarily due to the conflict of an objective with a subjective mind. But if some human frailty entered into their relations, especially from Manning's side, his weaknesses were redeemed by his philanthropic labors in behalf of the poor and oppressed, in which he showed an instinct for true Christian democracy that Newman seldom felt. The venerable dignitary, immured in the busy Midland city of Birmingham, was not often visible elsewhere. His honors came too late to be much more than an official vindication and a source of personal comfort. He was now a very old man, and not without the misfortunes and vapors of such an age; but as one to whom holiness had become a habit and not a phrase, despite encircling gloom, he gradually ascended the heights which led him up to God. On rare occasions his speaking countenance and red robed figure could be discerned in the pulpits of his communion; a figure on which a fierce light had beaten, on which there now shone a more ethereal radiance, inducing a host of memories which recounted the unsurpassed dramatic interest of his career, and left a sad and solemn music in many hearts. In describing an interview with him, in 1884, James Russell Lowell wrote: "The most interesting part of my visit to Birmingham was a call I made by appointment on Cardinal Newman. He was benignly courteous and we excellencied and eminenced each other by turns. A more gracious senescence I never saw. There was no monumental pomp, but a serene decay, like that of some ruined abbey in a woodland dell, consolingly forlorn." He died at Edgbaston on August 11, 1890, having practically covered the century of which he was a foremost personality and which he never suffered to forget that the things which are seen are temporal, the things which are not seen are eternal.

EPILOGUE

THE Tractarians who remained steadfast after Newman's departure were compelled to remodel their party. Undeterred by the accusations, invectives and taunts hurled at them from all quarters they still believed that Anglicanism had a Catholic origin, and that a synthesis could be effected between traditional ecclesiasticism and the Established Church. Under the guidance of Pusey, Keble, Mozley, and Marriott they gradually recovered from the shock of Newman's secession, and retained an unalterable love for their former associations with him. Nor could his "Lectures on Catholicism in England," which he considered his best effort, and in which he cast down and derided the ideals he had once exalted to the skies, separate the hearts of his former comrades from him. After some years, the old friendships with him and Keble were resumed; Dean Church became his confidant, at whose home Newman stayed when he visited London, and who probably knew more about the convert's opinions and sentiments than any other man except Father Ambrose St. John. When the Cardinal was over eighty he traveled to Oxford to see in his last illness Mark Pattison, a scholar widely apart from him and Pusey in matters of belief, but one with them in their love for the University and for each other. Newman does not seem to have formed an intimacy with any man, Roman or Anglican, who was not reared at Oxford.

Yet these personal exchanges could not affect the important fact that the Movement assumed other and very different forms, some of which fell behind and others went beyond the designs of its originators. The liberalism they hated and fought à *l'outrance* reasserted itself; the spirit of inquiry necessary to intellectual research and achievement was no longer proscribed; Oxford emerged from the backwash of medievalism, and resumed her true vocation as a University of unhampered learning. Religious barriers were thrown down, credal tests were abolished, academic honors were distributed without regard to Anglican preferences; in brief, the attempt to arrest the heavens and the earth in behalf of clerical control and dictation ended, as it deserved to end, in complete failure. Newman himself, despite his secession, received an honorary fellowship in Trinity College, and was congratulated upon the part he had played as a Roman Catholic doctor in rescuing the University from its former narrowness.[1] Viewed from this standpoint, the Movement was cut off from its base of supplies at Oxford. It could not be recruited as a matter of privilege from the ranks of her professors and students. The Alma Mater which had spurned Wycliffe and Wesley, also subordinated Anglo-Catholicism to her general purposes.

While the University was entering upon another era, which made Tractarianism seem almost as remote as Scholasticism, historical theology slowly undermined some basic teachings of the sacerdotalists. They were men of their own time, with their own methods, desperately opposed to those who would not concede, in the phrase of Abbé Loisy, that the past should remain the present and become the future. This attitude exposed them to the attacks of progressive scholarship, which divorced itself from many of their claims. It argued that there could be no greater fallacy than to identify the medieval Church with any species of Catholicism. Rather it was the parent stem of which modern communions are the branches. These afterwards developed on their specific lines, the static and centripetal elements being found in the stereotyped Roman Church, the active and cen-

---

[1] Lord Bryce, then a professor at Oxford, was the toastmaster who offered the congratulations to Newman.

trifugal in the various reformed Churches. Neither branch
entertained conceptions of liberty of conscience, or a critical
or scientific theology. To attribute such intellectual virtues
to Romans or Protestants of the sixteenth century did
violence to their psychology and their history. Those who
understood the inner spirit and structure of orthodoxy,
whether Genevan, Lutheran, Anglican, or Roman, ceased
to wonder that Socinians, Baptists, and Quakers, the step-
children of the Reformation, as they have been happily
called, fared nearly as hardly as the Huguenots of France or
the victims of the Spanish Inquisition. Investigations of
this radical character are still under way, and whatever else
they may accomplish, they will not produce anything ad-
vantageous to Tractarianism or its successors.

A far more serious matter for them was the impairment
of the theory of apostolic succession already mentioned in
the chapters on Wesley. Upon this unbroken ordination
all Catholicism rested its case, and Newman boasted that
whatever else may happen, not a link in the chain was miss-
ing. His position in this respect, whether as an Anglican
or a Romanist, was destined to be overthrown at the instance of a great English bishop and scholar. John Barber
Lightfoot of Durham, Newman's superior in the massive-
ness and extent of his learning, showed that there was no
threefold order in the church of the Apostles. The Syriac
Peshito, the first version into which the New Testament
was translated, and the "Didache," most venerable of
Christian documents recently recovered, verified Lightfoot's
argument. Pusey's defense of the Anglican succession was
questioned not only by fellow Churchmen but also by Newman, who maintained that his former colleague did not
affect to appeal to any authority but his own interpretation
of the Fathers. "There is," he said, "a tradition of High
Church and Low Church, but not what is now justly called
Puseyism." Baptismal Regeneration, the Real Presence in
the Holy Communion, and other dogmas which derive their

sacramental value from the validity of Anglican Orders, while still believed and taught by Anglo-Catholics, must eventually be affected by the large variations already felt at the heart of their creed. Its advocates were driven by the invidious nature of their claims to unearth material for the support of foregone conclusions. Their researches travestied the past, and supplied them with no key to the processes of Christian thought. They stood, and still stand, upon an imaginary platform, "from which," in the language of Principal Tulloch, "they proceeded to the condemnation of everybody else, or the apotheosis of themselves as the representatives of Christian antiquity."

Further, the publication of "Lux Mundi," a series of essays by a group of gifted High Churchmen, which was edited by the present bishop of Oxford, Dr. Gore, frankly recognized that the dogma of the inerrancy of Holy Scripture was another fallen fortress. Let it be granted that some speculative conclusions put forth by the modern view of the Bible are as mischievous as the letter-worship against which they are drawn. Yet these aberrations do not make a rational interpretation of Sacred Writ the less necessary, and if those who are competent to deal with such intricate questions could be deprived of their freedom to do so, the last state would be worse than the first. The setting aside of one of Newman's main postulates, the absolute infallibility of all parts of the Holy Scriptures, was extremely adverse to the authority of those records of Jewish priesthoods, rituals, and sacrifices which had been a plentiful storehouse for the language and customs of the Eucharistic altar.

The second phase of Tractarianism found expression in its modes of worship. Newman's religious temper was indicated in his preference for Palladian over Gothic architecture. He loved definition; the dim recessed spaces, pillared gloom, half lights and shadows of English cathedrals did not appeal to him. Neither he nor Pusey cared for a highly ornate service, but Pusey's disciples depended on its concrete visible means whereby to impart Catholicism through sign and symbol to the less receptive minds of their flocks. Here the Movement fell into the care of minor spirits, who were charged with deflecting the adoration of the worshipers from the proper objectives of faith. The use of vestments, incense, sacring bells, candles, crucifixes; the genuflexions, and adoration of the Host, which constituted what has been described as the sacred dance around the altar; the practice of celibacy and of confession; the observance of fasts and feasts and saints' days without stint, and the homage paid to the Virgin Mary, created considerable excitement in England and kept the bishops busy in their efforts to subdue a civil war within the Church, preserve discipline, and adjudicate the disputes of rebellious priests with their parishioners. Some Anglicans looked upon these innovations as well-meant vagaries, others, less complaisant, pointed out that they were not only a violation of the simplicity which is in Christ, but also of the Apostolic and patristic Christianity to which the Tractarians had first resorted, and of the Canon Law of the Church. As a matter of fact, they reproduced and almost transcended the later developments of Roman Catholicism. The Anglican Articles and Rubrics had enjoined no special type of faith and worship: the exposition of their doctrinal and liturgical standard was laid upon the conscience of the clergy as enlightened by Holy Scriptures. But this liberty was guarded by the Book of Common Prayer, which, after the Bible of 1611, was the noblest heritage of the Church, the finest example of pure vernacular English, the most complete expression of Christian truth and supplication, which recognized and included the laity with the clergy in their united approach to God. Possessed by all, accessible to all, these external guides, the Bible and the Prayer Book, sustained the Church in her gravest emergencies, and, despite her inconsistencies, helped to make her one of the greatest religious forces of the world. Ecclesiastical parties had flourished, fought, declined, having this in common, the authority of the two classics derived in their stated form from the Reformation period. If Erastians had frequently neglected the spiritual economies of the Church in behalf of her political utility, they had also saved her from the fantastic inspirations of zealots against her unity. Her efficiency as a national organization had not been intrusted to an apostolic succession, but to the necessity and the usefulness of her institutions. And her most dispassionate and weighty intellects, such as Hooker, had judged and approved her on that basis. Now the stupidity against which even the gods contend in vain had broken loose, and for the first time in Anglicanism there was a marked divergence between the clerical and laical mind.

A similar divergence had long been felt in Latin Christianity, but the counteraction of Puritanism had prevented its leaven from spreading in England. Authority and liberty were again at odds, and the arbitrary self-exaltation of the Ritualistic cult was a heady wine for the younger Tractarians to drink. They carried over the residue of conservative reaction in the late eighteenth century into another outbreak in the nineteenth, which enthroned the priest as the mediator of divine grace, and the representative of God to the congregation. This special ambassadorship was asserted in the pious rhetoric with which such pretensions are usually conveyed, but no phraseology could make them palatable to the average Briton. Prosaic as he appeared to be, he was not deceived by it. Ritualism remained a mere decoration, and its sensuous materialism, irrational attitude, and reckless bearing were deeply resented. Neither the ardor of its advocates, nor their affection for environments befitting Christian worship could avert the condemnation of the nation at large, or make amends for the actual peril of priestly control and monopoly of the Church. The opposition this peril encountered was not always wise or courteous. Good men entangled in

2 P

their own fancies were caricatured and maligned; accused of wilful and mischievous plottings against the peace and welfare of the communion for which many of them felt a sincere affection and served at considerable cost to themselves. But the persecutions which they endured and which advanced rather than retarded their cause, were only the surplusage of a widespread and justifiable objection to rabid extremists who furnished abundant cause for the adverse sentiments with which they were regarded.

Presently they displayed contempt for Anglicanism, and moderate High Churchmen perceived that sacerdotal partisans, conscious of their anomalous standing, were willing to dispense Christianity only on their own terms. The extent of this perversity was revealed in a recent occurrence at Oxford, when two Anglo-Catholic professors proposed to omit from the theological degree the title of "sacred" and to throw it open to Buddhists and other non-Christians. The Warden of Keble College supported the motion and the Regius Professor of Divinity asserted that he did not know in these days what constituted a Churchman.[1]

Yet ritualism had a brighter side; the slovenliness of early Victorian observances was abolished, fabrics which had fallen into disrepair were rebuilt, monuments of antiquity were preserved, abbeys and cathedrals which had been ravaged by previous "restorations" assumed their original beauty and became the sanctuaries of daily praise and supplication. And though the ceremonialists seemed to have little inclination for missionary efforts abroad, they adorned the superficial life of their own land with many tokens of their devotion.

The third phase of Tractarianism, and in many respects the best, is the present passion of Anglo-Catholics for humanity and for social service. Their disturbance of complacent officialism in 1833 finds its sequel in the agitation for a Christian democracy in 1915. The bishops, the majority

---

[1] A. H. T. Clarke: "Collapse of the Catholic Revival"; *The Nineteenth Century* for October, 1913.

of whom are High Churchmen, no longer live in aristocratic
aloofness, surveying with indifference or contempt the
struggle of the people.   They have exceeded the example of
Samuel Wilberforce and enlarged their office by allying it
with all classes in their dioceses; giving guidance and
succor to the outcast and the helpless with a persistency and an inspiration drawn from a fresh vision
of Christian truth and Christian institutions.   Nothing
more significant has been accomplished in modern Anglicanism.   The rank and file of the clergy have also experienced a renewal of spiritual life which manifests
itself in these admirable ways.   Thousands of them
are found ministering in obscure and depressing parishes
of city slums and rural regions, remote from notice, with
no desire for emoluments and benefices.   A self-denying,
consecrated pastoral force covers once neglected spots,
instituting daily services, catechizing the children, consoling
the sick and bereaved, and injecting into the most brutalized
and hopeless conditions a sense of eternal things.   The work
of Father Stanton in Holborn and Father Dolling in the
East End of London was typical of similar labors and laborers
throughout England.   Much that is said and done is questionable, but notwithstanding mistakes and retrogressions,
the war on unbelief, on godless wealth, on luxury, on ease,
and on the vices of drink and immorality goes steadily forward.   To agitate, to innovate, to succeed, are its mottoes.
Incensed by the misery they have witnessed, many of these
men are Socialists of a sort, and proclaim against the vicious-
ness of the present economic system with unsparing words.
Even the Establishment, that sacred organism in behalf of
which Keble uttered the indictment that began the Oxford
Movement, has been assailed, and Anglo-Catholics of the
pattern of the late Father Stanton are found in the libera-
tionists' camp, denouncing the injustice and disgrace of an
alliance of Church and State in terms which would have surprised and charmed Edward Miall.

Nonconformists and Low Churchmen, who for a time stood afar off and thanked Heaven they were not as those Romanizing fanatics, eventually imitated their zeal for the betterment of the nation, giving to it a renewed measure of that evangelical effort they have always and honorably bestowed on foreign territories. The great missions of Wesleyan Methodism in many cities and that of Whitefield's Tabernacle, London, with which the names of Hugh Price Hughes, Samuel F. Collier, F. L. Wiseman, George Jackson, J. Ernest Rattenbury, and C. Silvester Horne are signally associated, were organized and soon became living agencies for religious and social improvement. Those who have no sympathy with the clerical pretensions of Anglo-Catholics concede that their latest developments inspire a respect which has never been felt for their historical or logical positions. This respect is intensified by their opposition to the narrowness of that spurious liberalism which reduces the vital content of the Gospel to a bloodless phraseology, and views it as an ethical system shorn of any adequate religious dynamic. In such relations the Oxford Movement reverted to the Evangelicalism from which, in a measure, it originated, and against which it had set itself. The life animating both these historic parties was lodged beneath their deepest differences and could not be exterminated. They unitedly repudiated the half-hearted replica of the Christianity of Christ which costs little, involves few, forgets no prudences, runs no hazards, and at last incurs reproach and decay. Thus the Oxford Movement was more than a theological reform, and infinitely more than an emotional episode; "it was a protest against the loose unreality of ordinary religious morality" and in this, the summary of its wisest historian, is the explanation of its value for the universal Church.

Newman was a prime instance of the persistence of earlier traits in an unfriendly environment; and, as we have seen, other converts from Tractarianism to Rome were, like him, Evangelicals by birth and training. His strength and theirs lay in a quick sense of the supernatural, a profound consciousness of religion as a personal experience, to which his genius gave a historic setting. God and himself were the only two, almost coördinate realities, the fixed foci of an ellipse around which revolved the world with its staggering burdens, as so much nebula, dream-stuff, phantasmagoria. Myself, my God, my end: and all things else mere means to that end—such was Newman's plea. The struggle to maintain each member of this system in its due place, and to cultivate their spiritualities by subjecting the forces of conquered egotism to their service constituted his moral greatness. Making a serious account of obstacles, he yet accepted all turns of affairs, drawing them into his main current, and moving on towards his goal; a simple, humane, universal goal; the doing of God's will on earth. Ever and anon he relaxed his customary vigilance and the opposition of his regnant will was revealed. The conflict engraved its traces on his soul, and in all probability he remained unsatisfied to the end. "That which won his heart and his enthusiasm," said Dean Church, "was one thing, that which justified itself to his intellect was another." This striking verdict from one who appraised him best, conducts us as near to the mystery of his being as it seems possible to get. His ultimate sense of the life, the society, and the principles of action contained in the Apostolic fellowship constrained him to seek that organization in which they were most completely embodied. In the search he surrounded himself with distillations of all kinds and arguments orientalized to the last degree. Questions of logical legitimacy gave way to the all-important issue of a vital system of Christianity. The high ideal of a Church which lived and wrought as Christ and His Apostles had lived and wrought offered the only adequate object to his reason and faith alike. The pursuit of that ideal engrossed him as it had Wycliffe and Wesley; the historian and all else in him were made obedient to his endeavors to attain that object. His first effort was a confessed mistake. In language which fulfilled the highest standards of the writer's art; dignity of manner, persuasiveness, crystalline clearness, fervor with restraint, he bared the innermost chambers of his heart to the world's gaze, and admitted that he had theorized wrongly. In his second effort he theorized successfully, but great results were denied him. He had lost touch with the younger generation, and could no longer take account of the form and pressure of his times, or remake the stock of his conceptions, or cast aside the prepossessions of his life. Caught in the toils of his own personality, he settled nothing for the problems of human freedom and human thinking. Behind him lay a divided Anglicanism, before him a bewildered and apathetic Romanism. The most loyal of Englishmen and of Oxford's sons was drawn by his sense of duty and by the logic of his premises into "a great cosmopolitan association in which England counted for little and Oxford for nothing at all." With dexterity of argument he tried to account for the indisputable fact that Papal doctrine and discipline were in many essential respects far removed from the Church of the New Testament. But neither the Essay on Development nor aught else could soothe his own disquietude; his reasoning and his style were the images of his mind rather than of his subject. Their elusiveness gives rise to the mingled admiration and doubt of which his readers are aware. They watch the manifestations of his intellect with the suspicion that he engages it to confirm the demands of his heart. These distractions prevented in him the purest faith, and made his story a sad one even to the casual observer. Although historically he was an Oxonian, a Calvinist, an Evangelical, an Anglican, a Tractarian, a Roman Catholic; primarily he was none of these, but always a Newmanite. The rest could assert themselves through his complex personality; none could diminish or overawe it. This invincible individualism, expressed in ways which outvie romance in their interest, accounted for the strange fascination he exercised over disciple and opponent. It isolated him, as we have seen, in the most congenial or inquisitive societies to which he successively adhered.

Hence few of his official overseers understood him: Hawkins, Whately, the English bishops, the Roman hierarchy, were equally at fault in their judgments concerning him. He was practically driven out of Anglicanism, he was snubbed and neglected by the chief pastors of the Church of his adoption. In 1860 he wrote in his Journal: "I have no friend in Rome: I have labored in England, to be misrepresented, backbitten and scorned. I have labored in Ireland, with a door ever shut in my face." Seven years later he continued — "Now, alas! I fear that in one sense the iron has entered into my soul. I mean that confidence in any superiors whatever never can blossom again within me. I shall, I feel, always think they will be taking some advantage of me." This was both his misfortune and his fault. In the pithy phrase of the London *Spectator:* "as an Anglican he stood for medieval principles in a scientific age; as a Roman he stood for a measure of scientific thought in a Church committed to medieval theology." That which Oxford did he chided Rome for not doing, yet he had left Oxford because she did it. The liberalism he denounced in the one place, he assumed in the other. This may explain why Archbishop Cullen intercepted the mitre, and Manning nearly prevented the scarlet hat from being bestowed on him. Not until he was harmless was he permitted to take his place among the Princes of the Church, and it is doubtful if even Ward's biography contains the full account of his differences with the Curia, and with the Roman Catholic episcopacy of Great Britain and Ireland.

He saw the defects of systems more keenly than their merits, and his sensitiveness inclined him to despair of their permanence or usefulness. Because he never shared the delusion that England was hungering for the true Church and on the verge of conversion to Catholicism, he set about re-

forming instead of propagating it among his countrymen.
Here, as elsewhere, he was bound to make his brain consent
to what his heart approved. They cajoled each other,
and most conspicuously in his treatment of faith, in which
he reversed the usual order and dealt with the essential
truths of religion as neither known nor knowable in themselves
but guaranteed by the sufficient explanation they gave of
facts and by their practical values for human nature.
The rationalistic conception of faith as an intellectual act
of belief based on sufficient evidence, and the moral conception of faith as the carrying out by the will of that which
had been accepted by the understanding, Newman dis-
allowed; the first because it confounded faith with opinion,
the second because it confounded faith with obedience.
Thus faith was placed above the operations of intellect; the
early Christians, he said, believed first and were afterwards
instructed as to what they believed. Glacial intellect
construed the spiritual as though it were the physical and
were incapable of the love and reverence which colored faith.
To an evil heart these were no more than dark suspicions,
and it was prone to accept the shadows cast by its own reflections as realities. But to a humble mind love and reverence were clear trusts, in behalf of which reason ceased
its struggle for supremacy, and cast in its fortunes with their
higher possibilities. Such, according to Newman, was saving
faith: its judgments were intuitive, immediate, detached,
unsystematic, flashes in our gloomy depths; begotten in us,
not created by us. His own faith was an act of will, vetoing
reason, or perhaps to be more just to him, a moral act of the
reason, transcending the requirements of demonstration.
The logical sequence was, that an authoritative guardian of
faith became necessary as a protection against skeptical
desolation. Hence faith for him was a philosophy, Christianity an idea, truth a matter of impression; evidences
were presumptions, hypotheses, ventures, rather than substantiated realities; conclusions which provoked Fairbairn's

retort that Newman was an agnostic baptized with religious emotion.

In all probability he was the greatest apologist for the Roman Catholic Church since the days of Bossuet. Neither of them would endure the reconciliation of faith with reason; the one appealed to force, the other to imagination, against the process. But Newman succeeded in mitigating the irrational resentment which had prevailed against the Papacy in England. The silent force of his example, even more than the eloquence of his writings, gave pause to those ardent partisans who saw nothing good in Rome.

*   *   *   *   *   *

The breach between faith and knowledge is not healed, yet this is not as impossible as traditionalists declare. It was successfully attempted by Clement and Origen, unsuccessfully by Abailard, and actually accomplished by Aquinas. Scholasticism was formerly as strongly reprobated by the Curia as Modernism is now. The New Learning was rejected by the Council of Trent for definite and interested reasons. Yet the New Learning has returned as Modernism to find Scholasticism sanctioned and its own representative banned. Surely it is within the highest possibility that the Church which gave Aquinas to the most illustrious services any man could render by the will of God to his own generation, will produce from her living soul another great doctor who can make the bounds of lawful freedom wider yet. The premature and desultory efforts of Father Tyrell in this direction are not forever forfeited, and if history is any warrant, it is a safe prediction that the things for which he stood will yet bear fruit after their kind and in their season. So far as Anglicanism is concerned, it was founded on sound scholarship, and, considered broadly, has never departed from that basis. Its leaders have welcomed the pioneers of truth who were glad to find shelter at Canterbury and Oxford. Cranmer, Hooker,

Tillotson, Thirlwall, Lightfoot, Westcott, Hort, Stubbs, and Creighton, to mention but a few historic names, toiled for the unification of learning and piety. That obscurantism has been all too active and mischievous among certain groups of Anglicanism is beyond question. But this should not confuse the general situation. For Churchmen of every stripe, wherever found, have felt the weight of these inquiries concerning past, present, and future. The separation which has disfigured the loveliness of the Church of England, narrowed and embittered Puritanism, divided and weakened Christendom, and gathered Protestant peoples into numerous sects, cannot endure the pressure now brought to bear upon its misconceptions and errors, nor is it congenital to Protestantism when the issues are properly understood and balanced. This understanding and balancing enjoy favorable prospects because the battle is no longer one of prelates or divines in "a vast, dumb, listless, illiterate world," or waged between a few sequestered university dons. It is an open contention, fraught with religious and moral consequences which embrace the honorable dealings of internationalism, the perpetuity of a just and universal peace, social reconstruction, the reconciliation of various forms of truth, the maintenance of essential spiritualities, the simplification of credal statements; in a word, the preservation of the Kingdom of God upon earth. At this moment the ferocious cruelties of an unparalleled war are driving home these reflections; a war which has revealed the indescribable perils that knowledge and culture incur when they are separated from the control of genuine religion, and subjected to the dictates of hate and greed, and to the anarchy of physical violence. In such a crisis, the magnitude and horror of which baffle description, the Christian Church must restore civilization to the purposes from which it has been wantonly deflected. Whatever the errors, the rectifications, the risks, the losses, this obligation entails, Catholic and Protestant, Traditionalist

and Modernist, are bound to gird themselves for its fulfillment. Had they bestowed the same assiduous care upon
the realities of love, and mercy, and righteousness which
has been devoted to their respective peculiarities of belief,
mankind might have escaped the sickening catastrophe which
has overtaken it. And if the flamings of this wrath shall
purge the Church militant of her dross, and through
suffering and deprivation sanctify her for the noblest
ideals of her faith and the sacrifices necessary to attain
them, then even such a vial of destruction as the European
conflict will not have been poured out in vain.

BIBLIOGRAPHY

ABBOTT, E. A.   The Anglican Career of Cardinal Newman.
ABBOTT, E. A.   The Philomythus: an Antidote against Credulity.
ACTON, LORD.   The History of Freedom and other Essays.
ALLEN, A. V. G.   The Continuity of Christian Thought.
BARRY, WILLIAM.   Newman (Literary Lives).
BREMOND, HENRI.   The Mystery of Newman.
CARPENTER, BOYD-, BISHOP WILLIAM.   A Popular History of the Church of England.
CECIL, ALGERNON.   Six Oxford Thinkers: Gibbon, Newman, Church, Froude, Pater, Morley.
CHURCH, R. W.   The Beginning of the Middle Ages.
CHURCH, R. W.   Occasional Papers.
CHURCH, R. W.   The Oxford Movement: 1833–1845.
CORNISH, F. W.   A History of the English Church in the Nineteenth Century.
Dictionary of National Biography.   Articles on Newman, Froude, Pusey and others.
DONALDSON, A. B.   Five Great Oxford Leaders: Keble, Newman, Pusey, Liddon, Church.
DYKE, PAUL VAN.   The Age of the Renaissance.
Encyclopædia Britannica.   Article on Newman.   Vol. XIX.   11th edition.
FAIRBAIRN, A. M.   Catholicism: Roman and Anglican.
FISHER, GEORGE P.   The Reformation.
FLETCHER, J. S.   A Short Life of Cardinal Newman.
HUTCHINSON, W. G. (Editor).   The Oxford Movement.
HUTTON, R. H.   Modern Guides of English Thought in Matters of Truth.
LILLY, W. S. (Editor).   Characteristics from the Writings of John Henry Newman.
MARTINEAU, JAMES.   Essays, Reviews, and Addresses.
McGIFFERT, A. C.   The Rise of Modern Religious Ideas.
MOBERLY, C. A. E.   Dulce Domum.
MOZLEY, THOMAS.   Reminiscences.
NEWMAN, F. W.   Contributions chiefly to the Early History of Cardinal Newman.
NEWMAN, JOHN HENRY CARDINAL.   Works.   (See list.)
NICOLL, SIR W. ROBERTSON.   The Expositor: Fourth Series, Vols. II, V, VI.
PEROWNE, J. J. STEWART (Editor).   Remains Literary and Theological of Connop Thirlwall, Vol. I.

SAROLEA, CHARLES. Cardinal Newman and his Influence on Religious Life and Thought.
WALKER, WILLISTON. The Reformation.
WALSH, WALTER. The Secret History of the Oxford Movement.
WARD, WILFRED. The Life of John Henry Cardinal Newman.
WARD, WILFRED. Ten Personal Studies: Balfour, Delane, Hutton, Knowles, Sidgwick, Lytton, Ryder, Grant Duff, Leo XIII, Wiseman, Newman, Cardinals Newman and Manning.
WEDGWOOD, JULIA. Nineteenth Century Teachers, and Other Essays.
WHYTE, ALEXANDER. Newman; An Appreciation.

A LIST OF CARDINAL NEWMAN'S WORKS

Parochial and Plain Sermons (8 vols.).
Fifteen Sermons Preached before the University of Oxford.
Sermons Bearing upon Subjects of the Day.
Sermons Preached upon Various Occasions.
Lectures on the Doctrine of Justification.
An Essay on the Development of Christian Doctrine.
On the Idea of a University.
An Essay in aid of a Grammar of Assent.
Two Essays on Biblical and on Ecclesiastical Miracles.
Discussions and Arguments.
Essays Critical and Historical (2 vols.).
Historical Sketches (3 vols.).
The Arians of the Fourth Century.
Select Treatises of St. Athanasius in Controversy with the Arians.
Lectures on the Prophetical Office of the Church.
Certain Difficulties felt by Anglicans in Catholic Teaching Considered (2 vols.).
Theological Tracts.
Lectures on the Present Position of Catholics in England.
The Via Media of the Anglican Church (2 vols.).
Apologia pro Vita Sua.
Verses on Various Occasions.
Loss and Gain.
Callista.
The Dream of Gerontius.
Meditations and Devotions.
Letters and Correspondence (2 vols.).

INDEX

2 Q

Printed in the United States of America.

THE following pages contain advertisements of a
few of the Macmillan books on kindred subjects

Henry Codman Potter, Seventh Bishop of New York

By GEORGE HODGES

Cloth, 8vo, ill., $3.50

It will be a source of gratification to Bishop Potter's many friends to learn that the preparation of the official biography of Dr. Potter has been intrusted to Dean Hodges of the Episcopal Theological School. Long conversant with the large essentials of Dr. Potter's life, his training and sympathy have been such as to qualify him to do the task well. The biography that he has written describes Dr. Potter's career throughout his ministry, especially as rector of Grace Church and as bishop of New York. The great public services of Bishop Potter are also dealt with at length.

The Life of Clara Barton

By PERCY H. EPLER

Cloth, 12mo, ill., $2.50

From the wealth of material at his disposal Dr. Epler has made a most fascinating biography. Miss Barton's intimate friend, he has supplemented his own knowledge of her with a vast array of facts drawn from diaries, correspondence, and reports of lectures and addresses. It has been his purpose in so far as is possible to let Miss Barton tell her own story, which he does by means of direct quotations from her writings.

THE MACMILLAN COMPANY

Publishers   64-66 Fifth Avenue   New York

The Reconstruction of the Church

By PAUL MOORE STRAYER

Cloth, 12mo, $1.50

The circle of the church, the author maintains, ought to be widened to embrace and utilize the immense amount of unconscious and " anonymous religion " that exists outside the church, and that the church must be Christianized by bringing the daily life and business practices of its members into line with the law of Christ. To this task, Part I of Dr. Strayer's volume is addressed. In Part II he gives a diagnosis of the present situation of the church in the light of this larger purpose, and with special reference to its program and method. Part III points out the directions in which reconstruction is most needed, and offers suggestions for greater efficiency.

The Rise of Modern Religious Ideas

By ARTHUR CUSHMAN McGIFFERT

Cloth, 12mo, $1.50

In " The Rise of Modern Religious Ideas," Dr. McGiffert shows the relation of present-day religious thought to the theology of the past. He discusses the prevalence of the religious ideas which differ more or less completely from those of the past, and shows their origin, indicating the circumstances under which they have arisen and the influences by which they have been determined. His text is divided into two books: I. Disintegration, II. Reconstruction. Under the first of these he takes up such topics as Pietism, The Enlightenment, Natural Science, The Critical Philosophy; under the second, The Emancipation of Religion, The Rebirth of Speculation, The Rehabilitation of Faith, Agnosticism, Evolution, Divine Immanence, Ethical Theism, The Character of God, The Social Emphasis, and Religious Authority.

THE MACMILLAN COMPANY

Publishers   64-66 Fifth Avenue   New York

The Man of Nazareth

By FREDERICK LINCOLN ANDERSON, D.D.
Professor of New Testament Interpretation in Newton Theological Institution

Cloth, 12mo, $1.00

There is nothing in English just like this book. Written not for theologians, but for the average man and woman, it nevertheless grapples fearlessly and independently the most important modern questions about Jesus, his development, and his career, including many matters which are only rarely discussed. Yet the whole book is remarkable for its simplicity and clearness. While there is no display of ponderous learning, the author shows that he is at home in all the recent literature of the subject.

Dr. Gifford says, in *The Watchman-Examiner:* "Small in body, this book is great in spirit. It deals with a great subject in a great way. It is clear in analysis, simple in style, and profound in thought."

Columbus Journal: "We can conceive of no argumentative biography more convincing Quite the sanest thing in the way of popular theological literature."

The Standard (Chicago): "It gives one the impression that it was written at white heat. The mood is so reverent that it may be used for devotional purposes."

Men's Classes are already using it.

The Drama of the Spiritual Life: A Study of Religious Experience and Ideals

By ANNIE L. SEARS
Introduction by Josiah Royce

Cloth, 8vo, $3.00

The basis of this book is an empirical study of the prayers, hymns and general religious poetry and other expressions of religious experiences. In the opening chapter it is stated that "man is incurably religious" because as human, man is idealistic. Religion is, therefore, close to the common life, yet in religious idealism a problem is involved. This problem religious mysticism attempts to solve. In the second chapter the author seeks to make clear what are the universal elements of religious experience, and in the succeeding portions of the volume she traces the story of religious experience through its differences, oppositions, tensions, conflicts, compromises, and reconciliations. The problem of the work is to discover whether the conflicting elements and forms of religion can be harmonized and whether a significant spiritual experience results.

THE MACMILLAN COMPANY
Publishers   64-66 Fifth Avenue   New York

The Mighty and the Lowly

By KATRINA TRASK

Cloth, 12mo, $1.00

As "In the Vanguard" was a stirring plea for universal peace, so
"The Mighty and the Lowly" is a plea for social reform through a
right understanding of the teaching of Jesus. Writing with her
accustomed vigor and charm, Mrs. Trask combats the idea that Christ
was set against any particular class — rich or poor. The theme is
built around actual events in the life of Jesus, and the reader will find
his interest stirred by the dramatic power of the book as well as by its
argument.

What is a Christian?

By JOHN WALKER POWELL

Cloth, 12mo, $1.00

This is a clear, straightforward discussion of the qualities which to-
day characterize a man who believes in Christianity. Special emphasis is put upon the Christian's relation to war; "how far can a man lag
behind his Master in thought and practice without forfeiting his right
to the title" of Christian? Other chapters treat of the Christian and
Wealth, the Christian Church, the Christian Ideal. The book is well
balanced, and a distinct contribution to the subject of the relation of
the modern world to the religion of Christ.

Contents

I. The Faith of a Christian. II. The Ethics of Jesus. III. The
Christian and the War. IV. The Christian and Wealth. V. The
Christian Ideal. VI. The Christian Hope. VII. The Christian
Church.

THE MACMILLAN COMPANY

Publishers   64-66 Fifth Avenue   New York

Printed in the United Kingdom
by Lightning Source UK Ltd.
116506UKS00001B/88